Galilee through the Centuries

Duke Judaic Studies Series
Volume 1

Second International Conference on
Galilee in Antiquity

Galilee
through the Centuries

Confluence of Cultures

edited by

Eric M. Meyers

Eisenbrauns
Winona Lake, Indiana
1999

Library of Congress Cataloging-in-Publication Data

Galilee through the centuries : confluence of cultures / edited by Eric M.
Meyers.
   p.   cm. — (Duke Judaic studies series ; v. 1)
   Papers presented at the 2nd International Conference on Galilee in
Antiquity held at Duke University and North Carolina Museum of Art on
Jan. 25–27, 1997.
   Includes bibliographical references and index.
   ISBN 1-57506-040-X (cl. : alk. paper)
   1. Galilee (Israel)—History Congresses.   2. Jews—History—70–638
Congresses.   3. Judaism—History—Talmudic period, 10–425 Congresses.
4. Sepphoris (Extinct city) Congresses.   5. Galilee (Israel)—Church
history Congresses.   6. Excavations (Archaeology)—Israel—Galilee
Congresses.   I. Meyers, Eric M.   II. International Conference on
Galilee in Antiquity (2nd : 1997 : Duke University and North Carolina
Museum of Art)   III. Series.
DS110.G2G38   1999
956.94′5—dc21   99-25995
                                                                        CIP

Contents

Bronze and Iron Ages

Early Roman Period

Jewish, Rabbinic, and Epigraphic Sources

Byzantine and Christian Sources

Early Medieval Period

Indexes

Preface

Eric M. Meyers

This volume presents the papers given at the Second International Conference on Galilee in Antiquity held at Duke University in Durham and at the North Carolina Museum of Art in Raleigh on January 25–27, 1997. The conference was organized in conjunction with the exhibition "Sepphoris in Galilee: Crosscurrents of Culture," which was brought to the North Carolina Museum of Art under the aegis of the State of North Carolina Department of Cultural Resources and the Ministry of Foreign Affairs of the State of Israel. The North Carolina Museum of Art and The Center for Judaic Studies of Duke University sponsored the conference, which was held both on the Duke campus and at the North Carolina Museum of Art.

In preparing this volume for publication, some changes from the original program have been made. While it includes most of the papers delivered there (almost all of them were submitted for publication), several of them have been revised since the conference and in light of continuing discussion. Furthermore, three new papers have been added to the collection. This publication is a fitting sequel to the volume edited by Lee I. Levine, *The Galilee in Late Antiquity*, published in 1992 by The Jewish Theological Seminary of America and distributed by Harvard University Press. That volume represents the fruits of the First International Conference on Galilean Studies held at Kibbutz Hanaton on August 13–15, 1989. Several of the contributors to that volume are also represented here. In part because the chronological range and purview of the second meeting was considerably broadened, we have been able to bring new participants into the academic discussion concerning the significance of Galilee and its rich and diverse culture over a longer period.

The papers are grouped here in approximate chronological order, though their subjects overlap in multiple ways. The paper that focuses on the earliest discussed inhabitants of Galilee is the one by J. P. Dessel, on the recent Bronze and Iron Age excavations at Tel 'Ein Zippori, near the Greco-Roman site of Sepphoris; and the contribution with the latest subject is Seth Ward's, which brings us into the medieval, Arab period. The astute reader will note some lacunae; the conference did not presume to attempt an exhaustive treatment of all facets of Galilee studies. But we believe that this collection of papers significantly advances the state of the field, especially in regard to the interaction between Judaism and Christianity.

Many individuals helped to make this conference a reality. Dr. Rebecca Martin Nagy of the North Carolina Museum of Art was cocurator with me of the Sepphoris exhibition there and also coorganizer with me of the conference. The North Carolina Museum of Art, cosponsor of the conference, also served as administrative center for the conference. Its support at every stage of planning was essential to the success of the conference, as was its hosting of our keynote lectures on Sunday afternoon and the Saturday evening banquet. The banquet was cohosted by the Duke Divinity School, and I offer special thanks to then Dean Dennis Campbell for his generous support. Duke's Office of the Vice Provost for Academic and International Affairs awarded a major grant for the conference, for which we are most grateful. The support of Vice Provost Professor Peter Lange in this connection is gratefully acknowledged. Special thanks go to Professor Kalman P. Bland, Director of The Center for Judaic Studies, for generous support of the conference and this volume, which will be the first in a series of volumes sponsored by the Center.

It has been a special privilege to work with Dr. Rebecca Martin Nagy, Associate Director of Education at the North Carolina Museum of Art. She has been an able administrator, eloquent spokesperson on behalf of the Museum, and an academic colleague of unusual insight. All of the conference participants are in her debt, and, on behalf of them, I express great appreciation for all that she has done.

I also express my appreciation to Roberta Maltese, who began the copyediting of the manuscripts but who for personal reasons could not finish the work. Given the diversity of the ongoing research projects of the conference participants, some variation in place-name spellings and language transliterations have been allowed. I am also grateful to James Eisenbraun for his kind assistance at every stage of preparation of this volume.

Acknowledgments

REBECCA MARTIN NAGY

The Second International Conference on Galilee in Antiquity was held in conjunction with the exhibition "Sepphoris in Galilee: Crosscurrents of Culture," which opened at the North Carolina Museum of Art on November 16, 1996 and remained on view through July 6, 1997 as part of the Israel/North Carolina Cultural Exchange inaugurated by Governor James B. Hunt. In April 1994, Gov. Hunt signed a memorandum of intent with the State of Israel establishing the North Carolina–Israel Cooperation Committee. The alliance was formalized in September 1995, with the goal of strengthening our business, scientific, educational, and cultural ties. One of the objectives is to "increase cultural awareness, promoting a deeper understanding of shared values through the arts, humanities, and education." To help realize this goal, twenty-one of the state's leading arts institutions joined together to produce the Israel/North Carolina Cultural Exchange, a program of exhibitions, artist residencies, concerts, and a film festival devoted to Israeli art, archaeology, and culture.

As a result of Governor Hunt's initiative, a long-held dream finally could be realized. In 1987, when the glorious third-century Dionysos mosaic was discovered at Sepphoris, Professors Eric M. Meyers and Carol L. Meyers of the Department of Religion at Duke University and I initiated ambitious plans for an exhibition on the art and archaeology of Sepphoris. The time was not right for such an undertaking then, but almost a decade later, thanks to the new program initiated by Gov. Hunt, the development of a Sepphoris exhibition could go forward. The beautifully illustrated, 240-page exhibition catalog, *Sepphoris in Galilee: Crosscurrents of Culture*, published by the North Carolina Museum of Art and distributed by Eisenbrauns, was edited by Rebecca Martin Nagy, Carol L. Meyers, Eric M. Meyers, and Zeev Weiss. The exhibition subsequently traveled to the University of Michigan Museum of Art and the Kelsey Museum of Archaeology in Ann Arbor and to the Michael C. Carlos Museum at Emory University in Atlanta.

In planning the conference, Eric Meyers and I were assisted by Professor Lee Levine of The Hebrew University of Jerusalem. With the goal of examining the rich history of the Galilee, with its multifaceted cultural and religious traditions, colleagues from diverse academic disciplines were invited. They arrived from many locations in Israel, the U.S., and Europe and enthusiastically contributed their findings.

The exhibition was made possible through the generosity of the State of North Carolina, Department of Cultural Resources, and the State of Israel, Ministry of Foreign Affairs, together with numerous individual, foundation, and corporate donors, listed in the catalog. The conference was made possible by their gifts and by the generous support of Duke University, through its Office of the Vice Provost for Academic and International Affairs and the Judaic Studies Program. Sincere appreciation is extended to these supporters of the exhibition and conference. Special thanks go to the Judaic Studies Program of Duke University for publishing the proceedings of the conference.

Abbreviations

AASOR	Annual of the American Schools of Oriental Research
ABD	*Anchor Bible Dictionary*
AfO	*Archiv für Orientforschung*
AJS Review	*Association for Jewish Studies Review*
ANRW	*Aufstieg und Niedergang der römischen Welt*
ASOR Dissertation Series	American Schools of Oriental Research Dissertation Series
BA	*Biblical Archaeologist*
BAI	*Bulletin of the Asia Institute*
BAR International Series	British Archaeological Reports International Series
BARev	*Biblical Archaeology Review*
BASOR	*Bulletin of the American Schools of Oriental Research*
BASP	*Bulletin of the American Society of Papyrologists*
BE	*Bulletin épigraphique*
BJRL	*Bulletin of the John Rylands University Library of Manchester*
BJS	Brown Judaic Studies
CBQ	*Catholic Biblical Quarterly*
CCSL	Corpus Christianorum Series Latina
CII	*Corpus Inscriptionum Iudaicarum*
CRINT	Compendia Rerum Iudaicarum ad Novum Testamentum
CSCO	Corpus Scriptorum Christianorum Orientalium
CSEL	Corpus Scriptorum Ecclesiasticorum Latinorum
DMOA	Documenta et Monumenta Orientis Antiqui
EI^2	*Encyclopedia of Islam* (2d ed.)
EncJud	*Encyclopaedia Judaica*
ErIsr	*Eretz Israel*
ESI	*Excavations and Surveys in Israel*
ET	*Evangelische Theologie*
ExpTim	*Expository Times*
FRLANT	Forschungen zur Religion und Literatur des Alten und Neuen Testaments
GCS	Griechischen christlichen Schriftsteller
HR	*History of Religions*
HTR	*Harvard Theological Review*
HUCA	*Hebrew Union College Annual*
IEJ	*Israel Exploration Journal*
IG	Inscriptiones Graecae. Berlin: de Gruyter, 1924–
IGR	Inscriptiones Graecae ad res Romanas Pertinentes. Ed. R. Cagnat et al. 1906–27.
JAAR	*Journal of the American Academy of Religion*
JANESCU	*Journal of the Ancient Near Eastern Society of Columbia University*
JAOS	*Journal of the American Oriental Society*
JBL	*Journal of Biblical Literature*
JJA	*Journal of Jewish Art*

JJS   *Journal of Jewish Studies*
JNES   *Journal of Near Eastern Studies*
JPOS   *Journal of the Palestine Oriental Society*
JQR   *Jewish Quarterly Review*
JRASupp   Journal of Roman Archaeology Supplements
JRS   *Journal of Roman Studies*
JSJ   *Journal for the Study of Judaism in the Persian, Hellenistic and Roman
                    Period*
JSNTSup   Journal for the Study of the New Testament Supplement Series
JSOT/ASOR Monographs   Journal for the Study of the Old Testament and
                    American Schools of Oriental Research Monographs
JSOTSup   Journal for the Study of the Old Testament Supplement Series
JSP   *Journal for the Study of the Pseudepigrapha*
JSPSup   Journal for the Study of the Pseudepigrapha Supplements
JSQ   *Jewish Studies Quarterly*
JSSR   *Journal for the Scientific Study of Religion*
JTS   *Journal of Theological Studies*
LCL   Loeb Classical Library
Leš   *Lešonénu*
LSJ   Liddell-Scott-Jones. *Greek-English Lexicon*. Rev. H. S. Jones. Oxford:
                    Clarendon, 1968
MDOG   *Mitteilungen der deutschen Orient-Gesellschaft*
MGWJ   *Monatsschrift für Geschichte und Wissenschaft des Judentums*
NEAEHL   *New Encyclopedia of Archaeological Excavations in the Holy Land.*
                    4 vols. Ed. E. Stern. Jerusalem: Israel Exploration Society, 1993
NovT   *Novum Testamentum*
NTAbh   Neutestamentliche Abhandlungen
NTS   *New Testament Studies*
OEANE   *The Oxford Encyclopedia of Archaeology in the Near East.* 5 vols. Ed.
                    Eric M. Meyers. New York: Oxford University Press, 1997
OIP   Oriental Institute Publications
PAAJR   *Proceedings of the American Academy of Jewish Research*
PEQ   *Palestine Exploration Quarterly*
PL   Patrologia Latina. Ed. J. Migne. Turnhout: Brepols
QDAP   *Quarterly of the Department of Antiquities of Palestine*
RB   *Revue Biblique*
REG   *Revue des études grecques*
REJ   *Revue des Études Juives*
SB   Sammelbuch griechischer Urkunden aus Ägypten. Berlin: de Gruyter,
                    1974–
SBF   Studium Biblicum Franciscanum
SBLSP   Society of Biblical Literature Seminar Papers
SC   Sources chrétiennes
SEG   Supplementum Epigraphicum Graecorum. Leiden: Sijthoff, 1923–
SJLA   Studies in Judaism in Late Antiquity
SJOT   *Scandinavian Journal of Theology*
SPB   Studia Postbiblica
ST   *Studia Theologica*
StudOr   Studia Orientalia
TAPA   *Transactions of the American Philological Association*
TAVO   Tübinger Atlas das Vorderen Orients
T-S   Taylor Schechter Collection of the Cambridge University Library

VT	*Vetus Testamentum*
WBC	Word Biblical Commentary
WMANT	Wissenschaftliche Monographien zum Alten und Neuen Testament
WUNT	Wissenschaftliche Untersuchungen zum Neuen Testament
YCS	Yale Classical Studies
ZDPV	*Zeitschrift des deutschen Palästina-Vereins*

Tell ʿEin Zippori and the Lower Galilee in the Late Bronze and Iron Ages: A Village Perspective

J. P. Dessel

University of Tennessee

An Introduction to Village Archaeology

Much of what is known about the Late Bronze Age in the southern Levant is based primarily on the excavation of urban settlements and on textual sources such as the Hebrew Bible, Amarna Letters, and Ugaritic texts. Using these data, cultural reconstructions of the Late Bronze Age have a decidedly urban bias. This urban bias has helped foster a sense of sociocultural disjunction as marking the transition to Iron Age I.[1] However, missing from these interpretations is a consideration of multiperiod village sites, of which there are excavated examples in the Lower Galilee and Jezreel Valley.[2] They display an

Author's note: I would like to thank Eric Meyers, Carol Meyers, and Ken Hoglund for their encouragement and support in this research. I would also like to thank Linda Bregstein, Rachel Hallote, Alexander Joffe, and Gloria London for their comments on earlier drafts of this article. Beth Alpert-Nakhai, John Brodsky, and Carol Meyers assisted in the preparation of this article, and I am extremely grateful for their help. The author takes full responsibility for any errors of fact or interpretation.

1. This urbancentric view is clearly seen in earlier synthetic treatments of the Late Bronze–Iron Age transition; see, for instance, W. F. Albright, *The Archaeology of Palestine* (London: Penguin, 1954) 108–9, 112ff.; and Kathleen M. Kenyon, *Archaeology in the Holy Land* (4th ed.; London: Benn, 1979) 206–10, 229–32. More recently, see similar views in Amihai Mazar, *The Archaeology of the Land of the Bible 10,000–586 B.C.E.* (New York: Doubleday, 1990) 232–79; and Rivka Gonen, "The Late Bronze Age," in *The Archaeology of Ancient Israel* (ed. Amnon Ben-Tor; New Haven: Yale University Press, 1992) 211–57.

2. For examples in the Lower Galilee, see for Tell el-Wawiyat: Beth Alpert-Nakhai, J. P. Dessel, and Bonnie Wisthoff, "Tell el-Wawiyat," *NEAEHL* 4.1500–1501; for Tell ʿEin Zippori: J. P. Dessel, "Tell ʿEin Zippori," *OEANE* 2.227–28; and for Tell Yinʿam: Harold Leibowitz, "Excavations at Tel Yinʿam—The 1976 and 1977 Seasons: Preliminary Report," *BASOR* 243 (1981) 79–94; and Harold Leibowitz, "Tell Yinʿam," *NEAEHL* 4.1515–16. For the Jezreel Valley, see for Tell Qiri: Amnon Ben-Tor and Yuval Portugali, *Tell Qiri: A Village in the Jezreel Valley* (Qedem 24; Jerusalem: Israel Exploration Society, 1987).

unforeseen sense of rural complexity and internal stratification that suggests a more richly diverse sociopolitical landscape than has been previously envisioned. That a wider range of sociospatial arrangements existed in both the Late Bronze Age and Iron Age I has significant repercussions for our understanding of these periods.[3] Based on the preliminary results of two excavations conducted in the Lower Galilee of Israel, it is possible to suggest alternative readings of Late Bronze and Iron Age societies that emphasize the role of the village as opposed to the role of the city. The two sites that will be considered, Tell el-Wawiyat located in the Beit Netofa Valley and Tell ʿEin Zippori (Arabic ʿAin el-Qasal) in the Nazareth Basin, provide a rare opportunity to examine the transition from the Late Bronze to the Iron Age from a village or rural perspective.

How we define ancient settlements and the sociocultural assumptions implicit in these definitions primarily serve to create static interpretations of economic, social, and political interactions.[4] Sites with long cultural sequences are most often understood as urban. Morphological characteristics such as the presence of fortifications and the size of a site are used to define a settlement rather than its social and economic functions.[5] However, there is little consideration of nonfortified tell sites, in part because very few have been excavated. This reductionist premise limits our ability to appreciate fully the potential variability in a sociospatial landscape and thus directly affects the types of interpretations that can be made.[6] The Late Bronze Age is traditionally characterized by several themes echoed in most of the recent

3. See Gloria A. London, "A Comparison of Two Contemporaneous Lifestyles of the Late Second Millennium B.C.," *BASOR* 273 (1989) 42.

4. The topic of urbanism in the archaeological record is too great to discuss here. See, however, Robert McC. Adams, *The Evolution of Urban Society* (Chicago: Aldine, 1966); Robert McC. Adams and Hans Nissen, *The Uruk Countryside: The Natural Setting of Urban Societies* (Chicago: University of Chicago Press, 1972); Y. V. Andreev, "Urbanization as a Phenomenon of Social History," *Oxford Journal of Archaeology* 8 (1989) 167–77; Robert E. Blanton, "Anthropological Studies of Cities," *Annual Review of Anthropology* 5 (1976) 249–64; Linda Manzanilla (ed.), *Studies in the Neolithic and Urban Revolutions: The V. Gordon Childe Colloquium Mexico* (Oxford: B.A.R., 1986); and Paul Wheatley, "The Concept of Urbanism," in *Man, Settlement and Urbanism* (ed. P. J. Ucko, G. Dimbleby, and R. Tringham; London: Duckworth, 1972) 601–37.

5. For the classic articulation of this perspective, see V. Gordon Childe, "The Urban Revolution," *Town Planning Review* 21 (1950) 1–17. For classificatory schemes of Late Bronze Age and Iron Age settlements, see Jacob J. Baumgarten, "Urbanization in the Late Bronze Age," in *The Architecture of Ancient Israel* (ed. A. Kempinski and R. Reich; Jerusalem: Israel Exploration Society, 1992) 143–50; and Zev Herzog, "Israelite City Planning," *Expedition* 20/4 (1978) 38–43; and "Settlement and Fortification in the Iron Age," in *The Architecture of Ancient Israel*, 231–74.

6. See Brian Hayden, "Village Approaches to Complex Societies," in *Archaeological Views from the Countryside: Village Communities in Early Complex Societies* (ed. Glenn Schwartz and Steven Falconer; Washington, D.C.: Smithsonian, 1994) 198ff.; and Carol Kramer, "Scale, Organization, and Function in Village and Town," in *Archaeological Views from the Countryside*, 210–11. For an important discussion of the effects of stability and instability on sociospatial configurations, see Juval Portugali, "Theoretical Speculations on

synthetic treatments of the period.[7] Internationalism, Egyptian domination, a strictly hierarchical city-state organization, and the presence of an important nonsedentary / pastoral social element are characteristics that serve not only to define Late Bronze Age society but also act as systemic linkages that help to plug the southern Levant into the social, economic, and cultural fabric of a greater Eastern Mediterranean interaction sphere. Data such as imported Cypriot and Mycenaean pottery, cultic and monumental architecture, exotic local and imported small finds, Egyptian material culture and epigraphic data. and contemporary written sources, especially the Amarna Letters and Ugaritic texts, are used to support these characterizations. However, these data are derived from a narrow range of site types, most often tell sites that are implicitly understood as urban, port sites primarily associated with international exchange and sites with an Egyptian administrative and/or military component. All of these site types have a decidedly urban cast to their primary function—either as cities themselves or in their relationship to cities. This urban paradigm cannot help but lead to static and rigid models of cultural change that stress discontinuity and turmoil as evidence of cultural transition. Greater Pan-Mediterranean cultural episodes that shaped the world of the Bronze and Iron Ages are reduced to site-specific events, as viewed through the lens of a particular stratum, building, or ceramic assemblage found at a large fortified site. The enigmatic destruction of Ugarit is an example of this type of cultural historical reconstruction.[8] Thus, the Late Bronze Age is conveniently portrayed as a period of sophisticated internationalism, revolving around urban based palaces and warrior classes, which at the end fell victim to dark forces, such as the Sea Peoples.[9]

---

the Transition from Nomadism to Monarchy," in *From Nomadism to Monarchy: Archaeological and Historical Aspects of Early Israel* (ed. Israel Finkelstein and Nadav Naʾaman; Jerusalem: Israel Exploration Society, 1994) 204–15. For alternative definitions of urbanism, see Roderick McIntosh, "Early Urban Clusters in China and Africa: The Arbitration of Social Ambiguity," *Journal of Field Archaeology* 18 (1991) 199–212; and Susan McIntosh and Roderick McIntosh, "Cities without Citadels: Understanding Urban Origins along the Middle Niger," in *The Archaeology of Africa: Food, Metals and Towns* (ed. T. Shaw et al.; London: Routledge, 1995) 622–41.

7. See Mazar, *The Archeology of the Land of the Bible*, 232–79; Gonen, "The Late Bronze Age," 211–57; and especially Schlomo Bunimovitz, "On the Edge of Empires: Late Bronze Age (1500–1200 B.C.E.)," in *The Archaeology of Society in the Holy Land* (ed. Thomas E. Levy; New York: Facts on File, 1995) 320–31.

8. For a recent view on the destruction of Ugarit, see Marguerite Yon, "The End of the Kingdom of Ugarit," in *The Crisis Years: The 12th Century B.C., from beyond the Danube to the Tigris* (ed. William A. Ward and Martha Sharp Joukowsky; Dubuque, Ia.: Kendall/Hunt, 1992) 111–22. For a more general view, see also Z. Gal, "Iron I in Lower Galilee and the Margins of the Jezreel Valley," in *From Nomadism to Monarchy: Archaeological and Historical Aspects of Early Israel* (ed. Israel Finkelstein and Nadav Naʾaman; Jerusalem: Israel Exploration Society, 1994) 44.

9. For a general overview of issues related to the end of the Late Bronze Age, see James D. Muhly, "The Crisis Years in the Mediterranean World: Transition or Cultural Disintegration," in *The Crisis Years: The 12th Century B.C., from beyond the Danube to the Tigris*

More recently, sociocultural and processual models have emphasized aspects of cultural continuity from the Late Bronze Age to the Iron Age, pointing out an artificiality in interpretation that emphasizes sudden breaks.[10] But even these models, which focus more on cultural continuity embedded within a more dynamic and unstable sociopolitical matrix, maintain the position that the Late Bronze is a period of internationalism and urbanism.[11]

However, missing from these interpretations is a consideration of multiperiod village sites. Such villages are significantly different from either Bronze Age cities or single-period sites, particularly highland settlements of the Iron Age I.[12] The neglect of the these smaller settlements in well-watered areas is understandable. Textual accounts, such as Egyptian topographical lists, tend to ignore or underrepresent such sites, and biblical accounts tend to conflate them, in very broad terms referring to such secondary settlements as *bānôt* and stressing their relationship to major urban sites.[13] And while

---

(ed. William A. Ward and Martha Sharp Joukowsky; Dubuque, Ia.: Kendall/Hunt, 1992) 10–26. See also Nadav Naʾaman, "The 'Conquest of Canaan' in the Book of Joshua and in History," in *From Nomadism to Monarchy: Archaeological and Historical Aspects of Early Israel* (ed. Israel Finkelstein and Nadav Naʾaman; Jerusalem: Israel Exploration Society, 1994) 241.

10. See, for instance, Patrick E. McGovern, "Central Transjordan in the Late Bronze and Early Iron Ages: An Alternative Hypothesis of Socio-Economic Transformation and Collapse," in *Studies in the History and Archaeology of Jordan* (ed. Adnan Hadidi; Amman: Antiquities Authorities, 1987) 3.267–74; David Ussishkin, "Level VII and VI at Tel Lachish and the End of the Late Bronze Age in Canaan," in *Palestine in the Bronze and Iron Ages* (ed. Jonathan Tubb; London: Institute of Archaeology, University of London, 1985) 224–26; and William G. Dever, "The Late Bronze–Early Iron I Horizon in Syria–Palestine: Egyptians, Canaanites, 'Sea People,' and Proto-Israelites," in *The Crisis Years: The 12th Century B.C., from beyond the Danube to the Tigris* (ed. William A. Ward and Martha Joukowsky; Dubuque, Ia.: Kendall/Hunt, 1992) 99–108.

11. See Bunimovitz, "On the Edge of Empires," 320–31.

12. For a comprehensive analysis of the composition of these single-period settlements, see Lawrence E. Stager, "The Archeology of the Family in Ancient Israel," *BASOR* 260 (1985) 1–35. See also Adam Zertal, "'To the Land of the Perrizzites and the Giants': On the Israelite Settlement in the Hill Country of Manasseh," in *From Nomadism to Monarchy: Archaeological and Historical Aspects of Early Israel* (ed. Israel Finkelstein and Nadav Naʾaman; Jerusalem: Yad Yitzhak Ben Zvi, 1994) 47–69; and Israel Finkelstein, "The Emergence of Israel: A Phase in the Cyclic History of Canaan in the Third and Second Millennia B.C.E.," in *From Nomadism to Monarchy*, 151.

13. See, for instance, Josh 15:45, 47; 17:11, 16; Judg 1:27; and 2 Chr 13:19; 28:18. Also note the use of the term *ḥaṣerôt* in Gen 25:16. Yuval Portugali ("Arim, Migrashim and Ḥaserim: The Spatial Organization of Eretz Israel in the 12th–10th Centuries B.C.E.," according to the Bible," *ErIsr* 17 (Brawer Volume; 1984) 282–90 [Hebrew]) suggests that the Late Bronze Age settlement hierarchy was fully integrated, consisting of cities (*ʿirîm*), daughters (*bānôt*) and small sedentary settlements or farmsteads (*ḥaṣerîm*). However the degree of economic and political interaction within this settlement model has never been archaeologically demonstrated.

texts from Ugarit[14] and Alalakh[15] mention villages, it is again only as they relate to their respective urban centers.

Unfortunately, an urbancentric view helps mask the rural underpinnings that are being increasingly recognized in the Bronze and Iron Ages. Already in 1983, Carol Meyers[16] pointed to the significance of villages in the history of premonarchic tribal apportions and anticipated a number of the issues raised by their presence. More recently, Steven Falconer[17] has defined Canaanite society as one of rural complexity, not urban preeminence. In looking at settlement data for the Early and Middle Bronze Ages and building on the work of Rivka Gonen,[18] Falconer has begun to document an extensive village-based society comprised of small sites that display a surprisingly diverse and potentially independent character. Unfortunately, the lack of excavation of rural sites has marginalized this view.[19]

Along with this reassessment of village society, the understanding of the formation and function of Bronze and Iron Age cities is also undergoing some important revision. Israel Finkelstein has persuasively argued that Middle Bronze Age highland centers are essentially small, well-developed strongholds with very small populations.[20] Habitation at the nonelite level was found scattered throughout the hill country, comprised of both sedentary

---

14. See Michael Heltzer, *The Rural Community in Ancient Ugarit* (Wiesbaden: Reichert, 1976); and Michael C. Astour, "Ugarit and the Great Powers," in *Ugarit in Retrospect: Fifty Years of Ugarit and Ugaritic* (ed. Gordon D. Young; Winona Lake, Ind.: Eisenbrauns, 1981) 3–4.

15. See Bonnie Magness-Gardiner, "Urban-Rural Relations in Bronze Age Syria: Evidence from Alalakh Level VII Palace Archives," in *Archaeological Views from the Countryside: Village Communities in Early Complex Societies* (ed. Glenn M. Schwartz and Steven E. Falconer; Washington D.C.: Smithsonian, 1994) 37–47.

16. C. Meyers, "Of Seasons and Soldiers: A Topological Appraisal of the Premonarchic Tribes of Galilee," *BASOR* 252 (1983) 47–59.

17. S. Falconer, "The Development and Decline of Bronze Age Civilization in the Southern Levant: A Reassessment of Urbanism and Ruralism," in *Development and Decline in the Mediterranean Bronze Age* (ed. Clay Mathers and Simon Stoddart; Sheffield Archaeological Monographs 8; Sheffield: Sheffield Academic Press, 1994) 305–33; and Steven E. Falconer, "Village Economy and Society in the Jordan Valley: A Study of Bronze Age Rural Complexity," in *Archaeological Views from the Countryside: Village Communities in Early Complex Societies* (ed. Glenn M. Schwartz and Steven E. Falconer; Washington, D.C.: Smithsonian, 1994) 139.

18. Rivka Gonen, "Urban Canaan in the Late Bronze Period," *BASOR* 253 (1984) 61–73.

19. Amnon Ben-Tor ("Introduction," in Amnon Ben-Tor and Yuval Portugali, *Tell Qiri*, 2) has brought attention to the problem of the disappearance of village sites from the archaeological record.

20. Israel Finkelstein, "Middle Bronze Age 'Fortifications': A Reflection of Social Organization and Political Formations," *Tel Aviv* 19 (1992) 206–16. For more on the demographic aspects of fortified Middle Bronze Age sites, see Schlomo Bunimovitz, "The Middle Bronze Age Fortifications in Palestine as a Social Phenomenon," *Tel Aviv* 19/2 (1992) 230.

and semisedentary elements. In this case the city was primarily made up of public space with cultic, administrative, and redistributive functions.

Gösta Ahlström[21] and Gloria London[22] hold similar views of Iron Age cities. Ahlström interprets the archaeological data from many Iron Age II tells as indicating a relative dearth of domestic architecture. He suggests that much of the population was living in unfortified villages, while only the elite lived within the walls of the political and economic center. London pushes this interpretation back to Iron Age I and argues that the loci of industrial activities, such as pottery production, should be sought outside of the city.[23] When these views are taken together, a more limited role of the city against a backdrop of an extensive rural heartland can be advanced.

One of the factors contributing to an emphasis on urbanism in the Late Bronze Age is the lack of village sites identified through surveys or, more importantly, actually excavated. Unlike in the Middle Bronze Age and Iron Age, the literature gives an impression of a disturbing rural hiatus in the Late Bronze Age.[24] The Amarna Letters have helped reify this impression, as have certain aspects of the archaeological data.[25] Substantial amounts of Cypriot and Mycenaean pottery provide convenient markers for the movement of "elite" status imports,[26] and great emphasis has been placed on the production of other finished goods such as metal tools, ivories, and jewelry.[27] These

---

21. G. Ahlström, "Where Did the Israelites Live?" *JNES* 41 (1982) 133–38.

22. G. London, "Tells: City Center or Home?" *ErIsr* 23 (Biran Volume; 1992) 71*–79*.

23. See Bryant Wood, however (*The Sociology of Pottery in Ancient Palestine: The Ceramic Industry and the Diffusion of Ceramic Style in the Bronze and Iron Ages* [JSOT/ASOR Monographs 4; Sheffield: Sheffield Academic Press, 1990] 34–36), who cites examples of workshops from both urban and village contexts.

24. See n. 1 (above) and also Israel Finkelstein, *The Archaeology of the Israelite Settlement* (Jerusalem: Israel Exploration Society, 1988) 34–117, 339–45; and Rivka Gonen, "Urban Canaan in the Late Bronze Period," *BASOR* 253 (1984) 61–73. Bunimovitz ("On the Edge of Empires," 324) takes note of the rural perspective as articulated by Gonen ("Urban Canaan in the Late Bronze Period") and even London ("A Comparison of Two Contemporaneous Lifestyles") but also stresses the importance and ultimately the dominance of urban centers. Gonen's study was groundbreaking and introduced the significance of ruralism. Her primary interest was in using settlement data to gauge the economic condition of Canaan in the Late Bronze Age. However, she failed to appreciate fully the results of her own study, which serve to demonstrate the potential cultural and economic importance of rural villages as opposed to urban centers. In Gonen's later synthetic treatment, "The Late Bronze Age," she returned to a more traditional interpretation of the period.

25. See, for instance, Nadav Na'aman's historical reconstruction of Late Bronze Age Jerusalem, "Canaanite Jerusalem and Its Central Hill Country Neighbors in the Second Millennium B.C.E.," *UF* 24 (1992) 275ff.

26. See Barry M. Gittlen, "The Cultural and Chronological Implications of the Cypro-Palestinian Trade during the Late Bronze Age," *BASOR* 241 (1981) 49–59; and Albert Leonard, Jr. "Considerations of Morphological Variation in the Mycenaean Pottery from the Southeastern Mediterranean," *BASOR* 241 (1981) 87–101.

27. See Harold Leibowitz, "Late Bronze II Ivory Work in Palestine: Evidence of a Cultural Highpoint," *BASOR* 265 (1987) 3–24; Bunimovitz, "On the Edge of Empires," 325–26; Gonen, "The Late Bronze Age," 236–40, 246–49, 251–57; and A. Bernard Knapp,

are usually seen as the products of a stratified urban society. Conversely, the absence of these markers in the single-period highland sites dated to the Iron I has led to a characterization of that period as one of social and economic simplification.[28] However, it is only the lack of excavation of nonurban sites and the apparent disappearance of Middle Bronze Age single-period settlement systems that support the textual impression of the Late Bronze Age as a wholly urban society in step with the Greater Eastern Mediterranean Co-Prosperity Sphere.[29]

Is the settlement landscape of the Late Bronze Age truly restricted to urban centers? A careful reading of both the historical and archaeological data would argue otherwise. This does not appear to be the case at Ugarit, where texts make very clear references to a hinterland. At times, Ugarit controlled up to two hundred adjacent villages that had clear economic connections to the urban core.[30] However, does this same model apply to the southern Levant, where little is known about the hinterland? The internal organization of unfortified Late Bronze and Iron Age villages along with their relationship to urban centers can only be guessed, for few have been systematically excavated. The appearance of rural villages raises a number of important questions. What is the degree of complexity found at the village level and how might it affect our understanding of the social, political, and economic dimensions of Late Bronze Age city-states? Were villages the loci of cultural innovation or conservatism, continuity or dislocation? How will the archaeology of villages affect the models developed to explain culture change and systemic collapse during the Late Bronze II–Iron Age I transition? And how

---

"Response: Independence, Imperialism, and the Egyptian Factor," *BASOR* 275 (1989) 67. For specific comments on the condition of the Canaanite economy in the Late Bronze Age, see Nadav Naʾaman, "Economic Aspects of the Egyptian Occupation of Canaan," *IEJ* 31 (1981) 172–85; Shmuel Aḥituv, "Economic Factors in the Egyptian Conquest of Canaan," *IEJ* 28 (1978) 93–105; and A. Bernard Knapp, *Society and Polity at Bronze Age Pella: An Annales Perspective* (JSOT/ASOR Monographs 6; Sheffield: Sheffield Academic Press, 1993) 38, 50, 83–84.

28. See Finkelstein, *Israelite Settlement*, 355–56; also note that in part 3 ("Material Culture," 237–91), the only categories discussed are architecture and pottery, suggesting the limitations of "Early Israelite" material culture. See also Finkelstein, "The Emergence of Israel," 164–70. A similar impression of a very limited material culture assemblage is found in Amihai Mazar, "The Iron Age I," in *The Archaeology of Ancient Israel* (ed. Amnon Ben-Tor; trans. R. Greenberg; New Haven: Yale University Press, 1992) 287–94.

29. See Schlomo Bunimovitz, "Socio-Political Transformations in the Central Hill Country in the Late Bronze–Iron I Transition," in *From Nomadism to Monarchy: Archaeological and Historical Aspects of Early Israel* (ed. Israel Finkelstein and Nadav Naʾaman; Jerusalem: Israel Exploration Society, 1994) 198–99.

30. Heltzer (*The Rural Community in Ancient Ugarit*, 7) estimates there were between 180 and 200 villages under Ugarit's control. Marguerite Yon ("The End of the Kingdom of Ugarit," 113) estimates that in the thirteenth century there were approximately 150 villages with a rural population of 25,000 within the kingdom of Ugarit.

are we to understand the presumed shift in the ethnic landscape during this transition in the context of continually occupied villages?

These are the sorts of queries that the excavations of Tell ʿEin Zippori and Tell el-Wawiyat were designed to address. These sites provide rare opportunities to examine the transition from the Late Bronze to the Iron Age from a village or rural perspective and, based on the preliminary results of these excavations, it is possible to suggest an alternative reconstruction of the sociocultural landscape of the Late Bronze and Iron Ages in Israel.

Village Sites of the Lower Galilee: Tell ʿEin Zippori and Tell el-Wawiyat

The site of Tell ʿEin Zippori[31] is situated in the Nazareth Basin, 5 km northwest of the modern city of Nazareth and 8 km south of Tell el-Wawiyat (see fig. 1). Prominent Bronze Age tell sites in the area include Tell Hannaton (Arabic Tell Bedeiwiyeh), 6 km to the north, and Tell Gath-Hepher (Arabic Khirbet ez-Zurra), 2.6 km to the east. Tell ʿEin Zippori is located in an area of low sloping hills ranging in height from 200 to 300 m, referred to as Givat ʾAllonim.[32] The area is comprised of chalky soil with a *nari* limestone crust, which limits its agricultural potential. However, the site itself lies in a small alluvial valley along the Nahal Zippori, which is covered with *terra rosa* and rendzina soils. It is adjacent to one of the only currently active springs in the Galilee, giving the site its name, ʿEin Zippori.[33]

The site is one hectare in size and about 5 m in height (see fig. 2), with two distinct tiers. The northern quarter of the tell is between 2 and 3 m lower than the central, upper part of the site. Three fields of excavation have been opened, covering 305 sq.m. Field I is located on the upper tier, and Field II on the lower. Field III was opened on the western slope of the site in 1994. It appears that both the northern and western sides of the site have been artificially cut, probably during the last two hundred years, in order to increase the area of the valley under cultivation.[34] Other human modifications to the tell include the construction of a circular well located on its eastern slope. Based

---

31. J. P. Dessel, "Tell ʿEin Zippori," *OEANE* 2.227–28; J. P. Dessel, Eric Meyers, and Carol Meyers, "Tell ʿEin Zippori," *IEJ* 47 (1997) 268–71; and J. P. Dessel, Eric Meyers, and Carol Meyers, "Tell ʿEin Zippori," *IEJ* 45 (1995) 288–92. See also the preliminary discussion by Carol L. Meyers, "Sepphoris in Lower Galilee: Earliest Times through the Persian Period," *Sepphoris in Galilee: Crosscurrents of Culture* (ed. R. M. Nagy et al.; Raleigh, N.C.: North Carolina Museum of Art, 1996) 15–19.

32. See Zvi Gal, *Lower Galilee during the Iron Age* (ASOR Dissertation Series 8; trans. M. R. Josephy; Winona Lake, Ind.: Eisenbrauns, 1992) 2–3. For a general description of the environment and ecology of the Lower Galilee, see chap. 1, "Ecological Environment," 1–11; also see Efraim Orni and Elisha Efrat, *Geography of Israel* (Jerusalem: Israel Program for Scientific Translations, 1964) 61–64; and Denis Baly, *The Geography of the Bible* (rev. ed.; New York: Harper & Row, 1974) 157–63.

33. See Gal, *Lower Galilee*, 4–5, 10; and idem, "Iron I in Lower Galilee," 35.

34. See ibid., 42.

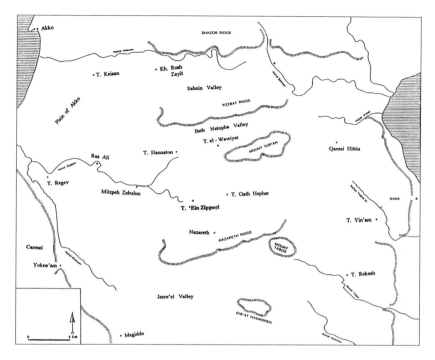

Fig. 1. Map of Lower Galilee (adapted from Gal 1992: fig. 6.1).

on the method and style of its construction and ethnographic data, we can determine that it was probably built within the last two hundred years. Closer to the center of the tell there are indications of another well of a similar date. It would appear that access to water was never a problem at the site.

The other site that is considered here is Tell el-Wawiyat.[35] It is located in the southwest quarter of the Beit Netofa Valley (Arabic Sahl el-Battof), about midway between Tiberias and Haifa. The Beit Netofa Valley is one of the largest valleys in the southern Levant, covering 46 sq. km. The alluvium in the Beit Netofa Valley is very rich, and the area receives sufficient water for dry farming, making it highly suitable for an agriculturally based economy.[36] A geomorphological study around the site has shown that a wadi probably ran through the valley north of the tell, providing an additional water source for an area in which springs are rare.[37]

35. See Beth Alpert-Nakhai, J. P. Dessel, and Bonnie L. Wisthoff, "Tell el-Wawiyat, 1986," *IEJ* 37 (1988) 181–85; Beth Alpert-Nakhai, J. P. Dessel, and Bonnie L. Wisthoff, "Tell el-Wawiyat, 1987," *IEJ* 39 (1989) 102–4; and Alpert-Nakhai, Dessel, and Wisthoff, "Tell el-Wawiyat," *NEAEHL* 4.1500–1501.
36. Gal, *Lower Galilee*, 2–3; and Orni and Efrat, *Geography of Israel*, 63.
37. Arlene Rosen, personal communication; and also see Gal, *Lower Galilee*, 5.

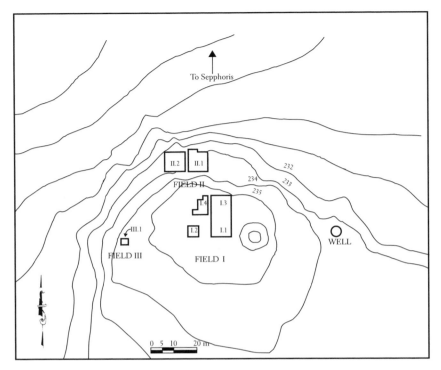

Fig. 2. Topographic plan of Tell ʿEin Zippori.

The valley itself is part of a series of four east–west intermontane valleys that comprise the Lower Galilee.[38] The Beit Netofa Valley was not a major east–west route in the Late Bronze Age, due to its topographic circumscription and winter flooding.[39] While the majority of east–west traffic flowed through the Jezreel Valley to the south, there was at least one route that passed through Tell Hannaton and on to the Sea of Galilee or the Jordan Valley.[40] The western end of the valley is dominated by Tell Hannaton (Tell

38. From north to south, the valleys of the Lower Galilee include the Beit Hakerem Valley (esh-Shaghur), Sakhnim Valley, Beit Netofa Valley, and the Turʾan Basin (or Rimmon Valley [Gal, *Lower Galilee*, 2]). See also Yohanan Aharoni, *The Land of the Bible: A Historical Geography* (rev. ed.; trans. A. F. Rainey; Philadelphia: Westminster, 1979) 28; Orni and Efrat, *Geography of Israel*, 64, fig. 37; and Baly, *Geography of the Bible*, map 56.

39. Gal, *The Lower Galilee*, 5; idem, "Iron I in Lower Galilee," 35; and personal observation.

40. An east–west route across the Beit Netofa Valley has been proposed but is somewhat problematic. Aharoni (*The Land of the Bible*, 61) and Bustani Oded ("Darb el-Hawarnah-

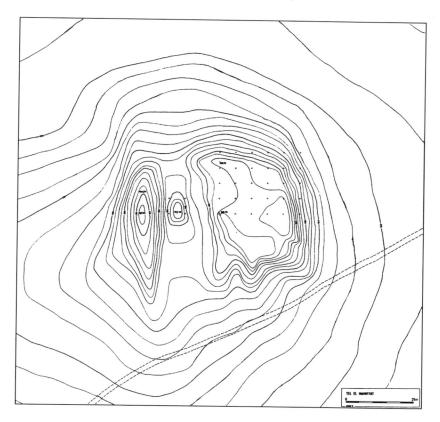

Fig. 3. Topographic plan of Tell el-Wawiyat.

Ancient Highway," *ErIsr* 10 [Shazar Volume; 1971] 191) discuss the importance of the Darb el-Hawarnah, an Ottoman road linking the Hauran and northern Transjordan to the Mediterranean Coast. Aapeli Saarisalo (*The Boundary between Issachar and Naphtali: An Archaeological and Literary Study of Israel's Settlement in Canaan* [Helsinki: Soumalaisen Tiedeakatemian Toimituksia, 1927] 23–24) had already suggested that a similar route was used in the Late Bronze and Iron Ages. Y. Aharoni and David Dorsey (*The Roads and Highways of Ancient Israel* [Baltimore: Johns Hopkins University Press, 1991] 105ff.) and Gal (*Lower Galilee*, 8–9) follow Saarisalo; however, this route probably did not actually go through the entire Beit Netofa Valley but rather, as Aharoni (p. 61) points out, only the western part of it. Dorsey's excellent study of ancient road systems in Israel suggests that this route, T1 (p. 105, map 5), ran from Akko through Hannaton to Rimmon and then over to either the Sea of Galilee via Carnei Hittin or the Jordan Valley and Tell 'Ubeidiya, through Tell Adami. In either case the position of Rimmon (Khirbet Rummana) is actually along a small pass leading from the southwestern part of the Beit Netofa Valley into the Tur'an Basin. Any Late Bronze or Iron Age road, along with the Ottoman road, probably followed the modern road, which ran through Tur'an Valley just to the south of the Beit

Bedeiwiyeh), a 5-hectare site identified as the Hinnatuni of the Amarna Letters.[41] Besides Hannaton, Tell el-Wawiyat is the only other archaeological site on the valley floor. Several small sites and sherd scatters ring the northern and southern edges of the valley, though they are always located on the limestone bedrock of the mountain chains.[42]

Tell el-Wawiyat is a low, flat mound 0.4 hectares in size and rising only 3.5 m above the valley floor (see figs. 1 and 3). Over the course of two field seasons, thirteen 6 × 6-meter squares were excavated, twelve of which are on the eastern half of the site. The site is ringed on all four sides by noticeable elevated areas, giving the site a characteristic tell profile. However, the northern and eastern rises were found to be walls constructed of large boulders comprising up to two courses, though they were found floating in Iron I debris. Both the northern and eastern walls' lines were constructed well after the Iron I abandonment and were probably formed in field-clearing activities by local farmers. Disassociating these walls from the site's Late Bronze and Iron Age history reduced the size of the site roughly by a third.

Each site has stratified deposits dating from the Middle Bronze Age through the Iron Age. Additionally, the excavation of both sites does not support the stratigraphic sequence suggested by Gal in his survey of the Lower Galilee.[43] This raises some concern regarding the accuracy of surface surveys and the subsequent derivation of settlement patterns.[44] Gal reported that a large percentage of the sherds recovered in survey from Tell 'Ein Zippori date to the Persian and Hellenistic periods.[45] Additionally, he reported that

---

Netofa Valley. Additionally, the Beit Netofa Valley was in all likelihood impassable during the winter and early spring because it usually was flooded (see above, n. 29). Thus, the predominant use of T1 was probably for summer and autumn traffic heading east from Akko and the Akko Plain. Hannaton probably was more vital as a node on the north–south route from Megiddo and Shimron north to Akko and Phoenicia (Dorsey, The Roads and Highways, 91–92, 105–6).

41. See EA 8 and EA 245 (William Moran, The Amarna Letters [Baltimore: Johns Hopkins University Press, 1992] 16–17, 299–300).

42. All of the following sites (followed by Gal's numbering) are described by Gal (Lower Galilee, 23–27) as located on fringes or bedrock outcroppings along the sides of the Beit Netofa Valley: Khirbet Ruma (1.39), Khirbet el-Lun (1.40), Khirbet Rigma [Rujma] (1.46), and Khirbet Netofa (1.47). See also Gal's settlement-pattern maps for the Late Bronze Age: fig. 4.2 (p. 57); Iron Age I: fig. 6.1 (p. 85); and Iron Age II: fig. 7.2 (p. 97). Similar conclusions were arrived at by Alexander Joffe ("An Archaeological Survey in the Area of Tell el-Wawiyat, Lower Galilee," unpub. MS, 1987).

43. Gal, Lower Galilee, 16, 25.

44. For a discussion of some of these problems, see Yuval Portugali, "A Field Methodology for Regional Archaeology (The Jezreel Valley Survey, 1981)," Tel Aviv 9 (1982) 170–88; and Amnon Ben-Tor, "Introduction," in Tell Qiri: A Village in the Jezreel Valley (Qedem 24; Jerusalem: Israel Exploration Society, 1987) 3.

45. Gal, Lower Galilee, 16. In the four seasons of excavation, only a very minimal amount of Persian pottery and no Hellenistic pottery has been found.

Fig. 4. Tell ʿEin Zippori: Area II.1—facing west, Stratum VI (Late Bronze I), top and right.

both sites yielded significant quantities of Iron Age II and Ottoman pottery.[46] Excavation did not support Gal's results, and his settlement-pattern maps must be used very carefully.

In the case of the tenth century B.C.E., Gal is not alone in positing a notable increase in the number of small sites.[47] However, the excavations of Tell el-Wawiyat and Tell ʿEin Zippori have shown that in situ Iron II material is either very scanty or entirely absent. Some reevaluation of the Iron II settlement pattern is warranted, especially in well-watered areas, where the effectiveness of survey techniques developed for arid lands might not be as appropriate.[48] In the Iron Age, survey results perhaps reflect the establish-

46. While Stratum II is dated to the ninth century, it appears to be a very small settlement limited to the western edge of the site. No in situ Ottoman remains have been found and almost no Ottoman pottery.

47. For example, see Avi Ofer, "'All the Hill Country of Judah': From a Settlement Fringe to a Prosperous Monarchy," in *From Nomadism to Monarchy: Archaeological and Historical Aspects of Early Israel* (ed. Israel Finkelstein and Nadav Naʾaman; Jerusalem: Israel Exploration Society, 1994) 102–6, figs. 5 and 6; and Israel Finkelstein, "The Emergence of Israel," 158–160, 163; see especially fig. 6.

48. See E. B. Banning, "Highlands and Lowlands: Problems and Survey Frameworks for Rural Archaeology in the Near East," *BASOR* 301 (1996) 25–27, 29ff.; and Portugali, "A Field Methodology for Regional Archaeology."

ment of isolated farmsteads and not actual village settlements, which would significantly affect our understanding of the tenth century B.C.E.

Eight strata have so far been identified at Tell ʿEin Zippori, with continuous occupation from the Middle Bronze II/III through the tenth century B.C.E. (Iron II), followed by a gap and then a brief reoccupation in the ninth century B.C.E. Periods represented by scanty sherd material include Roman, Hellenistic, Persian, and the Early Bronze IB. Five major strata have been identified at Tell el-Wawiyat, ranging from the Middle Bronze II/III to the eleventh century B.C.E. Other periods represented by pottery include substantial quantities of Late Bronze I material and a few Early Bronze I sherds.

The earliest securely stratified deposits at both sites date to the Middle Bronze II/II. Stratum VII at Tell ʿEin Zippori is represented by a beaten-earth surface and a mudbrick wall with a stone socle securely sealed by a Stratum VI (Late Bronze I) beaten-earth surface. A large pithos fragment points to a Middle Bronze II/III date and pushes back the temporal roots of the site several centuries. The earliest stratified deposits at Tell el-Wawiyat consist of two Middle Bronze II/III jar burials. Both jars contained poorly preserved infants and one sub-adult. Grave goods consisted of small ceramic vessels, including a Tell el-Yehudiyah juglet, a ceramic stopper, a basalt pestle, a flint blade fragment, and a few sheep/goat bones. Jar burials are relatively common in the Middle Bronze Age throughout Canaan,[49] and it does not appear that the site was actually occupied in the Middle Bronze Age. These burials might indicate close contact with Hannaton to the west.

Though there is no stratified Late Bronze I level at Tell el-Wawiyat, there is a considerable amount of Late Bronze I pottery, and it is likely that the site was first occupied in this period.

Significant remains of a Late Bronze I phase have been exposed at Tell ʿEin Zippori. In Stratum VI, a well-preserved beaten-earth surface was found throughout the four excavated rooms (see fig. 4). The most important feature is a long north–south wall, comprised of small- to large-sized boulders built on a foundation footing of cyclopean stones. The southern end of this wall has a niche on its eastern face. A storage jar was found resting in this niche, along with a basalt pestle.

To the east of this wall is a large open area. A thick layer of destruction debris, comprised of burned mudbrick and detritus, rests above a partially plastered surface. A concentration of small store jars and basalt pestles was found on this surface. Other finds include several pieces of worked pumice, a faience bead, and a possible bronze spear point. In the western half of the area, three rooms have been identified. A large group of restorable vessels was

---

49. In general, see: Rachel S. Hallote, "Mortuary Archaeology and the Middle Bronze Age Southern Levant," *Journal of Mediterranean Archaeology* 8/1 (1995) 97–98, 102; A. Mazar, *The Archaeology of the Land of the Bible*, 214; and David Ilan, "The Dawn of Internationalism—The Middle Bronze Age," in *The Archaeology of Society in the Holy Land* (ed. Thomas E. Levy; New York: Facts on File, 1995) 297–318, esp. 318, fig. 2.1d.

Fig. 5. Tell ʿEin Zippori: Area II.1—facing north, Stratum V (Late Bronze II) in foreground, Stratum VI (Late Bronze I) in lower right and top.

found in the middle room, along with fragments of imported pottery including LB I Bichrome Ware, Chocolate-on-White Ware, Cypriot White Slip I, and Cypriot Grey Burnished Bottles. It appears that the Late Bronze I settlement was destroyed.

The Late Bronze II is represented at both sites. In Stratum V at Tell ʿEin Zippori, a new building erected over the earlier Stratum VI structure exhibits a new orientation (see fig. 5). This building is 15 m in length, with rooms built up against its southern side. Parts of a Stratum VI wall (1079) appear to have been rebuilt in Stratum V. At Tell el-Wawiyat, Stratum IV architectural remains are limited to a narrow triangular area and include a tabun constructed from a typical Late Bronze II cooking pot.

Along with local pottery, both sites have a range of Cypriot imports including Base Ring I and II, Monochrome, White Shaved Ware, White Slip II, and White Painted VI. A few Mycenaean IIIB imports were also found. Tell el-Wawiyat also has examples of less-common Cypriot imports such as a White Painted VI rattle and a Base Ring II Bull (see fig. 6). At Tell el-Wawiyat the imports probably arrived via Tell Hannaton, an unobstructed 5-km walk to the west. Hannaton and even Tell Keisan in the Akko Plain could have been key redistribution nodes for Tell ʿEin Zippori (see fig. 1).

In 1996 an almost complete lead figurine was found at Tell ʿEin Zippori in a mixed debris layer, though most of the pottery dates to the Late Bronze

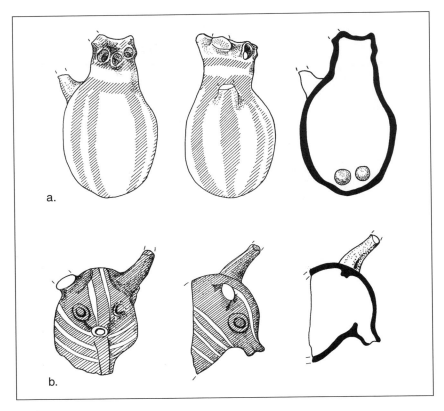

Fig. 6. Tell el-Wawiyat, Late Bronze II Cypriot imports.
a. White painted VI rattle. b. Base ring II bull.

II (see fig. 7a).[50] This figurine is only 6.5 cm long and does not conveniently fit into any existing typology.[51] Lead figurines are usually associated with an

50. See Carol L. Meyers, "Figurine of a Nude Female," in *Sepphoris in Galilee: Cross-currents of Culture* (ed. R. M. Nagy et al.; Raleigh, N.C.: North Carolina Museum of Art, 1996) 154–55.

51. Ora Negbi's *Canaanite Gods in Metal: An Archaeological Study of Ancient Syro-Palestinian Figurines* (Tel Aviv: Tel Aviv University Press, 1976) remains a very useful typological study of metal figurines. Unfortunately, the head and hair of the Tell ʿEin Zippori figurine are not clearly modeled, making their classification difficult. The placement of the figurine's hands, cupping her breasts, is a common motif in Levantine figurines; see, e.g., figs. 88 (#1567), 75 (#1525), 82 (#1542), and 87 (#1555). While the Tell ʿEin Zippori figurine does not seem to fit clearly into any of Negbi's types, it is somewhat reminiscent of Negbi's female figurines type I, class B, group d, the "Byblos" group (p. 73, fig. 88, pl. 43), which are described as bareheaded and have examples in which the arms support the breasts, two characteristics of the Tell ʿEin Zippori figurine.

Fig. 7a. Tell ʿEin Zippori: Late Bronze II lead figurine.
Fig. 7b. Tell el-Wawiyat: Late Bronze II mother and child plaque.

Anatolian tradition and are relatively uncommon in Israel.[52] Carol Meyers has suggested that this small figurine should be classified as an amulet or votive.[53] At Tell el-Wawiyat, a most unusual ceramic plaque was found (see fig. 7b). It depicts a mother, holding her child in her left arm. The degree of naturalism and the depth of the molding produce a striking effect, and while the mother-with-child motif is common throughout the Near East, this particular type of plaque figurine is unusual in the southern Levant.

Both sites continue into the Iron Age I, and there is no indication of any break in occupation at Tell ʿEin Zippori. The Stratum V building continued in use in Stratum IV, though with some modifications (see fig. 8). Three stone bins were found to the north of this wall in a large outdoor courtyard, along with several ceramic installations consisting of the inverted tops of collar-rim store jars. One of these installations appears to have been used as a

52. See ibid., 8, 60, 70, 73.
53. Meyers, "Figurine of a Nude Female," 155.

Fig. 8. Tell ʿEin Zippori: Area II.1 — facing east, Stratum IV (Early Iron I) building on right, Stratum III (Late Iron I) house on left.

tabun. The absence of imported pottery along with clear ceramic indicators point to the early twelfth century B.C.E. and suggest overall continuity from Late Bronze II to Iron I.

At Tell el-Wawiyat new structures are built along a different orientation in Stratum III . Building L13 is oriented to the cardinal directions and has unusual interior architectural elements, which point to a nondomestic function (see fig. 9). A poorly preserved tabun made from an inverted store-jar rim was set into the floor against the western wall. In the center of the room is an unusual circular installation made of used basalt grinding stones set above a soft limestone basin. North of the installation is a cylindrical stone column base. The architecture and installations within the room are all carefully aligned with the grinding stone / basin installation in the center as the focal point. The only evidence at the site of any hewn masonry and wall plaster is found in this room. In the southwest anteroom, a partially articulated butchered cow was found. Other finds include several restorable chalices and a geometric Hyksos scarab, which was probably a curated heirloom. Tentatively, a cultic or public function can be ascribed to this room.

The southern room of Building L13 is also unusual. It consists of a circular bin circumscribed by three right-angle walls. Small finds from the debris within the room include a steatite jewelry mold, a bronze spear, a delicate basalt tripod bowl, a fragment of an Astarte figurine, and a piece of gold leaf

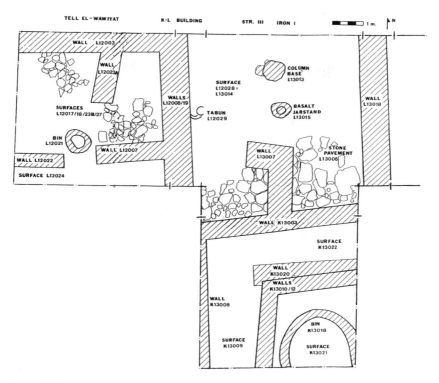

Fig. 9. Tell el-Wawiyat: Plan of Building L13—Stratum III (Iron I).

(see fig. 10a–c). A limestone mold used for agricultural tool production was also found at the site. Tell el-Wawiyat site was abandoned at the end of the Iron Age I, probably in the early eleventh century B.C.E.

It appears that Tell 'Ein Zippori was rebuilt in the late eleventh / early tenth centuries B.C.E., Stratum III, with some conscious attempt at intrasite spatial differentiation. Field II, which covers the lower terrace, was reserved as domestic space. A large rectangular structure appears to represent a partial version of a four-room house. The interior floor of the building is comprised of a well-constructed cobble surface, which served as a footing for a pier. Three stone pillar bases are oriented in an east–west alignment. In most four-room houses the central room is cobbled; however, the variability of this architectural type is so great that it mitigates against its value as a significant cultural feature.

To the west of the building, two cells were constructed and filled with small fieldstone boulders. These cells served to create an artificial fill used to raise the northern part of the tell. The entire area to the south of the building

Fig. 10. Tell el-Wawiyat: Small Finds from Stratum III (Iron I).
a. Steatite jewelry mold.   b. Basalt tripod bowl.   c. Limestone metal tool mold.

was open and sloped down from the vertical face at the foot of the upper terrace. The slope of the exterior open area must have created an erosional problem that was not solved by the construction of the narrow drain to the west of
the building. In a second phase, an additional drainage trough was added to
channel water around the southwest corner of the building.

This building originally extended further to the north. Excavation up to
the present edge of the tell suggests that this northern end was cut back
after the final abandonment of the site. The modification of the northern
edge of the lower terrace was probably undertaken in order to increase the
area of cultivation in the valley basin. A similar circumstance is found on
the western side of the site.

To the west of this building, in Area II.2, a series of three parallel walls
demarcates a minimum of three terraces, which climb the northern slope of
the site (see fig. 11). The southernmost terrace wall is over 11 m long and over
1 m wide. Rectangular rooms were built along both sides of this wall. There
are at least three distinct occupational phases, differentiated by the resurfac-
ing of both cobbled and beaten earth floors. The material culture found in

Fig. 11. Tell 'Ein Zippori: Area II.2—facing south, Stratum III (Late Iron I) domestic area.

this area is clearly domestic in nature. Some noteworthy small finds include a few thumb-impressed stamp handles (see fig. 12), a few metal fragments, and beads of carnelian and faience.[54]

In Field I, excavation focused on a large, well-constructed multiroom building complex, Building A, which measures at least 16 m × 14 m (see fig. 13). Building A can be divided into two units: a northern bench room and a southern enclosed area. It was built on an earthen foundation consisting of a deliberate deep fill that served to raise the level of Field I almost 2 m above that of Field II. This fill is almost sterile, with the latest material dating to the late eleventh century B.C.E. This raised fill would have made this building a very prominent feature on the site and also probably along the Nahal Zippori.

The focal point of Building A appears to be the large, open bench room, which measures at least 11 × 7 m. Its northern extent has not yet been reached. The bench itself lines the northern side of the back wall. In the northwest corner of the room, part of a rectangular platform was found. It is at least 3 sq. m and aligned with the bench. This installation is comprised of a low mudbrick platform lined with cobbles. A few very poorly preserved

54. See John S. Jorgensen, "Impressed Storejar Handles," in *Sepphoris in Galilee: Crosscurrents of Culture* (ed. Rebecca Martin Nagy et al.; Raleigh, N.C.: North Carolina Museum of Art, 1996) 158.

Fig. 12. Tell ʿEin Zippori: Impressed/stamped store jar handles—
Stratum III (Late Iron I).

traces of plaster were found on top of the mudbrick. In the southeast is a triangular room in which two large flat stones appear deliberately to have been
set into the beaten earth surface. The smaller stone is likely to have been a
seat and the larger one a work surface. The bench room communicates with
the southern part of the complex through a very well-made threshold that
uses hewn masonry for its door jambs and cobbling within the threshold area
itself.

The southern part of the complex is comprised of two interior walls abutting the southern wall, creating a nonsymmetrical tripartite division to the
large rectangular area behind the bench room. The central room has a second well-made threshold, which communicates with the eastern room. The
western room is much narrower than the eastern two rooms. Parallel to the
western room is a narrow corridor which stretches from the southern wall of
the complex into the bench room. Building A is surrounded to the southeast
by the corners of two other contemoraneous buildings.

A beaten-earth surface covers the interior of the structure. Thick deposits
of burned mudbrick debris were found within the building, suggesting that it
was destroyed sometime in the early tenth century B.C.E. Other than some restorable Iron I store jars, little else was left in any of the interior rooms, and it
appears to have been deliberately emptied prior to its destruction. The only
notable small finds are thumb-impressed stamped handles.

Field III was opened along the western slope of the tell, in part to answer
definitively any questions regarding the issue of fortification. The ridge along
the western side of the site represented an almost identical situation to that

Fig. 13. Tell 'Ein Zippori: Field I—facing southwest, Building A, Stratum III (Late Iron I–late eleventh / early tenth century B.C.E.).

found at Tell el-Wawiyat. It was an obviously late accumulation of well-aligned stones, probably reflecting field-clearing activities by local farmers. Part of a pillared structure was found, including the building's eastern wall, a stone bench, and a set of two stone pillars that served as roof supports (see fig. 14). A series of four beaten-earth surfaces were excavated, each containing restorable pottery. This building has a different orientation than the eleventh-century B.C.E. settlement found in Fields I and II. It appears that it was an isolated domestic structure on the western side of the tell. Stratum II represents the only in situ, ninth-century B.C.E. material as yet found on the site.

The Late Bronze Age:
A View from the Levantine Hinterland

The addition of permanent multiperiod village sites to the Bronze Age settlement spectrum is long overdue. It fills the conceptual void between stable, long-enduring urban settlements and highly volatile, relatively ephemeral single-period sites and thereby provides a means of more accurately assessing the level of complexity found at either extreme. That a wider range of sociospatial arrangements existed in both the Late Bronze Age and Iron Age I has significant repercussions for our understanding of these periods.

Fig. 14. Tell ʿEin Zippori: Field II—facing south, Stratum II (Iron II) pillared building.

The appearance of typical Late Bronze IIA Cypriot imports such as Base Ring I and II and White Slip II should not be unexpected at a village. The distribution of these vessels extends throughout the entire Levant, and their appearance in nonurban contexts helps reconfirm the impression that by the Late Bronze II, Cypriot pottery thoroughly saturated all levels of Canaanite society.[55] However, the appearance of relatively rare Late Bronze I Cypriot imports along with local fine wares, such as Chocolate-on-White ware, is unexpected, because this material is much less common in the southern Levant. This suggests that luxury goods circulated in a more complex manner than previously understood. Villages may well have been more fully integrated into the newly developing exchange system that began to emerge after the Egyptian destruction of many urban sites at the close of the Middle Bronze Age.[56] In the wake of those destructions and concomitant socio-economic dislocations, a range of new opportunities presented themselves, and the urban dominance over the Middle Bronze Age social landscape was given a severe jolt.

---

55. In general, see Gittlen, "Cultural and Chronological Implications," 52–55.

56. In general, see Bunimovitz, "Socio-Political Transformations in the Central Hill Country," 181–86, and bibliography.

There are some indications that the Egyptians did not allow destroyed urban centers, such as Megiddo, Lachish, and Jaffa, to be completely rebuilt.[57] This type of more intrusive Egyptian involvement in the southern Levant may have briefly shifted local attention toward new settlements that would escape Egyptian attention. Villages may have emerged that emulated or even replaced urban sites as important social and economic nodes. The exchange and distribution of imported and regional pottery may reflect these processes. Perhaps the success of imported pottery redistribution, in terms of local acceptance and distribution to the interior in the Late Bronze I, helped stimulate the Cypriot ceramic export industry, which reached its zenith in the Late Bronze IIA.[58] The redistribution of regionally made fine wares is also evident. Chocolate-on-White Ware, which according to Leonard[59] may have been produced at the site of Katarat es-Samra in the Jordan Valley, and Palestinian Bichrome Ware, which was produced both locally at Megiddo and in Cyprus,[60] are both found at Tell ʿEin Zippori.

There are other examples of village-based production of elite-status goods that have been overlooked, especially at specialized sites. At Nahariyah, figurines and molds were found, and ceramic production has been documented at Tell el-Hayyat.[61] Both are cult sites and should be understood in a somewhat

57. Gonen has suggested that in the cases of Megiddo, Jaffa, and Lachish monumental gates remained intact in the Late Bronze Age, though they were no longer connected to actual fortification walls. These gates would have functioned as key social, political, and economic loci within the unfortified city; see Gonen, "The Late Bronze Age," 218–19; and idem, "Urban Canaan," 69–70. See also Knapp, *Society and Polity at Bronze Age Pella*, 80. For Megiddo, see Gordon Loud, *Megiddo II* (Chicago: University of Chicago Press, 1948) figs. 381, 382. For Lachish, see David Ussishkin, "Excavations at Tell Lachish, 1973–1977: Preliminary Report," *Tel Aviv* 5 (1978) 45; and idem, "Excavations at Tell Lachish, 1978–1983: Second Preliminary Report," *Tel Aviv* 10 (1983) 169–70. For Jaffa, see Jacob Kaplan, "The Archaeology and History of Tel-Aviv-Jaffa," *BA* 35 /3 (1972) 78–82; and Jacob Kaplan and Haya Ritter-Kaplan, "Jaffa," *NEAEHL* 2.656–57. For an alternative view of the transition from the Middle to Late Bronze Ages, see Bunimovitz, "On the Edge," 322–23.

58. Gittlen, "Cultural and Chronological Implications," 51; Albert Leonard, Jr., "The Late Bronze Age," *BA* 52/1 (1989) 21, 31.

59. Ibid., 11; and idem, "Kattarat es-Samra 1985," *AfO* 33 (1986) 166.

60. Based on neutron activation analysis; see Michal Artzy, F. Asaro, and I. Perlman, "The Origin of the 'Palestinian' Bichrome Ware," *JAOS* 93(1973) 452ff.; Michal Artzy, F. Asaro, and I. Perlman, "The Tel Nagila Bichrome Krater as a Cypriot Product," *IEJ* 25 (1975) 133; and Michal Artzy, I. Perlman, and F. Asaro, "Imported and Local Bichrome Ware in Megiddo," *Levant* 10 (1978) 100–102, 106–7.

61. For Nahariyah, see Moshe Dothan, "The Excavation at Nahariyah: Preliminary Report (Season 1954/55)," *IEJ* 6 (1956) 20–21, pls. 5–6. For Tell el-Hayyat, see Steven E. Falconer and Bonnie Magness-Gardiner, with Mary C. Metzger, "Preliminary Report of the First Season of the Tell el-Hayyat Project," *BASOR* 255 (1984) 54–55; and Steven E. Falconer, "Village Pottery Production and Exchange: A Jordan Valley Perspective," in *Studies in the History and Archaeology of Jordan III* (ed. Adnan Hadidi; Amman: Department of Antiquities, 1987) 252ff.; idem, "The Development and Decline of Bronze Age Civilization," 133–34, 137; and idem, "Rural Responses to Early Urbanism: Bronze Age Household and Village Economy at Tell el-Hayyat, Jordan," *Journal of Field Archaeology* 22 (1995) 399–419.

different light from rural villages; however, these sites clearly demonstrate that craft production in the highly urbanized Middle Bronze Age was not confined to urban centers.[62] Katarat es-Samra and its production of Chocolate-on-White Ware is an excellent Late Bronze Age example of this same craft organization.[63] The manufacture of jewelry and weapons at Tell el-Wawiyat similarly demonstrates the economic vitality of villages down into Iron Age I.

In these cases villages played an important role in stimulating and supporting emerging interregional and international economic networks and by extension demonstrate some degree of social stratification.[64] The excavation results from Tell ʿEin Zippori and Tell el-Wawiyat suggest a level of rural complexity that challenges the notion of a narrowly construed urban society. The archaeological data presented here confirm that villages indeed functioned as both producers and consumers of elite-status goods.

Conquest and Continuity at the Rural Level

One of the most controversial topics in Bronze and Iron Age studies is the Israelite Settlement of Canaan. While the complexities of this question cannot be resolved by the excavations of Tell ʿEin Zippori and Tell el-Wawiyat, a village perspective can offer some new insights.

Israel Finkelstein's and Adam Zertal's surveys in the Central Highlands[65] have uncovered over 200 sites that they define as Israelite, in part based on a comparison to Late Bronze Age urban sites. The appearance of a large number of contemporaneous sites in a previously unoccupied area are compelling data for Finkelstein's interpretation that a new people, the Israelites, arrived at this time.[66] By contrasting the simplicity of these single-period highland villages to Late Bronze Age urban sites, Finkelstein recreates, yet again, the classic insider-outsider dichotomy that riddles the archaeological literature,[67] ultimately understanding culture change as the result of a new

62. See Knapp, *Society and Polity at Bronze Age Pella*, 71–72.

63. For the movement of Chocolate-on-White Ware, see ibid., 86.

64. For an alternative view on the nature of urban-village interrelationships, see ibid., 88.

65. See Finkelstein, *Israelite Settlement*, 25–204; and Adam Zertal, *The Israelite Settlement in the Hill Country of Manasseh* (Ph.D. diss., Tel Aviv, 1986) [Hebrew]; and idem, "To the Land of the Perrizzites and the Giants," 47–69.

66. Finkelstein, *Israelite Settlement*, 28, 337–38.

67. See, for instance, William F. Albright, "The Israelite Conquest of Canaan in the Light of Archaeology," *BASOR* 74 (1939) 11–23; Kenyon, *Archaeology in the Holy Land*, 43–45, 63, 66ff., 117–18, 119ff.; or Paul W. Lapp, *The Dhahr Mirzbaneh Tombs: Three Intermediate Bronze Age Cemeteries in Jordan* (New Haven: ASOR, 1966) 111–13. While these examples are dated, it is instructive to note the dependence on external elements as a stimulus of culture change. For an excellent discussion of the internal tensions within Canaanite society, what Alexander Joffe refers to as "Complementarity and Contradiction," see Alexander H. Joffe, *Settlement and Society in the Early Bronze I and II Southern Levant* (Monographs in Mediterranean Archaeology 4; Sheffield: Sheffield Academic Press, 1993) 90–93.

or, for Finkelstein, "reintroduced" peoples.[68] He does add a twist by claiming that these Iron I highland peoples are in some way related to the Middle Bronze II occupants of the same territory.[69] The Late Bronze Age occupational lacuna is dispensed with by claiming that the Middle Bronze Age villagers became pastoralists and (except for leaving a few isolated Late Bronze Age cemeteries) vanished, at least archaeologically.[70] Finkelstein's view, which alternately stresses both disjunction and continuity, very persuasively argues that a new people, the Israelites, did emerge at this time and can be traced archaeologically.

Gloria London, however, has pointed out that gross morphological differences in archaeological data may have more to do with economic, environmental, and social factors rather than ethnic ones.[71] Differences in pottery and architectural traditions may better reflect the demands of specific lifestyles, such as urban and rural. London quite correctly notes that nowhere in Finkelstein's data is there any archaeological reason to suspect the introduction of a new people. Her conclusions are supported by ethnoarchaeological data and follow the work of Carol Kramer, who over 15 years ago questioned whether pots equaled people, a query that needs to be revisited continually.[72]

From a village perspective, the transition from Late Bronze IIB to the Early Iron Age is marked by a sense of internal cultural persistence coinciding with external political and economic instability.[73] The breakdown of the Greater Eastern Mediterranean Co-Prosperity Sphere, as characterized by the cessation of Cypriot and Aegean imports, did not seem adversely to affect the internal organization of Tell ʿEin Zippori or dramatically affect the composition of rural Late Bronze Age material culture. At both Tell ʿEin Zippori and Tell el-Wawiyat, cultural continuity is evident, though not identical, and the results of these excavations suggest that the pace and scale of changes at the rural level are relatively indistinct.

Models pointing to cultural continuity are not without precedent but until now have been derived from a limited number of urban contexts.[74] At sites

68. Finkelstein, *Israelite Settlement*, 338.

69. Ibid., 339–41, 345ff.

70. Ibid., 341–45.

71. See Gloria A. London, "A Comparison of Two Contemporaneous Lifestyles of the Late Second Millennium B.C.," 42ff.

72. See Carol Kramer, "Pots and People," in *Mountains and Lowlands: Essays in the Archaeology of Greater Mesopotamia* (Bibliotheca Mesopotamica 6; ed. L. D. Levine and T. C. Young, Jr.; Malibu: Undena, 1977) 99–112.

73. See Niels Lemche, "From Patronage Society to Patronage Society," in *The Origins of the Ancient Israelite States* (ed. Volkmar Fritz and Philip R. Davies; JSOTSup 228; Sheffield: Sheffield Academic Press, 1996) 118; contra Gal, "Iron I in Lower Galilee," 44, 46.

74. See Patrick E. McGovern, "Central Transjordan in the Late Bronze and Early Iron Ages," 267ff.; Bunimovitz, "On the Edge," 324; Mazar, *Archaeology of the Land of the Bible*, 289–90, 296–300; Ussishkin, "Level VII and VI at Tel Lachish," 224–26; and Gösta Ahlström, *Who Were the Israelites?* (Winona Lake, Ind.: Eisenbrauns, 1986) 35–36, 57. For bibliography and general overviews of the competing schools of thoughts regarding the Israelite

such as Megiddo, Beth-Shean, Tell el-Far'ah (South), and Tell esh-Shari'a,
there can be no denying the continuity of Late Bronze Age cultural traditions
into the Iron Age.[75] This is not to suggest that juxtaposed against a backdrop
of sociocultural continuity there were not significant changes. Major urban
centers, such as Hazor, Lachish, Megiddo, Beth-Shean, Ashdod, Aphek, and
Gezer, were destroyed at the end of Late Bronze Age, though clearly these
destructions do not reflect a single episode; rather, they occurred over a period of a century, from 1250 to 1150 B.C.E.[76] Likewise, a new settlement system emerged in the Central Highlands, and the Philistines, an Aegean-based
people, were introduced to the area.[77] But whether these events should serve
as the defining characteristics of the Late Bronze–Iron Age transition is
unclear.

What is clear, however, is that at least some segment of the Canaanite
population lived in villages and continued to do so without significant interruption well into the Iron Age. This lack of interruption is critical toward understanding the interplay between ethnic and political designations. When
examining other Iron Age societies, etiological questions are not nearly as
problematic. Cultural continuity is assumed in explaining the origins of the
Phoenicians, who become tangible in the archaeological and historical
record only in the tenth century.[78] There is little, if any, discussion regarding

---

settlement and transition from the Late Bronze Age to Iron Age, see Finkelstein, *The Archaeology of the Israelite Settlement*, 295–314; and Richard Hess, "Early Israel in Canaan:
A Survey of Recent Evidence and Interpretations," *PEQ* 125 (1993) 125–42.

75. See Amihai Mazar, "The Emergence of the Philistine Material Culture," *IEJ* 35
(1985) 96–97; and idem, "The 11th century B.C. in the Land of Israel," in *Cyprus in the 11th
Century* B.C. (ed. Vassos Karageorghis; Nicosia: University of Cyprus Press, 1994) 41;
Frances W. James and Patrick E. McGovern, *The Late Bronze Egyptian Garrison at Beth
Shan: A Study of Levels VII and VIII* (Philadelphia: University Museum, 1993) 247–48;
Ram Gophna, "Tell el-Far'ah (South)," *NEAEHL* 2.441–43; Trude Dothan, *The Philis-
tines and Their Material Culture* (Jerusalem: Israel Exploration Society, 1982) 27 (see n. 20
for bibliography), 29; and Eliezer D. Oren, "Tel Sera'," *NEAEHL* 4.1330–31. Though
Megiddo and Beth-Shean clearly demonstrate the continuation of Canaanite society into
Iron Age I, both sites were destroyed.

76. See Mazar, *Archaeology of the Land of the Bible*, 288–90; and Gal, "Iron I in Lower
Galilee," 39.

77. Generally, see Finkelstein, "The Emergence of Israel," 150–78; and Lawrence E.
Stager, "The Impact of the Sea Peoples (1185–1050 B.C.E.)," in *The Archaeology of Society
in the Holy Land* (ed. Thomas E. Levy; New York: Facts on File, 1995) 332–48.

78. It is difficult to pinpoint a specific date for the "origin" of the Phoenicians. There
is some debate as to how early expressions of Phoenician material culture began. Archaeological data for the twelfth and eleventh centuries B.C.E. is relatively weak in the area of
what was to become the Phoenician heartland, the Levantine coast from roughly the area
of Tel Dor in the south to Tell Sukas in the north. However, it is becoming increasingly
likely that Phoenician "styles" in material culture, especially pottery, began to appear in
the eleventh century; see Ephraim Stern, "New Evidence from Dor for the First Appearance of the Phoenicians along the Northern Coast of Israel," *BASOR* 279 (1990) 27–34;
and idem, *Dor—Ruler of the Seas: Twelve Years of Excavations at the Israelite-Phoenician*

their ethnic origins. The appearance of Aramaeans in the tenth century B.C.E. and Arabs in the ninth century B.C.E. are also relatively unproblematic.[79] Why then are the Israelites the chosen people? Obviously a textual bias plays a role; however, an urban bias also plays an important role in shaping these perceptions.

New sites that demonstrate a continuity of "Canaanite village culture" into the Iron Age support the interpretation of overall cultural continuity from Late Bronze II. London's[80] functional reading of material culture assemblages based on their sociospatial contexts also supports a "Continuity Model." Additionally, it has not been satisfactorily shown that there are any good archaeological data that support the appearance of a completely new ethnicity or people[81] such as the Israelites in the late thirteenth century B.C.E. If in fact the rural population is as significant as Falconer, London, and Ahlström[82]

Harbor Town on the Carmel Coast (Jerusalem: Israel Exploration Society, 1994) 101–4; Patricia M. Bikai, "The Phoenicians," in *The Crisis Years: The 12th Century B.C., from beyond the Danube to the Tigris* (ed. William A. Ward and Martha Joukowsky; Dubuque, Ia.: Kendall/Hunt, 1992) 31, 35; and idem, "The Phoenicians and Cyprus," in *Cyprus in the 11th Century B.C.* (ed. Vassos Karageorghis; Nicosia: University of Cyprus Press, 1994) 133ff.; and William P. Anderson, "The Beginnings of Phoenician Pottery: Vessel Shape, Style and Ceramic Technology in the Early Phases of the Phoenician Iron Age," *BASOR* 279 (1990) 35–54. There seems to be a gap in Phoenician art in the twelfth and eleventh centuries B.C.E.; see Glenn E. Markoe, "The Emergence of Phoenician Art," *BASOR* 279 (1990) 13; Edith Porada, "Notes on the Sarcophagus of Ahiram," *JANESCU* 5 (1973) 360–64; and Irene J. Winter, "Phoenician and North Syrian Ivory Carving in Historical Context: Questions of Style and Distribution," *Iraq* 38/1 (1976) 21–22. By the tenth century B.C.E., there is a preponderance of archaeological and textual data directly relating to the Phoenicians; see, for instance, Zvi Gal, "Hurbat Rosh Zayit and the Early Phoenician Pottery," *Levant* 24 (1992) 173–86. For an excellent overview on historical and archaeological aspects of what is Phoenician, see James D. Muhly, "Phoenicia and the Phoenicians," in *Biblical Archaeology Today: Proceedings of the International Congress on Biblical Archaeology, Jerusalem, April 1984* (ed. Joseph Aviram; Jerusalem: Israel Exploration Society, 1984–85) 177–91.

79. While the origins of the Aramaeans in Mesopotamia and Syria is problematic, their appearance archaeologically in the southern Levant is more straightforward; see Glenn M. Schwartz, "The Origins of the Aramaeans in Syria and Northern Mesopotamia: Research Problems and Potential Strategies," in *To the Euphrates and Beyond: Archaeological Studies in Honour of Maurits N. van Loon* (ed. O. M. Chaex, H. H. Curvers, and P. M. M. G. Akkermans; Rotterdam: Balkema, 1989) 280–81, 285–86. For a historical overview on the Arabs, see Israel Ephʿal, *The Ancient Arabs: Nomads on the Borders of the Fertile Crescent 9th–5th Centuries B.C.* (Jerusalem: Magnes, 1984); and Nadav Naʾaman, "The ʿConquest of Canaanʾ in the Book of Joshua," 226.

80. London, "A Comparison of Two Contemporaneous Lifestyles," 42ff.

81. For a discussion of archaeological correlations to ethnicity, see Kathryn Kamp and Norman Yoffee, "Ethnicity in Ancient Western Asia during the Early Second Millenium B.C.: Archaeological Assessment and Ethnoarchaeological Perspectives," *BASOR* 237 (1980) (1980) 94–97; and Stephen Shennan, "Introduction: Archaeological Approaches to Cultural Identity," in *Archaeological Approaches to Cultural Identity* (ed. Stephen Shennan; London: Routledge, 1994) 14–16.

82. See above and nn. 15, 19, and 20.

suspect, the Late Bronze–Iron I transition must be recast, deemphasizing external agents as vehicles of change and supporting models that stress internal factors.

Rural Complexity in the Iron Age

While the Iron I villages in the Central Highlands are understood as reflecting a relatively unstratified society, the same cannot be said about the multiperiod village sites of Tell ʿEin Zippori and Tell el-Wawiyat. Ample evidence has been cited that suggests that villages exhibited a significant degree of social stratification. The circulation of imported pottery was one method by which Canaanite elites distinguished themselves and maintained an active dialogue with the rest of the eastern Mediterranean. Likewise, the metallurgical activities at Tell el-Wawiyat in the twelfth century B.C.E. suggest that access to valuable raw materials was not limited to urban settlements.

However, the most striking evidence for rural complexity is found at Tell ʿEin Zippori toward the end of Iron I, in the eleventh century B.C.E., with the construction of a large and probably public building. The internal features of Building A, such as the bench and well-hewn door jambs are frequently associated with nondomestic buildings both in the Late Bronze and Iron Ages.[83] Typical four-room houses and courtyard houses rarely include these features, and ashlar-like masonry is usually reserved for monumental buildings. A number of very simple stamped or impressed handles have been recovered, and perhaps this building served as a local administrative or small-scale redistribution center. There is also some indication of intrasite differentiation, with domestic units clustered on the lower terrace and the upper terrace reserved for public space. These are the type of data Bonnie Magness-Gardiner predicted would be found in communal or privately owned villages in the hinterland around Alalakh.[84]

The final phases at Tell ʿEin Zippori present an interesting set of historical possibilities. The site was partially destroyed in the early tenth century B.C.E. This destruction is seen clearly in Building A, where there are large quantities of burned mudbrick. An early tenth century B.C.E. date for this destruction places it within an historical context of the rise of a strong centralized state, the United Monarchy. A feature of this state was the construction

83. For ashlar masonry, see Yigal Shiloh, *The Proto-Aeolic Capital and Israelite Ashlar Masonry* (Qedem 11; Jerusalem: Israel Exploration Society, 1979) 60–68, 78–80, 82–87; and R. Naumann, *Architektur Kleinasiens* (Tübingen: Wasmuth, 1971) 38ff., 68ff. For the presence of benches in nondomestic buildings, see Amihai Mazar, "Temples of the Middle and Late Bronze Ages and the Iron Age," in *The Architecture of Ancient Israel: From the Prehistoric to the Persian Periods* (ed. Aharon Kempinski and Ronny Reich; Jerusalem: Israel Exploration Society, 1992) 161–87.

84. Magness-Gardiner, "Urban-Rural Relations in Bronze Age Syria," 44.

of administrative centers at Hazor, Jerusalem, Gezer, and Megiddo.[85] With the emergence of a centralized government, existing pockets of local power needed to be co-opted, controlled, or removed.[86] The existence of a rural elite at Tell ʿEin Zippori, with deep temporal roots, could have posed grave problems for a newly emerging authority bent on establishing a radically different political order from the one in place in Late Bronze or Iron Age I. Hanoch Reviv[87] notes that a drastic decrease in the roles and authority of rural elites is reflected in the Hebrew Bible precisely in the period of the United Monarchy. Was Tell ʿEin Zippori the victim of political consolidation and reorganization ?

Long-standing cultural continuity in the Lower Galilee may also be preserved in some of the tribal traditions found in 1 Chronicles.[88] According to biblical traditions, both the Beit Netofa Valley and the Nazareth Basin fell under the control of the tribe of Zebulon.[89] Naʾaman suggests that the area of Zebulon and elsewhere in the Galilee had a mixed Canaanite-Israelite population as late as the reign of David.[90] Ahlström[91] also argues that the Lower Galilee remained outside of Israel proper until the reign of David, at which time they entered into a political union with the newly emerging state.

These biblical traditions would seem to support the archaeological data and suggest that the Lower Galilee was an area marked by overall sociocultural continuity from the Late Bronze Age into the Iron Age.[92] This continuity was not disrupted until the development of a centralized political authority in the mid–tenth century B.C.E.

With the excavations of Tell ʿEin Zippori and Tell el-Wawiyat, a clearer picture of rural life in the Lower Galilee is beginning to emerge. Both sites are multiperiod tells, though clearly not urban in character. Tell ʿEin Zippori is a particularly good example of a settlement with a great deal of resiliency. It was continually settled for over 500 years, in part due to its position adjacent

85. See John S. Holladay, Jr., "The Kingdoms of Israel and Judah: Political and Economic Centralization in the Iron IIA–B (ca. 1000–750 B.C.E.)," in *The Archaeology of Society in the Holy Land* (ed. Thomas E. Levy; New York: Facts on File, 1995) 371ff., 368–98.

86. See Baruch Halpern, "The Construction of the Davidic State: An Exercise in Historiography," in *The Origins of the Ancient Israelite States* (ed. Volkmar Fritz and Philip R. Davies; Sheffield: Sheffield Academic Press, 1996) 73–74.

87. H. Reviv, *The Elders in Ancient Israel: A Study of a Biblical Institution* (trans. L. Plitmann; Jerusalem: Magnes, 1989) 188–90.

88. See, for instance, 1 Chr 6:77, 13:40.

89. Nadav Naʾaman, *Borders and Districts in Biblical Historiography* (Jerusalem Biblical Studies 4; Jerusalem: Simor, 1986) 119–43, map 4; and Gal, "Iron I in Lower Galilee," 43.

90. Naʾaman, *Borders and Districts in Biblical Historiography*, 198–99.

91. Ahlström, *Who Were the Israelites?* 64, 91–92, 95–96.

92. Contra Gal ("Iron I in Lower Galilee," 42–44, 46), who argues for a clear break between the Late Bronze II and Iron Age I, based on his settlement-pattern analysis for northern and southern Lower Galilee.

to a secure water source and arable land, but also perhaps due to the persistence of entrenched social groups. The presence of imported pottery in the Late Bronze Age and the construction of nondomestic architecture in the Iron I support the notion of an enduring tradition of independent rural elite formations.

Response to J. P. Dessel

JOHN S. JORGENSEN
Duke University Divinity School

The investigation of small, multiperiod tells in southern Syria–Palestine has begun to readdress the conceptual dichotomy of the urban tell on the one extreme and the one-period settlement site on the other. The contrast in the material cultures of these two settlement types has only furthered the preconception that *urban* necessarily equals *socially complex*, and *rural* necessarily equals *simple*. Notions such as this of the overall sociospatial landscape of southern Syria–Palestine in turn lend themselves, in a facile manner, to interpretive frameworks that envision tension and conflict in the relationship between two disjunctive social systems: one urban, bureaucratic, and elite and the other rural, agricultural, and socially undifferentiated. The excavations at Tell el-Wawiyat and Tel ʿEin Zippori in Lower Galilee, coupled with other recent archaeological and cross-cultural data, have begun to paint a more complex portrait of the landscape of southern Syria–Palestine.[1] This new portrait not only better reflects the sociospatial reality but has important implications for our interpretation of the period of the Late Bronze–Iron I transition and the crystallization of the population elements that in the early tenth century B.C.E. coalesced into the territorial state of Israel.

As a result of more recent understandings, sociological models that insist upon conflict or resistance as operative forces in urban-rural interaction are further undermined.[2] Rather than show a sharp distinction between a

---

1. See the series of articles in Glenn M. Schwartz and Steven E. Falconer (eds.), *Archaeological Views from the Countryside: Village Communities in Early Complex Societies* (Washington, D.C.: Smithsonian, 1994).

2. See Norman K. Gottwald, *The Tribes of Yahweh* (Maryknoll, N.Y.: Orbis, 1979). Much of Gottwald's reconstruction rests upon the assumption of urban-rural conflict and a peasant withdrawal from Canaanite society. Richard Horsley, a contributor to this volume (see pp. 57–74), also relies heavily on Gottwald's sociological framework in his own recent argument for a protracted history of Galilean resistance that culminates with the "Jesus movement" in the first century C.E. (*Galilee: History, Politics, People* [Valley Forge, Pa.: Trinity, 1995]; and idem, *Archaeology, History, and Society in Galilee: The Social Context*

Canaanite city and an outlying village, the results of these anc tions reveal social complexity at the village level. They suggest excava- volved integration of the village into the polity's socioeconomic core in- not simple urban exploitation of the hinterland. Urban and rural a and necessity, antagonistic to one another, but are, as J. P. Dessel and others suggested, interdependent elements within a complex and integrated economic system.[3]

Our excavations in Lower Galilee suggest the possibility of an operat. dynamic for the Iron I period that may compliment the model proposed by Israel Finkelstein for the settlement of the central hill country. The surveys of the central highlands, in particular those conducted by Israel Finkelstein and Adam Zertal, and the subsequent synthesis of these data by Finkelstein argue persuasively for a pastoral, nonsedentary background for large portions of the Iron I population of the central highlands.[4] Largely archaeologically invisible pastoralists who inhabited the highlands began a process of settling down in the Iron I period, thus accounting for the dramatic increase in the number of Iron I sites identified through survey. More recently, however, Finkelstein has nuanced his model, acknowledging the complexity of the Late Bronze II– Iron I landscape and a certain degree of settlement continuity between these two periods. Ecological differences between the moderate north with its broad intermontane valleys and steppe lands and the less hospitable south may, Finkelstein maintains, have played a significant role in affecting the limited Late Bronze II–Iron I settlement continuity. While he maintains that pastoralists constituted the bulk of the population of the highlands during Late Bronze II, the more agriculturally favorable, northern portion of the central highlands nevertheless also exhibited a concentration of permanent settlement. As one moves south, agricultural potential and permanent settle- ment diminish while the pastoral component in the highlands population in-

---

of Jesus and the Rabbis [Valley Forge, Pa.: Trinity, 1996]). For a critique of the sociological school, see, among others, Niels Peter Lemche, *Early Israel* (VTSup 37; Leiden: Brill, 1985); and the survey of scholarship in Israel Finkelstein, *The Archaeology of the Israelite Settlement* (Jerusalem: Israel Exploration Society, 1988) 306–14.

3. Glenn M. Schwartz and Steven E. Falconer, "Rural Approaches to Social Complex- ity," in *Archaeological Views from the Countryside: Village Communities in Early Complex Societies* (ed. Glenn M. Schwartz and Steven E. Falconer; Washington, D.C.: Smithsonian, 1994) 1–9. See also Bonnie Magness-Gardiner, "Urban-Rural Relations in Bronze Age Syria: Evidence from Alalah Level VII Palace Archives," in the same volume, pp. 37–47.

4. For a detailed presentation of his model, see Finkelstein, *Archaeology of the Israelite Settlement*; and more recently, idem, "The Emergence of Israel: A Phase in the Cyclic His- tory of Canaan in the Third and Second Millennia B.C.E.," in *From Nomadism to Monar- chy: Archaeological and Historical Aspects of Early Israel* (ed. Israel Finkelstein and Nadav Na'aman; Jerusalem: Israel Exploration Society, 1994) 150–78; see also Adam Zertal, "'To the Land of the Perizzites and the Giants': On the Israelite Settlement in the Hill Country of Manasseh," in the same volume, pp. 47–69.

creases. The few permanent Late Bronze Age settlements, located mostly in the agriculturally favorable northern portion of the highlands, thus rendered a degree of occupational continuity to the transformed Iron I landscape.[5]

The ecological factors that may have influenced the degree of demographic continuity in northern portions of the central highlands may also account in part for the emerging picture of continuity in Lower Galilee. Through intensive survey, Zvi Gal identified 22–25 newly founded sites dating to the Iron I period.[6] While these Iron I settlements might, at first blush, be interpreted as sedentarizing nomads, the results of the excavations at Tell el-Wawiyat and Tel ʿEin Zippori, as well as other recent excavations conducted at Tel Yinʿam and Beth-Gan,[7] have all revealed occupational continuity from the Late Bronze II to the Iron I periods. If the results of the excavations of these sites are typical of Lower Galilee as a whole, a high degree of demographic continuity with the Late Bronze Age is suggested, more so than in the northern portion of the central hill country. The ecology of Lower Galilee, with its moderate terrain, broad valleys, wadi systems, and relatively rich water resources, may have favored settled agricultural communities over a pastoral mode of existence to an even greater extent than the moderate northern portions of the central hill country did.[8] Thus, the inhabitants of Lower Galilee during the Iron I period may have had considerably more in common with sedentary Late Bronze Age culture than did the recently settled pastoralists of the Iron I central hill country.

While the limited excavation results suggest that Iron I Lower Galilee may have exhibited considerably greater continuity with the Late Bronze II than did the central hill country, Gal's survey data and the excavations at Tel ʿEin Zippori nonetheless point out material-culture affiliations between Lower Galilee and the central hill country during the Iron I period. These affiliations comprise certain ceramic forms and a distinctive architectural type. Lower Galilee, as Gal has noted, seems to mark the northern extent of the manufacture/distribution of the collar-rim jar and so lies within a larger material-culture isogram.[9] Other ceramic forms also show good parallels with the

5. Finkelstein, "The Great Transformation: The 'Conquest' of the Highlands Frontiers and the Rise of the Territorial States," in *The Archaeology of Society in the Holy Land* (ed. Thomas E. Levy; New York: Facts on File, 1995) 357.

6. Z. Gal, *Lower Galilee during the Iron Age* (ASOR Dissertation Series 8; Winona Lake, Ind.: Eisenbrauns, 1992); idem, "Iron I in Lower Galilee and the Margins of the Jezreel Valley, in *From Nomadism to Monarchy*, 35–46.

7. For the results of the excavations at Tel Yinʿam, see Harold Liebowitz, "Yinʿam, Tel," *OEANE* 5.379–81 with additional bibliography. For Beth-Gan, see also Harold Liebowitz, "Beth-Gan," in the same volume, pp. 301–2, with attendant bibliography.

8. See my forthcoming Ph.D. dissertation, Duke University Divinity School.

9. Finkelstein, *Archaeology of the Israelite Settlement*, 281–82; Douglas L. Esse, "The Collared Store Jar: Scholarly Ideology and Ceramic Typology," *SJOT* 2 (1991) 107–10; John S. Jorgensen, "The Collared-Rim Jar," in *Sepphoris in Galilee* (ed. Rebecca Martin Nagy et al.; Raleigh, N.C.: North Carolina Museum of Art, 1996) 156–57.

central highlands.[10] The excavations at Tel ʿEin Zippori have also revealed portions of a four-room house, an architectural type well-documented from the central hill country. In light of the apparent varied origin of the Iron I population (recently settled pastoralists and long-tenured, settled agriculturalists), consideration of these similarities in the Iron I material culture is perhaps instructive in identifying some of the pitfalls involved in attempting to draw inferences regarding ethnic affiliations or immediate socioeconomic background based on material culture.[11]

The large late-eleventh–early-tenth-century B.C.E. building complex uncovered at Tel ʿEin Zippori (Stratum III), with its implications for social complexity, and other similar contemporary sites like Tel Hadar[12] on the eastern shore of Lake Kinneret may suggest that following the collapse of many of the Late Bronze Age urban centers, small, independent polities arose briefly in Galilee in the political vacuum prior to the rise of an Israelite monarchy in the tenth century B.C.E. In a somewhat similar manner, Finkelstein, in his most recent book,[13] proposes viewing Tel Masos (Khirbet el-Meshash) as a short-lived chiefdom, occupying the political vacuum between the lapse in Egyptian control over southern Palestine and the rise of the Judean monarchy. While the desert polity centered at Tel Masos is interpreted as a "gateway community" controlling the southern trade routes, small centers like Tel Hadar and Tel ʿEin Zippori may have arisen for other reasons. Whatever the factors that brought about their nascence, neither Tel Masos, Tel ʿEin Zippori, nor Tel Hadar seem to have survived the rise of the more expansive Iron Age kingdoms of Israel or, perhaps in the case of Tel Hadar, Aram Damascus.

Finally, the excavations, principally those undertaken at Tel ʿEin Zippori, suggest that what later became incorporated into Israel was a rather more heterogeneous lot than much of biblical tradition would have us believe. Rather than an Israel that stems largely from a common social and cultural fabric, what is suggested instead by the archaeological data is that the political kingdom of Israel may have incorporated various peoples from varying backgrounds. Its core element most likely stemmed from the central highlands settlement sites, possibly from a recent pastoral, nonsedentary mode of exist-

---

10. While this analysis is still in its early phase, certain jars and bowls exhibit clear parallels with examples from excavated Iron I contexts in the central hill country. The full analysis of the ceramics from both Tell el-Wawiyat and Tel ʿEin Zippori will reveal the full degree of material-culture affiliation with the neighboring central highlands and Upper Galilee.

11. In this respect, see Israel Finkelstein, "Pots and People Revisited: Ethnic Boundaries in the Iron Age I," in *The Archaeology of Israel: Constructing the Past, Interpreting the Present* (JSOTSup 237; ed. Neil Asher Silberman and David B. Small; Sheffield: Sheffield Academic Press, 1997) 216–37.

12. See Moshe Kochavi, "Hadar, Tel," *OEANE* 2.450–52.

13. Finkelstein, *Living on the Fringe* (Monographs in Mediterranean Archaeology 6; Sheffield: Sheffield Academic Press, 1995) 103–26.

ence; other, peripheral elements exhibited demographic and cultural continuity with settled Late Bronze Age society.

It is the newly emerging picture of the urban-rural dynamic, the variable role of the village, and potential cultural persistence at the village level with which contemporary scholarship must now contend when constructing heuristic models. This new understanding is not a mere archaeological curiosity; it has direct bearing on the way in which biblical scholars, historians, and archaeologists wrestle with understanding the Late Bronze and Iron Ages and develop interpretive frameworks.

Behind the Names:
Galileans, Samaritans, *Ioudaioi*

SEAN FREYNE
Trinity College, Dublin

The fact that this is the second congress of Galilee studies is indicative of the importance of the region in recent discussions of Second Temple Judaism and early Christianity. This focus on Galilee is in no small measure due to the initiative and industry of Professor Eric Meyers over the last twenty-five or so years. He was the first to speak of the need to see Galilee within a larger regional context, pointing to the cultural continuities with the Golan on the one hand and the differences between Upper and Lower Galilee on the other.[1] Two recent books by Richard Horsley also indirectly highlight the issue of regionalism by positing tensions between the Judeans on the one hand and the Galilean Israelites on the other.[2] It is, perhaps, time for a consideration of Galilee not in isolation but in relation to other regions within first-century Palestine. Such an undertaking would constitute a useful hermeneutical exercise, refining or correcting the various hypotheses about Galilean society that have been proposed over the years. There are plenty of surface indicators—everything from geography to wine-making techniques—to suggest a rich cultural diversity within the borders of this relatively small territory; and our literary sources for the period are aware of such diversity also.

This paper focuses not directly on Judea, but rather on the in-between world of Samaria, which had fraught relations with both Galilee and Judea in our period. Samaria has been largely bypassed in discussion of Galilee, and yet two incidents, both with a strong religious coloring from the first century C.E. highlight the tensions in Galilean/Samarian relations. Luke states that

---

1. E. Meyers, "Galilean Regionalism as a Factor in Historical Reconstruction," *BASOR* 221 (1976) 93–101.

2. R. A. Horsley, *Galilee: History, Politics, People* (Valley Forge, Pa.: Trinity, 1995); idem, *Archaeology, History and Society in Galilee* (Valley Forge, Pa.: Trinity, 1996).

Samaritan villages rejected the emissaries of Jesus, "because his face was set toward Jerusalem" (Luke 9:52). In a similar vein, Josephus twice reports the civic turmoil occasioned by an attack on Galilean pilgrims on their way to Jerusalem by Samaritans from the village of Ginae (*Ant.* 20.118–36; J.W. 2.234–46). It is possible to interpret Luke's report as the construct of the evangelist in the light of his portrayal of Jesus and the early Christian missionary activity, but the episode reported by Josephus cannot be so lightly dismissed, despite the discrepancies between the two accounts. Tacitus also knows of these disturbances, which took place in the procuratorship of Cumanus (*Annals* 12.54).[3]

The fact that both incidents occur in the context of the pilgrimage to Jerusalem is surely significant. However, Richard Horsley repeatedly reminds us that religion was embedded in the real factors for conflict in agrarian societies—namely, the political, economic, and social dynamics. It is easy to suggest economic reasons for Samaritan resentment of Galilean pilgrims' bringing their produce to Jerusalem rather than to Gerizim. Pilgrims were a boost to the local economy in the ancient, no less than the modern, world. However, the Gerizim Temple was in ruins at this time, not having been rebuilt after its destruction by John Hyrcanus, more than 150 years earlier.[4] Thus, the economic explanation loses some of its cogency. Such an explanation begs a host of other questions in any event: why did the Galileans prefer Jerusalem? What circumstances led to their bypassing their natural cult center, if, as "Israelites" (as in Horsley's view), the Galileans were likely to have shared a common heritage with "the Israelites of Argarizein"? What does this tell us about the Galileans and the Judeans?

A survey of contemporary scholarship on Samaria and the Samaritans reveals two distinct, but cumulative, explanations given for their separateness from both Galilee and Judea: the Galileans and the Samarians suffered different fates at the hands of the Assyrians in the eighth century B.C.E., and these marked their relationships subsequently;[5] and the building of a temple on Mt. Gerizim and the process of hellenization represent two stages of the so-called Samaritan schism, whereby a final wedge was driven between Samarians and the adherents of the Jerusalem Temple, including, presumably, the Galileans. The following discussion reexamines critically these two explanations, conscious that they have both entered contemporary scholarship

3. S. Freyne, *Galilee from Alexander the Great to Hadrian* (Wilmington, Del.: Glazier, 1980; reprint, Edinburgh: T. & T. Clark, 1990) 73–74.

4. R. J. Bull, "An Archaeological Footnote to 'Our Fathers Worshiped on This Mountain,'" NTS 23 (1977) 460–62.

5. I propose to use the term 'Samarian' (*Samareis*) for the inhabitants of the region, irrespective of their religious affiliation, and to reserve 'Samaritan' (*Samareitai*) for the adherents of the Gerizim cult. There is good Josephan warrant for this, since he uses *Samareis* in *Ant.* 9.125, when speaking of the reign of Jehu. However, he uses *Samareitai* after the fall of the Northern Kingdom, since, as we shall see, in his biased view it is proper to date the origins of the Samaritan cult of his own day back to that moment (*Ant.* 9.290).

via the anti-Samaritan polemic of the Jerusalem priest Josephus, as expressed particularly in his *Jewish Antiquities*[6] — not the most reliable source in these circumstances.

The Assyrian Experience

Albrecht Alt in particular, drawing on the biblical account (2 Kgs 15:29, 17:23) as well as the Assyrian annals, proposes that, whereas the majority of the Galilean peasantry was left undisturbed when Tiglath-pileser III conquered the North in 733 B.C.E., Samaria suffered a very different fate 12 years later under Shalmaneser I (721 B.C.E.). The ruling aristocracy was taken into exile and replaced by people of non-Israelite stock. Galilee was then administered from Megiddo, the capital of one of three new provinces established by Tiglath-pileser and treated subsequently as a "kingsland." Samaria, however, with its own new governing elite and a cultic center was treated as a temple-state within larger imperial structures that continued into the Persian and Greek periods. This new elite, although it worshiped the god of the land, never fully enculturated with the peasantry in Samaria, who eventually felt more drawn to the Jerusalem Temple than to the one established on Gerizim.[7]

To this administrative-historical argument, Horsley has recently added a socio-economic component, as required by the materialist bias of his macromodel of agrarian empires.[8] In his view, Galilee was deprived of its local ruling officials and craftsmen (some of whom may not even have been of Israelite extraction) and was now ruled from Megiddo by imperial officials. Denuded of a native aristocracy, the Galilean Israelites were left free to conduct their own village affairs according to ancestral custom. By contrast, Samaria did have a "native" elite (presumably of non-Israelite stock) who, when ousted from the capital in the fourth century, resettled in Shechem and established a temple on Mt. Gerizim. Thus, unlike in Galilee, the changes in Samaria meant a ruling secular elite and a priestly and scribal retainer class. This latter was eventually to provide a legitimating version of the Torah that was intended to counter the Jerusalem hegemonic claims after the destruction of the Gerizim Temple. The Galileans had no such luck, or misfortune, depending on the point of view, maintaining and developing their traditions orally. Yet, they were resistant to any imposition of the laws of the Judeans, despite their common roots in Israelite tradition.[9] Several observations can be made about these two reconstructions, with respect to the question concerning the causes of later Galilean/Samaritan hostility.

6. R. J. Coggins, "The Samaritans in Josephus," in *Josephus, Judaism and Christianity* (ed. L. H. Feldman and G. Hata; Detroit: Wayne State University Press, 1987) 257–73.

7. A. Alt, "Die assyrische Provinz Megiddo und ihr Späteres Schicksal," in *Galiläische Probleme 2: Kleine Schriften zur Geschichte des Volkes Israels* (3 vols.; Munich: Beck, 1953–64) 2.374–84.

8. Horsley, *Galilee*, 8–9.

9. Ibid., 25–29.

The available evidence makes the reconstruction of the different experiences of Galileans and Samarians under the Assyrians problematic. Unless the findings of Zvi Gal's survey are disproven by detailed excavations, the evidence he produces for the depopulation of Lower Galilee in the sixth century B.C.E. must be taken into any account of the region's history, pace Horsley's too ready dismissal.[10] But even the literary sources do not support this scenario. The places listed in the Assyrian annals—Gabara, Hinatuma, Qana, Iatbite, Irruna—can all be confidently located in Lower Galilee. They neatly flesh out the more general statement in 2 Kgs 15:29 that lists "Galilee, all the land of Naphthali" as part of the devastated territory, together with such Upper Galilean strongholds as Ijon, Kadesh, and Hazor. Indeed, if Alt is correct in reading the oracle of Isa 8:23 as addressed to the three new Assyrian provinces of the North—Megiddo (including Galilee), Dor, and Gilead—it would seem to refute his own suggestion elsewhere that Galilee, as such, escaped the ravages of Tiglathpileser's conquest.[11] Where does that leave the Galilean Israelites? And, if they existed, why did they not make common cause with their Samarian peasant counterparts?

Even if the Alt/Horsley version of events is accepted, an additional question concerns the very notion of separate and separable Israelite traditions' being maintained by peasants over centuries. I also once espoused that position but have come to see its inherent improbability.[12] Morton Smith had long ago found plenty of evidence in the literary sources for what he calls "the syncretistic cult of Yahweh" throughout the whole country.[13] A more recent study by John S. Holladay, Jr., of the archaeological evidence distinguishes between what he describes as state cult centers and popular domestic religion in the divided monarchy and comes up with not dissimilar conclusions.[14] Working on the hypothesis that one of the major goals of state religious cult in antiquity was to promote national unity and a feeling of distinctiveness vis-à-vis neighboring states, Holladay looks at the evidence for

10. Z. Gal, *Lower Galilee during the Iron Age* (ASOR Dissertation Series 8; Winona Lake, Ind.: Eisenbrauns, 1992); Horsley, *Galilee*, 290 n. 13. For a recent discussion supporting Gal's conclusions, based on a new edition of the Assyrian annals by H. Tadmor (*The Inscriptions of Tiglath-Pileser III* [Jerusalem: Israel Academy of Sciences and Humanities, 1994]), see K. Lawson Younger Jr., "The Deportations of the Israelites," *JBL* 117 (1998) 201–27.

11. A. Alt, "Jesaja 8,23–9,6: Befreiungsnacht und Kronungstag," in *Galiläische Probleme 2: Kleine Schriften zur Geschichte des Volkes Israels* (3 vols.; Munich: Beck, 1953–64) 2.205–6.

12. Freyne, *Galilee*, 23–26; but see my *Galilee, Jesus and the Gospels* (Philadelphia: Fortress, 1988) 169–70.

13. M. Smith, *Palestinian Parties and Politics That Shaped the Old Testament* (New York: Columbia University Press, 1971; reprinted, London, 1987) 62–74.

14. J. S. Holladay, Jr., "Religion in Israel and Judah under the Monarchy: An Explicitly Archaeological Approach," in *Ancient Israelite Religion: Essays in Honor of Frank Moore Cross* (ed. P. D. Miller, P. D. Hanson, and S. D. McBride; Philadelphia: Fortress, 1987) 249–302.

cultic activity from eight different sites, north and south. He uses various criteria for distinguishing between conformist and tolerated nonconformist religious activities—these latter addressing the needs of excluded minorities or dealing with aspects of the divine world not adequately represented in the state, or conformist, cult. Of the Northern sites examined, Dan represents a national or regional cult center, Megiddo a conformist neighborhood shrine, and Hazor a domestic nonconformist profile. Samaria, on the other hand, is a nonconformist shrine, situated outside the walls and containing a significant number of small figurines and other objects. However, it lacks the incense altars associated with the establishment sites. The evidence of domestic religious objects of a nonconformist type from Stratum V at Hazor (i.e., eighth century B.C.E.) shows a marked increase over strata representing earlier periods. This suggests an intensification of such activity in periods of crisis, such as that of the Assyrian onslaught. On the basis of this analysis of the evidence, therefore, it appears that in situations in which the national cult was perceived to have failed, Galileans would have been more likely to turn to nonconformist religious practices in domestic settings not specific to the conformist Israelite cult.

Galilean Israelites might alternatively have been expected to frequent a national or local shrine, at which a sense of separate identity could continue to be fostered. Depending on its previous character, Dan might have provided such a center, at least until the arrival of the god Pan to nearby Banias in the Seleucid Period. There is evidence of at least two stages of building in the temenos area during the Hellenistic Period, and the tantalizing bilingual inscription "to the God who is in Dan."[15] Or, if the tradition of the priest from Bethel instructing the new arrivals in the worship of the god of the land has any substance, then some form of Yahwistic worship must have continued in Samaria (2 Kgs 17:28). Certainly, accounts from the Persian Period assume the presence of Yahweh-worshipers in Samaria whose overtures of help to Jerusalem were rejected (Ezek 4:1–5; *Ant.* 11.85–88). Presumably, one of the reasons why these possibilities are not explored by modern scholars is the common understanding that, in Samaria in particular, a new, syncretistic form of worship was thought to have been emerging that would have been inimical to Israelite Yahwism (see below). Or perhaps there is a danger of unconsciously imposing a far too-rigid notion of Yahwism as it was propagated later in the Deuteronomic reform onto an earlier, more fluid situation. Holladay's remark that "the uneasy thought that actual religious practice in ancient Israel might not have mirrored our texts in any recognizable fashion has disturbed many a scholar's ponderings" may sound somewhat dramatic. However, the impression I get from such scholars as William Dever and

---

15. A. Biran, "To the God Who Is in Dan," in *Temples and High Places in Biblical Times* (ed. A. Biran; Jerusalem: Hebrew Union College Press, 1981) 142–51. V. Tzaferis, "The 'God Who Is in Dan' and the Cult of Pan at Banias in the Hellenistic and Roman Periods," *ErIsr* 23 (A. Biran Volume; 1991) 128*–135*.

P. Kyle McCarter is that the understanding of Israelite religion needs to be broadened considerably in the wake of Kuntillet ʾAjrud and other discoveries, despite the ideological claims of the literary texts.[16]

The burden of the argument here so far is that a reconsideration of the circumstances of the Assyrian conquest of the North does not support the suggestion that later Galilean/Samaritan hostility had its roots in that experience. On the contrary, our putative Galilean Israelites should have been drawn to link up with their Samarian co-religionists—not just for religious reasons but because they can both be presumed to have suffered similarly under the foreign overlord in terms of economic and social pressures on their traditional way of life. To be sure, the imperial principle of "dividing and ruling" can be seen to be operative in the establishment of different provinces for the continued subjugation of conquered territories. Such a policy may have inhibited alliances between Israelite remnants in both Galilee and Samaria, but there is certainly no reason to suppose that Galilean and Samarian Israelites who survived the conquests should have regarded each other as enemies. Indeed, the fact that they were administered by new elites from Samaria and Megiddo should have strengthened the bonds between them. Perhaps modern scholarship has been unconsciously influenced by Josephus's anti-Samaritan handling of this episode, highlighting their foreign "Cuthean" origins and their devious and unfaithful character, as expressed in their religious rites "up to this day" (*Ant.* 11.290).

The Temple on Gerizim and Hellenization

A virtual consensus seems to have emerged among the most influential scholars of the Second Temple Period that the building of the Samaritan Temple on Gerizim should be linked to the arrival of Alexander and the Macedonians, as Josephus indicates (*Ant.* 11.303–8).[17] According to this consensus, the establishment of a Macedonian colony in the capital Samaria, either by Alexander or his governor, Perdicas, led to the dispersal of the ruling aristocracy, who re-established the ancient site at Shechem, which had previously been abandoned. Styling themselves the "Sidonians at Shechem," they set up their own sanctuary on Gerizim, not having received any support from Jerusalem. This dating is thought to be supported by both the Wadi Daliyeh

16. P. Kyle McCarter, Jr., "Aspects of Religion in the Israelite Monarchy: Biblical and Epigraphic Data," in *Ancient Israelite Religion: Essays in Honor of Frank Moore Cross* (ed. P. D. Miller, P. D. Hanson, and S. D. McBride; Philadelphia: Fortress, 1987) 137–56; W. Dever, "Will the Real Israel Please Stand Up? Archaeology and the Religions of Israel," *BASOR* 298 (1996) 37–58.

17. E. Bickerman, *From Ezra to the Last of the Maccabees* (New York: Schocken, 1962) 43–44; M. Hengel, *Jews, Greeks and Barbarians* (trans. J. Bowden; London: SCM, 1980) 8–9; J. Purvis, "The Samaritans," in *The Cambridge History of Judaism*, vol. 2: *The Hellenistic Age* (ed. W. D. Davies and L. Finkelstein; New York: Cambridge University Press, 1989) 591–693, esp. 602.

Samaritan papyri and the excavations at Shechem (Tel Balatah).[18] Though Yahweh-worshipers, their Cuthean origins and the possible presence of Greek trading elements in their midst made them prey to the hellenization process, to the point that they voluntarily requested Antiochus Epiphanes to establish the cult of Zeus in their sanctuary in the second century B.C.E.

In the light of the most recent findings, however, there are serious problems with this construal. It is unlikely that the Macedonians would have permitted the building of a fortified city at Shechem by the ousted Samarians. This is even less likely if the charred remains of more than three hundred people in the caves at Wadi Daliyeh are, as Frank Moore Cross has suggested, those of Samarians fleeing from the Greeks.[19] One dissenting voice to the consensus was that of Richard Coggins, who believed that the archaeological evidence from Tel Balatah was too imprecise to date its refounding to the time of Alexander. In addition, he considered the linking of the Gerizim Temple with Alexander as part of Josephus's anti-Samaritan bias of his own day and hence lacking historical credibility.[20]

Recently, Itzhak Magen proposed a different account of Samaritan origins based on his archaeological work on Mt. Gerizim since 1990.[21] What has been uncovered is not just a temple, but a fortified city with a sacred precinct at its center, both built at the same time. While there is evidence of habitation at the site from the Ptolemaic Period, Magen summarizes his findings to the effect that "the architectural, ceramic and numismatic evidence indicates that the hellenistic city on Mt. Gerizim and the sacred precincts were established during the reign of Antiochus III (early second century B.C.E.)."[22] Magen is aware that none of the literary sources mentions a city on Gerizim, but he attributes this silence to its destruction in fewer than a hundred years by John Hyrcanus; as a result, only the sacred character of the mountain was remembered. Apart from the material evidence, the suitable political circumstances for such a foundation need to be considered. It is unlikely that the inhabitants of the restored Shechem, whoever they may have been, built another city on Gerizim, let alone a temple. In fact, Magen believes that the restored Shechem was a Macedonian fortress, built to guard an important pass, and not the seat of the ousted Samarians. Antiochus III's well-known favorable treatment of the Jerusalem Jews (*Ant.* 12.138–53) appears to have

18. G. E. Wright, "The Samaritans at Shechem," *HTR* 55 (1962) 357–66.

19. F. M. Cross, "Aspects of Samaritan and Jewish History in the Late Persian and Hellenistic Times," *HTR* 59 (1966) 201–11. See also A. Crown, "Another Look at Samaritan Origins," in *New Samaritan Studies of the Société d'Études Samaritaines, IV–V* (Sydney: University of Sydney, Mandelbaum Publishing, 1995) 133–56.

20. R. J. Coggins, *Samaritans and Jews: The Origins of Samaritanism Reconsidered* (Oxford: Blackwell, 1985) 96–97, 103–6.

21. Y. Magen, "Mount Gerizim and the Samaritans," in *Early Christianity in Context: Monuments and Documents* (ed. F. Manns and E. Alliata; SBF Collectio Maior 38; Jerusalem: Franciscan, 1993) 91–147.

22. Ibid., 135.

extended itself to Samarian Yahweh-worshipers; the sacred precincts are modeled on the Jerusalem sanctuary, and in addition the material remains suggest a form of worship similar to the form in Jerusalem.

What is particularly suggestive about these considerations, hypothetical though Magen's reconstruction of the history may be at present, is the very different profile of the Samaritans and their Temple that results. This was not the building of ousted Samarians of Cuthean extraction whose religious affiliations were dubious at best in later Jewish estimation. It was, rather, the foundation of Yahweh-worshipers with strong Israelite connections. Josephus, despite all his anti-Samaritan bias, acknowledges that the Gerizim temple was modeled on the one in Jerusalem (*Ant.* 11.310, 13.235), something that Magen's discoveries seem to confirm.[23] That there were Yahweh-worshipers in Samaria in the Persian Period is amply documented in the books of Ezra and Nehemiah. It is to them, rather than to any possible syncretistic Samarians, that the foundations of Samaritanism as a discrete cultic community are to be attributed. The fact that Yahweh temples, other than the Jerusalem one, can be documented throughout the Second Temple Period demonstrates that the description "schismatic" for the Gerizim foundation is an anachronistic label.[24] Equally, the emergence of the Samaritan Pentateuch, the beginnings of which have been convincingly dated to the period following John Hyrcanus's destruction of their Temple, should not be seen as the sign of an obdurate sect that refused to accept the full and authentic canon of Jewish Scripture. This picture ignores the fluid state of the canonical process generally, as well as the debates in later rabbinic circles about the relative importance of various sections of the Tanakh, with the Prophets and Writings existing for the sole purpose of leading people back to the knowledge of the Torah.[25] Indeed, other archaeological evidence from Magen's work in the Samarian region develops this trajectory further. The remains of Samaritan synagogues as well as domestic and communal *miqva'ot* at various sites point to developments similar to those that occurred among Judean Yahweh-worshipers.[26] In addition, literary evidence from Josephus indicates a wider dispersal of Samaritans to Transjordan (*Ant.* 13.253–56; *J.W.* 1.62), as well as

23. Ibid., 102–3; and see p. 139 for a description of the northern gate in line with the description in the *Temple Scroll* from Qumran as well as other finds suggesting that "the sacred precinct was built according to the same sacred precinct of the Jerusalem temple which Josephus described."

24. Smith, *Palestinian Parties*, 69–70. See also J. Zangenberg, *Frühes Christentum in Samarien* (Tübingen and Basel: Franke, 1998), esp. 10–26, for a detailed discussion of the reent discoveries and their implications.

25. R. Boid (M. N. Saraf), "Use, Authority, and Exegesis of Mikra in Samaritan Tradition," in *Mikra: Text, Translation and Interpretation of the Hebrew Bible in Ancient Judaism and Early Christianity* (ed. Martin Jan Mulder; CRINT 2/1; Assen: Van Gorcum / Philadelphia: Fortress 1988) 595–633.

26. Y. Magen, "Qedumim: A Samaritan Site of the Roman-Byzantine Period"; idem, "The Ritual Baths (*miqva'oth*) at Qedumim and the Observance of Ritual Purity among the

to Egypt (*Ant.* 12.10, 13.74–76). More surprising still in the light of the usual stereotype of a beleaguered community around Gerizim is the second-century B.C.E. evidence from the island of Delos, in which we read of "the Israelites who make offerings to hallowed (*hieron*) Argarizein."[27]

This evidence points to a profile of the Samaritans as observant, loyal Yahweh-worshipers who availed themselves of the first political opportunity to build their own Temple. Furthermore, having been spurned for political, rather than religious, reasons by their Jerusalem co-religionists, they maintained their separate religious identity even after their Temple was destroyed by the Judeans' political leader. The reconstruction faces, however, the serious objection that, according to Josephus (*Ant.* 12.257–64), these Yahweh-worshipers were prepared, within a very brief period of time, to abandon their convictions, appealing directly to Antiochus IV to convert their worship into that of Zeus, the friend of strangers, and being prepared to abandon their Sabbath and other observances. This account differs from that of 2 Macc 6:2, where it is stated that worship of Zeus was imposed on both Gerizim and Jerusalem by Antiochus Epiphanes. It is only Josephus who describes them as "the Sidonians at Shechem," a description that has most often been taken to refer to a colony of traders present there as at Marissa in Idumea. Magen reports the remains of imported pottery at Tel Balatah, thus supporting the presence of such foreign traders, whose views need not have been shared by all at Gerizim—anymore than were the views of Jason and his followers shared by all in Jerusalem at the same time. Coggins, on the other hand, once again views the Josephan modifications of 2 Maccabees as a sign of his Jerusalemite, anti-Samaritan bias, an attitude that Josephus was by no means the first to portray, as can be seen from Sir 50:26, with its reference to "the foolish people who live in Shechem." Josephus earlier indicated that the Samaritans referred to themselves as Sidonians (*Ant.* 11.344) by way of dissociating themselves from the Jews—a constant ploy of theirs, according to him, when faced with a foreign threat. Thus, Coggins prefers a rhetorical rather than a historical referent to the description, especially in view of the fact that "Sidonian" is also already used as a highly derogatory term in Isa 23:2–3.[28]

Whichever explanation is to be accepted, it does not seem necessary to abandon the proposal for a revised understanding of the Samaritans as being descendants of Yahweh-worshipers in the region generally rather than just being the successors of the non-Israelite elite from the capital city. Their

---

Samaritans"; and idem, "Samaritan Synagogues," in *Early Christianity in Context: Monuments and Documents* (ed. F. Manns and E. Alliata; SBF Collectio Maior 38; Jerusalem: Franciscan, 1993) 167–80, 181–92, and 193–230.

27. A. T. Kraabel, "New Evidence of the Samaritan Diaspora Has Been Found on Delos," *BA* 47 (1984) 44–46.

28. Magen, "Mount Gerizim and the Samaritans," 141–42; Coggins, "The Samaritans in Josephus," 265–66.

understanding of Yahwism did not preclude worship outside of Jerusalem, but this did not necessarily make them syncretists or any less committed to their Israelite heritage, as their arrogation of the name "Israelite" makes clear. They may not have accepted the Deuteronomic ideal of the "Yahweh-alone" party in terms of worship in Jerusalem only, but they had a Deuteronomic warrant for their choice of sacred site (Deut 27:11–26; cf. 11:29–30)—a choice that could be discussed by the sages of the Mishna later (*m. Soṭa* 7:5) without any animosity toward the Samaritans of their own day, unlike the Josephan treatment we have encountered more than once.

This conclusion merely highlights the paradox of the Galilean/Samaritan animosity more forcibly. Far from finding the Gerizim cult center a threat, Galilean Israelites, as depicted by Horsley, should have been attracted to it, given this revised understanding of its social as well as its religious matrix among the older Samarian village community. Furthermore, the picture that emerges from Shimon Dar's survey of western Samaria is one of a village, peasant culture, consisting of small, family-sized farms of 5–25 dunams (20–100 acres), either freeholdings or leaseholdings. In all probability, there was a mixed land-owning pattern in Samaria as in Galilee.[29] The presence of more than a thousand field towers dating from the Ptolemaic to the Herodian periods in the area surveyed suggests a more organized pattern of cultivation and probably a trend toward larger estates. This development was intensified further in the Herodian Period, as Dar's study of Qarawat bene Hassan and its environs typifies. A large Herodian-style building has been identified and a number of local place-names still echo the region's Herodian connection. The village consisted of close to 200 family holdings, with individual plots marked off to an area of 2,500 acres and an extra 500 acres for pasturage. In all probability, the large building served as the estate manager's residence, and other building complexes in the vicinity may have served as granaries.[30] Just east of this site is the modern village of Haris, which has been identified as Josephus's Arus. One of Herod the Great's associates, Ptolemy of Rhodes, owned a village there as his private *ktema* (*Ant.* 17.189; *J.W.* 1.473), probably acquired as a grant from the king. In addition we hear that Herod planted six thousand veterans in the territory of Sebaste (*Ant.* 15.296; *J.W.* 1.403), presumably in this instance in small allotments, similar to the foundation at Gaba on the borders of Galilee (*Ant.* 15.294).

Social conditions for the Samarian peasantry may, if anything, have been worse than for their Galilean counterparts. It should also be remembered

29. S. Dar, *Landscape and Pattern: An Archaeological Survey of Samaria 800 B.C.E.–636* (BAR International Series 308/1–2; Oxford: BAR, 1986), with commentary by S. Applebaum, "The Settlement Pattern of Western Samaria from Hellenistic to Byzantine Times: A Historical Commentary," 257–69; D. Fiensey, *The Social History of Palestine in the Herodian Period* (Lewiston, N.Y.: Mellen, 1991) 31–43.

30. Dar, *Landscape and Pattern*, 230–54.

that the effects of urbanization came to Samaria earlier than to Galilee, with the presence of the Macedonian colony in the capital beginning in the Early Hellenistic Age. Herod the Great's establishment of Sebaste at this site continued the trend on a scale far greater than Antipas could have attempted at Sepphoris or Tiberias, even when these foundations put further pressure on the traditional Galilean way of life. In these circumstances, common politico-economic as well as socio-cultural factors, together with shared traditional values with a similar provenance, should have made for a coalition of Galileans and Samaritans—at least among those who continued to claim legitimation for that way of life from the Israelite memory. It might be hypothesized that the very intensity of the animosity that our sources indicate was due to the fact that, at least in the eyes of the Samaritans, Galileans were being deeply disloyal in not supporting them rather than the Judean/Jerusalem center, when social and religious experiences might be presumed to have dictated differently. Such a conclusion sharpens further the focus of the initial questions: why did the Galileans turn to Jerusalem? What role did Judea and Jerusalem play in determining relationships within this interregional network of Yahweh-worshipers with very different historical experiences? How were the rival claims and their embodiment in competing cultic centers legitimated through appeals to a shared religious story?

Galileans, Samaritans, and the Ioudaioi

Of all of the literary sources from the first century, the Fourth Gospel expresses the competing religious claims of the Samaritans and the Jews most sharply. The Samaritan woman is surprised that Jesus, a Jew, should ask her, a woman of Samaria, for a drink of water. Later in the dialogue she moves from water to worship, declaring: "our ancestors worshiped on this mountain, but you say that Jerusalem is the place where people must worship." In reply, Jesus makes the definitive statement: "salvation is from the Jews" (John 4:9, 20, 22). By contrast, Josephus, despite all of the anti-Samaritan bias noted from him, is not as definitive on the matter. Samaritans may have been disloyal, and they may have had dubious origins, but the Hasmoneans did not require them, as they had the Idumeans and Itureans, to be circumcised in order to be included in the Jerusalem cultic community; their illegitimate Temple had merely to be destroyed. Whereas the expulsion of Christians from the synagogue may explain the sharpness of the Johannine portrayal, the Jerusalem priest, Josephus, writing *Antiquities* in the nineties, at a time when the one center that mattered for him lay in ruins, seems anxious not to exclude any strand of Jew from the larger family.

For the purposes of this essay—to attempt to understand the complexity of the tangled relationships among Galileans, Samaritans, and *Ioudaioi*—Josephus's account of events in the Jewish community in Egypt during the reign of Ptolemy Philometer (180–145 B.C.E.) is quite significant.[31] First, the ousted Jewish priest, Onias IV, petitioned the king to be allowed to build a temple resembling the one in Jerusalem for his co-religionists, "because they are ill-disposed to one another, as is also the case with the Egyptians, because of the multitude of their temples and their varying opinions about the forms of worship" (*Ant.* 13.66). The message is clear: a multiplicity of places of worship creates social upheaval. Whatever the success of Onias's temple in other respects, it was unable to heal the divisions among Egyptian Jewry on the issue of the competing temples in the homeland. Jews and Samaritans appeared before the king in the very next episode, debating about whether the offerings should be sent to Jerusalem or Gerizim as the authentic Mosaic shrine (*Ant.* 13.74; cf. *Ant.* 12.10). Once again, the proponents of Jerusalem won out, and the defenders of Gerizim's claims were executed. The same message is delivered: adherence to the Jerusalem Temple alone can create national unity; anything else will cause destruction. And yet, in Josephus's treatment of the Samaritans in this episode, nothing of his bias displayed elsewhere occurs—neither their dubious origins nor their disloyalty are even mentioned. They, too, are Yahweh-worshipers, following the Mosaic dispensation, but their Temple lacked the legitimacy they claim for it. In other respects they are potential *Ioudaioi* (cf. *Ant.* 11.85–88).[32]

That this was Josephus's view is confirmed by his treatment of the offer by the Seleucid pretender, Demetrius, reported in 1 Maccabees. In order to win the favor of the Jews in his struggle with Alexander Balas for power, Demetrius offers to cede to Jonathan three border districts in Samaria (1 Macc 10:29–30). Josephus, however, transforms this into an offer of the three toparchies of Samaria, Galilee, and Perea—that is, the whole Jewish territory as it was later viewed in Herodian times and as Josephus himself describes it prior to the Great Revolt (*J.W.* 3.35–58). Furthermore, Demetrius is made to declare that "it shall be the concern of the High Priest that not a single *Ioudaios* shall have a temple to worship other than that at Jerusalem" (*Ant.* 13.50, 53). The irony that it was a Jerusalem Jewish leader, John Hyrcanus, not Demetrius, who achieved this goal was surely not lost on Josephus. Yet, he merely mentions the Temple's destruction in passing, unlike his detailed, gloating account of the fall of Samaria itself (*Ant.* 13.257, 281).

In his recent detailed study of Galilee, Horsley consistently translates *hoi Ioudaioi* as "the Judeans." He thus confines its meaning solely to its

---

31. S. Schwartz, "The Judaism of Samaria and Galilee in Josephus' Version of the Letter of Demetrius I to Jonathan (*Antiquities* 13,48–57)," *HTR* 82 (1989) 377–91, esp. 385–86; Coggins, "The Samaritans in Josephus," 263–64.

32. L. Feldman ("Josephus' Attitude towards the Samaritans: A Study in Ambivalence," *Studies in Hellenistic Judaism* [Leiden: Brill, 1996] 114–36) acknowledges Josephus's apparent ambivalence but finds no appreciable difference between the treatment in the *Jewish Antiquities* and the *Jewish War*, despite the former's more strident anti-Samaritanism. In this regard, he claims, Josephus's attitude is not dissimilar to the rabbinic attitude.

geographico-political reference to the Judean temple-state and does not acknowledge its more extended, religious significance in terms of a worshiper
at the Jerusalem Temple, irrespective of place of origin.[33] This restricted understanding then plays a major part in Horsley's treatment of the ongoing opposition between the Galilean Israelites and the Judean Jews in accordance
with his conflictual model, based on political-social-economic factors. The
remarks of John Ashton with regard to a similar interpretive attempt in respect to the *Ioudaioi* in the Fourth Gospel seem apposite here.[34] A term such
as *Ioudaios* does indeed continue to retain something of its geographic connotation, even when it is applied to people who no longer lived in Judea or
indeed may never have done so. When, for example, speaking of the Poles in
Britain or the Irish in America, while their place of origin (or their ancestors)
certainly is acknowledged, so is it also being affirmed that however long the
group in question may have lived elsewhere, "they can still be singled out by
the customs they share with the 'folks back home.'" And, further, those customs include, indeed primarily are, religious customs, as the examples of the
Poles and the Irish testify.

Significantly, Josephus himself seems to be aware that *Ioudaios* is not just
a geographic term: "This name (*Ioudaioi*) which they have been called from
the time when they went up from Babylon, is derived from the tribe of Judah;
as this tribe was the first to come to those parts, both the people themselves
and the country have taken their name from it" (*Ant.* 11.173). Presumably, the
processes were slow and by no means uniform whereby this group of return-
ing exiles from Babylon was able to impose its understanding of the national
sanctuary, as the struggles with the Samarian Yahweh-worshipers and the
Judean ʿam ha-ʾareṣ make clear. Thus, to restrict *Ioudaios* to a geographico-
political meaning, without attending to its very definite associations with worship in the Jerusalem Temple and acceptance of the customs, rituals, and
practices associated with this worship, is to ignore the powerful impetus that
religious belief and practice can give in transcending intolerable social and
economic factors, which from a secular post-Marxist perspective may be
judged as being thoroughly alienating. While agreeing with Horsley that "religion" as a discrete and separable aspect of life is an enlightenment construct, in dealing with the ancient world I prefer to speak of religious beliefs

---

33. Horsley (*Galilee,* 45 and passim) stresses Josephus's use of the term *ethnos ton Ga-
lilaion* in support of his theory of a radical separation of Galileans and Judeans in Josephus's mind, so that the former were never fully integrated into the Hasmonean-Judean
temple-state. Ironically, such a contention does not sit easily with Horsley's desire to see
the Galileans as Israelites, since, as Feldman has argued, the vast majority of Josephus's
uses of the term *ethnos* refers either to the Jewish nation as a whole or to other surrounding
peoples who are ethnically not Jews ("Josephus' Attitude towards the Samaritans," 117–18).

34. J. Ashton, "The Identity and Function of the *Ioudaioi* in the Fourth Gospel," *NovT*
27 (1985) 41–75.

and practices, especially Jewish ones, not just as being *embedded* but also as *embodying* the social and economic realities of that culture.[35]

The Samaritans are of course never called *Ioudaioi* by Josephus. They also seem to have continued to call themselves Israelites, in continuity with the name of the Northern Kingdom. Yet, by the logic of Josephus's own position they could have, indeed ought to have, been capable of being so designated, if only they had not behaved so obstinately with regard to their place of worship. The actual reality was quite different. Not all inhabitants of Samaria were Yahweh-worshipers, and presumably not all Yahweh-worshipers there were of old Israelite stock. They refused, however, to accept the ideology of only one place of worship espoused by the Judeans. The establishment of their own center of worship on Gerizim gave them a separate social, economic, and religious identity, however, that continued beyond the destruction of their Temple. The memory of that act of destruction by a Judean leader ensured that no reconciliation was possible between them and the Judeans—or those who, though geographically not Judeans, still espoused the cause of their temple as *Ioudaioi*. The memory also ensured that they could not participate in the struggle for political freedom from the Romans that was inspired by allegiance to the claims of Jerusalem, even when they themselves may have harbored similarly motivated aspirations (*Ant.* 18.85–89; *J.W.* 3.307–15). Undoubtedly, interests other than religious ones were operative in these tensions. It was, however, the differences about the proper understanding of the same religious tradition that ultimately gave rise to the emergence of two different political entities, recognition of which had to be made by various imperial ruling powers subsequently. Even when social and cultural patterns within the two communities were very similar indeed, these crystallized differently around the conflicting religious issues, and no rapprochement was possible.

This understanding of Samaritan/*Ioudaioi* tensions already points the way for an adequate explanation of the Samaritan/Galilean tensions with which this discussion began. These tensions were not based on events in the Assyrian Period. As has been seen, there is no warrant in the relevant accounts, when critically examined and correlated with the archaeological evidence, to suggest serious social or religious differences emerging at that time. Rather, the tensions belonged to more recent events. It is only with the Hellenistic Age and with the Hasmonean expansion in particular that Galilee as such comes into view in the literary sources. Even then Josephus is singularly lacking in information on how the expansion occurred in Galilee, in contrast to his treatment of Samaria and Perea. Is this silence merely because of a lack of sources or a lack of anything of note to report?[36] The hypothesis of enforced

---

35. Horsley, *Galilee*, 12, 129, and passim. In contrast, see J. Neusner, *The Social Study of Judaism: Essays and Reflections* (BJS 160; Atlanta: Scholars Press, 1988) esp. 1.3–23.

36. See Schwartz ("The Judaism of Samaria and Galilee," 384 n. 17), who suggests that the standard account of the all-conquering Hasmoneans based on Josephus and enshrined

Judaization of the Itureans has been developed by modern scholars to fill the gap but without any adequate basis either in the literary or archaeological evidence.[37] Once again, archaeology, not generalized macro-sociological models, will have to answer this question, independently of the literary sources. Quite a lot was at stake ideologically both for the author of 1 Maccabees and for Josephus in their portrayals of the Hasmoneans and their exploits.

The reports of various surveys suggesting a steady increase in settlements in Galilee from the Hellenistic to the Byzantine periods point to a much more gradual expansion than the model of a sudden and violent takeover based on a military campaign would suggest.[38] Furthermore, the more information that emerges on the nature of these settlements, the more adequately can their social role be interpreted. A reading of the evidence so far available does not find Horsley's claim, that the settlements have the nature of military outposts, convincing. Even if there is evidence that Gush Ḥalav was fortified, it was on the border with Tyre, as Horsley himself recognizes. Its role as a military outpost, if it was such, was therefore more likely to have been as a defense against invaders than as protection against recalcitrant elements of the older native population. In this regard, the absence of the round towers that were such a feature in the same period for western Samaria may be significant in assessing the Galilean situation.[39] In other words, if a colonization of Galilee is to be posited for this period, is it correct to see it as an imposition on an older, resistant native population giving rise to internal hostilities and the need for defensive arrangements for the new arrivals? What would the archaeological remains of such a process look like? In fact, the pattern of such hellenistic-style colonization going back to Alexander was, rather, one of

---

in Schürer-Vermes is in need of revision. See E. Schürer, *The History of the Jewish People in the Age of Jesus Christ* (ed. G. Vermes et al.; Edinburgh: T. & T. Clark, 1975–87) 2.7–10. In this regard Horsley's search for a more comprehensive category than conversion (*Galilee*, 46–52) is highly significant. However, his conflictual model encompassing resistant Galileans and exploiting Judeans seems to preclude the possibility of genuine enculturation, even though this seems to be the logic of such statements as: "their shared roots in Israelite traditions provided a basis for the incorporation of Galileans under the Judean temple-state" (p. 51).

37. Archaeological evidence for the Iturean expansion shows very little signs of either so-called Iturean ware or their characteristic style of habitation in Galilee, similar to those found in the Golan. See M. Hartel, "Khirbet Zemel, 1985–86," *IEJ* 37 (1987) 270–72; and idem, *Northern Golan Heights: The Archaeological Survey as Source of Local History* (Qazrin: Agaf ha-atiqot veha-muzeonim, 1989) [Hebrew].

38. M. Aviam, "Galilee: The Hellenistic and Byzantine Periods," *NEAEHL* 2.452–58.

39. See, however, Applebaum ("Settlement Pattern," 260), though Dar (*Landscape and Pattern*, 109–13) contends that the towers were not for defense purposes but for wine fermentation. R. Horsley ("Archaeology and the Villages of Upper Galilee: A Dialogue with Archaeologists," *BASOR* 297 [1995] 5–15, esp. 7–8) regards Gush Ḥalav as the site of a Hasmonean–Herodian fortress similar to Jotapata and Sepphoris, based on *m. 'Arak.* 9:6. But see E. Meyers's response, "An Archaeological Response to a New Testament Scholar," *BASOR* 297 (1995) 17–25.

encouragement to enculturate with the older population through inter-marriage and to adopt the local language, customs, and the like. Even the Herodians appear to have respected local sensibilities. Herod the Great's sub-sequent establishment of a colony of veterans at Gaba in the great plain and of Babylonian Jews in Batanea took the form, not of military outposts, but of village settlements, comprised of small landowners—in all probability not dissimilar in layout to Qarawat bene Hassan, but as far as we can tell, without the field towers.

Unlike what he calls the Samaritans, Josephus can call the inhabitants of Galilee *Ioudaioi*, even though, as is well known, his most frequent designa-tion, especially in *Life*, is *Galilaioi*. One very clear instance of particular im-portance for the argument here is *J.W.* 2.232, the episode in which the Samaritans attacked the Galilean pilgrims on their way to Jerusalem: "a Ga-lilean, one of a large company of *Ioudaioi* on their way up to the festival, was murdered."[40] This is precisely the extended meaning of the name already dis-cussed here: Galileans, insofar as they share in the customs—especially the religious ones—relating to worship in the single Temple in Jerusalem, are naturally designated *Ioudaioi*. Similarly, on the occasion of another festival, it is reported that people from Galilee, Idumea, Jericho, and Perea were gath-ered in Jerusalem, together with a great multitude from Judea itself (*auton te Ioudaion plethos*). A bitter confrontation arose between these people and the Roman troops. As Josephus relates the ensuing battle, he speaks simply of *hoi Ioudaioi*, on the assumption that all who had gathered from regions other than Judea could still be designated *Ioudaioi*, insofar as they shared common assumptions about the Temple and its sacredness (*Ant.* 17.254–58).

Several scholars have attempted to give a special meaning to the use of the term *Galilaioi* in *Life*, effectively identifying it with the alleged Zealot party opposed to Roman rule. The term is used virtually devoid of any geographic connotations, except insofar as the Galileans in particular were regarded as violently anti-Roman.[41] This stereotype of the Galileans is the result of Jose-phus's description of the people he was sent to command, as part of his self-glorification in *The Jewish War* (3.41–42). Furthermore, the use of the term *zealot* to cover all shades of Jewish nationalism in the first century C.E. is no longer admissible. Yet, a case can be made for a very special use of the term *Galilaios* in *Life*, namely to refer to the mainly village people who, Josephus claims, supported him against his local rivals for the command of Galilee,

---

40. The significance of this juxtaposition of *Galilaios* and *Ioudaion* seems to have been missed or overlooked by Horsley (*Galilee*, 146). While the account in *Ant.* 20.118ff. di-verges at several points from that of the *Jewish War*, nevertheless, it clearly assumes that Ga-lileans can call on *Ioudaioi* for their support in vindicating the murder of their kinsmen.

41. References in S. Freyne, "The Galileans in the Light of Josephus' *Vita*," *NTS* 26 (1980) 397–413, esp. 397–98 nn. 1–4; L. Feldman, "The Term 'Galileans' in Josephus," *Studies in Hellenistic Judaism* (Leiden: Brill, 1996) 111–13.

notably John of Gischala and Justus of Tiberias.[42] Several times they are designated as being "from the land," to distinguish them from the urban elites. Elsewhere I have attempted to interpret this characterization, for all of the signs of its Josephan special pleading, in terms of urban-rural tensions in the region in the wake of growing Herodian urbanization.[43] What cannot be doubted is that at least from Josephus's point of view, these Galileans are *Ioudaioi* in the sense discussed here. This is true even when this epithet is used to represent the strictly observant residents of Tarichaeae who insisted on refugee pagan noblemen's being circumcised before they could stay among them (*Life* 112–13).

The evidence that suggests that this picture of a Jewish Galilee is more than just Josephan rhetorical propaganda will not be reexamined here, though of course it is that also. Suffice it to say that I see no reason to change my overall views about a Jewish Galilee from at least the Early Roman Period, despite Horsley's critique. One of the reasons Horsley does not find any literary evidence to support the presence of Galilean pilgrims in Jerusalem may be that he virtually excludes the Gospels as sources for reconstructing Galilean life in the period, even though they may well be our best literary evidence for Jewish practices in the first century, despite all their well-established *Tendenzen*.[44] Such a view appears to be supported by the results of the present enquiry: namely, that first-century Galilean Israelites seem to be missing at those very times and places where they would be expected to show up, while Galilean Jews have left very clear traces of their presence in the archaeological as well as the literary evidence.

---

42. G. Jossa ("Chi sono I Galilei nella Vita di Flavio Giuseppe?" *Rivista Biblica Italiana* 31 [1983] 334–39), while essentially agreeing with the conclusions of my study (see previous note), namely, that Josephus uses the term *Galilaios* for his own supporters, wants to extend its range to the citizens of the major towns also. The opposition, in his view, was not between urban and rural but between traditionalists (Shammaites and Zealots) and *neoteristai*, that is, those who were prepared to compromise the ancestral customs for the Greek way. However, there is no evidence in the *Life* for characterizing the vast majority of Galileans in this way.

43. S. Freyne, "Urban-Rural Relations in First Century Galilee: Some Suggestions from the Literary Sources," in *The Galilee in Late Antiquity* (ed. Lee I. Levine; New York: Jewish Theological Seminary Press, 1992) 75–94; and idem, "Herodian Economics in Galilee: Searching for a Suitable Model," in *Modelling Early Christianity: Social-Scientific Studies of the New Testament in Context* (ed. Philip F. Esler; London: Routledge, 1995) 23–46.

44. Horsley, *Galilee*, 144–47. See his remarks on the use of the Gospels (p. 14). As Martin Goodman has suggested (personal communication), there is no great evidence for pilgrimage on a grand scale prior to Herod the Great, and it may be that Herod encouraged pilgrims from the diaspora as well as the homeland for economic reasons, in view of the vast expenditure involved in extending the Temple Mount and refurbishing the Temple itself. At all events, not just the Gospels but Josephus also attests to the Galileans' making the pilgrimage in the first century c.e.

Jesus and Galilee: The Contingencies of a Renewal Movement

RICHARD A. HORSLEY

University of Massachusetts, Boston

The independent individual isolated from historical contingencies and social relations is surely a modern middle-class enlightenment fiction. In the
same way, the "historical Jesus" we have been looking for as an individual
person is also a modern creation, filled with content by scholars who have
little sense of the history about which they are supposedly writing. The mis-
guided effort to establish Jesus' "authentic" sayings tears them from any intel-
ligible literary and historical context. Having no meaning in isolation from a
historically meaningful context, they are given meaning by modern scholars,
who usually group them by topic. The resulting "historical Jesus" thus resembles a museum exhibit, with his sayings on particular subjects displayed in
separate museum cases labeled with such categories as "the kingdom," "family," and "table fellowship" and with comments on each "artifact" written by
the curator who has arranged the exhibit.[1]

We have access to Jesus, however, only through the historical Jesus movements. We know of his sayings and doings only because certain people remembered and repeated them. The sayings and doings were remembered
and repeated only because they were significant in particular social connections and circumstances. Thus, the historically significant Jesus could not

---

1. Allusions in this paragraph and the next are primarily to John Dominic Crossan, *The
Historical Jesus: The Life of a Mediterranean Jewish Peasant* (San Francisco: HarperSan-
Francisco, 1991). Illustrations could be taken from a number of recent books on the historical Jesus. I focus on Crossan's work not to "pick on" it in particular but because it is
seminal, has been sold widely, and is familiar to many. The procedures followed by Crossan's and several other publications on the historical Jesus are further developments of
form criticism, which became standard in the study of Gospel traditions after Rudolf Bult-
mann and Martin Dibelius.

have been a teacher teaching teachings to everyone in general (and no one
in particular) about general subjects, nor would discrete individual sayings
have been remembered and transmitted in isolation from some concrete social context. Individual persons, moreover, do not act in isolation from social
relations, established social roles, and certain historical conditions and contingencies. Particular sayings and actions of Jesus had significance only in
connection with a person-in-role in a significant formative (therefore memo-
rable) movement in a people's history. On a quest for the historical Abraham
Lincoln, for example, it would be patently absurd to think the "Life of a
North American Illinois Farmer" had been written if only a few authentic
sayings of his wisdom had been established and discussed in topical groupings. Lincoln's sayings and Abraham Lincoln himself would be historically
insignificant if he had not become a senator, then president, and a martyred
hero at a particularly crucial juncture in the history of the United States of
America. The wit and wisdom of Jesus, like that of Lincoln, has no historical
significance and would not have been remembered if separated from the cul-
tural/societal role he played in a distinctive way in a particular history. What
the role was in Lincoln's case is well known. We are only beginning to be
able to establish it in the case of Jesus, although some scholars believe that we
know roughly what the possible roles were and the degree to which Jesus fit
one or more of them.

Jesus must be approached similarly, as a leader (and martyred hero) embedded in a movement in particular situations that began in Galilee around
30 c.e. but continued there and beyond for a period of twenty to thirty years
before the literature emerged that provides sources for our historical knowledge. If the historical Jesus is to be a historically connected or embedded ac-
tor and of historical significance—and not simply a cipher of Christian faith
or a historical peg on which to hang Christian christological constructs—the
historical circumstances that provide the conditions (in both senses) of Jesus'
role and movement must be understood.

Impact of Events on Galileans

A social movement arises in a concrete historical context that provides the
conditions for its emergence, the social forms and cultural contents with
which it works creatively in pursuing its purpose, and what it sees as the problematic situation or *institutions or* persons against which it is acting. In the
case of Jesus and his movement, this historical context was Galilee under the
Romans' client ruler, Herod Antipas.

To know about and interpret a movement in context, of course, evidence
and critically-formulated procedures are needed for dealing with it. Josephus
provides a great deal of information, most of it from more than a generation
later, during the Great Revolt of 66–67. Recent studies of Josephus and his
historiography have contributed importantly to a critical perspective from

which Josephus's histories can be read.[2] Rabbinic literature provides a wealth of evidence for Galilee in later centuries, some of which may be applicable to the time of Antipas and Jesus by critical extrapolation. Several recent studies have made important contributions to the ways in which rabbinic literature can be used as historical sources.[3] Jesus scholars are only beginning to avail themselves of these sources and the critical methods of using them to advantage.[4]

Ancient literature such as Josephus and the rabbis, however, generally comes from and reflects the interests of the social elite, whereas the Jesus movement almost certainly began among the Galilean peasantry. In this connection, the archaeology of Galilee may have a distinctive contribution to make to our understanding of the Jesus movement and its Galilean context.[5] The use of archaeological data and reports to reconstruct first-century Galilee and the Jesus movements that emerged there, however, may be problematic in several respects. Most archaeological data now available come from much later periods. Given the nature of the materials with which archaeology works, it necessarily deals in broad time periods, often of a century or more, in its stratigraphy of the Hellenistic, Early Roman, Middle Roman, and Late Roman periods. Archaeological reports based largely on Middle and Late Roman finds suggest that Galilee, far from being an isolated backwater, was in touch with broader political and cultural currents and was even politically and economically, if not culturally, integrated into the Roman Empire.[6] Ironically, these archaeological reports have fed into the tendency

---

2. Shaye J. D. Cohen, *Josephus in Galilee and Rome* (Leiden: Brill, 1979); Tessa Rajak, *Josephus: The Historian and his Society* (London: Duckworth, 1983); Per Bilde, *Flavius Josephus between Jerusalem and Rome: His Life, His Works, and Their Importance* (JSPSup 2; Sheffield: JSOT Press, 1988).

3. Shaye J. D. Cohen, "The Place of the Rabbi in Jewish Society of the Second Century," in *The Galilee in Late Antiquity* (ed. Lee I. Levine; New York: Jewish Theological Society, 1992) 157–73; Martin Goodman, *State and Society in Roman Galilee, A.D. 132–212* (Totowa, N.J.: Rowman & Allanheld, 1983); Lee I. Levine, *The Rabbinic Class of Roman Palestine in Late Antiquity* (New York: Jewish Theological Seminary Press, 1989); E. P. Sanders, *Jewish Law from Jesus to the Mishnah* (Philadelphia: Trinity, 1990).

4. There are exceptions, of course, a major one being the work of E. P. Sanders, such as *Jesus and Judaism* (Philadelphia: Fortress, 1985); and idem, *Judaism: Practice and Belief 63 B.C.E. to 66 C.E.* (Philadelphia: Trinity, 1992). The need to appropriate Josephan and rabbinic evidence for contextual study of Jesus and his movement is one of the principal motives for my own recent historical investigations, in *Galilee: History, Politics* (Valley Forge, Pa.: Trinity, 1995) and *Archaeology, History, and Society in Galilee: The Social Context of Jesus and the Rabbis* (Valley Forge, Pa.: Trinity, 1996).

5. This is one of the principal motives for the review of archaeological reports and evidence in my *Archaeology, History, and Society in Galilee*. The Historical Jesus Section and the Archaeology of the New Testament World Group held joint sessions at the SBL 1995 Annual Meeting.

6. Eric M. Meyers, "Galilean Regionalism as a Factor in Historical Reconstruction," *BASOR* 221 (1976) 95; idem, "The Cultural Setting of Galilee: The Case of Regionalism and Early Judaism," *ANRW* II.19.1 (Berlin: de Gruyter, 1979) 687–98.

among some Christian scholars to de-judaize or de-israelitize and to helle-
nize or "universalize" Jesus. This seems more defensible historically if the
cultural ethos he grew up in was already cosmopolitan. The key basis on
which J. D. Crossan justified his assumption that the pan-Mediterranean cultural ethos also dominated Galilee was a synchronic, general picture of a
cosmopolitan Sepphoris near which Jesus grew up: a "provincial capital of
considerable importance in late antiquity" that contained "courts, a fortress,
a theater seating three or four thousand, a palace, a colonnaded street on top
of the acropolis, two city walls, two markets, archives, the royal bank, and the
arsenal and a population around thirty thousand."[7] But what about the early
first century, not late antiquity? Were even half of these items in Sepphoris
during the early first century?

It is obviously important to work toward greater historical precision regarding the degree of Hellenistic and Roman influences in early first-century Galilee—that is, during the generation of Jesus and his earliest movement. And
such influences must be understood in relation to the traditional culture and
social forms of the area, in order to understand the conditions for the emergence of the Jesus movement(s). It would be particularly important to understand the forces affecting the traditional culture in Galilee in order to discern
how the Jesus movement(s) emerged from and responded to the situation. An
important aspect of an appropriate procedure in seeking greater historical
precision will be to avoid some of the essentialist interpretive concepts that
have been standard in the interrelated fields of ancient Jewish history, archaeology of Galilee, and Jesus studies.

It is possible to trace the impact on Galilee of three successive rulers—the
Hasmoneans, the Romans and their client king Herod, and the client-ruler
Antipas—in order to discern how and why the Jesus movement(s) arose toward the end of Antipas's reign. It seems likely that the Hasmonean takeover
in Galilee resulted in an ambivalent attitude among Galileans about their
Jerusalem rulers.[8] Galileans were now included under the same temple-state
with other descendants of Israel. Because the Northern tribes had lived independently of Jerusalem rule for eight centuries prior to the Hasmonean takeover, they had experienced centuries of separate development and history.
Galileans had not experienced the traumatic hellenizing reform or partici-
pated in the Maccabean Revolt. They may well have preferred coming under
the rule of the Hasmonean dynasty, which still carried the aura of being fellow Israelites who had resisted the Hellenistic imperial rule of the Seleucids,
to continuing under the domination of the Itureans to the north. Yet the Hasmoneans maintained garrisoned fortresses in towns such as Gush Ḥalav and
Yodfat, as well as Sepphoris, from which they "administered" the Galilean vil-

---

7. Crossan, *Historical Jesus*, 18–19.
8. I have attempted to work carefully through the extremely limited evidence for the
inhabitants and history of Galilee from the time of Solomon to the Hasmonean take-over,
in *Galilee: History, Politics, People*, chaps. 1–2.

lages. As Mordechai Aviam has recently delineated, the Hasmoneans also encouraged, and perhaps sponsored, an intensification of agricultural exploitation of Galilee in the form of olive-oil production.[9]

The Galilean descendants of the Israelites presumably had cultivated Mosaic covenantal teachings and other Israelite traditions, including the exodus narrative and stories of Elijah, Elisha, and other Northern prophets. But the Hasmoneans now required public affairs to be conducted according to the laws of the temple-state (what Josephus calls "the laws of the Judeans"; e.g., *Ant.* 13.257–58, 318–19, 397). These laws required payment of tithes and offerings to the Temple and priesthood, in addition to the taxes due to King Alexander Jannaeus. Thus the long-standing cultivation of their own sacred "little," or popular, Israelite tradition now became overlaid by the "great," or official, tradition from Jerusalem. While, with the Hasmonean takeover, Galilean Israelites were joined with other Israelites under the Jerusalem temple-state, they were also ruled and taxed by that temple-state, which imposed its own state law. Hasmonean rule in Galilee was intermittently attentive and distracted because of the internal struggles of the Hasmonean regime. As a result, Galilee was not rigorously ruled and politically and religiously resocialized, and affairs in the villages were not conformed to the same customs and regulations that prevailed in Jerusalem.

Rome's takeover of greater Judea in 63 B.C.E. touched off a quarter-century of repeated disruption and devastation in Galilee. The conflict between rival Hasmoneans only exacerbated the disastrous effects on life in Galilee. Roman armies repeatedly invaded the countryside and either killed or enslaved thousands of people in campaigns to put down successive attempts by rival Hasmonean leaders (and their Parthian backers) to seize power in greater Judea (e.g., *Ant.* 14.102; *J.W.* 1.177–78). In one of these campaigns, Cassius "fell upon Tarichea [Magdala] . . . and enslaved some thirty thousand men" (*Ant.* 14.120; *J.W.* 1.1 80; presumably, the number is exaggerated). Or, to support the ambitions of a Roman general for further conquests in the East, the Romans imposed an extraordinary levy of tribute, vigorously enforced in Galilee by the energetic young Herod, who also suppressed the "brigands" who had arisen out of the turmoil of periodic war and disruption (*Ant.* 14.159). The devastation of Galilee reached its greatest intensity in Herod's prolonged campaign, with the help of Roman troops, to take control of the "kingdom" given him by Roman decree in 40. The Galileans, already acquainted with Herod from his performance as military governor of the region, appear to have offered the most persistent and prolonged resistance to his kingship, rising repeatedly against Herod's partisans in the area and the officers he left in charge (*Ant.* 14.432–33, 450).

---

9. Mordechai Aviam, "Large-Scale Production of Olive Oil in Galilee," *Cathedra* 73 (1994) 26–35 [Hebrew]. Aviam also suggested, in recent conversation, that the Hasmoneans may have established numbers of Judeans in Galilee as part of their program of controlling and intensifying production in the area.

Once firmly in control, Herod ruled and taxed Galilee, along with the rest of his realm, with an iron fist, with well-garrisoned fortresses throughout the land. The resentment that built up during the three decades of Herod's repressive rule finally burst forth after his death in the form of popular messianic movements in Galilee, as in Judea and Perea. The Roman reconquest of these areas led by Varus was severe, particularly in Galilee, in and around Sepphoris, according to Josephus (see *J.W.* 2.68; *Ant.* 17.288–89). Given the usual Roman practices of retaliation against rebellions, it is highly likely that Varus wrought havoc with devastation and enslavement in the area around Sepphoris, even if archaeological excavation has not confirmed his report that "the Roman army burned Sepphoris" itself (*Ant.* 17.288–89).

The legacy of Rome's repeated conquest and Herod's rule in Galilee must have been a collective trauma of devastation and mass enslavement, symbolized particularly in the two massive enslavements by Cassius in and around Magdala in 52 B.C.E. and by Varus in and around Sepphoris in 4 B.C.E. In the aftermath of the twentieth-century Holocaust, historians now take more seriously the collective trauma of a people following mass slaughter, enslavement, and devastation. For early first-century C.E. Galilee, historians must take seriously the horrifying memories of murder or enslavement in Lower Galilean villages of friends and relatives by the Romans, one of the principal tactics in the Roman practice of "forceful suasion."

The regime of Herod Antipas had a major impact on Galilee, as is recently becoming recognized. The effect was partly cumulative, coming upon the Romans' devastation and Herod's political repression and economic exploitation. But Antipas's rule in Galilee itself had a direct, sudden, and dramatic impact on Galilean society. For all of Herod the Great's massive building projects, there is no indication that he carried out any major project in Galilee. He merely maintained fortresses and garrisons in key towns, the main administrative center being Sepphoris, site of the principal Herodian "royal fortress/palace/arsenal." This meant that the effect was all the more dramatic when Antipas began to "develop" Lower Galilee as the Romans' client ruler.

No sooner had Antipas rebuilt Sepphoris as his capital and "the ornament of all Galilee" than he began to build the completely new city of Tiberias on the lake. The two major building projects affected the Galileans in several interrelated ways. Most important perhaps was the cost of such major projects, paid for ultimately from Antipas's only basic source of revenue, taxation of the people. Whether he raised taxation rates is surely less important than the efficiency with which he collected them. In this connection, the unprecedented location of the rulers of Galilee directly on the scene made possible unprecedented efficiency in tax collection. It may be no exaggeration to say that most villages, which provided Antipas's economic base, were within sight (certainly within a few hours' walk) of one or another of the two cities. Peasants' usual tricks of sequestering part of the harvest before the tax collectors arrived at the threshing floors or wine presses were no longer as workable with the close surveillance of Antipas's officers.[10] Within two decades of Antipas's rule, the two cities of the Roman client-"king" were suddenly an immediate political-economic presence in Galileans' lives. The building of Tiberias, if not the rebuilding of Sepphoris, also apparently entailed the disruption of villages in the area. As Josephus writes, "the new settlers were a promiscuous rabble, no small contingent being Galilean, with such as were drafted from territory subject to him and brought forcibly to the new foundation" (*Ant.* 18.36). It appears that some villagers were virtually coerced into the settlement. It *is* worth noting that, in 66–67, Josephus found the riffraff of Tiberias making common cause with "Galileans" in the area against the "leading citizens" of Tiberias, who were clearly Herodian officials (*Life* 64–66).

If, analytically, the cultural impact can be distinguished from the politico-economic, there would appear to be little basis for the recent prominent claim by historical Jesus scholars of cosmopolitan cultural influences on Jesus in Lower Galilee.[11] It is difficult to find evidence for much cosmopolitan Hellenistic culture in the first three decades of the rebuilt Sepphoris and new foundation of Tiberias. The cultural style of building and the lifestyle of the ruling elite in both cities would have been set by Antipas himself, the Romans' client-ruler who had been raised in Rome. That is, the dominant cultural tone in both cities would have been an amalgam of Herodian royal and provincial Roman. Whether or not Antipas himself had the Roman theater built, it symbolizes what would have been the dominance of Roman political culture in these royal capital cities. But they were also royal, as symbolized by Antipas's having built a royal palace as the dominant structure in the new foundation of Tiberias. Antipas does not appear to have worried much about local or official Judean standards in his city-building. In Tiberias, for example, he built both city and palace without any scruples about violating Galilean or Judean sensitivities about a cemetery on the site of the city and animal decor in the palace. Yet, the stadium in Tiberias and possibly the theater in Sepphoris suggest more a provincial "Roman urban overlay"[12] than a truly cosmopolitan atmosphere.

Even three decades after Antipas, Tiberias does not appear all that cosmopolitan. The ten "principal men" (many with Latin names) who dominated the city politically and economically were apparently officers in Agrippa II's administration (of the toparchy centered there or of Agrippa's main court?).

---

10. See James C. Scott, *Weapons of the Weak: Everyday Forms of Peasant Resistance* (New Haven: Yale University Press, 1985).

11. On the following, see the further discussion in *Galilee*, chap. 7, esp. 174–81; and in my *Archaeology, History, and Society in Galilee*, chap. 2, esp. pp. 54–64.

12. See James F. Strange, "Some Implications of Archaeology for New Testament Studies," in *What Has Archaeology to Do with Faith?* (ed. James Charlesworth and Walter Weaver; Philadelphia: Fortress, 1992) 31–35.

Justus, professional intellectual and rival historian to Josephus, was dependent on the patronage of Agrippa II. Perhaps this tiny elite had cosmopolitan pretensions. They did resist the orders of the high-priestly provisional government in Jerusalem to tear down the royal palace because of the objectionable representations in its decor (*Life* 65–66). In 66–67, moreover, fifty years after the founding of the city, some "Greeks" were among the residents. Yet, they were not a substantial enough presence to avoid being easily wiped out by the resentful popular party led by the city archon, Jesus son of Sapphias (*Life* 66–67). Greek was apparently the language of administration in both cities, but at most the Hellenization was superficial, a mere cosmopolitan facade, if that. The "provincial" character of the recently rebuilt Sepphoris and Tiberias stands out more clearly by comparison with the larger and far more cultured cities of Caesarea on the coast (not that much older than Tiberias) and Scythopolis just to the south. Nothing close to their level of cosmopolitan imperial culture is found at Sepphoris and Tiberias, even after the more intense romanization of the latter during the second-century heyday of "urbanization" in the East. Thus, in the first three decades after their rebuilding, Sepphoris and Tiberias would hardly appear to have hosted the sort of cosmopolitan cultural atmosphere in which Cynic philosophers would have flourished and somehow influenced or provided models for Galilean villagers.

The political and economic impact of Antipas's regime on Galilee was probably far more important than the cultural impact in setting the conditions for the emergence of the Jesus movement(s). To fund his massive building projects, maintain his court, and support whatever ambitions led to his disastrous military venture against the Nabatean King Aretas, Antipas clearly had to intensify exploitation of the economic base of his tetrarchy—that is, the productive forces of his Galilean and Perean subjects. Viewed from a wider perspective of time and space, the shift from traditional freeholding families in semi-independent villages to sharecropping families or laborers dependent on large estates and perhaps even living around a manor house was an empire-wide development that happened at different paces in different areas. In Greece this development was well under way by Late Hellenistic times but was accelerated under Roman domination in the late republic and early empire.[13] In Anatolia the process appears to have been accelerated under Roman domination.[14] An extensive recent study identifies a new form of economic exploitation that appeared in Judea during the Early Roman Period under Herod: large agricultural estates, villas, or manor houses.[15] A review of the literary and archaeological evidence for "royal" (and other

13. As documented and analyzed by Susan E. Alcock, *Graecia Capta: The Landscapes of Roman Greece* (Cambridge: Cambridge University Press, 1993).

14. From archaeological surveys analyzed by Stephen Mitchell, *Anatolia: Land, Men, Gods in Asia Minor* (Oxford: Clarendon, 1993).

15. Yizhar Hirschfeld, "Changes in Settlement Patterns of Jewish Rural Populace before and after the Rebellions against Rome," *Cathedra* 80 (1996) 3–18 [Hebrew].

"large") estates, with attention paid to precise location, indicates that such large estates were not yet prominent in Galilee under Herod the Great.[16] Even at mid–first century, Queen Berenice derived her "income" from estates in the Great Plain, and Herodian officers in Tiberias, such as Crispus, had their estates not in Galilee itself but across the Jordan in Gaulanitis (*Life* 33). A century later, the situation had changed dramatically. To focus on only a sample of indicators of the situation in the next century or two, I would cite a recent survey, which indicates an increasing number of olive presses at many sites, implying production well beyond domestic use, in the Middle Roman Period;[17] and some of the most prominent rabbis of the third century are portrayed as having extensive fields between Sepphoris and Tiberias.[18]

It seems highly likely that the intensification of agricultural production begun by Antipas in Galilee appreciably accelerated the process by which many traditional freeholding peasant families in Galilee fell seriously into debt from which they could not recover. They eventually came into dependence upon wealthy figures who controlled large amounts of land devoted largely to production for sale and export trade. Surveys of sites in the Early and Middle Roman periods suggest that not only the population of already-settled sites, but the number of sites as well, was still expanding. There was still room for people who had lost control of their family inheritance to relocate. As elsewhere in antiquity, people who lost control of their land apparently shifted to a less-respectable status—as sharecroppers or laborers, often on what had been their ancestral land. Peasants were under intense economic pressure of indebtedness. Families and even village communities were disintegrating under the pressure. Village communities were still largely intact at the time of Antipas, but they were under pressure. That is, Galilee was not full of rootless people forced out of home, family, and land—villagers who were poised to become itinerant vagabonds in response to a compelling call from a Cyniclike Galilean peasant sage—but the fundamental social forms of family and village community were beginning to disintegrate from the severe economic pressure.

When the Jesus Movement Responded

It was thus not mere coincidence that the Jesus movement(s) arose in Galilee toward the end of Antipas's reign. For fifteen or twenty years I have been suggesting, implicitly or explicitly, that Jesus and his movement(s) can be fruitfully considered in comparison and contrast with other Judean and Galilean movements of distinctively Israelite form that took place within the

16. Horsley, *Galilee*, 207–16.

17. Aviam, "Large-Scale Production of Olive Oil in Galilee," 26–35.

18. Stuart S. Miller, "Intercity Relations in Roman Palestine: The Case of Sepphoris and Tiberias," *AJSReview* 12 (1987) 1–24; Lee I. Levine, "R. Simeon b. Yohai and the Purification of Tiberias: History and Tradition," *HUCA* 49 (1978) 173–74.

same two or three generations of Late Second Temple times.[19] There is the possibility that the distinctively Israelite social forms of the popular messianic movements and prophetic movements may help us to understand the "script(s)" that Jesus and his movement(s) were following and creatively adapting. The point to be emphasized here is that these other, parallel popular movements that resemble the Jesus movement(s) in significant ways occurred at precisely the same historical juncture, roughly within a generation of Jesus. Also suggestive is that similar movements of resistance to Roman imperial rule occurred among other ancient Mediterranean peoples at a corresponding point in their subjection to Rome. In Gaul and other western areas in the Roman Empire, what have been called native revolts occurred at a stage of romanization of agrarian societies corresponding to the same stage in Judea and Galilee in the first century.[20] As with the Judeans and Galileans, movements of protest, renewal, or revolt occurred not in response to the first impact of Roman conquest but after a few generations, during which the effects of romanization began to erode the traditional way of life. Then, another generation or two after such movements and revolts, such peoples no longer mounted the same movements and/or revolts. While the Judeans were unusually persistent in their resistance to Roman imperial rule and assimilation, the comparisons may be instructive with regard to the factors identified as significant for the emergence of protest and/or renewal movements.[21]

---

19. See esp. my "Popular Messianic Movements around the Time of Jesus," *CBQ* 46 (1984) 471–95; idem, "'Like One of the Prophets of Old': Two Types of Popular Prophets at the Time of Jesus," *CBQ* 47 (1985) 435–63; and idem, *Sociology and the Jesus Movement* (New York: Crossroad, 1989), chaps. 5, 6, 7.

20. See esp. Stephen L. Dyson, "Native Revolts in the Roman Empire," *Historia* 20 (1971) 239–74; and idem, "Native Revolt Patterns in the Roman Empire," ANRW II.3 (Berlin: de Gruyter, 1975) 138–75.

21. Studies of peasant movements in traditional agrarian societies in modern times, including peasant revolts, show that they happen not when the traditional peasant society has fallen apart—for example, when people have been turned off the land and village communities completely disintegrated. Rather they happen earlier in the disintegration process, when peasants accustomed to their traditional patterns of life become threatened by debts and loss of control of their family inheritance; not when they have all become share-croppers, but when becoming share-croppers looms as a threat to their semi-independent family and community life. Also, it is not the utterly poor and absolutely destitute peasants who join and lead protest or renewal movements but the "middle" peasants who discern that new political and economic forces or new arrangements pose a threat to their traditional way of life.

Let me reassure any scholars of ancient Jewish and Christian literature and religion who may be uneasy about such broad cross-cultural comparisons that in making them I am not interested in establishing any sort of social-scientific general law or in developing some cross-culturally valid model. The purpose is simply to elucidate the Jesus movement(s) in particular from what else we know from around the world in modern times as well as from around the Roman Empire in antiquity.

How the Jesus Movement(s) Responded:
Renewal of Israel in Village Communities

It is curious how many treatments of Jesus and his followers formulate his relationship to his context in terms of influences on him, as if peasants and other ordinary people were passively picking up influences, usually cultural ones, such as language and ideas. Galileans and other ordinary people, however, must also have been responding or reacting to the influences and impact of new forces and arrangements. And they must have been responding or reacting on the basis of, or in defense of, some culture and traditional way of life in which their concrete interests were embedded.

Some archaeologists have recognized that material remains do not necessarily yield evidence for ethnic and cultural identity.[22] In literary sources for Galilee in the first century, except for the Christian Gospels, there is precious little evidence for the popular culture and way of life. On the basis of the very limited historical evidence, it appears that the Galileans of Late Second Temple times were descendants of Northern Israelites.[23] Because imperial rulers in the ancient Near East tended not to interfere with the traditional way of life of their subject peoples, it seems likely on the surface of things that local Galilean community life must have been guided by Israelite customs and traditions, the particular Galilean case of what anthropologists call the little tradition or popular tradition.[24] That Galileans cultivated Israelite traditions such as circumcision and sabbath observance is confirmed by Josephus in reports of several incidents.[25] It is worth noting also that the rabbis, several generations later, while complaining about the Galilean peasants' lack of respect for their own rulings, assume that the variant customs operative in the different regions of Galilee, as well as in Judea, all belong in and are to be related to the heritage of Israel. Moreover, the Israelite traditions that Galilean village communities shared with the great, or official, tradition based in Jerusalem would have been reinforced during the century of direct rule from Jerusalem under the Hasmoneans and Herod. Thus, although Galilean culture would not have become closely conformed to Jerusalem culture (e.g., the official Torah), which is somewhat better known from extant Jewish literary sources, it would appear to have been solidly rooted in Israelite traditions.[26]

22. Colin Renfrew and Paul Bahn, *Archaeology: Theories, Methods, and Practice* (New York: Thames and Hudson, 1991); Eric M. Meyers, "An Archaeological Response to a New Testament Scholar," *BASOR* 297 (1995) 21; for the specific example of Nazareth in ancient Galilee, see my *Archaeology, History, and Society in Galilee*, 114–18.

23. Horsley, *Galilee*, chaps. 1–2.

24. A suggestive application of the concept is in James C. Scott "Protest and Profanation: Agrarian Revolt and the Little Tradition," *Theory and Society* 4 (1977) 1–39, 211–46.

25. Horsley, *Galilee*, 152–57.

26. The many popular movements near-contemporary with Jesus, at least the ones of the prophetic type and of the messianic type, were clearly informed by the distinctive Israelite

The Christian Gospels are full of references and allusions to Israelite traditions. The tendency (perhaps the agenda in some cases) of much of the recent analysis of Jesus' teachings rooted in form criticism has been to decontextualize, departicularize, de-israelitize, or de-judaize Jesus.[27] The most clearly Israelite elements in the Gospel tradition are determined to be secondary, created at later stages of the Jesus movements, such as a second, judgmental "apocalyptic" layer of Q or products of a synagogue reform movement.[28] The method by which such judgments are made, however, is blatantly circular. Individual sayings or stories are purposely isolated by type or form, so that broader patterns and connections are missed. Generically sapiential material is by definition primary; judgmental prophetic and apocalyptic material is by definition secondary. Not only are these mutually exclusive dichotomous categories the constructs of modern Christian scholarship (and not indigenous to ancient Jewish texts, in which sapiential and apocalyptic elements stand interwoven and side by side, as in *Enoch* 92–104),[29] but the agenda of finding a universalistic (and apolitical, spiritual) Jesus over against a particularistic (and political) Judaism is rooted in nineteenth century German theology and biblical scholarship.[30]

Because it is as methodologically indefensible to isolate Jesus traditions from their literary and social context as it is to isolate Jesus from the context of the movement and historical situation in which he had historical significance, the focus should be on what are, by a relatively broad consensus, the earliest identifiable documents produced by and used in Jesus movement(s): the Gospel of Mark and the series of Jesus' discourses (not simply sayings) known as Q.[31] Both represent Jesus and his followers as solidly rooted in Is-

---

historical traditions or figures such as Moses, Joshua, or David, although it must be acknowledged that only one of the movements, the one led by Judah son of Hezekiah, occurred in Galilee. See my "Popular Messianic Movements" and "Like One of the Prophets of Old."

27.   One thinks of many participants in the Jesus Seminar and certain interpreters of the Synoptic Sayings Source. A mild form is seen in Crossan, *The Historical Jesus*, chaps. 11–12. A wider-reaching form is in Burton L. Mack, *The Lost Gospel: The Book of Q and Christian Origins* (San Francisco: HarperSanFrancisco, 1993).

28.   The most influential hypothesis of strata in Q is by John S. Kloppenborg, *The Formation of Q* (Philadelphia: Fortress, 1987). The hypothesis of a synagogue reform movement is in Burton L. Mack, *A Myth of Innocence: Mark and Christian Origins* (Philadelphia: Fortress, 1988).

29.   See George W. E. Nickelsburg, "Wisdom and Apocalypticism in Early Judaism," and my "Wisdom Justified by All Her Children: Examining Allegedly Disparate Traditions in Q," both in *Society of Biblical Literature 1994 Seminar Papers* (Atlanta: Scholars Press, 1994) 715–32, 733–51.

30.   Often perpetuated in more recent Christian scholarship; e.g., Martin Hengel, *Judaism and Hellenism* (Philadelphia: Fortress, 1974) 303–9.

31.   That Q is a series of discourses and not simply a collection of sayings is the implication of Kloppenborg, *The Formation of Q*. See further my "*Logoi Propheton*? Reflections

raelite traditions. The indications are so many that they are grouped here for review, beginning with Q. First, the Q discourses mention or allude to a number of particular figures and events from Israel's history or cultural traditions, such as Sodom and Gomorrah, Solomon and the Queen of the South, Jonah and Nineveh, Abraham, Isaac, and Jacob (10:12, 11:31–32, 13:28–29, respectively). Second, the Q discourses utilize particular motifs from Israelite cultural traditions, such as allusions to prophetic articulations of the people's longings from Isaiah and "son of man" as a symbol of judgment (Luke/Q 7:22; 17:24, 26–27, 30). Third, John the Baptist and Jesus (even Q people themselves) are portrayed as the climactic prophets in a long line of Israelite prophets, many of whom were persecuted or even killed (Luke 6:23, 7:18–28, 11:49–51). Fourth, and usually missed because of the standard Christian theological agenda of Jesus versus Jewish law, is the Mosaic covenantal form as well as convenantal teaching contents in the Q "sermon" (Luke/Q 6:20–49)—which Q stratigraphers assign to the earliest, sapiential layer, Q1.

Similarly, in Mark, Jesus and his movement are squarely rooted in Israelite traditions. The gospel of the kingdom is the fulfillment of Israelite prophecy. Jesus is a prophet like Moses and Elijah, not simply in the transfiguration story, but in the cycles of miracle stories of healings, sea-crossings, and wilderness feedings (Mark 4:35–8:26). Again missed because of standard Christian insistence that Jesus stood against the law, the discourses in Mark 10 present, in effect, a renewal of Mosaic covenantal principles concerning marriage, egalitarian economics, and nonhierarchical politics, with direct reference to creation stories and the Decalogue. Not only that, many of the pronouncement stories defend, not deny, Israelite covenantal traditions such as Sabbath observance and principles of the Decalogue, against the official, or great tradition, and the scribal-Pharisaic "traditions of the elders" (especially Mark 7:1–13).

Indeed, the Israelite traditions are so prominent and strong in both Q and Mark that it is hard to resist the conclusion that they are portraying Jesus as spearheading the renewal of Israel. "The kingdom of God" being at hand is the keynote in Mark and is the persistent theme in virtually all of the discourses that comprise Q. It is a symbol and an overarching theme, but it refers to the restoration or renewal of Israel, as in such phrases as "entering" or "eating in" or simply "being in" the kingdom of God. The connection of the kingdom and renewal of Israel is explicit in what was apparently the concluding saying in Q, Luke 22:28–30 and its parallel in Matt 19:28. In Christian biblical scholarship and standard translations of the Gospels, this saying has ordinarily been misread, indeed read in almost the diametrically opposite sense that it must have had in Q. The saying portrays the twelve not "judging"

---

on the Genre of Q," in *The Future of Early Christianity: Essays in Honor of Helmut Koester* (ed. Birger Pearson et al.; Minneapolis: Fortress, 1991) 195–209; and idem, "Q and Jesus: Assumptions, Approaches, and Analyses," *Semeia* 55 (1991) 175–209.

(negatively) Israel but doing justice for or liberating Israel as the key meaning of the kingdom.[32]

If the prominence particularly of covenantal material in Mark and Q is further considered in connection with the fundamental social forms in which Israel existed, the thesis of Jesus as leading a renewal of Israel can take more precise contours in the historical mind's eye. The fundamental social forms in historical Israel, continuing into Late Second Temple times, were the household or family, the basic transgenerational unit of production and consumption and reproduction, and the local village community, comprised of a number of households. The monarchy, Temple, and high priesthood were added on, and in some Israelite traditions were not part of the original and ideal Israel.

The covenantal teachings of Jesus address precisely these fundamental social forms in an agenda of restoration and revitalization. He insists upon the indissolubility of the marriage bond (Mark 10:2–9, 10–12; Luke/Q 16:17; cf. Matt 5:31–32). Mark's Jesus even uses a familial image (albeit nonpatriarchal) for the larger community life he wants to renew (Mark 3:31–35). In a pronouncement story, Jesus defends the basic "commandment of God" that people should not be manipulated by the religious and political representatives of the temple-state into being unable to "honor their father and mother," in the sense of concrete economic support during their declining, nonproductive years (Mark 7:1–13). In the Q sermon, Jesus, after reassuring the poor that the kingdom of God is theirs, uses traditional covenantal exhortations in insisting that they overcome their current divisiveness amid the economic pressures on local interfamily relations and restore reciprocal socioeconomic practices in the village community: "Love your enemies, do good and lend!" (Luke/Q 6:20–36). The third petition in the Lord's Prayer (Luke/Q 11:2–4), in its more concrete earlier form of "forgive/cancel our debts as we herewith forgive our debtors," also expresses the covenantal, egalitarian economic ideal of reciprocity for the village community. In Mark 10, Jesus uses the inquisitive rich man as a foil, along with the saying about the difficulty of a rich man's entering the kingdom, to both promise and insist upon nonexploitative, egalitarian covenantal economic behavior in the renewal communities.

For the Jesus movement(s), the kingdom of God thus means the renewal of Israel, and the renewal of Israel means the revitalization of families and village communities along the lines of restored Mosaic covenantal principles. Other Jesus materials add to this same picture. The context indicated in the content of many of Jesus' sayings and discourses is the village community, and their subject is social relationships in the village community. Similarly,

---

32. For a criticism of the traditional misreading of this text as a judgment against Israel/Judaism and an alternative reading as a restoration or deliverance of Israel, see my *Jesus and the Spiral of Violence: Popular Jewish Resistance in Roman Palestine* (San Francisco: Harper & Row, 1987) 201–9.

the context indicated in Jesus' healing and exorcism stories is also the village community, and most healing stories, while focusing on two principal characters (Jesus and the person healed), also include other, supportive people, such as those who let the paralytic down through the roof.

That Jesus' mission focused on village communities finds yet another indicator in the recent recognition that the term *synagogai* in Mark (and Matthew and Luke), like the term *knesset* in the Mishna, refers to local village assemblies. Because archaeological exploration has found little evidence for synagogue buildings in Galilee until the third century and after,[33] it seems that *synagogai*, which means 'assemblies' anyhow, must refer not to buildings but to the assemblies in which the villagers met for all kinds of purposes, from communal prayers to assigning delegates to fix the village water source.[34] Rereading Mark with this in mind, it is surely significant that the context in which Jesus did his preaching and healing was the village assembly.

To take one more illustration, the mission discourses in both Mark and Q portray a prophetic movement engaged in the renewal of Israel focused on village communities rather than the begging by a bunch of itinerant charismatics for some food or the formation of a separate new community through table fellowship. The discerning readers of recent Jesus books will have noticed that the only social relations into which the Mediterranean Jewish peasant Cynic Jesus enters is occasional table fellowship, either in the form of the symposium of Greek philosophers featuring clever verbal repartee or in the form of an abstract, latinized, egalitarian ideal of "open commensality."[35] Ironically, Jesus' sayings offer no proof-text that directly portrays Jesus at table in anything like those forms. Jesus scholars, in fact, must resort to projecting or deducing such table fellowship from parables, from accusations leveled at Jesus, or from accounts of the Last Supper. Archaeological exploration, moreover, can provide no suitable concrete physical site for the presumed table fellowship. Houses and courtyards were too small for a group the size of J. D. Crossan's open commensality and would definitely have been too malodorous (of ox dung and whatnot) for the erudite symposia Burton Mack imagines as the catalysts of group formation and the site of Jesus' culture criticism. Indeed, one of the four kinds of saying from which Crossan either deduces or projects open commensality forms part of the mission discourses in Mark and

33. Among the critical evaluations of archaeological evidence that find little evidence for synagogue buildings until the third century are Lee I. Levine, "The Second Temple Synagogue: The Formative Years," in *The Synagogue in Late Antiquity* (ed. L. I. Levine; Philadelphia: American Schools of Oriental Research, 1987) 10–12; Paul V. M. Flesher, "Palestinian Synagogues before 70 C.E.: A Review of the Evidence," in *Approaches to Ancient Judaism* (ed. J. Neusner and E. Frerichs; Atlanta: Scholars Press, 1989) 6.75–80; and Lester I. Grabbe, "Synagogues in Pre-70 Palestine: A Re-assessment," *JTS* 39 (1988) 401–10.

34. So Howard C. Kee, "The Transformation of the Synagogue after 70 C.E.: Its Import for Early Christianity," *NTS* 36 (1990) 5–10; Horsley, *Galilee*, 222–33.

35. With reference to Mack, *The Lost Gospel*; and Crossan, *The Historical Jesus*, respectively.

Q (Mark 6:7–13; Luke/Q 10:2–16). These discourses deal not with the table fellowship of a large group but with the manner in which Jesus' envoys will be fed and housed during their stay in a given village. The social unit, or form, of the mission and group formation is the village community, which is disintegrating but which the workers are trying to revitalize in their extension of Jesus' program of preaching and healing.

While engaged in a renewal of Israel in its fundamental social forms of family and village community, the Jesus movement(s) took a sharply-critical stance toward Antipas and his cities. In their response to the cities and rulers of Galilee, the Jesus movement(s) appears as a less-violent form of opposition and parallels the more violent actions of other popular groups roughly 35 years before and after. Galilean peasants in the vicinity of Sepphoris launched an attack on the royal palace and arsenal upon the death of Herod in 4 B.C.E. Seventy years later, Galilean villagers exhibited active hostility both to the city of Sepphoris and to the Herodian elite in Tiberias. In attitude, the Jesus movement(s) appear to have been similarly resentful, with caustic comments about kings in their palaces and finery and sharply critical stories about the king's birthday banquets with the leading men of the realm (Luke/Q 7:24–25; Mark 6:17–29; cf. Luke 14:16–24). Insofar as John the Baptist is closely associated with the Jesus movement—albeit in a role carefully subordinate to that of Jesus—his prophecies against Antipas, as reported by Josephus (*Ant.* 18.116–19), may also express the critical attitude of the Jesus movement(s). Those involved in the Jesus movement seem to have studiously avoided dealings with the Herodian rulers, cities, and institutions as threatening to their interests. Several synoptic Gospel texts containing urban features express suspicion, if not hostility, about urban institutions such as the courts, councils, governors, and kings (e.g., Luke 12:57–59 and Matt 5:25–26; Mark 13:9b; Matt 10:17–19).[36]

Jesus and his movement(s), however, appear to have had a much more serious engagement with the Temple and high priests in Jerusalem than with Antipas and his cities—an engagement that led to Jesus' execution by the Romans for sedition. That their principal opposition was directed at the rulers and ruling institutions in Jerusalem, instead of against Antipas and his cities, is of considerable significance in discerning that the Jesus movements were indeed engaged in a renewal of Israel. As already noted, the Hasmonean takeover of Galilee had brought the Galilean Israelites together with other children of Israel under the same Israelite ruling institution for the first time in eight centuries. That would surely have increased the Galileans awareness of being part of Israel. Yet, the inherent conflicts entailed in coming under the Jerusalem rulers—who apparently demanded taxes, Temple dues, priestly tithes, and conformity to other laws of the temple-state—surely created am-

---

36. Strange ("Implications of Archaeology," 41–47) discusses a number of "urban features" in Q and Mark without finding any serious tension between villagers and the cities.

bivalent attitudes toward the ruling city and ruling institutions, the Temple and high priesthood. The subordination of both to Herod—who rebuilt the one in alien style and made the other into his creature through appointments to the high office from Babylonian and Egyptian Jewish families—may have exacerbated the conflict. The deeply-rooted difference in the historical experience of the Galileans and the Jerusalem ruling families surely compounded the political-economic-religious conflict inherent in the structure of the temple-state. In yet another possible factor, after only a century under the Jerusalem temple-state, Galilean Israelites, during Jesus' own generation, were no longer directly subject to the Jerusalem Temple and high priestly political jurisdiction. This separation from Jerusalem rule, along with the awareness that the Roman governors now appointed and dismissed wealthy priests to the high office at will, may have further delegitimated the ruling institutions in the already-skeptical eyes of Galileans.

Jerusalem, however, was the capital of Israel. Thus, Jesus' (and the movement's) agenda of renewing Israel required what must be seen as a challenge to illegitimate rulers and/or as an attempt to reach out to the rest of Israel from the capital. Israelite tradition was rich with prophetic precedents of challenge to and condemnation of—or simply laments over—the ruling institutions and families. These prophetic precedents informed the Gospel traditions of the face-off in Jerusalem, although it probably can never be known at what points, in the continuum between Jesus the charismatic prophet and the movements that focused on him in producing Q and Mark. Q's Jesus prophesies the eschatological gathering and banqueting of Israel explicitly without the ruling families who laid such stock in proper genealogies from Abraham, Isaac, and Jacob (Luke/Q 13:28–29). Q also portrays Jesus simply as the mouthpiece of God in a prophetic lament over the ruling house of Jerusalem, alluding clearly to early Israelite tradition in the Song of Moses (Luke/Q 13:34–35; cf. Deut 32:11). Christian interpretation, determined by its dichotomous opposition of Christianity and Judaism that simply blocks recognition of the class and regional divisions and diversity within greater Judea in Late Second Temple times, has understood these sayings to be Jesus' prophetic condemnation of all Israel or Judaism generally. The sayings are, rather, the expressions of a popular prophet and his movement deeply rooted in Israelite prophetic tradition against the ruling families and institutions. Mark not only features Jesus' prophecy of the destruction of the Temple with three references to it but includes his prophetic demonstration in the Temple precincts according to the paradigm of Jeremiah's famous Temple prophecy. Mark's Jesus also delivers a prophetic judgment against the high priests in the form of the parable of the wicked tenants. Similarly, these prophetic passages are not condemnations of Judaism or Israel generally, but the expressions of a popular movement against the ruling establishment.

The Galilean-based movement(s) led by Jesus of Nazareth, of course, was not alone in its prophetic judgment against the ruling city of Jerusalem. A decade or so later, the "Egyptian" Jewish prophet portrayed by Josephus as a new Joshua led his followers to the Mt. of Olives in anticipation that Jerusalem would fall like Jericho had of old (*Ant.* 20.169–71; *J.W.* 2.261–63). And thirty years later, the oracular peasant-prophet Jesus ben Hananiah delivered woes over Jerusalem that resembled the other Jesus' dirge in Luke/Q 13:34 (*J.W.* 6.300–309). Nor were peasant-prophets the only ones to condemn the incumbent high priests in Jerusalem, judging from the earlier scribal condemnation of the Hasmoneans in the *Psalms of Solomon* (especially *Psalms of Solomon* 2) and the continuing opposition to the Jerusalem priestly regime in various Qumran documents.

While some of the principal disciples of Jesus of Nazareth established a presence in Jerusalem following the martyrdom of their leader, as evident in traditions used by Luke in the book of Acts, other branches of the Jesus movement apparently continued the renewal of Israel in the villages and towns of Galilee. The polemic against Capernaum, Chorazin, and Bethsaida at the end of the mission discourse in Luke/Q 10:2–16 suggests that one branch of the movement experienced some ups and downs in the area opposite the city of Tiberias, around the lake to the north. At the end of the Last Supper discourse and in the final empty-tomb scene, Mark directs the disciples and the hearers/readers back to Galilee, presumably to continue the movement of renewal. Because both of these branches of the Jesus movement were focused on the revitalization of village communities in a program of renewing Israel, their enterprise never involved establishing anything like a church down the street from the synagogue, let alone of starting a new religion. In the case of Mark, the movement apparently spread into villages subject to other cities and rulers, such as Caesarea Philippi, Tyre, and the Decapolis. Nothing in Mark, however, suggests that this expanding movement ever thought of itself in opposition to Israel. It was, rather, simply the expansion of the gospel of the kingdom through the villages of Israel and beyond. Interpreters of the Gospel of Matthew have argued recently that it can be understood similarly as addressed to a movement that understood itself within Israel.[37] The communities of the Didache similarly understood themselves in continuity with the traditions of Israel.

The movement catalyzed by the prophetic message and practice of Jesus of Nazareth emerged in response to the disintegration of the fundamental social forms under the impact of the intensified exploitation by Herodian client-rule and its newly rebuilt cities. It focused its program of renewal of Israel on village communities in Galilee itself, both before and after Jesus' provocative prophetic adventure up to the capital of Jerusalem. What happened thereafter and elsewhere in other branches of a spreading movement is another story.

---

37. E.g., Anthony J. Saldarini, *Matthew's Christian Jewish Community* (Chicago: University of Chicago Press, 1994).

Mark and Galilee:
Text World and Historical World

CILLIERS BREYTENBACH
Institut für Urchristentum und Antike
Humboldt-Universität zu Berlin

Introduction

Mark and Galilee: since the groundbreaking work of Ernst Lohmeyer, *Galiläa und Jerusalem*,[1] it is general knowledge among scholars studying the Gospels that Galilee plays an important role in the Gospel of Mark. By *Mark*, however, I do not intend to refer to the Gospel of Mark but to the author implied by the text of the Gospel of Mark.[2] Although it is a commonplace in literary criticism on the Gospels that one should distinguish between the implied author and the historical author, this differentiation is not extremely important for the Gospel of Mark, since there is hardly anything that we know about the historical Mark that has not been inferred from the text of the Gospel. So in brief, *Mark*, the implied author, is a construct, engineered from the text through the process of reading. *Galilee*, the Galilee in the first century of the Common Era, is something similar, a construct that modern scholars made on the basis of the extant literary, geographical, archaeological, epigraphic, and iconographic data.[3] I thus intend to relate these two

1. E. Lohmeyer, *Galiläa und Jerusalem* (Göttingen: Vandenhoeck & Ruprecht, 1936). For more recent research, see Ernest van Eck, *Galilee and Jerusalem in Mark's Story of Jesus* (Hervormde Teologiese Studies Sup. 7: Pretoria: University of Pretoria Press, 1995) chap. 2.

2. On this, see Willem S. Vorster, "The Reader in the Text: Narrative Material," *Semeia* 48 (1989) 21–39; Robert M. Fowler, *Let the Reader Understand: Reader-Response Criticism and the Gospel of Mark* (Minneapolis: Fortress, 1991).

3. For the methodological issues at stake here, see the discussion on the theory of history in works, beginning with Gustav Droysen, *Historik* (Historisch-kritische Ausgabe von Peter Leyh 1; Stuttgart: Fromann-Holzboog, 1977), up through the three volumes by Jörn Rüsen, *Historische Vernuft—Grundzüge einer Historik I: Die Grundlagen der Geschichtswissenschaft; Rekonstruktion der Vergangenheit—Grundzüge einer Historik II: Die Prinzipien*

modern constructs, *Mark* and *Galilee*,[4] understanding the text world (Mark) in the light of the historical world (Galilee).

Within the space at my disposal, it will only be feasible to concentrate on one aspect of the relationship: How can our understanding of the spatial aspect of the world that can be constructed from the text of Mark benefit by taking cognizance of the relevant images of Galilean localities that historians construct from the remains of Galilee that have survived the last two millennia?

Since the work of Karl Ludwig Schmidt, biblical scholars have rightly been reluctant to use the narrative frame of Mark's Gospel to reconstruct the movements of the Jesus of history.[5] It is in fact important to take note of how the Markan discourse is structured. It is a literary composition, not an itinerary of Jesus of Nazareth's travels through Galilee. This becomes evident when one looks at the second part of the Gospel.

Mark presents his story to us in the form of a literary discourse. The omniscient narrator focuses from the outside on Jesus,[6] the main character in the story, but since he moves with Jesus, goes in and out with him, stands up and leaves with him, he lets the reader move with Jesus.[7] Thus Mark helps us to find our way in his story, enables us to construct scenes at specific locations that serve as settings for the actions he intends to narrate.

Let us have a look at the setting of the second main part (Mark 8:27–10:52) of the Gospel of Mark, the road to Jerusalem. The reader is taken along with the main character, Jesus—moves with him on the road from Galilee to Jerusalem, enters the house with him, and leaves it with him.[8] By creating this overarching setting, "Jesus and his disciples on the way to Jerusalem," Mark was able to find a meaningful setting for the minor stories within the larger context of the section.[9] Notwithstanding the variety of episodes, his overarch-

---

der historischen Forschung; and *Lebendige Geschichte—Grundzüge einer Historik III: Formen und Funktionen des historischen Wissens* (Göttingen: Vandenhoeck & Ruprecht, 1983–89).

4. For some methodological questions at stake here, see Sean Freyne, *Galilee, Jesus, and the Gospels: Literary Approaches and Historical Investigation* (Philadelphia: Fortress, 1988) 5–30.

5. Karl L. Schmidt, *Der Rahmen der Geschichte Jesu: Literarkritische Untersuchungen zur ältesten Jesusüberlieferung* (Berlin: Trowitzsch, 1919).

6. See Shlomith Rimmon-Kenan, *Narrative Fiction, Contemporary Poetics* (London: Methuen, 1983) 75–78, on "external focalisation." The narration, however, is a-perspectival. There is no description of space and locality from Jesus' or any other characters' spatial point of view. See Franz K. Stanzel, *Theorie des Erzählens* (6th ed.; Göttingen: Vandenhoeck & Ruprecht, 1995) 159–64.

7. See Stanzel (ibid.) on transition between the *Innenperspektive* and *Außenperspektive* in literary discourse.

8. On the basis of Boris Uspenskii, *A Poetics of Composition* (Berkeley: University of California Press, 1973), this has been investigated by Norman Petersen, "Point of View in Mark's Narrative," *Semeia* 12 (1978) 97–121.

9. In the following I make use of slightly revised previously published material. See my "Gospel of Mark as Episodical Narrative: Reflections on the 'Composition' of the Second Gospel," *Scriptura* (Special issue S4 of 1989) 18–20.

ing scene helps the reader not to lose track of the individual episodes. The journey starts among the villages of Caesarea Philippi (8:27). From there, Jesus travels through Galilee (9:30) and comes to the house (note the definite article!) of Peter and Andrew in Capernaum (9:33), where he sits down (9:35a) and talks to the disciples (9:35b–50). This locally specified scene has been embedded in the major scene "Jesus on his way to Jerusalem," to accommodate the speech. The episodes among the villages of Caesarea Philippi and the episode in the house of Peter and Andrew are the only episodes that have a more specified location before Jesus and his followers reach Jericho (10:46). How are we as readers to visualize these two, more-specific localities in the second part of the Gospel of Mark?

The Rural Spatial Perspective of the Gospel of Mark

We start with the *Caesarea of Philip*. As is well known, the city, originally called Panias, was named Caesarea by Herod's son, the tetrarch Philip. This had been an established πόλις long before the Gospel of Mark was written. In the second century B.C.E. the πόλις issued its own coins.[10] "It possessed from the first a large territory comprising Paneas, the region around the source of the Jordan, and Ulatha [= Kadesh], the region of the Lake of Semachonitis."[11] The narrator thus portrays the Markan Jesus as starting his journey from the villages that belong to the territory of Caesarea.[12] It is not implied that he entered this city, in which Jewish inhabitants must have been in the minority.[13]

In the first part of the Gospel, Mark 1:16–8:21, the narrator depicts the first day of Jesus' ministry as a Sabbath in Capernaum. Early in the morning of the next day Mark's Jesus leaves with the purpose of preaching in the neighboring towns (1:38). The reaction of the inhabitants of Jesus' hometown Nazareth is narrated in severe contrast to the way in which the response of the people of Capernaum to Jesus is depicted. Yet there is one clear similarity in the way the two stories are told. From Capernaum Jesus went to the neighboring towns; from Nazareth he went to the surrounding villages (6:6b). Although a big thriving city like Sepphoris was near Nazareth and Tiberias near Capernaum, the focus of the narrator moves from Capernaum and Nazareth to the surrounding villages. The author did not choose an urban setting for his depiction of Jesus' movements; he preferred rural localities.[14]

10. See Emil Schürer, *The History of Jewish People in the Age of Jesus Christ (175 B.C.–A.D. 135)* (ed. G. Vermes et al.; Edinburgh: T.& T. Clark, 1979) 2.170 n. 457.

11. Arnold H. M. Jones, *The Cities of the Eastern Roman Provinces* (2d ed.; Amsterdam: Hakkert, 1983) 282.

12. For details, see the "North" map from *Tabula Imperii Romani—Iudaea, Palaestina: Eretz Israel in the Hellenistic, Roman and Byzantine Periods* (ed. Yoram Tsafrir et al.; Jerusalem: Israel Academy of Sciences, 1994).

13. After the war, Vespasian and Titus rested here; Josephus *J.W.* 3.444, 7.23–24.

14. Even the healing of the blind Bartimaeus is located outside Jericho on the road to Jerusalem (Mark 10:46). See also Freyne, *Galilee, Jesus and the Gospels*, 41: "Though cities are mentioned, the perspective is outdoor and rural for the most part."

That Mark has a preference for rural locations can also be inferred from 7:24 and 31. According to Mark 7:24, Jesus left the house in Capernaum and went to the *"regions of Tyre."* It is neither said nor implied that Mark's Jesus visited the Phoenician city Tyre itself. "Tyran territory . . . stretched inland at least as far as a place which Josephus calls Kadasa or Kydasa, to the north of Gishala in Galilee" and "must have covered at least a large part of the northern half of the Galilean hills between the sea, the Leontes (Litani) River in the North, and the Huleh Valley to the east."[15]

The reading of the text of Mark 7:31 on *Sidon* is not as clear and text-critically established as one would wish. Admittedly, not as lectio difficilior but as a reading of which the origin cannot be explained easily, one could read[16] καὶ πάλιν ἐξελθὼν ἐκ τῶν ὁρίων Τύρου καὶ Σιδῶνος ἦλθεν εἰς. . . . Then Jesus would be leaving the regions of Tyre and Sidon in the direction of Lake Gennesaret, or as Mark puts it, the "Sea of Galilee." Josephus tells us that Sidon and Damascus shared a boundary.[17] This "makes it likely that Sidonian territory stretched across the Leontes (Litani) River and the southern end of the Bekaa Valley, and perhaps as far as some point on Mount Hermon."[18] The numerous difficulties concerning the reference to the *region of the Decapolis* in Mark 7:31 are well known.[19] Those who follow Pliny (*Natural History* 5.18) and say that Damascus belonged to the Decapolis have less difficulty in imagining the route Mark's Jesus took. Even though it is possible, although far from certain, that Damascus was part of the Decapolis,[20] for the purpose of our argument it suffices to say that the orientation is toward the *region of the Decapolis*, not to the cities themselves.

Even more problematic is the crux interpretum in Mark 5:1. Albeit impossible to infer whether the Gerasene, the Gadarene, or even the Gergesene were meant, Jesus went to the χώρα. It is essential to establish the reference of this expression. Since χώρα can have the sense of the Latin *regio*[21] or even *praefectura*,[22] it is possible to understand the phrase in the Nestle and Aland 27th edition in the sense that Jesus and his disciples went into the 'district of

15. Fergus Millar, *The Roman Near East, 31 BC-AD 337* (Cambridge: Harvard University Press, 1993) 292–93. See also Josephus *J.W.* 4.104–5.

16. Follwing papyrus 45, the codices Alexandrinus, Freerianus, 0131, families 1 and 13, and the majority text.

17. See Josephus *Ant.* 18.153.

18. Millar, *The Roman Near East*, 286–87.

19. See Friedrich G. Lang, "'Über Sidon mitten ins Gebiet der Dekapolis': Geographie und Theologie in Markus 7,31," ZDPV 94 (1978) 145–60; Thomas Schmeller, "Jesus im Umland Galiläas: Zu den markinischen Berichten vom Aufenthalt Jesu in den Gebieten von Tyros, Caesarea Philippi und der Dekapolis," BZ 38 (1994) 44–66.

20. See Hans Bietenhardt, "Die syrische Dekapolis von Pompeius bis Traian," in ANRW II.8 (Berlin: de Gruyter, 1977) 220–61, esp. 226; Lang, "Über Sidon mitten ins Gebiet der Dekapolis," 148–50; Millar, *The Roman Near East*, 410.

21. See LSJ, s.v.

22. See Hugh J. Mason, *Greek Terms for Roman Institutions* (Toronto: Hakkert, 1974) s.v.

the Gerasenes'[23] or 'region of the Gerasenes'.[24] Were the territory of the πόλις Γέρασα referred to here, one would have expected τὰ ὅρια Γεράσης. This would fit the use of τὰ ὅρια and the singular name of the πόλις in 7:24, 32. We thus have to look at another possibility. Since χώρα can mean 'a piece of land, an estate, farm' in the sense of *ager*,[25] it might be that Mark referred to a piece of land, farm or estate of the Gerasene, which then could have been on the eastern lakeside. That Mark uses χώρα to refer to 'a piece of land' is clear from 6:55. Here the phrase ὅλην τὴν χώραν ἐκείνην clearly refers back to *Gennesaret* in v. 53, denoting, as usual,[26] the fertile plain El Guwêr south of Capernaum.[27] The terminological subtlety of the Markan discourse, using χώρα in 5:1 raises the question whether the oligarchy of the Greek cities possessed estates and summer resorts at the lakeside. Were we to read the text in this way, there would be no need to alter the reading τῶν Γερασηνῶν in 5:1. From the external manuscript evidence, this reading is clearly to be preferred.

Even though we cannot but propose a possible solution for the difficulties of Mark 5:1, there is firm ground to say that 5:1–21, the narrative of the healing of the demoniac on the farming land of the Gerasenes, fits in the overall picture. The herdsmen went to the πόλις (Gerasa must be meant) and to the farms,[28] telling what had happened.

In the last two Galilean localities, the narrator also focuses on the rural areas.[29] According to 6:53, Jesus and the disciples came to land in *Gennesaret*. The people that recognized him as he disembarked and went to the El Guwêr plain were the rural people, as can be seen from 6:55. According to our narrator, the people living and working there left their work, fetched the sick at their homes, and carried them to Jesus wherever on the plain he was.

It is not as yet possible to locate *Dalmanutha* of Mark 8:10. Since the name does not occur elsewhere, it is unlikely that Mark, stating that Jesus and his disciples went into τὰ μέρη Δαλμανουθά, referred to a city. Rather, the parts of Dalmanutha, which probably is to be understood as referring to a region, were meant.

The manner in which Mark creates textual space demonstrates that the setting of his story, and the origin of the crowds flocking around Jesus, is the world of small villages, towns, fields, and the rural peasant people. Regarding

---

23. See Morna D. Hooker, *The Gospel according to St. Mark* (London: Black, 1991) ad loc.

24. See Robert A. Guelich, *Mark 1–8:26* (WBC 34A; Dallas: Word, 1989) ad loc.

25. See LSJ, s.v.; examples from Josephus given by Walter Bauer, *Griechisch-deutsches Wörterbuch zu den Schriften des Neuen Testaments und der frühchristlichen Literatur* (ed. K. Aland and B. Aland; 6th ed.; Berlin: de Gruyter, 1988), s.v.

26. See ibid., s.v.

27. See Josephus *J.W.* 3.516–21.

28. For this sense of ἀγρός, cf. LSJ, s.v.

29. See Gerd Theissen and Annette Merz, *Der historische Jesus: Ein Lehrbuch* (Göttingen: Vandenhoeck & Ruprecht, 1996) 163–64.

the way in which he focuses on localities, the local setting of Mark's story is quite close to the upper regions of the River Jordan, Lake Semachonitis, Lake Gennesaret. The detour to Nazareth is a clear exception.

The memory of the Jesus movement, which is reflected in the way Mark relates textual space to orient the reader of his story, should warn scholars studying the New Testament not to overestimate the bearing of discoveries like the ones in Sepphoris, Tiberias, and Caesarea Maritima for the construction of images of the Jesus movement in the interpretation of the Gospel of Mark. Mark orients his reader in such a way that, apart from the synagogue and Peter and Andrew's house in Capernaum, he or she is to construe a rural story world. I am not aware of first-century documents on early Christianity that could provide us with alternative conceptions on how we should imagine the localities Jesus visited and the type of people to whom he addressed his preaching.[30] Recent attempts to connect Jesus of Nazareth to urban movements (for example, cynic preachers) have no support in the way in which the earliest documents, Mark and Q, depict Jesus' movements in Galilee.

Peter and Andrew's House in Capernaum

Peter and Andrew's house in Capernaum is the second specific location in the second part of the Gospel. In Mark's story the second instruction of the disciples on the journey is located in that house (Mark 9:33–50). In the first part of the Gospel, Mark 1:16–8:21, the house of Peter and Andrew plays a more important role. Let us look at this part of Mark's discourse. There is little sense in arranging the first main part of the Gospel (1:16–8:26) according to geographic criteria. In Mark 1:16–8:26, Lake Gennesaret serves the purpose of orienting the reader within the ambit of the text.[31] The action is concentrated around the sea, and the boat motif together with the passage motif creates a common scenario for the many episodes.[32] It is less important on which side of the lake the action takes place;[33] the lake and its shore form the main scene. Since Capernaum is situated by the lake, this more precisely focused location fits in well with the scene. The narrator can launch several episodes directly in Capernaum and even describe a whole day in Capernaum (Mark 1:21–34). At Capernaum by the lake, he then zooms in on the

---

30. On Q, see John Kloppenborg, "City and Wasteland: Narrative World and the Beginning of the Sayings Gospel (Q)," *Semeia* 52 (1990) 145–60, esp. 154–57.

31. As the Temple does in Mark 11:1–13:37.

32. Mark 1:16–20; 2:13–14 (cf. πάλιν); 3:7–12; 4:1–34, 35–41, as well as 5:1–20, 21–43; 6:32–44, 45–52; 8:1–10, 11–13, 14–21, and 22–26 all take place around or on the lake.

33. For a different discussion of these local aspects in the Gospel, see Elizabeth S. Malbon, *Narrative Space and Mythic Meaning in Mark* (San Francisco: Harper & Row, 1986) 40–44, 76–79, 96–99; Elizabeth S. Malbon, "Galilee and Jerusalem: History and Literature in Marcan Interpretation," *CBQ* 44 (1982) 242–55.

house of Peter and Andrew as exact location.[34] The lake, its shore, and Capernaum with the house—all together form the basic points of reference for the reader, to enable him or her to visualize the spatial aspect of the story of the first main part. At the same time, it must be accepted that Mark assumes that the reader has some schematic knowledge about the region around the Sea of Galilee and knows where Capernaum is, or at least that it is situated on the shore of the sea.

The two localities in Capernaum on which the narrator focuses, the synagogue and the house, have been the subject of extensive archaeological excavation.[35] Lately the discussion on the so-called house of Peter has become quite controversial.[36] What is disputed are the conclusions drawn on the basis of the excavations of the central room in this house, the use of evidence from the levels dated in the Roman Period.[37] The bone of contention is whether the archaeological evidence allows the firm conclusion that the alleged house of Peter under the octagonal church has been a meeting place for Christians since the first century. That the identification between the house and Peter cannot be made on the basis of the epigraphic evidence found on the site has been shown by James Strange in his critique of the work of the Franciscan team.[38] Whereas Corbo and Loffreda claim that the central room of the house was converted into a veneration room by plastering its walls and paving the floor with beaten limestone by the end of the first century,[39] Joan Taylor recently argued that the beaten lime floors were not laid before the beginning of the third century.[40] An exegete would be ill advised

34. Mark 1:29–35, 2:1–12, 3:20–35; see also 9:33–34, 7:17 (doubtful), and twice the synagogue (Mark 1:21–28, 3:1–6).
35. See the four-part Studium Biblicum Franciscanum Publication 19: Virgilio C. Corbo, *Cafarnao I: Gli edifici della città* (Jerusalem: Franciscan, 1975); Stanislao Loffreda, *Cafarnao II: La ceramica* (Jerusalem: Franciscan, 1974); Augusto Spijkerman, *Cafarnao III: Catalogo delle monete della città* (Jerusalem: Franciscan, 1975); Emmanuele Testa, *Cafarnao IV: I graffiti della casa di S. Pietro* (Jerusalem: Franciscan, 1972); and Virgilio C. Corbo, "Sotto la sinagoga di Cafarnao un'insula della città," *Liber Annuus* 27 (1977) 156–72; S. Loffreda, "Potsherds from a Sealed Level of the Synagogue at Capharnaum," *Liber Annuus* 29 (1979) 215–20.
36. See *against* Corbo and Loffreda: Joan E. Taylor, *Christians and the Holy Places: The Myth of Jewish-Christian Origins* (Oxford: Clarendon, 1993) 268–94.
37. In the first fill that formed the foundation for the first pavement of the room, pottery from the second to first centuries B.C.E. was found. This Hellenistic layer need not occupy us here. See Corbo, *Cafarnao I*, 97; Taylor, *Christians and the Holy Places*, 281.
38. See James F. Strange, "The Herodian and Capernaum Publications (Part I)," *BASOR* 226 (1977) 65–73.
39. See Loffreda, *Cafarnao II*, 102–18; and Corbo, *Cafarnao I*, 105–6. See also ibid., 71–74, 79–98: "Questo fatto sta a dimostrare che la *domus ecclesia* era in uso al momento in cui furono abbattuti i muri per costruirvi le fondazioni della chiesa ottagonale" (p. 98). Cf. p. 106: "In conclusione, le nostre ricerche archeologiche vengono a confermare meravigliosamente i dati della tradizione. L'affermazione di Egeria (*parietes ita stant sicut fuerunt*) si è dimostrata di una accuratezza assoluta."
40. See Taylor, *Christians and the Holy Places*, 281–83.

GRANDE VÌA

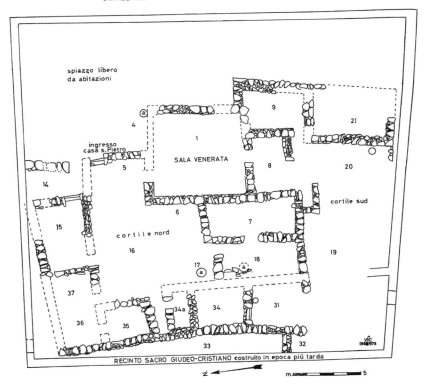

Fig. 1. *Plan of the* insula sacra *from the Early Roman Period (after Corbo).*

to become engaged in these disputes among archaeologists. Nevertheless, Markan scholarship might ask if the text of the Gospel of Mark has anything to contribute to the ongoing debate.

For the sake of the argument, *dato non concesso*, let us accept the verdict of Joan Taylor: "Veneration of the place known as the House of Peter appears to have begun in the fourth century."[41] That the house was used in this way at such a late date will go undisputed. The dispute circles around the question whether there is evidence to date the beginning of the veneration of the house earlier. We undoubtedly have a place identified as the house of Peter by the fourth century, as to be inferred from the well-known *Egeria Itinerarium* transmitted by Petrus Diaconus in his *De locis sanctis*.[42] According to Egeria, the walls of the house of the *princeps apostolorum* were, in her days, as they had

41. Ibid., 294.
42. See the *Egeria Itinerarium* as transmitted by Petrus Diaconus, *De locis sanctis*, 5.2.

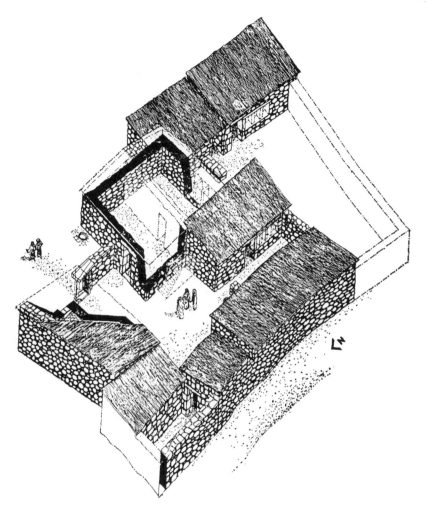

Fig. 2. Isometric view of the insula sacra *at the time of Jesus (after Loffreda).*

been (*parietes usque hodie ita stant, sicut fuerunt*).[43] Of course it is possible to argue that the veneration of this specific house in Capernaum originated from the time when Christians in Capernaum read the Gospels. Then we would have to argue that in the fourth century local Christians and pilgrims identified a certain house with the house of Peter because such a house was known from the Gospels. What cannot be explained in this way, however, is

43. Ibid.

the fact that Mark focuses his narrative in such a way that the house of Peter and Andrew becomes the primary center of spatial orientation in the first half of the Gospel. Why did Mark tell his story in such a way that this house becomes the place of healing and especially teaching of the disciples in his story? Most likely because Peter and Andrew's house had been a place of Christian gathering and teaching even before Mark wrote the Gospel. This does not prove the house excavated by the Franciscan archaeologists to be the same house that corresponds with the way Mark tells Jesus' story. What it does prove, however, is that the tradition about the house in Capernaum as the place of meeting of Christians dates back to the 60s of the first century c.e., when the Gospel of Mark was written. So it might just be that archaeology could benefit from the analysis of spatial focalization in Mark's discourse. The text world thus helps us to construct the historical world.

Can Markan exegesis profit from the construction of the historical site Capernaum? Evidently the Late Roman and Early Byzantine archaeological finds in the upper layers published by Corbo and Loffreda[44] do not help us in understanding Mark's discourse. It is undisputed that the house in question was originally built in the Late Hellenistic or Early Roman Period,[45] but it is not proven that this first-century house beneath the octagonal church really was the house of Peter. In order to pose our question though, it is not necessary to solve these disputes.

No matter whether the house excavated in Insula I was Peter and Andrew's house where Jesus is said to have resided, the houses that were excavated by the Franciscans date from, or even predate, the Early Roman Period and give us a clear impression of how the modern reader should construct the scene of Mark 1:33 and especially Mark 2:1–12 and 3:20, 31–33. Since this material is often utilized to explain the unthatching of the roof in the story about the healing of the leper,[46] let us rather have a look at the local aspect of the passages.

Of course Mark exaggerates when he tells us that on the evening of the *first day in Capernaum* (1:33), after the Sabbath, the whole city was gathering in front of the entrance. Nevertheless, the arrangement of the buildings excavated provides us with information on how the implied author might have wanted us to construct the scene from his text. As can be seen from the excavations, the houses were organized around two interior courtyards. Taking the so-called "house of Peter" as a mere example, we see that the eastern side of the house, where the entrance to the northern courtyard was identified,[47] was a free area. In such areas Mark could have imagined the crowd gathering.

44. Cf. above, n. 35.

45. According to Strange and Shanks, the house was built about 60 c.e. See James F. Strange and Hershel Shanks, "Has the House Where Jesus Stayed in Capernaum Been Found?" *BARev* 8/6 (1982) 26–37, esp. 37.

46. See ibid., 34.

47. See Tav. IX in Corbo, *Cafarnao I*; and see fig. 1 here.

The scene of the story on the healing of the *paralytic* (2:1–12) is set in a way that recalls 1:33. Again Jesus is in the house. "Many came together, so that no room was left, not even in front of the door" (2:2). This means that the whole courtyard was overcrowded. It was impossible to get into the house. (The way Mark tells the story requires that the house has one door only). The friends of the paralytic had to reach the roof over one of the walls that was not inside of the courtyard.[48]

Using the same archaeological information, we could imagine the following scene for Mark's version of the *Beelzebul controversy* (3:20–35). That the intercalation between the controversy on Beelzebul—the question who belongs to the household of God—was Mark's idea can be seen when one compares Mark's story with the independent parallel tradition in Q.[49] In Mark's story, Jesus was sitting either in the house or in one of the two courtyards, arguing with the Jerusalem scribes (3:20, 22). The crowd flocked into the courtyard. Consequently Jesus' family could not get into the courtyard. While standing outside they sent for him to call him (3:31), for because of the crowd in the courtyard, it was impossible to reach Jesus directly (3:32).

In this manner, constructions of the historical world, of localities in Galilee, supplement the linguistic information the author has encoded and facilitate the visualization of the spatial dimension of Mark's textual world. Allow me to thank those searching for the evasive house of Peter in the historical Capernaum and those constructing the historical Galilee for the help they have rendered in constructing Peter and Andrew's house and the Galilee as localities in the Gospel of Mark.

---

48. See Tav. X in Corbo, *Cafarnao I*; and see fig. 2 here.

49. See Jens Schröter, *Erinnerung an Jesu Worte: Studien zur Rezeption der Logien-überlieferung in Markus, Q und Thomas* (WMANT 76; Neukirchen-Vluyn: Neukirchener Verlag, 1997) 276–99.

Galileans, "Israelite Village Communities," and the Sayings Gospel Q

JONATHAN L. REED

University of La Verne, California

The identity of the Galileans in the first century is an important question for understanding Christian origins and the earliest layers of the Jesus tradition. While an earlier generation debated the issue under the shadow of Nazi racial theories and scurrilous attempts at an Aryan Jesus, the recent discussion's impetus is the recognition of diversity in early Judaism and regionalism as a factor in historical reconstruction.[1] The debate over the Galileans' identity has, for the most part, revolved around the significance of the Hasmonean annexation of Galilee and the identity of its prior inhabitants. Whether or not the Hasmoneans were enthusiastically received or bitterly resented turns on whether its inhabitants are construed as Gentile or Jewish, an issue that has divided scholars for some time.[2] Richard Horsley has reopened the

---

1. Most offensive is W. Grundmann's *Jesus der Galiläer und das Judentum* (Leipzig: Wigand, 1940); a distinct Galilean heritage was proposed by W. Bauer in 1927, "Jesus der Galiläer," reprinted in *Aufsätze und Kleine Schriften* (ed. G. Strecker; Tübingen: Mohr, 1967) 91–108; on the history of scholarship in general, see H. D. Betz, "Wellhausen's Dictum 'Jesus Was Not a Christian, but a Jew' in Light of Present Scholarship," *ST* 45 (1991) 83–100. On Galilean regionalism, see E. Meyers, "Galilean Regionalism as a Factor in Historical Reconstruction," *BASOR* 220–221 (1975–76) 93–101; and idem, "The Cultural Setting of Galilee: The Case of Regionalism and Early Judaism," *ANRW* II.19.1 (Berlin: de Gruyter, 1979) 686–702.

2. Earlier this century, E. Schürer argued for a Gentile (= Iturean) population, which converted (*The History of the Jewish People in the Time of Jesus Christ* [3 vols.; rev. and ed. G. Vermes et al.; Edinburgh: T. & T. Clark, 1973–87] 1.142, 216–18, 561–73). A Jewish population was proposed by S. Klein, *Galiläa vor der Makkabäerzeit* (Palästina-Studien 4; Berlin: Menorah, 1928). In the current debate, S. Freyne suggests that the Jewish (Israelite?) inhabitants of Galilee welcomed the Hasmonean annexation (*Galilee from Alexander to Hadrian: A Study of Second Temple Judaism* (Wilmington, Del.: Glazier, 1980) 43–44; and idem, "Bandits in Galilee: A Contribution to the Study of Social Conditions in First-Century Palestine," *The Social World of Formative Christianity and Judaism* (ed. J. Neusner et al.; Philadelphia: Fortress, 1988) 50–68.

87

debate by suggesting what he calls a third possibility, namely, "that during second-temple times most inhabitants of Galilee were descendants of the northern Israelite peasantry."[3] This thesis, not unlike Albrecht Alt's position of a generation ago, assumes that a good portion of the Northern Kingdom's population in Galilee both survived the Assyrian conquest and deportations of the late eighth century B.C.E. and cultivated its own traditions over the centuries there.[4] Horsley spells out the implications of this thesis for Christian origins: Jesus and his first Galilean followers, as expressed most notably in the Sayings Gospel Q, stood in the Northern prophetic tradition. As direct descendants of the Northern Israelites, they called for the revitalization of Israelite village communities and a return to covenantal principles as a means of redressing social, political, and economic injustices. Their antagonism toward Jerusalem—articulated in Q 11:49–51 and 13:34–35—stems from the pervasive Galilean hostility toward outside rule and from their role as inheritors of the ancient Northern prophetic critique of Jerusalem.[5]

Methodologically, Horsley rightly expands the discussion on Galilean identity to include the *longue durée* of Galilean history, from the Iron Age to the Roman Periods. But by too quickly dismissing the archaeological record, Horsley must eke out the Galileans' identity from the literary evidence, which is, as he admits, "fragmentary and cryptic."[6] New Testament passages with a likely Galilean provenience treat the identity of the Galileans as self-evident; those that were written outside of Galilee treat the terms *Galilee* and *the Galileans* as part of literary or theological schemes without offering clues on the Galilean social world.[7] The other relevant texts are likewise

---

3. R. Horsley, *Galilee: History, Politics, People* (Valley Forge, Pa.: Trinity, 1995) 40; see also idem, *Archaeology, History, and Society in Galilee: The Social Context of Jesus and the Rabbis* (Valley Forge, Pa.: Trinity, 1996).

4. A. Alt, "Zur Geschichte der Grenze zwischen Judäa und Samaria" and "Galiläische Probleme," reprinted in *Kleine Schriften zur Geschichte des Volkes Israel* (3 vols.; Munich: Beck, 1953–59) 2.346–62, 363–435; see also F. Loftus, "The Anti-Roman Revolts of the Jews and the Galileans," *JQR* 68 (1977) 78–98.

5. Horsley, *Archaeology, History, and Society*, 178–85; idem, *Galilee*, 280–81; and idem, "Archaeology of Galilee and the Historical Context of Jesus," *Neotestamentica* 29 (1995) 211–29. Horsley's archaeological reconstruction of Galilee fits his earlier statements in *Sociology and the Jesus Movements* (New York: Crossroad, 1989). The Lukan versification is used throughout this paper for Q—that is, Q 11:49–51 = Matt 23:34–36 // Luke 11:49–51.

6. Idem, *Galilee*, 39.

7. A point made by S. Freyne, "Galilee-Jerusalem Relations according to Josephus' *Life*," *NTS* 33 (1987) 600. E. Lohmeyer discussed the synoptic texts as part of his dichotomy between Galilean and Jerusalem Christianity (*Galiläa und Jerusalem* [FRLANT 34; Göttingen: Vandenhoeck & Ruprecht, 1936]); on Mark's use of Galilee from a redaction-critical perspective, see W. Marxsen, *Der Evangelist Markus: Studien zur Redaktionsgeschichte des Evangeliums* (FRLANT 49; Göttingen: Vandenhoeck & Ruprecht, 1956) 33–61; a more recent literary-critical perspective is found in E. Struthers Malbon, "Galilee and Jerusalem: History and Literature in Markan Interpretation," *CBQ* 44 (1982) 242–55; for John's use of Galilee, see J. Bassler, "The Galileans: A Neglected Factor in Johannine

problematic. 1 Maccabees was written before the annexation of Galilee and projects the ideals of Davidic kingship, deuteronomistic theology, and biblical phraseology onto the events it describes.[8] Josephus uses the term *Galileans* inconsistently, and his account that Aristobolus permitted Itureans to remain (in Galilee?) only if they circumcised themselves and obeyed Jewish laws is cited from Strabo, who in turn relies on Timagenes (*Ant.* 13.318–19).[9] The late or uncertain date of the rabbinic texts renders them especially problematic for reconstructing Galilee in Second Temple times.

The primary focus of this paper is the archaeological evidence relating to the Galileans' religious identity in the first century; the textual evidence will be treated only tangentially. The paper has four components. First, I will show that the Galilean settlement patterns from the Iron Age through the Roman Period rule out any direct continuity between the Northern Israelites and the first-century Galileans. Next, I will argue that the sudden rise in sites and overall material culture in Late Hellenistic Galilee, which coincides with the Hasmonean annexation, has its likeliest explanation in a Judean colonization of a scarcely inhabited Galilee.[10] Galilee and Judea's shared indicators of Jewish religious identity—stone vessels, ritual baths, burial practices, and a diet without pork—confirm this, even though the material culture cannot reveal the Galileans' religious *attitudes*, such as their loyalty to Jerusalem or devotion to its Temple. Third, the key literary texts will be examined briefly against the archaeological background. The implications

---

Community Research," *CBQ* 43 (1981) 243–57; on the history of scholarship as a whole and John in particular, see G. Stemberger's appendix, "Galilee: Land of Salvation?" in W. D. Davies, *The Gospel and the Land: Early Christian and Jewish Territorial Doctrine* (Berkeley: University of California Press, 1974) 409–38.

8. S. Schwartz, "Israel and the Nations Roundabout: 1 Maccabees and the Hasmonean Expansion," *JJS* 41 (1991) 16–38; and Horsley, *Galilee*, 40.

9. S. Freyne convincingly argues that in the *Life*, Josephus uses "the Galileans" to refer to his militant supporters from Galilee (perhaps somewhat nostalgically), while his *Jewish War* uses it to refer to its inhabitants in general without regard for their social location or loyalties ("The Galileans in the Light of Josephus' *Vita*," *NTS* 26 [1980] 397–413). S. Zeitlin argues that the term *Galileans* represented a particular group during the revolt and has no geographic connotation whatsoever ("Who Were the Galileans? New Light on Josephus' Activities in Galilee," *JQR* 64 [1974] 189–203); similarly F. Loftus, "A Note on σύνταγμα τῶν Γαλιλαίων B.J. iv 558," *JQR* 65 (1974) 182–83. A. K. Adam, "According to Whose Law?: Aristobulus, Galilee and the *Nomoi ton Ioudaion*," *JSP* 1996 (14) 15–21.

10. Admittedly, determining religious identity from archaeological evidence is not unproblematic, nor can religion be isolated from social, political, or economic concerns. Debates over what actually constitutes a religious indicator and the practical reality that not all excavations have collected or published such possible indicators is not denied. See the cautious remarks on this issue by E. Meyers, "Identifying Religious and Ethnic Groups through Archaeology," in *Biblical Archaeology Today, 1990* (ed. A. Biran and J. Aviram; Jerusalem: Israel Exploration Society, 1990) 738–45; see also W. Dever, e.g., "The Impact of the New Archaeology," in *Benchmarks in Time and Culture: An Introduction to Palestinian Archaeology—Dedicated to Joseph A. Callaway* (ed. J. Drinkard et al.; Atlanta: Scholars Press, 1988) 337–52.

specifically for the Sayings Gospel Q will be sketched at the conclusion of this study, namely, that the many apparently "Northern" references in Q do not imply *genealogical continuity* with the Northern Israelites but, rather, illustrate the *imaginative creativity* of the tradents of Q in fashioning their own communal identity.

Northern Israel and the Assyrian Conquest

The debate over the identity of the Galileans has its point of departure with the Assyrian advances into Palestine in the late eighth century B.C.E. Continuity between first-century Galileans and Northern Israelites depends on a sufficient number of the latter's surviving in Galilee the campaigns of Tiglath-pileser III in 733–732 B.C.E. The meager textual evidence consists of 2 Kings 15 and a few Assyrian texts. The former offers only that Tiglath-pileser III conquered Hazor, as well as "Gilead and Galilee and the whole land of Naphthali," and that he led "the population into exile in Assyria" (2 Kgs 15:29). The fragmentary Assyrian texts offer only the complete names of Hannathon and Merom and four numbers of exiles from Galilee (625, 650, 656, and 13,520).[11] These texts leave unanswered precisely which cities were destroyed, their location, and the extent of the deportations. The past decades' surveys and excavations in Galilee, however, permit a more comprehensive analysis of the actual situation on the ground. Most significant has been Zvi Gal's survey of the Lower Galilee, which, when coupled with the results of stratigraphic excavations in Upper and Lower Galilee, paint a picture of a totally devastated and depopulated Galilee in the wake of the Assyrian campaigns of 733/732 B.C.E.[12] Gal's surface survey of the Lower Galilee found no occupational evidence from the seventh and sixth centuries at any of the over eighty sites inspected, that is to say, after Tiglath-pileser III's expedition. The lack of seventh-century surface sherds *at any given site* can perhaps be attributed to the surveyor's vagrancy or the site's preservation history, but their lack *at each and every site* in such a large sample defies coincidence.

---

11. H. Tadmor, *The Inscriptions of Tiglath-Pileser III King of Assyria: Critical Edition, with Introductions, Translations, and Commentary* (Fontes ad res Judaicas spectantes; Jerusalem: Israel Academy of Sciences and Humanities, 1994); B. Oded, "The Inscriptions of Tiglath-pileser III: Review Article," *IEJ* 47 (1997) 104–8; and N. Naʾaman, "Population Changes in Palestine following Assyrian Deportations," *Tel Aviv* 20 (1993) 104–6. Horsley states that these documents, as products of the royal or priestly elites, are concerned only with the deportation of the upper classes and either assume or do not care whether or not peasants were left behind to work the land (*Galilee*, 25–29; *Archaeology, History, and Society in Galilee*, 22–23). B. Oded, however, stresses the reliability of the figures in the Assyrian bureaucratic lists (*Mass Deportation in the Neo-Assyrian Empire* [Wiesbaden: Reichert, 1979] 6–16).

12. Z. Gal, *The Lower Galilee during the Iron Age* (ASOR Dissertation Series 8; Winona Lake, Ind.: Eisenbrauns, 1992); and idem, "The Lower Galilee in the Iron Age II: Analysis of Survey Material and Its Historical Interpretation," *Tel Aviv* 15–16 (1988–89) 56–64.

Archaeological Period	Dates
Iron II	1000–733/732 B.C.E.
Iron III	733/732–586 B.C.E.
Persian	586–332 B.C.E.
Early Hellenistic	167–63 B.C.E.
Early Roman	63 B.C.E.–135 C.E.
Middle Roman	135–250 C.E.
Late Roman	250–363 C.E.

Fig. 1. Archaeological periods in Galilee.

A depopulated Galilee is verified by two corollary aspects of the survey's findings. First, while single-period sites existed between the twelfth and eighth centuries and subsequently in the fifth century, none have been found from the seventh or sixth centuries. If the Lower Galilee had been occupied after the Assyrian conquest, one would expect considerable instability among its resettled sites, with some having been occupied briefly until settlement patterns stabilized. But no such short-lived sites have been found. Second, the absence in Lower Galilee of Assyrian-style pottery or local imitations thereof is in stark contrast to their presence in Samaria and along the coast, areas that were populated in the seventh and sixth centuries.[13] Like the Lower Galilee, surveys show that the Upper Galilee, in spite of its terrain, was not spared by the Assyrians. Surface sherds from after 732 B.C.E. can be confirmed at only one site surveyed by the Meiron Excavation Project in the late 1970s, Gush Ḥalav.[14] A more recent survey of the Upper Galilee by M. Aviam

13. A point that also confirms Gal's ceramic chronology, upon which a deserted Galilee is based (*The Lower Galilee during the Iron Age*, 82).

14. The Meiron Project uses the designation "Iron 2" for the period 1000–586 B.C.E. and lists three sites with sherds from this period, Beer-sheba, Jotapata, and Gush Ḥalav (E. Meyers et al., "The Meiron Excavation Project: Archaeological Survey in Galilee and Golan, 1976," *BASOR* 230 [1978] 1–24). But not all sites contain sherds from what Gal calls Iron III, that is to say 733–586 B.C.E.: The current excavations at Jotapata report no seventh- or sixth-century B.C.E. evidence from their stratigraphic excavations (D. Adan-Bayewitz et al., "Yodefat 1992," *IEJ* 45 [1995] 191–97). Beer-sheba is very likely not from the seventh or sixth centuries, centuries that have only been confirmed in stratigraphic excavations at Gush Ḥalav. But this site is exceptional in Galilee. Horsley uses this one exception as evidence for continuity between the Israelites and the Galileans throughout Galilee but does not address the gap in occupation at all of the other sites (*Archaeology*, 97); his statement that the "Iron Age" pottery at Nazareth supports his notion of continuity cannot be right, since the published sherds are Iron I or possibly early Iron II; see B. Bagatti, *Excavations in Nazareth, Volume I: From the Beginning till the XII Century* (Jerusalem: Franciscan, 1969) 269–72.

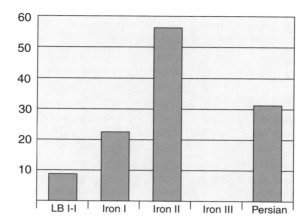

Fig. 2. Number of Lower Galilean sites per period (Gal).

reports limited evidence for the Persian Period in Upper Galilee and a significant resettlement only in the Hellenistic Period.[15]

Stratigraphic excavations in Galilee confirm the lack of seventh- and sixth-
century settlements.[16] Conflagration layers at the end of the eighth century
cover many sites in and around the Galilee, a phenomenon attributed to the
Assyrian conquest. The major urban sites south of Galilee—Megiddo and
Beth-Shean—were radically reduced in size. Assyrian-style administrative
buildings along with modest domestic dwellings were rebuilt at Megiddo,
and smaller sites were resettled toward the coastal plain near Megiddo (Qa-
shish, Qiri, and Jokneam), but this was outside the Galilee.[17] On the eastern
extremity of Galilee, Tel Kinneret on the northern shore of the Sea of Galilee
and Hazor in the Huleh Valley were also destroyed at the end of the eighth
century; *possible* Assyrian administrative buildings were then built, but without any evidence for a surrounding population.[18] In the Galilean heartland,
however, every single excavated site, including Tel Qarnei-Hittin and Gat-
Hepher in eastern Lower Galilee, Tel Mador abutting the Acco Plain, and

15. M. Aviam, "Galilee," *NEAEHL* 2.453.

16. A point made by Gal with regard to Tel Mador as early as 1989: "The presence and
absence of pottery types, as noted in our survey, were identical in the material from the
stratigraphic excavations" ("The Lower Galilee in the Iron Age II," 54).

17. A. Mazar, "Beth-Shean," *OEANE* 1.308; D. Ussishkin, "Megiddo," *OEANE* 3.467–
68; L. Herr, "The Iron Age II Period: Emerging Nations," *BA* 60 (1997) 167–68.

18. At Kinneret, it is difficult to determine the date of the structure; it could be either
Babylonian or Persian; V. Fritz, *Kinneret: Ergebnisse der Ausgrabungen auf dem Tell el-
'Oreme am See Gennesaret 1982–1985* (Wiesbaden: Harrassowitz, 1990) 18; and A. Ben-
Tor, "Hazor," *OEANE* 3.4–5.

Tel Harashim in Upper Galilee, was destroyed or abandoned at the end of the eighth century. Other Iron Age sites that have been excavated in Galilee, such as the villages of Tell el-Wawiyat, Sasa, and Tel ʿEin Zippori along the Beit Netofa Valley and the Phoenician fortress at Ḥorvat Rosh Zayit, were already abandoned in earlier periods.[19] Nor have excavators of the many Roman–Byzantine sites in Galilee published evidence, whether pottery, small finds, or architectural structures, that could be dated to the two centuries following the Assyrian campaigns—though pottery from the Bronze and Iron I Ages have often been found. This list includes Beth Sheʿarim, Capernaum, Chorazin, Hammath Tiberias, Ḥorvat Arbel, Jotapata, Khirbet Shemaʿ, Meiron, Nabratein, Nazareth, and Tiberias. Only Gush Ḥalav's few sherds, from fill in a Late Roman tomb, and one or two isolated structures near Hazor and on Tel Kinneret exist as evidence for the period in question. This should not obscure the fact, however, that the labor of all of the excavations and surveys in Galilee has produced literally only a handful of possible seventh- and sixth-century sherds. [20]

There is simply an insufficient amount of material culture in the Galilee from after the campaigns of Tiglath-pileser III to consider seriously any cultural continuity between earlier and subsequent centuries—there are no villages, no hamlets, no farmsteads, nothing at all indicative of a population that could harvest the Galilean valleys for the Assyrian stores, much less sustain cultural and religious traditions through the centuries.[21] The provincial capital of Megiddo southwest of Galilee was rebuilt and repopulated, but only on the fringes of Galilee have modest military or administrative outposts been found near Hazor at Ayyelet ha-Shahar and on Tel Kinneret. But both are without any significant domestic areas, both were abandoned after Assyrian domination was broken by Babylon, and neither continued into the Late

---

19. Gal, *Lower Galilee during the Iron Age*, 36–47; B. Zakkai, "Tell el-Wawiyat," *NEAEHL* 4.1500–1501; C. Meyers, "Sepphoris and Lower Galilee: Earliest Times through the Persian Period," in *Sepphoris in Galilee: Crosscurrents of Culture* (ed. R. M. Nagy et al.; Raleigh: North Carolina Museum of Art, 1996) 15–19; J. P. Dessel, "Tel ʿEin Zippori," *OEANE* 2.227–28; Gal, "Horvat Rosh Zayit," *NEAHL* 4.1289–90; for Tel Harashim and Sasa, see Gal, "Galilee," *NEAEHL* 2.451. The complexity of the stratigraphic situation at Bethsaida, because of extensive Syrian trenching, makes it difficult to show continuity between the Iron Age and the Persian Period; see R. Arav, "Bethsaida," *OEANE* 1.303–4.

20. At Gush Ḥalav, the excavators are clear that not much evidence and no structures have been found for the end of the Iron Age (*Gush Ḥalav*, 124). A surface survey of Shikhin has found a few pottery sherds that could be either eighth or *possibly* seventh century; the survey found virtually no sherds from the Iron Age 2C/3 when compared to the later Hellenistic and Roman Periods, and the one sherd in question (drawn as fig. 3:18 on p. 178) is parallel to seventh-century levels at Tanaach but is also present there in eighth-century assemblages (J. Strange et al., "Excavations at Sepphoris: The Location and Identification of Shikhin, Part II," *IEJ* 45 [1995] 178).

21. The Galilean ceramic traditions also show no continuity between the pre-732 and later periods, which derive their forms and types from elsewhere and closely parallel those of Judea in the Hellenistic and Roman Periods.

	Iron I	Iron II	Iron III	Persian	Hell I	Hell II	ER	MR–LR
Sasa	•						?	?
Tell el-Wawiyat	•							
Tel ʿEin-Zippori	•	•						
Tel Qarne-Hittin		•						
Tel Mador		•						
H. Rosh Zayit		•						
Tell Chinnereth	•	•	•	?	?			
Ayyelet ha-Shahar			?	?				
Tel Harashim	•	•		?	?			
Hazor	•	•		?	?			
Bethsaida	•	•		?	?			
Gush Ḥalav	•	•	•	•	•	•	•	•
Capernaum	•				?	•	•	•
Nazareth	•	?				?	•	•
Sepphoris		?		•	•	•	•	•
Tel Anafa					?	•	•	•
Gamla						•	•	
Jotapata						•	•	
Khirbet Shemaʿ						•	?	•
Hammath Tiberias						•	•	•
Meiron						•	•	•
Qatzrin		?				•	•	•
Horvat Arbel						•	•	•
Nabratein							•	•
Beth Sheʿarim							•	•
Chorazin							•	•
Tiberias							•	•

Fig. 3. *Strata from excavated sites in Galilee.*

Hellenistic or Early Roman Period.[22] We should imagine some way-stations
north of the lake along a road, with perhaps a branch crossing through Galilee at Gush Ḥalav.

A totally depopulated Galilee is in no way at odds with Assyrian imperial
policies. The Assyrian documentary evidence on mass deportation reveals
that policy varied from region to region and over time and that deportation
was never restricted to a single class. Often the lower classes, including peasants and farmers workers, were deported from peripheral regions to Assyria

22. R. Amiran and I. Dunayevski, "The Assyrian Open Court Building and Its Palestinian Derivates," *BASOR* 149 (1958) 25–32; V. Fritz, "Die Paläste während der assyrischen,
babylonischen und persischen Vorherrschaft in Palästina," *MDOG* 111 (1979) 63–74; and
R. Reich, "The Persian Building at Ayyelet ha-Shahar: The Assyrian Palace of Hazor?" *IEJ*
25 (1975) 233–37.

proper or other provinces for agricultural labor.[23] The Assyrians had an intense interest in *southern* Palestine, which served as a military base facing Egypt, the western terminus for spice trade, and a center for olive oil industries, as the excavations at Tel Miqne-Ekron have brought to light. The Assyrians also patronized the Phoenician maritime trade along the coast, so that Megiddo was oriented primarily toward the south and the coast, and Galilee, which did not figure in the Assyrians' resettlement plans, was neglected and deserted.[24] Stratigraphic excavations corroborate Gal's conclusion of a deserted Lower Galilee, a conclusion that can be extended to the entire Galilee. In his words,

> [t]he events of 732/732 B.C.E. provide a tragic landmark in the history of Israelite settlement in Galilee, particularly Lower Galilee. This was an extremely violent and almost total destruction. Whatever had not been destroyed by the wars was removed or laid waste by the exiles, and the region was not occupied during the seventh and sixth centuries B.C.E.[25]

Parallels in Galilean and Judean Material Culture

The absence of Galilean settlements for over a century after the conquest of Tiglath-pileser III rules out the hypothesis of an Israelite village culture spanning the Iron Age to Roman periods. But can the archaeological record say anything positive about the Galileans' religious identity in the first century? Previous scholarship has concentrated on the Galilean inhabitants prior to the Hasmonean annexation at the end of the second century B.C.E. However, since the number of sites and the overall material culture rose dramatically in the late second/early first century B.C.E., *who* the few inhabitants of the Galilee *had been* is less important than the fact that *Hasmonean rule coincided with an increase in sites and population growth.* Archaeological

23. Oded, *Mass Deportation,* 22 and 91. Horsley incorrectly assumes, without any evidence for the Galilee, that the situation there was analogous to the situation in Samaria, where in fact only the upper classes were deported (*Galilee,* 25–29; idem, *Archaeology, History, and Society in Galilee,* 21–24). Since the number and class of deportees varied within each region and between regions, the Samaritans and the Galileans do not have analogous histories.

24. E. Oren, "Ethnicity and Regional Archaeology: The Western Negev under Assyrian Rule," in *Biblical Archaeology Today, 1990* (ed. A. Biran and J. Aviram; Jerusalem: Israel Exploration Society, 1990) 102–5; N. Na'aman, "The Brook of Egypt and Assyrian Policy on the Border of Egypt," *Tel Aviv* 6 (1979) 68–90; S. Gitin, "Tel Miqne-Ekron: A Type Site for the Inner Coastal Plain in the Iron II Period," in *Recent Excavations in Israel: Studies in Iron Age Archaeology* (AASOR 49; ed. S. Gitin and W. Dever; Winona Lake, Ind.: Eisenbrauns, 1989) 59–79; and Na'aman, "Population Changes," 104–6.

25. Gal, *Lower Galilee during the Iron Age,* 108. Gal notes also that the legible numbers in the fragmentary Assyrian texts (the largest being 13,520) would have represented a substantial portion of the Galilean population (*Lower Galilee during the Iron Age,* 109). The paucity of Assyrian administrative documents dealing with Galilee confirms its insignificance and indirectly suggests its desertion.

surveys and excavations show that, after lying uninhabited following the Assyrian conquest, Galilee began to be sparsely settled during the Persian and
Early Hellenistic Periods. Persian administrative and economic interests concentrated along the coast and along the fertile Jezreel Valley, and only a modest pattern of ruralization can be detected in Galilee with many *very small*
sites clustered around the Beit Netofa Valley, perhaps centrally administered
at Sepphoris, a picture that continues in the Early Hellenistic Period.[26] The
religious identity of these people is difficult to determine, since their material
remains consist only of locally-made utilitarian pottery—whoever they were,
they were poor and traded little with the outside world.[27] The collapse of the
Seleucid Empire in the second century B.C.E. led to considerable shifts in
settlement patterns throughout the Levant, including the southward movement of the Itureans, who originated in southern Lebanon and expanded
toward the Hermon and northern Golan. Their distinct material culture is
characterized by unwalled farmsteads of field stones, brownish-pink heavily
tempered "Golan-ware" pottery, and (cultic?) standing stones; these sites,
however, never reached Galilee and hence, Schürer's hypothesis that the
Galileans were converted Itureans should be abandoned.[28]

In the Late Hellenistic Period, many new sites were also settled in Galilee
and in the Golan that have a material culture paralleling Judea's.[29] The vast

26. Two surveys by N. Zori show how several small settlements arose during the Persian
Period in the Jezreel Valley ("An Archaeological Survey in the Beth-Shean Valley," *The
Beth-Shean Valley: The Seventeenth Archaeological Convention* (Jerusalem: Israel Exploration Society, 1962) 135–98 [Hebrew]; and idem, *The Land of Issachar: An Archaeological
Survey* (Jeruslaem: Israel Exploration Society, 1977) [Hebrew]. On the Persian Period in
general, see E. Stern, *The Material Culture of the Land of the Bible in the Persian Period
538–332 B.C.* (Warminster: Aris and Philips, 1982); and idem, "Between Persia and Greece:
Trade, Administration and Warfare in the Persian and Hellenistic Periods," in *The Archaeology of Society in the Holy Land* (ed. T. Levy; London: Leicester University Press, 1995)
432–45; see also A. Berlin, "Between Large Forces: Palestine in the Hellenistic Period," *BA*
60 (1997) 3–4. The Galilee's Persian Period sites are almost all less than a single hectare
and are mostly scattered around the fertile Beit Netofa Valley (Gal, *Lower Galilee during
the Iron Age*, 12–35). The rhyton and the quadrilingual from Sepphoris suggest its administrative role, but no accompanying architecture has been found; R. M. Nagy et al. (eds.),
Sepphoris in Galilee: Crosscurrents of Culture (Raleigh, N.C.: North Carolina Museum of
Art, 1996). In light of the Zenon papyri and Hefzibah inscription, peasant farmers seem to
have lived in small villages, perhaps working the "king's land" in the larger valleys. The
Hefzibah inscription shows how even billeting by contingents of small traveling adminis-
trators upset the profits that the ruler took from *his* villages; see esp. lines 13 and 14 (Y. H.
Landau, "A Greek Inscription Found near Hefzibah," *IEJ* 16 [1966] 54–70; Berlin, "Between Large Forces," 14).

27. In contrast to the Galileans' urban neighbors along the coast and in some inland
cities such as Samaria or Scythopolis (ibid., 48).

28. Ibid., 36–38; S. Dar, "The History of the Hermon Settlements," *PEQ* 120 (1988)
26–44.

29. The Meiron Project reports a rise from zero to 10 sites at this time (of a total of 20).
A more recent survey of Upper Galilee reveals a jump to 39 sites (M. Aviam, "Galilee: The
Hellenistic to Byzantine Periods," *NEAEHL* 2.453).

majority of the Roman–Byzantine sites that have been stratigraphically excavated contain their earliest recoverable strata, that is to say the earliest architecture and first significant pottery assemblage, from the late second or early
first century B.C.E.: Capernaum, Gamla, Hammath Tiberias, Horvat Arbel,
Jotapata, Khirbet Shema', Meiron, Nazareth, Qatzrin, and Sepphoris (see
fig. 3).[30] In fact, the earliest traceable architecture at Sepphoris is a large military complex on the acropolis full of Jannaean coins in its foundation, suggesting that the site was fortified by the Hasmoneans. Other sites' first
significant settlements are a bit later, around the turn of the millennium or
in the first century C.E., such as Beth She'arim, Herod Antipas's Tiberias,
Nabratein, and Chorazin.[31] Pottery counts from Sepphoris, as recorded by
the University of South Florida excavation, most clearly illustrate the dramatic rise in material culture in the Late Hellenistic and Early Roman Periods: with virtually no sherds from the Persian and Early Hellenistic Periods,
to around one hundred in the Late Hellenistic Period, to nearly three thousand in the Early Roman Period, a pattern that is replicated at most sites in
the Galilee.[32] The numismatic profile of most excavated sites in Galilee mirrors the increase in ceramics. Beginning in the early first century B.C.E., the
number of coins proliferates, with an overwhelming Hasmonean—particularly Jannaean—component.[33] The emergence of Hasmonean coinage at
sites throughout Galilee points to its economic and political orientation toward Judea and strongly suggests that its subsequent population growth was
connected to Hasmonean policies.[34]

30. Meyers et al., *Excavations at Ancient Meiron, Upper Galilee, Israel, 1971–72, 1974–75, 1977* (Cambridge, Mass.: American Schools of Oriental Research, 1981) 155; idem, *Ancient Synagogue Excavations at Khirbet Shema', Upper Galilee, Israel, 1970–1972* (AASOR 42; Durham, N.C.: American Schools of Oriental Research, 1976) 2, 257; M. Dothan, *Hammath Tiberias: Early Synagogues and the Hellenistic and Roman Remains* (Jerusalem: Israel Exploration Society, 1983) 10; Z. Ilan, "Horvat Arbel," *ESI* 7–8 (1988–89) 8–9; and J. Strange, "Nazareth," *ABD* 4.1051; idem, "Nazareth," *OEANE* 4.113–14. At a few sites, handfuls of earlier, fourth- or third-century, sherds have also been found but at insufficient levels for the excavators to label them as a stratum. Horsley is at pains to suggest that the few possible third-century B.C.E. sherds in Nazareth argue against a Hasmonean refound-ing of the site, but he does not concede that there is no continuity with the Iron Age and that the earliest *significant* quantities of pottery, artifacts, and architecture coincide with the arrival of the Hasmoneans.

31. Y. Hirschfeld, "Tiberias," *NEAEHL* 4.1464–73. Meyers et al., "Preliminary Report on the 1980 Excavations at en-Nabratein, Israel," *BASOR* 244 (1981) 1–26; idem, "Second Preliminary Report on the 1980 Excavations at en-Nabratein, Israel," *BASOR* 246 (1982) 35–54. Z. Yeivin, "Chorazin," *NEAEHL* 1.301–4.

32. J. Strange et al., "Excavations at Sepphoris: The Location and Identification of Shikhin, Part II," *IEJ* 45 (1995) 180.

33. Meyers et al., *Ancient Synagogue Excavations at Khirbet Shema'*, 147–152; and *Excavations at Meiron*, 155.

34. A corollary to the Hasmonean settlement of Galilee is the destruction or abandon-ment of Gentile sites between Judea and Galilee, such as Gezer, Samaria, and Philoteria, and around Galilee, such as Tel Anafa; see Berlin, "Between Large Forces," 39.

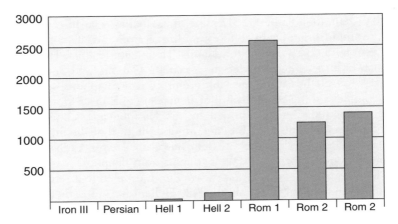

Fig. 4. USF pottery counts at Sepphoris.

The increase in sites and use of Hasmonean coinage point to economic and political connections between Galilee and Jerusalem. More importantly, archaeological indicators of Jewish identity point to a shared religious heritage with Judea. Scholars of Christian origins have devoted considerable attention to the extent of urbanization and Hellenization in Galilee—its language, public architecture, or symbols of Hellenistic culture and Roman rule. These, however, are determined primarily by the political and economic elites from above, and do not necessarily represent the broader population's identity.[35] Important for understanding the Galilee's religious character, however, is its domestic or private space, which is remarkably similar to that of Judea; in particular Galilee and Judea are united by four indicators of Jewish religious identity: (1) the so-called stone vessels, (2) stepped pools or *miqvaot*, (3) secondary burial in ossuaries in *loculi* tombs, and (4) bone profiles that lack pork. The first two items are particularly helpful because of their mundane everyday character and are used primarily in this study because they are typically identified by field archaeologists and published. Hand- or lathe-made vessels of chalk or limestone are easily identified in excavation—if they survive the more moist and acidic soils. Literary evi-

35. This is not to imply that public architecture is unimportant for understanding first-century Galilee, especially socioeconomic and political aspects; see J. Strange, "Some Implications of Archaeology for New Testament Studies," *What Has Archaeology to Do with Faith?* (ed. J. Charlesworth and W. Weaver; Valley Forge, Pa.: Trinity, 1992) 23–59; S. Freyne, "Jesus and the Urban Culture of Galilee," in *Texts and Contexts: Biblical Texts and Their Textual and Situational Contexts* (ed. T. Fornberg and D. Hellholm; Oslo: Scandinavian University Press, 1995) 596–622; J. Reed, "Population Numbers, Urbanization, and Economics: Galilean Archaeology and the Historical Jesus," *SBL 1994 Seminar Papers* (ed. David Lull; SBLSP 33; Atlanta: Scholars Press, 1994) 203–19.

dence ties them to a concern for ritual purity, but regardless of their owners' intentions, they are ubiquitous in Jerusalem and Judea, Galilee, and the Golan up to the first century c.e. but fade out of use in the early second century.[36] Plastered stepped pools, or *miqvaot*, are also frequent in Judea, Galilee, and the Golan but are not found where Jews are not known to have lived. They are found in the basements of houses and occasionally around olive press installations and are discussed in the Mishna as one of the means, in addition to bathing in a natural body of water, for ritual purification.[37] The two additional indicators of Jewish religious identity used in this study, burial practices and dietary habits, are less consistently excavated, recorded, or published. Secondary burial using soft limestone ossuaries inside so-called *kokhim*, or *loculi*, horizontally shafted family tombs underground, is a distinctly Jewish phenomenon at the end of the Second Temple Period.[38] Bone

36. Y. Magen, *The Stone Vessel Industry in Jerusalem in the Days of the Second Temple* (Tel Aviv: Society for the Protection of Nature, 1988) [Hebrew]; idem, "Jerusalem as a Center of the Stone Vessel Industry during the Second Temple Period," *Ancient Jerusalem Revealed* (ed. H. Geva; Jerusalem: Israel Exploration Society, 1994) 244–56; J. M. Cahill, "The Chalk Assemblages of the Persian/Hellenistic and Early Roman Periods," in *Excavations at the City of David 1978–1985 Directed by Yigal Shiloh*, vol. 3: *Stratigraphical, Environmental, and Other Reports* (ed. A. de Groot and D. T. Ariel; Qedem 33; Jerusalem: Israel Exploration Society, 1992) 190–274; and R. Deines, *Jüdische Steingefäße und pharisäische Frömmigkeit: Ein archäologisch-historischer Beitrag zum Verständnis von Joh 2,6 und der jüdischen Reinheitshalacha zur Zeit Jesu* (WUNT 2/52; Tübingen: Mohr, 1993).

37. At this point I am not arguing for a type of Judaism or religious belief associated with these *miqvaot* but, rather, that these stepped pools' presence is typical of a Jewish population. R. Reich has convincingly shown that these installations are uniquely Jewish, though not every plastered pool excavated is a *miqveh* ("The Hot Bath-House [*balneum*], the *Miqweh*, and the Jewish Community in the Second Temple Period," *JJS* 39 [1988] 102–7; idem, "Ritual Baths," *OEANE* 4.430–31). Y. Magen's suggestion, that he has found possibly another, Samaritan *miqveh* does not in my opinion seriously challenge Reich's conclusions ("The Ritual Baths [*Miqva'ot*] at Qedumim and the Observance of Ritual Purity among the Samaritans," in *Early Christianity in Context: Monuments and Documents* [ed. F. Manns and E. Alliata; Jerusalem: Franciscan, 1993] 181–92). The significance of the *miqveh* as a religious indicator is most clearly illustrated with the addition of such an installation to a house in Gezer when the Maccabees repopulated the area; see R. Reich, "Archaeological Evidence of the Jewish Population at Hasmonean Gezer," *IEJ* 31 (1981) 48–52.

38. Although elements of burial practices from the broader Hellenistic and Semitic world were adopted, Jews combined these into secondary burial in *kokhim* with ossuaries "in such a way that they created burial customs and rites that are uniquely Jewish" (R. Hachlili and A. Killebrew, "Jewish Funerary Customs during the Second Temple Period, in the Light of the Excavations at the Jericho Necropolis," *PEQ* 115 [1983] 129; see also the valuable summaries by B. McCane, "Ossuaries," *OEANE* 4.187–88; and idem, "Burial Techniques," *OEANE* 1.386–7). Recent examples near Jerusalem are reported by A. Kloner, "A Tomb with Inscribed Ossuaries in East Talpiyot, Jerusalem," *Atiqot* 29 (1996) 15–22; and S. Wolff, "A Second Temple Period Tomb on the Shu'afat Ridge, North Jerusalem," *Atiqot* 29 (1996) 23–28. Although the use of ossuaries and *kokhim* seems to be a democratization of elite burial, there were likely socioeconomic aspects within this type of burial that made it unaffordable for the poor, a point hinted at by Z. Greenhut, "Two Burial Caves of the Second Temple Period in Rehavia, Jerusalem," *Atiqot* 29 (1996) 41*– 46* (English Summary, p. 109).

profiles without pork confirm a Jewish presence, especially in combination with the other indicators. Together, this fourfold cluster offers a reliable indicator of Jewish religious identity.[39]

Although the number of sites with abundant first-century evidence is limited, the existing finds consistently mirror the finds of Judea and are remarkably homogenous with regard to religious indicators. At Sepphoris, the earliest recoverable stratum in the western domestic quarters, from about 100 B.C.E. to 70 C.E., includes over one hundred stone vessel fragments and over twenty *miqvaot*. Significant for the identification of the Sepphorean and other stepped pools as Jewish *miqvaot* is a single house at Sepphoris, occupied from the first through the fourth centuries, whose first-century strata include many stone vessels (mostly in the kitchen), four stepped, plastered pools, an absence of pork in the zooarchaeological profile, and a (slightly later) oil lamp decorated with a menorah. The other domestic units at Sepphoris, though at times less well preserved in the first century, contain stone vessels, *miqvaot*, and no pork. Outside of the city, typical Second Temple Jewish tombs have also been found.[40] In Tiberias, where the modern city precludes widespread excavation, work in mostly public structures has nevertheless uncovered stone-vessel fragments and a *miqveh*, as well as ossuaries in tombs. The scant Early Roman evidence under the synagogue at Hammath Tiberias also contains stone-vessel fragments.[41] At less urban sites with considerable first-century evidence the same pattern is repeated. At Jotapata, which was destroyed in the first Jewish war with Rome, about two hundred stone vessels have been found, as well as two *miqvaot* in the domestic quarters.[42] The limited Franciscan excavations at Nazareth published four stone

39. E. Goodenough's compilation and hypothesis make one weary of using allegedly "pagan" or "Jewish" symbols for religious identity. Hence I focus on domestic items and burial practices. Horsley is overly cautious in identifying any single item as Jewish for fear of essentialist reductionism. I would argue that the widespread use of stone vessels and the frequency of *miqvaot* indicate Jewish identity, especially where evidence for Jewish burial practices and an absence of pork exist. In this regard, see the important work by R. Vale, "Literary Sources in Archaeological Description: The Case of Galilee, Galilees and Galileans," *JSJ* 18 (1987) 209–26.

40. I am currently preparing the stone vessels of the western domestic quarters at Sepphoris for publication. The *miqvaot* are reported in E. Meyers, "Roman Sepphoris in the Light of New Archaeological Evidence and Research," *The Galilee in Late Antiquity* (ed. L. Levine; New York: Jewish Theological Seminary Press, 1992) 332; on the tombs in the Sepphorean hillsides, see Z. Weiss, "Hellenistic and Roman Sepphoris: The Archaeological Evidence," in *Sepphoris in Galilee: Crosscurrents of Culture* (ed. R. M. Nagy et al.; Raleigh: North Carolina Museum of Art, 1996) 35; B. Grantham, the zooarchaeologist of the Sepphoris Regional Project, reports a shift in diet (including pork) after the 363 C.E. earthquake and reports virtually no pork in any of the first-century domestic units.

41. Y. Hirschfeld, "Tiberias," *NEAHL* 4.1468; F. Vitto, "Tiberias: The Roman Tomb," *NEAHL* 4.1473; Dothan, *Hammath Tiberias*, 63, fig. 4, S; Deines, *Jüdische Steingefäße*, 147.

42. D. Adan-Bayewitz et al., "Yodefat, 1992," *IEJ* 1945 (1995) 191–97. M. Aviam and R. Urowitz have generously provided information on the soon-to-be-published stone vessels and *miqvaot* from Jotapata.

	Stone Vessels	Miqvaoth	Tombs	No Pork
Sepphoris	•	•	•	•
Nazareth	•	•	•	?
Tiberias	•	•	?	?
Jotapata	•	•	?	?
Gamla	•	•	?	?
Capernaum	•	○	?	?
H. Tiberias	•	○	?	?

Fig. 5. Sites with first-century C.E. *strata.*

vessels and a *miqveh*, and the tombs outside the ancient village are *kokhim* type with many ossuary fragments strewn about.[43] At Reina, a few kilometers from Nazareth and Sepphoris, a stone-vessel manufacturing site has also been found at a calcite outcropping; based on matches found in first-century contexts at Sepphoris, it certainly dates to the first century B.C.E. or C.E.[44] In Capernaum's Late Hellenistic and Early Roman loci, around one hundred fifty stone-vessel fragments have been uncovered. In each of the domestic units on the Franciscan side, including those under the synagogue and St. Peter's house, many stone-vessel fragments are present, attesting to their widespread distribution.[45] Little exists by way of tombs, other than the small Middle or Late Roman mausoleum with a few sarcophagi just to the north of the site. Strikingly absent at Capernaum are *miqvaot*, which I would attribute to the fact that the lake provided an alternative for acceptable bathing. At Gamla, which has its foundations in the late second or early first century, many stone vessels as well as two or possibly three *miqvaot* have been found, one connected with the synagogue, one with an olive press, and one in a house.[46]

At several sites where first-century remains are less well preserved, *miqvaot*, stone vessels, or tombs have been excavated. Particularly significant are

43. Bagatti reports stone vessels (p. 318), a seven-stepped *miqveh* filled in under a later mosaic, and *kokhim*-type tombs with ossuaries fragments strewn about (pp. 237–47), but no bone profile is reported (*Excavations in Nazareth*). Strange suggests a second-century date for the *miqveh* (ABD 4.1051).

44. Z. Gal, "A Stone-Vessel Manufacturing Site in the Lower Galilee," *'Atiqot* 20 (1991) 25*–26* (English summary, pp. 179–80).

45. I wish to thank S. Loffreda for his generosity in permitting an examination of all of the site's stone vessels. A study of these is in progress. The absence of *miqvaot* at Capernaum is notable and worthy of further study, especially since socioeconomic factors might also be involved. No bone profile is reported by the excavators.

46. S. Gutman, "Gamla," *NEAHL* 2.463; S. Gutman and D. Wagner, "Gamla: 1984/ 1985/1986," *ESI* 5 (1986) 41; and A. Berlin, personal correspondence.

stone vessels because they went out of use in the late first century, but their fragmentary presence in Middle or Late Roman Period fill indicates that they were present at the site in an earlier period. Stone vessels from Galilee have been found, in addition to the above-mentioned sites, in Bethlehem of the Galilee, Gush Ḥalav, Ibelin, Kfar Hananya, Kfar Kana, Khirbet Shemaʿ, Meiron, Migdal Ha-Emeq, and Nabratein; *miqvaot* at Chorazin, Beit Yinam, Beth Sheʿarim, Har Arbel (?), Khirbet Shemaʿ, and Sasa; and first-century *kokhim*-type tombs with ossuaries at the necropolis of Beth Sheʿarim, as well as at Kfar Kana and Huqoq.[47]

To summarize, the overall settlement history of Galilee shows a substantial gap after the Assyrian conquest in the eighth century, with an inkling of repopulation beginning in the Persian Period. Substantial settlement and population growth in Galilee begins with the Hasmonean rule of Galilee in the first centuries B.C.E. and continues through the first century C.E. Key aspects of the Galilean material culture of this period match the material culture of Judea: stone vessels, *miqvaot* in houses, lack of pork, and secondary burial with ossuaries in *kokhim*.[48] Therefore Hasmonean rule in Galilee should not be construed as a political-economic or administrative veneer over an indigenous Galilean population—wherever archaeologists have excavated, Jewish religious indicators permeate Galilean domestic space in the first century. Whether this was because the few previous inhabitants—and I stress their small number regardless of who they were—readily adopted Judaism and flourished as they adopted it or whether Judeans colonized the Galilee and overwhelmed the few prior inhabitants (who may have been earlier Jewish settlers), is difficult to determine. In either case, and I take the latter to be more likely, the crucial point is that Galilean religion was either overwhelmed by or originated in Jerusalem and Judea, in terms of the material evidence.

47. For stone vessels, see Meyers, *Ancient Synagogue Excavations at Khirbet Shemaʿ*, pl. 8.8, no. 18; idem, *Excavations at Ancient Meiron*, pl. 9.22, no. 15; D. Adan-Bayewitz, "Kfar Hananya," *ESI* 7–8 (1988–89) 108; and Y. Magen, *"Purity Broke Out in Israel:" Stone Vessels in the Late Second Temple Period* (Catalogue no. 9, The Reuben and Edith Hecht Museum; Haifa: University of Haifa, 1994) 24–25. *Miqvaot* are listed with varying degrees of probability in R. Reich, *Miqwaoth (Jewish Ritual Immersion Baths) in Eretz-Israel in the Second Temple Period and the Mishnah and Talmud Periods* (Ph.D. diss., Hebrew University, 1990) [Hebrew with English summary]; on burial sites, see B. Mazar, *Beth Sheʿarim: Report on the Excavations during 1936–1940, I–III* (2d ed.; Jerusalem: Israel Exploration Society, 1957) [Hebrew with English summary]; A. Berman, "Kfr Kanna," *ESI* 7–8 (1988–89) 107–8; and B. Ravani and P. P. Kahane, "Rock-Cut Tombs at Huqoq," *ʿAtiqot* 3 (1961) 121–47.

48. The homogeneity of Galilee with Judea is distinct from nearby sites on the coast (e.g., Strato's Tower) or to the north (e.g., Kedesh, Tel Anafa) or the south (e.g., Samaria). A point to be underscored is that the sites most closely associated with the Jesus tradition, Capernaum and Nazareth, share the same pattern in religious indicators as Galilee's two urban sites, Sepphoris and Tiberias.

Integrating the Literary Sources

Although a detailed exegesis lies beyond the scope of this paper, it is worth pointing out that none of the key literary texts undermines the notion of a sparsely populated Galilee prior to the Hasmonean Period, nor does any seriously challenge the idea of a shared Galilean-Judean material culture with regard to a common Jewish religious heritage.[49] To highlight just a few instances: Noticeable population growth in Judea in the third and second centuries B.C.E. is apparent in 1 Maccabees—demographic pressure in the South set the stage for immigration to Galilee.[50] Polybius reports that Antiochus III captured Philoteria and Scythopolis, then defeated the Ptolemaic army on Mount Tabor, but lists no other encounters in Galilee, I assume because there were no other significant settlements or fortifications there (*Hist.* 5.62).[51] The key to Schürer's argument for a non-Jewish Galilee, 1 Macc 5:14–5, reports that Simeon evacuated all of the Jews of Galilee and Arbatta to Jerusalem, a feat possible only if they were few in number. If the text is at all reliable, it means that a few Jews were in Galilee prior to the Hasmonean annexation; but certainly their *small* number does not imply a *large* number of Gentiles, as Schürer argued.[52] Josephus describes Hyrcanus's defeat of Scythopolis as leaving Galilee open for resettlement, implying that it was sparsely inhabited (*Ant.* 13.28; *J.W.* 1.64). Josephus's description of Ptolemy Lathyrus's attack on Sepphoris suggests that the Sabbath was observed in Galilee already in the early first century B.C.E. (*Ant.* 13.337–38). Finally, 1 Macc 13:43–48 casts the Hasmonean expansion into Galilee along the lines of the deuteronomistic account of the conquest, portraying a Jewish community "who observed the law" as driving out the Gentiles. In light of the archaeological evidence, the expulsion of a significant number of Gentiles is highly dubious but not its repopulation by Jews. The archaeological evidence also calls into question interpretations of Josephus that place the conversion of the Itureans in Galilee (*Ant.* 13.319). The text itself never specifies Galilee as the locale; moreover, no archaeological evidence exists for Itureans in Galilee.

49. See E. P. Sanders's notion of a "common Judaism," in *Judaism: Practice and Belief, 63 B.C.E.–66 C.E.* (Philadelphia: Trinity, 1992).

50. B. Bar-Kochva has convincingly argued for a demographic cycle under the Maccabees in which population pressure in Judea fostered the enlistment of young landless males, who were then resettled in conquered territories ("Manpower, Economics, and Internal Strife in the Hasmonean State," *Armées et fiscalité dans le monde antique* [Paris: Centre National de la Recherche Scientifique, 1977] 167–94).

51. M. Aviam reports having found fortifications dating to this period, but without any surrounding domestic area or village ("Mount Tabor," *OEANE* 5.152).

52. Schürer, *History*, 1.142, 216–18. Freyne suggests, based on the textual uncertainty and location of Arbella, that the Jews were removed only from Galilee's western fringe (*Galilee*, 37).

The alleged conversion is simply not a significant factor in assessing the ethnicity of Galileans.[53]

More generally, Josephus's ambiguous use of *Galileans* contrasts with his unequivocal description of Idumeans, Itureans, and Samarians as non- or half-Jews. He and the Jerusalem Council assumed that a priest from the Temple would have status among Galileans, and he writes that Galileans regularly visited the Temple ("as was their custom," *J.W.* 2.237 and *Ant.* 20.123). Josephus's writings tell us more about Jerusalemite expectations than Galilean loyalty, but the important point is that Galileans had an acceptable pedigree in Josephus's opinion, unlike Judea's neighbors.[54] In the rabbinic texts, although there were Galilean variations in a few details, such as the calendar or measurements, their basic halakic principles did not differ substantially from the Judeans.[55]

For these reasons the term *Jewish* is thoroughly appropriate for the inhabitants of Galilee in the first century. In fact, the term's geographical root (*Ioudaioi*) accurately grasps the Galileans' religious roots in Judea. To speak of *Galilean* Judaism or *Galilean* Jews is to add an important qualifier, but to juxtapose Galileans with Judeans and stress their geographical differences skews their common heritage and obscures their historical connections. Galilean Jews had a different social, economic, and political matrix than Jews living in Judea or the diaspora and even among themselves held diverse attitudes, practices, and goals—among them the ones preserved in the Sayings Gospel Q—but they were what we should call Jewish.

"Israelite" Components of the Sayings Gospel Q

The above analysis of the archaeological record does not, of course, solve the question of what kind of Judaism existed in first-century Galilee. The sig-

---

53. Berlin states the case stronger: "There is, in fact, no evidence that this area [south of Hermon and northern Golan] ever came under Hasmonean political or economic control. Nor is there evidence for Iturean settlement in Galilee itself. These discrepancies suggest that Josephus misrepresented the conquests of Aristobolus" ("Between Large Forces," 37). On the instability of the Itureans and their southern expansion in the Early Hellenistic Period, see W. Schottroff, "Die Ituräer," *ZDPV* 98 (1982) 125–47. Josephus's report of the enslavement of 10,000 inhabitants (*Ant.* 13.337) cannot be taken to indicate a substantial population in the Galilee—he elsewhere uses the term loosely, and here it likely simply means "a lot."

54. Freyne, "Galilee-Jewish Relations," 600–607.

55. L. Schiffman, "Was There a Galilean Halakhah?" *The Galilee in Late Antiquity* (ed. L. Levine; New York: Jewish Theological Seminary Press, 1992) 143–56. L. Levine, among others, has shown that the acrimonious rhetoric against the *ʿamme ha-ʾaretz* is not directed at Galileans in general; rather, he suggests that differences are due to social status and not a distinct Galilean religious character (*Rabbinic Class of Roman Palestine* [New York: Jewish Theological Seminary of America Press, 1989]); see also A. Oppenheimer, *The ʿAm Ha-aretz: A Study in the Social History of the Jewish People in the Hellenistic-Roman Period* (Leiden: Brill, 1977).

nificance or meaning attached by various people to the stone vessels or *miqvaot* cannot be determined by the artifacts alone, and certainly regional variations existed between Judea and Galilee. Yet the sketch of settlement patterns alone and the description of shared religious indicators drawn above have considerable implications for Christian origins. I will restrict my observations to the sayings material in Q, which can be located, as I have argued elsewhere, with reasonable certainty in Galilee, either originating with Jesus himself or with his first followers in Galilee.[56]

Much in the Sayings Gospel Q points to a generally Jewish religious milieu: appeal is to the Hebrew scriptures, faithful Torah observance is raised, and Jewish heroes are mentioned.[57] The specific archaeological items listed above are mostly ignored in Q, I assume because they were accepted as commonplace and somewhat of a moot point in the Q community's theology or disputes. General purity concerns at meals and the use of clean cups are specifically mentioned, but the alleged superficiality of the Pharisees is criticized without undermining the practice per se (Q 11:39–40). Likewise, Q does not comment on *miqvaot* or ritual washings, except to say that John's baptism should be accompanied by internal purity and should promote "fruits worthy of repentance" (Q 3:8). The practice of bathing in *miqvaot*, however, is not censured. Much the same can be said of burial practices and avoidance of pork. The former is not a topic in Q. The latter's omission is of note insofar as Jesus' laxity in selecting his dining company is defended but not his diet, which was apparently not under scrutiny by the Q community's critics. A more interesting phenomenon in Q, as Horsley observes, is the frequency of what can be described as Northern or Israelite traditions, in particular Israel's prophetic imagery. It is this gap, between the historical reality of the Galileans' southern origins on the one hand, and the Q community's epic imagination with the preponderance of Northern traditions on the other, that will conclude this paper.

Prophetic forms, themes, and allusions permeate the Sayings Gospel, many with particularly or possible Northern associations.[58] The term *Ioudaioi* 'Jews', or what Horsley translates 'Judeans', never appears in Q. Rather, the term 'Israel' is used, in Q 7:9 and notably in Q 22:30, where Jesus' followers

---

56. On the location of many of Q's sayings in Galilee, see my "Social Map of Q," in *Conflict and Invention: Literary, Rhetorical, and Social Studies on the Sayings Gospel Q* (ed. J. Kloppenborg; Valley Forge, Pa.: Trinity, 1995) 17–36. For the sake of simplicity, Q will be treated here in its final form, without any attempt to discern redactional layers.

57. W. Cotter, "Prestige, Protection and Promise: A Proposal for the Apologetics of Q2," in *The Gospel behind the Gospels* (ed. R. Piper; Leiden: Brill, 1995) 117–38, esp. 124–25.

58. Whether this is the result of a single prophetic redaction or due to the addition of a second, apocalyptic layer is beyond the scope of this paper. On the former see, e.g., M. Sato, *Q und Prophetie: Studien zur Gattungs- und Traditionsgeschichte der Quelle Q* (WUNT 2/29; Tübingen: Mohr [Siebeck], 1988); on the latter, see most prominently J. Kloppenborg, *The Formation of Q: Trajectories in Ancient Wisdom Collections* (Philadelphia: Fortress, 1987).

are promised ultimately to judge the *twelve tribes of Israel*, glancing nostalgically back to premonarchic times, when no specific tribe or locale had primacy.[59] Likewise in John's speech, religious identity is described in patriarchal terms of being "children of Abraham," a premonarchic concept (Q 3:9). Zion or its theology are also avoided. In Q 11:29–31 Jesus is compared to Jonah, a Northern prophet who is said to have originated in the Galilean village of Gad-Hepher and who was likely venerated as a local hero in first-century Galilee.[60] Allusions to the Northern prophets Elijah and Elisha also appear: Q 7:22–23, though quoting Isaiah, has close narrative parallels in the Elijah and Elisha cycles, with the cleansing of a leper and the raising of the dead (1 Kgs 17:17–24, 2 Kgs 4:18–37, and 2 Kings 5). Likewise, Q 7:21 quotes in part Mal 3:1, which yearns for a future Elijah *redivivus*. Jesus' call to discipleship in Q 9:57–62 echoes Elijah's call to his followers, and if Luke 9:61–62 is in Q, then there is a near verbatim quotation of 1 Kgs 19:19–21.[61] While prophets rank high on Q's scale of values, kings and priests—remarkably David and Moses—are absent in Q. Both had become localized in Jerusalem as the center for political and religious rule; the Davidic king would return to rule in Jerusalem, and the priests officiated in the Temple in Jerusalem. The prophet, however, was not localized; in fact, prophets served as moral and social critics of kings and priests, as well as of their centralization in Jerusalem in particular, a recurrent theme especially among Northern prophets and prophets outside of Jerusalem. In this vein Q criticizes the localization of the divine in Jerusalem: the Temple is described as deserted (Q 13:34–35), and the Temple's blood-stained past serves as a reminder of its current moral impurity (Q 11:49–51). The prophet was an understandable choice for a religious community in a Galilean setting. The prophetic role model did not succumb to the Jerusalemite hegemony and provided a traditional avenue for criticizing Jerusalem's religious and political structures in a way that justified rejection. As its adoption of the deuteronomistic theology makes clear, the Q community thought of itself as prophets in a way that justified past and anticipated future rejection (Q 6:23, 11:47–51, and 13:34–35; further somewhat also 7:33–35, 9:58, and 11:31–32).[62]

59. Horsley, "Social Conflict in the Synoptic Sayings Source Q," *Conflict and Invention: Literary, Rhetorical, and Social Studies on the Sayings Gospel Q* (ed. J. Kloppenborg; Valley Forge, Pa.: Trinity, 1995) 38–39.

60. J. Reed, "The Sign of Jonah (Q 11:29–31) and Other Epic References in Q," in *Reimagining Christian Origins: A Colloquium Honoring Burton L. Mack* (ed. E. Castelli and H. Taussig; Valley Forge, Pa.: Trinity, 1996) 130–43.

61. A possible allusion is 2 Kgs 4:29 in the prohibition against greeting anyone on the road (Q 10:4b); on Q's allusions to Elijah, see Sato, *Q und Prophetie*, 144–45; 376–77, 385, 400; on John as Elijah *redivivus* in early Jewish and Christian literature, see R. Webb, *John the Baptizer and Prophet: A Socio-historical Study* (JSNTSup 62; Sheffield: Sheffield Academic Press, 1991) 250–54.

62. On the development of deuteronomistic theology, see O. H. Steck, *Israel und das gewaltsame Geschick der Propheten* (WMANT 23: Neukirchen-Vluyn: Neukirchener Verlag,

These prophetic elements in Q with a particular "Northern" spin do not represent a revival of indigenous Northern Israelite traditions by their later genealogical heirs in Galilee, an idea the archaeological record rules out. Rather, they represent one particular Galilean community's carefully crafted epic imagination to locate themselves on their social map. They pictured themselves in the role of prophets proclaiming new rules for social intercourse, family structures, and personal relationships, and critiqued (like the ancient Northern prophets whose parallels Horsley accurately observed) aspects of the Galilean economic and political structures. Their yearning for the good old times, the cancelation of debts, and lending without requiring a return (or borrowing without repaying!) echoes much of what we have in the prophets.[63] The sayings in Q were crafted with the full plate of possibilities in the Hebrew Bible at the community's disposal. It is not surprising that a Galilean group would gravitate toward Northern passages and prophetic allusions, since they shared a common geographical and spiritual distance from the center, with the concomitant economic and political implications. The Q community linked itself with the Northern prophets, but we should not confuse their imagined origins with reality. In that sense, how they imagined themselves was not who they were.

There is, I think, an important difference between this view of Q's epic imagination and community formation and Horsley's notion of the early Galilean Jesus movement as the revitalization of Israelite village culture. In Horsley's view, Q represents the broader Galilean culture and attitudes, the "little tradition" as it were, which was later overwhelmed by the Judean rabbis, who forged Judaism around the book beginning in the second century in Galilee. Cast heavily in sociopolitical terms, Horsley pictures Jesus as representing the large lower classes, and the priests and Pharisees in or from Jerusalem representing the ruling elites or retainer class. Hasmonean rule and the subsequent (alleged) layering of taxes under the Herodians eroded the egalitarian Galilean village culture and stubborn resistance to outsiders. In Horsley's scenario, Jesus and his movement hoped to revive their ancient Israelite covenantal values in village communities. However, the Galileans' historical roots were Judean. The religious indicators show that Galileans and Judeans had much in common in their daily religious practices. The rabbis could interpret these common concerns and interests more readily after

---

1967). For various interpretations of its use in Q, see P. Hoffmann, *Studien zur Theologie der Logienquelle* (NTAbh n.s. 8; Münster: Aschendorff, 1972) 158–90; D. Lührmann, *Die Redaktion der Logienquelle* (WMANT 33; Neukirchen-Vluyn: Neukirchener Verlag, 1969). A. Jacobson, "The Literary Unity of Q," *JBL* 101 (1982) 365–89.

63. W. Arnal, "Gendered Couplets in Q and Legal Formulations: From Rhetoric to Social History," *JBL* 116 (1997) 75–94. See the provocative essay by R. Kessler on how studies on the Israelite prophets have in fact served as critiques of contemporary economic policies ("Frühkapitalismus, Rentenkapitalismus, Tributarismus, antike Klassengesellschaft: Theorien zur Gesellschaft des alten Israels," *ET* 54 [1994] 413–27).

the destruction of the Temple, which had likely been an earlier source of friction between Galilee and Jerusalem. The rabbis' codification of how to negotiate everyday life in the fields, farms, villages, and cities of Galilee was not an alien framework superimposed from outside and above onto Galileans but was an idealized codification of principles and an intellectual reflection on items and activities that had already been present in Galilean daily life. On the other hand, the Jesus movement and the Sayings Gospel Q were not, I think, representative of the Galileans in general, as several sayings in Q illustrate. The group felt most alienated from "this generation" (Q 7:31; 11:29, 31, 32, 51), a more holistic term for Israel or Jews. And three villages—Chorazin, Bethsaida, and Capernaum receive the most vehement condemnation because they rejected Q's message (Q 10:13–15). Although the Pharisees and scribes had historical connections with Jerusalem and are perceived as a threat in Q (3:7–9, 11:39–51), they are never directly connected with Jerusalem in Q. The Jerusalemite origins of the pharisaic movement is never the issue in Q. The Q community, I believe, marginalized itself and was never a major concern to Judaism as a whole in Galilee until after Constantine, when Christian political power came from outside to the Holy Land.[64]

64. See, among others, S. S. Miller, "The Minim of Sepphoris Reconsidered," *HTR* 86 (1993) 377–402.

Sepphoris on the Eve of the Great Revolt (67–68 C.E.): Archaeology and Josephus

Eric M. Meyers

Duke University

The tension between archaeological evidence and literary evidence has always been a major factor in the reconstruction of ancient history. For the earlier, preexilic historical periods in Syria–Palestine, a significant source of tension has been and continues to be between the Hebrew Bible and archaeological data. While this struggle was perhaps more visible in the 1960s and 1970s, the debates over the reliability of the Hebrew Bible in light of archaeology have reemerged as a major academic battleground today between the so-called "maximalists" and "minimalists."[1] While the dust has yet to settle in this struggle, a rather informed and sophisticated debate over the role of archaeology in reconstructing early Christianity and early Judaism has occurred in other circles, though increasing disagreement over the way archaeological evidence may be used in the debate is evident.[2] Often, however, the evidence is so complex that it is difficult to resolve an issue of historical importance definitively regardless of the archaeology and the literary data.

A major historical conundrum has arisen in the context of our recent excavations on the western acropolis at Sepphoris conducted between 1993 and 1997 by the Sepphoris Regional Project. This work has uncovered numerous items of great interest and importance. Of special significance is the area known as 85.3 or Unit I, which may be generally characterized as a military

---

1. See my forthcoming article "Ceramics, Chronology, and Historical Reconstruction," in *The Archaeology of Jordan and Beyond: Essays in Honor of James A. Sauer* (ed. L. E. Stager, J. A. Greene, and M. D. Coogan; Atlanta: Scholars Press, forthcoming). See also W. G. Dever, "Will the Real Israel Please Stand Up? Archaeology and Israelite Historiography Part 1," *BASOR* 297 (1995) 61–80.

2. See, for example, my response to Richard Horsley's work, "An Archaeological Response to a New Testament Scholar," *BASOR* 297 (1995) 17–26, and bibliography there.

Fig. 1. Photo of 85.3 looking south.

complex. Josephus recognized the unique strategic location of Sepphoris at a fairly early stage in his career and, after it was fortified, characterized its unique setting as being favorable for staging a major military move against Rome, had it been so inclined (*Life* 346–47). The thickened walls and unique ground plan of 85.3, indeed, stand in marked contrast to all of the structures around it. In addition to its unusual construction and configuration is the fact that its chronological history is also aberrant in terms of what happened on the acropolis. Its stratigraphic history begins approximately in 100 B.C.E., when its earliest attested use levels are associated with many coins of Alexander Jannaeus and Late Hellenistic pottery–though its origins may in fact be pre-Hasmonean–and continues to sometime after 53 C.E., when a massive artificial fill was intentionally brought in to bury and level the entire area. We are certain of the dating of this because the latest coin identified in the complex is a coin of Agrippa II that is dated to 53 C.E. and because of huge quantities of "Herodian" pottery, whose terminus ad quem is usually thought to be approximately 70 C.E. Thus the excavators are fairly certain that this filling activity occurred between 53 and 70 C.E.

To say the least, the historical circumstances at either end of the chronological spectrum are very complex. Although I want to concentrate on the possible reasons for putting in such a large artificial fill, I also want to discuss several aspects of the proposed Late Hellenistic dating for the complex. The earliest reference mentioning Sepphoris in Josephus notes that Ptolemy

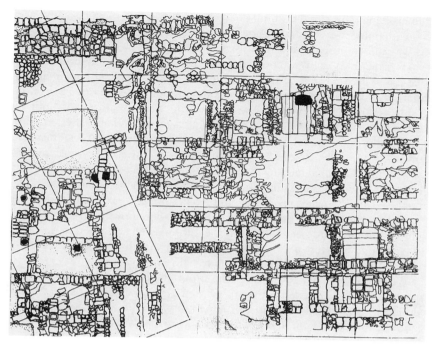

Fig. 2. Plan of 85.3 looking north; note Roman road in upper left.

Lathyrus, the former Egyptian king then ruling Cyprus, responded to Jannaeus's attack on the citizens of Ptolemais. Because of Jannaeus's threat, the city had turned to Ptolemy for help. He launched an unsuccessful campaign against Sepphoris in 103 B.C.E., after having raided nearby Asochis[3] on the Sabbath and having taken many prisoners and booty (*Ant.* 13.337–38). The battles between Alexander's troops and those of Ptolemy continued for a considerable time until Cleopatra, the mother of Ptolemy, sent her Egyptian army to Palestine to help Jannaeus (*Ant.* 13.348–56).[4] These wars between the Hasmonean armies and the Ptolemies, and subsequently between the Hasmoneans and others in Galilee and Transjordan, are important in understanding

3. Asochis has been identified with talmudic Shiḥin. This identification was already made in the 1943 Loeb edition of Josephus, vol. 7, p. 396 note a, and is adopted in *Tabula Imperii Romani: Iudaea–Palaestina — Maps and Gazetteer* (ed. Y. Tsafrir, L. Di Segni, and J. Green; Jerusalem: The Israel Academy of Sciences and Humanities, 1994) 70. See also most recently J. Strange, D. E. Groh, and T. R. W. Longstaff, "Excavations at Sepphoris: The Location and Identification of Shikhin," *IEJ* 44 (1994) 216–27; 45 (1995) 171–87.

4. For an account of these battles, see the revised edition of E. Schürer's *History of the Jewish People in the Age of Jesus Christ (175 BC–AD 135)* (ed. G. Vermes and F. Millar; 3 vols.; Edinburgh: T. and T. Clark, 1973–1987) 1.220–21.

the evolving ethnic and cultural character of the various peoples and places who inhabited these areas. For now, we may observe that, at the time, Sepphoris was sufficiently fortified to resist successfully the onslaught of Ptolemy, whereas nearby Asochis was not. I think we can safely infer from this reference that it is at least possible, if not probable, that some sort of settlement at Sepphoris had been there for some time—a supposition also supported by considerable ceramic data. Because the area of the western summit is built on bedrock, it is very difficult to recover all phases of use. What is attested stratigraphically, however, is Late Hellenistic (late second century B.C.E.–first century B.C.E.), while its date of construction and earliest use must remain conjectural. The character of the Galilee in the pre-Hasmonean era is hotly debated. Other papers in this volume consider and evaluate some of this material (see, e.g., Horsley, pp. 57–74, and Aviam, pp. 281–300). Suffice it to say that it is at least feasible that some of the population growth in the early Hellenistic period (third–second centuries B.C.E.) may be attributed to new Jewish settlements. Most of the data pertinent to this discussion comes from archaeological surveys, many of which remain unpublished.[5]

While there is a paucity of small finds from the Late Hellenistic Period, of special interest here is an ostracon, painted on a jar fragment with handle found on the western summit, just some meters to the west of what we are calling Unit I (85.3) and interpreting as having a possible military function. The inscription is in Hebrew square letters, written beneath the handle, in a script described as "typical of the second century B.C.E."[6] The first five letters read *'pmls*, probably from the Greek word *epimeletes*, which Naveh understands to come from the word 'manager' or 'overseer', that is, one who is in charge.[7] Though there are other letters after an apparent break, it is impossible to read them. Despite the absence of the letter *tet*, because the term is attested in a Palmyrene inscription and in rabbinic literature[8] Naveh concludes that the term may refer to a treasurer, manager, or *gabbay* of the Jewish community. But the term may also have a broader connotation, as it seems to have in several places in Josephus: Antipater, father of Herod the

---

5. See provisionally M. Aviam's entry, "Galilee: The Hellenistic to Byzantine Periods," *NEAEHL* 2.453; and also his article, "A Second–First Century B.C.E. Fortress and Siege Complex in Eastern Upper Galilee," in *Archaeology and the Galilee: Texts and Contexts in Graeco-Roman Galilee in the Graeco-Roman Periods* (ed. D. R. Edwards and M. Aviam; Atlanta: Scholars Press, 1997) 97–105. Aviam's work at Khirbet Hurrawi is particularly relevant to the question of the changing makeup of the Galilee in the Hellenistic Period. He suggests that the fortress there was built by the Seleucids to maintain control of the Huleh Valley settlements but became a Hasmonean fortress later and remained in Jewish hands through the reign of Herod Antipas until he was exiled by the Romans (p. 104 and notes).

6. See J. Naveh, entry no. 16, "Jar Fragment with Inscription in Hebrew," in *Sepphoris in Galilee: Crosscurrents of Culture* (ed. R. M. Nagy et al.; Raleigh: North Carolina Museum of Art, 1996) 170.

7. Ibid.

8. *T. B. Bat.* 10.5; *b. B. Bat.* 144b, *b. Menaḥ.* 85b.

Great is called *epimeletes* of the Jews, translated 'governor' in the Loeb edition (*Ant.* 14.127), though translated 'procurator' elsewhere (*Ant.* 14.139); Herod himself is appointed *epimeletes* of all Syria (*J.W.* 1.225), though he is called *strategos* elsewhere (*Ant.* 14.280);[9] and Marcellus, appointed temporary procurator of Judea when Pontius Pilate was called to Rome, is also called *epimeletes* (*Ant.* 18.89). It is therefore quite possible that there was in the time of Jannaeus a military presence at Sepphoris with its own quartermaster or leader or *epimeletes*; no doubt this leader was Jewish, else there would be no reason to use the Hebrew script for a Greek term. I would also lower the date of the inscription closer to approximately 100 B.C.E., in part because we are uncertain about the makeup of the community in the second century B.C.E. Also, the ceramic type might allow a slightly later date.

We have little information about the status of the area we are calling military until the time of Herod. Prior to then we know that Sepphoris was made one of five local councils or *synedria* from which the country was administered; these were organized by Gabinius, proconsul of Syria, in 57 B.C.E., shortly after Pompey conquered the land of Israel in 63 B.C.E. (*Ant.* 14.90–91). In the *Jewish War* (1.170) Josephus refers to these council as 'synods' (*sunodoi*).[10] The places of these councils were Jerusalem, Gadara, Amathus, Jericho, and Sepphoris. Sepphoris was the only location in Galilee, all of the others being in Judea, with Gadara emended to "Gazara," or biblical Gezer.[11] Apparently the purpose of this reorganization was to limit Hyrcanus's rule to sacerdotal functions only and to allow other forms of local rule to emerge. In any event, Sepphoris's unique role as the administrative and strategic center of the North of Israel was in place by the mid–first century B.C.E.

Another Hasmonean, Antigonus, the son of Aristobolus, was granted the title of king by the Parthians in 40/39 B.C.E. Antigonus had already installed a garrison in Sepphoris when Herod decided to capture his strongholds, including Sepphoris. Herod reached Sepphoris in a snowstorm, only to discover that Antigonus's garrison had already withdrawn; consequently, Herod succeeded in capturing the city and coming into possession "of a number of provisions" which undoubtedly were put to good use by his troops (*Ant.* 14.414–15). Consequently, Herod apparently used Sepphoris as a staging platform for pursuing brigands who were holed up in the nearby caves of Arbel (14.416). Sepphoris thus remained in Hasmonean hands in one way or

---

9. See R. Marcus (trans.), *Josephus* (LCL; Cambridge: Harvard University Press, 1986) 7.514–15, especially note d on *epimeletes*. There are numerous references in the Greek papyri and literature, where the overwhelmingly predominant meaning of the term is 'civic or military official'. The term appears no less than 461 times in the Duke papyri alone.

10. Cf. Josephus's use of the term in *Ant.* 14.235, where it refers to an association of the Jews of Sardis.

11. See Josephus *J.W.* 1.170, and pp. 77–79 note b in the Loeb edition, where this suggestion is made. Amathus, actually in Peraea, implies a "large" form of Judea.

another from approximately 100 B.C.E. during the reign of Jannaeus until Herod removed the city from Antigonus on the eve of his rise to power in 38 B.C.E. It is quite apparent already that during this period of more than six decades Sepphoris was involved in a number of key political developments and military encounters in which its strategic location high upon the hillside was of essential importance. None of these literary mentions, however, gives any clue about the character of the military presence there.

Herod's demise in 4/3 B.C.E. resulted in many attempts to prevent any form of Herodian rule from continuing, and at least one insurgency that was located in Sepphoris seems to have had royal pretensions. A revolt led by one Judas, son of the brigand Ezekias, was directed against the royal palace at Sepphoris, where Judas succeeded in arming his own soldiers with weapons that were stockpiled there (*J.W.* 2.56, *Ant.* 17.271). The Josephan account in *Jewish Antiquities* mentions that Judas succeeded in pulling off the revolt only by having first secured the help of "a large number of desperate men at Sepphoris." It is therefore quite possible that the Herodian years had not been good for all of the residents of Sepphoris. As a result of the insurrection there and elsewhere in Judea, Varus, the Syrian legate, set out to stifle further rebellion. At Sepphoris it is reported that he burned the city to the ground and enslaved its inhabitants (*J.W.* 2.68, *Ant.* 17.289); no doubt Josephus has exaggerated a great deal, since there is little or no evidence of burning at the entire site at this time.

Staying with the literary evidence of Josephus for now, whatever the truth of the report regarding Varus, Sepphoris is universally thought to have recovered and gained a good deal of its reputation under Herod Antipas (4 B.C.E.– 39 C.E.), who reportedly fortified the city, renamed it *autocratoris*, and made it "the ornament of all Galilee" (*Ant.* 18.27). It is not clear what *autocratoris* means, whether referring to the emperor or indicating that Sepphoris was granted autonomy.[12] The archaeology of the site provides no signs of the fortifications, unless we understand him to have rebuilt the garrison on the summit, possibly to house both troops and arms (see *Ant.* 18.251–52). But the archaeology of 85.3 shows conclusively that the area was already being transformed into nonmilitary space. The cache of weaving implements dating to the first century C.E. suggests a more industrial use for the area. Stuart Miller has convincingly clarified the meaning of 'ornament' (*proschema*) by explaining it as signifying the impregnable nature of the city.[13] Meanwhile, Antipas's reign as tetrarch in Galilee and Peraea ended in failure and tragedy. Emperor Caligula assigned Agrippa I the royal title and granted lands to Phillip in his second year of office (38–39 C.E.). Agrippa was the brother-in-

---

12. See H. W. Hoehner, *Herod Antipas* (Cambridge: Cambridge University Press, 1972) 86 n. 1.

13. See S. Miller's essay, "Hellenistic and Roman Sepphoris: The Historical Evidence," in *Sepphoris in Galilee: Crosscurrents of Culture* (ed. R. M. Nagy et al.; Raleigh: North Carolina Museum of Art, 1996) 22 and notes there.

law of Antipas; he went to Palestine that year, and his sister Herodias was jealous for her husband, wanting a royal title for him too. Agrippa, upon hearing this turn of events, set out to discredit Antipas, accusing him of collaborating with the enemy and of stockpiling weapons at Sepphoris (*Ant.* 17.252, J.W. 2.183).[14] Antipas and Herodias were both exiled, where they either died or were executed.

Unfortunately, Josephus reports nothing about Sepphoris between the reign of Herod Antipas and the outbreak of the Great Revolt in 66 C.E. Moreover, all information regarding the revolt is contained in his *Jewish War* and *Life*. In fact, the *Life* has considerably more references to Sepphoris than the *War*, which may be explained in terms of the city's unique pro-Roman policy, which became apparent in the year 67 C.E., a position Josephus himself came to adopt and advocate after serving for nearly two years as commander in chief of the Galilean forces. In light of this, we might have expected the historian to be consistent in his presentation of the facts regarding the war, if not the role of Sepphoris in it. Given the size of the city, it is possible that not all inhabitants were in accord regarding their role in the war against Rome. Though experts have been inclined to dismiss Josephus's inconsistencies regarding Sepphoris's[15] role and attitude-shift in 66–67 C.E., it is at least conceivable that the adoption of a pro-Roman stance was the result of much internal debate in the leadership of the city, and Josephus's writings reflect that lack of consensus, albeit in a very obscure way.

King Agrippa II was certainly pro-Roman throughout his tenure and even met Vespasian in Antioch when he was en route to Palestine with support troops. In this same report, Josephus notes that when Vespasian arrived in Ptolemais he was greeted by a like-minded group of Sepphoreans who already were committed to a pacific and pro-Roman course (*Life* 411–13). Vespasian's commander of the Twelfth Legion, Caesaennius Gallus, who had come to subdue Galilee in 66 C.E., had already granted to a group of Sepphoreans a Roman garrison to protect them (*J.W.* 3.29–34, 2.510–11). Cestius Gallus, governor of Syria, is credited with sending a first garrison of legionnaires to Sepphoris, whose citizens welcomed them with "open arms" (*J.W.* 2.507–12 and *Life* 394–97). But Josephus, still in charge of the Jewish Galilean forces, camped 20 furlongs away at Garis, possibly Cana of Galilee, and launched a night-time attack against the city, during which twelve Roman infantry were killed along with several Sepphoreans. These events occurred in 66/67 C.E., when Josephus was organizing the Galilean war.[16]

---

14. See Vermes and Millar (eds.), E. Schürer's *History of the Jewish People in the Age of Jesus Christ*, 1.352–53 n. 42.

15. Notably T. Rajak in *Josephus: The Historian and His Society* (Philadelphia: Fortress, 1984) 159 n. 31, where she refers to the inconsistencies in Josephus as being minor.

16. See Vermes and Millar (eds.), E. Schürer's *History of the Jewish People in the Age of Jesus Christ*, 2.175–76 and references there.

Particularly puzzling in Josephus's account of this period is his report that the residents of Sepphoris requested assistance in fortifying the city and were "eager for hostilities" against Rome (*J.W.* 2.574). Josephus credits himself with fortifying the city (*Life* 188), but he also reports that he had considerable trouble with John of Gischala (*Life* 203, 232–33; *J.W.* 2.168), who was prepared to attack him with assistance from some Sepphoreans and Justus of Tiberias (*Life* 346–54) who might have changed his position on the war after the traumatic suicide among Josephus's troops at Jotapata—the Tiberians ultimately appealed to Agrippa II for support (*J.W.* 2.636–45). Josephus goes on to question the accuracy and reliability of Justus's account of the war (*Life* 357–67). Both cities eventually joined hands in opposing Josephus's authority. Josephus's account of invading Sepphoris after Vespasian had promised military assistance (*J.W.* 3.59–62) and the story of his attack on Sepphoris (*Life* 373–80) before the Roman troops had arrived are very complicated, especially when Josephus himself is supposed to have fortified the city earlier. Ultimately, however, the role of Sepphoris in the Great Revolt more closely resembled that of Baneas, which was the home of Agrippa II (see below, especially n. 26).

In any case, the pro-Roman stance of the citizenry of Sepphoris is what eventually wins out. This ascendant view is best commemorated in the coins minted in 68 c.e., which bear the legend "Eirenopolis-Neronias-Sepphoris."[17] These coins date to the fourteenth year of Emperor Nero, during which time the inhabitants of Sepphoris declared loyalty to Vespasian and the senate. They provide striking visual testimonies to the unique role the city came to play in the course of the war. Moreover, Josephus's own change of heart vis-à-vis the war in 68 must be taken into account when evaluating the frequent mentions in *Life* of Sepphoris's support of Rome (30, 38, 104, 124, 232, 346–48, 373–80, 394–96, 411),[18] with which the *Jewish War* usually agrees (2.511; 3.30–34, 59). Along with the lingering doubts regarding the full meaning of the revolutionary attitudes attested among some of the inhabitants of Sepphoris (e.g., *J.W.* 2.629; *Life* 203; *J.W.* 2.574; and *Life* 188), at the very least Josephus's change suggests that some Sepphoreans supported the war effort early on. However, by the fourteenth year of Nero, Sepphoris had adopted as for-

---

17. There is a fairly substantial amount of literature on this subject, including most recently Y. Meshorer's restatement of his position in "Coins of Sepphoris," in *Sepphoris in Galilee: Crosscurrents of Culture* (ed. R. M. Nagy et al.; Raleigh: North Carolina Museum of Art, 1996) 195–96. A convenient summary of his views may be found in *Ancient Jewish Coinage* (Dix Hills, N.Y. : Amphora, 1982) 2.167–69 and notes on p. 221. See also H. Seyrig, "Irenoplois—Neronias—Sepphoris," *Numismatic Chronicle* 10 (1950) 284–89. It should also be noted that Caesarea Maritima, another pro-Roman city of mixed population, minted similar coins, paying appropriate respect to Vespasian. See G. F. Hill, *Catalogue of Greek Coins of Palestine* (London: British Museum, 1914) 16.

18. See Rajak, *Josephus*; and S. J. D. Cohen, *Josephus in Rome and Galilee* (Leiden: Brill, 1979) passim.

mal policy its pro-Roman political stance, one that had apparently predominated all along but that now became official.

It is precisely in this connection, in relation to some vacillation in attitude or internal disagreement, that we turn to the archaeology of the site. First, the numismatic evidence shows unequivocally that a unified position had been ironed out by 68 C.E. Adopting such an extraordinary position of peaceful cooperation with the enemy is truly reflected on the coins of Sepphoris. Although Seyrig thought that the sobriquet "City of Peace" was taken in honor of the closing of the Gate of Janus in Rome in 64 C.E. as an act of *pax romana*,[19] I accept the observation that it was adopted because Sepphoris alone of all cities and villages of Galilee welcomed Vespasian and his army in peace. It may also be a play on the expression in Zech 8:3, "City of Truth," which there is applied to Jerusalem.[20] Meshorer has correctly pointed out that Sepphoris certainly was a principal city of Agrippa II.[21] In this connection there were doubtless many royalists living there who supported an accommodationist stance vis-à-vis Rome. Moreover, the fact that both Caesarea Maritima and Sepphoris chose to honor Vespasian on their coins of 68 C.E. shows the extent of his popularity and power in the east.[22] Josephus's subsequent prediction, after he was taken prisoner, that Vespasian would become emperor after Nero (*J.W.* 3.399–401),[23] shows the pragmatic and political aspects of Josephus's persona. One other interesting point about the Sepphoris "City of Peace" coins is that they also mention Emperor Nero. Paneas (or Baneas), or Caesarea Phillipi, was dedicated to Nero in 61 C.E. and renamed Neronias and served as the capital city of Agrippa II (*Ant.* 20.211; cf. *Life* 95–96).[24] Though it was usual to continue to use the name of the emperor on coins for some years after his death, due to the fact of Nero's condemnation by the Senate and the Roman people, his name disappeared immediately after his death on June 9, 68 C.E.[25] Of special interest is the coin of Agrippa II struck at Paneas in 67 C.E.: it shares with Sepphoris the dedication to Nero, as well as including the symbols of the double cornucopia and caduceus. The coins of Sepphoris that bear the tripartite nomenclature in honor of Vespasian, Nero, and "City of Peace" also imitate the coin of Agrippa II from Paneas from the year before, 67 C.E., and hence send forth the message very clearly of the particular point of view of the city, which by 68 C.E. had

19. Meshorer, *Ancient Jewish Coinage*, 167.

20. For an extensive discussion of this epithet, see C. L. Meyers and E. M. Meyers, *Haggai, Zechariah 1–8* (AB 25B; Garden City, N.Y.: Doubleday, 1987) 408, 413–14. I should note, however, that Tiberias capitulated to Titus without a fight and Gadara, capital of Peraea, pulled down its walls before Vespasian arrived to demonstrate its peaceful intent.

21. Meshorer, *Ancient Jewish Coinage*, 167.

22. Ibid. See also Hill, *Catalogue of Greek Coins*, 16.

23. Suetonius *Vespasian* 4.5; Tacitus *History* 1.10 and 5.13.

24. Vermes and Millar (eds.), E. Schürer's *History of the Jewish People in the Age of Jesus Christ*, 2.474.

25. Meshorer, *Ancient Jewish Coinage*, 169.

resolved its internal political differences, at least for public consumption. Meshorer believes that the choice of symbols and absence of the image of the Roman emperor means that the Sepphoris coins and those of Paneas were struck by Jewish authorities, though in suggesting this he is inclined to understand the double cornucopia and caduceus symbols as being Jewish, because they were used by Herod and Herod Archaelaus.[26] These symbols, however, had a much broader usage in the Mediterranean world. What is most striking about the design is the absence of the image of Nero, no doubt omitted in deference to Jewish sensibilities.

The minting of these coins, especially the coins of Sepphoris, proclaimed the clear message that in addition to Agrippa II there were other important factions in Jewish society prepared to adopt a pacific stance vis-à-vis Rome in public. No doubt there were many in the Roman military and imperial administration who doubted that such a tendency could counterbalance the weight of rebellion being promulgated in virtually every quarter. Especially prior to the change in Josephus's own position, from a Roman perspective, the pro-Roman stand reflected in some of the teachings of some pious Pharisees or priests could hardly have been convincing evidence that the Jews were of a mixed mind on the Great Revolt.[27] Even in the case of Sepphoris, where we have found literary evidence of a divided opinion in the matter of collaborating with the Romans, the year 68 C.E. would have been an appropriate time for a public gesture from its inhabitants to convince the Romans that their city was united: such a public action might have been the intentional filling in of the area that had served for more than a century and a half as the castra or place of the military garrison. Such a hypothesis brings us back to the mute or anepigraphic side of archaeology, and it is to this we now turn.

The characterization of the group of thickened walls in area 85.3 or Unit I as a fortress or military area derives mainly from the width of the seven massive walls that enclose at least three rooms. In this complex four parallel, continuous, doubled, east–west walls intersect three parallel, doubled, north–south walls. As I have already noted, the ceramic and numismatic data from

---

26. Ibid., 1.67, 2.27–28. For a discussion of the recent excavations at Baneas, see John F. Wilson and Vassilios Tzaferis, "Banias Dig Reveals King's Palace," *BARev* 24/1 (1998) 54–61, 85. The palace in question is identified as belonging to Agrippa II, who reigned from 53–93 C.E. in Baneas. Although he was Jewish, he successfully maintained his standing with Rome during the Great Revolt (66–70 C.E.) by counseling a course of peace, as did the citizens of Sepphoris. We know very little about the ethnic or religious makeup of the city at this time. After Agrippa's death, the city was once again incorporated into the Province of Syria. For an extended discussion of the symbols on the coins, see Mark A. Chancey, *The Myth of a Gentile Galilee: The Population of Galilee and New Testament Studies* (Ph.D. dissertation, Duke University, 1999).

27. Josephus was not the only one who adopted a pacific, pro-Roman stance during the war: others were R. Hanina, deputy high priest (*m. 'Abot* 3:2), Yochanan ben Zakkai, and the majority of the people in Sepphoris, etc. On this point, see Rajak, *Josephus*, 166–67 and also 130–31.

the earliest strata in the area may be dated to approximately 100 B.C.E. Because these walls are laid on bedrock, however, we are not able to conclude decisively that they were founded at this time, that is, approximately 100 B.C.E. Indeed, in the crevices in bedrock and in the pockets of earth in them, pre-100 B.C.E. materials were regularly identified, including sherds from the Iron Age, Persian Period, and Early Hellenistic Period. Hence, we may refer to the Jannaean phase of use of this complex as the earliest attested "use" phase. A series of beaten earth floor levels attests to its continued use into the Early Roman Period.

There is very little evidence besides the double thickness of the walls (ca. 1.87 m) to bolster the idea that Unit I was a "castra," though among the small finds an arrowhead and some ballista stones are to be noted. In fairness, too, while it is possible that the entire area was filled in intentionally during the reign of Agrippa II and probably sometime around the Great Revolt, it could also have been filled in by the Romans (*Life* 411–13), though we have no way of knowing for how long or even if the Roman army was there during the war. The area is no doubt the location of the weapons that Antipas had stored, which got him in trouble earlier (see above). The interpretive crux thus seems to be whether the Sepphoreans took down the most visible element of their fortifications and invited in Roman troops, who accordingly took careful note of the implication of such a gesture, which in such a scenario led to an acknowledgment of the citizens as a "city of peace," or whether, on the other hand, the Romans systematically took down the fortifications or filled them in with dirt and forcibly made Sepphoris de facto a pro-Roman city. Josephus is certainly correct in pointing out that Sepphoris could have made great trouble for Rome had it adopted a war policy (*Life* 346). But, Josephus goes on to say, Sepphoris "forbade any of her citizens to take service with the Jews. . . ." The citizens "then voluntarily admitted a garrison provided by Cestius Gallus, commander in chief of the Roman legions in Syria. . . ." (*Life* 347). Moreover, the Sepphoreans did not send any sort of relief supplies to Jerusalem when it was besieged, "wishing to avoid all suspicion of having borne arms against the Romans" (*Life* 348). This particular account, along with the one a bit later (*Life* 373–80), where Josephus's own troops came to Sepphoris before Cestius Gallus and went wild, looting and burning down houses because the city had already become known for its pro-Roman views, makes the suggestion of a public gesture to cement its pacific stance on the war all the more likely.

The dating of two stepped pools or *miqvaot* from this same area (85.3) to the pre–68 C.E. period, recently proposed by one of the area's excavators,[28] also yields important information about the use of the castra before it was

---

28. I am grateful to Melissa Aubin and to Jürgen Zangenberg, excavators of this area, for their overall stratigraphic assessment and dating of the area. I am especially indebted to Ms. Aubin for access to the paper she read at the 1997 ASOR-SBL session on Rethinking Roman Period Judaism, "Two Sepphoris Mikvaot: Questions of Purity."

intentionally filled. While it is certainly unusual to find ritual baths in a military situation, it is not unlikely that a Jewish army would have had need for them. The eastern pool is the earlier of the two and may be dated to the Late Hellenistic Period. It is characterized by an entryway of five broad plastered steps descending into a plastered basin or pool with a surface of approximately 1 m × 0.7 m. A second stepped pool or *miqveh*, which abuts the eastern doubled wall of the fortress, contrasts with the former by having short, steep steps, each 26 cm high except for the last, which is 53 cm. It is quite clear from the northern balk that the eastern stepped pool fell into disuse before the construction of its western counterpart. In short, one of the ritual baths is Late Hellenistic, the other Late Hellenistic but used into the Early Roman Period.

Sometime before 68 C.E., both pools went out of use as ritual baths and were used for some industrial purpose, since a cache of weaving implements for various stages of manufacture was found in the eastern pool, its context being Early Roman or first century C.E. This important find means that the military character of the area was no longer apparent in the first century C.E., a surmise that we have inferred from literary-historical and numismatic information. That both *miqvaot* are clearly associated with the Late Hellenistic phases of the castra lends credibility to the notion that Sepphoris at this early time had a Jewish character. For the time being, that Jewish character seems to be best attested at the period of Hasmonean expansion, around the beginning of the first century B.C.E., or approximately 100 B.C.E.[29] While not everyone will accept the identification of these two stepped pools as *miqvaot*, especially without the attestation of an ‘*oṣar*,[30] there is no doubt that they were used for immersion. Whether such immersion was for hygienic or ritual purposes, at the very least it points up the distinctiveness of the inhabitants of this area, who went to extraordinary lengths to immerse bodily in water, which was in part captured from the rain and no doubt also transferred from nearby springs. Because these pools are so strikingly similar to the ones excavated by Avigad in the Jewish Quarter in Jerusalem,[31] I am confident that their identification as ritual baths will be upheld.

29. The period of Hasmonean expansion under Alexander Jannaeus has been the subject of considerable debate recently, especially in view of R. Horsley's assessment of it in his most recent books on Galilee. S. Freyne has taken quite a different view of this. See his essay, "Galilee in the Hellenistic through Byzantine Periods," OEANE 2.370–76; and also his "Town and Country Once More: The Case of Roman Galilee," in *Archaeology and the Galilee: Texts and Contexts in Graeco-Roman Galilee in the Graeco-Roman Periods* (ed. D. R. Edwards and M. Aviam; Atlanta: Scholars Press, 1997) 49–57.

30. Too much emphasis on the matter of an ‘*oṣar* may be observed in the comments of H. Eshel, who rejects the identification of a number of stepped pools at Sepphoris as *miqvaot*. See "A Note on 'Miqvaot' at Sepphoris," in *Archaeology and the Galilee: Texts and Contexts in Graeco-Roman Galilee in the Graeco-Roman Periods* (ed. D. R. Edwards and M. Aviam; Atlanta: Scholars Press, 1997) 131–33.

31. See N. Avigad, *Discovering Jerusalem* (Nashville: 1980) 139–42, figs. 143–45, 149.

ı of these pools as *miqvaot* also brings us back to the
per: why was this area systematically filled in during the
tween 53–68 C.E.? I have noted that the pools were al-
)ools sometime before the intentional filling, because a
ng implements was found in association with them. This
ımely, that at least parts of the castra were used for non-
ımetimes around the turn of the era—in archaeological
ı" era—means that the decision to fill in this area, proba-
of Sepphoris but also possibly by the Romans, who ulti-
ıped there for a time during the Great Revolt, was not as
as might be thought. For the Jewish residents who knew
ıtary character of castra but who also witnessed its conver-
pace, offering to fill in this space to convince Rome of its
ıs must have been a very easy decision. To any outsider,
ːks would still have looked like a military installation, and,
overtures to the Roman military had been made, all activi-
tary activities in the area had ceased. In other words, it was
ll and level an area that to any outside observer was clearly
tary usage. It is very hard to conceive of a situation in which
ıe of his troops would have come in, run loose, and done ex-
Life 373–80), especially to the area known as the castra. It is
equally difficult to imagine the troops of Cestius Gallus (*Life* 394–97; cf. 411–
13), once admitted to Sepphoris, leveling this area for their purposes. Hence,
the most likely scenario remains the one already proposed, namely, that the
citizens of Sepphoris purposefully filled in this area as part of a larger policy
of pacification. Such a gesture was accepted and recognized by the Roman
authorities, regardless of the fact that the garrison had not been used for some
time, possibly not since Late Hellenistic times when two functional ritual
baths were located in the heart of the area.

There is no doubt that the adoption of a pro-Roman stance by the Sepphoreans was not an easy thing to accomplish; nor can we assume that every resident would have been comfortable with such a decision. Nonetheless, at least
from the time of Herod Antipas, Sepphoris had harbored pro-Roman feelings
(*Life* 30–31); Agrippa II handed over the city to Nero as a present because of
such a policy, as a result of which it reverted to being the "seat of the royal
bank and archives" (*Life* 37–40). One can only wonder whether the success
of such a policy influenced Josephus himself, who ultimately adopted this
view, after surrendering his Galilean command at nearby Jotapata.[32] It is intriguing to speculate if Josephus's failure to defeat Cestius Gallus and his
troops (*Life* 394–97) and the subsequent recognition of Sepphoris by Nero as

---

32. For the latest report on the recent archaeological work there, see D. Adan-Bayewitz
and M. Aviam, "Iotapata, Josephus, and the Siege of 67: Preliminary Report on the 1992–
94 Seasons," *Journal of Roman Archaeology* 10 (1997) 131–65.

"City of Peace" made a far greater impact on him than previous scholarship on Josephus has recognized.

In any case, Sepphoris's unique stand vis-à-vis Rome during the Great Revolt has been described and several interpretive strategies offered. In a time of great political turmoil Sepphoris, as a result of its pro-Roman and pacific stance, was able not only to survive this important epoch in Jewish history but to develop as a major center of learning for centuries to come. Its pro-Roman policies of later times, especially during the time of Rabbi Judah the Prince, no doubt hark back to this extraordinary episode in Jewish history. It may well be that Sepphoris's early experience in resisting Ptolemaic interference (*Ant.* 13.338), attributed by Freyne to the role of the Hasmonean landed nobility,[33] became the very reason why Gabinius chose Sepphoris's native aristocracy to run the local assembly by means of which he administered the province (*Ant.* 14.91, *J.W.* 1.169–70). Similar parties within the Jewish leadership of Sepphoris in the first century C.E. were no doubt influential in bringing about the implementation of its policy of détente, but they no longer felt it necessary to use force. Such a policy of restraint has left an important legacy for all to ponder.

---

33. See Freyne, "Galilee in the Hellenistic through Byzantine Periods"; "Town and Country Once More"; and "Jesus and the Urban Culture of Galilee," in *Texts and Contexts: Biblical Texts in their Textual and Situational Contexts* (ed. T. Fornbery and D. Hellholm; Oslo: Scandinavian University Press, 1995) 597–622.

The Development of Synagogue Liturgy in Late Antiquity

LEE I. LEVINE

The Hebrew University of Jerusalem

There is no dimension more reflective of the growth and evolution of the synagogue in antiquity than its liturgy. This development is expressed in a variety of ways. Constituting one of many activities in its early stages, the synagogue's ritual component eventually became its dominant and definitive feature. At first including the reading of scriptures accompanied by their translation and some sort of homily or instruction, by late antiquity this religious element had evolved into a rich and varied worship setting containing not only these three components but also regular communal prayers and poetic renditions (*piyyut*), especially on Sabbaths and holidays.[1]

My examination of this evolution will focus on three different stages in the development of synagogue liturgy. The first was evident by the end of the Second Temple Period, ca. 50 C.E., about the time that communal worship first surfaced in our sources. The second emerged ca. 200 C.E., at the close of the tannaitic era and following a period of intensive liturgical creativity in the wake of the loss of Jerusalem and its Temple, while the third was in place by the end of antiquity, ca. 600 C.E.

The sources available for the study of this topic vary considerably from one period to the next. For the Second Temple Period, we are indebted primarily to the New Testament and Josephus, as well as to the valuable information found in Jerusalem's Theodotus inscription and several early rabbinic traditions. For the second period, we are totally dependent on a number of important sources in rabbinic literature that relate to the activity of the sages in this

---

1. The following remarks focus primarily (though not exclusively) on the synagogue liturgy of the Galilee, although they probably hold true for Palestine in general as well as for parts of the diaspora. Nevertheless, the situation in the diaspora seems to have been different in certain respects, but our evidence in this regard is woefully lacking. A full discussion of this and other aspects of the ancient synagogue may be found in my forthcoming *The Ancient Synagogue: The First Thousand Years* (New Haven: Yale University Press).

regard. How much these tannaitic traditions and decisions affected the contemporary second-century synagogue is an important question yet almost impossible to answer in light of the absence of corroborating material and the dearth of specific incidents. The last time-frame to be discussed reflects developments over the final four centuries of late antiquity and is illuminated not only by a rich trove of talmudic and midrashic material but also by epigraphical finds and other literary sources.

The 50 C.E. Stage of Development

The centrality of the Torah-reading ceremony in Jewish worship of the pre-70 synagogue should come as no surprise, since it is explicitly indicated by a plethora of sources from the Second Temple Period. The following are illustrative of the Torah-reading:

New Testament

> And he came to Nazareth, where he had been brought up; and he went to the synagogue, as was his custom, on the Sabbath day. And he stood up to read; and there the book of the prophet Isaiah was given to him. He opened the book and found the place where it was written. . . . (Luke 4:16–17)

> But when they departed from Perga, they came to Antioch in Pisidia and went into the synagogue on the Sabbath day and sat down. And after the reading of the law and the prophets the rulers of the synagogue sent unto them, saying. . . . (Acts 13:14–15)

> For Moses from time of old has in every city those that preach him, being read in the synagogues every Sabbath day. (Acts 15:21)

Archaeology

> Theodotus, son of Vettenos a priest and *archisynagogos*, son of an *archisynagogos* and grandson of an *archisynagogos*, built the synagogue for reading the Law and studying the commandments. . . .[2]

In addition to the above, Philo, Josephus, and rabbinic literature likewise focus on the Torah-reading aspect of liturgy in the first century.[3] Thus, there can be little question that at this time scriptural readings constituted the core of Jewish synagogue worship. Concerning when such readings became the central component in the nonsacrificial synagogue liturgy, the chronological parameters are probably to be fixed between the fifth and third centuries B.C.E. On the one hand, the terminus post quem is undoubtedly the period of Ezra and Nehemiah, when the first public Torah-reading took place. By

---

2. Jean-Baptiste Frey, *CII* (2 vols.; Rome: Pontifico istituto di archeologia cristiana, 1936–52) vol. 2, no. 1404.

3. Philo *Hypothetica* 7, 12; *Every Good Man Is Free* 81–82; Josephus *Ag. Ap.* 2.175; *t. Sukk.* 4.6 (ed. Lieberman, 273).

the third century, on the other hand, the existence of a regular communal Torah-reading framework was probably a prime factor in the creation of the Septuagint. Whatever may have been the original motivation for this translation, it would have served, among other things, the needs of the Alexandrian Jewish community, whose liturgical practice was probably brought to Egypt from Judea and was not the creation of the fledgling Alexandrian diaspora community. Moreover, there is no evidence of such a custom in the earlier Elephantine community, which flourished in Upper Egypt in the fifth century B.C.E. The brief account of the high priest Ezekias reading to his friends from the Torah (literally, scroll) upon his arrival in Egypt may well point to such a practice.[4]

By the first century C.E., a weekly ceremony featuring the communal reading and study of holy texts had become the common Jewish practice. Moreover, it was a unique liturgical feature in the ancient world; no such form of worship was known in paganism. True enough, certain mystery cults in the Hellenistic-Roman world produced sacred texts that were read on occasion.[5] However, it was indeed sui generis for an entire community to have devoted regular occasions to such activity. This, it appears, is the context within which one is to understand Josephus's and Philo's references to this practice, and while their tone may have been self-laudatory, it was not without cause. They were indeed trumpeting a form of worship that set the Jewish community apart from the surrounding cultures.

Moreover, by this time, readings from the Torah were accompanied by readings from the Prophets. The above-cited New Testament evidence here is pivotal: Jesus was asked to read from the book of Isaiah when he visited a Nazareth synagogue, and in a synagogue in Antioch in Pisidia, Paul delivered a sermon following readings from the Torah and the Prophets.[6] The third-century Tosepta has preserved a list of *haftarah*-readings for (and prior to) holidays, a series of passages not to be read in public at all, as well as norms governing such readings.[7] How much of this material is relevant to the pre-70 era is difficult to assess. Some of it probably is, since the material in this particular chapter appears to reflect practices of the first two centuries C.E.

Regarding the actual procedure for reading from the Prophets, it appears that only Luke can shed some light on the custom.

> And there was given to him the book of the prophet Isaiah. And when he had opened the book, he found the place where it was written. . . . And he closed the book, and he gave it again to the attendant, and sat down. And the eyes of

---

4. Josephus *Ag. Ap.* 1.183–89.

5. Arthur Darby Nock, *Conversion* (Oxford: Clarendon, 1933; reprint 1965) 26–32; Arnaldo Momigliano, *On Pagans, Jews and Christians* (Middletown, Conn.: Wesleyan University Press, 1987) 89–91.

6. Luke 4:17–19, Acts 13:14–15.

7. *T. Meg.* 3 (ed. Lieberman, 353).

all those in the synagogue were fastened on him. And he began to say unto them, "This day is this Scripture fulfilled in your ears." (Luke 4:17–21)

According to Luke, then, following the Torah-reading, Jesus was handed a scroll containing the book of Isaiah. Later rabbinic literature assumes that the prophetic readings were fixed and usually related in some fashion to the Torah-reading.[8] Was this true even at this early stage? The impression from the above passage is that Jesus chose at least the selection to be read (he "opened the book . . . found the place"). Furthermore, the prophetic reading seems to have consisted of only a few verses, and the amount quoted in Luke might indeed be indicative of the usual portion that was read.[9] Nevertheless, it is clear from Luke that, in this case at least, it was the prophetic reading— and not the reading from the Torah—that determined the nature of the sermon to be subsequently delivered.

It is impossible to say when the readings from the Prophets were introduced into synagogue worship. Since they followed and presumably related to the Torah portion, they most likely postdated the introduction of the Torah-reading. Abudraham (fourteenth century) dates the institution of the reading from the Prophets to the time of Antiochus IV's persecutions.[10] While this medieval source has no historical value for our purposes, the period designated may, in fact, not be far off the mark, since both Ben Sira and 2 Maccabees already speak of the Prophets as sacred literature alongside the Torah.[11] The Hasmonean era, with its many upheavals and dramatic political, military, social, and religious developments, gave rise to messianic expectations and hopes of renewed grandeur in certain circles; apocalyptic speculation emerged, and eschatological groups such as the Dead Sea sect combed the Prophets for contemporary allusions. The use of the prophetic corpus (or variations of it, as the apocalyptic mode appears to be) seems to have flourished at the time, and it may well have been this climate that gave rise to such recitations.

The New Testament evidence makes it crystal clear that the sermon was a recognized component of the Sabbath service. Jesus preached in Nazareth, as did Paul in Antioch in Pisidia. Moreover, Philo has furnished us with relatively detailed descriptions of communal Sabbath observance, at least among some Alexandrian Jews, and on each occasion he focuses on the sermon or exposition of the Torah:

> For it was customary on every day when opportunity offered, and preeminently on the seventh day, as I have explained above, to pursue the study of wisdom with the ruler expounding and instructing the people what they should say and

8. *B. Meg.* 29b: "one that resembles it (i.e., the Torah-reading)."
9. Luke 4:18–19. *T. Meg.* 3.18 (ed. Lieberman, 358) speaks of three, four, or five verses for the *haftarah*.
10. *Siddur Abudraham* (ed. Wertheimer, 172).
11. Ben Sira, prologue; 2 Macc 15:9.

do, while they received edification and betterment in moral principles and conduct. (Philo *Moses* 2.215)

And indeed they do always assemble and sit together, most of them in silence except when it is the practice to add something to signify approval of what is read. But some priest who is present or one of the elders reads the holy laws to them and expounds them point by point till about the late afternoon, when they depart, having gained both expert knowledge of the holy laws and considerable advance in piety. (Philo *Hypothetica* 7.13)

A second activity that appears to have accompanied the Torah- and *haftarah*-readings was the oral recitation of the targum. It is generally assumed that this custom of translating scriptures into the vernacular in the synagogue service already existed in the Second Temple Period.[12] Given the increasing dominance of Aramaic throughout the Near East from the Persian Period onward and the fact that this language is reflected in books, official documents, personal names, and the speech of Jews in the Late Second Temple Period, it is not at all surprising that the need arose to make the reading and study of scriptures accessible to the people at large. This phenomenon had been preceded by similar, though accelerated, developments within the Jewish communities of Greek-speaking countries during the Hellenistic and Early Roman Periods. It was in Egypt that the Torah was translated into Greek, following the large-scale settlement of Jews there in this era, and this was closely followed by the translation of other biblical books as well. Thus, it appears that in many, if not most, places in the Roman diaspora, no targum was necessary, since the readings themselves may have been in the vernacular. This, however, is far from certain, and it may be that the Septuagint translation (or variations thereof) was used after the Hebrew reading, parallel to the Aramaic targum practice in Judea.[13]

It is impossible to assess when the first Aramaic translations made their appearance. It has generally been assumed that the editing process of the targums occurred over centuries, from late antiquity into the early Middle Ages. Much material was added and adapted over time, although some traditions may well be early, deriving from the first century C.E., if not earlier.[14] While scholars are still at odds about how much early material is, in fact, embedded in the targums, there is a consensus regarding several matters: (1) the targums

---

12. Martin McNamara, *Palestinian Judaism and the New Testament* (Wilmington, Del.: Glazier, 1983) 17–89, 171–210; Philip S. Alexander, "Jewish Aramaic Translations of Hebrew Scriptures," in *Mikra* (CRINT 2/1; ed. Martin Jan Mulder; Assen: Van Gorcum, 1988) 242–50.

13. Charles Perrot, "La lecture de la Bible dans la diaspora hellénistique," in *Études sur le Judaisme Hellénistique, Congrès de Strasbourg (1983)* (ed. Raymond Kuntzmann and Jacques Schlosser; Paris: du Cerf, 1984) 118–21.

14. Émil Schürer, *The History of the Jewish People in the Age of Jesus Christ* (rev. ed.; 3 vols.; Edinburgh: T. & T. Clark, 1973–87) 1.99–114; Paul Kahle, *The Cairo Geniza* (London: Oxford University Press, 1947) 191–208.

already existed in the first century C.E. in both written and oral form. The fact that an Aramaic targum of Job was found on the Temple Mount in the days of Rabban Gamaliel the Elder (first half of the first century C.E.) would indicate that other such works of the Torah and the Prophets were also in circulation, and not only at Qumran;[15] (2) much of the material in the extant targums originated in the synagogue setting. No one doubts that some of these traditions had their origin in a later literary *beit midrash* context, but others are quite different in both form and content and are best explained as having a more popular, synagogal Sitz im Leben.

The most problematic area in the study of synagogue worship in the Second Temple Period is that of communal prayer. Private prayer was, on the one hand, a well-known phenomenon in biblical and Second Temple times; on the other, it is universally acknowledged that steps were taken within rabbinic circles at Yavneh, soon after the destruction of the Temple, to institutionalize communal prayer (see below). The question today, however, is whether communal prayer as a regular and obligatory worship framework already existed in the pre-70 era and, if so, to what degree it found expression. For the most part, discussion in this regard has focused on the Shemoneh 'Esreh or 'Amidah, the central prayer in Jewish liturgy.

Over the past century, a broad consensus has prevailed that the activity of Rabban Gamaliel and his colleagues in Yavneh was one of editing and organizing an already extant public prayer. Scholars differ on the degree of editing involved, from a minimalist position of "touching up" or slightly reformulating an existing version to a position advocating a serious reworking of earlier materials by the Yavnean sages.[16]

Until recently, the lone dissenting voice to this consensus was Zeitlin. Decades ago, he argued that no public prayer was known in Judea in the pre-70 period and that the institution of communal synagogue prayer is a post-70 phenomenon. Of late, I have adopted this line of argument, and now Fleischer and Reif have as well.[17]

The case against the existence of institutionalized communal prayer in the Second Temple synagogue rests squarely on the evidence at hand (or lack

---

15. *T. Šabb.* 13.2 (ed. Lieberman, 57).

16. See the range of opinions from the minimalist position of Naomi Cohen ("Shimon Hapakuli's Act regarding the Eighteen Blessings," *Tarbiz* 52 [1983] 547–55 [Hebrew]) through that of Ismar Elbogen (*Jewish Liturgy: A Comprehensive History* [trans. Raymond P. Scheindlin; Philadelphia: Jewish Publication Society, 1993] 201–2) and Joseph Heinemann (*Prayer in the Talmud: Forms and Patterns* [Berlin: de Gruyter, 1977] 13ff.).

17. Solomon Zeitlin, "The Tefillah, the Shemoneh Esreh: An Historical Study of the First Canonization of the Hebrew Liturgy," *JQR* 54 (1964) 208–49; Lee I. Levine, "The Second Temple Synagogue: The Formative Years," in *The Synagogue in Late Antiquity* (ed. Lee I. Levine; Philadelphia: ASOR, 1987) 19–20; Ezra Fleischer, "On the Beginnings of Obligatory Jewish Prayer," *Tarbiz* 59 (1990) 397–441 [Hebrew]; Stefan Reif, *Judaism and Hebrew Prayer: New Perspectives on Jewish Liturgical History* (Cambridge: Cambridge University Press, 1993) 44–52, 82–87.

thereof). With all their diversity, extant sources are unanimous in this respect; all pre-70 sources—the New Testament, the Theodotus inscription, Philo, Josephus, and what appear to be early rabbinic traditions—speak only of scriptural readings and sermons. None mentions public communal prayer. Moreover, the few extant buildings usually identified as synagogues would seem to indicate not only a range of plans and styles but the lack of any discernible or distinctive orientation toward Jerusalem.[18] First-century Judean synagogues all focus on the center of the hall, with benches on four sides. This is significant, because facing Jerusalem was the physical orientation of the devotee that was associated with prayer early on and with prayer halls in late antiquity.[19]

Nevertheless, the issue of communal prayer in Judea requires a more nuanced approach. While there is no evidence for communal prayers in the typical synagogues of Judea throughout this period, it did, in fact, exist in certain specific settings. For example, it is clear from extant literary sources (Josephus and Philo) and from the Qumran scrolls that the Essenes and related groups conducted regular communal prayer sessions.[20] In addition, prayer services were held in the Temple every morning by the officiating priests, as attested by the Mishna,[21] and Beit Hillel and Beit Shammai are said to have disputed the precise number of blessings that were to be recited on holidays and on Rosh Hashanah that fell on the Sabbath.[22] It would appear, therefore, that certain religious groups had developed some sort of communal prayer setting already in the pre-70 period.

The 200 C.E. Stage of Development

There is no question that a major shift in the nature of religious worship in Palestinian synagogues was precipitated by the destruction of the Temple. For all the controversy that surrounded this central institution in the late Second Temple Period, the Temple remained, to its very end, the central and preeminent religious framework of Jewish life. Thus, it is no wonder that with its disappearance there was an urgent need to fill the vacuum, among other ways, by incorporating certain Temple practices within the synagogue framework, as well as by creating additional avenues of religious expression. Under the leadership of Rabban Yoḥanan b. Zakkai and particularly of Rabban

---

18. See my "Second Temple Synagogue," 10–19.

19. Dan 6:11. Some sort of communal prayer seems to have been a feature of the diaspora synagogue, to wit the widely-used term *proseuche* ('house of prayer').

20. Philo *Contemplative Life* 81–83; CD XI 21; Shemaryahu Talmon, *The World of Qumran from Within: Collected Studies* (Jerusalem: Magnes / Leiden: Brill, 1989) 241–42; Esther Chazon, "On the Special Character of Sabbath Prayer: New Data from Qumran," *Journal of Jewish Music and Liturgy* 15 (1992–93) 1–21.

21. M. *Tamid* 5:1, and comments of Reuven Hammer, "What Did They Bless? A Study of Mishnah Tamid 5, 1," *JQR* 81 (1991) 305–24.

22. See, for example, t. *Roš Haš.* 2.17 (ed. Lieberman, 320–21). See also Acts 3:1.

Gamaliel, the sages at Yavneh (ca. 70–132) addressed this issue in a variety of ways; their work was continued in subsequent generations, at Usha (ca. 140–180) and in the era of R. Judah I (ca. 180–225). This period of approximately 150 years produced the first clear-cut evidence of a synagogue prayer liturgy, which eventually evolved into what has become normative Jewish worship.

Torah-Reading

The one worship element that was clearly carried over from the pre-70 worship context was the Torah-reading. Evidence from throughout the entire first millennium C.E. attests to the fact that Palestinian practice employed a triennial cycle that was loosely defined and that varied from one locale to the next. Evidence from the second half of the millennium indicates that a triennial cycle may have been divided into 141, 154, 167, or 175 portions (*sedarim*).[23] The annual Torah-reading cycle, associated primarily with Babylonia in late antiquity, is evidenced in late Byzantine Palestine as well but appears either to have been limited to Babylonian Jews living there or to reflect a period in which Babylonian customs began making inroads in Palestine. Two statements from later antiquity relate explicitly to this triennial cycle. One appears in the Babylonian Talmud: "those in the west [i.e., Palestine] who finish reading the Torah in three years."[24] The second is from the *Differences in Customs*, which reflects the very end of late antiquity:

> Those in the east [Babylonia] celebrate Simḥat Torah (marking the conclusion of the reading of the Torah) every year; those in Eretz-Israel (celebrate the holiday once) every three-and-a-half years.[25]

Despite this rather explicit evidence, we are nevertheless ill-informed about precisely how the triennial cycle worked. Several tannaitic statements give us some idea, although they relate only to specific instances during the year:

> When the New Moon (*Rosh Ḥodesh*) of Adar falls on the Sabbath, we read *Parashat Sheqalim*. When it falls in mid-week, we move [the reading] up to the previous [Sabbath] and skip (i.e., suspend the usual reading for) the following Sabbath. On the second [Sabbath, we read] *Zakhor* (Deut 25:17), on the third, the "Red Heifer" (Num 19:1), on the fourth "This month will be to you" (Exod 12:1), on the fifth we return to the regular order. For all (special occasions) we

23. These numbers appear in lists of *sedarim* found in Genizah manuscripts and early Torah scrolls (Issachar Joel, "A Bible Manuscript Written in 1260 [with two facsimiles]," *Kiryat-Sefer* 38 [1962] 126–29 [Hebrew]), as well as Tractate *Sop.* 16:8 (ed. Higger, 291–92). Avigdor Shinan ("Sermons, Targums and the Reading from Scriptures in the Ancient Synagogue," in *The Synagogue in Late Antiquity* [ed. Lee I. Levine; Philadelphia: ASOR, 1987] 97–110) has argued that the variation within the triennial cycle should not be limited only to the known lists of *sedarim*, but that, in fact, there were many more variations, as reflected in midrashic homilies.

24. *B. Meg.* 29b.

25. *Differences in Customs*, no. 48 (ed. Margalioth, 172–73).

interrupt [the regular order]: for New Moons, for Hanukkah, and for Purim, for fast days and *ma'amadot*, and for Yom Kippur.[26]

Although the Babylonian Talmud records a dispute between two Palestinian sages originally from Babylonia over what the phrase "regular order" refers to—the reading of the Torah or the *haftarah*—it seems rather clear that the subject of this mishna is the Torah-reading. Postponing the regular readings so frequently could never work out if an annual cycle was being practiced,[27] but it was the Babylonian annual cycle that may have prompted R. Jeremiah to interpret the above tradition as referring to the *haftarah* cycle.

With regard to the Torah-reading, the Tosepta fills out the picture sketchily drawn by the Mishna. For example, it adds the *haftarot* to be recited on special Sabbaths and holidays and also spells out the Torah-readings for the intermediate days of the Passover and Sukkot festivals.[28] Of more interest, however, is the fact that the Tosepta also notes alternative Torah-reading customs to those listed in the Mishna. For Shavu'ot, for example, instead of the selection from Deuteronomy 16, another custom of reading Exodus 19–20 is noted; with regard to Rosh Hashanah, some replace the reading from Leviticus 23 with Genesis 21.[29] The difference between these alternative practices is far from insignificant, because the contents of each is radically different; knowing the Sitz im Leben of each custom would be an enormous boon to understanding the different emphases among various second-century congregations. On the one hand, according to the Mishna and the main tradition cited in the Tosepta, the Torah selections are what we might have expected for special occasions, namely, passages that address these particular holidays. The alternative readings, however, introduced by the phrase "others say," focus on a very different type of reading, namely narrative portions: the revelation on Mt. Sinai in one case and the story of Abraham and his seed in the other. Was this choice based on ideological or religious considerations, or were these readings simply more appealing and popularly oriented? Unfortunately, we simply have no way of knowing.

Tannaitic material knows of other instances of competing customs revolving around the reading of the Torah. For example, two Ushan sages, R. Meir and R. Judah, had a difference of opinion with regard to the weekday Torah-readings. According to R. Meir, each reading was to be consecutive. Thus, the reading on Monday morning would pick up where the Sabbath afternoon Torah-reading left off, and the readings on Thursday and the following Sabbath would follow suit. R. Judah, on the other hand, was of the opinion that the readings on these three occasions should repeat themselves, and then on the following Sabbath the same portion should be read once again and more

---

26. *M. Meg.* 3:4.
27. Such was the case with R. Ami in *b. Meg.* 30b.
28. *T. Meg.* 3.1–7 (ed. Lieberman, 353–55).
29. *T. Meg.* 3.5–6 (ed. Lieberman, 354).

added to it.[30] The implication of these different procedures seems to be that synagogues might well have read different sections of the Torah on any given Sabbath, not to speak of weekdays.

It is difficult to say how much the sages themselves had a hand in shaping the Torah-reading service at this stage. Many customs practiced in the second century C.E. most likely originated in the pre-70 era, rendering the sages' influence on synagogue worship unknown (and probably minimal) — unless we limit ourselves to Pharisaic practice in this regard, of which we know next to nothing. Moreover, it is difficult to gauge the degree to which the Mishna and Tosepta simply recorded common practices or, alternatively, the degree to which they record rulings that the sages themselves made.

Finally, it is impossible to determine how much change took place in the Torah-reading in the second century. Most relevant rabbinic traditions are anonymous (in sharp distinction from the prayers; see below), and most pericopes seem to describe known practice without much discussion of change, tension, or conflict. We thus tend to assume that the above practices were widespread, at least in Palestine, and aroused relatively little controversy either among the sages or in the community at large.

Prayer

In contrast to the ambiguous rabbinic role in the shaping of the Torah-reading ceremony, the second major area of Jewish liturgy, communal prayer, is markedly different. One basic component of later Jewish prayer that crystallized at this time was the Shemaʿ and its accompanying blessings. Here the rabbis clearly adopted a Temple-based custom. The sages, however, were not satisfied with mere adoption but set about to supplement, amplify, and even eliminate some of the paragraphs preceding and following the three biblical passages. The Mishna reports that the prayer service recited in the Temple every morning was composed of four parts: (1) a call for reciting a blessing and its recitation, (2) recitation of the Decalogue, (3) three paragraphs from Deuteronomy and Numbers, and (4) three blessings for the people.

Assuming the veracity of this report, the sages consciously reworked this Temple prayer unit, transforming it into an integral part of the daily prayer ritual they were promoting. The three Pentateuchal paragraphs retained their centrality, although why precisely these three passages had been selected in the first place, and why in this particular order, is unclear.

According to the Mishna, the relationship between the three paragraphs is both ideological and technical. The link between the first two is ideological; one first accepts the yoke of God's kingdom and then the yoke of His commandments. The tie between the second and third is more technical in nature: the former deals with commandments relevant to both day and night;

---

30. *T. Meg.* 3.10 (ed. Lieberman, 355).

the latter only to daytime commandments.[31] A widely-accepted view is that the three blessings preceding and following the Shema[c] focus on the three basic themes of Creation, Revelation, and Redemption, and some suggest that the three biblical paragraphs may also be understood in this light.[32]

Thus, building on the Temple liturgy as described in *Mishna Tamid*, the sages added a second blessing before the Shema[c] (and possibly changed the content of the first, which is left undefined in the Mishna), while developing the above-noted thematic triad. The Decalogue was eliminated—probably by the sages themselves—despite the fact that the Decalogue-Shema[c] combination appears to have been widely used in the late Second Temple Period. They appear together (though not always contiguously), first in Deuteronomy and then in the Nash Papyrus from Hellenistic Egypt, in the *tefillin* from Qumran, as well as in the above-noted priestly prayer from the Temple. The coupling of these two sections remains enigmatic. Weinfeld opines that the Decalogue and Shema[c] parallel ancient Near Eastern loyalty oaths and vassal treaties, similar to those found in connection with Nabonidus and Esarhaddon, while Goldstein suggests that they parallel the oath (*sacramentum*) taken by a Roman soldier in allegiance to the emperor.[33] The sages attribute the elimination of the Decalogue to an attempt to counter sectarian polemics.[34] Nevertheless, the association of the Shema[c] with the Decalogue continues in a number of rabbinic expositions as well as in later Palestinian synagogue traditions.

The formulation of the three paragraphs surrounding the Shema[c] was far from fixed, either in tannaitic times or later. A number of versions seem to have been in circulation. For example, although the benediction following the Shema[c] was intended to highlight the theme of redemption, this was not the case at the outset, and by the turn of the third century a number of different historical references were being used:

31. *M. Ber.* 2:2.

32. See, for example, Heinemann, *Prayer in the Talmud*, 33–36; Reuven Kimelman, "The Shema[c] and Its Rhetoric: The Case for the Shema[c] Being More than Creation, Revelation and Redemption," *Journal of Jewish Thought and Philosophy* 2 (1992) 111–56, and the literature cited therein.

33. Moshe Weinfeld, *Deuteronomy 1–11* (AB 5; New York: Doubleday, 1991) 352–54; Jonathan Goldstein, *I Maccabees: A New Translation* (AB 41; Garden City, N.Y.: Doubleday, 1976) 133 n. 171.

34. *B. Ber.* 12a; *y. Ber.* 1, 8, 3c; and Louis Ginzberg, *A Commentary on the Palestinian Talmud* (4 vols.; New York: Jewish Theological Seminary, 1941–61) 1.166–67 [Hebrew]. For later rabbinic references, see *y. Meg.* 3, 8, 74b; 4, 2, 75a; as well as the comments of Ephraim E. Urbach, "The Role of the Ten Commandments in Jewish Worship," in *The Ten Commandments in History and Tradition* (ed. Ben-Zion Segal; Jerusalem: Magnes, 1990) 182–89. See also Reuven Kimelman, "The Shema and the Amidah: Rabbinic Prayer," in *Prayer from Alexander to Constantine* (ed. Mark Kiley et al.; London: Routledge, 1997) 109–10.

He who reads the Shema᷃ must mention the Exodus from Egypt in (the paragraph) "True and certain." Rabbi (Judah I) says: "He must mention [God's] sovereignty." Others say: "He must mention the slaying of the firstborn and the splitting of the sea."[35]

᷃Amidah

The key prayer formulated at this time was the ᷃Amidah, and here a rabbinic stamp is most clearly documented. Ironically, however, only one statement refers explicitly to this event:

ת״ר: שמעון הפקולי הסדיר הסדיר י״ח ברכות לפני רבן גמליאל על הסדר ביבנה.

Our sages taught: Simeon Hapaquli arranged eighteen benedictions before Rabban Gamaliel according to [their] order at Yavneh.[36]

As noted, most scholars working under the assumption that some form of the ᷃Amidah already existed in the Second Temple Period have debated the nature of Simeon's work in Yavneh; was it mostly editorial in nature, or did it involve a more creative integration of the contents, patterns, and structure of earlier prayers? Over the past decade, a number of views concur in their assertion that the ᷃Amidah was in reality a creation of the Yavnean period. Working from very different perspectives, Fleischer, Zahavy, and Kugelmass have all found in the post-70 historical context, and each on the basis of very different sources, support for assuming that the sages of this period were responsible for this major liturgical innovation.[37] Finally, Reif has charted a somewhat more balanced approach. Reckoning with the rich mosaic in the public and private expressions of prayer in the first century C.E., he points to the delicate balance between continuity and creativity as well as variety and uniformity in the evolution of Jewish prayer from the Second Temple to tannaitic eras.[38]

Thus, what is called for is an approach that takes into account much of the primary data that has been brought to bear on the subject, as well as the ostensibly contradictory claims by scholars for the existence of pre-70 communal prayer on the one hand, and the far-reaching measures adopted in Yavneh on the other. Needless to say, an attempt to synthesize such data is not merely a question of setting them down side by side and somehow trying to create an amalgam; these views, in their present formulation, are clearly

---

35. *T. Ber.* 2.1 (ed. Lieberman, 6); *y. Ber.* 1, 9, 3d; *Exod. Rab.* 22:3.

36. *B. Ber.* 28b; *b. Meg.* 17b; *Midraš Hagadol*, Exod 40:32 (ed. Margalioth, 790).

37. Fleischer, "Beginnings of Obligatory Jewish Prayer," 397–441; Zvi Zahavy, "Three Stages in the Development of Early Rabbinic Prayer," in *From Ancient Israel to Modern Judaism: Intellect in Quest of Understanding—Essays in Honor of Marvin Fox* (ed. Jacob Neusner et al.; Atlanta: Scholars Press, 1989) 1.233–65; Harvey J. Kugelmass, "Jewish Liturgy and the Emergence of the Synagogue as House of Prayer in the Post-Destruction Era," in *"Où demeures-tu?" (Jn. 1, 38): La maison depuis le monde biblique* (ed. Jean-Claude Petit; Quebec: Fides, 1994) 289–301.

38. Reif, *Judaism and Hebrew Prayer*, 53–87.

irreconcilable. However, recognizing the valid points in each of the approaches may enable us to integrate them into a plausible theory.

What, then, are these basic points of reference? There is no question that public prayer existed in pre-70 Judea, but, as we have seen, these instances were restricted to specific circles: at Qumran, in the Jerusalem Temple, and among the Pharisees. Public prayer (as distinct from prayer recited in public—see Matt 6:5) did not exist in the ordinary community synagogue of pre-70 Judea—whether in Jerusalem or the Galilee.

Moreover, the sages of Yavneh did not work in a vacuum but drew on a reservoir of earlier traditions and practices. Adopting phrases and ideas borrowed from scriptural verses (Nehemiah 9 or Ps 103:2–6), perhaps from earlier Pharisaic practice (for example, the dispute between Beit Hillel and Beit Shammai)[39] or from Ben Sira, would not have constituted any sort of problem for the Yavnean sages. Interestingly, however, not all of the traditions that may have constituted potential sources for the ʿAmidah stem from settings or groups with whom the rabbis would necessarily have wished to associate themselves. The priestly liturgy from the Temple or the Qumran parallels are cases in point. How some of these ideas and formulations reached Yavneh is impossible to determine, though the fact that so many threads of different origins appear to have been interwoven is intriguing. Thus, we can assuredly posit a great deal of continuity in Jewish liturgy if we understand that this corpus evolved as a result of rabbis drawing significantly from earlier literary and nonliterary traditions. In this sense, what they created was as much a continuation as it was an innovation.

Nevertheless, there is little question that something very new was developing in Yavneh as a result of the new circumstances and historical exigencies of the post-destruction period. However, it would be wholly gratuitous to assume that Rabban Gamaliel's initiatives brought about a sudden and total revolution by creating ex nihilo an obligatory prayer liturgy for both individuals and community alike. It is most improbable that the prayers discussed by the rabbis took shape all at once or that they immediately became the normative practice among Jews. The creation of an obligatory daily worship framework in Yavneh was a dramatic initiative that required decades, perhaps centuries, to reach some sort of final form.

Perhaps the most important source (other than the one quoted above) attesting to the fact that the ʿAmidah seems to have been an innovation of the Yavnean period is recorded in the Mishna:

Rabban Gamaliel says: "One must recite the Shemoneh ʿEsreh (i.e., the ʿAmidah) daily"; R. Joshua says: "[It suffices to recite] a shortened Shemoneh ʿEsreh (מעין שמונה עשרה)." R. ʿAqiva says: "If one knows the prayer well (שגורה בפיו), he should recite the (entire) Shemoneh ʿEsreh; if not, a shortened Shemoneh

39. For example, *t. Ber.* 3.13 (ed. Lieberman, 15).

ʿEsreh." R. Eliʿezer says: "One who makes his prayer fixed (i.e., routine — קְבַע),
his prayer is no longer a supplication."[40]

The span of ideas reflected in this source is indeed wide. Rabban Gamaliel
wished to institute a full recitation of the ʿAmidah's eighteen blessings, with
set themes and a fixed order. R. Joshua advocated a shortened version of the
above. What precisely he had in mind is unclear. The fact that over a century
later sages had differing opinions regarding what exactly was meant by a
"shortened Shemoneh ʿEsreh" indicates its inherent ambiguity.[41] R. ʿAqiva
took a middle-of-the-road approach: recitation of the complete or shortened
version would be dependent upon the knowledge of the particular individual. R. Eliʿezer, however, adopted a radically different position, opposing any
imposition of a set framework. The statement attributed to him juxtaposes
two different and seemingly contradictory elements: fixed prayer on the one
hand and prayer as supplication on the other. According to this view, the two
do not mix. Prayer requires spontaneity, and any attempt at regimentation is
self-defeating. Moreover, this view is articulated by another Yavnean sage,
R. Simeon b. Netanel, a student of R. Yoḥanan b. Zakkai, who is quoted as
saying: "And when you pray, do not make your prayers fixed, but rather [a
plea for mercy and] supplications before God."[42] Thus, taking into account
the approaches of Rabban Gamaliel at one extreme and R. Eliʿezer and
R. Simeon at the other, as well as the two middle positions, we have evidence
of a wide spectrum of attitudes regarding this innovation.

In addition to the above two sources, a number of discussions and statements about prayer by Rabban Gamaliel and his colleagues at Yavneh are
best interpreted in light of the fact that the institution of obligatory prayer had
been introduced only recently. Such discussions appear to be a working-out
of the implementation and ramifications of this new framework.[43]

As has been recognized for generations and has received particular emphasis in the writings of Heinemann, the prayer formulas of the ʿAmidah and
Shemaʿ benedictions (on the latter, see below) that began in Yavneh were not
"etched in stone." Concerning the ʿAmidah, for example, what was promulgated in Yavneh probably involved the overall framework, sequential topics,
and the number of blessings.[44] Even some of these elements were, in fact,
fleshed out only over time; the Tosepta notes that certain competing themes
should be combined, thus alluding to the fact that various combinations of
themes were still being recited in different locales:

40. *M. Ber.* 4:3–4a.
41. *B. Ber.* 29a.
42. *M. ʾAbot* 2:13. Some manuscripts omit the words in parentheses (רחמים).
43. As, for example, *m. Ber.* 4:7; *m. Roš Haš.* 4:9; and *t. Roš Haš.* 2.18 (ed. Lieberman,
321); *b. Ber.* 28b; *b. ʿAbod. Zar.* 7b–8a.
44. Heinemann, *Prayer in the Talmud*, 23–30.

The eighteen benedictions that the sages fixed are parallel to [the use of the Divine name in Psalm 29], "Give praise to the Lord, sons of gods. . . ." One should incorporate [the reference to] heretics (מינים) in [the blessing about] sectarians (פרושין), proselytes in [that relating to] elders, and David in "He Who builds Jerusalem."[45]

Before I conclude this discussion on the ʿAmidah prayer, several important caveats are in order. In the first place, for all the innovation of the Yavnean generation of sages, we must remember that what has been discussed in these sources was the daily prayer, the Shemoneh ʿEsreh or eighteen benedictions. In terms of the Pharisaic-rabbinic tradition, the Sabbath and holiday ʿAmidah may have already been known and practiced by Beit Hillel and Beit Shammai in the first century, although the tradition attesting to this is problematic.[46] If its historicity is granted, then within their own circles, Rabban Gamaliel and his colleagues were extending a known practice to the weekday—a not-insignificant move yet, at the same time, one that was not totally revolutionary.

Nevertheless, these Yavnean sages were taking a very significant step vis-à-vis Jewish society generally by obligating every Jew to recite weekday prayers, and although admittedly not stated, this certainly included Sabbath and holiday prayers. Moreover, much of the discussion in *Mishna Berakot* seems to deal with the obligation of prayer, regardless of where it was conducted. Very little is said of prayer in a public setting. One might therefore gain the impression that synagogue worship was almost entirely irrelevant or superfluous. It is only when we take other tannaitic sources into account that the importance and centrality of public prayer, presumably but not necessarily in the synagogue, is emphasized.

At some point in the course of the second century, there appears to have been a move toward combining the Shemaʿ and ʿAmidah into one prayer service. Here, however, the sages made a distinction. While they were willing to consider the recitation of the morning Shemaʿ in the synagogue as fulfilling one's obligation of saying it upon waking, this was not true with regard to the evening. Rather, the Shemaʿ had to be recited upon retiring as well.[47] It was left to the third-century R. Yoḥanan to take the next step and advocate that the evening Shemaʿ should be combined with the ʿAmidah (see below).

The contours of synagogue liturgy as it evolved in the second century may well be reflected in several tannaitic sources that speak of the liturgical elements requiring a quorum of ten men, a minyan. The Mishna speaks in the following vein:

---

45. *T. Ber.* 3.25 (ed. Lieberman, 17–18).
46. *T. Roš Haš.* 2.17 (ed. Lieberman, 320), and the discussion of this tradition in my *Ancient Synagogue*, chap. 16.
47. *Y. Ber.* 1, 1, 2a.

We do not recite the Shema‘ responsively (as a congregation), nor [have the prayer-leader] pass before the ark (i.e., recite the ‘Amidah), nor [have the priests] lift their hands (in blessing), nor read the Torah, nor recite the *haftarah* . . . with less than ten [males].[48]

A *baraita* expands this list somewhat differently:

As was taught [in the Mishna]: We do not recite the Shema‘ responsively with less than ten men [present]. If we begin with ten and some leave, one completes [the recitation]. We do not recite the ‘Amidah congregationally with less than ten; if we begin with ten and some leave, one completes [the ‘Amidah]. We do not recite the priestly blessing with less than ten; if we begin and some leave, one completes [the benediction]. We do not read the Torah with less than ten; if we begin and some leave, one completes [the reading]. We do not recite the *haftarah* with less than ten; if we begin and some leave, we complete [the reading].[49]

Thus, by the end of the second century, the rabbinic Sabbath and holiday liturgy seems to have featured five elements, three of which occurred daily, one weekly, and one several times a week. The Shema‘, ‘Amidah, and priestly blessing (included as part of the ‘Amidah but singled out owing to its uniqueness and importance) constituted the basic liturgical framework, with the Torah-reading supplementing this basic ritual twice on the Sabbath (morning and afternoon) and once on Monday and Thursday. Reading the *haftarah* was a Sabbath and holiday addition. Elsewhere in the Mishna, a similar listing appears, although without the reading of scriptures that was dealt with in the previous and subsequent paragraphs. The following mishna seems to imply that one person could often lead in all of the above:

He who recites the passage from the Prophets leads in the recitation of the Shema‘ and leads the congregation in the ‘Amidah and raises his hands (in blessing).[50]

To these lists we should add prayers such as the Hallel for holidays and private penitential prayers, which appear to have been fairly widespread, at least in rabbinic circles. Moreover, a number of short responses were used in the liturgy, although we cannot be certain of their precise context. *Sipre Deuteronomy* lists a number of these. Following the formal call to prayer, ‘Praise the Lord Who is blessed’ (ברכו את ה' המבורך), the congregation responds, ‘Praised is the blessed Lord forever’ (ברוך ה' המבורך לעולם ועד); “Amen” is said after every benediction; ‘Blessed be the name of His glorious kingdom forever’ (ברוך שם כבוד מלכותו לעולם ועד) is recited, presumably following the

---

48. M. *Meg.* 4:3. See also Tractate *Sop.* 10:6 (ed. Higger, 212–14); *Yal. Šim. Leviticus, Emor,* 643 (ed. Hyman, 700).

49. Y. *Meg.* 4, 4, 75a; *Pesiq. R.* 40 (ed. Friedmann, 167b) adds one further element: “When one arises, he immediately goes to the synagogue and recites the Shema‘, the ‘Amidah, listens to the Torah, and listens to the elder (preach).”

50. M. *Meg.* 4:5.

opening verse of the Shemaᶜ; those who say, 'May His great name be praised' (יהא שמו הגדול מבורך), and others respond, 'forever and ever' (לעולם ולעולמי עולמים).[51] The former praise, which eventually became the central refrain in the Qaddish prayer, is reported elsewhere in connection with the second-century R. Yosi (b. Ḥalafta) as being regularly recited in synagogues and academies.[52]

The 600 C.E. Stage of Development

Our knowledge of Jewish liturgy increases immeasurably in late antiquity as a much larger and more variegated array of sources became available, not only from within rabbinic circles, as before, but supplemented now by other sources as well. The Jerusalem and Babylonian Talmuds replace the Mishna and Tosepta, and the amoraic midrashim, almost exclusively aggadic in nature, replace their tannaitic predecessors, which were far more focused on halakic issues. The change in the rabbinic genres not only reflects internal rabbinic literary proclivities but may also be a response to the external needs of the Jewish community. The rabbinic agenda appears now to have been expanded to include types of intellectual-religious endeavors that would appeal to a wider public. A statement by the third-century R. Isaac is most revealing in this regard:

> Once, when money was available, a person would want to study mishnah and talmud. Now, when there is no money, and especially when we suffer from the [rule of the wicked] kingdom, one prefers to study scriptures and *aggadah*.[53]

It may not coincidental, therefore, that late antiquity witnessed a significant degree of rabbinic involvement in delivering public sermons and, later, in compiling midrashic material into literary corpora. Even within rabbinic literature itself, we can detect traces of (liturgical?) poetry, which a few sages at least seem to have been inclined to create.

Late antiquity witnessed a number of significant developments in Jewish communal worship. On one level, there was the continued crystallization, consolidation, and amplification of the basic prayer frameworks that had been inaugurated at an earlier period. The cluster of blessings and prayers around the Shemaᶜ and the ᶜAmidah was further refined, and new components were added, either to the body of these prayers or as prefatory and concluding sections.

The third century witnessed an accelerated rabbinic involvement in communal life generally and in the synagogue in particular, a development that opened numerous lines of communication between this elite group and the people at large. A by-product of their increased involvement may well have

---

51. *Sipre Deut.* 306 (ed. Finkelstein, 342).
52. B. *Ber.* 3a. See also *b. Ber.* 21b; *Midr. Prov.* 14, where the context given is that of a *beit midrash*.
53. *Pesiq. Rab Kah.* 12:3 (ed. Mandelbaum, 205); see also *Cant. Rab.* 2, 5, 1.

been that, on the one hand, the sages were more responsive to congregational needs and proclivities while, on the other, the community was more sympathetic to rabbinic opinion, thus enabling rabbinic liturgical traditions more readily to penetrate synagogue ritual.

While many third- and fourth-century sages contributed to the evolving liturgical tradition, two pairs of rabbis, one in Babylonia and the other in Palestine, seem to have been unusually active in this area. Both pairs lived in the third century, Rav and Samuel in the first part of the century in Babylonia, and the slightly younger Palestinian amoraim, R. Joshua b. Levi and R. Yoḥanan, toward the middle of the century in Palestine.

A second focus of synagogue liturgy in 600 C.E. was, of course, the Torah-reading ceremony. This component continued to be varied, including readings from the Torah and the Prophets (*haftarah*), targum, and sermons. None of these elements, of course, was new at this time, since all had existed within the synagogue setting for centuries. Nevertheless, a large number of sources relating to these dimensions of synagogue worship stem from late antiquity, and thus our knowledge of each is far greater for this period than for earlier ones. Ironically, very little new information is available with regard to the pivotal component—the Torah-reading itself. Both talmuds, our primary sources in this regard, essentially relate to mishnaic and toseptan discussions, and little new material is added. The additional readings required for the second days of a holiday in the Babylonian diaspora (and possibly elsewhere, although this cannot be verified) are one notable exception to this generalization.

Both the targum and sermon continued to be integral parts of the worship service in late antiquity. The *haftarah* continued to be translated along with the Torah-reading, although the rabbis at least were much less stringent about the former.[54] The system of translation as noted in various rabbinic sources was as follows: a translation must be made orally (although targumic texts seem to have existed) immediately following the Torah-reading; it is to be recited verse by verse with regard to the Torah, but as many as three verses at a time for the *haftarah*. The goal was to render a passage as faithfully as possible to the original, yet not too slavishly; as formulated by the second-century R. Judah b. ʾIlai: "He who translates a verse according to its simple meaning (כצורתו) is a liar, and he who adds [to it] is a blasphemer."[55]

In contrast to targumic activity, where rabbinic involvement remains somewhat enigmatic, there is little question that a number of sages, at the very least, were actively involved in delivering sermons in synagogues; rabbinic literature has preserved a number of interesting references in this regard, as we have noted above. Besides known rabbis, we hear of itinerant preachers who would travel from place to place and address congregations. We are told of one such preacher, identified simply as a *ḥaver*, who came to

---

54. M. Meg. 4:4; t. Meg. 3.18–20 (ed. Lieberman, 358–59); b. Meg. 21b.
55. T. Meg. 3.41 (ed. Lieberman, 364); b. Qidd. 49a.

a synagogue and, having expounded a scriptural lesson, was accorded much respect and material support.[56]

With the emergence of a rabbinic center in Babylonia, we are now witness to the evolution of rabbinic forms of worship in more than one locale. This affords an opportunity to compare and contrast the similarities and differences between these centers. As a result, the continued evolution and consolidation of tannaitic initiatives now proceed along parallel tracks, with some striking instances of accommodation of liturgical practices to local conditions or the adoption of certain forms owing to different historical contexts.

These differences were manifest in the main body of the liturgy as well as in its ancillary customs. For example, the Babylonian sages expanded the ʿAmidah from eighteen to nineteen prayers by creating a separate blessing for the seed of David (literally, 'plant of David' צמח דויד). Whether this was a gesture intended for the Exilarch, who claimed to have descended from the Davidic line, or merely an expression of theological yearnings for redemption that the Babylonians wished to emphasize further, is difficult to assess. With regard to the Torah-reading, the Babylonians instituted an annual cycle, which stood in sharp contrast to the Palestinian triennial one; they also added readings for the extra festival days, as was indeed the practice at least in Babylonia.[57] These are probably the three most salient differences between Babylonian and Palestinian synagogue practice, but there were others as well, as for example:

1. Babylonians would sit when reciting the Shemaʿ; in Palestine, people would stand.

2. Babylonian elders would face the congregation, as had been the practice in the tannaitic period; in Palestine, the elders would face the ark along with the rest of the congregation.

3. Babylonians would conclude the blessing following the Shemaʿ with the phrase, "Who has redeemed Israel" (past tense); in Palestine the concluding phrase was formulated in the present tense: "Rock of Israel and its Savior."

4. Babylonians would recite the daily ʿAmidah silently; in Palestine this prayer would be said aloud so as "to familiarize the people."[58]

With the growth of the rabbinic center in Babylonia, we find that in a number of cases Babylonian customs penetrated into Palestine. For instance, there seems to be evidence attesting to the appearance of the Babylonian annual Torah-reading cycle in Palestine. Whether this custom took root among

---

56. *Tanḥuma, Terumah* 1 (ed. Buber, 45a).

57. *Torah-Reading: Differences in Customs*, no. 48 (ed. Margolioth, 172–73); *b. Meg.* 29b; *Two days: Differences in Customs*, no. 41 (ibid., 161–64); *b. Meg.* 31a; *y. Dem.* 4, 2, 23d; *y. ʿErub.* 3, 9, 21c; and elsewhere.

58. *Differences in Customs*, nos. 1, 36, 43 (ed. Margolioth, 91–94, 156, 165–67); and Elbogen, *Jewish Liturgy*, 210.

the indigenous population or only among Babylonians living in the country is unclear. Nor is it clear how smooth and harmonious such practices were. One piece of evidence, from the Babylonian Pirqoi ben Baboi around 800 c.e., relating to the practice of reciting the Qedushah prayer, indicates that it often may have been accompanied by a considerable degree of tension and conflict:

> Until now the Qedushah and Shema᷄ are said in Palestine only on Sabbath and holidays and only in the morning (Shaḥarit) service, with the exception of Jerusalem and all cities where there are Babylonians who pressure (lit., cause controversy and dispute) until they (the Palestinians) take upon themselves [the custom of] saying the Qedushah daily. But in the other cities and towns of Palestine where there are no Babylonians, they only recite the Qedushah on the Sabbaths and holidays.[59]

The third basic component of Jewish liturgy in the Byzantine era, and the one entirely new element in synagogue worship at the time, is the *piyyut*. Derived from the Greek ποιήτης, the *piyyut* was a liturgical poem that may have been introduced into any one of a number of worship frameworks: the Shema᷄ section (*yotzer*), the morning ᷄Amidah (*qerovah*, and especially featuring the Qedushah, that is, the *qedushta*), on Sabbath and festival evening services (*shiv᷄ata*), the Mussaf ᷄Amidah, and on special occasions such as the ᷄Abodah service on Yom Kippur and on Tish᷄a b'Ab. Written in Hebrew for the most part, the *piyyut*'s rich and often complex poetic presentation draws heavily on Bible and Midrash. Hekhalot traditions played a role in setting the religious and literary framework for these compositions, as did contemporary Christian liturgical tradition.[60] The *piyyutim* at hand all stem from Palestine. Babylonia does not seem to have produced any such compositions in late antiquity and, judging from the attitude of several *geonim* from ensuing centuries, there was not a great deal of enthusiasm for this genre, at the least within Babylonian rabbinic circles.

We know very little about who the poets (*paytanim*) of these early compositions were or what their social and religious standing was within the communities in which they lived and functioned. In contrast to earlier generations, which dated the beginnings of *piyyut* to anywhere between the second and ninth centuries, there is a general consensus today that this form of religious expression emerged in Palestine at some point during the Byzantine era.

The *piyyut* focused on the basic components of the service (the Shema᷄ and ᷄Amidah); in fact, these compositions indicate further what constituted

---

59. Louis Ginzberg, *Geniza Studies* (3 vols.; New York: Jewish Theological Seminary, 1928–29) 2.555–56 [Hebrew].

60. Philipp Bloch, "Die יורדי מרכבה, Die Mystiker der Gaonenzeit, und ihr Einfluss auf die Liturgie," *Monatsschrift für Geschichte und Wissenschaft des Judentums* 37 (1893) 18–25, 69–74, 257–66, 305–11; Ithamar Gruenwald, "Yannai's Piyyutim and the Literature of יורדי מרכבה," *Tarbiz* 36 (1967) 257–77 [Hebrew]; Joseph Yahalom, "Piyyut as Poetry," in *The Synagogue in Late Antiquity* (ed. Lee I. Levine; Philadelphia: ASOR, 1987) 112.

the formal public prayer service at the time. The *piyyut* was intended from the outset for public recital by the *ḥazzan*. We know of no such poetry for private use. As a matter of fact, the silent recitation of the ʿAmidah was probably retained even when the *piyyut* incorporated and replaced the public repetition of the ʿAmidah.

It is far from clear what sort of reality lay behind this liturgical phenomenon. While thousands of *piyyutim* have already been identified, it is not clear how widespread or frequent their recitation was. For example, how many synagogues would have had such a poetic recitation on any given Sabbath, and how often would it have occurred in any particular place? While Fleischer's theory that the early *piyyut* (in contrast to its later stages and to the practice today) was intended to replace the public prayer service for that particular morning has often been quoted,[61] one may ask whether this was always true or whether there were different concurrent practices in this regard.

Of more consequence is the issue of comprehension, noted above. Even today, when one studies the *piyyut* and utilizes the various apparatuses available, it is not an easy task to understand the language of these poems or their allusions, metaphors, and nuances. If the intended audience was the ordinary synagogue congregant, then comprehension of this genre speaks wonders for the intellectual level of the typical Jewish worshiper! Perhaps, however, these poems were to be enjoyed primarily for their esthetic value—that is, the melodies to which they were sung. Alternatively, are we to assume that these compositions were recited when only a very few in attendance could understand their language? Or were the *piyyutim* intended primarily for certain types of audiences in which the participation of the learned was more pronounced (for example, an academy setting)? Whatever the case, the contrast between the attempt to make the Torah-reading and sermon comprehensible to a wider audience on the one hand and the complexity of most *piyyutim* on the other is most puzzling. We are not in a position to provide definitive answers to any of the above questions at present. While the *piyyut* has led to a new appreciation of the variety of components in Jewish worship in late antiquity, it has also left us with a series of intriguing questions.

✴ ✴ ✴ ✴ ✴

It is thus clear that there was constant growth in synagogue liturgy throughout the six centuries that we have been examining. Beginning with an almost exclusive focus on the reading of scriptures (at least in Second Temple Judea) along with other activities intended to enhance this experience, synagogue liturgy expanded over the course of late antiquity to include other basic components. The prayer dimension developed in the second and third centuries, while the *piyyut* emerged as a significant factor in late antiquity.

---

61. Ezra Fleischer, *The Yozer: Its Emergence and Development* (Jerusalem: Magnes, 1984) 11–15 [Hebrew].

The liturgical dimension witnessed alternating periods of centripetal and centrifugal forces. There were periods of consolidation and others of increasing differences and variation. The nonsacrificial component of Jewish worship during the Second Temple Period appears to have been diffuse and largely dependent on local initiative. This was certainly the case with respect to the prayer component in Palestine and, even then, only within certain circles, such as the Temple priesthood or sectarian groups. On the other hand, the tannaitic period witnessed a serious rabbinic effort to create a prayer framework that integrated some of what had existed earlier, while adding new material as well. This effort, which lasted about a century, seems to have created a degree of unity while still allowing for some significant diversity.

With the emergence of a Babylonian rabbinic center in the third century, some significant variations emerged in synagogue liturgy. Each tradition developed not only within its own religious and social setting but was also influenced by its immediate non-Jewish historical context. This is particularly evident in the *piyyut* and the expanded targumic tradition (*Pseudo-Jonathan*) which developed in Byzantine Palestine; in contrast, Babylonian liturgy exhibited little of these last-mentioned components. An important caveat, however, ought to be made in this regard. Our knowledge of synagogue practice in late antiquity is far more extensive for Palestine than for Babylonia. Archaeological finds, combined with aggadic midrashim and *piyyutim*, reveal a far richer and more varied range of synagogue practice in Palestine than in Babylonia. Palestinian Torah-reading patterns varied greatly (compared to Babylonia's fixed annual cycle), homiletical material and practices were multifaceted (little is known about Babylonia in this regard), and many different types of targums were in circulation in Palestine (compared to the rabbinically-authorized *Targum Onqelos* in Babylonia). Whether these differences indeed reflect a striking difference in these two locales or whether they merely reflect the fact that sources for Palestinian practice are far richer requires further investigation.[62]

Thus by late antiquity the pendulum had swung in the opposite direction, and diverse customs and practices had proliferated considerably. This called for a renewed period of consolidation, a process which was to continue for several centuries, reaching its apogee with the appearance of the first siddurim composed by Rav ʿAmram and Rav Saʿadiah Gaon in the ninth and tenth centuries.[63]

62. See Avigdor Shinan, "Synagogues in the Land of Israel: The Literature of the Ancient Synagogue and Synagogue Archaeology," in *Sacred Realm: The Emergence of the Synagogue in the Ancient World* (ed. Steven Fine; New York: Oxford University Press, 1996) 130–52.

63. Salo Baron, *A Social and Religious History of the Jews* (2d ed.; 18 vols.; New York: Jewish Publication Society, 1952–83) 7.111–18; Lawrence Hoffman, *The Canonization of the Synagogue Service* (Notre Dame, Ind.: University of Notre Dame Press, 1979) 160–71.

New Perspectives on the History of Sepphoris

STUART S. MILLER

University of Connecticut at Storrs

The interest of the Jews of the Late Second Temple and Talmudic Periods in urban matters does not compare to the interest in urban matters taken by their Greco-Roman contemporaries or later by Christians and Muslims. Josephus, of course, is somewhat of an exception because he often furnishes accurate details, especially with regard to Herodian centers such as Jerusalem and Caesarea.[1] Nevertheless, neither he nor the rabbis share the same interest in civic institutions and urban affairs displayed by Greco-Roman writers. Certainly there was no Pausanius (ca. 150 C.E.) among the Jews to describe the topography and social life of the towns in which they lived, no Vitruvius (first century B.C.E.) to relate the layout and buildings of their cities, and no Dio Chrysostom (40–112 C.E.) to reflect upon urban problems.[2] When relating details of their schools, bishoprics, and martyrdoms, Christians would often reveal important information about the cities in which they resided.[3]

---

1. Josephus on Jerusalem: *J.W.* 5.136–247 and *Ant.* 15.380–425; on Caesarea: *J.W.* 1.408–15 and *Ant.* 15.331–41.

2. See *Pausanius' Description of Greece* (trans. J. G. Frazer; 6 vols.; New York: Biblio and Tannen, 1965) and Vitruvius, *On Architecture* (ed. and trans. F. Granger; 2 vols.; LCL; Cambridge: Harvard University Press, 1970–83). On Dio Chrysostom, see C. P. Jones, *The Roman World of Dio Chrysostom* (Cambridge: Harvard University Press, 1978); and cf. my "Those Cantankerous Sepphoreans Revisited," in *Ki Baruch Hu: Ancient Near Eastern, Biblical, and Judaic Studies in Honor of Baruch A. Levine* (ed. R. Chazan, W. W. Hallo, and L. H. Schiffman; Winona Lake, Ind.: Eisenbrauns, 1999) 543–73.

3. See G. Downey, "The Christian Schools of Palestine: A Chapter in Literary History," *Harvard Library Bulletin* 12 (1958) 297–319; and L. I. Levine's discussion of the Christian community at Caesarea in idem, *Caesarea under Roman Rule* (Leiden: Brill, 1975) 113–34. St. Augustine's view of the earthly city is, of course, well known. See his *City of God* and cf. L. Storoni Mazzolani, *The Idea of the City in Roman Thought: From Walled City to Spiritual Commonwealth* (trans. S. O'Donnell; Bloomington: Indiana University Press, 1970) 242–79.

Muslim writers would do even better, preserving recollections of the construction of Baghdad, local histories of Medina, and descriptions of the topography and government of Mecca.[4]

We certainly have no comparable accounts of the cities in Eretz Israel that were either founded by Jews or populated by them. Indeed, Jacob Neusner may well be right when he characterizes the city as "a useless symbol in Late Antique Judaism." The Jews may have formed distinct communities in the metropolises of the Mediterranean world and may also have constituted the majority in large towns such as Tiberias and Sepphoris, but by and large, as Neusner says, "they entered no encounter with the city either as an abstraction, or as something concrete and ominous in their lives."[5] Indeed, for the Pharisees and later the rabbis, the internalization of the Halakah may have provided the Jew with a sense of *politeia* that transcended the physical parameters and idea of the city, as Ellis Rivkin claims.[6]

4. Baghdad: S. Ah. El-Ali, "The Foundation of Baghdad," and J. Lassner, "The Caliph's Personal Domain: The City Plan of Baghdad," in *Papers on Islamic History I: The Islamic City, A Colloquium* (ed. A. H. Hourani and S. M. Stern; Oxford: Cassirer, 1970) 87–101 and 103–18. Mecca and Medina: F. Wustenfeld, *Chroniken der Stadt Mekka* (Leipzig: Brockhaus, 1857–61); and F. Rosenthal, *A History of Muslim Historiography* (2d ed.; Leiden: Brill, 1968) 150–75.

5. When he uses the word *city*, Neusner means metropolises such as Alexandria. He tends to refer to the larger places in Eretz Israel where Jews were a sizable proportion of the population as either "towns" or "villages." His point is that the rabbis, for the most part, lived in such places (with few exceptions, such as R. Abbahu of Caesarea) and viewed them in their halakic discussions as "economic units" consisting of "a group of households made up of individual households." So, even though Neusner has in mind the larger metropolis in the statement quoted here, it still reflects his observation that the rabbis had little interest in the concept of the city per se. Neusner suggests that it was only when Jews found themselves in larger metropolises living among a majority of non-Jews that they experienced the self-consciousness that results in self-differentiation. See J. Neusner, "The City as Useless Symbol in Late Antique Judaism," *Major Trends in Formative Judaism 1: Society and Symbol in Political Crisis* (BJS 60; Chico, Calif.: Scholars Press, 1983) 29–40, quotation from p. 29. In this regard, Philo's observations on city life are especially interesting. The Alexandrian Jewish philosopher comments on the evils of the city and regards Moses as the lawgiver to the urban centers. See B. W. Winter, *Seek the Welfare of the City: Christians as Benefactors and Citizens* (Grand Rapids, Mich.: Eerdmans, 1994) 205–7. Cf. Storoni Mazzolani, *The Idea of the City in Roman Thought*, 77–79. On Philo's view of Jerusalem, see below.

6. E. Rivkin, "The Internal City: Judaism and Urbanization," *JSSR* 5 (1966) 225–40. This, of course, has not prevented modern historians from attempting to reconstruct the history of the Jewish centers of Eretz Israel. Most recently, Levine (*Caesarea under Roman Rule*) and J. Schwartz (*Lod (Lydda), Israel: From Its Origins through the Byzantine Period, 5600 B.C.E.–640 C.E.* [Oxford: Tempus Reparatum, 1991]) have written comprehensive views of Caesarea and Lod. A closer look, however, reveals that both of these works are more selective than their titles would suggest. Levine, for example, wisely chose to concentrate on the Herodian and First Revolt administrative center that emerges in the writings of Josephus and then on the distinct Jewish and non-Jewish communities of Caesarea alluded to in the later rabbinic, pagan, and patristic materials. Schwartz ambitiously titles one section of his work "the story of Lod" and attempts also to provide a physical description of the

With regard to Sepphoris, this lack of sustained interest in urban developments has made historical reconstruction hazardous. True, our richest source, talmudic literature, provides hundreds of references to the city—not to mention the names of people, mostly rabbis, who actually lived there. Moreover, Josephus comments on various episodes in the history of the city. These sources, however, pose serious challenges to the historian, who must consider the obvious textual difficulties, while keeping in mind that Josephus and the rabbis wrote in distinct periods and had different interests. In *Studies in the History and Traditions of Sepphoris* and subsequent efforts,[7] I intentionally concentrated on select topics and on the methodological issues they present with the hope of gaining better control over the evidence.

I would like to revisit and expand upon some of my findings to emphasize the advantages of such an approach. To begin, a review of earlier inquiries into the history of Sepphoris and some of the more influential and enduring misconceptions that have resulted is in order. Sepphoris has long been of interest to talmudic historians. Two in particular, A. Büchler and Samuel Klein, wrote at length about the city. In 1909 Büchler, who trained in Budapest and Breslau before becoming the principal of Jews' College in London in 1907, published *The Political and Social Leaders of Sepphoris in the Second and Third Centuries*.[8] This influential work explored social tensions within Sepphorean society and generally painted a picture in which the aristocrats and rabbis were at each others' throats. The wealthy leaders of Sepphoris refused to support the sages and also took advantage of the poor. The sages accused these leaders of corruption and also charged them and, for that matter, the commoners, with licentious behavior. Büchler further promoted this theme in his relatively unknown "Familienreinheit und Sittlichkeit in Sepphoris im zweiten Jahrhundert," which appeared in 1934.[9] In this article, Büchler describes the moral life of the Sepphoreans, who he claims indulged in all sorts of forbidden sexual liaisons.

After reading Büchler, one is likely to ask why the rabbis would have moved to Sepphoris in the first place! Indeed, one cannot help wondering whether Büchler's known difficulties with the Anglo-Jewish community and with the chief rabbinate of England colored his perspective of ancient Jewish communal life. Büchler was known for his insistence on the scholarly preparation of students for the ministry, which led him to question the competence of ministers appointed by the chief rabbinate who were not graduates of Jews'

---

city, which he calls its "morphology." Here, too, an interesting but, of necessity, selective account emerges. Likewise, B. Z. Rosenfeld, *Lod and Its Sages in the Period of the Mishnah and the Talmud* (Jerusalem: Yad Itzhak Ben-Zvi, 1997). For historical writing on Sepphoris, see below.

7. S. S. Miller, *Studies in the History and Traditions of Sepphoris* (Leiden: Brill, 1984). Other relevant articles will be cited below.

8. Büchler, *Political and Social Leaders of Sepphoris* (London: Jew's College, 1909).

9. Idem, "Familienreinheit," *MGWJ* 78 (1934) 126–64.

College.[10] I have dealt with Büchler's portrayal of the Sepphoreans at length elsewhere.[11] Suffice it to say that his conclusions are based on a rather imaginative reading of the sources. In addition, Büchler resorts to statements attributed to rabbis who had only the scarcest connection with Sepphoris. The societal tensions he assigns to the city, therefore, have been much exaggerated and, in any event, could have been found in any of the larger towns of Galilee and the Roman Near East.

Similar methodological problems apply to Büchler's "*Minim* of Sepphoris and Tiberias in the Second and Third Centuries."[12] Again, as I have pointed out in my studies on the *minim*,[13] Büchler resorts to much evidence that has little or nothing to do with either Sepphoris or Tiberias. Interestingly, despite the fact that this essay is often alluded to by those wishing to prove that Jewish Christians could be found in the cities of talmudic Galilee, Büchler never says that the *minim* were to be so identified. Rather, he claims, most *minim* were "Bible reading heathen" and antinomian Gnostics—a view that points to the difficulty in fine tuning our understanding of the few *minim* associated with Sepphoris and Tiberias.

Klein's approach to the history of Sepphoris was considerably different. A Hungarian-born historical geographer trained in Berlin, Klein, in 1929, was appointed to the faculty of the Hebrew University in Jerusalem. His approach to the history of settlement ("Siedlungsgeschichte") in Eretz Israel was driven by his determination to foster knowledge of the ancient homeland of the Jews among the residents of the *yishuv* of his day. Indeed, for Klein, knowledge of the land (*yedi'at ha-'arez*) was essential to national rejuvenation.[14] Klein devoted himself to an intensive investigation of place references in rabbinic literature. He discusses Sepphoris most comprehensively in a little-known

10. See A. M. Hyamson, *Jews' College, London: 1855–1955* (London: Jews' College, 1955) 85–88; and A. Tobias, "Adolf Buechler," *EncJud* 4.1459.

11. See my "Cantankerous Sepphoreans Revisited."

12. Originally published as Büchler, "Über die Minim von Sepphoris und Tiberias im zweiten und dritten Jahrhundert," *Judaica: Festschrift zu Hermann Cohens siebzigstem Geburtstage* (Berlin: Cassirer, 1912) 271–95. The English version appeared in A. Büchler, *Studies in Jewish History: The Adolf Büchler Memorial Volume* (London: Oxford University Press, 1956) 245–74.

13. S. S. Miller, "The *Minim* of Sepphoris Reconsidered," *HTR* 86 (1993) 377–402; and idem, "Further Thoughts on the Minim of Sepphoris," *Proceedings of the Eleventh World Congress of Jewish Studies*, division B, vol. 1: *The History of the Jewish People* (Jerusalem: World Union of Jewish Studies, 1994) 1–8.

14. Klein especially wanted to show that Eretz Israel remained settled even after the destruction of the Temple and the Bar Kokhba Revolt. See S. Klein (ed.), *The Book of the Settlement: The Settlement and Its Locations from the Days of the Destruction of the Second Temple until the Arab Conquest of 'Erez Yisra'el* (reprint ed.; Jerusalem: Yad Itzhak Ben-Zvi, 1977) 1.14 [Hebrew]. Also cf. D. S. Levinger, "Professor Shemuel Klein (1886–1940)," in *The Wisdom of Israel in Western Europe* (ed. S. Federbusch; Jerusalem/Tel Aviv: Nyuman, Ogen, 1963) 2.240–48 [Hebrew]; and especially Klein's introductory remarks to "Zippori," *Various Essays Pertaining to the Study of 'Erez Yisra'el* (Vienna: Menorah, 1924) 44–47 [Hebrew].

article of 1924, "Zippori."[15] Unlike Büchler, who looked to reconstruct aspects of society at Sepphoris that are not explicitly described in the sources, Klein confined his interests to realia that were more evident. He categorizes and discusses the information provided by the sages under the following rubrics: location, physical description and buildings, historical notices, the sages, residents, Sepphoris and Tiberias, the city environs, and, finally, the geographic limits of Sepphoris. Klein often resorted to epigraphic and archaeological evidence to further an understanding of these categories, often to much advantage. While his harmonization of the literary sources would be regarded as uncritical by today's standards, Klein did succeed in providing a useful collection and assessment of the materials, one that has clearly served as an inspiration for others. Here the recent effort of Yehuda Ne'eman to describe Sepphoris in the Second Temple and Talmudic Periods immediately comes to mind.[16]

Despite advances in talmudic methodology and Josephean studies, the temptation to harmonize the sources, now including the archaeological data, continues to result in gross and misleading generalizations. Thus we hear that first-century Sepphoris, the "ornament of all Galilee"[17] as Josephus refers to it, maintained a large priestly community and was primarily an aristocratic center, which is the reason it chose to sit out the First Revolt.[18] Jesus, a resident of the small nearby village of Nazareth, would have known about the city and perhaps even spent time there.[19] The *minim*, or "heretics," who resided in the city are thought to have constituted a well-defined and significant group of Jewish Christians.[20] The city once again had a special relationship with Rome in the late second and early third centuries when Rabbi Judah ha-Nasi and the 'holy council' (ἱερᾶς βουλῆς) entered into an "alliance" with Rome.[21] Local tensions with Tiberias, which Josephus describes for the period leading up to the First Revolt,[22] endured. Thus, we hear that

---

15. See previous note. Cf. S. Klein, *Beiträge zur Geographie und Geschichte Galiläas* (Leipzig: Haupt, 1909) 26–45.

16. See the table of contents in Y. Ne'eman, *Sepphoris in the Period of the Second Temple, the Mishnah and the Talmud* (Jerusalem: Shem, 1993) [Hebrew], where many of the chapter headings are similar to Klein's.

17. Josephus *Ant.* 18.27.

18. See S. Freyne, *Galilee from Alexander the Great to Hadrian, 323 B.C.E. to 135 C.E.* (Wilmington, Del.: Glazier, 1980) 126–28.

19. The idea that Jesus had some connection with the city was first put forth in the early part of the century and has most recently been resuscitated by R. A. Batey, *Jesus and the Forgotten City: New Light on Sepphoris and the Urban World of Jesus* (Grand Rapids, Mich.; Baker, 1991).

20. See, for example, F. Manns, *Essais sur le judéo-christianisme* (Jerusalem: Franciscan, 1977) 165–90; J. F. Strange, "Sepphoris," *ABD* 5.1090–93; and E. M. Meyers, E. Netzer, and C. L. Meyers, *Sepphoris* (Winona Lake, Ind.: Eisenbrauns, 1992) 16.

21. Y. Meshorer, "Sepphoris and Rome," *Greek Numismatics and Archaeology: Essays in Honor of Margaret Thompson* (Wetteren: NR, 1979) 166–70.

22. Josephus *Life* 36–39.

the two cities were rivals until Tiberias eclipsed Sepphoris sometime in the
third century.[23] Earlier, during the time of Judah, Sepphoris was in its heyday.[24] Just the same, the city was never able to shake its image as a center of
cantankerous and ill-willed personalities.[25] Sepphoris is regarded as a predominantly Jewish city, despite its recasting as Diocaesarea in the second century. We are especially reminded that by the time of Judah ha-Nasi there were
some eighteen synagogues in the city.[26] Indeed, the Hellenistic veneer that
has been revealed by the excavations still comes as a surprise to those whose
impression of Sepphoris is one of a rabbinic center that achieved its glory in
the early third century when the Sanhedrin and patriarchate moved there.

I have dealt with many of these perceptions elsewhere. The question of
Jesus and the city has been sufficiently addressed by me and others.[27] My recent study of Sepphorean society will hopefully shift the discussion away
from the negative characterization of the population.[28] In *Studies in the History and Traditions of Sepphoris*, I showed that the rabbis' use of the term
castra clearly indicates that they were cognizant of a Roman presence at Sepphoris, especially within the fortified acropolis where Roman soldiers were
stationed after 67 C.E. Other rabbinic traditions make it clear that the Jews
constituted the majority within the city but were very much aware that they
had Gentiles as neighbors.[29] The number of synagogues in Sepphoris and in
other cities of Eretz Israel is the subject of another of my recent studies.[30] In

23. See M. Goodman, *State and Society in Roman Galilee, A.D. 132–212* (Totowa, N.J.:
Rowman & Allanheld, 1983) 134; L. Levine, "R. Simeon b. Yoḥai and the Purification of
Tiberias: History and Tradition," *HUCA* 49 (1978) 176; and R. Kimelman, *Rabbi Yoḥanan
of Tiberias: Aspects of the Social and Religious History of Third Century Palestine* (Ph.D.
Diss., Yale University, 1977) 51, 54, and 84 n. 39.

24. See A. Oppenheimer, *Galilee in the Mishnaic Period* (Jerusalem: Shazar, 1991) 69
[Hebrew].

25. See especially, A. Büchler, *The Political and Social Leaders of the Jewish Community of Sepphoris in the Second and Third Centuries* (London: Jew's College, 1909); and
S. Lieberman, *Texts and Studies* (New York: Ktav, 1974) 124, 146, and 186.

26. Most recently, Z. Weiss and E. Netzer, *Promise and Redemption: A Synagogue Mosaic from Sepphoris* (Jerusalem: The Israel Museum, 1996) 11.

27. See my "Sepphoris, the Well Remembered City," *BA* 55 (1992) 74–83; S. Freyne,
Galilee, Jesus and the Gospels: Literary Approaches and Historical Investigations (Philadel-
phia: Fortress, 1988) 140; and E. P. Sanders, "Jesus' Relation to Sepphoris," in *Sepphoris in
Galilee: Crosscurrents of Culture* (ed. R. M. Nagy et al.; Raleigh, N.C.: North Carolina
Museum of Art, 1996) 75–79.

28. See my "Cantankerous Sepphoreans Revisited."

29. See Klein, "Ẓippori," 52–53, 61; and Ne'eman, *Sepphoris in the Period of the Second Temple, the Mishnah and the Talmud*, 290–303. A further consideration of the non-
Jewish presence will appear in my forthcoming *Ancient Sepphoris and Historical Memory*
(tentative title).

30. Miller, "On the Number of Synagogues in the Cities of ʾErez Israel," *JJS* 49 (1998)
51–66. Cf. idem, "The Rabbis and the Non-existent Monolithic Synagogue," in *Jews, Christians and Polytheists in the Ancient Synagogue* (ed. S. Fine; London: Routledge, forthcoming) 57–70.

brief, the tradition in *y. Kil.* 9.32b that has been understood to mean that there were eighteen synagogues in Sepphoris in fact is open to other more convincing interpretations and has to be understood in the context of rabbinic accounts pertaining to the numbers of synagogues in other cities of Eretz Israel.

Some of the remaining perceptions, although discussed in my earlier work, can bear further discussion. There is no question that first-century Sepphoris, situated at the crossroads of Lower Galilee, is an important link in appreciating the milieu of early Christianity. Nevertheless, there is little direct evidence of any kind connecting the city with Christianity before the Byzantine Period.[31] Attempts to identify distinct groups of Jewish Christians in the Galilee of the rabbis remain forced and are largely dependent on the reading of later Byzantine sources that report the existence of such groups back into the earlier period. The *minim* of rabbinic literature are mostly individuals who maintained heretical views or practices and not well-defined groups of Christians or Gnostics. Moreover, to project these persons onto the epoch of Jesus is often an anachronistic usage of the references. The single source that unequivocally refers to a *min* at Sepphoris who espoused a teaching of Jesus, *t. Ḥul.* 2.24, actually refers to a person visiting from elsewhere in the early second century and hardly points to a *community* of like-minded people in the city then or earlier. Rather, it suggests that *individuals* who either taught in the name of Jesus or found teachings attributed to him attractive could be found in Galilee. What the *minim* passages do drive home is that there were individual Jews in Galilee who harbored nonrabbinic views. Whatever the extent of rabbinic influence in Galilee, the rabbis reveal an awareness that Jewish society included others besides themselves, which is precisely the point. Sepphoris may very well have been primarily a Jewish city, but this in no way rules out diversity within its population. Rabbis, Jews, Jewish Gnostics, and Jewish Christians may be distinguishable as distinct types and groups in our minds but were less so in the eyes of first-century Galileans.[32]

---

31. Late fourth- early fifth-century sherds with Byzantine cross monograms are the earliest Christian artifacts found so far. See Meyers et al., "Ornament of All Galilee," *BA* 49 (1986) 18; and Nagy, *Sepphoris in Galilee*, 66, 208. The Council at Chalcedon (451 C.E.) included a bishop from Diocaesarea, Dorotheus. See G. D. Mansi, *Sacrorum conciliorum nova et amplissima collectio* (Florence and Venice: Zatta, 1759–98) 6.1091E. For bishops of the sixth century in Diocaesarea, see Mansi, 8.1071C and 8.1174C. Cf. M. Avi-Yonah, "A Sixth Century Inscription from Sepphoris," *IEJ* 11 (1961) 187. Also see B. Bagatti, *The Church from the Gentiles in Palestine* (trans. E. Hoade; Jerusalem: Franciscan, 1971) 94; and Manns, *Essais sur le judéo-christianisme*, 165–90, 179. For a recently-found inscription mentioning "Eutropius the Episcopus" and the remains of a late fifth- or sixth-century church at Sepphoris, see E. Netzer and Z. Weiss, "New Evidence for Late-Roman and Byzantine Sepphoris," *The Roman and Byzantine Near East: Some Recent Archaeological Research* (JRA Supp. 14; Ann Arbor, Mich.: JRA, 1995) 171–73.

32. See my "*Minim* of Sepphoris Reconsidered," 377–402. Freyne contends that the Jewish Christians described by Epiphanius (315–403 C.E.) had "definite similarities with the

Interestingly, we see a similar tendency to project a later situation into the first and earlier centuries with regard to the priests. Recent studies by Dalia Trifon have corroborated my earlier finding with regard to Sepphoris that there is no evidence for the removal and consolidation of the priestly *mishmarot* from Judah to Galilee before the third century, at the very earliest.[33] This is not to say that there were no *kohanim* in first- and second-century Sepphoris. Rather, like the *minim*, the priests in the city at that time were *individuals* who did not necessarily represent a larger group—in this instance Yed'ayah, the *mishmar* later associated with Sepphoris. During this earlier period, the proportion of priests to other residents at Sepphoris was probably similar to the proportion elsewhere in Galilee. It follows that the *supposed* preponderance of priests in the city at this time cannot be used to explain the great number of structures tentatively identified as *miqva'ot* from the Early Roman Period.

The assumed persistence of a rivalry between Sepphoris and Tiberias is a good example of the forced conflation of information provided by Josephus and the Talmud. Josephus's *Life* 36–39 describes the demotion of Tiberias during the reign of Nero, when Sepphoris replaced it as the capital of Galilee. Josephus attributes to Justus of Tiberias a speech in which he expresses the resentment felt by the Tiberians toward Sepphoris as a result of their city's loss of status. Attempts to find hints in talmudic literature of an ongoing rivalry of the type that is known to have existed between cities in the Roman Near East are futile. Rather than support the notion of a rivalry, the talmudic materials that mention both Tiberias and Sepphoris in the same context present them in a harmonious relationship.[34] Evidently, there was room in

Galilean *minim/noẓrim* from Sepphoris and Kefar Sekhanyah." This, however, reads much too much into *t. Ḥul.* 2.24 and is an example of the generalization from later to earlier periods. Freyne does, however, admit that "the literary evidence leaves many unanswered questions about Christians in Galilee . . ." and that "it has not yet been possible to trace fully a . . . trajectory for Christians at Sepphoris." See S. Freyne, "Christianity in Sepphoris and in Galilee," in *Sepphoris in Galilee: Crosscurrents of Culture* (ed. R. M. Nagy et al.; Raleigh, N.C.: North Carolina Museum of Art, 1996) 67–73. Nor does the allusion to 24 divisions (*kittot*) of *minim* in *y. Sanh.* 10.29c, which is attributed to the third-century sage R. Yoḥanan of Tiberias, suggest the existence of such groups. See my "Further Thoughts on the Minim of Sepphoris," 5. For a recent discussion of the difficulty in locating Jewish Christians in Galilee, see J. E. Taylor, *Christians and the Holy Places: The Myth of Jewish-Christian Origins* (Oxford: Clarendon, 1993). Again, my point is that Jews who held views associated with Christianity could be found in Roman Palestine, but there is no indication that they thought of themselves as belonging to distinct social groupings. In all likelihood, they did not.

33. See my *Studies in the History and Traditions of Sepphoris*, 62–132. Cf. D. Trifon, "Did the Priestly Courses Move from Judah to Galilee after the Bar Kokhba Revolt?" *Tarbiz* 59 (1990) 77–93 [Hebrew]. Trifon's article is based on her unpublished doctoral dissertation.

34. See my "Intercity Relations in Roman Palestine: The Case of Sepphoris and Tiberias," *AJS Review* 12 (1987) 1–24.

Much has been written about the removal of the patriarchate from Beth She'arim to Sepphoris and the seventeen-year tenure of Judah ha-Nasi in Sepphoris.[35] We especially hear that there must have been more to Judah's move than the claim of the Talmud that the pleasant air of Sepphoris was beneficial to the ailing patriarch, who moved there for his remaining years.[36] Thus, it is presumed that the *nasi* wished to elevate the status of the patriarchate by associating with an urban center.[37] In turn, the patriarch brought prestige to the city, not only through the presence of his court, but also by virtue of his work on the Mishna, which he is presumed to have completed there.[38]

While Judah's move to Sepphoris undoubtedly had important implications for the city and especially for the rabbinic class, it should not be seen as the single development that, all of a sudden in the early third century, catapulted the town to center stage of rabbinic history. This, in fact, is an inversion of the actual state of affairs. Sepphoris was already a great rabbinic center by the time Judah arrived. This in no small way was the achievement of R. Yose ben Halafta, who appears some three hundred times in the Mishna of Judah. Indeed, it is likely that the *nasi* resorted to a preexisting collection of views attributed to Yose in his final, composite work.[39] In later, Babylonian traditions, Judah reversed his own halakic decisions in favor of those of Yose and referred to him with titles of respect.[40] This perception of Yose seems premised on that of the Jerusalem Talmud, which has Judah contrast the generation of Yose with his own. The difference between the two, Judah reportedly said is, "like that between holy things and profane."[41] Yose's son, Ishmael,

---

35. See *y. Kil.* 9.32b; *y. Ketub.* 12.35a; and parallels. Cf. Y. Cohen, "Did the Patriarchate Move to Tiberias and [if so] When?" *Zion* 39 (1974) 114–22 [Hebrew]; and S. Safrai, "Beit She'arim in Talmudic Literature," reprinted in idem, *In Times of Temple and Mishnah: Studies in Jewish History* (Jerusalem: Magnes, 1994) 1.187–90 [Hebrew].

36. *B. Ketub.* 103b.

37. See the discussions of Cohen, "Did the Patriarchate Move?" and Safrai, "Beit She'arim."

38. See Oppenheimer, *Galilee in the Mishnaic Period*, 68–69.

39. It should be recalled that Yose was a disciple of Akiva, whose mishna collection was also utilized by Judah. On Yose's contribution to the Mishna, see J. N. Epstein, *Introduction to the Literature of the Tanna'im* (Tel Aviv: Devir, 1957) 126–47 [Hebrew].

40. See *y. Git.* 6.48b. Judah reverses his decision in *b. Šabb.* 51a (= *b. Sanh.* 24a), where he reportedly says, *kevar horeh ha-Zaqen* 'the elder (*zaqen*) already decided'. Also see *b. Hul.* 137a, where the title *beribbi* is used by Judah in reference to Yose and cf. *b. Yebam.* 105b, where the term is again applied to him. *Beribbi* apparently connotes a great scholar. It appears in both Greek (βηρεβι) and Aramaic synagogue inscriptions. See J. Naveh, *On Mosaic and Stone: The Aramaic and Hebrew Inscriptions from Ancient Synagogues* (Jerusalem: Erets Yisrael ve-Atikoteha, 1978) 72, 74, and 116. In Palestinian sources, *beribbi* is frequently used by R. Simeon ben Gamaliel, Judah's father, in reference to Yose. See *t. Ber.* 5.2; *t. Dem.* 3.14; *t. Sukk.* 2.2 (= *y. Sukk.* 2.53a). These sources clearly convey the impression that Yose was remembered as a scholar who was held in esteem by the patriarchal house. Cf. D. Zlotnick, *The Iron Pillar-Mishnah: Redaction, Form, and Intent* (Jerusalem: Bialik, 1988) 172.

41. *Y. Git.* 6.48b.

who passed on his father's traditions, would become a prominent member of Judah's circle at Sepphoris.[42] In all likelihood, it was the renown of the already-existing rabbinic infrastructure at Sepphoris—even more than the desire to be where the administrative authorities and institutions were—that enticed Judah there.

The truth is, there is little information regarding the activities of the patriarch at Sepphoris. Only two halakic decisions attributed to Judah explicitly mention the city. One pertains to sabbatical year produce, another to the *kashrut* of meat purchased in the city's *macellum* (meat market). These appear in the Jerusalem Talmud.[43] The Babylonian Talmud preserves reports of the chief butcher of Sepphoris before Rabbi Judah, but the Palestinian parallel fails to mention the patriarch.[44] The Babylonian also has a discussion of a report that Rabbi Judah once bathed in the spring of Sepphoris on a fast day, when such ablutions were ordinarily prohibited.[45] Aside from accounts pertaining to Judah's last testament and death at Sepphoris,[46] the only other aggadic passage in which he appears has him studying Torah before the synagogue of the Babylonians in the city.[47] Nowhere is it stated that Judah completed work on the Mishna at Sepphoris, however logical that frequently-heard assertion may seem. Interestingly, in its list of the leading *battei din* of Eretz Israel, *b. Sanh.* 32b assigns the *yeshivah*, here meaning 'court', of R. Yose ben Ḥalafta to Sepphoris and that of Judah to Beth She'arim. The passage draws our attention once again to the acclaim that Sepphoris had received before the *nasi* arrived and reminds us that for the better part of his life he was associated with Beth She'arim. Only a much later letter of Sherira Gaon (ca. 906–1006), found in the Cairo Genizah, reworks the narrative so that the court of Judah not only is assigned to Sepphoris but also represents the apogee of rabbinic history in the city.[48]

Sherira had his reasons for emphasizing the importance of Judah's court, reasons I explore in a forthcoming article.[49] I do not wish to suggest here that Judah's presence at Sepphoris was of little consequence. As the *nasi*, he un-

---

42. See J. Neusner, "An Aristocrat of the Intellect," *History and Torah: Essays on Jewish Learning* (New York: Schocken, 1965) 103–21.

43. Y. Šeb. 6.37a; y. Šeqal. 7.50c.

44. See b. Ḥul. 50b and 58b and the parallel in t. Ḥul. 3.2 (ed. Zuckermandel).

45. B. Meg. 5b.

46. y. Ta'an. 4.68a; Qoh. Rab. 7:7; and y. Kil. 9.32b. See my "R. Hanina bar Hama at Sepphoris," in *The Galilee in Late Antiquity* (ed. L. I. Levine; New York: Jewish Theological Seminary, 1992) 194–97.

47. Gen. Rab. 33:3.

48. T-S. 10 J1. See S. Schechter, *Saadyana: Genizah Fragments of Writings of R. Saadya Gaon and Others* (Cambridge: Deighton and Bell, 1903) 119; and B. M. Levin (ed.), "Various Collections," *The Letters of Rav Sherira Ga'on* (Haifa: Ittskoviski, 1921) xxvii [Hebrew]. See next note.

49. S. S. Miller, "Sepphoris and the Diaspora: The Lasting Influence of a Galilean Talmudic Center" (ed. I . Gafni, L. H. Schiffman, and A. Baumgarten; Jerusalem: Zalman Shazar, forthcoming) [Hebrew].

doubtedly enhanced the prestige and academic standing of the city. His move to Sepphoris, however, should not be seen as a surprising development, and his death hardly marked the decline of the city as a rabbinic center. The rabbis would continue to thrive at Sepphoris just as before. R. Ḥanina bar Ḥama, one of Judah's disciples, would emerge as the leading sage.[50] Indeed, with the exception of Yose ben Ḥalafta, Hanina appears in far more Sepphoris-related passages than any other sage, certainly more than Judah. Ḥanina's students at Sepphoris included R. Yoḥanan and Resh Laqish, who would eventually bring fame to Tiberias. These sages also kept the lines of communication open with their counterparts in Sepphoris. Thus, rabbinic sources preserve accounts of third-century sages "going up" from Tiberias to Sepphoris.[51] Furthermore, certain *Zippora'ei* ('Sepphoreans') appear to have served at Tiberias as a conduit for traditions that emanated from Sepphoris.[52] In the late third and fourth centuries, R. Huna *Rova* ('the great') *De-Zipporin*, R. Ḥiyya *Zippora'ah*, R. Ḥanan/Ḥanin *De-Zippori*, R. Avdima *De-Zipporin*, R. Mana, and R. Ḥanina *De-Zippori* were associated with Sepphoris.[53] While Tiberias emerged in the late third century as the most influential rabbinic center, this was in no small part due to the earlier flourishing of the rabbinic class at Sepphoris. Despite the ascendancy of Tiberias, the academies in Sepphoris continued to prosper, much as those at Caesarea and Lud did.[54]

The relationship of Sepphoris to Rome also requires a more nuanced appreciation. To be sure, Sepphoris gained a reputation as a "City of Peace," not only according to those who minted coins in 67 C.E. with the title *Eirenopolis*, but also in the eyes of Josephus, who generally presents the city as pro-Roman. But was it really so? Most historians discount statements in the *Jewish War* that ill will toward Rome existed in Sepphoris, preferring instead the supposedly more consistent account in the *Life*.[55] The *Jewish War* relates (2.574)[56]

50. For what follows, see my "R. Ḥanina bar Ḥama at Sepphoris."
51. See my "Intercity Relations in Roman Palestine," 12–13.
52. Other Zippora'ei appear to have been mere commoners. Still others had more informal contacts with the sages. See my "*Zippora'ei, Tibera'ei* and *Deroma'ei*: Their Origins, Interests and Relationship," *Proceedings of the Tenth World Congress of Jewish Studies*, division B, vol. 2: *History of the Jewish People* (Jerusalem: World Union of Jewish Studies, 1990) 16–17; and idem, "R. Ḥanina bar Ḥama at Sepphoris," 181–84.
53. See H. Albeck, *Mavo' La-Talmudim* (Tel Aviv: Devir, 1969) 233 (R. Huna Rova'), 325 (R. Ḥiyya *Zippora'ah*), 385 (R. Avdima *De-Zipporin*), 393 (R. Ḥanina *De-Zippori*), and 398 (R. Mana). R. Ḥanan *De-Zippori* appears in *Gen. Rab.* 10:4 and 13:9. The large number of sages who are designated 'of Sepphoris' (*de-Zippori*, etc.) may reflect the perspective of the Tiberian editors of many of the documents and traditions in which these sages appear. Cf. my "*Zippora'ei, Tibera'ei* and *Deroma'ei*," 20.
54. See Levine, *Caesarea under Roman Rule*, 86–97; and Schwartz, *Lod (Lydda), Israel*, 101–20.
55. See, especially, S. J. D. Cohen, *Josephus in Galilee and Rome: His Vita and Development as a Historian* (Leiden: Brill, 1979) 245–48.
56. Translations of the *Life* and *Jewish War* of Josephus follow H. St. J. Thackeray (trans.) (LCL; Cambridge: Harvard University Press, 1926–28).

that Josephus found the city "eager for hostilities," so he allowed the Sepphoreans to erect their own walls. Later in the same work (3.59–62), Josephus relates that he had a difficult time capturing Sepphoris when Vespasian sent along support for its inhabitants because he himself had fortified the city "before it had abandoned the Galilean cause."

In the *Jewish War* Josephus might have wanted to emphasize the military challenge he faced and the lengths to which he went to get Sepphoris to join the revolt, as Shaye J. D. Cohen contends.[57] However, Josephus is not immune to exaggeration in his *Life* either. Nor is the presentation in his autobiography entirely consistent. Thus, *Life* 346–48 records that the Sepphoreans failed to send assistance to Jerusalem when the capital was under siege "to avoid all suspicion of having borne arms against Rome." Does this mean that they actually contemplated helping the Jerusalemites? A closer reading of the *Life* reveals that Josephus contrasts pro-Roman Sepphoris with Tiberias, which ultimately joined the revolt. He clearly exaggerates to heighten the effect. *Life* 30 reports that upon Josephus's first arrival at Sepphoris, he found the *Sepphorites* in distress. The Galileans, he says, were planning to attack the city because of its "overtures of loyalty and allegiance" to the Romans. Josephus then says (31) that he intervened with the Galileans and further calmed the fears of the *Sepphorites* by allowing them to communicate with their fellow citizens held hostage by Cestius Gallus at Dor. At this point, Josephus pointedly turns to the situation at Tiberias, which had already "proceeded to hostilities." In the ensuing narrative Justus, who was "eager for revolution," recalls that Sepphoris had been promoted to capital of Galilee at the expense of Tiberias.[58] In his harangue against the Tiberians, Justus urges them to "take up arms" along with the Galileans against Sepphoris. Thus in the *Life*, written long after the *Jewish War*, Josephus would have us believe that he maintained the peace at Sepphoris while Justus inflamed passions at Tiberias. One way or another, the situations at Sepphoris and Tiberias are contrasted in the extreme.[59]

Perhaps Sepphoris really did make "overtures" to Rome but had at one time inclined toward revolt, as the *Jewish War* suggests. Otherwise, it is difficult to explain why the Romans took hostages, who were ordinarily seized to guarantee the allegiance of the conquered.[60] There must have been factions in the city that indeed sympathized with the Galilean cause and/or a period

---

57. Cohen, *Josephus in Galilee and Rome*, 214.

58. See discussion above.

59. Cf. S. Freyne, "Galilee-Jewish Relations in the Light of Josephus' Vita," *NTS* 33 (1987) 603; and T. Rajak, *Josephus: The Historian and His Society* (London: Duckworth, 1983) 153.

60. See A. D. Lee, "The Role of Hostages in Roman Diplomacy with Sasanian Persia," *Historia* 40 (1991) 366–374; and my "Josephus on the Cities of Galilee: Factions, Rivalries and Alliances in the First Jewish Revolt" (forthcoming).

in which the *Sepphorites* as a whole leaned in that direction.[61] Do a couple of coins minted by elites within the city really refract the sentiments of others beside the powers that be?[62] Moreover, is it likely that Sepphoris was so different from other towns, such as Gischala, Gamla, and Tiberias, all of which had both prorevolt and propeace factions?[63] True, the prorevolt party would prevail in these towns, but all this means is that the peace party in Sepphoris may have been more pronounced and more influential. It does not preclude the likelihood that Sepphoris too had rebellious factions—at least at the outset of the war.[64]

Once again, the temptation to generalize from one period to another must be resisted. Talmudic sources preserve various conversations between Judah ha-Nasi and one Antoninus, presumably a high Roman official, often thought to be Caracalla or some other emperor.[65] While these encounters are of doubtful historicity, they should not be seen as an indication that the peaceful proclivity of the Sepphoreans persisted or resurfaced long after the First Revolt. The Antoninus traditions serve to glorify the patriarch, who we hear is even consulted by the emperor on all sorts of governmental and personal matters. Why, Antoninus even studies Torah with Judah and helps him into bed![66]

True, legends appearing on coins of Caracalla and Elagabalus from Sepphoris have been interpreted as references to an alliance between the Roman Senate, the people of Rome, and the holy council of Sepphoris. Although the "holy council" has been taken to mean the court, or even the Sanhedrin, of the patriarch R. Judah ha-Nasi,[67] the phrase more likely refers to the Roman Senate, as it does on other imperial issues. Properly read, these issues also do not refer to a formal alliance. Instead, they allude to Sepphoris as a "friend and ally" of the Romans and their Senate, a common boast of urban elites throughout the empire. At most, the Sepphoreans who minted these coins

---

61. H. W. Hoehner (*Herod Antipas: A Contemporary of Jesus Christ* [Cambridge: Cambridge University Press, 1972] 87) is almost certainly wrong that the people of Sepphoris had learned their lesson in 4 B.C.E., when Varus burned the city and enslaved its inhabitants. If anything, those who remembered the destruction would have harbored resentment and distrust of the Romans.

62. Cf. L. Feldman, "Flavius Josephus Revisited: The Man, His Writings, and His Significance," *ANRW* II:21.2 (1984) 850.

63. See P. Bilde, *Flavius Josephus between Jerusalem and Rome: His Life, His Works, and Their Importance* (Sheffield: JSOT Press, 1988) 40–41.

64. For a fuller discussion, including the situation at Tarichaeae, see my "Josephus on the Cities of Galilee."

65. See S. Krauss, *Antoninus und Rabbi* (Vienna: Israel-Theologische Lehranstalt, 1910) and M. Avi-Yonah, *The Jews of Palestine: A Political History from the Bar Kokhba War to the Arab Conquest* (New York: Schocken, 1976) 39–42.

66. B. *'Abod. Zar.* 10b.

67. Meshorer, "Sepphoris and Rome," 168–70; idem, "The Coins of Sepphoris as an Historical Source," *Zion* 43 (1978) 194–99 [Hebrew].

would have based their claim on the ultimate faithfulness of the city during the First Revolt, or perhaps upon a more recent display of support for Rome.[68] Even so, the pacifism of yesteryear would have been no more than a well-kept memory, rather than an enduring characteristic of the residents of the city.[69]

We have reviewed a number of assertions regarding Sepphoris that, upon investigation, needed revision. In particular, we have sought to show that many generalizations have resulted from the tendency to harmonize the evidence of Josephus and the rabbis. Furthermore, we have argued for a closer reading of these and other sources, one that first attempts to understand what it is our sources are saying before their historical worth is even considered.

Our sources may not tell us as much as we would like to know about Sepphoris, but what Josephus and the rabbis provide us is not insignificant. While neither affords a chronological, in-depth treatment of the institutions and people who once lived in the city, we should not forget that we certainly would be left in the dark without them.

Only one city in antiquity captured the attention and imagination of all Jews and, for that matter, many others. That, of course, was Jerusalem, the city that Philo regarded as the "Metropolis"[70] of all Jews, and Pliny the Elder called "by far, the most famous city of the East."[71] In a remarkable passage in

68. See my "Intercity Relations in Roman Palestine," 6–7; and the more lengthy discussion of the legend in my "Cantankerous Sepphoreans Revisited." Cf. H. Lapin, *Early Rabbinic Civil Law and the Social History of Roman Galilee: A Study of Mishnah Tractate Baba' Meṣi'a'* (Atlanta: Scholars Press, 1995) 12 n. 28. K. Harl (*Civic Coins and Civic Politics in the Roman Near East, A.D. 180–275* [Berkeley: University of California Press, 1987] 81) suggests that the coins point to the possibility that the Diocaesareans supported Caracalla in the Parthian War, perhaps by providing supplies or recruits. Harl further speculates that the Diocaesareans later helped Elagabalus in his attempt to depose Emperor Macrinus.

69. Although the role of Sepphoris and, for that matter, of Galilee in the Bar Kokhba Revolt remains an open question, it should be remembered that the city certainly had periods in which opposition to the Romans was pronounced. This, of course, would be true of the insurrection of 4 B.C.E. and, if the argument presented above is correct, at the start of the First Revolt. Whatever the extent of the Gallus Revolt of 352 C.E., the whole incident points to the presence of anti-Roman sentiments in the city in the fourth century. On Bar Kokhba and Galilee, see my *Studies in the History and Traditions of Sepphoris*, 58–59, esp. n. 292; and M. Mor, *The Bar-Kokhba Revolt: Its Extent and Effect* (Jerusalem: Yad Izhak Ben-Zvi, 1991) 103–21 [Hebrew]. On Gallus, see B. Geller Nathanson, "Jews, Christians, and the Gallus Revolt in Fourth Century Palestine," *BA* 49 (1986) 26–36.

70. Cf. *Exod. Rab.* 23:10, which claims that Jerusalem will be the metropolis for all of the world (*likhol ha-arẓot*) in the time to come. See Urbach, "Jerusalem Below and the Heavenly Jerusalem," reprinted in *From the World of the Sages: A Collection of Studies* (Jerusalem: Magnes, 1988) 380 [Hebrew].

71. Pliny *Natural History* 5.70, as translated by H. Rackham (LCL; Cambridge: Harvard University Press, 1962). See M. Stern, *Greek and Latin Authors on Jews and Judaism* (Jerusalem: Israel Academy of Sciences and Humanities, 1976) 1.477–78; and idem, "Jerusalem the Most Famous of the Cities of the East," *Jerusalem in the Second Temple Period:*

the Babylonian Talmud that extols the virtues of Jerusalem and speaks of its future appearance and size, Resh Lakish, an erstwhile resident of third-century Sepphoris, says that, in the time to come, the Holy One, blessed be He, will add to Jerusalem thousands of gardens, towers, palaces, and monumental archways (*tetrapyla*). He then comments, "and each of these will be equal to those of Sepphoris in its period of tranquility."[72]

Sepphoris may not have had a historian in antiquity, but the legacy of the "Ornament of all Galilee" and of the city that, according to the rabbis, "sat on a hill like a bird,"[73] would endure just the same.

Abraham Schalit Memorial Volume (ed. A. Oppenheimer, U. Rappoport, and M. Stern; Jerusalem: Yad Izhak Ben-Zvi, 1980) 257–70 [Hebrew].

72. See *b. B. Bat.* 75b. The passage has a number of obscure terms, but the gist has been conveyed here. Cf. *Midr. Ps.* 48 and *Yal. Zech.* 568, neither of which has the gloss concerning Sepphoris. The passage in the Babylonian Talmud continues with the remark of R. Yose (ben Halafta) that he had seen Sepphoris in its period of tranquility and "it had a hundred and eighty thousand markets for potted meats."

73. *B. Meg.* 6a.

The Aqueducts to Sepphoris

Tsvika Tsuk
Nature and National Parks Protection Authority, Israel

> Rabbi Judah said: "Concerning the aqueduct that
> went from Avel to Zippori. . . ." (*b.* '*Erub.* 87a)

The ancient water systems that brought the precious fluid over long distances to cities of the known world in antiquity were a phenomenon of the first millennium B.C.E. In the kingdom of Urartu, the Menua channel was dug a distance of 56 km (35 miles) to Tuşpa, capital of King Menua; it is considered the world's first aqueduct.[1]

This technology was subsequently borrowed by their neighbors, the Assyrians. During the reign of Sennacherib, at the end of the eighth century B.C.E., the Assyrians brought water a distance of 54 km (34 miles) to Nineveh, their capital.[2] Although Nineveh was located on the banks of the Tigris River, the Assyrians brought water from a long distance away to ensure that the city would always have high-quality water at a level high enough to supply every place in the city where it was needed.

During the Persian and Hellenistic Periods (sixth–first centuries B.C.E.), many cities enjoyed aqueducts that brought perpetual running water, often from quite far away. It was not until the Roman Period, however, that most cities were served by aqueducts, and then to such an extent that the concept became one of the symbols of the Roman Empire. Frontius, water commissioner for the city of Rome sometime during the first century C.E., praised its aqueducts and commented on the difference between them and other constructions: "With such an array of indispensable structures carrying so many

---

1. Gunther Garbrecht, "The Water Supply System at Tuşpa (Urartu)," *World Archaeology* 11 (1980) 306–12.

2. T. Jacobsen and S. Lloyd, *Sennacherib's Aqueduct at Jerwan* (OIP 24; Chicago: University of Chicago Press, 1935).

waters, compare if you will, the idle Pyramids or the useless, though famous, works of the Greeks!"[3]

In the first century B.C.E. and the first century C.E., the Eternal City reached one of the peaks of its tumultuous history. During this time, nine aqueducts (with a total length of 425 km, or 264 miles) brought fresh, sweet water to the sovereign city-state from a variety of sources.[4]

In the first century B.C.E., the renowned Roman engineer and architect Vitruvius (ca. 90–20 B.C.E.) wrote the oldest extant Western treatise on architecture, *De Architectura* (the *Ten Books*), an invaluable document of Roman and Greek architectural history and building practices that for many centuries was the architectural textbook of the Classical world.[5] In book 8 he describes how to build water systems, including a number of canons that were the cornerstone of constructing and installing water systems in the ancient Roman world. Vitruvius discusses how to locate a spring or some other source of water and, if necessary, raise it to potable level; how to build a particular aqueduct in a specific topological location; how to ascertain the aqueduct's proper angle of descent, and with what instrument; how to overcome the problem of valleys by using arched bridgelike structures; and how to surmount the difficulties presented by a mountain along a route by tunneling through it; where to build reservoirs; how to distribute the water within a city; and more. Reading *De Architectura* today makes the reader feel he or she is taking part in creating a masterpiece. There is no doubt that the publication of Vitruvius's books and the dissemination of their construction theories enabled many an engineer in the Roman world to convert theory into practice.

The expansion of the Roman Empire into Mediterranean lands and into the vast areas of western Europe transmitted scientific and technological know-how throughout the provinces. Aqueducts sprang up like mushrooms all over the empire, bringing fresh water to many dozens of cities. It is absolutely certain that the source from which these were copied was the mighty water system of Rome itself.

Sepphoris was one of the Roman cities to which aqueducts were constructed. Like many other cities, Sepphoris existed as a settlement long before the time when its water system was planned. Bringing water by gravitation to a city built on a hill was no easy task. In a number of cities, the solution lay in using a stone or lead conduit whose point of origin was higher then the city, thus permitting water to be brought to the city's highest point. It was also possible to construct a high, arched bridge to carry the aqueduct at the required height. At Sepphoris, the aqueduct could not supply the very top of

3. Sextus Julius Frontius, *The Stratagems and the Aqueducts of Rome*, vol. 1/16: *The Aqueducts of Rome* (LCL; trans. C. E. Bennett; London: Heinemann, 1980) 356–59.

4. Gunther Garbrecht, "Rom," in *Die Wasserversorgung antiker Städte* (Geschichte der Wasserversorgung 2; Mainz am Rhein: von Zabern, 1987) 208–13.

5. Vitruvius, *On Architecture* (LCL; trans. F. Granger; London: Heinemann, 1980) book 8.

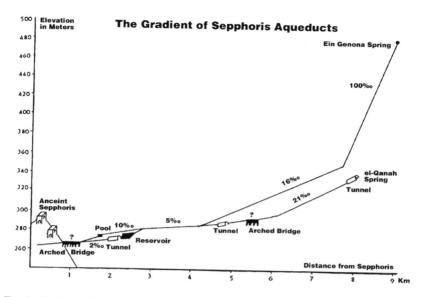

Fig. 1. *Section of the gradient of the Sepphoris aqueducts.*

the city (fig. 1). Why the engineers did not bring the water to the top of the city by an arched bridge or a stone siphon is a difficult question to answer. The reason may be purely technical, or it may be that it would have been too expensive. Whatever the explanation, the decision was made that Sepphoris would be one of the few cities in the Holy Land whose aqueduct did not conduct water to its highest point.

Research into the system of aqueducts to Sepphoris was begun in 1872 by the Palestine Exploration Fund, which investigated the Sepphoris reservoir and aqueduct.[6] In 1931, parts of Sepphoris were excavated by the University of Michigan expedition, which also explored the adjacent water system.[7]

I first heard about the reservoir at Sepphoris from a local resident named Buki in 1975. He described an underground reservoir some 200 m long and 10 m deep—seemingly a flight of fancy worthy of the brothers Grimm. In the summer of 1975, full of wonder, I stood in the middle of it and visually measured the vast dimensions that had been related to me. My host, Buki, added that the place had never really been investigated. The challenge implicit in

6. C. Conder and H. Kitchener, *The Survey of Western Palestine, 2: Galilee* (London: Palestine Exploration Fund, 1881) 330–34.

7. L. Waterman, *Preliminary Report of the University of Michigan Excavations at Sepphoris, Palestine, in 1931* (Ann Arbor: University of Michigan Press, 1937) 14–16.

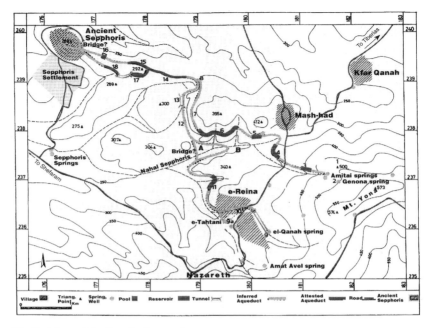

Fig. 2. Map of the Sepphoris aqueducts.

his words pushed me to intensive research concerning the Sepphoris aqueducts. From 1975 to 1991, we were busy with a field survey of the aqueducts
that included exploratory excavations, measurements, mapping, and locating the overall water system from ground-surface features. We also carefully
scrutinized the archives of the Israel Antiquities Authority and of Merkot, the
national water company. The results of these research efforts and excavations
have enabled us to reconstruct the system of aqueducts carrying water to
Sepphoris.[8]

The system comprises four aqueducts whose total length is 13.5 km (8.5
miles). The first two consist of two branches, one originating at Mash-had
and the other at e-Reina (see fig. 2), some 5 km (3 miles) from their respective
sources. The two branches are joined. They flow thereafter as a single conduit to a point near the city, where the conduit divides once again; the northern branch terminates in a pool, and the southern branch flows into the
underground reservoir.

The Mash-had aqueduct begins at the Amitai and Genona springs (fig. 2,
no. 2), situated at the northern foot of Mt. Yona. The aqueduct remains can

8. Tsvika Tsuk, *The Aqueducts to Sepphoris* (M.A. thesis, Tel Aviv University, 1985) [He-
brew with English summary].

Fig. 3. The Mash-had
aqueduct carved in the
bedrock.

first be seen about 300 m to the west (fig. 2, no. 3). Later, the channel can be followed parallel to a bend in the old main road from Nazareth to Tiberias (fig. 2, no. 4; fig. 3). The channel continues along the north bank of Sepphoris Creek (Nahal Zippori), where sections carved into the bedrock can be followed for almost 2 km (1 mile; fig. 2, nos. 5–7); the aqueduct then disappears. Parts of the aqueduct were lined with grayish plaster. The dilapidation of the Mash-had aqueduct and its higher topographical position attest to its being the older of the two; it can be dated to the first century C.E.

The e-Reina aqueduct was the main channel. It begins in the el-Qanah spring, located inside the village of e-Reina (fig. 2, no. 9; fig. 4). The spring is housed in a well-built subterranean springhouse of excellent-quality ashlar masonry. Most of the aqueduct has been completely obliterated in land-development work; it may be assumed, however, that the aqueduct was carried over the valley of the Sepphoris Creek on an arched bridge (fig. 2a). A constructed section of the aqueduct about 100 m long, 30 cm wide, and

Fig. 4. The el-Qanah springhouse (blocked by a modern concrete wall).

25 cm deep was found north of the creek (fig. 2, no. 12). Farther along, the aqueduct crossed a saddle by means of a tunnel, now destroyed (fig. 2, no. 13). Later, the aqueduct was raised above the ground by a foundation wall preserved to a height of 1.5 m (fig. 2, no. 14). In the saddle of Mt. Yeda'aya (fig. 2, no. 15) the aqueduct branched into two channels: one, as mentioned, terminated in a pool, and the other flowed into the underground reservoir.

The pool aqueduct is only 1 km long. It begins with a section still roofed with large stone slabs (fig. 2, no. 15; fig. 5). It can be followed for about 350 m, at which point it disappears. It becomes visible again adjacent to the pool (fig. 2, no. 16). The open pool is 21 m long and 14.5 m wide. Based on the nature of the pool, the level, the plastered surface that surrounds it, and its proximity to the city, it is logical to assume that it was used for swimming in the spring and early summer, when water from the springs was plentiful.

The reservoir aqueduct can be seen as two short sections of channel appearing 100 m southwest of the saddle of Mt. Yeda'aya. The first section is constructed and covered with two stone slabs. The second is hewn and served

Fig. 5. The pool aqueduct: A section near Mt. Yeda'aya.

as a foundation course for the constructed channel (fig. 6). This section is about 3 m long. The bottom of the carved channel is divided into three sections of 30, 31, and 31 cm, respectively. The center section is 2 cm lower than the sections on the sides. This small section is a microcosm of the engineering methods used in constructing the aqueduct. The hewn channel, serving as foundation and support for the conduit later constructed on top of it, was marked for the mason: the two side sections for the walls and the lower, center section for the masonry-lined bottom. It appears that the unit of measurement used here was the Roman foot.

About 100 m away is the famed subterranean reservoir, the most interesting and impressive installation in the entire water-supply system (fig. 2, no. 17; fig. 7). It is long and narrow, rather sausage-shaped, and located about 1.5 km (a mile) east of the city. Its function was to store water and to regulate its flow to the city. The reservoir is approximately 250 m long, 10 m deep, and 3 m wide, on average. Its water-storage capacity was in the vicinity of 4,300 cu. m. The reservoir was hewn from the bedrock—a soft, chalky, native limestone, whereas the north wall is supported by a harder limestone bedrock. The location of the reservoir was determined by the point closest to the city at which the appropriate depth of soft limestone bedrock could be found. The water entered the reservoir from the upper end in one side, filled it, and exited from a port at the lower end on the other side.

Fig. 6. The
reservoir
aqueduct,
carved in
bedrock.

In 1993–94, I led a team from the Tel Aviv University Institute of Archaeology to excavate the reservoir.[9] The excavations were sponsored by the Israel
National Parks Authority and the Government Tourism Company. The main
objectives were to locate and unearth the openings through which water
from the aqueduct entered and exited the reservoir—neither of which was
known. We exposed the entrance to the reservoir in an open, rocky area;
other than a single point at which a small cut had been made in the bare
rock, there was no hint of its existence. We dug there and were very pleased
to expose the end of the aqueduct, from which the water flowed into a sedimentation basin—the entrance of the reservoir (fig. 8).

We deepened the excavation to the floor of the basin, about 5 m. The water had flowed into the reservoir about a meter above the bottom, through a
narrow opening in the western wall. A large number of ceramic vessels found
on the bottom of the sedimentation basin were dated to the end of the Byzantine period (seventh century C.E.).

The sedimentation basin opens into the grotto of the reservoir itself. The
length of the reservoir is approximately 250 m, of which the first 190 m have
a storage depth of about 8 m; the remaining 60 m consists of a low, narrow
tunnel that leads to the outlet of the reservoir.

Two distinct layers of plaster could be recognized along the entire length
of the reservoir. In a number of places the plaster had been applied over potsherds that were dated to the fourth century CE. The first layer can be dated
to the first or second century C.E.

Nine openings in the ceiling of the reservoir apparently belonged to the
primary rock cutting; these openings served in the removal of hewn material

9. Tsvika Tsuk, A. Rosenberger, and M. Peilstocker, *The Ancient Reservoir of Sepphoris:
Excavations 1993–1994* (Tel Aviv, 1996) [Hebrew].

Fig. 7. The reservoir.

and gave access to the interior for maintenance, repair, and drawing water. Two of the openings had obviously been used as the main accesses for descending to the level of the water (fig. 9).

The excavation at the western end of the reservoir was designed to locate the reservoir's exit; this also proved fascinating. To begin, the last entrance opening was excavated. Steps discovered within it were followed; with the help of a small Bobcat tractor, the area adjacent to the steps was widened. We continued digging by hand until a small opening was discovered that led to a tunnel sealed off for some thirteen hundred years. Crawling inside on hands

Fig. 8. The sedimentation basin.

and knees, we came almost immediately to a place large enough to stand erect. We quickly advanced along the length of this imposing tunnel, whose side walls held projections for holding lamps. The last section of the tunnel was very low, and once more we were compelled to crawl on all fours. We eventually reached a wall closing off the tunnel, in the center of which was a lead pipe (the end of the reservoir; fig. 10) 10.5 cm in diameter and 5.8 m long. It was necessary to close off the exit, or the water entering the reservoir (about 36 cu. m per hour) would not have accumulated but would all have run out. We considered this discovery, deep below, to be the high point of the expedition. The location of the other end of the pipe was still a mystery. Only after several more months of excavation did we come upon it from the other side.

Approximately 200 m west of the reservoir, the continuation of the reservoir aqueduct was found facing the city of Sepphoris (fig. 2, no. 18; fig. 11). The aqueduct must have run underground along the length of that section.

There were no visible surface signs of either tunnel or shafts, except for a small hole in the ground. Excavation continued into a steeply angled and irregular shaft that did not appear promising but that revealed a small opening. It was the first opening discovered. One of our party, equipped only with a flashlight, went inside. He did not return soon. To our relief, he finally did and reported that he was able to walk erect for a long way along a remarkable tunnel that led to a water channel on its bottom (fig. 12). Thus shaft 3 was discovered in the 6–shafts tunnel.

Fig. 9. The central
entrance to the reservoir.

The tunnel was approximately 235 m long, with a gradient of 4‰. The area's surface declivity was somewhat greater. The shafts were filled with stones and soil down to their bases, but a little to the side, sections were found to be clear.

At the base of shaft 1 (fig. 13), the pipe terminated a little above the floor of the plastered channel, coinciding with the end of the stairs in the shaft. Approximately 50 cm from the end of the pipe, we discovered a metal lug solidly fastened to the floor. It appears that there was a gate valve in this section that could be opened or closed as required to fill the reservoir and supply the needs of the town. This valve disappeared in the distant past, but it very likely resembled the bronze valve discovered by John Oleson at Humayma, in southern Jordan.[10]

The 6–shafts tunnel is a typical example of Roman rock-digging technique as described in Vitruvius's book. The shafts were cut at a steep angle

10. John P. Oleson, "Nabataean and Roman Water Use in Edom: The Humayma Hydraulic Survey, 1987," *Echos du Monde Classique/Classical Views* 32 n.s. 7 (1988) 117–29.

Tsvika Tsuk

Fig. 10. The end of the reservoir: The lead pipe.

Fig. 11. The reservoir aqueduct west of the reservoir.

Fig. 12. The 6–shafts tunnel.

that reflects a compromise between ease of descent and the need to raise the hewn material nearly vertically.[11] From the bottom of each shaft, the digging crew tunneled in two directions, so as to meet the workers cutting their way toward them from the adjacent shafts (fig. 12). Four of the places where the

11. Klaus Grewe, "Zur Geschichte des Wasserleitungstunnels," *Antike Welt* 17, Sondernummer 2 (1986) 65–76.

Tsvika Tsuk

*Fig. 13. The edge of
the lead pipe in the
6–shafts tunnel.*

teams of cutters met were evident because of the deviations they made to correct the cumulative directional error.

The modern excavating team discovered many niches along the tunnel
walls in which oil lamps had been placed. The water conduit emerges at the
surface to the west of the tunnel, appearing suddenly out of the rock. From
this point, the water conduit continues in the direction of the town.

The aqueduct can be traced for some 400 m (fig. 2, no. 18) to a point also
400 m from the city. The gradient of the aqueduct at this point is 2.1‰
(fig. 1). The elevation of the aqueduct at this point (approximately 272 m
above sea level) enables it to enter the city at an elevation at least 265 m
above sea level. Thus, the aqueduct served only the sections of the city that
were lower than this line of elevation, which was more than 80% of the city.
Less than 20% of the city (the Acropolis area) was unable to obtain its water
directly from the aqueduct. Many cisterns that substituted for the aqueduct
were found in the upper part of the city. Within the city of Sepphoris, the
main line of the aqueduct has not yet been discovered. However, many water
installations have been found in the vicinity of the city's Nile Festival building, indicating that the aqueduct's main water conduit passed through the
area. It may be that this line was destroyed in the past and thus is no longer
visible in this sector. It is even possible that an arched bridge here carried the
aqueduct to the center of the city, which was on the slope of the hill.

The aqueducts can be dated according to both historical sources and archaeological data. The sources mention the existence of the aqueduct in the
time of Rabbi Judah Bar-Ila'ai (mid–second century C.E.). The types of plaster and pottery we found in the excavations permit the dating of the Mash-

had aqueduct to the first century c.e. The e-Reina aqueduct (the main aqueduct in the system) and the reservoir can be dated to the second century c.e.

The potsherds found in the plaster on the walls of the reservoir date to the fourth century c.e. and may be connected with repairs made after the well-documented earthquake of 363. It appears that in the early period of Moslem rule, concomitant with the decline of the city, the water stopped flowing in the aqueducts of Sepphoris.

The system of aqueducts at Sepphoris is noted for the small quantity of water carried. Those who designed and built the aqueducts knew how to exploit every last drop. Therefore, a very special reservoir was devised to store the water, releasing it to the city only according to need. A similar reservoir is known from the city of Capitolias in northern Jordan. It is very similar to the one at Sepphoris and thus was probably designed by the same engineer.

The research on the aqueducts of Sepphoris goes on and will continue until the discovery of the main water line in the city enables delineation of the municipal water-supply system. The eastern area of the city, like other substantial parts of the excavations at Sepphoris, is now included in a well-arranged national park that features the underground reservoir, significantly restored and open to visitors.

Incense Shovels at Sepphoris?

LEONARD VICTOR RUTGERS

University of Utrecht

During the recent excavations on the acropolis of Sepphoris, a series of small and intriguing pottery artifacts came to light that have been identified by the excavators as incense shovels.[1] Surprisingly, these artifacts have failed to attract the attention they deserve. The purpose of this contribution is to discuss briefly the formal characteristics of these artifacts, to detail the stratigraphic context from which they derive, and to explore the implications of their identification as incense shovels on the basis of an analysis of references to incense in contemporary literary sources.

The shovels from Sepphoris are unique in various respects. While all other ancient incense shovels known today were made of bronze, the shovels from Sepphoris are the first known examples of shovels made of pottery. No less importantly, while practically all of these other shovels derive from illegal excavations, the Sepphorean shovels came to light in carefully monitored excavations. As a result, it is possible for the first time to fix the chronology of these shovels and to start reconstructing how these artifacts may have been used.

An investigation of the shovels from Sepphoris is also worthwhile because of the many references to incense in the surviving literary sources, including the Hebrew Bible, Josephus and Philo, and rabbinic literature. Allowing us to determine how incense was handled, by whom, and in what context, these references take on special importance when we compare them with the archaeological evidence uncovered in Sepphoris. As we will see, the pottery incense shovels from Sepphoris present us with several anomalies. In the concluding section to this essay, I will propose an explanation for these anomalies.

---

1. E. M. Meyers, E. Netzer, and C. L. Meyers, *Sepphoris* (Winona Lake, Ind.: Eisenbrauns and Joint Sepphoris Project, 1992) 25; R. M. Nagy et al. (eds.), *Sepphoris in Galilee: Crosscurrents of Culture* (Raleigh: North Carolina Museum of Art, 1996) 205, nos. 78–79.

Description and Identification

Among the pottery shovels found in Sepphoris, two types can be distinguished: rectangular and round shovels.[2] Rectangular shovels have a rectangular pan. While the long sides of this pan and one short side with an attached handle flare upward, the other short side does not display any rim at all, as a result of which these artifacts could in fact be used as shovels. Several of the rims of these rectangular shovels have been decorated with small round discs ("cups"). These are arranged on top of the rims, in the corner where the rims of the long and short sides meet one another.

Round shovels display an upstanding rim on all sides. Thus a shallow bowl was created, to which a handle could be attached. Circular shovels were not shovels in the proper sense of the word, inasmuch as the upstanding rim on all sides probably prevented its users from shoveling up coals or other substances. It should be noted, however, that the presence of a rim on all sides did not in itself make it impossible to use these artifacts as shovels. It is quite conceivable that coals were not shoveled onto the round shovels but put on them by means of tongs or some other bronze object designed for the purpose.

That both round and rectangular shovels nevertheless belong to the same class of artifact is borne out by two facts. First, both round and rectangular shovels were made of the same type of clay. This clay is different from other clay objects found in the excavations at Sepphoris, marked by its reddish-brown color. The color that all pottery incense shovels from Sepphoris have in common is so distinctive that, even when tiny and seemingly unrecognizable fragments of shovels are brought to light in the excavations, it is possible to identify them as shovel fragments on the basis of their reddish-brown color. This suggests that all of these shovels were fired in a similar way. It also suggests that the clay from which they were made derives from a single clay source. Hopefully, the DCP spectrometry tests that have been performed on a few samples will enable us to determine in the near future the location of the clay source used to fabricate these shovels.[3]

The second reason round and rectangular shovels should be considered in the same class of artifacts concerns their use. Both round and rectangular shovels were found in association with perforated lids made of the same

2. For depictions, see the publications cited in n. 1. Most of the incense shovels from Sepphoris have not yet been published. The present investigation is based on an inspection of all pottery incense shovels found in the excavations carried out in the framework of the Sepphoris Regional Project.

3. These tests have been carried out by Eric Lapp. On pottery production in and near Sepphoris, see D. Adan-Bayewitz's classic study *Common Pottery in Roman Galilee: A Study of Local Trade* (Ramat Gan: Bar-Ilan University Press, 1993); and see James F. Strange, "Excavations at Sepphoris: The Location and Identification of Shikhin, Part II," *IEJ* 45 (1995) 171–87.

reddish-brown clay used to make the shovels themselves. The lids have been preserved especially well in the case of the round shovels. In their centers these lids display a small round projection which enabled the users of these shovels to remove the lid easily.

That the rectangular shovels were also equipped with lids follows from the presence of small, perforated lid fragments that are also rectangular in shape and whose dimensions are such that they fit precisely on the rectangular shovels. Even though only a few rectangular lid fragments survive and even though the fragments in question are tiny, there can be no doubt that both round and rectangular shovels were normally equipped with perforated lids. It is important to take these lids into consideration, because they help us to identify the Sepphorean artifacts as shovels—as we will now see.

The identification of the pottery artifacts from Sepphoris rests on their similarity to objects that appear frequently in Jewish art from late antiquity. These objects appear, for example, on a series of mosaic floors belonging to Jewish[4] and Samaritan synagogues,[5] on lead sarcophagi found in Beth She'arim,[6] on pottery oil lamps of the Beit Nattif and the Samaritan types,[7] and on sculpted objects, including a Corinthian capital from the Capernaum synagogue[8] and an Ionic capital from 'Ein Nashot on the Golan,[9] a rather unusual stone relief from Beth-Shean,[10] further stone reliefs from synagogues

---

4. They include the synagogues of Beth Alpha, Beth Yeraḥ, Gerasa, Hammath Tiberias, Hulda, Isfiya, and Ḥorvat Susya. For further references, see F. Hüttenmeister and G. Reeg, *Die antiken Synagogen in Israel*, vol. 1: *Die jüdischen Synagogen, Lehrhäuser und Gerichtshöfe* (Beihefte zum Tübinger Atlas des Vorderen Orients, Reihe B, Nr. 12/1; Wiesbaden: Reichert, 1977) s.v. For the mosaic floor of the newly discovered synagogue at Sepphoris, see Z. Weiss and E. Netzer, *Promise and Redemption: A Synagogue Mosaic from Sepphoris* (Jerusalem: Israel Museum, 1996) 18.

5. Including the Samaritan synagogues at Beth-Shean and el-Khirbe; see F. Hüttenmeister and G. Reeg, *Die antiken Synagogen in Israel*, vol. 2: *Die samaritanischen Synagogen* (Beihefte zum Tübinger Atlas des Vorderen Orients, Reihe B, Nr. 12/2; Wiesbaden: Reichert, 1977) s.v.; and Y. Magen, "Samaritan Synagogues," in *Early Christianity in Context: Monuments and Documents* (ed. F. Manns and E. Alliata; Studium Biblicum Franciscanum: Collectio Maior 38; Jerusalem: Franciscan Printing Press, 1993) 197–200 and pl. 1.

6. N. Avigad, *Beth She'arim: Report on the Excavations during 1953–1958*, vol. 3: *Catacombs 12–23* (Jerusalem: Israel Exploration Society and Bialik, 1971) fig. 89 and pl. 63.

7. V. Sussman, *Ornamented Jewish Oil-Lamps: From the Destruction of the Second Temple through the Bar Kokhba Revolt* (Warminster: Aris & Phillips, 1982) 11. For a depiction of a Samaritan lamp, see Magen, "Samaritan Synagogues," 225, fig. 47. And see E. R. Goodenough, *Jewish Symbols in the Greco-Roman Period* (Princeton: Princeton University Press, 1953) vol. 3, figs. 293, 334–37.

8. M. Fisher, "The Corinthian Capitals of the Capernaum Synagogue: A Revision," *Levant* 18 (1986) 131–42, esp pl. 34.

9. D. Urman, "Public Structures and Jewish Communities in the Golan Heights," in *Ancient Synagogues: Historical Analysis and Archaeological Discovery* (ed. D. Urman and P. V. M. Flesher; Leiden: Brill, 1995) 2.441 and pl. 31a.

10. For a depiction of the Beth-Shean relief, see G. Foerster, "Beth-Shean," *NEAEHL* 1.234; or Goodenough, *Jewish Symbols in the Greco-Roman Period*, vol. 3, fig. 444.

at Ashkelon,[11] Koḥav ha-Yarden,[12] Nawa,[13] Peqiʿin,[14] Sanabir,[15] and Kafra,[16] and possibly on a menorah lintel from Danna.[17]

These objects usually occur in close association with objects that together constitute the standard Jewish iconographic repertoire of late antiquity: the menorah, lulav, ethrog, and shofar. The representations listed above are remarkable in that they include only remains found in Roman Palestine or in areas directly adjacent to it. Even if one follows Goodenough, who believed that representations of the incense shovel appear at least twice in the diaspora[18] (in renderings that are so rudimentary that they make the identification doubtful), these two examples are simply but an exception to the rule that only in Late Roman Palestine did incense shovels become part and parcel of the iconographic repertoire current among the Jews of late antiquity. A depiction of a shovel in Panel WB 4 of the Dura-Europos synagogue can probably also be discerned among the objects that lie scattered in front of the Temple of Dagon.[19] Because the Temple of Dagon is a pagan temple, this representation does not inform us about the use of shovels by Jews or as a Jewish symbol in art from the diaspora.

When, in the early 1930s, scholars first started to encounter these representations, they were quite confused about the identification of these rectangularly shaped objects.[20] Several suggestions circulated until M. Narkiss marshaled all of the evidence then available to argue that the objects in question were snuff-shovels (מחתות) of the type known from the Hebrew Bible as having served in the Jerusalem Temple to clean the menorah.[21] Narkiss's identification of these objects with the biblical *maḥtah* has won general acceptance, albeit in slightly modified form. Scholars now believe that the object in question symbolizes the *maḥtah*, but they also hold that

11. Hüttenmeister and Reeg, *Die samaritanische Synagogen*, 23.

12. Ibid., 273.

13. Ibid., 338

14. Ibid., 351.

15. Ibid., 381.

16. Z. Gal, "Ancient Synagogues in the Eastern Lower Galilee," in *Ancient Synagogues: Historical Analysis and Archaeological Discovery* (ed. D. Urman and P. V. M. Flesher; Leiden: Brill, 1995) 1.169, fig. 16.

17. See G. Foerster ("A Menorah Lintel from Danna," *ʿAtiqot* 3 [1966] 66–67 and pl. 16), who identifies the objects in question as stylized lulavim. See also Gal, "Ancient Synagogues in the Eastern Lower Galilee," 168 and fig. 14.

18. Goodenough, *Jewish Symbols in the Greco-Roman Period*, vol. 3, figs. 703 (Monteverde catacomb, Rome) and 873 (Carthage).

19. C. H. Kraeling, *The Synagogue—The Excavations at Dura-Europos: Final Report VIII, Part I* (New Haven: Yale University Press, 1956) 101–2.

20. E.g., E. L. Sukenik, *The Ancient Synagogue of Beth Alpha* (Oxford: Oxford University Press, 1932) 27–32; idem, "Designs of the Lectern (ἀναλογεῖον) in Ancient Synagogues in Palestine," *JPOS* 13 (1933) 221–22.

21. Exod 25:38 and 37:23; Num 4:9. See M. Narkiss ("The Snuff-Shovel as a Jewish Symbol," *JPOS* 15 [1935] 14–28), who also summarizes the various interpretations put forward by the scholars preceding him.

the term should be translated 'incense shovel' rather than 'snuff-shovel'. This translation conforms to the Biblical Hebrew usage of *maḥtah* in the majority of cases.[22]

Narkiss's interpretation (in its modified form) is especially attractive because it enables us to link all elements that appear in a standard way in the Jewish iconographic repertoire of late antiquity to the Jerusalem Temple in general and to the Jewish holidays that were initially celebrated in that Temple in particular. Just as the menorah could serve as a reference to the Temple menorah and perhaps more specifically to the role played by priests in Temple worship, the lulav and ethrog symbolized the festival of Sukkoth, and the shofar, Rosh Hashanah. The incense shovel stood for the festival of Yom Kippur when, during one of the most significant and holy moments of the festival, the high priest would enter the Holy of Holies carrying an incense shovel. Given the strong religious connotations inherent in the other ritual objects represented in mosaics and on stone reliefs belonging to the ancient synagogue, it seems reasonable to suppose that the shovels represented alongside them were not regular shovels but incense shovels used by priests on various occasions during worship in the Jerusalem Temple. In this way the ancient synagogue expressed visually what its users saw it to be, a successor to the Jerusalem Temple.

There is another reason why Narkiss's identification of objects such as incense shovels is convincing. In Hebrew illuminated manuscripts from the tenth to late fifteenth centuries and from various countries around the Mediterranean, it was customary to include a "frontispiece" with a representation of all of the objects that had once belonged to the tabernacle or to the Temple of Solomon.[23] These representations are especially interesting because, next to the objects represented in them, short inscriptions can be found that allow us to identify each object precisely.[24] Studying the *maḥtoth* that appear regularly in these manuscripts, we observe that later generations also visualized the biblical *maḥtah* as a shovel not unlike the ones depicted in ancient synagogues.[25] Of course, the artists responsible for these splendidly illustrated manuscripts could not have been familiar with the representations found in the Palestinian synagogues of late antiquity. They based their depictions directly on a reading of the biblical text. Though seemingly self-evident,

---

22. See the remarks of A. Reifenberg, "Jüdische Lampen," *JPOS* 16 (1936) 167–68. On incense shovels in art in general, see Goodenough, *Jewish Symbols in the Greco-Roman Period*, 4.195–208; and R. Hachlili, *Ancient Jewish Art and Archaeology in the Land of Israel* (Leiden: Brill, 1988) 257–66. For more information on the *maḥtah*, see below.

23. T. Metzger, "Les objets du culte, le sanctuaire du désert et le temple de Jérusalem, dans les bibles hébraïques médiévales enluminées, en Orient et en Espagne," *BJRL* 52 (1969–70) 397–436; 53 (1970–71) 167–209. Metzger distinguishes six different subtypes (p. 406).

24. For a brief discussion, see ibid., 431–33.

25. For pictures of the so-called Perpignan Bible of 1299, see J. Gutmann, *Hebrew Manuscript Painting* (New York: Braziller, 1978) pls. 6–9.

these observations are especially important because they imply that through time there apparently existed a consensus: the biblical *mahtah* was evidently always believed to be some sort of a shovel.[26]

The pottery artifacts from Sepphoris, and the lids in particular, provide us with further evidence that these artifacts must have been used for burning fragrant substances. As has already been observed, the lids have been perforated with little round holes. Such holes are characteristic of artifacts used for fumigation because they were designed to control the flow of oxygen. Not only do the Sepphorean examples display holes, Christian incense burners dating to a later period also regularly have perforated covers, as do pagan burners dating to the early Empire (*acerrae*).[27] The holes allow enough oxygen in to keep coals burning while reducing the oxygen flow enough to keep the coals burning for long periods of time.

The presence of these lids from Sepphoris is not only important for identifying the artifacts in question as having served for fumigation but also for explaining an iconographic peculiarity that has puzzled scholars for several generations. Little black dots appear on several shovels that were represented on the mosaic floors of the synagogues referred to above. Similar dots also appear on the stone relief from Beth-Shean. Goodenough believed these dots to represent either draft holes in the bottom or coals on the censer.[28] More recently scholars have tended to regard the latter interpretation as the more credible.[29]

The pottery artifacts from Sepphoris now allow us to determine what these black dots actually represented. They were neither draft holes in the bottom nor coals on the censer. They were the holes in the shovels' lids.

Another similarity exists between the artifacts discovered in Sepphoris and the representations in the synagogues of late antiquity in Palestine. Remarkably, on the mosaic floors that carry representations of the shovel (for ex-

---

26. Metzger ("Les objets du culte," 435) believes one can detect the influence of medieval rabbinic exegesis (Rashi, Maimonides) in some of these manuscripts.

27. For a depiction of a Christian incense burner, see the exhibition catalog *Ägypten—Schätze aus dem Wüstensand: Kunst und Kultur der Christen am Nil* (Wiesbaden: Reichert, 1996) 216, no. 224. For a short history of Christian incense burners, see F. Witte, "Thuribulum und Navicula in ihrer geschichtlichen Entwicklung," *Zeitschrift für Christliche Kunst* 13 (1910) 101–12, 139–52, and 163–74.; cf. K. Wigand, "Thymiateria," *Bonner Jahrbücher* 122 (1912) 93–97; H. Leclercq, "Encensoir," *Dictionnaire d'archéologie et de liturgie chrétienne* 5 (Paris: Letouzey, 1922) 22–33. For such a burner found near Hebron, see R. Peled, "Clay Incense-Burner," ʿ*Atiqot* 7 (1974) 99 [Hebrew]. For other Christian incense burners from the Syro-Palestinian area, see K. Weitzmann (ed.), *Age of Spirituality* (New York: Metropolitan Museum of Art, 1979) 626–27, nos. 563 and 564; and L. Y. Rahmani, "Palestinian Incense Burners of the Sixth to Eighth Centuries C.E.," *IEJ* 30 (1980) 116–22.

28. Goodenough, *Jewish Symbols in the Greco-Roman Period*, 2.174.

29. Y. Yadin, *The Finds from the Bar Kokhba Period in the Cave of Letters* (Jerusalem: Israel Exploration Society, 1963) 58; M. Dothan, *Hammath Tiberias: Early Synagogues and the Hellenistic and Roman Remains* (Jerusalem: Israel Exploration Society, 1983) 38–39.

ample, the synagogues of Hammath Tiberias, Tell Istaba, Beth Alpha, and Sepphoris), the shovels have always been depicted by means of reddish or brown *tesserae*. Thus, these shovels look surprisingly similar to the artifacts discovered in Sepphoris, not just in formal appearance but also in terms of color. It seems reasonable to assume, therefore, that the two-dimensional shovels of late antiquity were directly inspired by the kind of pottery artifact found at Sepphoris. Conversely, if one agrees with Narkiss that the shovels rendered on the floors of late ancient synagogues are representations of incense shovels or *maḥtoth*, then it makes sense to suppose that the artifacts from Sepphoris must be regarded as incense shovels too.[30]

It is true that all other incense shovels known today were made of bronze. However, because none of these bronze incense shovels was found in situ (one exception will be discussed below), we do not know whether Jews used them as incense shovels. That it was not unusual for Jews to use incense shovels made of pottery is beyond doubt. This follows from a rabbinic discussion about purity, in which pottery *maḥtoth* are referred to.[31] In addition to the archaeological evidence discussed above, this literary reference shows that pottery shovels must have been a fairly common occurrence in the material culture of Roman Palestine.

How such shovels were used is another, rather complex, question. To answer it, we need to turn to the literary sources. Before we do so, let us pause and briefly continue our investigation of the formal aspects of the pottery artifacts from Sepphoris.

Formal Parallels and Their Relative Importance

Even though the pottery shovels from Sepphoris were made from a different material than the other shovels that have come to light in the ancient Near East, they do have have much in common with their bronze counterparts in terms of formal appearance.

We have already seen that the rims of the shovels from Sepphoris were decorated with small discs. In this way they imitate bronze shovels such as the ones discovered by Y. Yadin in the Cave of Letters, next to Babatha's archive.[32] The use of such appliqués is characteristic of artistically decorated artifacts made of bronze. There can be little doubt that the rectangular shovels from Sepphoris were modeled on rectangular bronze shovels, examples of which are listed in the appendix.

---

30. This is, of course, not the only possible conclusion one can draw. For a more detailed discussion of this issue, see below.

31. *M. Kelim* 2:3 and 7.

32. Yadin, *Finds from the Bar Kokhba Period*, 37, 40, 42–58; and idem, *Bar-Kokhba: The Rediscovery of the Legendary Hero of the Last Jewish Revolt against Imperial Rome* (London: Weidenfeld & Nicolson, 1971) 94–51, 108–9.

Rectangular bronze shovels clearly enjoyed a great deal of popularity in the Hellenistic and Roman Periods, when they were used by various groups throughout the Mediterranean for burning frankincense. One of the earliest examples of how they were used can be found in the form of a two-dimensional representation on an Etruscan bronze basket from Palestrina, near Rome, dating to the Hellenistic Period.[33] It depicts a *thymiaterion*, or altar, for frankincense, with a rectangular shovel attached to it. The use of rectangular shovels with an attached handle—*batilla*, as Roman writers called them—was widespread. Not only worshipers of Serapis used them, as an inscribed Hellenistic shovel in the Brooklyn Museum makes clear,[34] but Christians too, as for example in Sardis, where excavations have brought to light a rectangular shovel decorated with a cross.[35] Bearing in mind the widespread occurrence of such bronze shovels, we have reason to accept Yadin's contention that the shovels discovered in the Cave of Letters are not necessarily Jewish but should be interpreted as booty deriving from the Roman auxiliary forces that had been stationed at ʿEin Gedi in the years directly preceding the Bar Kokhba Revolt.[36]

It is conceivable that all of the rectangular shovels of the Hellenistic and Roman Periods derive from earlier examples. Rectangular bronze shovels appear as early as the eighth century B.C.E. at Tell Dan, where three were discovered next to an altar in what appears to have been a private residence. Another rectangular shovel, this one carrying a small sculpted lion on top of the handle, was found at Makmis. It dates to the Persian Period.[37] In Egypt, too, the use of such shovels predates the Hellenistic Period by many centuries.[38] Although such parallels are interesting, they need not concern us here, primarily because we do not know how such early examples relate to shovels used by Jews in the Roman Period. Incidentally, the fact that these Roman-Period shovels from Sepphoris are similar in formal appearance to contemporary shovels used by non-Jews should not surprise us. As I have argued at length elsewhere, the exchange between Jews and non-Jews on an artistic level in both Palestine and the diaspora was intense, at least in the Roman Period.[39] The shovels from Sepphoris are just another example of how Jews

33. Wigand, "Thymiateria," 35 and pl. 2.
34. K. Herbert, *Greek and Latin Inscriptions in the Brooklyn Museum* (Brooklyn: The Brooklyn Museum, 1972) 14, no. 5 and pl. 5 = SB XII, 11085. The inscription reads Σαρά-πιος.
35. G. M. A. Hanfmann, "Excavations at Sardis, 1958," *BASOR* 154 (1959) 26, fig. 11; and J. C. Waldbaum, *Metalwork from Sardis: The Finds through 1974* (Cambridge: Harvard University Press, 1983) 98–101, no. 588.
36. Yadin, *Finds from the Bar Kokhba Period*, 44–45.
37. See N. Avigad, "Excavations at Makmish, 1958," *IEJ* 10 (1960) 95.
38. Wigand, "Thymiateria," 13–15 and pl. 1, nos. 24–36. And see, in general, O. Keel, "Kanaanäische Sühneriten auf ägyptischen Tempelreliefs," *VT* 25 (1975) 413–69.
39. L. V. Rutgers, *The Jews in Late Ancient Rome: Evidence of Cultural Interaction in the Roman Diaspora* (Leiden: Brill, 1995) 49–99.

adapted artifacts that were commonly available in the Roman world to their own requirements.

The finds from the Cave of Letters are also important in another respect. Next to bronze rectangular shovels, several round hollow dishes were also found. These dishes, which were likewise made of bronze, belong to a class of artifacts known as pateras.[40] Originating in sixth-century B.C.E. Greece,[41] pateras were widely used in the Roman world for libations, as many a marble statue or relief makes clear.[42] The use of pateras was so widespread that they rapidly became standard symbols on the side of Roman funerary altars. Several years ago it was even suggested that certain representations of pateras should be taken as relating directly to one of Rome's four major priesthoods, the *septemviri epulonum*.[43] Whether or not this proposal is convincing, we see that pateras continued to enjoy popularity well into late antiquity. This is evident from the Paris patera (among other examples), which belongs to the famous mid-fourth-century Esquiline treasure.[44]

This evidence shows that it cannot be purely coincidental that we encounter this same circular shape among the shovels from Sepphoris. Just as rectangular shovels from Sepphoris were modeled on bronze counterparts, so the round shovels imitated bronze (or silver) examples. The round pottery shovels from Sepphoris are, therefore, similar to the rectangular ones in that they also document, on the level of material culture, the intensity of exchange between Jews and the larger world of late antiquity.

It is quite unfortunate that most of the bronze shovels included in the appendix do not derive from carefully-monitored excavations but were acquired on the antiquities market. Only a few of these shovels were found in situ, and most of them were found in contexts that are clearly pagan. This applies to a shovel deriving from the votive deposits of a Hellenistic temple discovered at Tell Beer-sheba,[45] as well as to several others originating in graves found at

40. Yadin, *Finds from the Bar Kokhba Period*, 46–63.

41. M. Gjødesen, "Bronze Paterae with Anthropomorphous Handles," *Acta Archaeologica* 15 (1944) 101–87, esp. pp. 170–74.

42. For examples, see P. Zanker, *The Power of Images in the Age of Augustus* (Ann Arbor: University of Michigan Press, 1990) 85, fig. 68; 125, fig. 101; 323, fig. 253. Another excellent example can be found on two helmets decorated in relief and deriving from the necropolis of Nawa, where a bronze incense shovel was also found, see S. Abdul Hak, "Rapport préliminaire sur des objets provenant de la nécropole romaine située à proximité de Nawa (Hauran)," *Les annales archélologiques de Syrie* 4–5 (1954–55) 176 and pl. 6. See also W. Altmann, *Die römischen Grabaltäre der Kaiserzeit* (Berlin: Weidmann, 1905) and R. von Schaewen, *Römische Opfergeräte, ihre Verwendung im Kultus und in der Kunst* (Berlin: Ebering, 1940).

43. Cf. the remarks of T. Hölscher, "Actium und Salamis," *Jahrbuch des deutschen archäologischen Instituts* 99 (1984) 205 and 209 n. 110.

44. K. J. Shelton, *The Esquiline Treasure* (London: British Museum, 1981) esp. 78 (Paris patera).

45. See Y. Aharoni ("Excavations at Tel Beer-Sheba: Preliminary Report of the Fifth and Sixth Seasons, 1973–1974," *Tel Aviv* 2 [1975] 165 and pl. 36:1), who does not discuss this plate in the text (!).

Nawa in Roman Syria[46] and at Hesban (Jordan).[47] Isolated finds such as these suggest that rectangular shovels were used by pagans for fumigation during worship as well as for funerary gifts—practices for which there exists a wealth of literary[48] and independent archaeological evidence.[49] The evidence for pateras is slightly better. They too are often found in funerary contexts.[50] Unambiguous archaeological evidence for the use of incense shovels by Jews, however, is more wanting.

In one of the side rooms of a building on Tell Istaba, some 300 m north of the Byzantine city wall of Beth-Shean, a small tower-like incense burner was found that looks quite different from the Sepphorean shovels. Scholars disagree as to whether the building was a Jewish or a Samaritan synagogue.[51] Upon closer consideration, the evidence seems to favor a Samaritan identification. Clues are an inscription in Samaritan script and the fact that the incense burner discovered at Tell Istaba is nearly identical to an incense burner found recently during the excavations of the Samaritan site of Qedumim.[52]

Something similar applies to the so-called incense burner of Auxanon, originally discovered somewhere in Egypt and now on display in the Brooklyn Museum.[53] Not only does this object differ from the shovels we have been studying so far, but Roger Bagnall's suggestion that it once belonged to a synagogue and that it was used there for burning incense remains purely hypothetical.[54]

Still another censer was found in shop E6 in Sardis. This shop, whose owner seems to have been a Jew by the name of Jacob, was built against the synagogue's outer wall. It was explained by the excavators as an object used to

46. Hak, "Rapport préliminaire sur des objets provenant de la nécropole," 185 and pl. 9.

47. S. H. Horn, "The 1971 Season of Excavations at Tell Hesban," *Annual of the Department of Antiquities of Jordan* 17 (1972) 22 and pl. 5, no. 13; D. Merling and L. T. Geraty, *Hesban: After 25 Years* (Berrien Springs, Mich.: Andrews University, 1994) 285 and 298.

48. See the abundance of materials collected in the excellent entree by W. W. Müller, "Weihrauch," *Paulys Realencyclopädie der classischen Altertumswissenschaft* (Munich: Druckenmiller, 1978) supp. vol. 15, pp. 700–777, to which can now be added N. Groom, *Frankincense and Myrrh: A Study of the Arabian Incense Trade* (London: Longman, 1981).

49. For the archaeological evidence, see, for example, F. Drexel, "Ein Rauchfaß aus Ägypten," *Römische Mitteilungen* 28 (1913) 183–92.

50. A. Radnóti, *Die römischen Bronzegefässe von Pannonien* (Dissertationes Pannonicae 2/6; Budapest: Pazmany Universität, 1938) 83–93.

51. For pictures, see Foerster, "Beth Shean," *NEAEHL* 1.223–35.

52. Y. Magen, "Qedumim—A Samaritan Site of the Roman-Byzantine Period," in *Early Christianity in Context: Monuments and Documents* (ed. F. Manns and E. Alliata; Studium Biblicum Franciscanum, Collectio Maior 38; Jerusalem: Franciscan Printing Press, 1993) 175.

53. Herbert, *Greek and Latin Inscriptions*, 61, no. 32 and pl. 19. And see W. Horbury and D. Noy, *Jewish Inscriptions of Greco-Roman Egypt* (Cambridge: Cambridge University Press, 1992) 225, no. 134.

54. R. S. Bagnall, *Egypt in Late Antiquity* (Princeton: Princeton University Press, 1993) 276 n. 105. Cf. *SB* XII, 11100: "Herkunft unbekannt."

counter the stench that accompanies the operation of a dye shop.[55]

To my knowledge, there exists only one example that derives from an archaeological context that is indisputably Jewish, namely, a fragmentary piece of a bronze rectangular shovel discovered by Benjamin Mazar in the early 1970s during the clearing of some tombs on French Hill in Jerusalem.[56]

Given the limited amount of information that can be derived from archaeological evidence bearing on incense shovels, it is necessary to turn to literary sources to explain what function the Sepphorean examples could have fulfilled in the domestic context in which they were found.

The Use of Incense and Frankincense among Jews

The Bible is relatively forthcoming in its discussion of the use of aromatic substances[57] by Jews and of the use of shovels. Throughout the Bible, in the strata that date to the postexilic period, a clear distinction is drawn between incense (קטורת) on the one hand and frankincense (לבונה) on the other.

According to the Bible, *ketoreth* consisted of seven ingredients (including *levonah*) but, according to later traditions, the total number of ingredients amounted to thirteen or even to sixteen.[58] The Bible is specific regarding who was permitted to handle *ketoreth* and on what occasions: only priests — that is, descendants of Aaron — were supposed to do this, and they were allowed to do so only when *ketoreth* was used in the worship of the God of Israel.[59] To underscore this point, the Bible includes several accounts of people who tried to usurp the priestly prerogative of offering *ketoreth* or who tried to appropriate *ketoreth* for uses other than sacrificial and who were then struck with leprosy, as in the case of King Uzziah, or who had to pay for the act with their lives, as happened with Nadab and Abihu, and the Levite Korah and his congregation.[60]

No such restrictions were imposed on the use of *levonah* in the Bible. Frankincense could be used on various occasions, including the bringing of

55. J. Stephens Crawford, *The Byzantine Shops at Sardis* (Cambridge: Harvard University Pres, 1990) 15 and 61; cf. pp. 71, 74, and 98.

56. A. Mazar, "A Burial Cave on French Hill," *ʿAtiqot* 8 (1982) 41–45 [Hebrew].

57. For surveys of the biblical materials, see K. Nielsen, *Incense in Ancient Israel* (Leiden: Brill, 1986); and see the much more detailed and comprehensive study of W. Zwickel, *Räucherkult und Räuchergeräten: Exegetische und archäologische Studien zum Rauchopfer im Alten Testament* (Göttingen: Vandenhoeck & Ruprecht, 1990). Also important is M. Haran, "The Uses of Incense in the Ancient Israelite Ritual," *VT* 10 (1960) 113–29.

58. Exod 30:34–37; Josephus *J.W.* 5.218; *t. Yoma* 41d, 27–36; *b. Ker.* 6a–b.

59. The locus classicus is Exod 30:1–10. And cf. Num 17:1–5.

60. 2 Chr 26:16–19 (Uzziah — the term used here is מקטרת rather than מחתה; on this term, see the important discussion in Zwickel, *Räucherkult und Räuchergeräten*, 239–44); Lev 10:1 (Nadab and Abihu — ibid., 280); Num 16:6 and 17 (Korah). On the misappropriation of *ketoreth*, see also Ezek 16:18 and 23:41.

meal offerings and firstfruits.[61] Frankincense was commonly sprinkled on the Table of Shewbread, but it was also one of the seven ingredients that formed *ketoreth*.[62] Offerings brought on the occasion of adultery or purification offerings were valid only when they did not include *levonah*.[63]

It is particularly interesting to note that when the Hebrew Bible speaks of *ketoreth*-offerings, it often refers to *mahtoth*.[64] In the Hebrew Bible the term *mahtah* is used to describe a utensil used to clean the menorah in the inner sanctuary of the Jerusalem Temple.[65] Much more frequently, however, the term *mahtah* refers to an object that the Septuagint and Philo translate as πυρεῖον, or 'firepan'.[66] These pans served a double purpose. They were used to carry coals from the altar of burnt offering to the altar of incense that was located inside the tabernacle and later inside the Temple of Jerusalem. The pans also functioned as incense shovels for carrying coals on the occasion of the High Priest's entering the Holy of Holies on the Day of Atonement.[67]

We need not ask who was responsible for these passages in the Bible, what the purpose behind them was, or even when exactly they were redacted.[68] What matters here is how Jews in the Roman Period reacted to these passages. To judge on the basis of the surviving evidence, all of these biblical traditions were vividly remembered. Thus, Josephus not only follows the Hebrew Bible in his descriptions of the tabernacle and Jerusalem Temple, how incense was used and by whom,[69] he also retells the stories of Uzziah, Nadab

---

61. Lev 2:1–2 and 2:14–16.

62. Lev 24:7 and Exod 30:34–37.

63. Num 5:15 and Lev 5:11.

64. E.g., Lev 16:13. And cf. Ezek 8:11.

65. Exod 25:38 and 37:23; Num 4:9. We do not know what these snuffers looked like. The artists responsible for the illuminated manuscripts discussed earlier represent them either in the form of spoon with elongated handles, or as shovels identical to the incense shovels discussed in this paragraph, see the pictures in Gutmann, *Hebrew Manuscript Painting*.

66. LXX, see E. Hatch and H. A. Redpath, "מחתה," *A Concordance to the Septuagint and the Other Greek Versions of the Old Testament* (Oxford: Clarendon, 1897) . In one case, the LXX translates מחתה with θυΐσκη, but normally this term is used to translate the Hebrew כף. The term מקטרת (2 Chr 26:19 and Exod 8:11) is translated as θυμιατήριον in the LXX. Philo *De spec. lib.* 1.72 (reference to the high priest with his brazier or πυρεῖον). In *De congress. erud.* 114, Philo likewise renders כף with θυΐσκη. While Josephus generally prefers to use the word θυμιατήριον to refer to the מחתה, he uses the term θυισκη twice, in referring to the tabernacle (*Ant.* 3.150 and 220).

67. Lev 16:12–13. The incense was carried in a jar (בוז) below which a ladle (כף)was held.

68. On such questions, see Zwickel (*Räucherkult und Räuchergeräten*, passim, and esp. pp. 171–72, 269–70, and 282–83), who maintains that most of the biblical texts discussed in this article document an attempt to centralize the offering of incense during the period following the Babylonian Exile. A similar view can be found in Nielsen, *Incense in Ancient Israel*, 51, 71, and 78.

69. Josephus *J.W.* 5.218 (Temple); *J.W.* 13.282 (Hyrcanus as Highpriest); *Ant.* 3.199 (incense offered twice daily); *Ant.* 3.220 (tabernacle) and 8.92 (shovels). The number of

and Abihu, and of Korah in some detail.[70] The same holds true, more or less, for Philo. Not surprisingly, Philo prefers to imbue these practices with symbolic meaning.[71] The New Testament also affords a glimpse into the practices surrounding the Day of Atonement and into the respective uses of incense and frankincense.[72]

No less importantly, the rabbis also considered the biblical accounts relevant to their own time. According to one tradition, the rabbis stressed the expiatory qualities of *ketoreth* in an attempt to prevent people who were familiar with the awesome biblical stories from developing excessive fear of *ketoreth*.[73] The rabbis also specified that those who prepared *ketoreth* in the same amount as was used in the Temple were liable to flogging.[74] Elsewhere they added that they considered the compounding of *ketoreth* one of the 36 transgressions that entailed excision.[75] According to rabbinic literature, the compounding of *ketoreth* was a prerogative of the house of Abtinas.[76] This clan was singled out in rabbinic literature for its unwillingness to share the secrets of its trade with contemporaries, out of fear that the procedure might lead to idol worship.[77]

It should come as no surprise that in its discussions of *ketoreth* and *mahtoth* rabbinic literature closely followed the specifications contained in the Bible.[78] According to rabbinic literature the *mahtah* was used for offerings on the altar of incense twice daily (the *tamid* offering)[79] and once a year by the High Priest,[80] and it was always *ketoreth* that was used for fumigation on these occasions.[81] Rabbinic literature also follows the Bible in drawing a

---

passages in which Josephus links the use of incense with worship in the tabernacle or Temple abound; see, e.g., *J.W.* 1.150, 3.199, 6.390, 8.101, 9.155; *Ant.* 3.220.

70. Josephus *J.W.* 9.223 (Uzziah); *Ant.* 4.11–12; cf. esp. 4.32 (Korah).

71. E.g., Philo *Quis rerum div.* 226 (description of Temple vessels and symbolic interpretation), *De spec. lib.* 1.72 and 171 (offerings twice daily and once on Yom Kippur); *De vita Mosis* 2.101 and 105 (symbolic interpretation).

72. Luke 1:10–11 on the Day of Atonement when incense (θυμίαμα = קטורת) was offered; Matt 2:11 on the birth of Jesus when frankincense (λίβανος = לבונה)was presented. In its terminology, the NT parallels the usage of these terms in the LXX, in which λίβανος is likewise used to translate לבונה and θυμίαμα to render קטורת.

73. *Midr. Rab. Num.* 4:20.

74. *T. Mak.* 4.2.

75. *M. Ker.* 4:4.

76. *M. Yoma* 3:11; *t. Yoma* 2.6; *y. Yoma* 41a, 54–63; *b. Yoma* 38a.

77. N. Avigad (*Discovering Jerusalem* [Nashville: Thomas Nelson, 1980] 131) has suggested that incense may have been produced in the workshop of Bar Kathros. In light of the rabbinic materials discussed in this article, however, this suggestion does not seem very convincing.

78. See in particular *m. Tamid* passim.

79. *M. Yoma* 3:5, 7:4; *m. Menah.* 4:4 (morning and afternoon sacrifices).

80. *M. Yoma* 4:3–4, 5:1; *t. Yoma* 3.3 (Day of Atonement).

81. *M. Yoma* 5:1 and 7:4 (*ketoreth* on a *mahtah*). That such *mahtoth* were different from frankincense dishes belonging to the table of Shewbread follows from the term used to

clear distinction between *ketoreth* and *levonah*. According to this literature, *levonah* was used in worship but unlike *ketoreth* it was used for fumigation on very different occasions, such as meal offerings.[82] Even Gentiles who were willing to pay for it could offer *levonah*.[83] The many passages in the Mishnah that mention *ketoreth* locate its use, without exception, in cultic worship practices in the Jerusalem Temple—never in practices taking place elsewhere.[84]

In short, rabbinic literature is amazingly consistent in discussions in which *ketoreth* and *levonah* appear. The rabbis might disagree on all sorts of details concerning the use of incense, for example, on the Day of Atonement.[85] But as far as we know, no rabbi ever questioned what was self-evident to all—namely, that the use of *ketoreth* and priestly worship in the Temple in Jerusalem were of a kind. Aromatic substances were clearly used on a variety of occasions—to perfume cloths, during blessings said over spices after dinner, or on the occasion of funerals—but they were systematically referred to in rabbinic literature with the term מוגמר.[86] In this way, a clear linguistic distinction was drawn (and maintained) between the practices characteristic of Temple worship and the practices of daily life.

This brief discussion shows how rabbinic literature may help to determine why incense shovels were represented on the mosaic floors of a number of late ancient synagogues: the *maḥtah*—a utensil designed exclusively for the burning of *ketoreth*—could easily be read as a reference to the Jerusalem Temple in general and to some of the most significant elements in the priestly worship of God in particular. Whether the meaning of the incense shovels from Sepphoris can be interpreted along similar lines is an intriguing possibility but one that becomes plausible only after a brief discussion of the archaeological and stratigraphic context from which these shovels derived.

---

designate the latter: בזיכי לבונה, cf. for example, *m. Tamid* 2:4–5; *m. Yoma* 2:5; *m. Zebaḥ.* 13:6; *t. Menaḥ.* 11.12. And cf. *t. Zebaḥ.* 12.5.

82. *T. Menaḥ.* 7.1 and 1.16–17; *t. Zebaḥ.* 9.6 and 11.3 (establishes a link between Temple worship and the use of *ketoreth*); *m. Zebaḥ.* 13:4 and *t. Zebaḥ.* 5.2 (distinguishes between *ketoreth* and *levonah*). And cf. *m. Soṭa* 2:1 and *t. Soṭa* 1.11 (adultery: follows the specifications of the Hebrew Bible) and *m. Menaḥ.* 13:3 (special vows). Note also the discussion in *m. Menaḥ.* 5:3 that is clearly based on Leviticus and that details which offerings need or do not need frankincense.

83. *T. Šeqal.* 1.7. But cf. *m. ʿAbod. Zar.* 1:5.

84. *M. Šeqal.* 4:5; *m. Yoma* 1:2, 2:4, 3:4–5, 3:11, 4:4, 5:1, 7:4; *m. Zebaḥ.* 4:3, 4:5, 9:5, 13:4; *m. Menaḥ.* 4:4; *m. Ker.* 1:1; *m. Meʿil.* 2:9; *m. Tamid* 3:8, 5:2, 5:4, 6:3; *m. Kelim* 1:9 and 17:11.

85. See, for example, the evidence discussed by J. Z. Lauterbach, "A Significant Controversy between the Sadducees and the Pharisees," *HUCA* 4 (1927) 173–205.

86. *M. Ber.* 6:6 (meals); *t. Nid.* 9.16 and *b. Moʿed Qaṭ.* 27a–b (funerary customs); *b. Šabb.* 18a (to perfume clothes).

The Shovels from Sepphoris:
Stratigraphic Context

The pottery shovels from Sepphoris constitute a body of evidence whose importance cannot be overestimated. On the acropolis of the city, in Area 84.1, 41 round or rectangular shovels or shovel fragments were recovered, and 14 or 15 additional fragments survive in areas adjacent to this part of the site.[87] Still other incense shovels brought to light in the same general area on top of the city's acropolis can be added, but their exact number is as yet unknown.[88] Thus the collection of incense shovels from Sepphoris represents the largest corpus of its kind anywhere in the Roman world.

All of these incense shovels were discovered in what appears to have been a domestic area. Many are in fragments, a result of the fact that they were discarded at one point and thrown into a series of huge cisterns where the majority survived until their discovery ten years ago. Even though these cisterns were not sealed right away but were used over long periods of time, it is possible roughly to estimate the period of time when these shovels were used.

In critical loci, incense shovels appear with materials dating to the Early and Middle Roman Periods.[89] In other loci, such as a sealed locus under a floor, incense shovel fragments were found mixed together with ceramic materials dating to the Early through Late Roman Periods.[90] In a number of cases, incense shovel fragments were found in association with chalkstone vessels,[91] suggesting a date in the first and possibly also in the second century.[92] In one case, an incense shovel handle was found in fill in a *mikveh* that had evidently gone out of use.[93] This evidence suggests that shovels and *mikvaot* were used at roughly the same time and possibly by the same people.

87. Areas 83.3, 84.2, 85.1, 85.3, 86.1, and 95.1.
88. J. Strange of the Univerity of South Florida Excavations kindly informs me that he has discovered a series of incense shovel fragments too. These have not yet been published.
89. Most clearly in cistern 84.1068.
90. Locus 1048.2 and 5; locus 1179.6. And cf. locus 1209.
91. E.g., 84.1068, 84.1173, and 84.1209.
92. On such vessels, see J. M. Cahill, "Chalk Vessels Assemblages of the Persian/Hellenistic and Early Roman Periods," in *Excavations at the City of David 1978–1985, Directed by Yigal Shiloh*, vol. 3: *Stratigraphical, Environmental, and Other Reports* (ed. A. de Groot and D. T. Ariel; Qedem 33; Jerusalem: Israel Exploration Society, 1992) 190–272; Y. Magen, *The Stone Vessel Industry in Jerusalem during the Second Temple Period* (Tel-Aviv: Ḥevrah la-Ḥaganat ha-Teva, 1988) [Hebrew]. The most comprehensive study is that of R. Deines (*Jüdische Steingefäße und pharisäische Frommigkeit: Ein archäologisch-historischer Beitrag zum Verständnis von Joh 2,6 und der jüdischen Reinheitshalacha zur Zeit Jesu* [WUNT 2/52; Tübingen: Mohr, 1993]), who argues on the basis of an impressive database that the majority of stone vessels were produced in the pre-70 era but that some continued to be used well into the second century C.E. A preliminary inspection of the chalkstone vessels discovered in Sepphoris shows that the pattern there is very similar to the one sketched by Deines.
93. 84.1209.

not even one displays evidence of having been used. Had they been used, one would have expected the coals to leave traces of soot—just as the spouts of pottery lamps that have been used are black with soot from burning. Of all of the fragments, only one shovel fragment is black; however, not only is this fragment atypical, its blackness can be ascribed to factors other than fumigation.[102] Shovels found elsewhere on the acropolis of Sepphoris neatly conform to this pattern in that they too lack traces of wear and tear.[103]

Bearing in mind the injunctions against the use of *ketoreth* outside of the Temple of Jerusalem both in the Hebrew Bible and in later rabbinic sources, we should not be surprised by the absence of soot on the shovels from Sepphoris. In fact, the absence of traces provides yet another bit of evidence in support of the argument that the shovels found in Sepphoris are incense shovels. What they were doing in Sepphoris and why they were not used are questions that we cannot answer beyond speculation. Were these shovels manufactured to symbolize Jerusalem and its Temple? Did priests actually carry the shovels with them to Jerusalem when it was their turn to serve in the Temple? What role was played by artifacts that do not seem to have been used and that *could not* be used—at least not by Jews who observed biblical and rabbinic regulations?

One explanation is that the shovels from Sepphoris were used for burning unspecified spices rather than incense. One could point to a set of literary sources according to which Jews burned spices (מוגמר) in domestic settings, on Sabbaths, and in the house of Rabban Gamaliel,[104] using vessels for this purpose variously described as כנונא, פרדיסקים, מגופה, or ערדסקאות של ברזל.[105] According to this line of reasoning, the shovels from Sepphoris were not incense shovels at all but utensils. This suggestion, however, is not convincing. The shovels from Sepphoris do not seem to have been used, as I have pointed out.

If we argue that the shovels were used, we must dispute the identification of the Sepphorean shovels as incense shovels because the use of incense shovels was a priestly prerogative. We would have to explain why the shovels

102. The piece in question is entirely black and does not display traces of black, as one would expect had it been used for burning coals. The black slip of this piece can be ascribed to the way this fragment was fired (little oxygen was let into the oven and thus the entire piece turned dark). It is also conceivable that the piece was burned at a later point in time (it fell into a fire or was thrown into one on purpose). Eric Lapp writes me that, in his view as well, the shovels appear "brand-spanking new."

103. I would like to thank J. Strange for providing me with this information.

104. *M. Beṣa* 2:7; *m. ʿEd.* 3:11; *b. Beṣa* 22b. Cf. *b. Ber.* 43a.

105. For מגופה and פרדיסקים, see *t. Beṣa* 2.14; for כנונא, *b. Šabb.* 47a and *b. Beṣa* 22b and cf. Rashi's commentary, ad. loc. On the possible etymology of this term, cf. S. Krauss, *Talmudische Archäologie* (Leipzig: Fock, 1910) 410 n. 274. S. Krauss (*Griechische und Lateinische Lehnwörter im Talmud, Midrasch und Targum* [Berlin: Calvary, 1898–99] 479–80) believes פרדיסקים to be an adaptation of the Greek πυργίσκος. On ערדסקאות של ברזל, see *b. Beṣa* 22a. This term is usally translated 'brazier'.

from Sepphoris look so similar to ones represented on later mosaics floors. Of course, one could maintain that the mosaic shovels were copies of the Sepphorean shovels and that the Sepphorean shovels were used for purely secular purposes. But, in light of the rabbinic sources, this idea seems farfetched. After all, it amounts to hypothesizing that (1) "secular shovels" existed next to shovels reserved for worship in the Temple, and (2) the secular examples then entered the iconography of the synagogue several centuries later, where their connotation changed from secular to sacred. This is unlikely. The relationship between the shovels in the Jerusalem Temple, the ones from Sepphoris, and the shovels on the mosaic synagogue pavements can, in my view, be explained in a much more coherent and evolutionary manner (see below, conclusion).

Finally, we do not know what the מגופה, פרדיסקים, כנונא or ערדסקאות של ברזל looked like. Given the function that they served (they were filled with burning coals and spices and then sealed up to be opened on the Sabbath or on holidays),[106] one may reasonably speculate that they differed from the shovels found in Sepphoris, since they were considerably larger.

Another explanation is also not convincing, for reasons similar to the ones just cited. Supposing that the shovels from Sepphoris are incense shovels, one might argue that they were used for burning incense by people who did not care about the rabbinic injunctions. Again, this is hardly likely in light of the fact that the shovels in question do not display traces of use.

Finally, the suggestion that the shovels from Sepphoris are *maḥtoth* as understood by Narkiss (that is, snuff-shovels for cleaning menorahs) rather than incense shovels, properly speaking, is also not very helpful. This explanation leaves the perforated lids of the Sepphorean shovels unexplained. The function of the perforated lids becomes inexplicable as soon as one supposes that the shovels were snuffers.

Conclusion

Although it is exceedingly difficult to explain why pottery shovels appear in such abundant numbers in Sepphoris, I believe that the "priestly explanation" is the best explanation. This explanation enables us to interpret not only the shovels but also some of the other finds discovered in association with the shovels in a more comprehensive manner than all of the other explanations I have explored.

The above analysis of the archaeological evidence provided by the Sepphorean shovels themselves, by the iconography of the late ancient synagogue, and by rabbinic literature shows that the shovels from Sepphoris are likely to have been incense shovels. Our analysis of the rabbinic materials in particular shows that the incense shovels inevitably document some sort of connection with the priestly establishment. It should also be recalled that,

106. Cf. *b. Beṣa* 22b.

while shovels play a prominent role in the art of late ancient Palestine, they are entirely absent from Jewish art found in the diaspora.[107] This serves as a reconfirmation of what literary and epigraphic sources likewise indicate — namely that, in Late Roman and Byzantine Palestine, descendants of priests continued to make a mark on society in general and on the synagogue in particular while, in the diaspora, priests simply were never a force with which to reckon.

It has often been argued that the use of frankincense in Christian liturgy derives from Jewish synagogal worship.[108] I have found no evidence that suggests that frankincense (or incense) was ever used in the ancient synagogue.[109] The only indications of *incense* offerings in a synagogue are the *maḥtoth* represented in a two-dimensional format on synagogue floors. This representation does not, of course, in any way prove that incense was actually used in the ancient synagogue. Evidence for such a practice actually does not predate the High Middle Ages.

It seems conceivable that the two-dimensional mosaic *maḥtoth* in the synagogues of late antiquity represent the third and final stage in a development that started with the use of three-dimensional *maḥtoth* in the tabernacle and in the Jerusalem Temple. The incense shovels from Sepphoris can be regarded as representing the second and intermediate stage in this development: establishing a link between the functional, three-dimensional incense shovels used in the Temple and the shovels represented two-dimensionally in the ancient synagogue; the Sepphorean shovels were still three-dimensional but no longer functional.

Taking the shovels from Sepphoris as evidence for the presence of people with priestly connections shows how archaeological finds from Sepphoris can throw light on one of the most discussed questions in the modern study of Galilean Jewish history: how did Galilee and its inhabitants relate to other parts of Roman Palestine on a social, economic, political, and cultural level?[110] Before we can answer this question, much work still needs to be done. There can be little doubt, however, that the forthcoming final report on the excavations carried out on the acropolis of Sepphoris in the framework of the Sepphoris Regional Project will profoundly affect the way we look at this question in the future.

107. Note that this observation is not *e silentio*: enough Jewish archaeological evidence has been discovered in the diaspora to ascertain that the incense shovel did not belong to the standard iconographic repertoire among diaspora Jews.

108. See, e.g., K. Gamber, *Sacrificium Vespertinum: Lucernarium und eucharistisches Opfer am Abend und ihre Abhängigkeit von den Riten der Juden* (Regensburg: Pustet, 1983) 16 and 62–67, referring to *m.* and *t. Ber.* 6.6.

109. To this may also be added the fact that Christian incense burners seem to derive from *acerrae* or incense containers rather than from *batilla* or incense shovels; see Leclercq, "Encensoir," 22.

110. Most recently, R. A. Horsley, *Galilee: History, Politics, People* (Valley Forge, Pa.: Trinity, 1995).

Appendix

This appendix contains a list of *rectangular bronze shovels* that were published in the years following the publication of similar lists by E. R. Goodenough, in *Jewish Symbols in the Greco-Roman Period* (New York: Princeton University Press, 1954) 4.197; and Y. Yadin, *The Finds from the Bar Kokhba Period in the Cave of Letters* (Jerusalem: Israel Exploration Society, 1963) 54–57. This supplement to Goodenough and Yadin does not claim to be exhaustive. A visit to any antiquities dealer in Jerusalem or New York or to archaeological museums such as the one in Aleppo, Syria makes clear that lists of the type included here are destined to remain incomplete, since unpublished incense shovels outweigh published examples by far.

1. French Hill, Jerusalem, Israel. Incense shovel fragment from a Jewish tomb. Hellenistic Period.[111]
2. Jerusalem, Israel. Incense shovel in the collection of the Bible Lands Museum. Provenance and date not known.[112]
3. Tell Beer-sheba, Israel. Incense shovel from a votive deposit. Hellenistic Period.[113]
4. Hesban, Jordan. Incense shovel from a Roman tomb.[114]
5. Nawa, Syria. Incense shovel found in a funerary (but disturbed) context. Late first, early second century C.E.[115]
6. Aleppo, Syria. Three incense shovels on display in the archaeological museum. Provenance and date unknown. Unpublished (?).
7. Damascus, Syria. Four bronze incense shovels referred to summarily already by Yadin. The shovels are on display in the museum. Exact provenance and date unknown.[116]
8. Beirut, Lebanon. Incense shovel in the collection of the American University of Beirut. Provenance and date unclear.[117]
9. Ontario, Royal Ontario Museum, Canada. Six shovels, first–second century C.E. From the Eastern Empire but exact provenance unknown (possibly of Egyptian origin).[118]

111. Mazar, "Burial Cave on French Hill."
112. O. S. Muscarella (ed.), *Archäologie zur Bibel: Kunstschätze aus den biblischen Ländern* (Mainz am Rhein: von Zabern, 1981) 313 no. 274.
113. Aharoni, "Excavations at Tel Beer-sheba."
114. Horn, "The 1971 Season."
115. Abdul Hak, "Rapport préliminaire sur des objects."
116. M. Abu-l-Faraj Al-Ush, in *A Concise Guide to the National Museum of Damascus* (ed. A. al-Jundi and B. Zuhdi; Damascus, 1980) 90 nos. C 2554; C 4048; 4567 and 3078.
117. D. MacKay, *A Guide to the Archaeological Collections in the University Museum (American University of Beirut)* (Beirut: American University of Beirut, 1951) 63 and pl. 8.
118. J. W. Hayes, *Greek, Roman and Related Metalware in the Royal Ontario Museum: A Catalogue* (Toronto: Royal Ontario Museum, 1984) 100, no. 159 and 163; 104, nos. 164–68.

10. Cambridge Mass., Harvard University, Dept. of Classics. First-century shovel of unknown provenance.[119]
11. Raleigh, North Carolina Museum of Art. First- or second-century shovel of unknown provenance.[120]
12. Bethsaida, Israel. Incense shovel from a refuse pit. First century C.E.[121]

119. D. G. Mitten, "Two New Bronze Objects in the McDaniel Collection: An Etruscan Strainer and a Roman Incense Shovel," *Harvard Studies in Classical Philology* 68 (1965) 164–67.
120. Nagy et al., *Sepphoris in Galilee*, 179, no. 27.
121. R. Arav and R. A. Freund, "An Incense Shovel from Bethsaida," *BARev* 23 (1997) 32.

The Sepphoris Synagogue: A New Look at Synagogue Art and Architecture in the Byzantine Period

ZEEV WEISS AND EHUD NETZER
The Hebrew University of Jerusalem

Many synagogues were built in Sepphoris during the Roman and Byzantine Periods, as befitted a city populated largely by Jews. According to the Palestinian Talmud, there were eighteen synagogues in the city during the time of Rabbi Judah the Patriarch (beginning of the third century C.E.).[1] Several are even mentioned by name in the talmudic literature.[2] One can assume that these structures were scattered throughout Sepphoris. A synagogue was discovered on the western side of the city at the beginning of this century, but very little is known about its art and architecture. The Aramaic and Greek dedicatory inscriptions found near the Crusader church on the site are the sole evidence of its existence.[3] Other fragments of dedicatory inscriptions revealed on the summit by the Joint Sepphoris Project (but not in situ) indicate the presence of another synagogue on the site.[4]

The first complete synagogue was excavated by the Hebrew University team during the 1993 excavation season.[5] Its importance lies not only in its

---

1. Y. *Kil.* 94.32b.

2. For example, the "Great Synagogue of Sepphoris"; see *Pesiq. Rab Kah.* 18:5 (Mandelbaum 792). Other synagogues are also mentioned by name; see *y. Ber.* 3, 1, 6a; *Gen. Rab.* 52:2 (Theodor-Albeck 345).

3. P. Viaud, *Nazareth* (Paris: Picard, 1910) 179–84; and see also J. Naveh, *On Mosaic and Stone* (Jerusalem: ha-Ḥeverah le-Hakirat Erets Yisrael ve-Atikoteiha, 1978) 51–52 [Hebrew]. For the Greek inscription, see L. Roth-Gerson, *The Greek Inscriptions from Synagogues in the Land of Israel* (Jerusalem: Yad Yitshak Ben-Tsevi, 1987) 105–10 [Hebrew].

4. E. M. Meyers, E. Netzer, and C. L. Meyers, *Sepphoris* (Winona Lake Ind.: Eisenbrauns, 1992) 21.

5. Additional work was carried out in the synagogue area during the summers of 1994, 1996, and 1997 in order to complete the excavation of the building and its surroundings. The first two seasons were directed jointly by both authors, while during the last two seasons

art and architecture, which in themselves are significant, but also in the fact that it is one of the few examples in which the integration of a synagogue into the city infrastructure is clearly seen. In addition, this synagogue demonstrates the stylistic influences of other mosaics unearthed at the site.

The Architecture of the Synagogue

The synagogue is located not far from the city center. Although the building was most likely rectangular in shape, it was not constructed symmetrically. It was divided into an entrance room (narthex) at the narrow eastern end of the rectangle and a main hall that occupied the rest of the space (fig. 1). The entrance to the synagogue was not located along the building's longitudinal axis but on the narrow southern side of the narthex. Also lacking symmetry is the structure of the main hall, which is divided into an elongated nave and a narrower aisle of equal length on its northern side. This is one of the very few examples of a synagogue with only one aisle.[6] It is reasonable to assume that the narrowness of the building was due to the limited dimensions of the plot available to the community that erected it. Traces of the rectangular bema, the focus of the prayers in the synagogue, were found on the western side of the building, facing away from Jerusalem. According to the numismatic evidence, this synagogue was probably built during the first half of the fifth century C.E. and destroyed at the end of the Byzantine Period.

As mentioned above, the main entrance to the building was on the narrow southern side of the narthex. The narthex probably jutted out into the north–south street located adjacent to the synagogue. Entry was thus directly from the street. The street's fairly steep slope and perhaps also its width, in effect, prevented entry along the building's longitudinal axis. The narthex was rectangular in shape and decorated with a colorful mosaic floor featuring geometric designs. To the best of our knowledge, it lacked any installations or items of furniture. A cistern measuring 5.8 × 2.0 m is located below most of the area of the narthex (fig. 3). The ceiling of this cistern evidently consisted of wooden beams with branches, reeds, or straw mats above them that sup-

---

work was carried out under the sole direction of Zeev Weiss. The excavations were financed by the Israeli Ministry of Tourism and the National Parks Authority, in cooperation with the Galilee Foundation, headed by Bini Shalev, who assisted us in many ways during those years. We wish to thank all of those who helped uncover the building and its mosaic. The photos of the mosaic were taken by Gabi Laron, and the drawings are by Penina Arad. For previous publications, see Z. Weiss and E. Netzer, *Promise and Redemption: A Synagogue Mosaic from Sepphoris* (Jerusalem: The Israel Museum, 1996); idem, "The Synagogue Mosaic," in *Sepphoris in Galilee: Crosscurrents of Culture* (ed. R. M. Nagy et al.; Raleigh: North Carolina Museum of Art, 1996) 133–39.

6. See G. Foerster, "The Ancient Synagogues of Galilee," in *The Galilee in Late Antiquity* (ed. L. I. Levine; New York: Jewish Theological Seminary of America Press, 1992) 289–319; R. Hachlili, *Ancient Jewish Art and Archaeology in the Land of Israel* (Leiden; Brill, 1988) 141–60.

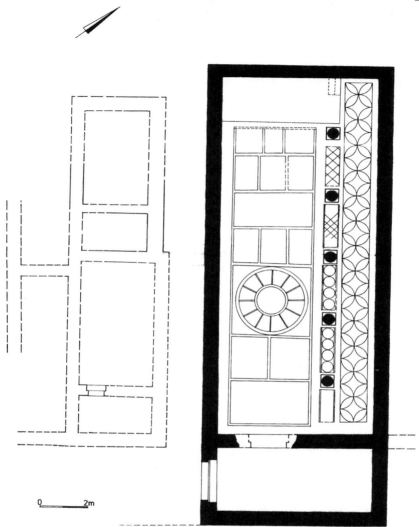

Fig. 1. Sepphoris—plan of the synagogue.

ported the bed of the mosaic floor of the narthex. Fragments of this floor were found in the cistern. Since the cistern's deepest point was below the north-western corner of the entrance room, it can reasonably be assumed that the opening through which water was drawn was located here. The cistern itself was fed either by water that flowed in the street or, as seems more reasonable, by water from drainpipes from the roof of the synagogue. The most logical lo-cation of the cistern's opening rules out the hypothetical possibility of a door offering access from the narthex to the aisle on the north of the nave. It can thus be assumed that the sole entrance from the narthex to the main hall was via a doorway located along the nave's central axis—opposite the centers of the zodiac and the bema.

The main hall, including the aisle, measured 16.0 × 6.6 m (a length-to-width ratio of 5:2), whereas the size of the nave itself was 16.0 × 4.6 m (a length-to-width ratio of 7:2). These narrow dimensions raise the question of the significance of the row of columns that divided the main hall into two parts. A room 6.6 m wide (the combined width of the nave and the aisle) could easily be roofed without additional support from columns. This partition may stem from a special use of the aisle that is not clear to us, but it obviously did not serve as a women's section, the first possibility that comes to mind.[7] Apparently we should disregard the possibility that the row of columns was built according to the dictates of tradition, since here we are dealing with only a single row and not the customary two. Another possibility is that the row of columns was needed to provide the building's interior with better illumination (see below).

The synagogue's main hall can in fact be divided into three units: the major part of the nave, the floor of which was covered by a central mosaic "carpet" (13.8 × 4.6 m in size); the bema (5.0 × 2.2 m in size); and the aisle (16.0 × 2.0 m in size). We may assume that the planning of the synagogue's mosaic floor was carried out when the building was under construction—that is, the building's planners were aware of the floor's main features. Not only has no evidence of earlier floors been revealed, but both of the main "carpets" (the one in the nave and the one in the aisle) neatly occupy the entire floor area at the disposal of the designers.[8]

The boundaries of the bema can actually be defined, and its original height was ca. 60–80 cm. Its front side, facing east, flanks the western face of the westernmost column's pedestal, and its northern side continues the line of the northern face of the same pedestal. Ascent to the bema was probably from the north (that is, from the aisle), and some of the surviving stones there could have formed part of this staircase. It is difficult to determine whether the bema was also paved with mosaics or was covered by some other material.

7. S. Safrai, "Was There a Women's Gallery in the Ancient Synagogue?" *Tarbiz* 32 (1963) 329–38 [Hebrew]. The separation of men and women and the construction of women's galleries began only at the end of the Byzantine Period or in the early Arab Period; see Z. Safrai, "Dukhan, Aron and Teva: How Was the Ancient Synagogue Furnished?" in *Ancient Synagogues in Israel* (ed. R. Hachlili; BAR International Series 499; Oxford: BAR, 1989) 78–79; L. I. Levine, "From Community Center to 'Lesser Sanctuary': The Furnishings and Interior of the Ancient Synagogue," *Cathedra* 60 (1991) 48–50 [Hebrew].

8. Theoretically, the structure of the floor, with its relatively numerous bands, could have led to the planning of the nave (and of the entire main hall) with such a small width, since the many bands called for maximum length, and the customary length:width ratio would have led to a considerable increase in the synagogue's size, which was not the intention of the community and/or would have been beyond its means.

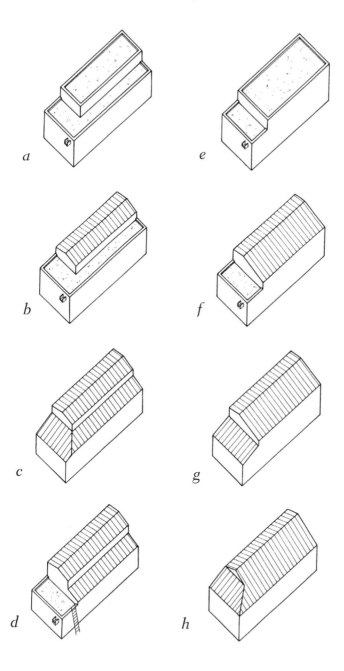

Fig. 2. *Schematic proposals for the reconstruction of the synagogue roof.*

We also lack information about any permanent furniture (for example, a Torah ark) within the area of the bema.

In order to reconstruct the missing upper part of the synagogue, one should take into consideration the significance of the row of columns separating the nave from the aisle. There are no grounds for assuming that the aisle was topped by a gallery, both on account of the absence of any signs and because of the narrowness of the aisle and the nave. In our opinion, the main and perhaps only reason for introducing a row of columns within the Sepphoris synagogue's main hall was to provide better illumination of the nave, especially its splendid mosaic floor. With the aid of the row of columns it was possible to install clerestory windows close to the nave on the northern side. Evidently there were similar windows also on the southern side, but there the nave bordered on a narrow alley (or courtyard), thus making possible the insertion of similar apertures, apparently also at the same height, in the main hall's southern wall, even though there was no aisle there.

One of the major questions relating to the reconstruction of the synagogue is the design of its roofs. In view of the building's dimensions and its rectangular shape, it would have been easy to cover the main hall with a simple roof supported by the two longitudinal outer walls of the building, the distance between which was only about 6 m. However, since the row of columns between the nave and the aisle was evidently intended to bear a wall into which clerestory windows were cut, the more reasonable possibility is that the roof of the nave was borne on one side by the conjectured wall above the row of columns and on the other side by the southern wall of the building.

An analysis of the building's architectural remains has led to 8 different schematic proposals (see fig. 2) for the reconstruction of the synagogue's roofing. Four of them (*a–d*) are based on the principle that the nave was higher than the aisle and that a wall with a row of clerestory windows was located above the row of columns. The other four proposals (*e–h*) are based on solutions in which there is no wall above the row of columns. The narthex in all of the suggested reconstructions had a lower roof.

- Proposals *a* and *e* are characterized solely by flat roofs.
- Proposals *b*, *d*, and *f* are based on a solution in which one part of the building (in any event, including the nave) was covered by a sloping tiled roof, and the other part by a flat roof.
- Proposals *c*, *g*, and *h* are based solely on sloping tiled roofs, but in each of them the layout of the slopes is different.

Other solutions could be suggested, but they appear to be further removed from reality. For example, we have not presented the seemingly simple proposal that the building had a single flat roof, since this would give the narthex an exaggerated height. Similarly, we have omitted the proposal that the entire building was covered by a symmetrical, gabled tile roof. It should also be mentioned that in each of the above solutions it is possible to propose different absolute and relative heights (the relationship between the heights of the

Fig. 3. General view of the synagogue area, looking southward, with the building in the foreground. Water cistern to the left under the narthex. Bema's foundation to the right, behind the reconstructed column. Photo by G. Laron.

narthex, the nave, and the aisle). In each of these solutions it is also theoretically possible to suggest two different combinations with regard to the supporting structure above the row of columns—flat beams (of stone or wood) or, alternatively, arches. However, it seems to us that support by means of arches is not only unattested at the site but also is not in accord with the relatively small dimensions of the synagogue. In any event, the beams above the columns were probably made of wood.

We tend to regard solution *b*—with wooden beams above the row of columns—the most reasonable one. It provides illumination of the nave from above; the roof above the nave is gabled and tiled, as was customary in most synagogues. According to this proposal, the roofs above the narthex and the aisle were flat, a solution that was logical and easily implemented in a synagogue of this size. Also meriting serious consideration are solution *a*, in which all of the roofs are flat, but the one above the nave is higher than the others; and solution *c*, in which the nave is higher, but the gabled roof and the sloping roofs of the aisle and narthex are tiled. It is self-evident that the flat roofs were based on wooden beams covered by organic materials, as mentioned above, and finally a layer of earth of a composition that was fairly impermeable. In any event, even though a number of tile fragments were found within the synagogue, its ruinous state does not permit a clear determination of their origin.

The two most prominent features of the structure and location of the Sepphoris synagogue are its unusual plan and its orientation toward the west-northwest rather than toward Jerusalem. The latter feature is also shared by a number of other synagogues located in the northern part of the country—at Japhia, Ussfiyeh, and Horvat Sumaqa.[9] Although it cannot be established indisputably, this orientation may have been a regional custom or tradition. It seems that, despite the rabbinic ruling reflected in the midrash[10] and the fact that many synagogues excavated so far do face Jerusalem, the direction toward which people prayed had not yet been ruled upon in this period.

The Sepphoris synagogue, like other buildings uncovered recently, demonstrates that the architecture of ancient synagogues including synagogues constructed during the Byzantine Period was characterized by variety and that synagogues did not have a single, definitive, regular plan or form. There were several principles that influenced their design, but they were applied independently in each case.

Several questions regarding the architecture of this synagogue still await an answer. Were the capitals of the columns Doric, Ionic, or Corinthian? What was the shape of the windows? Were there stucco or fresco decorations on the walls? Was the building plastered on the outside, or were the hewn stones of which it was probably built visible? The lack of uniformity of the masonry in the surviving sections suggests that the walls were originally coated with plaster. The finds at our disposal do not provide answers to these questions.

The Layout of the Mosaic

The most significant remnant of the synagogue is the mosaic floor of the nave, which was designed like a single, long "carpet." This mosaic has a figurative design, whereas the mosaic in the aisle features geometric designs, including thirteen circles arranged in a single row, and encompasses several Aramaic inscriptions. Another five, small, geometric "carpets" were inserted at the intercolumniations, a customary phenomenon in synagogues and churches of that time.[11] Each of these carpets contained a dedicatory

9. E. L. Sukenik, "The Ancient Synagogue at Yafa near Nazareth: Preliminary Report," *Louis M. Rabinowitz Fund Bulletin* 2 (1951) 6–24; N. Makhouly and M. Avi-Yonah, "A Sixth-Century Synagogue at Isfiya," *QDAP* 3 (1934) 118–31; S. Dar, "The Synagogue at Hirbet Sumaqa on Mt. Carmel," in *Synagogues in Antiquity* (ed. A. Oppenheimer et al.; Jerusalem: Yad Yitshak ben Tsvi, 1988) 213–30 [Hebrew].

10. *Sipre Deut.* 29 (Finkelstein 47).

11. See Hammath Tiberias, for example: M. Dothan, *Hammath Tiberias* (Jerusalem: Israel Exploration Society, 1983) 51, pl. 25; M. Aviam, "Horvat Hesheq: A Church in Upper Galilee," in *Ancient Churches Revealed* (ed. Y. Tsafrir; Jerusalem: Israel Exploration Society, 1993) 62.

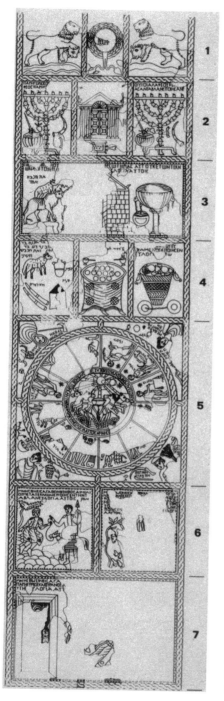

Fig. 4. Diagrams of the synagogue mosaic unearthed in the nave. Drawing by P. Arad.

Fig. 5. One of the Aramaic inscriptions found in the aisle, reading: "May be remembered for good: Yudan, son of Isaac the kohen, and Paregri, his daughter. Amen. Amen." Photo by G. Laron.

inscription, which was inserted at its edges in the space left between it and the geometric carpet of the aisle.

The carpet in the nave is divided into seven bands, with a zodiac in the center (fig. 4). Some of the bands have internal subdivisions. Each panel depicts a different scene, although all are thematically connected. The placement of the zodiac in the center of the floor, with additional panels on both sides, resembles the layout of other mosaics, such as the ones at Hammath Tiberias and Beth Alpha.[12] The number of registers and their subdivision in the Sepphoris mosaic floor differentiate it from the others. An arrangement of this type appears in the frescoes that decorated the walls of the Dura-Europos synagogue in Syria, dated to the mid–third century C.E.[13] The various biblical scenes depicted there are organized in three horizontal zones of unequal height, with an internal subdivision. This layout was implemented in the Sepphoris synagogue but in a different medium. The manifestation of this tradition in Sepphoris suggests that it does not characterize just the art of the Dura-Europos synagogue, which was influenced by Palmyrene or Mesopotamian art, but that the tradition was given wider expression in Jewish art, even in ancient Palestine.[14] This does not mean that the frescoes in the Dura-

12. Dothan, *Hammath Tiberias*, 33–52; E. L. Sukenik, *The Ancient Synagogue of Beth Alpha* (Jerusalem: Hebrew University Press, 1932) 21–43.

13. C. H. Kraeling, *The Synagogue: The Excavations at Dura-Europos* (Final Report 8/1; New Haven: Yale University Press, 1956) 66–70.

14.   The mosaic in the main hall of the sixth-century C.E. synagogue at Gaza was probably arranged similarly. Several panels made up the central carpet, but it is not clear from the actual remains whether they were also subdivided; see A. Ovadiah, "The Synagogue at

Europos synagogue directly influenced or inspired the planning of the Sepphoris mosaic floor or others like it, but it does indicate the existence of this artistic tradition in this region.

The Inscriptions

A notable feature of the synagogue is the many inscriptions. A number of Hebrew and Greek inscriptions accompany some of the mosaic's depictions and serve as their captions—for example, in the case of a season of the year, signs of the zodiac and certain scenes connected with the tabernacle and the Temple. Most of the inscriptions on the floor are dedicatory, honoring various donors. The inscriptions in the aisle are in Aramaic, while the dedicatory inscriptions in the nave are in Greek, except for two in Aramaic. This division is very interesting but not easy to explain. Nevertheless, it is clear that both languages were used by the members of the community in the early fifth century C.E., when the synagogue was built.

The dedicatory inscriptions incorporated into the floor of the Sepphoris synagogue have a fairly uniform format. The texts of the blessings, whether in Aramaic or Greek, are quite similar to texts known from other synagogues in ancient Palestine. The donors are mentioned by name and their deeds are blessed, but almost no other details pertaining to the people of the synagogue are provided. In most cases the named donors are fathers of families and their children, but the sums they contributed for the laying of the mosaic are not specified. From the variety and quantity of inscriptions, we learn that many members of the community donated sums for the construction or embellishment of this synagogue.

The wording of the Aramaic inscriptions is brief. They open with the customary phrase: "May he/they be remembered for good," followed by the name(s) of the donor(s), without any mention of the actual contribution, and end with the word "Amen," which sometimes appears twice. For example, one of the inscriptions reads: "May be remembered for good: Yudan, son of Isaac the *kohen*, and Paregri, his daughter. Amen. Amen" (fig. 5).

The texts of the dedications in the Greek inscriptions are slightly more varied and differ from panel to panel. Each of the panels of the mosaic was donated by a family whose members are mentioned by name in the inscription at the top. These inscriptions often state the motive of the donation—the fulfillment of a vow or the hope for redemption. Some of them first give the names of the donors, and others begin with the blessing: "May he/they be remembered for good," which is actually a literal translation of the Hebrew or Aramaic blessing. In such cases the blessing is followed by the names of the donors. Most of the Greek inscriptions end with the words "a blessing upon him/them," a phrase that also appears in Hebrew and Aramaic dedicatory

Fig. 6. The zodiac. Photo by G. Laron.

inscriptions in synagogues. For example, the dedication on the left-hand panel of the sixth band of the mosaic, which features the two youths left behind Abraham at the foot of Mount Moriah, reads: "May he be remembered for good, Boethos (son) of Aemilius with his children. He made this panel. A blessing upon them. Amen" (fig. 8).

The Depictions in the Mosaic and Their Meaning

A zodiac was incorporated into the center of the mosaic (fig. 6). The design featured two concentric circles inside one, bigger square. Zodiacs, as a central theme of ornamentation, can be found in several synagogues — for example, Hammath Tiberias, Beth Alpha, and Naʿaran.[15] The inner circle of

15. For a more detailed study of the zodiac in ancient Jewish art, see R. Hachlili, "The Zodiac in Ancient Jewish Art: Representation and Significance," *BASOR* 228 (1977) 61–77;

Fig. 7. *Scorpio, the sign of Marheshvan. Photo by G. Laron.*

the Sepphoris zodiac, which is bordered by a Greek dedicatory inscription, depicts the chariot of Helios (the sun-god), drawn by four galloping horses. Blue, wave-like lines fill the lower section of this circle, resembling a body of water, possibly the sea, from which the chariot emerges. The sun, moon, and a star are depicted above the chariot on a dark-blue background. The sun replaces the image of Helios, which is notably missing in the Sepphoris zodiac. It has been placed in the center of the sky, its rays extending in all directions. The lowest ray projects downward, toward the chariot, a detail creating the illusion that the sun is riding in the chariot.

The outer circle depicts the twelve signs of the zodiac. The signs are arranged counterclockwise. All of the figures are portrayed with their feet outward and their heads toward the inner circle. A young male figure accompanies most of the signs (fig. 7). Most are clothed in cloaks covering the upper part of their bodies. The names of the signs, as well as the names of the respective months, appear in Hebrew. A star appears at the top of each of the signs.

Personifications of the four seasons appear in the four corners of the square. The seasons are represented by female busts shown frontally. Several artifacts symbolizing the agricultural activities of each season are depicted beside these busts. Inscriptions in both Hebrew and Greek, indicating the

and G. Foerster, "Representations of the Zodiac in Ancient Synagogues and Their Iconographic Sources," *ErIsr* 18 (Avigad Volume; 1985) 380–91 [Hebrew].

seasons, also appear within these corners. The placement of the seasons corresponds with the matching months.[16]

The zodiac, including its various components, was a popular theme in synagogue floor mosaics for a long period. Depictions of seasons, signs, and Helios within a zodiac were common subjects in pagan and Christian art. The unification of these three elements is representative only of synagogue art.[17] Despite stylistic changes over the course of time, the subject and basic composition with which we are familiar did not change. The Sepphoris synagogue mosaic represents a significant exception. Although its basic layout remains true to the traditional format, its additional iconographic details and even more so, the missing details, make it exceptional. The design of the seasons, signs, and chariot differs stylistically from previously found zodiacs. The number of symbols representing each season is greater than on other floors, and the Hebrew names of the month are unique to the Sepphoris zodiac. The array of details that creates each sign differs from the common format, and the Greek dedicatory inscription around the central circle makes its first appearance at Sepphoris. But the absence of Helios, the sun-god (*Sol Invictus*), who is traditionally portrayed as a charioteer riding his chariot, is the most significant element of this zodiac and raises several questions.

Many scholars have explored why a zodiac was located in the center of several ancient synagogue floors and what exactly it symbolized. It is clear that this motif had special significance, which dictated its central placement. Some scholars suggest a link between the zodiac and the Jewish calendar.[18] Others point to cosmic or even astrological symbolism.[19] Another opinion connects the zodiac with *piyyutim* (liturgical poems) recited in the synagogue.[20] It seems that the zodiac represented the blessing implicit in the divine order of the universe, which is expressed in the depictions of the seasons, the months, and the celestial bodies, which are responsible for nature's cyclical patterns, for growth and harvest.[21] Helios in the center of the zodiac symbolized the sun's central place in the entire universe, an idea that also finds expression in talmudic literature.[22] But was this the main reason for the placement of such a design in the center of a synagogue? Was it merely in-

16. For detailed descriptions of the signs and seasons, see Weiss and Netzer, *Promise and Redemption*, 26–29.

17. Foerster, "Representations of the Zodiac," 382.

18. M. Avi-Yonah, *Art in Ancient Palestine* (Jerusalem: Magnes, 1981) 396–97; Dothan, *Hammath Tiberias*, 47–49.

19. E. R. Goodenough, *Jewish Symbols in the Greco-Roman Period* (Princeton: Princeton University Press, 1958) 8.167–218.

20. Y. Yahalom, "The Zodiac in the Early Piyyut in Eretz Israel," *Jerusalem Studies in Hebrew Literature* 9 (1986) 313–22 [Hebrew].

21. G. Foerster, "The Zodiac in Ancient Synagogues and Its Place in Jewish Thought and Literature," *ErIsr* 19 (Avi-Yonah Volume; 1987) 225–34 [Hebrew].

22. *Num. Rab.* 12:4; *Seper Ha-Razim* 4:61 (M. Margalioth 99).

tended to represent the sun's central role in nature, or did it represent a more significant concept with a deeper message?

In the course of a discussion in the Palestinian Talmud regarding the scepter and the orb, which symbolize the power of the creator over the universe, a sermon by Rabbi Ze'ira, son of Rabbi Abbahu, is cited, in which he says: "A mortal king has a patron to whom he is subservient. In this region he does not truly rule. Is it possible that he rules in another? And if you would claim that there is *cosmocrator*, he rules over land, but does he rule over sea? But the Holy One, blessed be He, is not so. He rules over sea and land. . . ."[23] The contrast between the power of Caesar, the *cosmocrator* (ruler of the world), and the power of God is at the root of this sermon. The power of Caesar is false. He is unable to rule everywhere. In other words, Rabbi Ze'ira is saying that God is the true *cosmocrator*. He rules over both land and sea and is omnipotent. Although the sun is central in the universal order, as is demonstrated in the Sepphoris mosaic and elsewhere, it is God who ultimately rules over the entire creation. These depictions do not aspire to portray God in human terms, presenting as it were, His likeness. The picture allegorically symbolizes the power and ability of God in our world. Just as the *cosmocrator* is employed in the sermon as a metaphor to illustrate God and His power, Helios's chariot, emerging from the sea toward heaven, expresses the same idea, though in an artistic medium.[24]

Helios or the chariot (in the case of Sepphoris) in the center of the zodiac represents the power and actions of God as the sole ruler of the universe and of creation. It was by no means accidental that the zodiac, with all its significance, was located in the center of the floor. It was the focus point in the iconographic layout of the mosaic and served as a link between the various themes portrayed in the floor (see below).

The three panels below the zodiac are partially destroyed (Bands 6–7). The first panel, located adjacent to the doorway of the main hall, depicts the Visit of the Three Angels to Abraham in Mamre, described in Gen 18:1–15. Only small fragments are preserved. One figure, standing in a rectangular structure, can be seen on the left of the panel. Traces of two other figures can be identified next to it. One is standing to the right of the rectangular structure, and the other is depicted in a reclining position farther to the right and below the previous one. Traces of a cloth with a fringed hem, which probably covered a table that stood in the picture's foreground, are visible below the reclining figure. Although this scene is poorly preserved, the analysis of its remains in the light of a close parallel in Christian art makes its reconstruction possible.

23. Y. 'Abod. Zar. 3, 1, 42c.

24. In Roman art, Helios riding a chariot harnessed to four horses symbolized the god ruling the universe. The emperor is depicted in later Roman art as ruler of the world, in the form of Sol Invictus, the invincible sun-god riding the chariot; see C. Letta, "Sol," *Lexicon iconographicum mythologiae classicae* (Zurich: Artemis, 1986) 4.1–2, 592–625.

The hospitality of Abraham and the annunciation of the birth of a son symbolized a prefiguration of the incarnation, the holy trinity, or the Annunciation to Mary in Christian art.[25] Various depictions of this story are known in Christian art and can be grouped according to several iconographic traditions. The earliest one, dating to the fourth century C.E., was discovered in the Via Latina catacomb, but it represents only the first phase of the biblical story—Abraham's meeting with the angels.[26] A more detailed portrayal is found on a mosaic wall in San Marco, Venice, which is based on a late fifth- or early sixth-century illuminated manuscript.[27] The three angels are shown seated behind a table in the foreground of the picture, with Abraham next to them, whereas the tent, with Sarah inside it, appears behind them. Another example representing a different tradition, which is the closest parallel to the Sepphoris panel, is in the presbytery in St. Vitale, Ravenna, dating to the mid–sixth century C.E.[28] The three angels seated behind a rectangular table are in the central part of the picture. Abraham is shown to the left, approaching them with food, whereas Sarah, who stands in the tent, is depicted behind him. An analysis of the remains of the Sepphoris panel leads us to base its reconstruction on the Ravenna example. The figure on the left in our panel is Sarah standing in the tent, designed as a rectangular structure with a flat roof. The vestigial figure visible to the right of the tent is Abraham, whereas the traces of a reclining man belong to one of the three angels seated next to the table in the foreground of the panel.

The story of the Binding of Isaac (Gen 22:1–19) is depicted in the other two panels forming the sixth band of our mosaic, above the previous one. In the left panel appear two youths, whom Abraham has left behind, together with an ass, at the foot of Mount Moriah (fig. 8). The ass stands in the foreground of the scene; behind it is one of the youths, holding a spear in his left hand. The other youth is seated on the left beneath a tree whose branches spread above him, and he holds the rein of the ass. The story continues in the badly damaged right panel. Discernible on its left margin is a tree with a few branches, to which a ram (only its head has been preserved) is tethered by a

25. L. Thunberg, "Early Christian Interpretations of the Three Angels in Gen. 18," *Studia Patristica* 8 (1966) 560–70; U. Schwab, "Proskynesis und Philoxenie in der altsächsischen Genesisdichtung," in *Text und Bild* (ed. C. Meier and U. Ruberg; Wiesbaden: Reichert, 1980) 209–63; H. M. von Erffa, *Ikonologie der Genesis* (Munich: Deutsche Kunstverlag, 1995) 2.91–103.

26. A. Ferrua, *Le pitture della nuova catacombs di via Latina* (Rome: Pontif. istituto di archeologia cristiana, 1960) 50; L. Kötzsche-Breitenbruch, *Die neue Katakombe an der Via Latina in Rom* (Jahrbuch für Antike und Christentum Ergänzungsband 4; Münster: Aschendorf, 1974) 56–60.

27. K. Weitzmann and H. Kessler, *The Cotton Genesis* (Princeton: Princeton University Press, 1986) 79–80; and see also K. Weitzmann, "The Genesis Mosaics of San Marco and The Cotton Genesis Miniatures," in *The Mosaics of San Marco in Venice* (ed. O. Demus; Chicago: University of Chicago Press, 1984) 2/1.128–29.

28. F. W. Deichmann, *Ravenna: Geschichte und Monumente* (Wiesbaden: Steiner, 1969) 1.235–38.

Fig. 8. The Binding of Isaac. Photo by G. Laron.

reddish-colored rope. Below it are visible two pairs of upturned shoes, removed by Abraham and Isaac when they reached the site of the sacrifice, a
detail not appearing in other depictions of this episode.[29] Another small part
of the mosaic is preserved in the center of the panel, in which one can identify the blade of a hefted knife and, to its right, the remains of a cloak.

29. The removal of shoes due to the sanctity of a particular place originates in the Bible
but was further developed in talmudic literature as expressed in one midrash: "Wherever
the *Shekinah* (divine Presence) appears, one must not go about with shoes on. . . ." (*Exod.
Rab.* 2:6). It is reasonable to assume that the design of our panel was probably influenced
by the same tradition. The presence of the *Shekinah* in the form of a cloud enveloping the
mountain (*Gen. Rab.* 56:2; Theodor-Albeck 595) necessitated the removal of shoes. The
artist or the iconographic sources he used realized that Abraham and Isaac would have removed their shoes at the site chosen for the binding, where the *Shekinah* dwelled. For
more details on the issue, see Weiss and Netzer, *Promise and Redemption*, 32.

The story of the Binding of Isaac appears twice in early Jewish art.[30] The two examples, which differ from one another in iconography and style, do not resemble our example. Therefore they cannot serve as a model for reconstructing the original scene in our panel. It is in early Christian art that this story makes its major appearance, in rich and varied forms.[31] Several stages of the biblical story are presented in early Christian art prior to the adoption of Christianity as the official religion of the Byzantine Empire, whereas from the fourth century C.E. onward the depictions focus mainly on the moment of the binding itself. The strong emphasis on this aspect is related to Christian theology, which reinterpreted the biblical story as a prefiguration of Jesus—his willingness to sacrifice himself in order to deliver humans from their evil deeds.[32]

A close study of the preserved parts of our panel and their comparison to similar early Christian scenes found mainly in the Roman and Byzantine East, such as the pyxis which is now in the Museum of Bologna, indicate that Abraham was portrayed standing in the forefront of the original panel, holding a knife in his left hand.[33] Isaac most likely appeared next to him, on the right, beside an altar that was located on the panel's right side. The ram on the left of the panel completes the scene of the Binding of Isaac, which resembles other similar depictions.

The two narratives are jointly dedicated to the patriarchs. This combination has a close parallel in the above-mentioned presbytery in St. Vitale, Ravenna, but in ancient Jewish art this is its first appearance.[34] Together, they form a complete iconographic unit with one clear message in the Sepphoris synagogue mosaic. The promise to the children of Abraham is at the core of these depictions. In other words, God promised Abraham not only that his son Isaac would be worthy of succeeding him but also that he would bless all

30. The story of the Binding of Isaac is depicted above the holy ark in the Dura-Europos synagogue, dated to mid–third century C.E.; see Kraeling, *Dura-Europos*, 56–58. In the mosaic of the Beth Alpha synagogue, which is dated to the sixth century C.E., it is located below the zodiac in front of the building's main entrances; see Sukenik, *The Ancient Synagogue of Beth Alpha*, 40–42.

31. I. Speyart van Woerden, "The Iconography of the Sacrifice of Abraham," *Vigiliae Christianae* 15 (1961) 214–55; J. Gutmann, "The Sacrifice of Isaac: Variations on a Theme in Early Jewish Art and Christian Art," in *Thiasos ton Mouson* (ed. D. Ahrens; Cologne: Bohlau, 1984) 115–22.

32. J. Danielou, *From Shadows to Reality* (Westminster, Md.: Newman, 1960) 115–30; K. Wessel, "Abraham: Das Opfer A's," *Reallexikon zur Byzantinischen Kunst* (Stuttgart: Hiersmann, 1963) 15.

33. D. V. Ainalov, *The Hellenistic Origins of Byzantine Art* (New Brunswick, N.J.: Rutgers University Press, 1961) 94–97, fig. 49. Other depictions based on a similar tradition are known from a fourth-century tomb excavated in El Bagawât, Egypt and a pyxis that is now in the museum of Berlin; see A. Fakhry, *The Necropolis of El Bagawât in Kharga Oasis* (Cairo: Government Press, 1951) 72–73; A. Clair, "The Iconography of the Great Berlin Pyxis," *Jahrbuch der Berliner Museen* 20 (1978) 5–27.

34. Deichmann, *Ravenna*, 1.235–38.

Fig. 9. *Architectural facade, menorahs, and other Jewish symbols. Photo by G. Laron.*

of Abraham's innumerable offspring. God promised to protect the descendants of Abraham and shield them from danger in the future. The depictions in the mosaic are not intended just to relate the biblical story. The promise of the future is implicit in these scenes and constitutes a key element in the iconographic layout of the entire mosaic.

Several panels arranged in four bands are located above the zodiac. The first two bands portray themes that were well known in Jewish art, while the other two feature themes that here made their first appearance in the synagogue art of ancient Palestine.

The first band, adjacent to the synagogue's bema, contains three panels. In the central panel is a round wreath of stylized leaves with a Greek dedicatory inscription at its center. The words "blessed be he" are discernible in the surviving part of this inscription. A lion with its head facing the center is depicted in each of the side panels. The left front paw of both lions grips the head of a bullock. The upper part of the band has been destroyed completely as the result of the looting of the bema sidewall. The motif of two lions in heraldic pose flanking some sort of central motif is very common in Jewish art.[35] A good parallel to our mosaic, although not a complete one, is preserved at Hammath Gader, where a panel depicting two lions flanking a dedicatory inscription encircled by a wreath is located next to the synagogue's bema.[36]

The second band also contains three panels (fig. 9). The middle one, which is only partly preserved, depicts the facade of a building with two doors.

35. For the use of this motif in ancient Jewish art, see Hachlili, *Ancient Jewish Art and Archaeology in the Land of Israel*, 321–28.

36. E. L. Sukenik, *The Ancient Synagogue of El-Hammeh (Hammath by Gadara)* (Jerusalem: Mass, 1935) 35–36.

Below the gabled building is a single incense shovel, in contrast to the pair appearing in the synagogue mosaics at Hammath Tiberias and Beth Alpha.[37]

A menorah (seven-branched candelabrum) and other Jewish symbols appear on each of the panels flanking the facade. At the top of the menorah is a horizontal bar on which rest seven receptacles from which flames emerge, all of them extended toward the left. The Four Species are depicted on both panels to the left of the menorah, and a single shofar is shown on its right. The palm branch, myrtle, and willow are bound together and located within a round bowl, whereas the citron is next to them. Fire-tongs were added on the two panels to the right of the menorah, but only the one on the right-hand panel is preserved completely. This detail, rare in ancient Jewish art, appears frequently next to a menorah in Jewish manuscripts from the thirteenth and fourteenth centuries C.E.[38]

Architectural facades flanked by two menorahs and other Jewish symbols are known from various sites throughout ancient Palestine, but their significance remains uncertain.[39] It is not clear whether this depiction of two menorahs reflects arrangements in synagogues in which the Holy Ark was flanked by two menorahs[40] or whether the decorated facade itself symbolized the tabernacle or the Temple, which was once the focus of national religious life.[41] Another possibility is that they represent the Holy Ark of both the synagogue and the Temple simultaneously.[42]

The last group of panels was set aside thematically and deals with the tabernacle or the Temple. The single panel forming the third band features a scene with three components that should be viewed from right to left. On the right is a water basin standing on a column with an Ionic capital (fig. 10). Two heads (of bullocks?) project from the basin's left side, and streams of water flow from their mouths into an adjacent hemispherical bowl. In the center of the panel is a large altar, only half of which has been preserved. It is built of dressed stones and apparently stands on a stepped base. Two of its corners are decorated with horns, and the destroyed part should be reconstructed similarly. Aaron, the high priest, stands next to the altar, as attested

---

37. Dothan, *Hammath Tiberias*, pl. 27; Sukenik, *The Ancient Synagogue of Beth Alpha*, pl. 8.

38. B. Narkis, *Hebrew Illuminated Manuscripts in the British Isles: The Spanish and Portuguese Manuscripts* (2 vols.; Oxford: Oxford University Press, 1982) figs. 326, 333, 335. A pair of fire-tongs appears between the branches of the menorah in the mosaic of the Samaritan synagogue at El-Hirbeh; see I. Magen, "Samaritan Synagogues," *Qadmoniot* 25 (1993) 70–72 [Hebrew].

39. Hachlili, *Ancient Jewish Art and Archaeology*, 234–85.

40. J. C. Sloane. "The Torah Shrine in the Ashburnham Pentateuch," *JQR* 25 (1934) 1–12; Dothan, *Hammath Tiberias*, 33–39; E. M. Meyers and C. L. Meyers, "The Ark in Art: A Ceramic Rendering of the Torah Shrine from Nabratein," *ErIsr* 16 (1982) 176–85.

41. E. Revel-Neher, "L'Alliance et la Promesse: Le symbolisme d'Eretz Israel dans l'iconographie juive du Moyen Age," *JJA* 12–13 (1986–87) 135–46.

42. C. Roth, "Jewish Antecedents of Christian Art," *Journal of the Warburg and Courtauld Institutes* 16 (1953) 22–24.

Fig. 10. The right side of the panel, describing the Consecration of Aaron for Service in the Tabernacle. Photo by G. Laron.

by the inscription to the left of the remains of a human figure dressed in a robe. On the left side of the panel a bullock with a lamb above it is depicted, and next to the lamb is an inscription with an excerpt from the Bible: "one lamb . . ." (Num 28:4; cf. Exod 29:39).

The continuation of this scene is found in the panel on the left side of the fourth band of the mosaic (fig. 11). It features four objects portraying the perpetual sacrifice offered daily, both in the tabernacle and the Temple. A lamb (in addition to the one on the previous panel) is depicted on the upper left side, with an inscription above it, reading, "And the other lamb . . ." (Exod 29:41). To the right of the lamb is a black storage jar with the Hebrew word *shemen* (oil) on its right, indicating its contents. Below the jar is a yellowish vessel containing fine flour, as indicated by the word *solet* on its right. To its left is a pair of trumpets accompanied by the word *ḥatzotzrot*. The juxtaposition of the two trumpets with the second lamb, oil, and flour in the mosaic reflects actual practice during the Second Temple Period, as recorded in early rabbinic tradition, according to which two trumpets were blown when the daily offering was sacrificed.[43]

43. *Sipre Zuta, Behaʾaloteka* 10:10 (H. S. Horovitz 262); *m. Sukk.* 5:5.

Fig. 11. Four objects portraying the perpetual sacrifice offered daily, both in the tabernacle and in the Temple. Photo by G. Laron.

Scenes such as ours, relating to Aaron and the tabernacle, find a close parallel in the Dura-Europos synagogue—the panel depicting the Consecration of Aaron for Service in the Tabernacle.[44] Although these two panels appear to be similar at first glance, a careful comparison reveals that there are also many differences. An analysis of the Dura-Europos panel indicates that it is not a narrative depiction but, rather, a collection of scenes connected with

44. Kraeling, *Dura-Europos*, 125–31.

the tabernacle rites that were joined together in one frame.[45] The Consecration of Aaron for Service in the Tabernacle (Exodus 29) is portrayed in the center together with the commandment to make silver trumpets for calling the assembly (Num 10:1–3) and the story of the burning of the red heifer (Numbers 19). Not only does it combine several scenes but it excludes the daily sacrifice, which is clearly incorporated in our depiction.

The tabernacle and its utensils also appear in the *Topography of Cosmas* (a sixth-century C.E. work devoted to cosmography),[46] in the Octateuchs (illustrated Greek translations of eight biblical books)[47] and in Jewish manuscripts from as early as the tenth century C.E.,[48] but these depictions differ significantly from the one in Sepphoris. These miniatures show the plan of the tabernacle and its utensils but without any direct connection to the sacrifices that took place there, a detail that is specially highlighted in the Sepphoris mosaic.

In contrast to the previous examples, the themes depicted in the Sepphoris mosaic seem to serve as a narrative description of Exodus 29, a chapter that deals with the story of the Consecration of Aaron and His Sons for Service in the Tabernacle and that ends with the commandment about the daily sacrifice. The three essential phases of this biblical text are depicted in the two panels from Sepphoris.

The water basin on the right side of the large panel symbolizes the first stage of the purification ceremony (Exod 29:4). Then come the sacrifices. First, the sacrifice of the bullock opposite the door of the tabernacle is depicted in the middle of the panel (Exod 29:10–11). Aaron the high priest stands next to the altar, which is located in the court of the tabernacle. The daily sacrifice, the inspiration of the Divine Presence, and the promise of continuity appear in the last part of the biblical chapter (Exod 29:38–45). The "other lamb" along with the other sacrificial components appearing in the smaller panel symbolize the continuity of worship in the tabernacle and the Divine Presence in the chosen place.

The other two panels next to the depiction of the daily sacrifice complete the fourth band. They deal with other elements of Temple worship but are

---

45. Ibid, 130–31; K. Weitzmann and H. L. Kessler, *The Frescoes of the Dura Synagogue and Christian Art* (Washington, D.C.: Dumbarton Oaks, 1990) 59–62.

46. E. Revel-Neher, "Some Remarks on the Iconographical Sources of the Christian Topography of Cosmas Indicopleustes," *Kairos* 32–33 (1990–91) 78–96; B. Kuhnel, "Jewish Symbolism of the Temple and the Tabernacle and Christian Symbolism of the Holy Sepulchre and the Heavenly Tabernacle," *JJA* 12–13 (1986–87) 147–68, esp. 160–62.

47. L. Brubaker, "The Tabernacle Miniatures of the Byzantine Octateuchs," *Actes du XVᵉ Congrès International d'Études Byzantines, 1976* (Athens: Association Internationale des Études Byzantines, 1981) 2.73–92.

48. T. Metzger, "Quelques caractères iconographiques et ornementaux de deux manuscrits hébraïques du Xᵉ siècle," *Cahiers de civilisation médiévale, Xᵉ–XIIᵉ siècles* 1 (1958) 205–13; C. O. Nordström, "Some Hebrew Miniatures in Hebrew Bible," in *Synthronon: Art et archéologie de la fin de l'antiquite et du moyen age* (ed. A. Grabar; Paris: Klincksieck, 1968) 89–105, esp. figs. 4, 14.

not directly connected with the panels relating to Aaron and the sacrifice. The Table of Shewbread is depicted in the middle panel (fig. 13). It is a rounded table with three legs and is covered by a tablecloth on which the twelve loaves of unleavened bread, shown as round objects, are placed. Two censers containing frankincense are depicted above the table, on either side of it. It is evident that this is the Table of Shewbread, although it is unclear why the artist chose to present the table as round furniture instead of rectangular, as portrayed elsewhere[49] and described in literary sources.[50]

A wicker basket of firstfruits, including grapes, a pomegranate, and a fig, appears in the panel on the right (fig. 12). Suspended from the rim of the basket are a pair of birds with their heads hanging downward. A pair of cymbals joined together by a chain is located below the basket of firstfruits. The commandment to bring the firstfruits to the priest is enunciated in Deuteronomy 26, although the depiction in the mosaic is clearly in the spirit of talmudic literature. Not only the placement of the Seven Species of fruit in a woven basket, as was the practice of the poor who brought their firstfruit to the Temple,[51] but even the adornment of the basket with young pigeons and the tying of them to the rim reflect rabbinical tradition in a very special way: "R. Yose taught: They did not put pigeons on top of the basket, so as to avoid dirtying the firstfruits, but suspended them outside of the basket."[52] This detail and others in the mosaic indicate the centrality of rabbinic literature and the scope of its influence in the iconographic design of the Sepphoris synagogue mosaic.

What is the idea behind the last four depictions mentioned above (The Consecration of Aaron, Perpetual Sacrifice, Table of Shewbread, and wicker basket of firstfruits; fig. 13), and is there a thematic connection between them? Although Band 3 and the left side of Band 4 are interconnected and flow with the biblical narrative, it is not clear why the theme of the other two panels was chosen to complement them. If the intention of the artist was to depict the tabernacle utensils, why did he choose the basket of firstfruits, and if he sought to present the different types of sacrifices, why did he include the Table of Shewbread?

These choices were not made by chance. The depiction of all three subjects clearly reflects an iconographic layout with a single defined theme, which can be explained in the light of the following midrash:

---

49. See, for example, the incision (executed *in graffito*) of the sanctuary implements found in Jerusalem: N. Avigad, *Discovering Jerusalem* (Oxford: Blackwell, 1984) 147–49 [Hebrew]; and B. Narkis, "A Scheme of the Sanctuary from the Time of Herod the Great," *JJA* 1 (1974) 6–14.

50. Exod 25:23–30 and 37:10–16. This is repeated by Josephus as well as by the talmudic sources that describe the Table of Shewbread of the Second Temple; see: Josephus *Ant.* 3.139–43; *m. Menah.* 11:5 and parallels.

51. *M. Bik.* 3:8.

52. *Y. Bik.* 3.4, 65d.

Fig. 12. The basket of firstfruits. Photo by G. Laron.

The Holy One said "When you offered the shewbread you would sow a little and reap plenty, but now you sow plenty and reap little . . . and the fig will not bud since the offering of the firstfruit has ceased; there is no yield on the vine since libation has ceased; the olives have failed, since olive oil is no longer used for lighting . . . the sheep have vanished from the fold, since daily sacrifices have ceased; and there are no cattle in the shed since the bull [sacrifices] have been canceled." Rabbi Shimon Ben Gamliel said that, since the destruction of

Fig. 13. *Bands 3–4, depicting themes related to the tabernacle and the Temple. Photo by G. Laron.*

the Temple, a day does not pass without a curse . . . , but in the world to come the Almighty will restore the blessings that He has provided, as cited: "But you, O mountains of Israel, shall yield your produce and bear your fruit for my people Israel, for their return is near."[53]

The Temple and sacrifices were a source of inspiration and blessing for the entire universe, according to the midrash. Once the Temple was destroyed, this bounty in the world ceased to exist, but the Almighty promised His people that in the future He will restore his blessings. The daily sacrifice, the Table of Shewbread, and the firstfruits play a dominant role in this sermon, and all appear in the Sepphoris mosaic. These three items reflect all of the needs of man in this world, but this is not the reason for their presentation in the mosaic. They were chosen not only to depict the plenteousness during the time of the Temple but also to serve as the focus of the religious and eschatological message that is intertwined throughout the mosaic. It reflects religious aspirations that prevailed among the Jews of Palestine regarding redemption and the rebuilding of the Temple, the message that is also at the heart of the midrash cited. Just as in the past God filled his world with an abundance of good because of the worship in the Temple, so in the future He will redeem His people, rebuild the ruined Temple, and return his bounty to the world.

53. *Midr. Tanḥ., Tezaveh* 10 (Buber 52).

The entire floor is made up of various scenes, but an examination of the relationship between them brings to light three focal points within the mosaic. First is the rendering of the Hospitality of Abraham and the Binding of Isaac, representing God's covenant. The zodiac in the center symbolizes the centrality of God in the universe, in the promise and the process of redemption. The various Temple and tabernacle scenes symbolize redemption. The main theme of this mosaic is that God is the center of creation, has chosen His people, the people of Israel, and in the future, due to His promise to Abraham on Mount Moriah, He will rebuild the Temple and redeem the children of Abraham. It was not by chance that the zodiac, expressing the strength and sovereignty of God in the universe, was placed in the center of the floor. It is actually the link between the past—the promise given to Abraham on Mount Moriah—and the future redemption and the rebuilding of the Temple. It is in the power of the true ruler of the world, who had made a promise in the past, eventually to keep this promise.[54] This idea, which appears in Jewish prayers, in the rabbis' sermons, and in liturgical poetry, was meant to convey a clear message to the community through art about the rebuilding of the Temple and the future redemption.[55] The depictions in the Sepphoris synagogue mosaic may also be an artistic reflection of the Judeo-Christian dialogue regarding the identity of the chosen people, the rebuilding of the Temple, and the Messiah, during whose time redemption will occur.[56] Allusions to this dialogue can be found in rabbinic literature as well as in the works of the church fathers.[57]

Summary

The architecture of the Sepphoris synagogue, the abundance of dedicatory inscriptions both in Aramaic and Greek in the floor, and above all, the variety of depictions incorporated into the mosaic and their iconographic richness accord this find an important place in Jewish art and history. Some of the narrative depictions presented on the central carpet of the mosaic have not been found to date in any other synagogues in ancient Palestine. The various scenes included in the mosaic and the interpretation of their iconographic layout shed new light on synagogue art and, in certain cases, lead to a reconsideration of previous interpretations.

54. For a broader discussion of the subject with regard to the Sepphoris mosaic, see Weiss and Netzer, *Promise and Redemption*, 34–39.

55. R. Kimelman, "The Daily Amidah and the Rhetoric of Redemption," *JQR* 79 (1989) 165–97, esp. 180–82; Y. Yahalom, "The Temple and the City in Hebrew Liturgical Poetry," in *The History of Jerusalem, 1: The Early Islamic Period (638–1099)* (ed. J. Prawer; Jerusalem: Yad Yitshak Ben-Tsvi) 215–33 [Hebrew].

56. Weitzmann and Kessler, *The Frescoes of the Dura Synagogue and Christian Art*, 178–83.

57. See, for example, E. E. Urbach, "Rabbinical Exegesis and Origens' Commentaries on the Song of Songs and the Jewish-Christian Polemics," *Tarbiz* 30 (1960) 148–70 [Hebrew].

Our analysis of the architecture of the Sepphoris synagogue building and our study of the iconography of its mosaic and its implications for ancient Jewish art leave many unanswered questions. Although we are unable to answer all of these questions, this important find certainly broadens our knowledge and will prove valuable to many archaeologists and art historians, as well as to scholars studying the history of Jewish society and its literature in Late Antiquity.

Art and the Liturgical Context of the Sepphoris Synagogue Mosaic

Steven Fine

Baltimore Hebrew University

This essay is dedicated to Professor Dov Noy,
the father of Jewish folklore study in Israel
and a dear friend

The discovery of a fifth-century synagogue mosaic during the construction of a parking lot in Sepphoris National Park in 1993 created immediate excitement among scholars. It is no wonder. No discovery of Jewish narrative art in Israel has matched this one since kibbutzniks digging a water channel uncovered the Beth Alpha synagogue mosaic and brought it to the attention of Eliezer Lippa Sukenik in late 1928.[1] In fact, the Sepphoris synagogue mosaic is the single most important discovery of late antique narrative art from a Jewish context in Israel since the Beth Alpha synagogue. Here in one mosaic are unique images, not only of a Torah shrine and zodiac wheel, but of the Visit to Abraham by the Divine Messengers, the Binding of Isaac, "Aaron" in the Tabernacle, and images drawn from the sacrificial cult itself. Zeev Weiss and Ehud Netzer, excavators of this monument, describe this floor in their preliminary report. The authors show a number of instructive parallels to this mosaic from late antique Christian art and cite literary parallels for each of the panels from rabbinic literature. This series of iconographic interpretations is then woven into an all-encompassing global theory that connects

Author's note: I would like to thank Selma Holo, Stuart Miller, Lawrence Schiffman, and Rhoda Terry for their valuable insights at various stages of this project.

1. On the discovery of Beth Alpha, see N. Silberman, *A Prophet from amongst You: The Life of Yigael Yadin—Soldier, Scholar, Mythmaker of Modern Israel* (Reading, Mass.: Addison-Wesley, 1993) 21; E. M. Meyers, "Ancient Synagogues: An Archaeological Introduction," in *Sacred Realm: The Emergence of the Synagogue in the Ancient World* (ed. S. Fine; New York: Oxford University Press, 1996) 3–6.

each of the images, which Weiss and Netzer call "Promise and Redemption."[2] In the conclusion of the handsome exhibition catalog, the authors sum up their approach as follows:

> When the mosaic is read as a whole, as a single structured scheme, the significance of each of its foci in the overall message becomes clear: the Angels' Visit to Abraham and Sarah and the Binding of Isaac symbolize the promise; the zodiac expresses God's centrality in creation, in his promise, and in redemption; and the architectural facade and other symbols associated with the Tabernacle and Temple represent the future redemption.

The search for a global interpretation and the choice of the messianic idea as the unifying theme have a long history in the historiography of Jewish art. Rachel Wischnitzer, for example, adopted the messianic stance in her 1948 study *The Messianic Theme in the Paintings of the Dura Synagogue*.[3] The messianic interpretation continues to have currency, primarily among art historians, to this day.[4] Other scholars have suggested differing metatexts for interpreting Jewish narrative art. Herbert Kessler, for example, sees the paintings at Dura as polemical documents that represent a messianic theme in response to an ascendant Christianity.[5] John Wilkinson[6] interprets the Beth Alpha mosaic as a neo-Platonic projection of the Jerusalem Temple. E. R. Goodenough, working almost exclusively from Hellenistic Jewish sources, constructed an interpretive schema for ancient Jewish art based on Jungian psychology and an errant notion that a non-rabbinic mystical Judaism is preserved in the material remains of synagogues.[7]

2. Z. Weiss and E. Netzer, *Promise and Redemption: A Synagogue Mosaic from Sepphoris*, (Jerusalem: Israel Museum, 1996) 38. See also Weiss and Netzer, "The Synagogue Mosaic," in *Sepphoris in Galilee: Crossroads of Culture* (ed. R. M. Nagy et al.; Raleigh: North Carolina Museum of Art, 1996) 133–39.

3. R. Wischnitzer, *The Messianic Theme in the Paintings of the Dura Synagogue* (Chicago: University of Chicago Press, 1948). P. V. M. Flesher, "Rereading the Reredos: David, Orpheus and Messianism in the Dura Europos Synagogue," in *Ancient Synagogues: Historical Analysis and Archaeological Discovery* (ed. D. Urman and P. V. M. Flesher; Leiden: Brill, 1995) 2.346–66.

4. See, for example, A. St. Clair, "God's House of Peace in Paradise: The Feast of Tabernacles on a Jewish Gold Glass," *Jewish Art* 11 (1985) 6–15; E. Revel-Neher, "L'Alliance et la Promesse: Le symbolism d'Eretz Israël dans l'iconographie juive du moyen âge," *Jewish Art* 12–13 (1986–87) 135–46; L. Roussin, "The Beit Leontis Mosaic: An Eschatological Interpretation," *Jewish Art* 8 (1981) 6–19. Against this approach at Dura, see Flesher, "Rereading the Reredos." Flesher in turn underestimates the messianic content of the Dura-Europos synagogue wall paintings.

5. K. Weitzmann and H. Kessler, *The Frescoes of the Dura Synagogue and Christian Art* (Washington, D.C.: Dumbarton Oaks, 1990). See the critique of A. J. Wharton, "Good and Bad Images from the Synagogue of Dura Europos: Contexts, Subtexts, Intertexts," *Art History* 17/1 (1994) 7–9.

6. J. Wilkinson, "The Beth Alpha Synagogue Mosaic: Towards an Interpretation," *Jewish Art* 5 (1978) 16–28.

7. E. R. Goodenough, *Jewish Symbols in the Greco-Roman Period* (Princeton: Princeton University Press, 1953–68). For reviews of Goodenough's work, see M. Smith, "Goodenough's

I myself can think of at least one alternative metanarrative that could cred-
ibly explain the Sepphoris mosaic utilizing mainly contemporaneous Palestinian Jewish literature that is radically different from the *Promise and
Redemption* model. One might suggest, for example, that the mosaic treats
the synagogue as a replacement for the Temple, as an institution that replaces
the sacrificial system (represented in the Binding of Isaac panel and Aaron
before the Altar) with prayer and the study of Scripture. The zodiac wheel
could represent, as Shaye Cohen has somewhat tentatively suggested about
earlier discoveries, the centrality of the synagogue in Jewish life. In Cohen's
words: "Perhaps some Jews attempted to attribute this centrality [of the
Temple] to the synagogues by depicting the zodiac and the sun chariot in the
middle of mosaic floors, as if to say, 'here is the center of the cosmos; our
synagogue performs the role once performed by the temple.'"[8] In this paper,
I will make a first attempt at a more multivalent interpretive hermeneutic
than the ones that have been proposed to this point. The approach that I will
suggest stresses the factor that unifies all of the images: their relationship to
the liturgically recited and enacted sacred texts of the synagogue. I will argue
that the synagogue mosaic of Sepphoris must be interpreted primarily in
terms of the various liturgical expressions that took place upon it.

The approach that I am suggesting has, in fact, been used with considerable results by scholars of Christian art. A number of scholars, foremost
among them Thomas Mathews and Peter Brown,[9] have interpreted the late
antique church building as the backdrop for the liturgical life of a community. The most extreme proponent of the liturgical interpretation of Christian
art is the Norwegian scholar Soren Sinding-Larsen. Sinding-Larsen has suggested, with much justification, that the art of late antique and Medieval
churches actually took on different meanings depending on the liturgy
pronounced before, within, or upon it. That is to say, "Liturgy determines

Jewish Symbols in Retrospect," *JBL* 86 (1967) 66. The most important discussion of Goodenough to appear since then is R. Brilliant, "'Jewish Symbols': Is That Still Good Enough?"
in *Commentaries on Roman Art: Selected Studies* (London: Pindar, 1994) 233–44.

8. S. J. D. Cohen, "The Temple and the Synagogue," in *The Temple in Antiquity* (ed.
T. G. Madsen; Provo: Brigham Young University Press, 1984) 170–71. I have argued against
this approach in my book, *This Holy Place: On the Sanctity of the Synagogue during the
Greco-Roman Period* (Notre Dame, Ind.: University of Notre Dame Press, 1997) passim,
esp. 7–8; see also my "Did the Synagogue Replace the Temple?" in *Bible Review* 12/2
(1996) 18–26, 41.

9. T. F. Mathews, *The Early Churches of Constantinople: Architecture and Liturgy* (University Park: Pennsylvania State University Press, 1971); P. Brown, "Art and Society in Late
Antiquity," in *The Age of Spirituality: A Symposium* (ed. K. Weitzmann; New York: Metropolitan Museum of Art, 1980). For a survey of scholarly approaches to this issue, see S. De
Blaauw, "Architecture and Liturgy in Late Antiquity and the Middle Ages: Traditions and
Trends in Modern Scholarship," *Archiv für Liturgie-Wissenschaft* 33/1 (1991) 1–34. A similarly contextual approach was applied by Linda Safran to the Theodosian obelisk base in
the Hippodrome of Constantinople. See L. Safran, "Points of View: The Theodosian Obelisk Base in Context," *Greek, Roman and Byzantine Studies* 34 (1993) 409–35.

specific modes of relationship in action and idea between the onlooker or
congregation and the subject illustrated in the liturgical iconography."[10]
Sinding-Larsen goes so far as to see the meaning of church art changing according to the progression of a given liturgy. He makes his position clear in
his discussion of the apse of the Medieval church of San Clemente in Rome:
"The figure of Christ [in the apse at San Clemente] obtains a complete sense
only when evaluated in its functional context, which is that of the altar, and
the point is that this meaning is changing, consisting as it does of multiple
elements in varying relations to one another—rather like molecules in reaction."[11] According to this approach, the art and architecture of churches in
late antiquity were a "backdrop" for the liturgical life of its community, a
"set" on which the priests and the rest of the community were the "actors."
Like every good stage set, of course, the architecture and art of the church
were a reflection, reaction, and complement to the variety of performances
that took place there.

While synagogue remains in Palestine are not nearly as rich as the
churches of Rome, Ravenna, and Constantinople, many of the insights of
scholars of Christian art are applicable to the Sepphoris mosaic. The question that I will address is how this mosaic functioned within the total liturgical space of the synagogue. I begin by discussing the organization of the floor
and some of its relationships with Christian iconography. I will then turn to
the meaning of the floor itself. It is my belief that the Sepphoris synagogue
floor does not encode a self-evident global meaning that can be summed up
in a kerygma-like statement—at least not one that we can uncover with any
degree of reliability. Rather, this floor should be interpreted in terms of the liturgical life of the synagogue community that was enacted upon it, which included prayer, Scripture reading, and homiletics.

The general characteristics of the Sepphoris synagogue mosaic fit well
with the synagogue discoveries that preceded it. As in the fourth-century mosaic of Ḥammath Tiberias and the sixth-century floors at Beth Alpha and
Naʿaran, the center of the nave is dominated by a large zodiac wheel.[12] Close
to the *bemot* of these synagogues is the image of a Torah shrine flanked by

---

10. S. Sinding-Larsen, *Iconography and Ritual: A Study of Analytical Perspectives*
(Oslo: Universitetsforlaget, 1984) 95; G. Hellemo, *Adventus Domini: Eschatological
Thought in 4th-Century Apses and Catecheses* (Leiden: Brill, 1989) esp. xx–xxi. Hellemo's
corrective of Sinding-Larsen's disinterest in object-centered analysis is quite in order: "We
agree with Sinding-Larsen's theoretical considerations but do, at the same time, maintain
that the complicated 'dogmatical and doctrinal concepts expressed in the liturgy,' can only
be captured by a sort of iconological investigation" (p. xxi). "Iconology" is a term made
popular by E. Panofsky in his seminal essay, "Iconography and Iconology," in *Meaning of
the Visual Arts* (Garden City, N.Y.: Doubleday, 1955) 26–54.
11. Sinding-Larsen, *Iconography and Ritual*, 38.
12. The most convenient survey of synagogue archaeology is R. Hachlili, *Ancient Jewish Art and Archaeology in the Land of Israel* (Leiden: Brill, 1988). On the zodiac wheel, see
pp. 301–9.

two seven-branched menorahs. The discovery of the Nabratein Torah shrine aedicula[13] and remains of free-standing seven-branched menorahs at Hammath Tiberias, Eshtemoa, Maon in Judea, and Khirbet Susiya[14] make this more than just a hypothesis. The menorahs from the Judean Hills region, from Eshtemoa, Maon, and Khirbet Susiya, are quite similar in conception and execution and may represent a regional type. A parallel phenomenon in Christian art, where we find the furnishings of church apses illustrated on floor mosaics, confirms this interpretation.[15] The Torah shrine, flanked by lampstands, was the most important feature of the synagogue interior, the menorahs serving as spotlights for the *bema* and providing light for reading Scripture.[16] The selective reverse mirroring of the Torah shrine and menorahs in the mosaics at Sepphoris, Beth Alpha, Na'aran, Horvat Susiya, Beth-Shean A, and Hammath Tiberias B served to emphasize the central significance of the Torah shrine within the hall in much the same way that a reflecting pool added grandeur to many an ancient Roman building[17] and does so to public buildings today. At Sepphoris the shrine was reflected not only in the Torah ark panel but also in the image of the Tabernacle that was just below it. This visual alignment of the gabled Torah shrine and the partially gabled Tabernacle altar may suggest a conceptual tie between them, paralleling numerous literary sources. The earliest of these presents the synagogue as

13. E. M. Meyers, J. Strange, and C. Meyers, "The Ark of Nabratein: A First Glance," *BA* 44 (1981) 237–43; E. Meyers and C. Meyers, "Finders of the Lost Ark," *BARev* 7/4 (1981) 24–39.

14. *Hammath Tiberias*: N. Slouschz, "Hammath-by-Tiberias," *Journal of the Jewish Palestine Exploration Society* 1 (1921) 32 [Hebrew]; S. Fine (ed.) *Sacred Realm: The Emergence of the Synagogue in the Ancient World* (New York: Oxford University Press, 1996) 168, pl. 25.

Eshtemoa: in a letter dated 3 March 1992, Z. Yeivin, excavator of this synagogue, informed me: "The Eshtemoa menorah fragment was not discovered within its niche — rather, nearby among the ruins. It is our suggestion that the holy ark stood in the central niche and that in the two side niches were two menorahs, pieces of which were discovered also in the synagogue of Horvat Susiya" [my translation].

Maon in Judea: D. Amit, "A Marble Menorah from an Ancient Synagogue at Tel Ma'on," *Proceedings of the Tenth World Congress of Jewish Studies (1989)*, division B, vol. 1: *The History of the Jewish People* (Jerusalem: World Union of Jewish Studies, 1990) 53–60 [Hebrew]. The menorah was reconstructed under the direction of Y. Israeli at the Israel Museum and is illustrated in S. Fine (ed.), *Sacred Realm*, 37.

Khirbet Susiya: Z. Yeivin, "Reconstruction of the Southern Interior Wall of the Khorazin Synagogue," *ErIsr* 18 (Avigad Volume; 1985) 272 [Hebrew]; idem, "Khirbet Susiya, the Bima, and Synagogue Ornamentation," in *Ancient Synagogues in Israel* (ed. R. Hachlili; Oxford: BAR, 1989) 94–95, figs. 12–13.

15. See Fine (ed.), *Sacred Realm*, 173, pl. 9; G. Foerster, "Christian Allegories and Symbols in the Mosaic Designs of 6th Century Eretz Israel Synagogues," in *Jews, Samaritans and Christians in Byzantine Palestine* (ed. D. Jacoby and Y. Tsafrir; Jerusalem: Yad Yitzhak Ben-Tsvi, 1988) 198–200 [Hebrew].

16. See my *This Holy Place*, 116; D. R. Dendy, *The Use of Lights in Christian Worship* (London: SPCK, 1959) 17.

17. For example, the garden peristyle of the Villa of the Papyri in Herculaneum. See J. J. Deiss, *Herculaneum: Italy's Buried Treasure* (Malibu: Getty Museum, 1989) 62–63.

a kind of small temple and the latest of them understands the Jerusalem
Temple as a kind of big synagogue.[18] The image of the Binding of Isaac at
Sepphoris is also not unheralded. A less-refined version from about a century
later was discovered at Beth Alpha.[19] The rest of the biblical scenes, while
unique and exciting, fall into well-established categories. Biblical narrative
scenes were discovered at a number of sites: Noah's Ark was uncovered at
Gerasa, Daniel in the Lions' Den at Naʿaran and probably at Khirbet Susiya,
and David the Sweet Singer of Israel at Gaza[20]—not to mention the geographically and chronologically distant wall paintings at Dura-Europos,
which were destroyed around 256 C.E.[21] Significantly, the only distinctively
Jewish contents that can be identified in the Sepphoris mosaic are the Torah
shrine panel and the images of vessels from the Temple cult. In fact, without
the menorahs and the Hebrew and Jewish Aramaic inscriptions, the synagogue floor might be mistaken for a church mosaic! All of the imagery has
clear Christian parallels. Weiss and Netzer have shown important parallels to
the Binding of Isaac in the Ravenna wall mosaics, and close parallels can be
found as well for the Table of Shewbread,[22] the image of Aaron before the
Tabernacle,[23] and the zodiac.[24] The image of Aaron before the Tabernacle at
Sepphoris is well designed with concern for perspective and spacing. This
depiction is ultimately drawn from general Greco-Roman iconography,
where images of priests sacrificing before temples are common. A similar
image was discovered in the Dura-Europos synagogue,[25] though there is no
direct relationship between these depictions.[26] Below the Aaron register are

18. See my *This Holy Place*, 35–94; idem, "From Meeting House to Sacred Realm: Ho-
liness and the Ancient Synagogue," in *Sacred Realm: The Emergence of the Synagogue in
the Ancient World* (ed. S. Fine; New York: Oxford University Press, 1996) 24–34.
    19. On Christian parallels to the Beth Alpha Binding of Isaac, see J. Gutmann, "The
Sacrifice of Isaac: Variations on a Theme in Early Jewish and Christian Art," in *Sacred
Images: Studies in Jewish Art from Antiquity to the Middle Ages* (Northampton, Mass.:
Variorum Reprints, 1989) 115–22; and idem, "Revisiting the Binding of Isaac Mosaic at
Beth Alpha," *BAI* 6 (1992) 79–85.
    20. Hachlili, *Ancient Jewish Art and Architecture*, 297–98. On the supposed identifica-
tion of David in the Meroth mosaic, see S. Fine, *Sacred Realm*, 166–67.
    21. See S. James, "Dura-Europos and the Chronology of Syria in the 250s A.D.," *Chi-
ron* 15 (1985) 111–24; D. MacDonald, "Dating the Fall of Dura-Europos," *Historia* 35/1
(1986) 45–68.
    22. Weiss and Netzer, *Promise and Redemption*, 24–25.
    23. Ibid., 20–23.
    24. G. Hanfmann, "The Continuity of Classical Art: Culture, Myth and Faith," in *The
Age of Spirituality: A Symposium* (ed. K. Weitzmann; New York: Metropolitan Museum of
Art, 1980) 79–82.
    25. On images of sacrifice at Dura, see Kessler in Weitzmann and Kessler, *The Frescoes
of the Dura Synagogue and Christian Art*, 156.
    26. K. Weitzmann and his school posit the existence of an illustrated Jewish manuscript
tradition that preceded and ultimately connected the paintings of Dura Europos to medieval Jewish and Christian book illumination. See K. Weitzmann, "The Illustration of the
Septuagint," in *No Graven Images: Studies in Art and the Hebrew Bible* (ed. J. Gutmann;

three panels portraying cult objects from the Tabernacle/Temple. To the right is a basket of firstfruits and in the center panel the table for showbread. To the left is an assemblage of four elements of the Temple sacrifice: a lamb, a jar of oil, two horns, and a container of flour. Each of the four is labeled in Hebrew. The registers are connected explicitly through the truncated citation of Num 28:4 (or perhaps Exod 29:39). A lamb in the upper register is labeled *et ha-keves ehad* 'the one lamb', and the lamb in the lower register is labeled *ve-et ha-keves ha-sheni* 'and the second lamb'. This register reflects no attempt at perspective and so is very different from the Aaron register above. The awkward attempt by the Sepphoris artisans to connect the image of Aaron before the Tabernacle with the cultic paraphernalia in the register below reflects poorly on the skill level of the designer(s) of the Sepphoris mosaic, or their sources.[27]

The organization of the various images on the floors at Ḥammath Tiberias, Beth Alpha, Naʿaran, Ḥorvat Susiya, and Sepphoris reflects the creativity both of the local artisans and of the communities that they served. While the large zodiac was always placed in the center and the ark near the bema, the biblical scenes were placed in a number of different arrangements. At Beth Alpha the Binding of Isaac appears near the northern entrance to the basilica; at Naʿaran Daniel appears immediately before the ark in an orans position that may be reminiscent of a synagogue prayer position in late antiquity.[28] At Susiya the organization was entirely different because the hall was a broadhouse and not a basilica. The organizing principle at Sepphoris, it seems to me, was first and foremost the placement of the zodiac near the center of the long nave and of the Torah shrine image near (though not adjacent to) the

---

New York: Ktav, 1971) 201–31; J. Gutmann, "The Illustrated Jewish Manuscript in Antiquity: The Present State of the Question," also in *No Graven Images*, 232–48; Weitzmann and Kessler, *The Frescoes of the Dura Synagogue and Christian Art*. This approach is accepted implicitly by Weiss and Netzer, *Promise and Redemption* (e.g., p. 32) and is refuted persuasively by Gutmann, "Illustrated Jewish Manuscript in Antiquity," 232–48; idem, "The Illustrated Midrash in the Dura Europos Synagogue Paintings: A New Dimension for the Study of Judaism," *PAAJR* 50 (1983) 100–104.

27. On pattern books, see: B. Goldman, *The Sacred Portal: A Primary Symbol in Ancient Judaic Art* (Detroit: Wayne State University Press, 1966) 143–44; C. M. Dauphin, "Byzantine Pattern Books and 'Inhabited Scroll' Mosaics," *Art History* 4 (1988) 401–23; M. Piccirillo, "The Mosaics of Jordan," *The Art of Jordan, Treasures from an Ancient Land* (ed. P. Bienkowski; Stroud, England: Sutton, 1991) 129; L. A. Hunt, "The Byzantine Mosaics of Jordan in Context: Remarks on Imagery, Donors and Mosaicists," *PEQ* 126 (1994) 121–23 and n. 28.

28. G. Alon, *Studies in Jewish History* (Tel Aviv: ha-Kibuts ha-Meuḥad, 1967) 181–84 [Hebrew]; Y. Deviri, *Light in the Sayings and Aphorisms of the Sages* (Holon, Israel: Deviri, 1976) 112–15 [Hebrew]; E. Zimmer, *Society and Its Customs: Studies in the History and Metamorphosis of Jewish Customs* (Jerusalem: Zalman Shazar, 1996) 78–88 [Hebrew]; D. Sperber, *The Customs of Israel* (Jerusalem: Rav Kook, 1994) 3.88–91 [Hebrew]; S. Fine, *This Holy Place*, 125.

ark. The Abraham narrative was then grouped together below the zodiac and the Temple/tabernacle above the zodiac and below the Torah shrine due to the architectural resonances shared by the synagogue ark.

What does all of this mean? The answer is difficult, specifically because I am not willing to conjecture an intricate global interpretation of the mosaic, apart from the thesis that Scripture and liturgy were the unifying glue of the composition. I imagine that the imagery of the Binding of Isaac had different meaning on Rosh Hashanah than it did at other times, just as the Temple imagery would have been seen differently on Passover than on *Tishah be-Av*, the anniversary of the destruction of the Jerusalem Temple. Fortunately, literary sources provide some relief. Large quantities of more-or-less contemporaneous local literature, with which we may interpret this floor, is extant, much of it discovered in the Cairo Genizah. Many examples are cited by Weiss and Netzer. The rich "literature of the synagogue," as Joseph Heinemann and Jakob Petuchowski call it, ranges from homiletical midrashic collections to liturgical texts to Aramaic paraphrases of Scripture (the targums).[29] What unites all of this literature is not only its apparent synagogue context but also its focus on the biblical text.[30] While it is useful to draw parallels from the rabbinic corpus to interpret individual images, this practice creates a kind of textual free-for-all when one then attempts to construct a unifying interpretation. Fortunately, the large number of extant liturgical poems, piyyutim (from the Greek *poietas*), provides a kind of control. Written by individuals, these poems can be roughly dated. The piyyutim differ markedly from the midrashic collections, with their long and often difficult redactional histories and their unclear *Sitzen im Leben*. They also differ from the targums, which were also the work of numerous hands. Reading through one poet's corpus of work, one can observe how a single Jew in late antique Palestine formulated and reformulated traditions in the synagogues of his day. The best example for our purposes is Yannai the *Paytan*, a sixth-century poet whom Menahem Zulay aptly called *Raban shel ha-Paytanim*, the 'master of the piyyut writers'. Z. M. Rabinowitz, the most recent editor of Yannai's corpus, assembled 165 poems from the Cairo Genizah to be recited on the Sabbath according to the

---

29. J. Heinemann and J. J. Petuchowski, *The Literature of the Synagogue* (New York: Behrman House, 1975). See A. Shinan's survey of this literature, "Synagogues in the Land of Israel: The Literature of the Ancient Synagogue and Synagogue Archaeology," in *Sacred Realm: The Emergence of the Synagogue in the Ancient World* (ed. S. Fine; New York: Oxford University Press, 1996) 130–52. On midrashic literature in general, see H. L. Strack and G. Stemberger, *Introduction to the Talmud and Midrash* (trans. M. Bockmuehl; Edinburgh: T. & T. Clark, 1992) 254–393. On targum, see P. Alexander, "Jewish Aramaic Translations of Hebrew Scriptures," in *Mikra* (ed. M. J. Mulder; Philadelphia: Fortress, 1990) 217–53. On prayer and piyyut, see I. Elbogen, *Jewish Liturgy: A Comprehensive History* (trans. R. P. Scheindlin; Philadelphia: Jewish Publication Society, 1993); E. Fleischer, *Hebrew Liturgical Poetry in the Middle Ages* (Jerusalem: Keter, 1975) 23–275 [Hebrew].

30. To these may be added traditions that are preserved in the Mishna, the Tosepta, and the Palestinian and Babylonian Talmuds.

so-called triennial cycle and another 15 or so for special days.[31] The striking fact is that all of the issues that appear in the Sepphoris mosaic are dealt with by Yannai, from the Binding of Isaac to Aaron in the Tabernacle to the Table of Shewbread to the firstfruits, menorah, and zodiac.[32] By reading how this author understood these subjects, we can construct a picture of how one Jew (who could have visited the Sepphoris synagogue) understood the themes that were set in stone by the mosaicist.

For the purpose of this essay, I will cite one poem by Yannai that within just a few lines utilizes many of the themes represented on the Sepphoris floor. The poem was recited on Rosh Hashanah. This extended poem, like the rest of Yannai's poetry, reflects on the liturgical themes of the day as it poetically embellishes the themes of the central Tefillah prayer that it celebrates. While I am in no way suggesting that this particular poem influenced the design of the mosaic on the floor (or vice-versa), it is my contention that the selection and arrangement of themes to decorate the Sepphoris mosaic and the selection and arrangement of themes by the liturgical poet are each reflections of how Jews constructed the synagogue environment through image and word during nearly the same time period.[33] The literary and the visual artists assembled similar building blocks in constructing their individual artistic creations for synagogue settings. The section of Yannai's poem that concerns us translates as follows:[34]

Then the shofar will be blown for the Complete [One],
Desiring complete [shofars] just as he desires the complete sacrifice [in
   the Temple].

Hence any shofar that has a fissure,
Is not fit, for it interrupts the sounding.

Come forth with a broken soul and not with a broken horn,
With a broken heart and not with a broken shofar.

Lovers drawn after Him (God) and, as the girdle, cleave—
They will sound a long shofar that has no adhesions.

---

31. Z. M. Rabinowitz (ed.), *The Liturgical Poetry of Rabbi Yannai* (Jerusalem: Bialik, 1985–87); S. Lieberman, "Ḥazanut Yannai," *Sinai* 4 (1939) 221–50 [Hebrew]; M. Zulay, "Rabban shel ha-Paytanim," in *Eretz Israel and Its Poetry* (ed. E. Hazan; Jerusalem: Magnes, 1995) 85–94 [Hebrew].

32. For example, see Rabinowitz (ed.), *The Liturgical Poetry of Rabbi Yannai*: firstfruits, 2.175–82; menorah, 1.340–45, 2.35–40, 242; zodiac, 1.83–89, 2.242.

33. The relationship between synagogue mosaics and piyyut literature has been discussed by A. Mirsky, "Aquarius and Aries in the Ein Gedi Inscription and in Early Piyyutim," *Tarbiz* 40 (1970) 376–84 [Hebrew]; and most pointedly by J. Yahalom, "The Zodiac Wheel in Early Piyyut in Eretz-Israel," *Jerusalem Studies in Hebrew Literature* 9 (1986) 313–22 [Hebrew]; idem, "Piyyut as Poetry," in *The Synagogue in Late Antiquity* (ed. L. I. Levine; Philadelphia: ASOR, 1987) 111–26. See most recently Shinan, "Synagogues in the Land of Israel," 146–52.

34. Rabinowitz (ed.), *The Liturgical Poetry of Rabbi Yannai*, 2.204, and Rabinowitz's comments there.

For from the ram come the horns,
To remember the merit of the ram stuck by its horns [at the Binding
    of Isaac].

Sound, O sons of might, Sound to the God of might,
Who covers over and removes from them all sins.

A time of concealment when the moon is concealed,
To conceal sins well, just as the moon [is concealed].

The sun, how can it bear witness [to the new month] alone.
When one witness is not enough [for a court] to inflict the death
    penalty?

The [heavenly] array of the seventh month, its constellation is Libra,
For sin and righteousness God will lay upon the scales.

His hand will remove sin and we will proclaim the day with the shofar,
To the scale of utter righteousness He will incline.

I have cited enough of this text, which is very difficult to translate, to show that the themes of the shofar, the Binding of Isaac, the sun, moon, and astronomical symbols are among the building blocks for Yannai's Rosh Hashanah liturgy. Elsewhere in his corpus, Yannai weaves these themes and many others together in other ways, depending on the reading for the day and the festival context. It is important to note, however, that the Binding of Isaac, representing the doctrine of "merits of the ancestors,"[35] the zodiac, representing both the heavens and the Jewish solar-lunar calendar,[36] and the sacrificial system[37] are extremely common throughout Yannai's corpus due to their centrality within the Tefillah prayer upon which he artistically expands.[38] Yannai, reflecting on the Scripture readings of Rosh Hashanah, the ceremonies of that day, and the calendrical cycle, brings together images that give texture to his liturgical creation. That all of this imagery appears on our floor is no accident. These themes were central in Jewish liturgical life during this period.

To my mind, the Sepphoris floor is a preeminently liturgical piece. Its iconography, drawing from a tradition of synagogue art that was highly influ-

35. S. Schechter, *Aspects of Rabbinic Theology* (New York: Macmillan, 1909) 170–98; G. F. Moore, *Judaism in the First Centuries of the Common Era* (Cambridge: Harvard University Press, 1927–30) 1.538–46.

36. See Yahalom, "The Zodiac Wheel in Early Piyyut in Eretz-Israel."

37. On the significance of the sacrificial system in rabbinic prayer, see the sources cited in n. 35 above.

38. On the development of the Amidah, see I. Elbogen, *Jewish Liturgy: A Comprehensive History* (trans. R. P. Scheindlin; Philadelphia: Jewish Publication Society, 1993) esp. 24–54; J. Heinemann, *Prayer in the Talmud* (trans. R. S. Sarason; Berlin: de Gruyter, 1977) 13–24, 33–36, 50; R. Kimelman, "The Daily Amidah and the Rhetoric of Redemption," *JQR* 79 (1988–89) 165–97. Cf. E. Fleischer, *Eretz-Israel Prayers and Rituals as Portrayed in the Geniza Documents* (Jerusalem: Magnes, 1988) 14–15 [Hebrew].

enced by the iconographic possibilities of late antique Christian art, was organized so as to complement and give visual expression to the biblically infused prayers, Scripture reading, and homiletics of the synagogue. Did the artist have a metanarrative in mind? The sort of intense conceptual planning of a floor that is envisioned by Weiss and Netzer seems highly unlikely. I suspect that the iconography of the floor was chosen by consensus, based on convention, availability of models, the preferences of the community as a whole, and the preferences of the patrons whose names appear prominently at the top of each panel.[39] What unified the composition was the biblical text that stood within the ark at the focal point of the hall, which, through the refractive lenses of the literature of the synagogue, was projected onto the synagogue pavement.

In the end, however, it is important to remember that this pavement is just a floor. The images of Aaron, the sacrificial cult, Abraham, Sarah, Isaac, the angels, and even citations of biblical verses were regularly trodden upon by the Jews of Sepphoris.[40] Imagine what the synagogue would look like if the walls, the ark, the menorahs, and the other lamps that illuminated this synagogue were extant:[41] we would barely notice the pavement below, covered with furniture and perhaps with reed mats.[42] Walls painted with images like the ones in the Dura-Europos synagogue or covered with mosaics as in the churches of Ravenna and Bethlehem would require of us a completely different and considerably less grand attitude toward the Sepphoris floor mosaic and toward its ultimate "meaning"—both as an art object and as testimony to the rich liturgical life of late antique Palestinian synagogues.

39. See C. Dauphin, "Mosaic Pavements as an Index of Prosperity and Fashion," *Levant* 12 (1980) 112–34.

40. See my *This Holy Place*, 125. On Christian attitudes, see Y. Tsafrir, *Eretz Israel from the Destruction of the Second Temple to the Muslim Conquest: Art and Archaeology* (Jerusalem: Yad Yitshak Ben-Tsvi, 1984) 416–17 [Hebrew].

41. On remains of wall decoration, see Hachlili, *Ancient Jewish Art and Archaeology*, 224.

42. Genizah documents speak of "reed mats" within Fatamid-period synagogues, some of which were "large" and used for seating on the floor. See S. D. Goitein, "Ambol: The Raised Platform in the Synagogue," *ErIsr* 6 (Narkiss Volume; 1960) 166 [Hebrew]; idem, "The Synagogue Building and Its Furnishings according to the Records of the Cairo Geniza," *ErIsr* 7 (Mayer Volume; 1964) 82, 90–92 [Hebrew]; idem, *A Mediterranean Society* (Berkeley and Los Angeles: University of California Press, 1971) 1.149–50.

Palestinian Inscriptions and Jewish Ethnicity in Late Antiquity

Hayim Lapin

University of Maryland

This paper is offered as a contribution to current attempts to rethink the problem of Jewish ethnicity in late antiquity, by using Palestinian Jewish inscriptions as the basis for discussion. At the most general level, my argument is that, although lines of continuity between various communities over long periods of time can be drawn (and these should not be minimized), the study of Jewish ethnicity must seriously consider ethnicity as constructed and "ascribed." Part of the task is thus to explore change or even disjunctures in the constructions of "Jewishness" and in the term in which "Jewishness" was ascribed in concrete historical circumstances. More specifically, I argue that Palestinian inscriptions may be read as demonstrating the emergence of a new ethnic discourse marked by the fact that "Jewishness" was made explicit in epigraphic contexts for the first time. Furthermore, I will argue (more tentatively) that the expression of ethnicity is complementary to the development of Palestinian synagogues and communal ideals, which are also reflected in the inscriptions. After a brief discussion of some methodological issues, I will present a profile of the inscriptions, describing some of the kinds

Author's note: An earlier version of some of this material appeared as part of my doctoral dissertation, *Text, Money and Law: A Study of Mishnah Tractate Baba' Meṣi'a'* (Ph.Đ. diss., Columbia University, 1994) §III.A.2. An expansion of that study was presented as "Palestinian Epigraphy and the World of Judaism in Late Antiquity," at the 1994 American Academy of Religion / Society of Biblical Literature Annual Meeting (November 21, 1994). The present paper represents a substantial revision of this earlier material and was completed while I was NEH Fellow at the Albright Institute for Archaeological Research (Jerusalem) in 1996–97. Several people have read or discussed parts of this project and are due thanks: Daniel Boyarin, Leah Di Segni, Maxine L. Grossman, Lee I. Levine, Miriam Peskowitz, Jonathan Price, and Zeev Weiss. Special thanks are due to Kenneth G. Holum and C. M. Lehmann for allowing me to make use of a typescript of their editions of Caesarea inscriptions. The edition of Golan inscriptions by Gregg and Urman (cited occasionally below) arrived too late to be reviewed critically or utilized fully.

of social interactions that are presented in (or absent from) the inscriptions. Against this background I will attempt to tease out some of the themes of "Jewishness" in the inscriptions.

Some Methodological Problems

Before I turn to the inscriptions themselves, a brief discussion of methodological problems and presuppositions is in order. First, I have relied primarily on standard collections, and although I have made an effort to supplement them, I make no claims to completeness. For that very reason, much of the argument that I make will have to be provisional. In addition, within that body of inscriptions that are conventionally dated from the second or third century to the seventh century c.e., I have found it difficult to make any chronological distinctions that would allow for a developmental scheme. Naveh has long argued that Aramaic synagogue inscriptions are difficult or impossible to date paleographically because of conservatism in script.[1] Scholars working with Greek inscriptions are generally more comfortable making guesses based on paleography, but more frequently dating must rely on the archaeological context. Yet archaeological context too has become a problematic issue. Recent work on Beth She⁽arim, the locus for much of the funerary material, has stressed that the town was occupied and possibly made use of the necropolis long past the middle of the fourth century,[2] and the dating of synagogues continues to be problematic.[3] As a result, this study risks collapsing multicentury processes into a single phenomenon.

1. J. Naveh, *On Stone and Mosaic* (hereafter cited as Naveh; Jerusalem: Maariv, 1978) 4–6 [Heb.].
2. Z. Weiss, "Social Aspects of Burial in Beth She⁽arim," in *Galilee in Late Antiquity* (ed. L. I. Levine; New York: Jewish Theological Seminary, 1992) 370–71; F. Vitto, "Byzantine Monuments from Bet She⁽arim: New Evidence for the History of the Site," ⁽*Atiqot* 28 (1996) 115–46, esp. 137–41.
3. For a discussion of the problems of stylistic dating, see E. M. Meyers, "The Current State of Galilean Synagogue Studies," in *The Synagogue in Late Antiquity* (ed. L. I. Levine; Philadelphia: American Schools of Oriental Research, 1987) 127–37; idem, "Synagogue," *ABD* 6.251–60; cf. the restatement of the typological chronology in G. Foerster, "The Ancient Synagogues of the Galilee," in *Galilee in Late Antiquity* (ed. L. I. Levine; New York: Jewish Theological Seminary, 1992) 289–320. In particular, the claim of late dating (that is, not before the late fourth century) of the "early" type Capernaum synagogue has problematized the chronology (see the bibliography in Foerster, "Ancient Synagogues," 316–17; and Y. Tsafrir, "On the Source of the Architectural Design of the Ancient Synagogues of Galilee: A New Appraisal," in *Ancient Synagogues: Historical Analysis and Archeological Discovery* [ed. D. Urman and P. V. M. Flesher; SPB 47; Leiden: Brill, 1995] 79–93); see also Z. Ilan, "Synagogue and Study Hall at Meroth," in *Synagogues in Antiquity* (ed. A. Oppenheimer, A. Kasher, and U. Rappaport; Jerusalem: Yad Yitshak ben-Tsvi, 1987) 231–66 [Heb.]; and Y. Tsafrir, "The Synagogues at Meroth and Capernaum and the Dating of the Galilean Synagogues: A Reconsideration," *ErIsr* 20 (Yadin Volume; 1989) 337–44 [Heb.] (see also the response to Ilan, in Foerster, "Ancient Synagogues," 301–2). For an attempt to reassess the chronological development of synagogue forms, see D. E.

Second, I have relied almost exclusively on inscriptions and their context as the basis of my argument in order to talk about ethnicity, despite the fact that there are more expressive sources, particularly rabbinic material, to which appeal could be made. Rabbinic literature, although offering us well-articulated notions of Israel and its place in the world, is the product of an intellecutal and religious elite and therefore not necessarily reflective of a wider population; thus, it poses a complex of problems for historical reconstruction.[4] In contrast to literary remains, Palestinian Jewish inscriptions have two advantages for the present purposes. First, they are not, by and large, the product of rabbis.[5] Second, they are the concrete products of specific, and

---

Groh, "The Stratigraphic Chronology of the Galilean Synagogue from the Early Roman through the Early Byzantine Period (ca. 420 C.E.)," in *Ancient Synagogues*, 51–69. J. Magness ("Synagogue Typology and Earthquake Chronology at Khirbet Shema', Israel," *The Journal of Field Archaeology* 24 [1997] 211–20) has argued that there was no mid-third-century "broadhouse" synagogue at Khirbet Shema', as E. Netzer has it ("Review of the Synagogues at Gush Ḥalav and Khirbet Shema'," *ErIsr* 25 [Aviram Volume; 1996] 450–55 [Heb.]); he also assigns a fourth-century date to the synagogue at Gush Ḥalav. In the same volume as Netzer's essay, Z. U. Ma'oz ("When Were the Galilean Synagogues First Constructed?" 416–26 [Heb.]) argues that the primary period for Galilean synagogue-building should be seen as the late second or early third century.

4. See L. I. Levine, *The Rabbinic Class of Roman Palestine in Late Antiquity* (New York: Jewish Theological Seminary, 1989).

5. The presence of a rabbinic text from a synagogue in Rehov (Naveh no. 49) and of a lintel from Dabura in the Golan stating "this is the *bêt midraš* of R. Eliezer ha-Qappar" (Naveh no. 6) are sufficient to alert us to the spread of the rabbinic movement in Palestine. Nevertheless, it is well to be cautious. The Rehov inscription is from the sixth or seventh century, and it sheds no light on earlier phenomena. The Dabbura inscription is dated to the third century entirely on the basis of the similarity of the name on the inscription to the name of the rabbinic figure. Yet even if the named figure were the rabbinic Eleazar ha-Qappar, it remains possible that this is a later attribution to an earlier sage (note that the only analogies Naveh provides for this form of inscription are funerary, that is, commemorative: N. Avigad, *Beth She'arim,Volume III: Catacombs 12–23* (hereafter cited as BS III; New Brunswick, N.J.: Rutgers University Press, 1976) 5: "these sarcophagi, the inner and the outer . . ."; 17; there are more examples of this formula, including an abbreviated form, with the subject omitted: *zô šel* 'this [is the burial place] of . . .' or 'this belongs to . . .', e.g., BS III nos. 9, 10). The identification with the rabbinic Eleazar ha-Qappar (at least as an active figure) is made problematic by the fact that he is generally not associated with the Galilee or Golan in rabbinic texts, although D. Urman ("*Lĕ-šĕ'ēlat mĕqôm battê ha-midrāš šel bar qappārā' wĕ-r. hôša'yâ*," in *Ummâ wĕ-tolĕdôtehā* [ed. M. Stern; Jerusalem: Merkaz Zalman Shazar, 1983] 169–71) has attempted (unpersuasively) to place him in the Golan. It remains possible that the person named in this inscription is not identical to the Eleazar ha-Qappar known from rabbinic texts. D. Urman ("Jewish Inscriptions from Dabura in the Golan," *Tarbiz* 40 [1970–71] 407 [Heb.] = *IEJ* 22 [1972] 22), in suggesting that the ha-Qappar may be based on the [modern] name of the nearby village of Qefire, has laid the foundations for supposing that a local Eliezer, not necessarily identical with the rabbinic figure, is meant. I would similarly hesitate to identify the occupants in Catacomb 14 of Beth She'arim with Judah the Patriarch and his circle (for a detailed argument for identification, see BS III 62–65); Lifshitz (in M. Schwabe and B. Lifshitz, *Beth She'arim, Volume II: The Greek Inscriptions* [hereafter cited as BS II; New Brunswick, N.J.: Rutgers University Press,

generally quite localized, social relationships. As a result, inscriptions allow us, at least initially, to sidestep the dominance of the particular concerns of rabbinic texts. I am not claiming that rabbinic texts have no relevance for the study of Jewish ethnicity. Still less would I argue that literary texts are elite products while inscriptions put us in touch with the "masses," or that inscriptions are any more "objective" or ideologically "neutral" (this will become clear below). My argument is merely that, since inscriptions allow us to talk about nonrabbinic groups in communal contexts—no small thing—they deserve separate treatment.[6]

Third, I should point out the circularity of the project of studying Jewish ethnicity in antiquity, particularly through inscriptions. We recognize inscriptions as "Jewish" because they make use of symbols (*lûlab*, menorah), terminology (*rabbî*, *arkhisynagōgos*), or an onomasticon that we already recognize as Jewish, that are found in association with other inscriptions that do those things, or that are part of an installation (for example, a synagogue) that we recognize as Jewish. The circularity takes place in the modern (not unpoliticized) identification of what is truly or significantly Jewish. It also (and perhaps more significantly) results from the fact that we can only ask questions about ethnicity where, in antiquity, the social conventions that produced the inscriptions already structured the evidence as "Jewish." However, precisely because Jewish inscriptions are already structured as "Jewish," they can be used to give the impression that Jewish ethnicity was, in antiquity, a simple, obvious, and unproblematic thing. There are clearly good reasons to take such a view, such as the existence of a large body of literature produced by Jews and Gentiles over centuries and over a wide geographical area that knows precisely who "Jews" are. However, ethnicity in general and Jewish ethnicity in particular is a complex cultural construct built up over time through the lived experience of people by themselves and in communities and, as such, is a shifting, historically-conditioned social product. A view that begins with "Jewishness" as essentially knowable risks ignoring the shifting of the centers and boundaries of communities as people struggle with conditions that are only partially of their own making and, indeed, risks missing, even in the literary texts themselves, the investment in the creation, alteration, or maintenance of boundaries (as in the insistence in rabbinic texts on speaking to and for all of "Israel," or in a variety of Christian attempts in antiquity to create a disourse about "Jews").[7]

1974] 148 n. 6) questions the identification. For the whole question, see S. J. D. Cohen, "Epigraphical Rabbis," *JQR* 72 (1981) 1–17.

6. This is not to say that inscriptions and rabbinic texts cannot be profitably brought to bear upon one another. See, for example, L. I. Levine, "Synagogue Officials: The Evidence from Caesarea and Its Implications for Palestine and the Diaspora," in *Caesarea Maritima: A Retrospective after Two Millenia* (ed. A. Raban and K. G. Holum; Documenta et monumenta Orientis antiqui 21: Leiden: Brill, 1996) 392–400.

7. See "Introduction: Locating Ethnicity and Religious Community in Later Roman Palestine," in *Religious and Ethnic Communities in Later Roman Palestine* (ed. H. Lapin;

This circularity is inevitable, at least initially, if we are to say anything about questions of ethnic identity in antiquity as it is expressed in inscriptions. A funerary inscription, for example, that commemorates Zoila, her relations, the fact that she was devoted to her husband (*philandros*), her age at death, the date of her death, and the nondescript wish that she 'be of good courage' (*tharsei*)[8] gives no toehold, despite the fact that it was included in the *Corpus Inscriptionum Iudaicarum*. There is no way of knowing from the inscription whether the deceased and the person who provided the inscription were Jews or not, or if they were not, how they might have identified themselves or even, ultimately, how they might have understood that identity; we know only that they made none of this explicit. Yet, if we focus on "Jewish" inscriptions, the question of who was Jewish in late antique Palestine, how "Jewishness" was expressed, and what its implications were for the way in which people lived their lives is already partially answered before we have even begun.

These problems are unavoidable and ultimately insoluble and should not be wished away. In an effort to keep them in view, I have attempted not to assume that Jews would mark their inscriptions as Jewish. Instead, I have drawn attention to this marking precisely as a feature of late antique "Jewish" inscriptions. In examining synagogue inscriptions, in particular, I have also tried to ask what claims to community were being staked on the walls, columns, and floors of this developing Jewish institution. If there is any utiltity to this approach, the inscriptions serve as an index, if not to Jewish ethnicity in all its complexity, at least to a new pattern in the material display of Jewishness as an aspect of individual or communal identity in Palestine.

Profile of the Inscriptions

"Jewish" inscriptions from late antique Palestine are primarily the remains of ancient burials and of dedications in buildings collectively known as synagogues.[9] The burial inscriptions are almost exclusively exercises in naming:

Studies and Texts in Jewish History and Culture 5; Bethesda, Md.: University Press of Maryland, 1998) 1–28.

8. J. B. Frey, *Corpus Inscriptionum Iudaicarum* (hereafter cited as *CII*; Rome: Pontificio istituto di archeologia cristiana, 1936, 1952) no. 891, from Apollonias.

9. Two are explicitly so labeled in ancient Aramaic inscriptions (Hammath Gader, in an inscription found in situ [Naveh no. 34]; and a column section from Bet Guvrin [Naveh no. 71]). The Greek examples are either from too far afield (for Gerasa, see L. Roth-Gerson, *The Greek Inscriptions for the Synagogues in Eretz Israel* [hereafter cited as Roth-Gerson; Jerusalem: Yad Yitshak ben-Tsvi, 1987] no. 10) or exceptional in terms of both chronology and language (Jerusalem, Roth-Gerson 19). Z. Ilan argued that an inscription found north of Tiberias (and perhaps to be associated with Tiberias) mentioned a *kĕništā'* (Z. Ilan, "Ḥammat [Rakkath]: Aramaic Dedicatory Inscription," *Excavations and Surveys in Israel* 6 [1987–88] 110; idem, *Ancient Synagogues in Israel* [Tel Aviv: Misrad ha-Bitaḥon, 1991] 145 [Heb.]), but J. Naveh ("The Aramaic and Hebrew Inscriptions from Ancient Synagogues," *ErIsr* 20 [Yadin Volume; 1989] 307 [Heb.]) found this reading "difficult." The so-called

the name of the deceased, with or without titles, family connections, pious wishes, or other items.[10] Similarly, while synagogues may contain "literary" inscriptions—of which the most obvious example is surely the passage of a rabbinic text from Rehov[11]—even then, listing the names of donors is the most regular recurrent feature, and it is to these lists that I will pay particular attention. This naming, moreover, is embedded within specific and different social practices through which their "meaning" was constructed. To the extent that burial places, say, at Beth She'arim were private property, the funerary inscriptions announced the names of the deceased and other messages primarily to other family members on the occasion of the death of new members or on other visits.[12] The synagogue inscriptions, on the other hand, were aimed at a different section of the community, those who attended the synagogue and commemorated the donation of money or labor to the construction of the synagogue.[13] In both contexts (although in different ways) the inscriptions thus

---

"house of Leontis" at Beth-Shean (Roth-Gerson nos. 6–7) need not be a synagogue but is nevertheless some sort of public building (see the text of no. 7 and Roth-Gerson's discussion on pp. 37–38).

10. Exceptions include, for example, prohibitions against tampering with the tomb, as in BS II nos. 129, 134, 162; BS III nos. 1, 2, 3; or wishes for the deceased, as in BS II no. 194. I have taken formulas such as wishes accompanying the name or even more elaborate compositions, such as the Greek verse epigram for Ioustos (BS II no. 127), as extended examples of "naming." See further J. Naveh, *On Sherd and Papyrus* (Jerusalem: Magnes, 1992) 192–98 [Heb.].

11. The Rehov inscription is Naveh no. 49. For this distinction, applied to the synagogue inscriptions, see Naveh, *Sherd*, 118. The "literary" inscriptions also include the verse fragments used as labels in the scene of the binding of Isaac at Beth Alpha (Naveh no. 44), the greeting on the lintel inscription (Ilan, "Hamat [Rakkath]," 254), and the mosaic label based on Isa 11:6 (ibid., 257 and 259, fig. 12); and the verse fragments or labels on the Sepphoris synagogue mosaic (Z. Weiss and E. Netzer, *Promise and Redemption: A Synagogue Mosaic from Sepphoris* [Jerusalem: Israel Museum, 1996]). *Literary* may be something of a misnomer, since the names for signs of the zodiac, whether in a list (as at 'Ein Gedi; Naveh no. 70) or as labels in a zodiac mosaic (as at Hammath Tiberias, Beth Alpha, and Naaran: Naveh nos. 27, 45, 67, respectively), which Naveh includes in this category, are not necessarily based on a specific literary source as much as on shared cultural knowledge. The same may be true of the lists of the 24 priestly courses (Caesarea [Naveh no. 51]; Ashkelon [Naveh no. 52]; possibly Kisufim [Naveh no. 56]; see also Urman, "Jewish Inscriptions from the Mishnah and Talmud Period from Kazrin in the Golan," *Tarbiz* 53 [1983–84] 518 [Ahmadiye; cf. the suggestion of Naveh no. 109]; H. Eshel, "A Fragmentary Inscription of the Priestly Courses?" *Tarbiz* 61 [1993] 159–61 [Heb.], who proposes reading a block with eight preserved letters as a list of this type) or the lists of the first ten human generations, the months, the patriarchs, and Hananiah, Mishael, and Azariah at 'Ein Gedi (Naveh no. 70, lines 1–2, 5–8), as well. Nor does the dichotomy between "literary" and "dedicatory" adequately categorize the curse formula at 'Ein Gedi (Naveh no. 70).

12. See Weiss, "Social Aspects," 357–71. At least Catacombs 14 and 20 were built with meeting-places above, suggesting occasions for their use (see BS III 56–62, 111–14, and figs. 23, 24, 35, 51).

13. For a discussion of this aspect of the inscriptions and the terminology, see Z. Safrai, "Financing Synagogue Construction in the Period of the Mishnah and the Talmud," in

refer back to and make claims upon whole networks of relationships on the level of households, larger familial units, communities, and wider frameworks.

Two other broad categories by which the inscriptions can be grouped are worth examining: geographic and linguistic distribution. Geographic distribution is particularly difficult to evaluate. In the case of funerary inscriptions from Joppa or Beth Sheʿarim, both of which have foreign burials as well as Palestinian ones, it is impossible to determine the extent to which the burial places with which the inscriptions are associated primarily served a circumscribed local or a wider regional population.[14] The apparent centrality that sheer numbers of published inscriptions might suggest may be the result of political, economic, or religious processes centered elsewhere or the absence (not likely to be corrected soon) of systematic excavation and publication of other Jewish necropolises.[15] Synagogue inscriptions may be somewhat easier to evaluate: more synagogues with inscriptions are attested from the Beth-Shean Valley, the Golan, and the Galilee than from elsewhere in Palestine.[16] This, in turn, mirrors what is frequently thought to be the demography of Jewish settlement in late antique Palestine: concentration in Galilee, a band of settlement in "the south" (Aramaic *dārômā*ʾ; Greek *Darōmas*), and scattered settlement elsewhere.

Language is no easier a category with which to work. The inscriptions use Hebrew, Aramaic, and Greek almost exclusively. In synagogue inscriptions, the use of Hebrew is usually restricted to "literary" inscriptions (such as the inscription at Rehov or inscriptions citing scripture) but is used occasionally

---

Synagogues in Antiquity (ed. A. Oppenheimer, A. Kasher, U. Rappaport; Jerusalem: Yad Yitshak ben-Tsvi, 1987) 77–95 [Heb.]; see also Naveh, Introduction, 9–12. On donations themselves, see further below.

14. For possible "foreign" burials, see n. 25 below. At the very least, rabbinic traditions tell of the transportation of R. Judah the Patriarch from Sepphoris to Beth Sheʿarim (a distance of more or less 16 km as the crow flies but effectively probably closer to 20 km): *y. Kil.* 9.4 (32a–b); *y. Ketub.* 12.3 (35a); cf. *Qoh. Rab.* to 7:11; and *b. Ketub.* 103b, 104a.

15. See the brief comments on cemeteries around Sepphoris in Z. Weiss, "Sepphoris," *NEAEHL* 4.1328.

16. This can be seen most easily from the respective tables of context and maps in Naveh iii, 12 and Roth-Gerson 9–10, 14; the occasional addition since then (see, for example, Naveh, "Aramaic and Hebrew Inscriptions"; Weiss and Netzer, *Promise*) has not altered this picture. By contrast, once we remove from the section on Palestine in *CII* the subsections on Joppa, Beth Sheʿarim, and Jerusalem and its vicinity (where "Jewish" remains are likely to be earlier than the period under consideration), areas likely to be Samaritan, and the synagogue inscriptions republished by Naveh and Roth-Gerson in their collections, what remains is a series of scattered funerary inscriptions that are clearly not concentrated in any part of the country (minimally: Haifa [*CII* nos. 882–83], Caesarea [nos. 886–90], Apollonias [no. 891], Gaza [no. 968], Maiumas of Gaza [no. 970], Hammath Tiberias [nos. 985–86], Nazareth [no. 988], Sepphoris [no. 990], Lydda [nos. 1171–72], Khirbet Ḥabra [no. 1175], Beer-sheba [no. 1196], Soar [nos. 1208–9]). This should remind us that to discuss Palestinian Judaism in Late Antiquity is not to discuss only the Galilee and adjacent areas, although the inscriptions are not a firm basis for studying the actual distribution of the population.

in dedicatory inscriptions.[17] Aramaic is the language of the bulk of the dedicatory inscriptions. Notably, Greek dedicatory inscriptions tend to be concentrated in cities, so that the new cluster of inscriptions from Sepphoris enlarges the number of Greek synagogue inscriptions substantially but changes the map not at all. However, in funerary inscriptions, at least at Beth She'arim and Joppa where there is a substantial cluster, Greek clearly predominates.[18] The presence of Greek in synagogue inscriptions from Dabura and Capernaum and what are possibly dedicatory inscriptions from Beth She'arim is sufficient warning against a simple linguistic contrast between town and country, the former open and the latter impermeable to Greek.[19] Nor is there any sure way of generalizing more broadly from the inscriptions to degrees of linguistic competence or literacy: we are not in a position to judge—at least not on the basis of the inscriptions alone—when conventions other than language (narrowly defined) might have determined the differential patterns of choice of epigraphic language in funerary and dedicatory inscriptions.[20] Class, place of origin (local, from cities or villages, or, for example, transported burials from the diaspora), and notions of appropriateness may all be factors.

Let me now attempt to spell out some of the relationships that may be expressed (explicitly or implicitly) in the inscriptions, as well of some of the limits of this documentation. There is not enough evidence to allow one to generalize "typical" and "nonnormative" families, although the combined study of human remains, epigraphy, and archaeology might tease out a certain amount of information about the population.[21] Nor is the role of slaves and

---

17. See Naveh (*Sherd*, 25; idem, "Hebrew versus Aramaic in the Epigraphic Finds after the Bar Kokhba Revolt," *Leš* 57 [1992–93] 17–38 [Heb.]) for the transition from Hebrew to Aramaic in inscriptions, linked to change in the vernacular.

18. For instance, by my rough count, at Beth She'arim Greek inscriptions (more than 200) vastly outnumber Hebrew/Aramaic (some 66) or Palmyrene (8) inscriptions. The inscriptions from *CII* nos. 892–969 for Joppa yielded approximately 55 Greek and 9 Aramaic inscriptions (which might be expanded somewhat if one included inscriptions ending with *šalôm*). This is in contrast to the numbers based on L. Y. Rahmani, *A Catalogue of Jewish Ossuaries in the Collections of the State of Israel* (Jerusalem: Israel Antiquities Authority, 1994) 304–7 (table 2): by my count there are 115 Hebrew or Aramaic inscriptions, only 62 Greek ones (with another 10 bilingual inscriptions), and one Palmyrene inscription. As a group, these are likely to be earlier than the burials at Beth She'arim, and they are also concentrated in the south (especially near Jerusalem but, particularly after the late first century, from elsewhere as well; ibid., 21–25) and are open to both chronological and regional comparison.

19. Roth-Gerson 11, 20, appendix, inscriptions I–VI.

20. For characteristics of Greek inscriptions as opposed to Hebrew or Aramaic inscriptions, see L. Roth-Gerson, "Similarities and Differences in Greek Synagogue Inscriptions of Eretz-Israel and the Diaspora," in *Synagogues in Antiquity* (ed. A. Oppenheimer, A. Kasher, U. Rappaport; Jerusalem: Yad Yitshak ben-Tsvi, 1987) 133–44 [Heb.]; see also Roth-Gerson 147–62; Levine, "Synagogue Officials," 392–400.

21. For a discussion of burial in Palestine, see B. R. McCane, *Jews, Christians, and Burial in Roman Palestine* (Ph.D. diss, Duke University, 1992) 40–86, with a catalog, pp. 87–92; anthropological study of skeletal remains supplementing a study of burial practice has

freedpersons in the master's household or in the wider community at all clear, beyond the fact that this status was occasionally deemed important enough to state in inscriptions.[22] However, some relationships can be pursued in greater depth. Beyond the identification of a man or woman as the offspring of the father, funerary inscriptions from Beth She'arim also testify to the persistence of multigenerational family structures.[23] Synagogue dedications, too, sometimes reflect the presence of the family within the community.[24]

---

been supplied, for example, in the appendix (by R. Arensburg and P. Smith) to R. Hachlili and A. Killebrew, "Jewish Funerary Customs during the Second Temple Period in the Light of the Excavations at the Jericho Necropolis," *PEQ* 115 (1983) 133–36. The vexing problem of defining family at all is discussed in M. Peskowitz, "'Family/ies' in Antiquity: Evidence from Tannaitic Literature and Roman Galilean Architecture," in *The Jewish Family in Antiquity* (ed. S. J. D. Cohen; BJS 289; Atlanta: Scholars Press, 1993) 9–36; D. B. Martin, "The Construction of the Ancient Family: Methodological Considerations," *JRS* 86 (1996) 40–60.

22. Di Segni, "*Kĕtôbôt ṭĕberyâ*" [hereafter cited as Di Segni], in *Ṭĕberyâ mē-yissûdāh 'ad ha-kibbûš ha-mûslĕmî* (ed. Y. Hirschfeld; Jerusalem: Yad Yitshak ben-Tsvi, 1988) no. 8 (= M. Schwabe, "*Lĕ-tôldôt ṭĕberyâ*" [hereafter cited as Schwabe], in *In Memoriam Iohannis Lewy* [ed. M. Schwabe and J. Gutman; Jerusalem: Magnes, 1949] no. 10): the (unnamed) *threptoi* of "our master Sirikios" dedicate some sort of funerary monument; BS II no. 200: Kalliope is identified as the freedwoman (*apeleuoeras, l. apeleutheras*) of Procopius. The proper translation of *threptos*, which appears again at Hammath Tiberias (Roth-Gerson nos. 16, 18 [Di Segni nos. 29, 30]: "Severos the *threptos* of the illustrious patriarchs") is difficult (see the literature collected in Martin, "Ancient Family," 46 n. 25). One common meaning is 'slave' (and this seems to fit with Di Segni no. 8: the *threptoi* have a master [*despotos*]), but 'pupil' is also possible (so Di Segni 93, with the note: "not necessarily Jewish learning"). The latter interpretation seems unlikely (another noun, such as *mathētēs*, might have been more appropriate). Perhaps 'freedman' is intended (in which case, however, *apeleutheros* would have been the expected term) or, in keeping with the root meaning of the term, someone who regularly was fed by (merited or was dependent upon the hospitality of) the patriarchs. S. Schwartz (personal communication) suggests that *threptos* means 'adopted son' (cf. BS II no. 131, which commemorates an uncle, *ho ethrepsen hēmas*, i.e., 'who raised us'), but in that case, "*threptos* of N the illustrious patriarch" rather than the collective *tōn patriarkhōn* would be expected. Whatever *threptos* means, in the Hammath Tiberias inscriptions it is clearly a status of which the bearer can be proud and presumably does not emphasize "servility" even if it means slave; on the other hand, it does emphasize dependence and thus reflects some kind of patronage. At Hammath Gader, the word *mynwk* appears (Naveh nos. 33, 35 [twice, one of which is restored], a close literal approximation to *threptos*; Naveh took the term to mean 'offspring'). Could this term, too, refer to a dependent (or adoptive) relationship?

23. See Weiss, "Social Aspects," 358–61. In some cases, such as at Catacomb 1 Hall G of Beth She'arim (see BS II 13), a family stemma can be constructed. (See also BS II 71 and nos. 94, 96; and the attempt at BS II 27.)

24. The best example of this is Naveh no. 32 from Hammath Gader: "Remembered (singular) for good: *qyrs* (Greek *kyros*) Hoples and *qyrh* (Greek *kyra*) Proton and *qyrs* Sallustius his son in law, and the *comes prwrws* (Pheroras? Phrouros?) his son and *qyrys* Photios his son-in-law, and *qyrs* Hanina his son, they and their sons . . ."; see also no. 2 (Kfar Baram): the sons of Eleazar b. Yudan; no. 20 (Khirbet Kanaf): Yoezer . . . and Simeon his brother; no. 59 (Naaran): Rebecca the wife of Pinhas (immediately below a commemoration of Pinhas, no. 58); no. 65 (Naaran): *mrwt*[±4]*tynh* and Jacob his son; no. 81 (Khirbet Susiye): Leazar

That certain kinds of relationships are given greater prominence in inscriptions in the context of commemorations of the dead or of dedications to synagogues is not simply a result of the accidents of preservation. Consider how issues such as class or gender might play a role in the distribution of the inscriptions. In the case of synagogue inscriptions, we are after all dealing with donors. Judging by the range of the donations recorded in the inscriptions, these donors were not poor, although the amounts are small enough that we cannot say they only represent the activity of the wealthy few. Nor do funerary inscriptions necessarily give us a view that cuts across all classes: burial in the monumental tombs of Beth She'arim was presumably not cheap, and a portion of the funerary inscriptions may even reflect costly transportation from areas outside of Palestine.[25] In both funerary and dedicatory

---

and Isi the sons of Simeon b. Leazar (other members of the same family may be represented here); no. 34 (Hammath Gader) may reflect the donation of a married couple. Roth-Gerson no. 2 (Ashkelon): "Menamos and Marona [Roth-Gerson: Ma(t)trona] his wife [(?) after emendation] and Samuel their son"; no. 7 (Beth-Shean): "for the salvation of himself and . . . his brother"; no. 20 (Capernaum): Herod, Justus his son, "together with the children"; no. 21 (Gaza) a dedication by two brothers; no. 28 (Caesarea): a dedication "for the salvation of" a daughter; nos. 4 and 5 (Beth Alpha, Beth-Shean) have dedications by the same father-son team of craftsmen. See, in addition, Naveh, "Aramaic and Hebrew Inscriptions," 307 (Ilan, "Hammat [Rakkath]," 10; idem, *Ancient Synagogues*, 144–45), "R. 'Ula' and his brothers." Weiss and Netzer (*Promise*, 41) quote the inscription (from the aisle mosaic) reading: "May Tanhum b. Yudan and Sumaqa and Nehorai the sons of Tanhum be remembered for good, amen"; and by connecting this with two other inscriptions, one from the same synagogue and another from elsewhere at Sepphoris (Naveh no. 29), propose "a four-generation genealogy of a single family that lived in Sepphoris." Of the five Aramaic dedications remaining from the aisle, at least four add offspring (in one case a daughter), to the commemoration. Family relationships occur in the inscriptions from the nave mosaic as well, as in the right-hand panel of Band 2 (see Weiss and Netzer, *Promise*, 19), which begins "The sons of Alapheos . . . ," with "the sons" in the nominative case (for a discussion of this inscription, see below, n. 31).

25. The phenomenon is most frequently discussed in connection with Beth She'arim (transportation was often a reflection of the desire to be buried with the patriarchs; see Weiss, "Social Aspects," 366–67; Naveh, *On Sherd and Papyrus*, 200), but origin in foreign places is also attested in other Palestinian inscriptions. See the indexes of "ethnica" in BS II 228; BS III 297 (where Sidonios, p. 40, may also be a patronymic); see also *CII* no. 882 (Haifa), no. 889 (environs of Caesarea; *babylōnarios*, taken by Frey as a local name but perhaps better taken as a craft-related term), nos. 901, 910, 916, 925, 928, 931, 934, 950 (Joppa), no. 1175 (Khirbet Hebra); Schwabe no. 5 (restored, and slightly emended), no. 7 (Di Segni nos. 14, 16 respectively; both from Tiberias). BS II no. 141, mentioning "Aidesios the gerousiarch, Antiochian," may (with nos. 142–44) be something of a special case, since Lifshitz has connected him with the ancestor of "Ilasios son of Eisakios *arkhisynagogos* of the Antiocheans," known from an inscription from Apamaea (B. Lifshitz, *Donateurs et fondateurs dans les synagogues juives* [Cahiers de la Revue Biblique 7; Paris: Gabalda, 1967] no. 39; see also nos. 38 and 48 and the commentary to BS II no. 144). This identification is attractive but far from certain. Not all the geographic terms need to imply the transportation of the dead, but sometimes they seem to quite clearly (e.g., BS II no. 183 [p. 157], Catacomb 18). For a discussion of the custom, see A. Oppenheimer, *Galilee in the Mishnaic Period* (Jerusalem: Merkaz Zalman Shazar le-Toledot Yisrael, 1991) 103–6 [Heb.]; I. Gafni

inscriptions, a craft occasionally accompanies a name.[26] Participation in a craft (rather than landed wealth) need not imply poverty.[27] Indeed, in the case of people dealing in perfume, or of a goldsmith whose son attained the imperial post of *palatinus*, or of the father of a scribe who donated the mosaic floor and the plastering of the walls, the opposite seems more likely.[28] By contrast, the people who may have been successful independent peasant producers or tenant farmers are invisible as such.[29] Why this should be so—whether, for

---

("Reinterment in the Land of Israel: Notes on the Origin and Development of the Custom," in *Jerusalem Cathedra I* [ed. L. I. Levine; Jerusalem: Yad Yitshak ben-Zvi, 1981] 96–104), who dates the beginning of this practice to the third century.

26. See *CII* no. 928, (small wares-seller, see LSJ, s.v. *grytopōlēs*) no. 929 (a fuller, according to Frey's correction; Frey reads the description *kymina* of the father as a short form of *kyminopōlēs* 'cumin dealer'), no. 940 (baker); *BS II* no. 61 (goldsmith), no. 79 (perfumer), no. 89 (doctor), no. 124 (teacher), no. 168 (perfumer), no. 188 (cloth-dyeing? [so, *BS II* 173]), no. 189 (dealer in fine linen), no. 200 (a woman steward); Roth-Gerson no. 4 (artisans), nos. 6, 7 (*kloubas* 'maker of bird-cages'?, 'oven maker'?; see the discussion of Roth-Gerson 165), no. 14 (marble worker), no. 21 (wood dealers); Naveh no. 3 (*'wmnh* 'artisan'), no. 47 (artisan), no. 75 (scribe). In addition, the following appear to occur in connection with burials brought to Palestine from elsewhere: *CII* no. 902 (baker), no. 931 (linen seller); *BS II* no. 92 (banker). J. B. Frey, following M. Schwabe ("*Kĕtobet yĕwwānît-yĕhûdît šel mišpaḥat dayyāgîm mi-yapô*," in *Sēper ha-yôbel le-propessôr šĕmû'ēl qroys* [Jubilee volume for Samuel Krauss; Jerusalem: R. Mass, 1937] 80–86 [Heb.]) wanted to read *CII* no. 945 as referring to a family organization of fishers, but I remain unpersuaded.

27. See the brief comments of C. Roueché (*Aphrodisias in Late Antiquity* [hereafter cited as *Aphrodisias*; Journal of Roman Studies Monographs 5; London: Society for the Promotion of Roman Studies, 1989] 229–30) on the apparently greater prominence and status of traders and artisans in the late antique city.

28. For references, see n. 26 above. For goldsmiths, cf. C. B. Welles, "The Inscriptions," in *Gerasa, City of the Decapolis* [hereafter cited as *Gerasa*] (ed. C. H. Kraeling; New Haven: American Schools of Oriental Research, 1938) 335 (611 C.E.; a dedicatory inscription), 353; and M. Sartre, *Inscriptions grecques et latines de la Syrie, Tome XIII. 1: Bostra* [hereafter cited as *Bostra*] (Bibliothèque archéologique et historique 113; Paris: Geuthner, 1982) no. 9129 (*pronoētai* of the goldsmiths involved in public building), as well as nos. 9161–63 (restored). Especially in the case of the inscription of the father of the scribe (Naveh no. 75), which uses the verbs *'āśâ* ('made') and *ṭaḥ* ('plastered'), my interpretation depends on the metaphorical use of these terms (i.e., that the donor provided for the making of these items). For the possibility that verbs of "making" in the inscriptions may refer to actual labor, see Safrai, "Financing," 91–92; cf. Naveh nos. 9–10. For examples where provision of labor is commemorated, see Naveh no. 3 (the same person is mentioned in Naveh no. 1), 47; Roth-Gerson no. 4 (the same people are referred to in no. 5, where their handiwork [*khirothesia*] is identified), no. 14.

29. Naveh no. 43 (Beth Alpha), a very fragmentary inscription, apparently refers to donations of wheat; whether this reflects donations by peasants is far from clear. Safrai ("Financing," 90) saw this as involving donations of wheat for resale (see also Naveh 74). This is certainly possible, but the inscription is not well preserved and this interpretation must remain tentative. If the Greek term *phrontistēs* refers to managers of estates (whether private or imperial), at least that aspect of production is reflected: *CII* no. 919: a grave of two (?) *phrontistai* (*phrotitōn*, Frey emends: *phro⟨n⟩ti⟨s⟩tōn*); Roth-Gerson no. 27 (Caesarea). See also *CII* no. 918, which refers to the phrontistes (*phrontisti*, *l. phrontistē*) of Alexandria There is much material on *phrontistai* on both private and (in Kehoe) imperial estates in

instance, because a large majority of the population was involved in agricultural production and that therefore such activity was unremarkable, because the agrarian population had not the means to participate in dedications or to pay for elaborate burials and inscriptions, or because of issues of status and prestige—is far from clear.

Among these relatively well-off people, women also are clearly underrepresented. By my very rough count, at Beth She'arim some 56 women are acounted for, as opposed to 105 men (a ratio of 1 : 1.88); and at Joppa as many as 16 women to 58 men (1 : 3.63).[30] Low though these figures may be, women are even more poorly represented in synagogue inscriptions: I have counted some 8 women in 4 synagogues.[31] Once again, just what accounts for the dis-

---

Egypt in D. Rathbone, *Economic Rationalism and Rural Society in Third-Century Egypt* (Cambridge Classical Studies; Cambridge: Cambridge University Press, 1991); D. P. Kehoe, *Management and Investment on Estates in Roman Egypt during the Early Empire* (Papyrologische Texte und Abhandlungen 40; Bonn: Habelt, 1992). However, *phrontistēs* (Latin *procurator*) may reflect one of a number of imperial posts, including the official responsible for carrying out the manpower levy for the army (A. H. M. Jones, *The Later Roman Empire, 284–602: A Social, Economic, and Administrative Survey* [Oxford: Blackwell, 1964] 615–16; for further references, see the index, s.v. *procuratores*). Roth-Gerson 114, following B. Lifshitz ("Fonctions et titres honorifiques dans les communautés juives," RB 74 [1967] 59), who discusses the possiblity that the term has a Jewish communal referent (which seems a reasonable reading of CII no. 918, cited above).

30. Over and above the problem of textual reconstruction, the accuracy of these numbers is complicated by a number of issues, not least of which are (1) the fact that where the same name is repeated in a tomb it is unclear whether the same person is referred to; and (2) occasional uncertainty over whether a particular name refers to a male or a female. The matter requires further study. For the present, see T. Ilan, "Notes on the Distribution of Jewish Women's Names in Palestine in the Second Temple and Mishnaic Periods," *JJS* 40 (1989) 186–200 (whose data on inscriptions does not extend to Joppa or Beth She'arim). I had initially intended to supplement this paper with a comparison with the distribution of women in C. M. Lehmann and K. G. Holum, *The Greek and Latin Inscriptions from Caesarea Maritima* [hereafter cited as *Caesarea*] (forthcoming); *Bostra*; *Gerasa*; and *Aphrodisias* as a way of comparing "Palestinian Jewish" with "Roman, civic" epigraphic practices. In practice, however, these four cities themselves had rather different distributions by gender. For instance, Caesarea had a fairly even representation of funerary inscriptions for women or girls among what were likely to be pagan or Christian inscriptions, but only about 5 examples (I counted *Caesarea* nos. 167, 174, 187, 189, 191), compared to some 22 commemorating males, among Jewish inscriptions. By contrast to *Caesarea*, *Aphrodisias* had a smaller percentage of funerary inscriptions commemorating females. The methodological problems involved in comparing the corpora (indeed, with comparability in general) seemed sufficiently complex to warrant withholding this comparison.

31. Ashkelon (Roth-Gerson nos. 2, 3); Hammath Gader (Naveh nos. 32, 34); Naaran (Naveh nos. 59, 60). At least one inscription discussed by Weiss and Netzer (*Promise*, 41) mentions the daughter of a donor. In a photo (see p. 41 in the Hebrew section), one inscription contains the sequence *brtdy*/[(?); whether in fact this should be read as *brt dy*[or *br tdy*[will have to await full publication by the excavators. M. Avi-Yonah ("A Sixth Century Synagogue at 'Isfiyā," *QDAP* 3 [1933] 129) took line 1 of what is now Naveh no. 39 (Huseifa) to

tribution is far from clear. To name just a few possibilites, none of them mutually exclusive, the near silence in synagogue inscriptions might be due to outright exclusion on the part of men, disinterest on the part of women, or (since the inscriptions commemorate donors) a differential distribution of wealth. The Babatha papyri have shown, in a way that would have been difficult to imagine before their discovery, how effectively a second-century Jewish woman from southern Judea could pursue her own interests despite legal disabilities.[32] We should therefore be cautious in translating epigraphic remains into facts about the physical or social invisibility of women. Still, the paucity of women in inscriptions implies that not only in the communal arena of the synagogue but in the sphere of family commemoration as well, this was a society in which it was easier for men, in a literal way, to make a name for themselves. That this gender differential is embedded in other social expectations is, I think, reflected in the fact that, like men, women were known occasionally as "blessed" or "holy" (in funerary inscriptions) or bore the title *kyra* ('lady'),[33] and appeared regularly as the mothers of their children or the wives of their husbands,[34] but only rarely as playing another social role.[35]

Synagogue inscriptions in particular refer back to the use of wealth for communal purposes, and the communal naming of the donor is presumably linked to claims to prestige and honor. The rhetoric of the social use of wealth can be quite explicit, as in the inscriptions that clearly state the

---

refer to a woman (Klein, cited in n. 4 of Avi-Yonah, read the name of the woman), but Naveh (p. 67) favors an entirely different reading. A name ending in *-eina* is preserved in Roth-Gerson no. 23, which may refer to a woman.

32. Still only partially published: N. Lewis, Y. Yadin, and J. C. Greenfield (eds.), *The Documents from the Bar Kokhba Period in the Cave of Letters* (Jerusalem: Israel Exploration Society, 1989); Y. Yadin, J. C. Greenfield, and A. Yardeni, "Babatha's *Ketubba*," *IEJ* 44 (1994) 75–101; H. M. Cotton (alone or with collaborators) has published a number of documents related to this same archive in various journals, but see H. M. Cotton, "The Guardianship of Jesus Son of Babatha: Roman and Jewish Law in the Province of Arabia," *JRS* 83 (1993) 94–108.

33. 'Holy' (*hosia*): BS II no. 34; 'blessed' (*makaria*): BS II nos. 176, 183; 'lady' (*kyra*): BS II nos. 39, 57, 66 70, 130, 151 (*kyris kyra*; possibly one or both are personal names; cf. no. 170: *kyrias* the wife of Symmakhos, which the editors take as a proper name, 'of Kyria', rather than the title of an unnamed wife), nos. 165, 191, 219; BS III nos. 19, 20, 24; Naveh nos. 32, 34; Roth-Gerson no. 3. See also BS II nos. 136, 137, Greek forms of the Latin *matrona*.

34. E.g., BS II no. 48 (*CII* no. 1061): Rheouth [= Ruth?] the daughter, the mother of Ioudas; no. 129: "I Hesykhis lie here with my wife (*symbios*)"; Schwabe no. 6 (Di Segni no. 15): "Thaleththi Mara, daughter of Samuel, wife of Le[ontius (?)]." See further the use of forms of *gynē*: BS II nos. 101, 170, 149; *symbios*: Roth-Gerson no. 2 (after emendation); *mēter*: BS II nos. 22, 27, 130, 183; and *'iššâ* (or the Aramaic equivalent): BS III no. 24; Naveh no. 59.

35. BS II no. 200: Kalliope the steward (?) (*mizotera*) and freedwoman of Procopius. For *CII* no. 945, where, based on the interpretation of Schwabe and Frey, a woman's connection with a fishing guild is mentioned, see n. 26 above.

amount that a donor (or group of donors) has given[36] or when the installation
built or paid for is specified[37] or through the frequent use of verbs denoting
some form of giving.[38] Perhaps most striking is the fact that these inscriptions,
particularly the Hebrew and Aramaic ones, are rarely proclamations of one's
own benefaction[39] but, rather, are framed as public prayers for the well-being
of the donors.[40]

36. Naveh nos. 32–35 (Hammath Gader), no. 57 (Maon), no. 74 (Eshtemoa); Naveh,
"Aramaic and Hebrew Inscriptions," 307 (Ilan, "Ḥammat [Rakkath]," 10; idem, *Ancient
Synagogues in Israel*, 144–45) (Tiberias). Currency terms almost certainly correspond to
whole or fractional solidi. For a sense of scale, consider that a pre-Constantian aureus was
minted at 60 to the pound and consisted of 25 denarii at a time when a round figure for a
day-laborer's wage might be given as one denarius (for this last figure, see Matt 20:1ff.;
m. B. Meṣ. 7:5; and my brief discussion in *Early Rabbinic Civil Law and the Social History
of Roman Galiee* [BJS 307; Atlanta: Scholars Press, 1995] 214 n. 208). Solidi were minted
at 72 to the pound. Assuming that, in terms of gold, prices for labor remained more or less
stable, this would be roughly equivalent to 21 days' worth of day labor. See D. Sperber, *Roman Palestine 200–400: Money and Prices* (Ramat Gan: Bar-Ilan University Press, 1974) 34
and 194 n. 28 for *dînār* as solidus and 149–53 for stability of prices in terms of gold; see further S. Lieberman, *Tosefta Ki-Fshutah* (New York: Jewish Theological Seminary of America, 1955–88) 8.843. For questions of currency, see A. H. M. Jones, *The Later Roman
Empire* (Oxford, 1964) 438–45; R. S. Bagnall, *Currency and Inflation in Fourth Century
Egypt* (Bulletin of the American Society of Papyrologists Supplement 5; Chico, Calif.:
Scholars Press, 1985). To the comparatively modest Palestinian synagogue donations,
compare the scale in *Aphrodisias* 74, involving a donation of 3000 solidi.

37. See Safrai, "Financing," 93–95. Once again, the scale is quite worth noting. In Oc-
tober of 1996, a stone-cutter working on renovations of the North Theater in Gerasa told
me that a large ashlar block took him two days to complete and that one of the large elaborate columns (6–8 m high) took three months. Presumably, the somewhat smaller columns dedicated in synagogues (e.g., Naveh nos. 12, 18, 40; Roth-Gerson no. 20) amount to
the equivalent of stone and several days' labor. Dedicating a "stoa" (e.g., Naveh no. 17,
Roth-Gerson no. 17) or a large section of mosaic floor (e.g., Naveh no. 75; Roth-Gerson
nos. 7, 21, 27) would account for rather more outlay on the part of the donor.

38. Safrai ("Financing," 93–95) summarizes the Hebrew and Aramaic evidence for this
as well. For the Greek inscriptions see: Roth-Gerson no. 3 (Ashkelon), no. 21 (Gaza): *pros-
pherō*, no. 8 (Beth-Shean), no. 9 (Beth-Shean): *prosphora*, no. 7 (Beth-Shean, House of
Leontis): *psēphoō*, no. 11 (Dabura, restored), no. 15 (Tiberias), no. 20 (Capernaum): *ktizō*
(restored); no. 13 (Hulda): *kistēs. Poieō* (Roth-Gerson nos. 16, 17 [Hammath Tiberias]) presumably reflects donation by wealthy benefactors (if a dependent of the patriarchs is any
indication), although it could refer to contributed labor; see also no. 27 (Caesarea): a large
donation is "made" by an *arkhisynagogōs* and *phrontistēs. Teleō* in Roth-Gerson no. 18
(Hammath Tiberias) may refer to oversight (with Severus and Ioullos in charge of the construction?) but may also merely refer to donation of funds. 'Founding' (*ktizō, ktistēs*) is part
of the standard vocabulary of Greek euergetism; however, D. Urman ("Dabura" [English
ed., 18–19; Hebrew ed., 400–403]) and more recently, R. C. Gregg and D. Urman (*Jews,
Pagans, and Christians in the Golan Heights* [Atlanta: Scholars Press, 1996] 126) and
Naveh (p. 27) took the appearance of this term at Dabura as referring to the actual builder
(cf. Roth-Gerson 52). I leave Roth-Gerson no. 23 (Gaza), no. 24 (Sepphoris), no. 26 (Caesarea), and no. 29 (Caesarea) out of consideration here, because of problems of reading.

39. See, for instance, Naveh no. 3 (Alma) and no. 28 (Afeq), which are both first-person
inscriptions; note also that some inscriptions (e.g., Naveh no. 20 [Ammudim; corrected in

Prestige, or the claim to it, is also expressed through the use of titulature. Like funerary inscriptions,[41] synagogue inscriptions utilize more or less generalized titles for men, much like those for women just mentioned, but also a range of more specific ones corresponding to functions in Jewish communal institutions or the Roman imperial government.[42] Although an occasional

---

Naveh, "Aramaic and Hebrew Inscriptions," 307]: "Yoezer . . . made this place ((')*tr*') of the Lord of heaven"; no. 54 [Gaza B], which merely has the name of the donor in Greek and Aramaic) do not explicitly include the aspect of public prayer and might be taken as individual proclamations. In Greek inscriptions this is a bit more common, especially where these inscriptions designate that the gift was made by the donor 'for the sake of the salvation' (*hyper sōtērias*) of someone: Roth-Gerson nos. 2, 7 (Beth-Shean, House of Leontis), no. 23 (Gaza), no. 28 (Caesarea); two inscriptions from Beth-Shean merely announce the gift, *prosphora*, of the donor: Roth-Gerson no. 8 (Beth-Shean), no. 9 (Beth-Shean).

40. See the use of the formula "let PN be remembered for good": for the Hebrew and Aramaic examples, see Naveh, index, s.vv. *dkr* (Aramaic), *zkr* (Hebrew); and idem, *On Sherd and Papyrus*, 130–43; for the Greek, see Roth-Gerson nos. 1, 4, 7, 17 (the phrase recurs in the Sepphoris synagogue mosaic in both Greek and Aramaic; see Weiss and Netzer, *Promise*, 41–42 and photos throughout). See also Roth-Gerson no. 6 (with abbrevations expanded): *k(yri)e b(o)ēth(ei)* . . . 'Lord help . . .'.

41. The titles for women are discussed above. Like the women, deceased men too are 'holy' (*BS* II nos. 35, 126, 163, 173, 193), as well as 'lord' (*kyris/-ios*, *BS* II nos. 130, 151 [?]; cf. no. 204, *mar*). See also the epithet 'the poor' (*BS* II nos. 99, 206 [restored]). The most obvious communal title is *arkhisynagōgos*, as in *BS* II no. 203. *Presbeutēs* (emmisary; possibly for *presbeuteros* 'elder' or even *presbys* 'old'?) may refer to a communal function in *CII* no. 949 (in no. 883 the term is applied to a *comes*, and may reflect an imperial position). For *presbeuteros*, see also L. Di Segni, "A Jewish Greek Inscription from the Vicinity of Caesarea Maritima," *'Atiqot* 22 (1993) 133–36. The following relate to communal officials of non-Palestinian communities: *BS* II no. 164 (*arkhisynagōgos* from Beirut), no. 141 (*gerousiarkhēs* from Antioch), no. 221 (*arkhisynagōgos* from Sidon or: Yose the *arkhisynagōgos*, the son of Sidon⟨i⟩os?); *BS* II no. 203 can be read in this sense as well (see Roth-Gerson, appendix, no. II and p. 138). Imperial service is represented not only by a *centenarius* (*CII* no. 920; given the continuation ['of the camp'], this is presumably a military officer rather than a grade of the equestrian order, for which see Jones, *Later Roman Empire*, 525, 530, 584) but also a *palatinus* (*BS* II no. 61) and a *comes* (*CII* no. 883). The epithet *kratistos* (*BS* II no. 189) may reflect equestrian status (*egregius*), but this is denied (without explanation; presumably it is because Benjamin is a fine linen dealer) by the editors, who take the term instead as a "moral" one (p. 174). If this is correct, it suggests that other occurences of epithets known from the imperial administration may be used in a nontechnical sense in Jewish inscriptions, as in *BS* II no. 164 (*lampros* for *lamprotatos*). At any rate, *BS* II no. 179, where the editors read *l(a)m(p)ros*, a simpler reading—one not assuming that the superlinear letters, here shown in parentheses, were added in reverse order—is La(za)ros. In addition to the preceding, as noted earlier, men are twice referred to as chiefs of *collegia* of craft associations (*CII* no. 931; *BS* II no. 188).

42. Forms of *rabbî* (Naveh nos. 6, 15, 33, 43, 60, 75; Roth-Gerson, appendix, no. I); *kyris/-ios* (Naveh nos. 32, 34, 71; Roth-Gerson nos. 3, 6, 7, 9, 25, 30); *kohēn, kahana'* (Naveh nos. 58, 74, 85, 88, 89); "artisan" (Naveh no. 3, see also no. 47; Roth-Gerson no. 4); *kômēs* (*comes*) (Naveh no. 32; Roth-Gerson no. 24) Among Aramaic or Hebrew terms, those that most likely refer specifically to communal service are *ḥazzān* (Naveh nos. 20, 28; Naveh also reports an unpublished inscription mentioning a *ḥazzān* from 'Ein Gedi, Naveh p. 12; idem, "Aramaic and Hebrew Inscriptions," 308) and *parnas* (Naveh no. 63; cf. also Greek

inscription may be dated to the term in office (Naveh no. 13, Roth-Gerson no. 25), and although it may be that the use of the title *arkhisynagogos* reflects growing institutionalization on the part of Palestinian synagogues, no clear picture of a hierarchical organization of synagogue function, much less a sense of how one might come to be an office-holder, can be gotten from the inscriptions. Indeed in both examples of a dedication dated to a term of office, no specific office title is mentioned.[43]

As a result, precisely how the connections between wealth, communal authority, and local prestige played themselves out in the day-to-day workings of the communities and their synagogues is impossible to tell, since the structures of power and patronage may be complex.[44] In addition, the inscriptions are too terse to lay out exactly what went on in synagogues or how and whether prestige was acknowledged. Nevertheless, the presence of a chair with an inscription honoring a donor who "made" the stoa and its steps—if indeed it was used for sitting—is instructive.[45] The fact that the bearers of titles in the synagogue inscriptions generally appear as donors

---

pronoētēs 'administrator', Roth-Gerson no. 18). *Pronoumenos*, from the same root as *pronoētēs* (Roth-Gerson no. 18) but used as a participle and associated with the same person, occurs in Roth-Gerson no. 16, together with several other dedications. Since 6 of the remaining 7 dedications in Roth-Gerson no. 16 have the form *eukhomenos epoiēsen* '. . . vowing, made' but Ioullos *pronoumenos panta etelese* 'having forethought [or: "administering"], completed all', it may be that what Ioullos administered had to do with the building of the synagogue. In Greek the most obvious communal officials are *arkhisynagogoi* (Roth-Gerson nos. 19, 24, 27, appendix, no. II [*BS* II no. 203]; see also appendix, no. IV [*BS* II no. 212], where this is restored but perhaps overconfidently). Some of the Greek terms may refer either to communal or noncommunal roles (*phrontistēs*, Roth-Gerson no. 27 [see above, n. 29]; *mizoteros, l. meizoteros*, Roth-Gerson no. 16; cf. *BS* II no. 200 [see the editor's commentary, p. 186: perhaps either a communal or a household steward; *skholastikos*, Roth-Gerson no. 24]). Naveh nos. 75 and 77, from Khirbet Susiya have peculiar concentrations of titles. In no. 75 the main donor is labeled *qĕduššat marî rabbî 'Issî ha-kohēn ha-mĕkubbād, bĕrabbî* ('his holiness, my lord, my master Issi the priest, the honored, my master' [perhaps: 'son of a master']); his son is *rabbî yôhanan ha-kohēn bĕrabbî* ('my master Yohanan the priest, my master'). Naveh no. 77 commemorates people with the title "witness" (notary?) and advocate (?) (see Naveh's commentary, pp. 118–19).

43. The relevant term in Naveh no. 13 is *bi-sĕrar*. Perhaps on analogy with the Dura-Europos synagogue, in which an inscription is dated *bi-qĕšîšûtēh* 'in the eldership [or: presbytership]' of Samuel (Naveh nos. 88, 89a, 89b), one should read this inscription as referring to officers who held the title *śar*. At any rate Roth-Gerson no. 25, if it is properly read, does not mention a title.

44. For instance, in Roth-Gerson nos. 16, 18, it is not the patriarchs themselves who are commemorated in the inscriptions from Hammath Tiberias but a member of their household, although the connection with the patriarchs surely accounts, at least in part, for the wealth of Severus, as well as for his prestige.

45. Naveh no. 17 (Chorazin). For other chairs (the so-called "seats of Moses"), see M. S. Chiat, *Handbook of Synagogue Architecture* (BJS 29; Chico, Calif.: Scholars Press, 1982) 91 (Capernaum), 105 (Hammath Tiberias A), 221 ('Ein Gedi). For the argument that such chairs were not used for sitting, see L. Y. Rahmani, "Stone Synagogue Chairs: Their Identification, Use and Significance," *IEJ* 40 (1990) 192–214.

suggests that, whatever else it may have been, the synagogue was a locus for appropriating or expressing power through the public display and commemoration of patronage. The presence in the dedicatory inscriptions of true local aristocrats (for example, those who had attained the rank of *comes* 'count') may be another expression of the playing out of local power through synagogue dedications.[46]

It is not only relationships between individuals and communities that are reflected in the inscriptions but also connections across communities, regions, and countries.[47] The use of the same artisans in two nearby synagogues (as in Beth-Shean and Beth Alpha, and again in Bar'am and Alma) may testify to the economic linkages between communities and possibly, by extension, to other contacts as well.[48] Synagogue dedications may also imply regional or local interconnections with Galilee, such as patronage by the elites of other communities or the honoring of foreign dignitaries.[49] It has

46. References to people with the title *comes* were given in nn. 41 and 42 above. I am assuming that in Roth-Gerson no. 24, Elasios (not Gelasios) *skho(lastikou) kō(mētos)* [*l. komētos*] *lam(protatou)* is one of the donors (against the emendation of Lifshitz, *Donateurs*, 74).

47. In addition to the material below, note the following epigraphic examples of Palestinian Jews in the diaspora: a Tiberian is attested from Rome (*CII* no. 502) as is a Sepphorian (*CII* no. 362); for other Palestinian Jews in Rome, see H. J. Leon, *The Jews of Ancient Rome* (Philadelphia: Jewish Publication Society, 1960), 239. See also *CII* no. 680 (the provenence is given as Daloma in Dalmatia, but cf. L. Robert ["*Un corpus des inscriptions juives*," *REJ* 101 (1937) 80], who notes that the inscription was found in Senia [Zengg]); *SEG* XVIII 775 (Carthage); *IG* VI 1256 (B. Lifshitz, "Prolegomenon" to *CII* [New York: Ktav, 1975] 86, no. 721a, Taenarum in Laconia). These inscriptions presumably reflect emigration and not necessarily permanent intercommunal connection.

Other epigraphic material relative to Palestine should not be considered as evidence of "Jewish" supralocal or supraregional relationships. For instance, the presence of a "Tiberian" in an execration text from Beth-Shean (H. Youtie and C. Bonner, "Two Curse Tablets from Beisan," *TAPA* 58 [1937] 73–75, with a note by L. Robert, *BE* no. 13 in *REG* 52 [1939] 450; Schwabe no. 22; Di Segni no. 24) may testify to personal dealings between residents of both cities (if Judas the Tiberian [?] and the second [?] Tiberian mentioned later were not residents of Beth-Shean) but need not reflect communal connections. Similarly, the appearance of a *statio* of Tiberias in Rome reflects the role Tiberias played as a city within the Roman Empire. See *IGR* I 111, 132 (Schwabe nos. 16, 15). In the latter inscription, Schwabe restored 'Tiberias' (*statiōn [Tibe]rieōn tōn kai Klaudiopolitōn Syria Pale[s]tinē*; Cagnat read [*tōn Tyr]ieōn*), but this restoration seems secure. Compare the official name of the city on its coins, which bore the legend *Tiber() Klau()* or the equivalent from the reign of Trajan onward, and which under Commodus (180–92) bore the longer version *Tiber() Kla() Syr()pal()* or the equivalent; the revised edition of Schürer (E. Schürer, *The History of the Jewish People in the Age of Jesus Christ* [rev. G. Vermes et al.; Edinburgh: T. & T. Clark, 1973–87] 2.181–82 n. 532) dated the inscription to "before A.D. 194."

48. Roth-Gerson nos. 4, 5; Naveh nos. 1, 3. Economic linkage between communities in later Roman Palestine (that is, the reliance of Galilean towns on pottery produced in one place) is addressed in D. Adan-Bayewitz, *Common Pottery in Roman Galilee* (Ramat Gan: Bar-Ilan University Press, 1993).

49. See Naveh no. 4 (Alma): the dedication by "NN the Tiberian"; no. 21 (Abelin), if the reading ⟨'l⟩ks⟨n⟩dryy 'Alexandrian' for *ksdryy* is accepted; Roth-Gerson no. 8 (Beth-Shean):

been suggested that Rabbi Yudan b. Tanhum (?) (*rby ywdn* [*br tn*]*ḥwm*) on an inscription in Sepphoris and Yoseh b. Tanhum b. Buta on a synagogue inscription in nearby Kfar Kana (Cana) were brothers, and the same Sepphorean Yudan b. Tanhum has recently been connected with a Tanhum b. Yudan now known from the new Sepphoris synagogue mosaic.[50] If this were so, we could begin to speculate on the role of urbanites in village dedications and multigenerational traditions of patronage. Unfortunately, there is no firm evidence for connecting these epigraphic figures—even the two Sepphorean ones—other than the similarity of names, and both the names Judah and Tanhum are known from elsewhere.[51] Intercommunal connections may be in evidence in the form of foreign burials in Palestine, mentioned earlier, not only from Phoenicia and Trachonitis but also from such areas as Palmyra and Himyar in Southern Arabia (see n. 25 above). Finally, I would like to note the occasional presence within communities of subcommunities linked apparently by geographic origin. At Beth Sheʿarim an inscription (perhaps a synagogue dedication?) names a Pamphylian *arkhisynagōgos* from Caesarea.[52] An inscription from Sepphoris, dating to the fourth century at the earliest, commemorates an *arkhisynagōgos* of Tyre.[53] The first of these inscriptions might be taken as evidence of a Palestinian synagogue whose membership was based on regional origin (i.e., a Pamphylian synagogue at Caesarea).[54] However, similar claims on the basis of the hopelessly problematic inscription

---

donation of "Nonnos . . . the Cyzicene." In all three cases, however, it is possible that the donors now lived in Almah, Abelin, and Beth-Shean, respectively (and this may well be the point of *dhkh* 'of (?) here' in Naveh no. 21). If so, synagogue inscriptions, like the burial inscriptions, may reflect immigration to Palestine. See also Roth-Gerson no. 24: "for the sake of (*yber* for *hyper*) . . . illustrious *arkhisynagōgos* of Tyre" (in this respect my reading differs from Roth-Gerson and agrees with the initial reading of M. Schwabe, "*Kĕtobet bēt ha-kĕnessest še-bĕ-ṣippôrî*," in *Festschift für David Yellin* (Jerusalem: R. Mass, 1935) 100–103.

50. Naveh 29, 30 (see p. 52, comment to no. 29, lines 3–4; Y. Neʾeman, *Sepphoris in the Period of the Second Temple, Mishna and Talmud* [Ph.D. diss., Hebrew University, 1987] 163–64 and n. 37 [Heb.]; Neʾeman's transcription of no. 29 does not yield good sense); Weiss and Netzer, *Promise*, 41.

51. Judah and other forms are ubiquitous, and I will not document this here. In addition to Naveh no. 29 (restored) and no. 30, Tanhum occurs in dedicatory inscriptions on nos. 33, 35, 87. It also appears at least once in Greek transcription: *CII* no. 920. L. I. Levine ("Excavations at the Synagogue at Ḥorvat ʿAmmudim," *IEJ* 32 [1982] 8–9) and Naveh ("Aramaic and Hebrew Inscriptions," 306) restore *br t*]*nḥ*[*wm* in line 2; although based on the photo alone, the mosaic appears blank after *ḥ*.

52. Roth-Gerson, appendix, no. II (*BS* II no. 203): *Iakōs Kaisareus arkhisynagōgos Pamphylias*. The phenomenon itself is not peculiarly "Jewish": see, e.g., *Aphrodisias* 196, 197 (restored); and Roueché's comment, *Aphrodisias* 236.

53. Roth-Gerson no. 24 (*CII* no. 991).

54. *BS* II no. 203. Schwabe (p. 217) saw a similar phenomenon in *CII* no. 931 (Joppa), which he took as evidence of both a "Tarsian" and "Cappadocian" community in Joppa. Above I have treated this as a transported burial. See, for example, the description of first-century Jerusalem in Acts 6:8; and the references in the Yerushalmi to a *kĕnîštāʾ dĕ-bābel* ('synagogue of Babylonia') at Sepphoris (e.g., *y. Ber.* 5.1 [9a]).

from Sepphoris as well as the funerary inscription for Leontina from Tiberias remain unsubstantiated.[55]

Inscriptions and Palestinian Jewish Ethnicity

These social contexts, in which relationships are highlighted or obscured, in which status or prestige is claimed, also occasioned the epigraphic expressions of ethnic identity and are not separable from them. It is for this reason that I have devoted so much space to "profiling" the inscriptions. "Jewishness" here is, to put it overly simplistically, a Jewishness predominantly of men wealthy enough to pay for the privilege of having their names inscribed in communal or semiprivate spaces. The inscriptions, in other words, are not the crystalization of what "the Jew" said, did, thought, or felt but expressions made by or for select Jews in the context of and in reference to religious, social, and communal contexts.

Moreover, in talking about a "Jewishness" in late antique Palestine, we are not discussing a pure and easily definable essence that can easily be distinguished from "Greco-Roman." In fact, the emergence of what I would like to think of as a new form of Jewish ethnicity in late antique Palestine is inextricably tied to its more general context. In the first place, the widespread use of

---

55. Roth-Gerson no. 24, from Sepphoris, has been read in a number of different ways, in part because of manifest errors in writing in the beginning of line 3 (cf. the discussions of Schwabe, *Kĕtobet*, 100–112; Frey, *CII* 991; F. Hüttenmeister, *Die antiken Synagogen in Israel* [Wiesbaden: Reichert, 1977] part 1, 407–9; Lifshitz, *Donateurs*, 74; Roth-Gerson 105–9; Ne'eman, "Sepphoris," 166, 235). *Sidoniou* in line 2 is likely to be a personal name and not a toponym; by contrast *Tyrou* in line 4 does seem to refer to Tyre. In neither case, however, does the toponym necessarily imply that we are dealing with an "ethnic" synagogue in Sepphoris itself. Still less do lines 3–4 give evidence of a synagogue peopled by the African community from Tyre at Sepphoris. What influenced Schwabe, *"Kĕtobet,"* 104–9 (and with him, more recently, Ne'eman, "Sepphoris," 166, 235, against Schwabe's own assessment of the most straightforward meaning [*lĕ-pî ha-pĕšāṭ*, 104]) was the coincidence of four personal names based on toponyms (Judah, Sidon, Tyre, and Aphro[ ]), which Schwabe considered too many to be likely. Judah, however, is a commonplace name; Aphros (?) is not really a toponym; and the coincidence of a reference to the city of Tyre, in connection with one person, with someone else named Sidonius does not tax the imagination.

For Tiberias, see the inscription discussed as Schwabe no. 7 (pp. 216–21). There is not enough left of the inscription to restore with certainty [*arkhisynagog(ou)*] *Antiokh(eōn)* (line 4), which Schwabe based on an unwarranted analogy with *CII* no. 803 (Apamaea): that an *arkhisynagogos* of Antiocheans is mentioned in the Apamaean inscription does not mean that the same is true of the inscription from Tiberias, especially since no claim is being made of any relationship between the individuals mentioned in the inscriptions and since the actual expansion of *Antiokh( )* is unknown, so that the syntactical relationship with the preceding word cannot be determined. The proposed corrections in B. Lifshitz, "Varia Epigraphica" (*Euphrosyne* 6 [1973–74] 25–26), do not alter these difficulties. In any case, even if the inscription were to be restored as Schwabe suggests, it would not exclude the possibility that relatives of an *archisynagogos* from Antioch had been brought to the vicinity of Tiberias for burial.

Greek, noted above, is a case in point. Whatever the implications of the use of Greek in funerary inscriptions for assessing the linguistic competence of Palestinian Jews, clearly those who paid for inscriptions found the complex of personal, communal, and ritual obligations centering on burial and an attendant inscription to be an appropriate occasion for using Greek. Although less well represented, dedicatory inscriptions in Greek imply much the same thing. In addition, a review of the inscriptions, both funerary and dedicatory, shows a substantial number of names of Greek or Latin origin.[56] None of this should be taken for granted. Naming and language, in general, and particularly in the kinds of formalized and ritualized contexts from which inscriptions stem, can be highly charged and can form a primary marker of identity.[57]

Moreover, much the same could be said about other aspects of the inscriptions and mosaics. There is nothing particularly "Jewish" about warnings not to tamper with tombs, or about the phrase *tharsei . . . oudeis athanatos* 'be of good courage . . . no one is immortal'. In fact both are attested elsewhere in non-Jewish contexts.[58] Synagogue floors displayed Helios in his chariot, surrounded by the signs of the zodiac, borrowing themes from Greco-Roman art and mythology; an analogous composition, although with important differences, occurs in the Monastery of the Lady Mary in Beth-Shean.[59] If the "House of Leontis" served a Jewish communal function, it is worth noting the presence of the nilometer motif in a church at Tabgha, as well as at what may

56. The recently published mosaic from Sepphoris has, for instance, provided masculine and feminine forms of Paregorios (both Greek and Aramaic), as well as a Boethos son of Aemilius (Weiss and Netzer, *Promise*, see Band 6, left). See, for example, the indexes of personal names in BS I–III (BS I = B. Mazar, *Beth She'arim, Volume I: Catacombs 1–4* [Jerusalem: Israel Exploration Society, 1973]); Naveh; and Roth-Gerson. I offer a few striking examples: literary names: Sappho (BS II no. 27) and Socrates (BS II no. 185); imperial names: Domna (Roth-Gerson no. 3, *Domna Iou[*, restored *Iou[lianou*, perhaps a bit hopefully), Iulius (and related forms; BS II nos. 13, 14, 58, 61, 72; Roth-Gerson nos. 16, 18, 26; Naveh no. 13 [*lwly'n'*]; cf. *CII* no. 919, *Loulianou*), and Antoninus (*CII* no. 970; BS II no. 208).

57. See S. Honigman, "The Birth of a Diaspora: The Emergence of a Jewish Self-Definition in Ptolemaic Egypt in the Light of Onomastics," in *Diasporas in Antiquity* (ed. S. J. D. Cohen and E. S. Frerichs; BJS 288; Atlanta: Scholars Press, 1993) 93–127.

58. E.g., *Gerasa* nos. 227, 236; *Bostra* nos. 9230, 9268, 9315, 9352, 9366 (restored), 9394, 9416; see also no. 9381 (partially restored); *Caesarea* no. 150 (see also no. 151); see the index of Gregg and Urman, *Jews, Pagans, and Christians*, s.v. *tharsei* (some of the examples cited are restored) and, for the full formula, nos. 175, 177, 178, 179, 181 (restored), 183 (restored), 185 (explicitly Christian), 201, 203, 224; see also nos. 36, 206.

59. G. M. Fitzgerald, *A Sixth Century Monastery at Beth-Shan (Scythopolis)* (Philadelphia: University of Pennsylvania Press, 1939) 6–7, and its frontispiece. For synagogue mosaics (Hammath Tiberias, Naaran, Huseifa, and Beth Alpha, to which add the Sepphoris mosaic) and their relationship to Greco-Roman representations and as Jewish compositions, see R. Hachlili, "The Zodiac in Ancient Jewish Art: Representation and Significance," *BASOR* 228 (1977) 61–77; G. Foerster, "Representations of the Zodiac in Ancient Synagogues and Their Iconographic Sources," *ErIsr* 18 (Avigad Volume; 1985) 380–91 [Heb.].

have been a public building at Sepphoris without specific religious markings.[60] Late antique synagogues also saw what are probably best understood as late antique borrowings from church architecture: apses and chancel screens.[61]

My point here is not that there was no "Jewishness" in late antique Palestine but that it was articulated in the context of a wider world and that attempts to isolate an essential Jewish core risk missing the far more interesting phenomenon of negotiation. The writing of names of Greek or Latin origin in Semitic characters and the transcription of Hebrew names into Greek[62] both suggest ways in which people might make what are identifiable to us as "Jewish" gestures in a complex linguistic and onomastic situation. Weiss and Netzer have recently made a valuable, if by their own admission preliminary, contribution to understanding how a Helios and zodiac theme might be incorporated into a "structured scheme" that tells an identifiably "Jewish" story to Jews.[63] Apses and chancel screens were incorporated in ways that drew attention to the Torah and its liturgical use within the synagogue.[64]

60. See N. Zori ("The House of Kyrios Leontios at Beth Shean," *IEJ* 16 [1966] 123–34), who considered it a private house (p. 132); A. M. Schneider, *The Church of the Multiplying of the Loaves and Fishes* (trans. E. Graf; London: Ouseley, 1937); E. Netzer and Z. Weiss ("New Evidence for Late-Roman and Byzantine Sepphoris," in *The Roman and Byzantine Near East* [ed. J. H. Humphrey; JRASupp 14: Ann Arbor: Journal of Roman Archaeology, 1995] 166–71), noting the possible use of the building in a harvest water festival; C. L. Meyers and E. M. Meyers ("Sepphoris," *OEANE* 4.535) connect the building with a *maiumas* festival.

61. Y. Tsafrir, "The Byzantine Setting and Its Influence on Ancient Synagogues," in *The Synagogue in Late Antiquity* (ed. L. I. Levine; Philadelphia: American Schools of Oriental Research, 1987) 146–57.

62. Greek or Latin names in Semitic characters: e.g., *BS* I no. 38 (= *CII* no. 1041): *prygry* (again in Greek, *Parēgoris, BS* II no. 31); a feminine version of the same name is transcribed in Hebrew characters in the aisle mosaic from the Sepphoris synagogue (see Weiss and Netzer, *Promise*, 41); Naveh no. 34 (= *CII* no. 858): *ly'ntys* (Leontis), *qlnyk* (Kallinike), *'ntwlyh* (Anatolia [?]; cf. the comments of Naveh 61) (Hammath Gader). Hebrew names in Greek: e.g., *CII* no. 920: *Thanoum, Simōn, Beniamin* (Joppa); *CII* no. 943: *Naoum; BS* II no. 69 (= *CII* no. 1086): *Anania, Ioudas* (Beth She⁽arim); Roth-Gerson no. 14: Abramios (Tiberias); Weiss and Netzer, *Promise*, Band 2: Alapheos (right-hand inscription and possibly left-hand as well: line 2 begins *pheos*). Also worth noting in this regard is the fact of bilingual commemoration, that is, the name written out in both Greek and Aramaic or Hebrew; for example, Roth-Gerson no. 22 (= *CII* no. 967).

63. Weiss and Netzer, *Promise*; see also Hachlili, "Zodiac"; and G. Foerster, "Representations of the Zodiac." See also the contributions of Zeev Weiss and Steven Fine in this volume (pp. 199–44 and 227–237).

64. See Tsafrir, "Byzantine Setting," 151–12. For screens in particular, see, J. R. Branham, "Sacred Space under Erasure in Ancient Synagogues and Early Churches," *Art Bulletin* 74 (1992) 375–92; Branham, "Vicarious Sacrality: Temple Space in Ancient Synagogues," in *Ancient Synagogues: Historical Analysis and Archeological Discovery* [2 vols.; ed. D. Urman and P. V. M. Flesher; SPB 47; Leiden: Brill, 1995] 2.319–45. Part of Branham's position is critiqued in S. Fine, "'Chancel' Screens in Late Antique Palestinian Synagogues: A Source from the Cairo Genizah," in *Religious and Ethnic Communities in Later Roman Palestine* (ed. H. Lapin; Studies and Texts in Jewish History and Culture 5; Bethesda, Md.: University Press of Maryland, 1998), but these screens remain problematic. If,

In what follows, I wish to draw attention to some of the ways that "Jewishness" is articulated in the inscriptions. Beginning with the funerary inscriptions, the first thing to note is that it was expressed at all, as in the Greek inscription from Zoar, which apparently commemorates Aeneas the Jew.[65] Who would have seen this monument, and to whom does it proclaim ethnic or religious affiliation? The inscriptions use other explicit "Judaizing" markers, such as the supplement of Greek inscriptions with the Hebrew šālôm.[66] Like other formulas added to names, such as wishes for good luck in the resurrection, the addition of "peace" presumably was a pious wish.[67] However, I suspect that like the representation of a menorah, which Avigad suggested "primarily represented affiliation and identification with the Jewish people,"[68] these additions also served to identify the commemorated as Jewish. The analogy with the menorah is particularly striking, since both markers emerge in the context of later Roman inscriptions; in earlier Palestinian contexts both are rare, if inscriptions on ossuaries are any indication.[69] Avigad sought to ex-

---

in Tsafrir's words, "the bêmâ, apse, and chancel screen were not imbued with special status, as they were in the church" (Tsafrir, "Byzantine Setting," 152), why would synagogue builders have screened off part of the synagogue area?

65. CII no. 1209. The inscription is dated; assuming it is dated to the era of the foundation of the province of Arabia (106 C.E.), it should be dated 389/90. Lines 1–2 of the inscription read mnēmion Aini|ou Ioudeou. It is possible that Ioudeou is a patronymic, but Judah is usually represented by forms of Ioudas (genitive Iouda), and the interpretation of the word as an ethnic identifier (Ioudeos for Ioudaios) seems a more likely alternative. The possibility exists that this fatherless Jewish man with a Roman name is a convert to Judaism (see R. S. Kraemer, "On the Meaning of the Term Jew in Greco-Roman Inscriptions," HTR 82 [1989] 85–53), but this is only a possibility.

66. Šalôm is of course added to Hebrew/Aramaic inscriptions as well, but the addition to Greek inscriptions strikes me as particularly interesting. See, e.g., CII nos. 903, 908, 914, 920, 922, 933, 934, 937, 943, 951, 956, 959; BS II nos. 28, 29, 69, 178, 203, 219. See also the use of eirēnē 'peace' in much the same way (CII nos. 930, 942), presumably translating šālôm. In addition to the foregoing, BS II has a number of examples of šālôm written in Greek characters (salom): nos. 21, 25, 28, 72, 91.

67. For a wish regarding resurrection, see BS II no. 194; see also BS II no. 162 for a reference to resurrection in the context of a warning to tomb violators. For "peace" as part a wish for the dead, see BS II no. 173 (restored): [en ei]r[ē]/nēi hē kymēsis (l. koimēsis) tou hosiou Aristeou; BS III no. 5. In CII no. 887, Frey prints the restoration šlwm '[l yśr'l, 'peace upon Israel', but '[l mškbw 'on his deathbed' is a workable alternative.

68. Avigad, BS III 268.

69. For the earlier rarity of menorahs, see Avigad, BS III 268; Rahmani, Ossuaries, 51–52; see also R. Hachlili, Ancient Jewish Art and Archaeology in the Land of Israel (Leiden: Brill, 1988) 251–55. Of the examples listed by Rahmani for the usage of šālôm as a wish rather than a name, only two are more plausibly taken as a wish: Rahmani, Ossuaries, no. 3 (where šlm appears to accompany a name); and since šlwm is a woman's name (Salome), while no. 217 contained the bones of a male, "the female name Shalom could not have been intended" (Rahmani, Ossuaries, 130). Note however, that Rahmani listed no. 217 (with a question mark) in the index of names with the vocalization šallûm, a masculine name (cf., e.g., 2 Kgs 15:10–5, Neh 3:12). Of the others, most have the use of šlm/šlwm alone, with no indication of whether it should be taken as a wish or a name (Rahmani, Ossuaries, nos. 66,

plain the spread of the use of the menorah in the period represented at Beth
Sheʿarim with reference to the foreign burials at Beth Sheʿarim.[70] However,
this is likely to be only a partial explanation of the phenomenon since, clearly,
the menorah was used in purely Palestinian contexts as well and came to be a
central iconographic feature in synagogue art.[71] Another dimension of the explanation may well be that, as in diaspora communities, the Jewishness of late
antique Palestinian Jewish communities emerged as an aspect of personal and
communal identity that needed to be expressed both on the semipublic familial level of the funerary inscriptions and the communal level of the synagogue
dedications.

Two other epigraphic practices that occur in both funerary and dedicatory contexts make the emergence of ethnicity more explicit as a theme in
Palestinian Jewish inscriptions. The first is the use of the wish "peace upon
Israel" or a similar prayer, which rhetorically links the fate of the individual
or individuals commemorated with the fate of "Israel."[72] The second—most
often in funerary inscriptions—is the use of formulas dating the inscription
to the year in the sabbatical cycle or the year of the destruction of the Jerusalem Temple.[73] Like counting from creation, which also occurs once,[74] the

---

286, 682 [very worn, reading uncertain], 694. In no. 226 *šlwm* (*šlwm brt šʾwl*) clearly appears
as a woman's name in line 1; Rahmani wanted to read the second occurrence of the word,
in the expression *šlwm brtʾ*, as 'Peace, daughter', but I wonder if the inscription does not
merely repeat "*Šālôm* the daughter". The remainder of the uses of forms of *šlm* almost certainly refer to a woman (as in the first line of no. 226); see Rahmani, *Ossuaries*, index III.A.1
(p. 293).

70. Avigad, *BS* III 268–69: "Evidently Diaspora Jews felt a stronger need to display their
Jewish identity on tombstones than did Palestinian Jews who lived among their own people
in their own country, and whose national identity did not require supplementary affirmation." See also Rahmani, *Ossuaries*, 51.

71. See, e.g., R. Hachlili, "Late Antique Jewish Art from the Golan," in *The Roman and
Byzantine Near East* (ed. J. H. Humphrey; JRASupp 14: Ann Arbor: Journal of Roman Archaeology, 1995) 184–85 and catalog nos. 4–24. It may be worth noting the use at Beth
Sheʿarim of menorahs in conjunction with a monumental doorway (see Hachlili, *Ancient
Jewish Art*, 247, fig. 7), which becomes a well-attested feature in Palestinian synagogue mosaics (Weiss and Netzer, *Promise*, 18 for a recent example; see also the mosaic from the Samaritan synagogue from el Khirbe, Y. Magen, "Samaritan Synagogues" [Heb.], *Qadmoniot*
25 (1993), for example, the figure on p. 70, for a similar combination of elements but in a
different compositional scheme).

72. Funerary inscriptions: E. L. Sukenik, "Jewish Tomb Stones from Zoar," *Kedem* 2
(1945) 87 [Heb.]; Naveh, *Sherd*, 203; synagogue inscriptions: Roth-Gerson no. 12 (Hul-
dah); Naveh no. 1 (Kfar Baram), no. 3 (Almah), no. 38 (Huseifa), nos. 68, 69 (Jericho),
no. 75 (Khirbet Susiye).

73. Sabbatical cycle: Naveh no. 76 (Khirbet Susiye); *CII* no. 1208; Sukenik, "Jewish
Tomb," nos. 2–3 (85–88; no. 1 is *CII* no. 1208); see also two additional examples from Soar
in Naveh, *Sherd*, 203–6 (figs. 142–43). All but the first are also dated to the destruction of
the Temple, another example of which occurs in Naveh no. 13 (Nabratein). With the exception of the sixth-century inscription from Nabratein, all are from the southern part of the
country.

74. Naveh 76 (Khirbet Susiye).

utilization of the sabbatical cycle organizes time around connectedness with biblical tradition and also perhaps around the sanctity of the land of Israel, over which Jews no longer had control. To begin the reckoning of time with the loss of the Temple and priesthood similarly projects powerlessness and perhaps hostility as well, since it is the Romans who were responsible for the Temple's destruction. The occasional use of other dating conventions more firmly rooted in Greco-Roman ideology and convention (emperor and regnal year, civic era, provincial era, or year in the indiction cycle[75]) suggests that an ideological choice was made to use a formula that was self-consciously Jewish and also suggests possible contradictions (acculturation and difference, appropriation and resistance) at play in the decision-making.

These choices may be present in other, more subtle ways as well. For example, while imperial military or administrative posts may on occasion be reflected in Jewish inscriptions, a comparison of two epitaphs, one clearly involving someone with a "Jewish" name and the other generally thought to commemorate someone who was not Jewish, may expose one kind of Jewish strategy in self-commemoration.[76] The Jewish inscription identifies the deceased as Tanhum (*Thanoum*) b. Simeon b. Benjamin, "the *centenarius* of the camp." In contrast, the inscription from Tiberias, generally deemed "non-Jewish," identifies both the dead centurion and his wife as Aurelii (i.e., draws attention to their "Romanness") and specifies the legion.[77] Similarly, two Greek funerary epigrams found at Beth She'arim testify to the influence of still another Greco-Roman convention, but only one epigram, from Tiberias,

75. Regnal year: Naveh no. 43 (Beth Alpha); civic era: Roth-Gerson no. 2 (Ashkelon); provincial era: *CII* no. 1209 (Zoar); indiction: Roth-Gerson no. 23 (Gaza).

76. See *CII* no. 920 (Joppa) for the Jewish inscription; Di Segni no. 10 (cf. the reading of Schwabe no. 17) for the "Gentile" inscription. The inscription from Joppa presumably dates from no earlier than the third century (see Jones, *Later Roman Empire*, 634 on *centenarius*) and is perhaps much later. In earlier versions, I suggested that the near absence of the use of Aurelius in Jewish inscriptions reflected a general tendency with respect to "Roman" identity. I am no longer quite as confident of this conclusion. It is true that nearby Near Eastern cities have more Aurelii than "Jewish" inscriptions (see, e.g., *Bostra* nos. 9008, 9009, 9190, 9276–78, 9399, 9408–9; see also two additional inscriptions with an official character, no. 9083 [*officialis*, that is, a member of the provincial adminstration (?), in a dedication for the provincial governor], no. 9169 [a list of soldiers, probably from before the *constitutio Antoniniana*), and a string of inscriptions naming the provincial governor, nos. 9060, 9062, 9078, 9079, 9101, 9108]; *Gerasa* nos. 137, 233; and in a more official vein, nos. 72, 155–58, 189–90). Part of the distinction may have to do with the nonofficial context of the "Jewish" inscriptions (in which case, the absence of typical Greco-Roman forms remains interesting), but much may depend upon the dating as well. At any rate, it may be possible to add at least one Aurelii. Based on the photo for Roth-Gerson, appendix, no. VI (p. 143; *BS* II no. 212), the letter read by Schwabe and Lifshitz (and accepted by Roth-Gerson) as *iota* in line 1 (i.e., Αὐιτο[) is identical to the *rho* in line 2. The first line of that inscription should therefore perhaps be read Αur() Τρ[.

77. For a somewhat more fulsome and complex pagan military epitaph, see *Caesarea* 147.

reflects (twice) close connection to the *polis*.[78] It is not by accident (although the conclusion may be the result of the kind of circularity discussed above) that commentators have doubted that the deceased commemorated in this inscription and in the second military epigraph were Jewish.[79]

The explicit marking of inscriptions as Jewish increases in late antiquity (at least when compared to material from the Second Temple Period). This process parallels the development of architecturally distinct (and expensive) synagogues in Palestine. By way of concluding this discussion of ethnicity in Palestinian Jewish inscriptions, I would like to examine briefly how dedicatory inscriptions from synagogues might reflect an emerging Palestinian Jewish ethos. Consider briefly the recently published synagogue floor mosaic from Sepphoris. Based on the dedicatory inscriptions that survive—and there has clearly been much damage to the inscriptions—at least two features are striking. First, the inscriptions, both Aramaic and Greek, are highly formulaic and betray almost no individuality on the part of the donors.[80] Second, there is, as far as I can see, no indication of officialdom within the organization of the synagogue. This, of course, is not to claim that there was no communal organization. I wonder, for instance, if the removal of a Greek

78. For Beth She'arim, see *BS* II nos. 127, 183 (the latter is a transported burial); for Tiberias, see Di Segni no. 27.

79. Schwabe 225; Di Segni no. 91.

80. The formulaic elements in these inscriptions are all known, to a greater or a lesser degree, from other Palestinian Jewish inscriptions. *Děkîr lĕ-ṭab; mnēsthei eis agathon* 'may . . . be remembered for good' (Band 5, dedicatory inscription, and Band 6, left-hand inscription, may include expansions of this formula) is ubiquitous (see above, n. 40; note, however, its use in a church from Ḥorvat Ḥesheq in western Galilee; L. Di Segni, "Ḥorvat Ḥesheq: The Inscriptions," in *Christian Archaeology in the Holy Land, New Discoveries: Essays in Honor of Virgilio Corbo, OFM* [ed. G. C. Bottini, L.\Di Segni, and E. Alliata; Studium Biblicum Franciscanum, Collectio Maior 36; Jerusalem: Franciscan Press, 1990] pp. 379–80, no. 1). *Hyper sōtērias* (Band 3; see Roth-Gerson, "Similarities and Differences," 138–40): for Palestinian Jewish examples, see Roth-Gerson, *Greek Inscriptions*, no. 3 (*CII* no. 964, Ashkelon); nos. 7, 8 (Beth-Shean); p. 100 (marble basin with inscription, associated with Gaza A); no. 23 (*CII* no. 966; Gaza B, [*hyper sōtēri*]*as* restored); no. 28 (Caesarea). *Euxamenos epoiēsen* 'having taken a vow, made . . .' (restorable in Band 4, right-hand inscription, and Band 5); see Roth-Gerson no. 26 (Caesarea); cf. Roth-Gerson no. 16 (Hammath Tiberias). *Eulogia autō* (Band 5, Band 6, left-hand inscription; restorable in Band 1, Band 3, Band 4, right-hand inscription, Band 6, right-hand inscription, Band 7): cf. *tĕhê lēh birkĕtāh* or similar formula in Aramaic dedications, Naveh no. 10 (Dabura), no. 12 (Gush Ḥalav), no. 18 (Capernaum), no. 26 (Hammath Tiberias), no. 30 (Kfar Kana), no. 35 (Hammath Gader), no. 39 (Huseifa, restored); and see Roth-Gerson nos. 16, 17, 18 (Hammath Tiberias). Finally, *'āmēn*, written at least once in Hebrew characters at the end of a Greek inscription (Band 6, left-hand inscription) and ocurring with the Aramaic inscriptions as well: see Roth-Gerson nos. 16, 17 (Hammath Tiberias; in both, *amēn* is written in Greek characters); see also no. 10 (Gerasa; Greek characters); some Aramaic inscriptions are collected in Roth-Gerson 160 n. 42. For the lack of intentionality as a feature particular to the Hebrew and Aramaic inscriptions as opposed to Greek inscriptions, see Roth-Gerson, "Similarities and Differences," 140–41; see also Roth-Gerson 150–52.

inscription and its replacement with an Aramaic one was not due to the fact that the floor was paved by a subscription for specific panels, suggesting some kind of organization.[81] However, the absence of both individuality and officialdom may reflect the cultivation of an egalitarian ethos that pointedly deemphasized hierarchical structures.

It is in this context that I would explain the relative paucity of inscriptions dated by the officership of synagogue officials (mentioned above), in contrast, for example, to the frequent dating of church inscriptions by bishops or other church officials.[82] Within the dedicatory inscriptions, identifiable synagogue officials are actually quite rare and generally appear as donors, not as officers.[83] And while, as noted above, the Jewish inscriptions do make use of honorary titles (*rabbî*, *kyrios*, and so on) and designations of official status (*lamprotatos*, *comes*), there is nothing like the inscription from Sepphoris (in this case, apparently an example of public benefaction) that is dated to the

81. Note *tēn tablan* 'the panel' in Band 6, left-hand inscription, and in the inscription around the inner ring of the zodiac mosaic (Band 5), *tēn pasan tablan* 'the whole panel'. I would propose that this phrase means that the donors "made" (i.e., paid for) this specific panel. Presumably, in Band 2, right-hand inscription, line 2, the restoration should be *tēn pa]san tablan* as well, although I am not certain that those letters ought to be placed at the end of line 1. Band 2 in general poses some problems. Neither the right-hand nor the left-hand inscription begins with the expected formula. Line 2 of the right-hand mosaic ends mid-formula, the final *epsilon* apparently introducing *e[ulogia autois]*, although there is no room for an additional line. Perhaps the central and right-hand panels bore a single inscription, the end of which would have been concluded in the center panel. The restored *tēn pa]san tablan* might then refer to the larger panel. Given that there is a possible connection between the]*pheos* in line 2 of the left-hand inscription and the Alapheos of line 1 of the right-hand panel, might there not be a connection between all three panels? (Admittedly, this is entirely speculative; in addition, as the design in the center panel is reconstructed, there is no room for a corresponding third line to complete the formula beginning in line 2 of the right-hand inscription.)

82. See L. Di Segni, "The Involvement of Local, Municipal and Provincial Authorities in Urban Building in Late Antique Palestine and Arabia," in *The Roman and Byzantine Near East* (ed. J. H. Humphrey; JRASupp 14; Ann Arbor: Journal of Roman Archaeology, 1995) 312–13; some of the inscriptions cited by Di Segni in the pages that follow are relevant. See also *Gerasa*, e.g., 292, 298, 304, 309; M. Avi-Yonah, "An Addendum to the Episcopal List of Tyre," *IEJ* 16 (1966) 209–10 (Khirbet Karkara); Gregg and Urman, *Jews, Christians, and Pagans*, 17, 22, 47, 68; Fitzgerald, *Mosaic*, 16, inscriptions VI and VII (Beth-Shean); C. H. Kraeling, "The Mosaic Inscriptions," in *A Byzantine Church at Khirbet al-Karak* (ed. P. Delougaz and R. C. Haines; OIP 85; Chicago: University of Chicago Press, 1960), and the contributions of Di Segni in Bottini, Di Segni, and Alliata (eds.), *Christian Archaeology in the Holy Land*: "The Monastery of Martyrius at Maʿaleh Adumim (Khirbet al-Muraṣṣa): The Inscriptions," no. 2, restored (p. 154); no. 6 (p. 158); "Nuṣeib ʿUweishîra: The Inscription," 201; "Khirbet el-Beiyûdât: The Inscriptions," no. 3 (p. 268).

83. Reading Eiouda the *arkhisynagogos* in Roth-Gerson no. 24 (Sepphoris) as other than the donor seems to me to involve too much emendation; the *arkhisynagogos* of Roth-Gerson no. 27 (Caesarea) is explicit. For a possible exception (commemoration of the *pronoētēs* for the management of a building project see Roth-Gerson nos. 16, 18, and the discussion in n. 42 above).

time of "our most holy father Eutropios the bishop."[84] The nearest example in a roughly contemporaneous Jewish context is the commemoration of "his holiness, my lord, my master, Issi, the priest, the honored, my master [perhaps: 'son of a master'] . . ." (Khirbet Susiye, Naveh no. 75). This is an exceptionally fulsome inscription by Jewish epigraphic standards, but even here the man so recognized is making a donation in honor of the marriage of his son. Whatever these titles mean, they are not the graphic expressions of elaborate hierarchical organizations. In fact, far from recording a fixed hierarchical structure and a formal clergy, the dedicatory inscriptions give the impression of institutions built, managed, and run by local lay donors. Throughout this period, the epigraphic use of *rabbî* and related forms is probably almost always merely honorific ('my master'), but even if it had more specific reference to members of the rabbinic movement, these "epigraphical rabbis" do not appear to have had any role in the synagogues other than donor.[85] Similarly, while the status of priest (*hiereus, kôhēn*) is sufficiently significant to bear mentioning in inscriptions,[86] as in the inscription from Khirbet Susiye just mentioned, and while several fragments of lists of the priestly courses have been discovered,[87] dedicatory inscriptions do not imply a special place in the hierarchy for actual living priests.

84. See Netzer and Weiss, *Promise*, 172 and fig. 13.
85. See Cohen, "Epigraphical Rabbis," 1–17. See also my "Rabbi," ABD 5.600–602; F. Millar (*The Roman Near East 31 B.C.–A.D. 337* [Cambridge: Harvard University Press, 1993] 380) notes that this use of *rabbî* as a title is peculiar to Jewish inscriptions, but this has no direct bearing on whether the bearers of the title are "rabbinic." To Cohen's approach, compare D. Urman, "Kazrin," 543–44.
86. Synagogue inscriptions: Naveh no. 58 (Naaran); no. 74 (Eshtemoa); no. 75 (Khirbet Susiyeh), all from Judea; see also Naveh no. 88, copied in no. 88a, b (Dura-Europos); Roth-Gerson no. 19 (Jerusalem; arguably from the first century). Burial inscriptions: see, e.g., BS I nos. 62, 67 ("This [burial] place belongs to priests"); BS II nos. 66 ("Sara . . . the mother of the priestess") 180, 181 (funerary inscriptions) identify individuals as priests. BS II no. 148, *khoēn buritios*, which, if the editors' translation 'a priest from Beirut' is correct, is a strange inscription, if for no other reason than that a proper name is expected. Perhaps *khoēn*, like the Aramaic *kahanā'* served as a proper name. In any case, it may reflect the custom of bringing the dead for burial in Palestine and, therefore, may shed no light on priests in Galilee.
87. S. Klein, *Sēper ha-yiššûb* (Jerusalem: Bialik, 1939) vol. 1/part 1, pp. 102–7, summarizing earlier work; T. Kahane, "The Priestly Courses and Their Geographical Settlements," *Tarbiz* 48 (1978–79) 19–26 [Heb.]. See also the discussion and references in S. S. Miller, *Studies in the History and Traditions of Sepphoris* (SJLA 37; Leiden: Brill, 1984) 62, 120–27. The list is reconstructed from partially preserved Byzantine Palestinian liturgical poems and from fragmentary inscriptions (Naveh no. 51 [Caesarea]; no. 52 [Ashkelon, from the late fourth or early seventh century, the uncertainty stemming from the era according to which to date an inscription associated with the same synagogue, Roth-Gerson no. 3, commentary]; and from the proposed reading of Eshel, "Fragmentary Inscription." See also Naveh no. 106 (from Yemen, fifth or sixth centuries [?], R. Degen, "An Inscription of the Twenty-Four Priestly Courses from the Yemen," *Tarbiz* 42 [1973–74] 303 [Heb.]). If the attribution to R. Levi were both correct and reliable, we could date the earliest reference to

Moreover, Palestinian Jewish dedicatory inscriptions are generally not in the first person but are frequently expressed as a prayer by the community (as in "may he/she be remembered for good who made . . .").[88] Just what to make of this is by no means clear. Since none of the synagogues for which we have inscriptions appears to have been built in its entirety by one person or household,[89] it is possible that the synagogue donors were not the very wealthy members of Palestinian Jewish society, who, if they played a communal role, did not do so in synagogue buildings. However, the presence in the inscriptions of people who are likely to be real aristocrats (Roth-Gerson no. 24, from Sepphoris, if Elasios is to be take as a donor; the family in Naveh no. 32, from Hammath Gader) makes this conclusion far from inevitable. As an alternative, perhaps we should see this as the cultivation of a communal rhetoric of inclusiveness, in which outright and complete patronage is de-emphasized in favor of a communitarian ideal.[90] The recurring congratulations to the entire community for its participation in the building of the synagogue that are expressed beginning in the late fourth or early fifth century are susceptible to much the same interpretation.[91] Let me stress that I am not proposing a romanticized picture of egalitarian and democratic Jews over and against stratified and aristocratic Gentiles. The seat from Chorazin (mentioned above) is evidence against this, as is the rhetoric of the inscription just cited from Khirbet Susiye, and I have no doubt that community members knew precisely who the "truly" important people were. Rather, I am suggesting that it was precisely the elites of late antique Palestine who cultivated this inclusive approach. It is in this sense that I would take the rarity of outright demonstrations of "ego" that sometimes occur in, for example, late antique church dedications.[92]

---

this list to the very end of the third century (y. Ta'an. 4.5 [68d]). For a cautious assessment of the evidence of these lists for settlement pattern, see D. Trifon, "Did the Priestly Courses (Mishmarot) Transfer from Judaea to Galilee after the Bar Kokhba Revolt?" Tarbiz 59 (1990–91) 77–93 [Heb.].

88. Naveh (Sherd, 126) understands this as due to the fact that synagogue officials (parnāsîm) formulated the inscriptions. I am inclined to attribute greater importance to communal rhetoric: one could easily imagine a situation where officials asked donors what they wanted their dedicatory inscription to say. See Naveh nos. 3, 28 for examples of first-person dedications (the former appears to name the artisan).

89. Even the "house of Leontios," if it was a synagogue, in addition to the mention of Leontios in the floor mosaic (Roth-Gerson nos. 6, 7), apparently included an inscription naming another donor (Roth-Gerson no. 8). Zori ("House of Leontios," 132) described this as a lintel; Roth-Gerson 39 as a marble plaque; both associate it with the "house of Leontios."

90. See M. P. Bonz ("Differing Approaches to Religious Benefaction: The Late Third-Century Acquisition of the Late Sardis Synagogue," HTR 86 [1993] 139–54), who argues for a communal mode of benefaction at Sardis.

91. Naveh no. 39 (Huseifa), no. 43 (Beth Alpha, partially restored), no. 46 (Beth-Shean), no. 57 (Maon), no. 69 (Jericho), no. 70 ('Ein Gedi), no. 83 (Khirbet Susiye), no. 84 (Khirbet Susiye, partially restored). See also Roth-Gerson no. 12 (Hulda), no. 25 (Caesarea).

92. See, for example, Gerasa nos. 315, 316, labeling portraits of the donors. If the priest Aeneas was responsible for the elaborate inscription in the Church of St. Theodore, Gerasa

Conclusions

I have been arguing that in Palestinian Jewish inscriptions ethnicity ("Jewishness") emerged in late antiquity as an item to be noted, even stressed. When this appears in funerary inscriptions, it seems to me that it is not to be understood merely as the presence of burials transported from the diaspora or even as the influence of diaspora practices on Palestinian Jews. Instead, it may reflect the development of ethnic discourse in Palestine analogous to the language of Jewish communities in the diaspora. In this way, the complex of ethnic and religious connections that we label "Jewish" was an element in the way that at least some Palestinian Jews quite literally made names for themselves. This is paralleled by the very emergence of the synagogue, whatever its prehistory, as a distinctive and archaeologically recognizable institution to which communities and individuals committed funds and resources.[93] Some traces of an inclusive communal ethos may be teased out—tentatively—from the synagogue inscriptions themselves.

We should not allow familiarity and hindsight to make us take ethnicity for granted or view it as merely the outward expression of an ethnic identity and a communal ethos that had "always" existed. The emergence of local community may itself be a late antique phenomenon in the Roman East, of which local lay-run synagogues may be but one manifestation.[94] Moreover, the spread of urbanization in Palestine and the subordination of rural territories including Lower Galilee to urban administration, the demographic changes that affected Palestine in Late Antiquity (population growth in absolute terms but a decline and regional shift, especially to Galilee, of the Jewish

---

no. 299 is a particularly good example of self-advertisement in Christian dedications. See also the inscriptions from the Monastery of the Lady Mary, published by Fitzgerald. Some are mere formulas, analogous in that respect to synagogue inscriptions (nos. I–III, VI–VII). But two emphasize both the importance of the Lady Mary to this institution and the authority of Elias (nos. IV–V).

93. Cf. L. I. Levine, "The Nature and Origins of Palestinian Synagogues," *JBL* 115 (1996) 425–48.

94. See the brief comments in R. S. Bagnall, *Egypt in Late Antiquity* (Princeton: Princeton University Press, 1993) 137–38. On the other hand, note the evidence for active institutionalized village life in Syria in G. M. Harper, "Village Administration in the Roman Province of Syria," YCS 1 (1928) 116–45; H. I. MacAdam, "Epigraphy and Village Life in Southern Syria during the Roman and Byzantine Periods," *Berytus* 31 (1983) 107–8; idem, *Studies in the History of the Roman Province of Arabia: The Northern Sector* (BAR International Series 295; Oxford: British Archaeological Reports, 1987); M. Sartre, "Villes et village du Hauran (Syrie) du Ier au IVe siècle," in *Sociétés urbaines, sociétés rurales dans l'Asie Mineure et la Syrie hellénistiques et romaines* (ed. E. Frézouls; Strasbourg: AECR, 1987) 240–57; J. D. Grainger, "'Village Government' in Roman Syria and Arabia," *Levant* 27 (1995) 179–95. It should be noted that nothing like this epigraphic body of material from Roman Syria exists for Palestine, but the epigraphic study of rural Palestine is still in its infancy (cf. S. Dar and N. Kokkinos, "The Greek Inscriptions from Senaim on Mt. Hermon," *PEQ* 124 [1992] 9–25, especially their final remarks, citing F. Millar; and Gregg and Urman, *Jews, Christians, and Pagans*, 24, 34, and possibly 219).

population following the collapse of two failed revolts[95]), the rise to official prominence of Christianity, and its implications for the legal status of Jews and their institutions and for the reconfiguring of the landscape of the Holy Land[96] — all this meant that Palestinian Jews were living in a world whose horizons had palpably shrunk. If, in the time of Josephus (first century) an elite Jerusalemite priest could still speak of Palestinian Jewry as constituting a kind of polity, despite the loss of political independence and the repeated fragmentation of Judea into several subterritories and despite the destruction of the Temple and its developed structures of both extraction and integration, that impression had long since passed. Like rabbinic literature, which reimagines Jewishness as a community gathered around a tradition, Palestinian inscriptions, particularly dedicatory inscriptions, may reflect the emergence of a new "imagined community," a new Judaism.[97]

95. For growth during the Roman and Byzantine Periods, see M. Broshi, "The Population of Western Palestine in the Roman Byzantine Period," *BASOR* 236 (1979) 1–10, and the general comments of Y. Tsafrir, "Some Notes on the Settlement and Demography of Palestine in the Byzantine Period: The Archaeological Evidence," in *Retrieving the Past: Essays on Archaeological Research and Methodology in Honor of Gus W. Van Beek* (ed. J. D. Seger; Winona Lake, Ind.: Eisenbrauns, 1996) 269–83. Y. Portugali ("The Settlement Pattern in the Western Jezreel Valley from the 6th Century B.C.E. to the Arab Conquest" [Heb.], in *Man and Land in Eretz Israel in Antiquity* [ed. A. Kasher, A. Oppenheimer, and U. Rappaport; Jerusalem: Yad Yitshak ben-Tsvi, 1986] 7–19) argues that, at least in the area covered by his survey, the population curve peaked before the Byzantine Period; cf. Z. Safrai, "The Influence of Demographic Stratification on the Agricultural and Economic Structure during the Mishnaic and Talmudic Periods" [Heb.], in *Man and Land*, 20–48. For specifically Jewish demographic patterns, see G. Alon, *Tôldôt ha-yĕhûdîm bĕ-ʾereṣ yiśrāʾēl bi-tĕqûpat ha-mišnâ wĕ-ha-talmûd* (2 vols.; Tel Aviv: Hotsaat ha-Kibbuts ha-Meuḥad, 1953–57) 2.242–62, especially 243–48; M. Avi-Yonah, *The Jews of Palestine: A Political History from the Bar Kokhba War to the Arab Conquest* (Oxford: Blackwell, 1976) 15–20. J. Schwartz (*Jewish Settlement in Judaea after the Bar Kochba Revolt until the Arab Conquest* [Jerusalem: Magnes, 1986] Heb.) argues for the persistence of Jewish settlement in Judea, although he too deals with decline, on pp. 42–46.

96. See, for legal status, A. Linder, *The Jews in Imperial Roman Legislation* (Detroit: Wayne State University Press, 1987); J. Cohen, "Roman Imperial Policy toward the Jews from Constantine to the End of the Patriarchate," *Byzantine Studies* 3 (1976) 1–29. For the invention of a Christian Holy Land, see R. L. Wilken, *The Land Called Holy: Palestine in Christian History and Thought* (New Haven: Yale University Press, 1992); J. E. Taylor, *Christians and the Holy Places* (Oxford: Clarendon, 1993).

97. The expression "imagined community" is borrowed from B. Anderson, *Imagined Communities: Reflections on the Origin and Spread of Nationalism* (rev. ed.; London: Verso, 1991). The argument that rabbinic texts are in this sense analogous to the development of synagogues is beyond the scope of this paper and deserves a full-length study of its own. I have made a partial argument, based on the rabbinic development of a "Jewish" civil law, in my "Early Rabbinic Civil Law and the Literature of the Second Temple Period," *Jewish Studies Quarterly* 2 (1995) 149–83.

Social Magic and Social Realities in Late Roman and Early Byzantine Galilee

C. Thomas McCollough
Centre College, Danville, KY

AND

Beth Glazier-McDonald
Centre College, Danville, KY

Over the past two decades, archaeology and archaeologists have made great strides toward re-creating ancient Galilee. Archaeological excavations at urban sites such as Sepphoris and others have uncovered the remains of the monumental structures that give striking visual evidence of the extent of the wealth and cultural synthesis once at work. But archaeology has rightfully prided itself on displaying the evidence, not only of the elite and the monumental, but also of the ordinary. In the material remains, one may catch a glimpse of the convictions and outlines of life patterns of people either not represented or misrepresented in the literature. Such evidence provides critical elements of a more inclusive social history. For this task, the monumental structures have to be supplemented by the likes of domestic structures, industrial installations, small finds (for example, jewelry, cosmetic bottles, and spoons), household god/goddess statues, and certain types of epigraphy. To this evidence the University of South Florida Excavations at Sepphoris had the good fortune of adding two metal amulets.[1] The amulets and their incised incantations help pry open a window into the fears and convictions of the population of Sepphoris in the Late Ancient Period and so aid in the effort to describe the social realities of the people of this ancient city.

The two amulets, one of bronze and one of silver, were found in the soil and among the debris of the Early Byzantine occupation of the large basilica

---

1. The University of South Florida Excavations are under the direction of James F. Strange. The Associate Directors are Dennis Groh and Thomas Longstaff. Tom McCollough is the Assistant Director. The amulets were found in the course of the excavation of Field V (the basilica building) in 1992 (bronze amulet) and 1993 (silver amulet).

building to the east of what was likely the center of the Roman city of Sepphoris. Their location within the building (near the northwest corner) and
their relation to the mosaic floor (in soil approximately 45 cm above the
floor) were similar. The related finds of pottery and coins and the stratigraphy
date the amulets to the early fifth century C.E.

When found, both amulets were still tightly rolled, and the silver amulet
was still in a case made of copper. Both were remarkably well preserved. In
fact, despite the fact that the bronze amulet was out of its case, its original
borders (which showed jagged edges, as if it had been cut from a larger sheet
with an instrument with serrated edges) were still visible. The extraordinarily
difficult task of unrolling the amulets was given to the staff of the Israel Museum, in particular Joseph "Dodo" Shenhav.

The language of the incantations is similar, though the one on the bronze
amulet is more consistently Aramaic, while the silver one utilizes Hebrew
with occasional Aramaicisms. These several points of similarity (location,
date, language) do not carry over, however, to the content of the incantations.
In the case of the bronze amulet (fig. 1), the incantation falls into the category of formulas whose intent is, in the most general sense, protective. This
type of formula is part of the largest subcategory, that of providing protection
from disease. The incantation on the silver amulet (fig. 2), on the other hand,
is social, rather than protective. That is, its intent is to capture and direct
power outward, in order to manipulate a situation or a person. The more narrow typology in this case is the curse text. Thus, we have two amulets from
roughly the same period and found very near each other but representing two
poles on the spectrum of incantational magic. This is good fortune, since it
allows one to speak more broadly about the upsurge in the magical arts in this
period and the range in the intent of the magical incantations.

The Bronze Amulet

Unrolled, the bronze amulet measures 3.5 cm in width and 8.2 cm in
length. The amulet was partially broken at the bottom, but it is unlikely that
the inscription continued beyond the row of *šins* partially exposed.
The incised incantation reads:

Text	Translation
1. קמיע לאשתה	1. An amulet against fever
2. רבתה דאזיה	2. protracted that burns
3. ולא שבקה	3. and does not cease
4. (three magic signs)	4. (three magic signs)
5. ננן והיהאו (one magic sign)	5. (one magic sign)NN(final)N WHYHAW
6. אאאששש	6. AAAŠŠŠ
7. קמיע לאשתה	7. An amulet against fever
8. רבתה דאזיה	8. protracted that burns

Fig. 1. *The bronze amulet. Draw-ing by Ada Yardeni.*

9. (one magic sign) ‏ולא שבקה‏   9. and does not cease (one magic sign)
10. (three magic signs)   10. (three magic signs)
11. (one magic sign) ‏ננן והיה‏   11. NN(final)N WHYH
12. ‏אואאא‏   12. AWAAA
13. [‏ש‏]‏שש‏   13. ŠŠ[Š]

The incantation is obviously intended to ward off a serious and persistent fe-ver. We note at the outset of the incantation that, unlike most of the Aramaic amulets studied by Naveh and Shaked, this one has no personal reference.[2] That this incantation is generic suggests that it was made for a mass market,

2. For example, in J. Naveh and S. Shaked, *Amulets and Magic Bowls: Aramaic Incan-tations of Late Antiquity* (2d ed.; Jerusalem: Magnes, 1987) 99, amulet 2.1 begins with the phrase, "an amulet proper to heal Ya'itha." See also, J. Naveh and S. Shaked, *Magic Spells and Formulae: Aramaic Incantations of Late Antiquity* (Jerusalem: Magnes, 1993).

incised for those who could not afford the more detailed, personalized type or perhaps could not wait. Fevers are by far the health problem most frequently addressed by amulets of this period. The term used for fever, אשתה, is according to Naveh and Shaked, "well known in all Aramaic dialects as 'the fire' or 'the fever.'"[3]

The second line is interesting in that the incantation attempts to discriminate the type of fever being combatted. The addition of רבתה to distinguish the severity of the fever appears on only one other Aramaic amulet.[4] Greek amulets, on the other hand, regularly incorporated phrases from Greek medical vocabulary to distinguish the severity or duration of the fever.[5] Here we agree with Naveh and Shaked, who suggest that the Aramaic is borrowing Greek medical terminology.[6] A common designator in Greek for a severe fever, μέγας πυρετός, is then translated into the Aramaic incantation as אשתה רבתה.[7] That the phrase has been borrowed may also account for the clarifying phrase that follows the reference to אשתה רבתה. That is, a severe fever is one that burns (דאזיה) and does not cease (ולא שבקה).

This relatively unique effort in constructing an incantation against fever is most intriguing when seen in conjunction with the magical signs or figures drawn on the amulet. These figures, which have been identified most often as *charaktêres*, appear with some regularity on Greek, Hebrew, and Aramaic amulets, magical bowls, defixiones, and in texts. At times, they are mingled with the written formula, as in this case, while at other times they stand alone and become the unique instrument to empower the object or the text. As John Gager noted, "they [charaktêres] had taken on a life of their own and were seen as personifying, representing, and embodying great power."[8]

Despite the frequency and apparent importance of *charaktêres* for the magical vocabulary, their meaning or symbolic reference is uncertain. Most recently, and we think most persuasively, the theory has been advanced that they are linked to astrology. In this regard, Gager suggested that "they represent various planetary powers, powers that were in turn commonly identified with angels and archangels by late Roman astrologers."[9] A clue to the connection between fever, astrology, and incantational magic practiced in Sepphoris is provided by the apocryphal work *Testament of Solomon*. While the origin of this work is yet to be firmly established, a recent editor, David Dul-

---

3. Naveh and Shaked, *Amulets and Magic Bowls*, 47.

4. Amulet 19 in Naveh and Shaked, *Magic Spells and Formulae*, 60.

5. See, for example, the fever amulets cited in R. Daniel and F. Maltomini, *Supplementum Magicum I* (Abhandlungen der Rheinisch-Westfälischen Akademie der Wissenschaft: Sonderreihe Papyrologica Coloniensia 16/1; Opladen: Westdeutscher, 1990).

6. Naveh and Shaked, *Magic Spells and Formulae*, 60–61.

7. For a discussion of the use of the Greek phrase, see R. Kotansky, "An Incised Copper Amulet from ʿEvron," *ʿAtiqot* English Series 20 (1990) 81–87.

8. J. Gager, *Curse Tablets and Binding Spells from Antiquity and the Ancient World* (New York: Oxford University Press, 1992) 11.

9. Ibid.

ing, has argued for a late third-century C.E. date and a provenance of Galilee.[10] *Testament of Solomon* 18 contains a lengthy discussion of the "thirty-six heavenly bodies" and their activities. Each of these bodies, identified as "decans of the zodiac," ruled over 10 degrees of the 360° zodiac. The 16th decan, identified as Katrax, is responsible for inflicting severe or possibly incurable fever on men. In the case of the amulet, the *charaktêres* would cojoin with the formula to identify the origin and nature of the disease.

The series of letters that follows the *charaktêres* is also not an uncommon feature of amulets. In some cases these strings of letters have an apparent referent to a divine name or power, while in other cases they have no clear meaning. In the latter case this veiled intelligibility may either be a signal of the perceived power of the letters as such or a manifestation of the related concept of *voces mysticae*. In this instance, the first series of letters, NNN, has no known meaning, nor is this a common set for Aramaic amulets. The next series, WHYH, may represent the divine name. Such a rendering occurs in the Cairo Geniza. The next series of letters is difficult to decipher. A possible reading is AW, AAA, ŠŠŠ. If AW is a contraction of the divine name, the series of *alephs* and *šins* could be an elaboration on the root of fever, that is, 'Š. This would give a reading that in part invokes the divine name and fire or fever.

Later Qabbalistic writings are also suggestive, wherein initial letters of biblical verses were used as *shemoth*. In a list developed by Schrire, based on several Qabbalistic books, the letters *yod, aleph,* and *šin* serve as pointers to Deut 6:4–9 and also serve as an allusion to Num 11:2, where invoking Yahweh (אי) results in a dying down of fire/fever (אש).[11] Taken together, the letters suggesting the divine name, the disease, and efficacious biblical verses became a powerful instrument. The power of the sacred was drawn onto the amulet and, accordingly, into the sphere of the amulet owner to effect the cure or prevent the onset of the illness. This seemingly simple amulet thus presents us with a complex interrelationship of a written formulaic identification of the disease joined with a symbolic identification of its astrological origin ultimately brought into intersection with the sacred power that protects one from or ultimately extinguishes this horrible fever.

The Silver Amulet

The second amulet, the silver amulet, was found still enclosed in its copper case. Bound in its case, it measured about 10 cm in length. When removed from the case and unfolded, it measured 11.2 cm long and 3.1 cm wide. The copper wrapper appears to have been incised (a not uncommon practice), but these incisions could not be deciphered. There is a fold in the center of the

---

10. D. C. Duling, "Testament of Solomon," in *The Old Testament Pseudepigrapha* (ed. J. H. Charlesworth; Garden City, N.Y.: Doubleday, 1983) 1.935–87.

11. Theodore Schrire, *Hebrew Amulets: Their Decipherment and Interpretation* (London: Routledge & Kegan Paul, 1966).

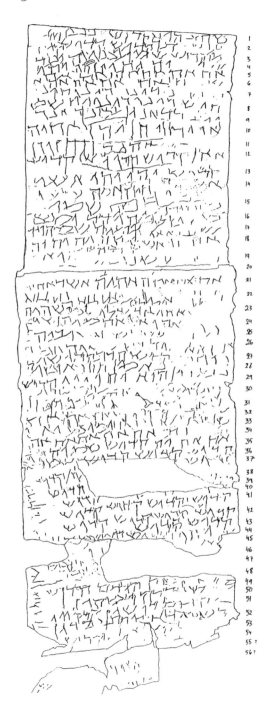

Fig. 2. The silver amulet.
Drawing by Ada Yardeni.

amulet, so that it could be folded over before being rolled and placed inside the case. The amulet itself is made from a thin sheet of silver foil.

As one can see from the drawing (fig. 2), unlike the bronze amulet, the incantation on the silver amulet is densely packed onto and ultimately fills the surface of the amulet and, in fact, at points is written sideways into the small margin. This is a much longer text, some 55 lines. For this study it is unnecessary to analyze all of the lines; instead, we have isolated key lines in terms of content or lines that are indicative of the pattern of the incantation.

In part, the text of the incantation reads:

Text	*Translation*
1. ‏[י]‏מחא הוא הקדוש אפבנ אי‏	1. He will smite! He is the holy one. (magic names)
2. בטוש שתך קדוש קדוש יאי‏[ר]‏	2. With a rod, he will crush. Holy, holy
3. בקדוש שמו בנייה יצוד	3. By his holy name, he gives light. With a hempcord he lies in wait.
7. ‏[חיש הקדוש]‏ דינו דינו חיש	7. Quickly, O Holy one[s]! Execute judgment, execute judgment quickly!
8. חיש דינו דינו יה שמו	8. Quickly execute judgment, execute judgment, YH is his name.
9. ‏[יגער]‏ באנין באנך אנך	9. May he rebuke the murmurer (oppressor). With a plumb line he plumbs.
14. ‏[אשבע ב]‏יה אמח. עלעלי	14. I adjure YH. Blot out my misfortune.
15. יה שמו	15. YH is his name.
16. שמו יה יה אדיר ומש	16. His name is YH. YH, magestic is his name. (letters reversed)
28. נוהו . . . נאמן תות אושו	28. His dwelling . . . The mark of his foundation is trustworthy.
29. נגש‏[יה]‏ הוא יהו ייי קדוש	29. [YH] draws near. He is YHW. YYY is holy.
33. ‏[כ]‏תש געש פעא ומצ‏[יא י]‏	33. YA strikes, thrusts, bellows, and squeezes.
50. ש קבל הט . . . ילקו‏	50. Charges are brought. They are smitten.
51. . . . יקוו בטושין קלק ייי	51. The crushers gather; YY throws down.
52. דא. ‏[יותיב]‏ דין	52. He will restore justice.

It should be noted at the outset that selecting lines creates the impression of a more coherent set of appeals and descriptions than is the case. In actuality, lines of appeal for action against the antagonist(s) (for example, 'quickly execute judgment') are often followed by several lines of repeated forms of the divine name (YAH) or the word 'holy' (קדוש), which create more the effect of a formulaic magical chant.

This incantation is clearly of a different type than the one on the bronze amulet. This sort of incantation utilizes the power beckoned or captured to manipulate some person or situation external to the holder of the amulet. Such social incantations might be used, for example, to bring on disease, ill luck at the racetrack, defeat in an athletic competition or, in a more constructive mode, to persuade one's love to return the affection. While a protective amulet like the bronze one would likely be worn, a social amulet like this silver one might be deposited near the person or persons to whom the power is directed.

The incantation itself is replete with formulaic elements of the sort identified and analyzed by Michael Swartz's work on the Cairo Geniza.[12] For example, Swartz identified a common adjuration formula among the Geniza texts, "I adjure you . . . ," followed by a set of instructions to be carried out by the deity or an agent of the deity (for example, an angel). This formula appears as well on this amulet: 'I adjure YH, blot out my misfortune' (line 14). We also note the appearance of such conventions as drawing a box around the divine name and reversing letters. The appearance of these formulaic elements and conventions is at once indicative of the transition of this sort of magical art from the hands of the magician to the scribe or, if you will, the technician. The conventions facilitated the construction of the incantation because the scribe employed prescribed units of text or symbols (as found for example in the Greek magical papyri) to address the problem at hand.[13] This also properly located the scribe in the chain of power. He served merely as the facilitator; the power as such was then clearly resident in the formula or symbols. Once turned over to the client, he or she had immediate and, in a sense, autonomous access to the highest powers. A second point about the presence of these conventions is that they also indicate the high demand for these implements in late antiquity. Such a demand created the sort of cottage industry wherein amulet makers using these formulas could produce them in the number and type sufficient to meet what appears to have been a growing demand. More will be said about this growing demand below.

Beyond the formula and conventions, the content of this incantation falls into the larger category of curse texts, and we suggest that it may be located

12. M. Swartz, "Scribal Magic and Its Rhetorical Formal Patterns in Medieval Hebrew and Aramaic Incantations from the Cairo Geniza," *HTR* 83 (1990) 163–80. See also the discussion in L. Schiffman and M. Swartz, *Hebrew and Aramaic Incantation Texts from the Cairo Geniza* (Semitic Texts and Studies 1; Sheffield: Sheffield Academic Press, 1992) 52–58.

13. For the Greek magical papyri, see H. D. Betz (ed.), *The Greek Magical Papyri in Translation* (Chicago: University of Chicago Press, 1986).

more narrowly in a category of incantations that H. S. Versnel identified as judicial prayers.[14] Versnel noted: "in the typical curse text, a person desires to harm an enemy without argumentation or justification for the action; the demons or gods who carry out the curse are manipulated rather than persuaded. In the judicial prayer, however, an individual supplicates the gods in a subservient way and asks for divine assistance for an injustice suffered."[15] The latter seems applicable to this incantation, as we have God or God's agents identified by way of various names and epitaphs and then supplicated by way of a formula of invocation. The wrong suffered is identified only vaguely as "my misfortune." The references to the offending person or party are equally vague and are identified as "murmurers" or "oppressors." The revenge sought is sometimes given straightforward appellation (for example, "execute judgment"), while at other points there seems to be implicit reference to the judgment formulas of Hebrew prophets. Line 9 is especially relevant in this regard. The first word, יגער, which we translate 'rebuke', implies prophetic judgment (e.g., Zech 3:2). Indeed, as Naveh and Shaked have noted, "Zech 3:2 is the most commonly used verse in magic texts."[16] The term באנין, translated 'murmurer', is the denominative form of אנן that appears in mishnaic and later literature. A prophetic reference is suggested as well with the concluding phrase באנך אנך, which may allude to the text of Amos 7:7–8, where the plumb line is symbolic of irrevocable and sure destruction decreed by God.[17] In sum, by way of a cluster of biblical references (drawn predominantly from the prophetic corpus), the incantation invokes the deity to bring irrevocable judgment on a murmurer who has caused misfortune.

Precisely who the amulet has in mind as the enemy (that is, the murmurer, line 9) is unclear. The text is too vague to allow a specific referent to be identified with any confidence. It seems worthwhile, nonetheless, to offer two of what we take to be the more likely options. The first is that the enemy may be malignant spirits (as is often the case with disease) who have caused the misfortune and need to be flushed out and destroyed. A second, less ethereal, option suggests itself. The late fourth and early fifth centuries were a time of transition in the life of Sepphoris. More aggressive efforts at Christianization, combined with a redefining of the *polis* in the aftermath of the destructive battles and earthquakes of the mid–fourth century, might very well have created an environment in which this forceful language of judgment — indeed apocalyptic imagery — percolated. Perhaps the murmurers were the

---

14. H. S. Versnel, "Beyond Cursing: The Appeal to Justice in Judicial Prayer," in *Magika Hiera: Ancient Greek Magic and Religion* (ed. C. A. Faraone and D. Obbink; New York: Oxford University Press, 1991) 60–106.

15. Ibid., 90.

16. Naveh and Shaked, *Magic Spells*, 22.

17. We are aware of the problematic nature of the concluding phrase of Amos 7:7–8 and thus offer the translation and suggestion of a connection with appropriate reservations.

Christians, or those who had succumbed to Christianization.[18] At the very least, a small clue to tensions building in the city, to a landscape tinged with a certain angst, is given.

Conclusion:
From Artifact to Social World

The corpus of amulets so far recovered from the soil of ancient Galilee is overwhelmingly dated to the period of the late fourth through the sixth centuries C.E.—in archaeological terms, the Early Byzantine Period. This may be an accident of recovery, but we suspect otherwise. It may speak to the social realities of this time and place, and we offer three observations in this regard. The first takes into account the incantations' mix of magical signs and constructs, with language and images drawn from the religious vocabulary of Judaism. This opens the door to the tangled debate over the relationship of religion and magic. This is not the place to enter fully into this question. We simply assert that we have found that a sociological approach makes the most sense of our data. This approach to magic and religion tends to see magical practice as "practice alternate to those normally sanctioned by the dominant religious institution."[19] This is helpful because it avoids discriminating on the basis of content and it also correlates with evidence from rabbinic and patristic texts—that is, the texts of the dominant institutions. Religious authorities, faced with the reality of the burgeoning trade in the magical arts, and of amulets in particular, either condemned the practice outright or, more often, attempted to bring it under their control by designating appropriate symbols or practice.[20] The latter is clearly the dominant tone in the early rabbinic texts, many of which are associated with Judah's residence in Sepphoris. The recovery of these amulets is a reminder that religious practice and the employment of sacred language goes on in a wider circle than is encompassed by sanctioned texts. This means, among other things, that the task of describing the religious life of this city must pay heed to such artifacts as revelatory of a way in which religion was perceived and practiced, if not necessarily sanctioned by authorities.

---

18. The references to the *minim* of Sepphoris may also be indicative of the tensions between Jews and Jewish-Christians, although S. Miller has argued otherwise ("The *Minim* of Sepphoris Reconsidered," *HTR* 86 [1993] 377–402). For a different view on this question, see S. Goranson's response to Miller in this volume (pp. 145–159).

19. D. Aune, "Magic in Early Christianity," *ANRW* II:23.2.1515.

20. For a recent discussion of the response to magic in patristic literature, see M. Dickie, "The Fathers of the Church and the Evil Eye," and H. Maguire, "Magic and the Christian Image," in *Byzantine Magic* (ed. H. Maguire; Washington, D.C.: Dumbarton Oaks, 1995) 9–34, 51–71. The classic and still frequently referenced study of magic and rabbinic literature is L. Blau, *Das altjüdische Zauberwesen* (Strasbourg: Trübner, 1898). More recently, see the helpful discussion in J. Neusner, *A History of the Jews in Babylonia* (5 vols.; Leiden: Brill, 1965–70) especially 2.147–50; 3.110–26; 4.330–62; 5.174–96, 217–43.

Second, we note that the incantations brought to life by the recovery of these amulets witness to the persistence of local languages, cultures, and religions, even in the face of the tremendous transformations wrought by hellenization and massive Roman overlay. Indeed, as the amulets weave together Aramaic and Hebrew expressions of biblical epithets for God with references to biblical passages and phrases and symbols drawn from the wider sphere of Greco-Roman magical practice, we catch a glimpse of the phenomena on which Eric Meyers has commented.[21] Building on the work of G. W. Bowersock, Meyers argued that hellenization should be seen, not as a destructive force, but as a force that loaned local religions (and the Judaism of the Galilee in particular) a framework for creative expression.[22] Ramsey MacMullen made a similar point when he commented on what he characterized as the tenacious staying power of local culture:

> The number and artistry of amulets in the fourth century is testimony to the tenacious conservatism characterizing beliefs in the supernatural. . . . As Celtic, a language living only among the poor and isolated, found its way into books in the form of an incantation, so the last inscriptions in Phyrigian are predominantly curse formulas. . . . Archaeologists working with a totally different kind of evidence report parallel findings. The dominant culture of the empire exerted its strongest influence on the material plane, while nonmaterial aspects such as cults and superstitions remained less affected.[23]

The Greek and Roman cultures had indeed proved potent additions to the cultural mix of Galilean Judaism, and the monumental structures in Greco-Roman style certainly had dominated the architectural horizons of Sepphoris, but the tenacious and creative response of the local to the imposed can be detected in these amulets. This leads to our third and final observation.

The incantation on the silver amulet, appealing directly to God to establish justice, is suggestive of what Peter Brown, among others, has described as a growing sense of alienation from political and legal sources of power and a concomitant erosion of classical institutions. Brown, commenting on the rise of the holy man, remarked that "on every level of life the institutions [of the later Roman Empire] that had seemed capable of receiving the awesome charge of permanence and divinity in classical times either declined or exploded."[24] New sources of power like the holy man or, as Brown himself notes, magical objects such as amulets arose to provide a means to resolve the dilemmas of everyday existence. The magician/amulet-maker, with his tools

21. E. Meyers, "The Challenge of Hellenism for Early Judaism and Christianity," *BA* 55 (1992) 84–91.
22. The work by Bowersock to which Meyers makes reference is, *Hellenism in Late Antiquity* (Ann Arbor: University of Michigan Press, 1990).
23. R. MacMullen, *Enemies of the Roman Order: Treason, Unrest and Alienation in the Empire* (Cambridge: Harvard University Press, 1966) 245–46.
24. P. Brown, "The Rise and Function of the Holy Man in Late Antiquity," in *Society and the Holy in Late Antiquity* (Berkeley: University of California Press, 1982) 149.

and formulas, linked the autonomous client with the power needed to address illness or a grievance. In the late fourth century, the crust of the Roman overlay had cracked in the wake of natural disaster and revolutionary causes. Several of the monumental buildings that had played such a key role in defining the Roman *polis* of Sepphoris were vandalized for stone and reconfigured for other purposes or filled in and then reused (for example, the theater). Significant new buildings were going up on the plain below and to the east of what had been the center of the *polis*. Building patterns suggest that neighborhoods replaced the *polis* as defining realities for the citizen of Sepphoris. So also magical incantations incised on amulets, to be used by individuals to manipulate their physical and social world, are indicators of greater individuation and atomization. As the structures of the *polis* crumbled, the citizens of Sepphoris looked to another set of support structures. From *polis* to neighborhood to autonomous client using an amulet to ensure justice, these small artifacts are critical testimony to changing social realities in late antique Galilee and Sepphoris.

Christian Galilee in the Byzantine Period

MORDECHAI AVIAM

University of Rochester and Israel Antiquities Authority

In 324 C.E., Emperor Constantine declared Christianity to be the official religion of the Roman Empire. This single event led to a monumental change in the status of the land of Israel. The rebellious peripheral province suddenly and forever changed into "the Holy Land" and assumed a central role in the development of Christianity.

Lower Galilee Christian Cult Centers

In Galilee, two main Christian cult centers developed—both in Lower Galilee. The first center was located along the shores of the Sea of Galilee where the earliest churches in the Galilee were identified, such as the *domus ecclesia* at Capernaum and the early chapel at Tabgha. The second center was in Nazareth.

At Capernaum, on the western shore of the Sea of Galilee, on top of the ruins of a late Hellenistic private house, a larger room was built and identified by its excavator as an early "Judeo-Christian" community gathering place. The excavators suggest that some of the graffiti found on the wall's plaster may be identified as ancient Christian prayers and blessings. One graffito carries the Hebrew name Shimeon (Simon), and they suggest that the building should be identified as the traditional location of the house of St. Peter.[1] It appears that this *domus ecclesia*, or 'house-church', at Capernaum was built in the center of a Jewish village, which continued to be Jewish all during the Byzantine Period. In addition, the nearby synagogue continued to exist and to remain in use. Further evidence of the Jewishness of the village is that no Christian remains, other then the church itself and Late Roman Red Ware with Christian crosses, have been found in the large excavated areas—finds

---

1. V. Corbo, "The Church of the House of St. Peter at Capernaum," *Ancient Churches Revealed* (ed. Y. Tsafrir; Jerusalem: Israel Exploration Society, 1993) 71–76.

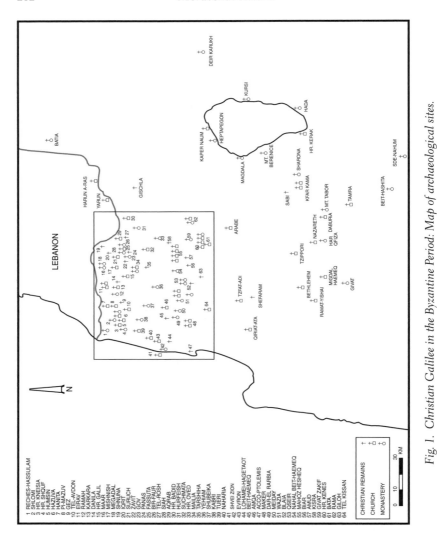

Fig. 1. Christian Galilee in the Byzantine Period: Map of archaeological sites.

such as architectural elements decorated with crosses or Christian inscriptions. This fact can help to explain the unusual phenomenon of this fortified church, or *insula sacra*. The church of the "house of St. Peter" was surrounded by a wall with only two modest entrances, to define and guard it as an island from the buildings around it. The early chapel at Tabgha, which is a small building (9.5 × 12.5 m) with one apse, was dated by the excavators to the end of the fourth or beginning of the fifth century C.E.[2]

2. A. M. Schneider, *The Church of the Multiplying of Loaves and Fishes* (London: Coldwell, 1937).

The second early Christian center was in Nazareth, the hometown of Jesus, and the villages surrounding it, where Jesus performed some of his miracles. Nazareth appears from excavations, however, to have been a small, typical Jewish Galilean village all through the Byzantine Period.[3] Our knowledge about the cult center comes from pilgrims who visited Nazareth in the fourth century C.E.[4] The archaeological finds of early Christianity in Nazareth are probably not earlier than the fifth century. There are a few poor remains of a small church (an apse, parts of walls, and some sections of mosaic floor), probably the one that memorialized the traditional location of the annunciation.[5]

This site, traditionally believed to be part of the rooms of the house of Joseph and Mary, is made of a few rock-cut chambers, typical of sites in the chalky regions of ancient Israel: it had cisterns, storage cavities, and secret underground hideaways.[6] Graffiti were found carved on the walls, a few of which are blessings for Mary. It does appear that worship during the Early Byzantine Period was mainly directed to Jesus' mother. No other Christian remains were found at the site.

There is also no archaeological evidence earlier than the end of the fifth century or beginning of the sixth century C.E. from the other sites that developed in this area during the Byzantine Period, Cana and Mt. Tabor, whereas the historical evidence begins in the fourth century C.E.[7] On the summit of Mt. Tabor are remains of a Byzantine church (a few architectural elements, poor remains of a mosaic floor, and Byzantine potsherds) and a few caves that were probably used by hermits. In the villages around the mountain, a few churches have been surveyed and excavated, including two churches in Kfar Kama,[8] a church in Daburia,[9] a church in Tamra, and the remains of a church mentioned by Guerin in Nin. In February 1998, a stone tomb door decorated with a cross was found in the village in a salvage excavation by the Israel Antiquities Authority.

Thus far there are no archaeological remains in the Galilee of Christianity prior to the fourth century C.E. However, it is very clear that some of the first Judeo-Christian groups were located in Jewish Galilee during the second and third centuries C.E. All of the Galilee finds are from no earlier than the fifth

---

3. V. Corbo, "La chiesa-sinagoga dell'annonziata a Nazaret," *Studium Biblicum Franciscanum Liber Annuus* 37 (1987) 335–48.

4. J. Wilkinson, *Jerusalem Pilgrims before the Crusades* (Warminster: Aris & Phillips, 1977).

5. Ibid., 81, 109.

6. M. Aviam, *Jews, Pagans and Christians in the Galilee* (Atlanta: Scholars Press, forthcoming).

7. Wilkinson, *Jerusalem Pilgrims*, 52, 81.

8. A. Sarissalo and H. Palve, "A Byzantine Church at Kafr Kama," *StudOr* 30 (1966) 3–15.

9. A. Ovadiah, *Corpus of the Byzantine Churches in the Holy Land* (Bonn: Hanstein, 1970) 45, no. 29.

Fig. 2. Cathedral (left) and baptistery church (right) at Hippos.

century C.E., and they represent concrete evidence for the vast development of Christianity in the fifth and especially during the sixth century C.E.

Beginning in the late fifth century C.E., when Christianity was more widely practiced throughout the Holy Land, especially in Galilee, an octagonal church was built at Capernaum over the house of St. Peter. This church is atypical of churches in the country. The only two others that are similar are on Mt. Gerizim[10] and at Mar Elias, north of Jerusalem.[11] The octagonal church of St. Peter was decorated with mosaic floors and a depiction of a peacock, a symbol of immortality, in the center. At a later stage, a baptismal font was built in the center of the apse.[12]

At the same time, a large basilica with beautiful mosaic floors was built at Tabgha.[13] This cross-shaped building, the only one known in the area, was probably part of a monastery, since it had adjacent rooms, one of which contained an oil press. A cathedral and a baptistry church were built at Susita-Hippos,[14] and a large fortified monastery was erected at Kursi beside a small chapel in a cave and a large natural rock that was surrounded by a wall. The cave and the wall probably memorialized the location of the "miracle of the

10. Y. Magen, "The Church of Mary Theotokos on Mount Gerizim," *Christian Archaeology in the Holy Land* (Studium Biblicum Franciscanum Collectio maior 36; ed. G. C. Bottini et al.; Jerusalem: Franciscan Press, 1990) 333–42.

11. R. Avner, "Mar Elias," *Excavations and Surveys in Israel* 13 (1993) 89–92.

12. Corbo, "The Church of the House of St. Peter."

13. Schneider, *The Church of the Multiplying of the Loaves and Fishes.*

14. C. Epstein, "Hippos (Sussita)," *NEAEHL* 2.634–36.

Fig. 3. Aerial photo of Akko.

swine."[15] Special note should be taken of the defense wall of the monastery, which had only one gate and a watchtower. Another monastery was built near Kibbutz Haon. A church with a chapel was also built at Beth Yeraḥ-Philoteria,[16] as was a monastery at Magdala. A large monastery was built on the summit of Mt. Berenice (see below).

Although the area of Beth Sheʿarim is known as a Jewish area because remains of ancient synagogues and burial caves were found in the vicinity, a few Christian remains have also been found. In Ramat Yishai a small section of a mosaic floor with a Christian Greek inscription was excavated, probably the remains of a church or a monastery.[17] And in nearby Beit Leḥem Ha-Glilit (Bethlehem in Galilee), a church with a mosaic floor was excavated and dated to the sixth century C.E.[18]

Western Galilee Christian Settlements

In Western Galilee, Christian public buildings were probably first erected during the fourth century C.E. in Akko-Ptolemais, since it was the metropolis

15. V. Tzaferis, *The Excavations at Kursi-Gergesa* (ʿAtiqot 16; Jerusalem: Department of Antiquities and Museums, 1983).

16. P. Delougaz and R. C. Haines, *A Byzantine Church of Khirbat al-Karak* (OIP 85; Chicago: University of Chicago Press, 1960).

17. Aviram Oshri, personal communication.

18. A. Oshri, "Beit Lehem Haglilit," *Hadashot Arkheologiot* 106 (1996) 42–43 [Hebrew].

Fig. 4. The church in Shavei Tzion: A cross covered with a table.

of the region. However, no remains have been found there so far. Unlike the Lower Galilee, only two sites in Western Galilee were mentioned by pilgrims during the Byzantine Period. These were Akko, since it is a port of entry, and a village named Perisima, mentioned by Johanes Moschus (*Pratum Spirituale* 56, *Patrologia Graeca* 87). The earliest church thus far excavated is in ʿEvron, where a Greek inscription dates the first stage of the church to the beginning of the fifth century C.E.[19] This evidence supports the suggestion that early Christian churches developed around Akko, the metropolis and bishopric town. The excavators of a church in Shavei Tzion dated it to the end of the fourth or beginning of the fifth century C.E., mainly because of the appearance of crosses on the floor, covered later by tables. They suggested this date because they assumed that the covering of the crosses was related to the prohibition of drawing crosses on floors in the beginning of the fifth century C.E.[20] In fact, however, drawing crosses on floors did not disappear in the fifth century, as is evident from excavations of several other churches. Two crosses appear on the mosaic floor of Ḥorvat Shubeika (see below), dated to the sixth and seventh centuries C.E. Consequently, there is no reason to date the church in Shavei Tzion as early as the fourth century C.E.

19. V. Tzaferis, "The Greek Inscriptions from the Early Church at ʿEvron," *ErIsr* 19 (Avi-Yonah Volume; 1987) 36*–53*.

20. M. Prausnitz, *Excavations in Shavei Zion: The Early Christian Church* (Rome: Centro per le antichita e la storia dell'arte del Vicino Oriente, 1967).

Fig. 5 (left). Overall view of Ḥorvat Hesheq.

Fig. 6 (below). The dated inscription at the main door of Ḥorvat Hesheq.

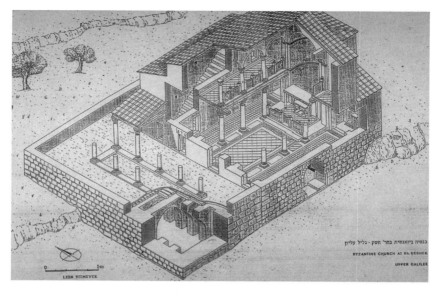

Fig. 7. Reconstruction of Ḥorvat Hesheq.

A large and richly decorated church has been located in Naharia.[21] All of the pillars, capitals, and chancel screens are made of white marble, and the mosaic floor is surrounded with multicolor "peopled scrolls" depicting hunting scenes. Other churches that have been excavated over the years in Western Galilee are: Suhmata, Hanita, Tel Keisan, ʿArabe, Rama, and ʿEirav.[22]

From 1980 to 1990, I conducted a survey in the Western Galilee to identify remains of churches and Christian villages.[23] During this and other surveys, 140 sites from the Byzantine Period were located in Western Galilee. evidence for churches was found at 51 sites: architectural elements, some of which were decorated with crosses, remains of mosaic floors, pillared build-

21. C. Dauphin and G. Edelstine, *L'eglise byzantine de Nahariya (Israel)* (Thessalonike: Kentro Uyzantinon Ereunon, 1984).

22. Shumata: M. Avi-Yonah and N. Makhouly, "The Byzantine Church at Suhmata," *QDAP* 3 (1932) 92–105; Hanita: M. Prausnitz, "The Byzantine Church at Hanita," *Ma'aravo shel Galil* (ed. M. Yedayah; Tel Aviv: n.p., 1961) [Hebrew]; Tel Keisan: J. Briend and J.-B. Humbert, *Tell Keisan (1971–1976): Une cité phenicienne en Galilee* (Fribourg: Éditions universitaires, 1980); ʿArabe: V. Tzaferis, "Byzantine Churches and Inscriptions Found in Eretz-Israel," *ErIsr* 10 (Shazar Volume; 1971) 241–44 [Hebrew]; Rame: V. Tzaferis, "Churches Discovered in Israel," *Qadmoniot* 9/33 (1976) 22–25 [Hebrew]; ʿEirav: Z. Ilan, "The Excavation at the Western Church at Hr. Eirav," *Qadmoniot hagalil hama'aravi* (ed. M. Yedaya; Tel Aviv: Misrad haBitaḥon, 1986) 503–15 [Hebrew].

23. M. Aviam, *The Christian Settlement in the Western Galilee in the Byzantine Period* (M.A. thesis, Hebrew University of Jerusalem, 1994).

Fig. 8. *A scene from the mosaic floor fragment at Ḥorvat Wazia.*

Fig. 9. *Overall view of the excavated church at Ḥorvat Kenes.*

ings with an east–west orientation, tiles, and architectural elements made of marble and clay roof-tiles. This number includes the churches that are mentioned above and the seven that will be discussed below. The survey also provided a large amount of additional information regarding the undecided

Fig. 10. Ḥorvat Shubeika: The bema, inscriptions, and crosses.

issue of monasticism in the Western Galilee, since twelve of the sites were identified as monasteries.

Starting in 1985, remains of seven churches were excavated. (1) Ḥorvat Hesheq is an unusual structure in the Tephen region.[24] It is a small, isolated building (21 × 17 m) 250 m north of the remains of a large Christian village (Ḥorvat Mahoz) dated to the Byzantine Period, where the remains of two other churches are located. A small barrel-roof burial room and a water reservoir formed its lower floor. On the upper floor a small basilica was built, having all of the typical elements of basilicas: atrium, narthex, nave, and two aisles. The site was probably abandoned in the beginning of the seventh century, probably during the Persian conquest, as were most of the other churches in this area. The building subsequently collapsed, but all of the architectural elements were found in situ, including the second-story galleries, an unusual phenomenon in Israeli archaeology. According to four of the inscriptions found on the simple geometric mosaic floors, this was a private family church built by a deacon, Demetrius, and his son Georgius in honor of their family and St. George. The inscription in the main doorway says that all of the work was finished in the month of April, year 582 in the twelfth

24. M. Aviam, "Horvat Hesheq—A Unique Church in Upper Galilee: Preliminary Report," *Christian Archaeology in the Holy Land* (Studium Biblicum Franciscanum Collectio maior 36; Jerusalem: Franciscan Press, 1990) 351–77.

Fig. 11. Horvat 'Ureib: The narthex mosaic.

Fig. 12. Overall view of the monastery chapel of Horvat Meidav.

Fig. 13. Oil press at the
monastery at Ḥorvat
Qseir.

indiction, 527 C.E., according to the Pompeian era. A fifth inscription in the
northern doorway is a verse from Ps 97:2.

(2) Just as Ḥorvat Hesheq is one of the smallest churches in the region, the
church at Ḥorvat Wazia, 5 km east of Akko, between the hills, is the largest
that was excavated, measuring 47 × 42 m. This measurement does not include the atrium and the narthex, since they were not excavated. This church
was once covered with a very large mosaic floor, of which only a small part
has survived. It consisted of a beautiful, multicolored depiction of animals
and hunting scenes on a black background.[25] Remains of ashes and destruction on the floor and in the storage room, and the blocking of the side door
of the storage room provide vivid evidence of the violent end of the church in
the beginning of the seventh century C.E.

25. Aviam, *The Christian Settlement in the Western Galilee in the Byzantine Period*,
53–60.

(3) The church at Ḥorvat Kenes in Karmiel in the Beit Kerem Valley was built on a hill north of a fortified village, Ḥorvat Bata, that is dated to the Byzantine Period. The church was probably part of a monastery. It is a large basilica (25 × 50 m) with an annexed baptistry hall in the south and a large, paved atrium (western side destroyed). In the baptistry, the adjacent rooms in the north and south were paved with geometrically-patterned mosaic floors, as were the two aisles. The central nave was paved with *opus sectile* white and red pavers. Five donation inscriptions were found on the mosaic floors. Three tombs were cut through the floors of the church—an unusual phenomenon in Galilean churches.[26]

(4) The small church at Ḥorvat Shubeika, on the southern margin of the road climbing to Galilee from Naharia eastward, is a monastery church, according to the inscription "Prokopius the abbot" found in the mosaic floor. The floor was decorated with geometric patterns and an amphora and included some crosses. The building is dated to the sixth and seventh centuries C.E. Some of the crosses and one of the inscriptions were later covered by the bema that extended into the main hall.[27] On the other side of the road, remains of other buildings were uncovered and should probably be identified as the monastery itself, on the basis of its plan, the association with the church and its inscription, an oil press, an inscribed oil lamp dedicated to St. Sabas, and a tomb under the buildings in which a heap of skulls was found.[28]

(5) Poor remains of a church were excavated at Ḥorvat ʿUreib at Kibbutz Matzuva, northeast of Naharia. The most interesting element of the building is the narthex, which was covered with a very simple and unusual mosaic floor decorated with floral patterns and a parade of animals around it.

(6) Remains of another chapel were excavated at Ḥorvat Meidav, east of Akko, near Kfar Yasif. The chapel, containing a mosaic floor with a geometric pattern, was badly damaged by agricultural activity and bears no inscription. Three rock-cut sarcophagi were found under the mosaic floor. Since no bases for columns were found, it appears that the chapel was roofed by a vault. Sections of four rooms paved with mosaic floors were excavated along the southern wall of the chapel. The latest dated pottery at the site is from the sixth or seventh century C.E.

(7) And finally, architectural remains of a church were found along with remains of a monastery at Ḥorvat Gov (see below).

The above survey and excavations revealed features in common that characterized the Western Galilean churches: about half of the churches are tri-apsidal; others are mono-apsidal; only two have square pastophoria rooms on

---

26. D. Avshalom-Gorni and M. Aviam, "Ḥorvat Kenes," *Excavations and Surveys in Israel* 15 (1996) 25–26.

27. A. Tatcher and D. Syon, "Khirbet esh-Shubeika—1993," *Excavations and Surveys in Israel* 15 (1996) 21–22.

28. A. Tatcher and D. Avshalom-Gorni, "Khirbet esh-Shubeika," *Excavations and Surveys in Israel* 13 (1993) 15–17.

Fig. 14. *The laura at the Mt. of Precipitation.*

the sides of the apse. There are also characteristics in the mosaic patterns that distinguish them from groups of mosaic floors in other regions. Lack of an ambo and shifting of the chancel screen from the facade of the bema into the main hall created more space in the area of the bema. Some of the characteristics of the churches of Western Galilee are also characteristic of churches in southern Lebanon.

Western Galilee Monasteries

Small structures (up to 2 or 3 dunams) that were square in shape and included a church, oil presses, and a series of rooms I have identified as monasteries. The remains of Ḥorvat Qseir, Ḥorvat Maʾar, and Ḥorvat Gov are the best examples of this type of monastery and are in some ways similar to the small monasteries in the Judean Desert.[29]

Ḥorvat Qseir is located in the Tephen region and includes two different complexes. Each one includes 2 or 3 oil presses, rooms on both sides of a small alley, and decorated Christian elements. A few of the oil presses were excavated, and the complexes were dated to the late Byzantine Period.[30]

29. Y. Hirschfeld, "List of the Byzantine Monasteries in the Judean Desert," *Christian Archaeology in the Holy Land* (Studium Biblicum Franciscanum Collectio maior 36; Jerusalem: Franciscan Press, 1990) 1–90.

30. R. Frankel, "Some Oil-Presses from Western Galilee," *BASOR* 286 (1992) 39–71.

Fig. 15. A hermit cave in the Tephen region.

At Ḥorvat Gov a central courtyard was excavated, on which marble architectural elements were found, together with many pieces of mosaic floor. Half of a eucharistic bread stamp decorated with crosses and a blessing for Jesus was found nearby. In two other areas, dwellings and an oil press were uncovered. All of these elements point to the existence of a monastery.

Ḥorvat Maʾar is a square structure with one or two entrances, five oil presses, a central courtyard and a church. Although it was not excavated, most of the pottery at the site is from the late Byzantine Period.

There are hermits' caves and lauras in various places in the Galilee. A small laura existed in a cave on Har Haqfitza (the Mt. of Precipitation), south of Nazareth. Remains of walls and potsherds from the Byzantine Period were found in a small cave and the building in front of it and in the prehistoric caves on the other side of the wadi. Another hermit cave, 2 × 3 m, with crosses on its walls and a cistern, was found in the cliffs of Nahal Beit Haʿemeq in the Tephen region. A large group of hermit caves was partly surveyed in the cliffs of Nahal Aviv near the Lebanese border.

Jewish and Christian Communities
Juxtaposed in Galilee

I turn now to the very challenging question of what type of Christian presence existed in the two Jewish cities of the Galilee, Sepphoris and Tiberias. In the city of Tiberias itself, no remains of churches have been located, although

Fig. 16. Hermit caves at Naḥal Aviv.

the suggestion has been made to identify the Roman basilica that was excavated in the center of the city as a church from the fourth century C.E.[31] In the
sixth century, the town was surrounded by a wall that also climbed up to the
summit of Mt. Berenice. On top of the mountain, adjacent to the wall, a
church and another building have been found. The excavator suggested that
the building was a monastery and that it was built with the church, high above
the central Jewish city of the Galilee as a result of an ideological and religious
struggle between Jews and Christians. This appears to be the correct interpretation. He also suggested that this church is the "anchor church." This term
alludes to the symbolic basalt anchor that was found under the altar's location
as well as to the Christian tradition that Jesus' activities in the Sea of Galilee
were the core of his work.[32] In my opinion, the symbolic cultic anchor was
there on the highest point, in front of the lake, as the cult focus of the small
Early Bronze village that was found a few meters below the church, to the east.
In the Byzantine Period, the cultic stone was found near the place where the
church was erected, and because it had a large hole in its center, it was reused
in the church as the receptacle for a relic under the altar. I do not think that
there is a connection between the fact that the Early Bronze period cultic
object was designed as an anchor and the fact that it was reused by Christians
as an anchor symbolic of Jesus' activities on the Sea of Galilee.

31. Y. Hirschfeld, "Tiberias," *NEAEHL* 4.1464–70.
32. Idem, "The 'Anchor Church' at the Summit of Mount Berenice near Tiberias,"
Qadmoniot 26 (1993) 120–27 [Hebrew].

Fig. 17. An oil press (front) and the monastery (back) at Mt. Berenice-Tiberias.

At Sepphoris, Christian remains have been evident for a long time, including an inscription of a bishop[33] and a tomb with a cross east of town. New excavations revealed two Christian inscriptions on the mosaic floors of the cardo's sidewalks, which point to very heavy involvement of Christians in the public life of the Jewish town. The remains of two churches in the center of the town also raise the question of how Jewish the town was in the sixth century C.E.; the answer to this question can deeply affect our understanding of Christian and Jewish life in the Galilee.

A map of Christian sites in the Galilee is indicative of the historical situation during the Byzantine Period (fig. 1). In the Upper Galilee there is a sharp borderline between Jewish and Christian communities. East of an imaginary line stretching from Fassuta in the north to Baqa in the center to

---

33. M. Avi-Yonah, "A Sixth-Century Inscription from Sepphoris," *IEJ* 11 (1961) 184–87.

Monasteries were built between and inside the villages, mainly in close proximity to the Jewish area in Eastern Galilee. In the central part of Upper-Western Galilee, a Christian site of the Byzantine Period can be found in every square kilometer. In Lower Galilee, the situation was much different. There were many large Jewish villages and the two Jewish towns, Tiberias and Sepphoris, that prevented Christian expansion. Churches and monasteries were mainly built at Christian holy sites, which were all located in Lower Galilee.

This work is an example of the ability of archaeology to define ethnic identities and borders and their development. A similar survey conducted by Z. Ma⁽oz in the Golan yielded similar conclusions. Another survey of the same type conducted in Samaria (by M. Yitah; not yet published) defined the ethnic borders between Christians and Samaritans. There is still much of this kind of research to do in the Carmel, Judea, and the Negev.

Identifying Jews and Christians in Roman Syria–Palestine

REUVEN KIMELMAN

Brandeis University

The Problem

The subject of Jewish-Christian relations in Late Antiquity in general and in Syria–Palestine in particular could easily fill a book. Recent research has in fact produced a slew of books on this subject. Nonetheless, there is little consensus on the subject. The disagreement extends to almost every aspect of this relationship, including the facts, the interpretation of texts, the explanation of social phenomena, and even the definition of *Jew* and *Christian*.

This study focuses on the last, namely, the difficulty in defining Jews vis-à-vis Christians, specifically Bible-true Christians. It is not concerned with Judaism and Christianity per se. This needs to be underscored, since the relationship between Jews and Christians is not simply a function of the relationship between Judaism and Christianity, however that might be defined. The texts that concern us are the ones that shed light on the problem of definition.

Much of the problem lies in the fact that most of what we know about Judaism and Christianity is circumscribed by the literary remains of their respective authorities, namely rabbis and the Church fathers. Much of this literature is more concerned with advocating normative policies than reflecting social realities. Part of this policy sought to widen the gap between Christians and Jews in order to maintain the boundary between them. The crystallization of Palestinian Judaism, primarily under a rabbinic formulation, and of Gentile Christianity, primarily under a Pauline formulation, succeeded in marginalizing and eventually eliminating the "dangerous ones in between," to use Gager's (1992) formulation: Christianizing Jews and Judaizing Christians.[1] Much of what survived reflects the victory of this policy, not

---

1. As Marcel Simon observed, "At the two ends of the religious spectrum the two orthodoxies, the rabbinic and the catholic, were radically opposed to each other. . . . But the intermediate groups between these two extremes formed a continuous spectrum" (Simon

the actual situation in antiquity. Nonetheless, these groups had staying power
far beyond what could be gathered from only the statements of their detrac-
tors. There is even evidence of their survival into the Islamic Period.

It does not follow from the above that our interest lies with Jewish Christianity or Christian Judaism per se, or any other group that shared characteristics of rabbinic Judaism and Catholic Christianity but, rather, with the
phenomenon of boundary-blurring caused by that which is both similar and
alien. For Catholic Christianity the major problem was with Judaizing Christians; for rabbinic Judaism the major problem was Christianizing Jews. Both
problems persisted into the fourth century.[2]

Despite the apparent symmetry of the problem, there is no equivalency in
the data available. Christian literature is so full of references to Jews and Judaism that the phrase *obsessed with* may be in order. In contrast, the data on
Christianity in rabbinic literature is comparably sparse. In fact, there is not
even an explicit reference to the Christian take-over of the Roman Empire in
pre-fifth-century rabbinic literature. The one possible candidate, *m. Soṭa*
9:15 המלכות תהפך למינות ('the kingdom will turn to heresy'), is in actuality a
reformulation of a statement by the early-fourth-century rabbi, R. Isaac,[3]
cited in *b. Sanh.* 97a.[4] Its presence in the aggadic conclusion is not probative,
since such conclusions to chapters of the Mishnah were appended long after
the legal material was redacted.[5] Thus the rabbinic literature redacted in Roman Palestine by as early as 350, or as late as 400, makes no mention of Christianity as the religion of the Roman Empire. The literature under discussion
includes Mishnah, Tosepta, tannaitic midrashim, *Genesis Rabbah*, *Leviticus
Rabbah*, and *Lamentations Rabbah*, none of which contains citations of fifth-
century rabbis.[6] With the accession of Christianity in the Roman Empire,
this dictum was added to appear as a prophecy, following the widespread
practice of inserting post facto prophetic oracles in order to enhance the authority of religious works.[7] The absence of the impact of Constantinian

---

1996: 95). For the variety of relationships between believers in Jesus and Judaism, at least
for the first century, see the four-part typology of Brown (1983). For the persistence of this
multiform phenomenon, see J. E. Taylor (1990). The use of the term *Jewish Christian* frequently correlates with one's understanding of Christian origins.

2. For the considerable attraction of things Jewish for Christians through the fourth
century, see Feldman 1993: 356–82.

3. The same R. Isaac polemicizes against the Christian claim that Israel is now God's
divorcée, having been replaced by the Church (*Cant. Rab.* 1, 6, 3); see Kimelman 1980: 593.

4. The association of *minut* with the government is made elsewhere in the Babylonian
Talmud (*b. ʿAbod. Zar.* 17a, line 13): הרחק מעליה דרכך' —זו מינות והרשות'. Since the parallel to this exegesis in *ʾAbot R. Nat.* 3, versions A and B, makes no mention of the government, the association of the two is probably a later development of the Babylonian Talmud.

5. See Epstein 1964: 976; and Albeck 1969: 394.

6. Thus nothing can be derived from their silence on the Christianization of the Empire.

7. This is precisely the charge that pagans brought against Christian claims of fulfilling
the prophecies of Isaiah, Daniel, Jeremiah, and other prophets; see Augustine, *Commentary on John* 35.7.

Christianity on Palestinian Judaism confirms evidence from elsewhere that the Christianization of the Empire begins in earnest after 380, with the ascension of Theodosius I, and is not significantly accomplished until the sixth century (see Wilken 1983: 66–73). Thus it is not surprising that the infamous prohibition against Jewish entry into Jerusalem attributed to Constantine cannot be traced to him (so Irshai 1995).

In order to get at the actual situation between Jews and Christians, as opposed to what became the historical reality, the documents of the two great traditions have to be read against their rhetoric. The goal is to hear what they sought to uproot, not what they sought to plant in their stead.

In order to describe the relations between Jews and Christians in the Roman Empire in general and in Roman Palestine in particular, we must be able to distinguish them. Attempts at formulating the dividing line have been plagued by a methodological monothetism that relies on a single indicator or criterion to define them, such as circumcision for a Jew or loyalty to Jesus for a Christian. Neither characteristic is readily visible in regular social discourse, and circumcision is a male-limited criterion.[8] More fundamentally, it assumes a fixity of identity in a world rife with protean identities. If there ever was a world in antiquity in which identity was in formation, it was the Roman world. There is thus a need for a polythetic approach that focuses on a cluster of features and perceptions that in Late Antiquity identified one as Jew or Christian (see Smith 1980: 8–10). One approach could be to ask who was born Jew or Christian, who was called Jew or Christian, and who called himself or herself Jew or Christian. It could then be said that only a person with two of the three criteria would qualify as such. So, for example, only were one born a Jew and called a Jew could one be categorized as one.

The present morass is based on a social reality in which the borders between Christianity and Judaism were far more porous than desired by the authorities of either side. The fact that so much effort was invested in boundary maintenance itself attests to the lack of effective boundaries. Since, as deviance theory argues, a society is significantly formed by what it rejects, establishing criteria for insiders versus outsiders becomes a decisive factor in self-definition and community formation (see J. T. Sanders 1993: 129–49). As Segal writes:

> When the conflict cannot be handled within the society, division of the community into two parts becomes necessary. The positive function of the division is to contain the problem by excluding the opposition and protecting the members remaining inside the group by careful education about the crucial points of difference. (Segal 1992: 161)

In the socially permeable world of the Roman Empire, identities of birth were exchanged for identities of choice. Such a world is indicated by the

---

8. As noted by Justin, *Dial.* 23, indeed most discussions of the subject are limited to males. A female-focused study is a *desideratum*.

comments of Baruch to God, in which he notes persons who abandoned their Judaism, "many of Your people who separated themselves from Your statutes and who have cast away from them the yoke of Your Law" (41.3), as well as persons who abandoned their paganism for Judaism, "others who left behind their vanity and who have fled [i.e., sought refuge] under Your wings" (41.5).

Alternatively, it could be said that, sociologically, a Jew was one whose primary reference group was the Jewish People, and a Christian was one whose primary reference was the Christian community, or a Jew was Torah-centered and a Christian—Jesus-centered. The word *or* needs to be emphasized, for these considerations did not always converge. In other words, membership among the Jewish People and the Christian community were not always mutually exclusive. The same applies to being Torah-centered or Jesus-centered.

The issue gets further complicated by asking whose perspective should be determinative. Should it be the rabbinic, the patristic, or the pagan? For example, from the perspective of other Romans, Jews were often recognized by their exclusive monotheism, circumcision, Sabbath, and diet as well as by their new moon and festival celebrations, purifications after sexual relations, and the wearing of fringes and phylacteries. Considered most admirable was their monotheism, their ethics, and the antiquity of their scriptures. Thus Jews could be distinguished by the distinctiveness of their worship, bodies, work/rest schedules, diet, clothing, and celebrations. This image of Jews is surprisingly consistent through both pagan and Christian literature. Whatever differences may have prevailed among Jews from the inside, they were perceived as similar from the outside.

Significantly, many of these Jewish identifiers were subject to debate among Christians. Circumcision is an issue in Gal 5:2, as apparently were Sabbaths, new moons, and festivals in Gal 4:10 and Col 2:16, which adds food and drink (see 2:20). This debate was to be expected since, as Sanders points out, these were membership issues (E. P. Sanders 1983: 20).

The more the boundaries became blurred, the more Rabbinic Judaism and Catholic Christianity focused on boundary maintenance. In this regard both were exceptional. In an Empire where the adding of cults and loyalties was the norm, Jews and Christians were noted for their exclusive loyalty. This needs to be emphasized, since the maintaining of boundaries was not just a problem of Jewish-Christian relations but a problem of the relationship of the two with everything else. In a world of multiple loyalties, the acquisition of new loyalties outdistanced the surrendering of old ones (see Garnsey 1984; 1992). Typical of this phenomenon is the observation of Tertullian in 197 C.E. that some Gentiles kept a type of Sabbath and Passover while presumably continuing to worship at pagan altars (*To the Nations* 1), whereas *The Apostolic Canons*, cited below, prohibited Christians from frequenting both heathen and Jewish places of worship.

As we shall see, there are parallels in the way Jewish and Christian authorities maintained the boundaries between them and in the way they sought to ostracize the ones blurring the boundaries. It is commonly thought that a low Christology, focusing on Jesus as messiah, as opposed to a high Christology, focusing on Jesus as divine-like, ultimately caused the separation of the two communities. It follows, it is similarly thought, that intermediate groups such as Jewish Christians who held to a low Christology would less likely be excluded by the rabbis, since only a high Christology would be subject to the charge of the heresy of ditheism or "two Authorities," as the rabbis called it.

While distinctions between low and high Christology may be of utmost consequence to contemporary theologians and to their ancient, especially post-Nicean, counterparts, they are unlikely to have been decisive for the lay Christian or Jew who defined others more by life-style and reference groups than by theological conviction. Thus Trypho tells Justin that were he to be circumcised, observe the Sabbath, feasts, and new moons, "in brief, fulfill the whole written law," he would "then probably . . . experience the mercy of God" (*Dial.* 8). No statement is made about his Christology. Similarly, a medieval Jewish writer, Jacob ben Ephraim, when asked about a Christian sect that followed Jesus yet kept the Jewish calendar, replied: "We do not repel those who ascribe prophetical power to those who were not prophets, Jesus, Muhammed, and Abu Isa — because they agree with us about the festival calendar" (cited in Wilken 1983: 92). Since a religious community is a community of common celebration, people who celebrate together will perceive each other as part of the same community. One who celebrates as a Jew functions as a Jew. Because the blurring of boundaries is more dependent upon ritual than belief, it is unlikely that the boundary itself was predicated on a high or low Christology. This does not negate the assumption that change in belief can generate change in ritual — only that it is the change of ritual itself that brings about a shift in the boundary markers of religious community. This phenomenon is superbly illustrated by the conflicts over changes in the calendar.

Moreover, it is not even clear that low Christology characterized Jewish Christianity (see Saldarini 1992: 78). If anything did characterize Jewish Christianity as a whole, it was the privileging of Matthew's Jesus over Paul's (see Luedemann 1989) and the concomitant proposition that loyalty to the God of the Bible entails loyalty to the Law of the Bible, as is made clear in Matt 5:17–19:

> Do not think that I have come to abolish the Law or the Prophets. I have come not to abolish, but to fulfill them. I tell you solemnly, till heaven and earth depart, not one iota, not one stroke of letter, shall disappear from the Law until all is accomplished.

For Matthew, Jesus is primarily the messiah of Israel, the son of David, the exemplary Jew who has come to "save his people" (1:21) by bearing away the diseases of Israel (8:17, citing Isa 53:4). For one branch of Jewish Christianity, Jesus was also the true prophet who determined the validity and meaning of scripture. Even the eternity of scripture, they contended, is by virtue of Jesus' teaching in Matt 24:35.[9] For Jewish Christianity, Sabbath or dietary compliance in daily social intercourse may have been at least as self-defining as theological affirmation.

Moreover, as long as Christianity was an illicit religion, Christians would tend to be restrained about publicly proclaiming their theology except under secure conditions. This would explain the sparse evidence of an active missionary campaign in the second and early third century. The assumption of such a campaign is the result of generating a trajectory from Paul, who it turns out was more the exception than the rule.[10]

Since the patristic evidence for Jewish-Christian interaction is so much more ample than the rabbinic evidence, let us begin with it. But let us again emphasize that what authorities define as Jewish or Christian may not be identical with self-definition. After all, how is a Sabbath-observing circumcised believer in Jesus to be defined and by whom? The problem of definition is not limited to Jewish Christians or, better, Christianizing Jews, but also to Judaizing Christians. For example, to rephrase the previous question, were a Gentile to accept Jesus as savior and then go on to emulate the life of Jesus or the primitive church as portrayed in Matthew and become a Torah-citing Sabbath observer,[11] what would he be and according to whom? If many Church leaders could not always distinguish between Judaizing Christians and Jewish Christians, it is no wonder that we have such difficulty (see Wilken 1983: 69–72).

The practice by converts to Christianity of adopting Jewish ways was not rare; neither should it be expected. Converts are not known for their restraint. With a motivation as powerful as the expiation of sin (see 2 Tim 3:6), why limit the purging process and not go the whole way, especially when the scriptural warrant was so compelling. From a Gentile's perspective the process of Judaizing was already set in motion when Christianity accepted Judaism's Bible, God, and cosmology, as pointed out by both Marcion and Celsus.

Justin is a good witness to how porous the situation was in the first half of the second century. In chap. 47 of the *Dialogue*, he speaks of Gentile Christians who have become Law-abiding as well as those who have gone over to Judaism totally. The first he attributes to Jewish persuasion when he says: "Some of your race, who say they believe in this Christ, compel those Gen-

---

9. *Pseudo-Clementine Recognitions* 36.2; *Epistula Petrii* ("The Kerygmata Petrou") 2.4–5.

10. See Goodman 1994: 94. MacMullen states, "After New Testament times and before Constantine, very little open advertising of Christianity is attested. . . . Missionaries are just not mentioned"(1984: 111). This helps explain the widespread ignorance of Christianity and its scriptures (1984: 131–32 nn. 13–14).

11. See Saldarini 1991. In another book, *Matthew's Christian-Jewish Community* (1994), Saldarini argues that "Matthew is a Jew who believes in Jesus" and thus to be understood as "a Christian-Jew" (1994: 203). Note that it is precisely Matt 5:17–18 that is cited in the Talmud (*b. Šabb.* 116b).

tiles who believe in this Christ to live in all respects according to the Law given by Moses." With regard to the second, he says: "Such as have confessed and known this man to be Christ, yet who have gone back for some reason or another to the legal dispensation and have denied that this man is Christ" (*Dial.* 47). In sum, Justin's awareness extends to onetime pagans who are now Christians, to non-Law-abiding Christians who became Law-abiding ones, and to onetime Christians who are now Jews.

Justin does not proffer an explanation for those who left Christianity for the "legal dispensation." One explanation may be that they despaired of making sense of the Christian rhetoric vis-à-vis Judaism. Irenaeus describes Jews as "imagining that they could know the Father (apart) by Himself, without the Word, that is without the Son" (*Against Heresies* 4.6.1, 4.7.4). Cyprian says: "We Christians, when we pray, say our Father; because He has begun to be ours, and has ceased to be the Father of the Jews who have forsaken Him" (*On the Lord's Prayer* [*De oratione Dominica*] 10). Crossovers to Judaism must have rejected both contentions, believing that they could know the Father by Himself and that He had not forsaken the Jews.

It is also possible that those pagans initially interested in Judaism converted to Christianity upon encountering a form of Judaism, as it were, more acceptable to their Roman sensibilities. What could be better than getting written scriptures, antiquity, morality,[12] and monotheism,[13] along with the salvific power of a divine man (*theios aner*),[14] without having to adopt an alien nation, land, and temple, all of which had recently undergone upheaval?

In any event, there were Gentile Christians who argued that as members of *verus* Israel they were obliged to observe God's commandments such as circumcision, Sabbath, and dietary laws. For them such practices were not only not incompatible with allegiance to Jesus but are required by his precedent. Judaizers saw themselves as "imitators of Christ" (Origen *Commentary on Matthew*, sermon 79). As they said: "It suffices for the disciple to be like his teacher. . . . Since Christ lived according to the law; therefore you do the same" (Epiphanius *Panarion* 28.5.1–2). Even Emperor Julian cited Matt 5:10 and 17 to prove that Jesus taught men to observe Jewish Law (see Wilken 1984: 193). These grounds were used to justify aspects of Sabbath and Passover observance from early-third-century Caesarea (Origen *Homily on Jeremiah* 12.13; *Commentary on Matthew*, sermon 79) to late-fourth-century Antioch (Chrysostom *Homilies against the Jews* 3.4).

This thesis gains support from the abundant evidence in patristic sources that Christians were frequenting the synagogues annoyingly often.[15] Such

---

12. On the attractiveness of Jewish antiquity and virtue in the Roman world, see Feldman 1993: 177–232.

13. Even in the Golan Heights, converts from pagan polytheism are identified by their "One God" inscriptions; see Gregg and Urman 1996: 318, 321.

14. On the significance of this image in the spread of Christianity, see Tiede 1984.

15. On the general Gentile interest in the synagogue, see Overman 1988.

evidence indicates a Christian problem, not a Jewish one. That Church leadership was striving to keep Christians away from the synagogue points to the lack of exclusion on the parts of the host. Such receptivity on the part of the synagogue makes it highly unlikely that the synagogue liturgy contained a curse against Christians.[16] The issue of the synagogue, however, looms far larger than just attendance. Christians were attracted to synagogues for a variety of reasons, including its awesomeness (Chrysostom *Homilies against the Jews* 1.3), holiness as a place of "the Law and the books of the prophets" (1.5), by virtue of the prestige of its leaders and the "superhuman purity" of their judges (Origen *Contra Celsum* 4.31), or by their capacity to heal, do wonders, or exorcise demons (8.5–7). Whatever the motivation, they would be subject to the biblical lectionary and exposition that characterized synagogue services. This exposition would surely focus on the significance of observance of the Law for the life of the spirit and the salvation of the soul.[17] It is thus unlikely that a synagogue-attending Christian would adhere to an understanding of Jesus as the sole means of salvation. Moreover, the exorcism of demons was in the popular mind bound up with salvation, and if rabbis could exorcise, could they not save? Indeed, as Wilken has argued, the conflict between Chrysostom and the Judaizers was precisely about whose religion was more powerful and whose rites were more effective (Wilken 1983: 83–88).

The issue of exorcism is a classical case of Wilken's observation that competition among religions was often over the power of their rites. Exorcism is of special import in the light of the aforementioned attractiveness of the rabbis as exorcisers.[18] In his *Commentary* on Cant 1:5, "I am black and/but beautiful," Origen states: "Black refers to the ignoble birth of the Gentile, while beautiful refers to the Gentiles coming to Christ" (2.1), whereas his contemporary and Palestinian compatriot, R. Yoḥanan, glosses "I am black" "with

---

16. See Kimelman 1982. Despite all of the subsequent literature on the subject (see, e.g., Horbury 1998: 67–110), I have not seen any evidence that would undermine my thesis that *birkat ha-minim* was directed only against Christianizing Jews. I hope to take up the issue anew and focus on how and why the need for an anti-Christian Jewish prayer serves more the needs of Christian historiography than the needs of historical accuracy. As Setzer has noted, "The Blessing against the Heretics (Birkat ha-Minim) has loomed large as an issue in the Jewish context of early Christianity, partly because it seems to represent a certain specific measure taken by Jews" (1994: 2). Since there are so many anti-Jewish measures on the part of Christianity, Christian scholars pounce on anything that can somehow right the balance; see the conclusion of M. S. Taylor (1995: 189–96).

17. Philo describes the activities of the synagogue as follows: "The Jews every seventh day occupy themselves with their ancestral philosophy. . . . For what are our prayer places throughout the cities but schools . . . of piety and holiness and virtue as a whole, by which one comes to recognize and perform what is due to men and God" (Philo *The Life of Moses* 2.216). The rabbis claimed "that anyone who enters synagogues . . . in this world deserves to enter them in the world to come" (*Deut. Rab.* 3:1).

18. On Jewish magic and its impact on Christians, see Wilken 1983: 83–88.

the act of the (golden) calf; but beautiful with the act of (constructing) the Sanctuary" (*Agadat Shir Ha-Shirim*, ed. Schechter, p. 5, line 371).[19]

By applying the word "beautiful" to Christ and to the sanctuary, respectively, Christianity and Judaism are not only promoting their respective means of atonement but, in line with third-century religiosity, also the means of exorcism or casting out of demons. What for first-century Christianity was the expiation of sin became in the third century the expulsion of demons. As Nock notes, "for the Apologists as a group . . . the redemptive operation of Christ lay in deliverance from demons rather than in deliverance from sin" (Nock 1933: 222). Indeed, "For the mind of Post-Apostolic Christianity, the core of the problem lay in the traditional idea that the overthrow of the daimonic-powers must have been caused by the death of Jesus."[20] The seed of such an understanding of Jesus is already noted in Matt 7:22, where the name of Jesus is used in the casting out of demons. By the third century, Origen boasts that "Christians make no use of spells, but only of the name of Jesus" (*Contra Celsum* 1.6). Thus, he argues, "demons . . . are able to do nothing to us who are devoted to the person that is alone able to help all those who deserve it" (7.36). For Origen, as for so many others, the reward of devotion to Jesus is salvation from demons. Exorcists were thus in great need by Christians. This function discharged by the *prophetai* survived in the Order of Exorcists, who are listed among the clergy of the Roman Church about the middle of the third century (Eusebius *Ecclesiastical History* 6.43.11).

Such concern with exorcism was not limited to Christianity. Religion of Late Antiquity was touted for its apotropaic capacity, of which exorcism was a major expression. On this, Christianity and paganism concurred. The question was only whose medicine was stronger. As Dodds says, "The main formal difference between Christian and pagan magic was one of nomenclature" (Dodds 1965: 125 n. 2).

The rabbis were not unaffected by the obsession with demons in Late Antiquity. The same development from Christ as a means of atonement to Christ as a means of exorcism can be discerned in their understanding of the Sanctuary. Thus the third-century R. Yoḥanan is cited as saying: "with the construction of the Sanctuary the demons vanished from the world" (*Pesiq. R.* 5, 21b; see Friedmann 1880: 21b, n. 105). All one has to do now is make the classical rabbinic shift, in which the synagogue serves as the Sanctuary's surrogate and the synagogue becomes a place of deliverance from demons (see Fine 1996: 30–32). What was perceived by Christianity and Judaism in the first century as a means of deliverance from sin became by the third century the means also for the deliverance from demons.

---

19. On the dispute between the two on the meaning of Canticles, see Kimelman 1980.
20. Werner 1957: 97; see Harnack's chapter "The Conflict with Demons" (1908: 1.95–106).

Since Church fathers who condemned compliance with biblical injunctions frequently took note of church-goers who were also synagogue-goers, it
is unclear whether complying with the Bible generated synagogue attendance or vice versa. In other words, was Judaization the catalyst or the result?
In any case, they were mutually reinforcing. In view of Chrysostom's com-
plaint that there were days when the churches were empty because Christians
were filling the synagogue and were keeping the Sabbath with the Jews (Chrysostom *Homilies against the Jews* 1.5, 8.8; see Wilken 1983: 178), we have to
ask who these people were and how they would define themselves. Surely,
one's place of worship has to be factored into one's religious membership.

The Church Fathers

With regard to the Christian evidence, we shall focus on the extra-NT evidence. The NT is only cited[21] when it sheds light on a problem outside of it.
An example of this is the book of Revelation, whose problem with Judaizers
overlaps with the same problem in the writings of Ignatius of Antioch. The
book of Revelation, likely addressed to the churches in Smyrna and Philadelphia, was composed during Domitian's reign in the nineties of the first century, apparently by a Jewish apostate to Christianity. He writes:

> I know the slander (or blasphemy) on the part of those who say that they are
> Jews and are not, but are a synagogue of Satan. (Rev 2:9)

> I will make those of the synagogue of Satan who say that they are Jews and are
> not, but are lying—I will make them come and bow down (*proskyne*) before
> your feet. (Rev 3:9)

The identity of the subject of this text has generated much speculation.[22]
Whatever the correct identification, it should account for the term "synagogue
of Satan," the nature of the blasphemy, and the nature of the punishment.

An identification that meets all three tests is Christian Gentiles who
claimed the designation *Ioudaioi*, a claim that the book of Revelation denies
them.[23] The claim was not unique. Gentiles who followed Jewish practice
were dubbed *Ioudaioi* elsewhere, as noted by the contemporaneous Epictetus:

> Why, then, do you call yourself a Stoic, why do you deceive the multitude, why
> do you act the part of a Jew, when you are a Greek? Do you not see in what
> sense men are severally called Jew, Syrian, or Egyptian. For example, whenever
> we see a man hesitating between two faiths, we are in the habit of saying, "He
> is not a Jew, he is only acting the part." But when he adopts the attitude of mind

---

21. For evidence of Gentile Christians' Judaizing in the NT, see Galatians, the pastoral
letters (1 Tim 1:6, 2 Tim 3:6 with Titus 1:10, 14), Colossians (2:16–22), and Ephesians.

22. For three recent treatments, see Collins 1985: 204–10; Setzer 1994: 99–104; and
Wilson 1995: 162–65.

23. For those scholars who are in general agreement that the exponents of Judaizing
were Gentile rather than Jewish Christians, see M. S. Taylor 1995: 29.

of the man who has been baptized and has made his choice, then he both is a *Ioudaioi* and is also called one. (*Discourses* 2.9.19–20)

Despite Epictetus's disapproval, those acting like Jews were called Jews. Even Epictetus concedes that one who underwent baptism became a Jew.[24] "Jew" here served as an identity of choice as well as one of birth. Similarly, Suetonius writes of "people who followed the Jewish way of life without formally professing Judaism, and people who concealed their Jewish nationality and thereby avoided paying the taxes levied on their race" (*Domitian* 12.2).[25] Around the same time, Josephus noted that Samaritans described themselves as kinsmen of the Jews when it suited them and as Gentile when it did not (*Ant.* 9.291). A century later Dio Cassius notes that those who complied with biblical law were called Jews: "This title *Ioudaioi* is also borne by other persons who, although they are of other ethnicity, live by their laws" (*Dio* 66.1.4; and see 37.17.1). Finally, in a study of the inscriptional evidence, Kraemer suggests that *Ioudaios* was applied especially to Gentiles who adopted Jewish ways. Thus "Jew" could have an ethnic ("Jew"), geographic ("Judean"), or an affiliate ("Jew sympathizer") sense—the latter as a self-designation (Kraemer 1989: 51).

The book of Revelation calls their place of gathering a "synagogue of Satan," an expression redolent of "the synagogue of heretics" in the *Apostolic Constitutions* cited below.[26] If a synagogue of Satan was tantamount to a synagogue of heretics, then its frequenters were, from the author's view, Christian heretics, namely, defectors from his type of Christianity. Jews who were never Christians can no more qualify as Christian heretics than Christians who were never Jews can qualify as Jewish heretics (*minim*).[27] Only those *in* can be read *out*. Only onetime members of a group who have "chosen" an undesirable path are deemed heretics, as Jerome notes:

> Until now a heresy is to be found in all parts of the East where Jews have their synagogues. They believe in Christ . . . but since they want to be both Jews and Christians, they are neither Jews nor Christians. (*Epistle to Augustine* 112.13)[28]

24. Since the subject is the perception of the Jew, it is irrelevant whether or not baptism sufficed for conversion. Incidentally, with regard to Epictetus's knowledge of things Jewish, note that he hails from Phrygia and was a slave of Epaphroditus, who was probably Josephus's patron, as noted in *Against Apion* and *Jewish Antiquities*. On the Jewish community of Phrygia, see Trebilco 1991.

25. See Smallwood (1981: 376–85) for this citation and a discussion of the issues involved in the Roman identification of Jews.

26. That is, the reference to Satan is a term of negation, not a technical term; cf. Collins 1985: 209–10. Ephrem also takes note of the impious men who urged his flock to desert the Church of Christ and cross over to the synagogues of Satan (*Opera Syriaca*, ed. Mobarek 1.558; cited in Goodman 1994: 144).

27. On terms for heretics in Judaism, see Sussman 1989: 53–55 n. 176.

28. This text is apparently directed against Christian Jews rather than Judaizing Christians and thus to be classed with the people mentioned by Justin (*Dial.* 47). Similarly, Justin's somewhat contemporary, Celsus, noted those who "accept Jesus although they still

According to him, Jews who believed in Christ qualified as Christians; wanting to remain Jews qualified them as heretics.

Let us return to the text of Revelation and ask which Christian heretics would claim to be Jews if not converts to Christianity who subsequently became Law-abiding Jews? And of which synagogue-attending Jews would Christian leaders deny their Jewishness if not previous converts to Christianity who went on to accept the whole Torah? For Revelation, once a Christian, always a Christian. One cannot go on and become Jewish and remain Christian. It remans unclear whether this group saw themselves as remaining Christian though practicing Judaism or whether they left Christianity totally for Judaism.

What about the charge of slander or, better, blasphemy? What would non-Law-abiding Christians consider slanderous or, better, blasphemous from the mouths of Law-abiding Christians/Jews? Surely it is the claim that loyalty to the God of the Bible entails compliance with His Law, thereby negating the Pauline-based understanding of Christology as the sole salvific path. As the contemporaneous Ignatius says: "If we continue to live until now according to Judaism, we confess that we have not received grace" (Ign. *Magn.* 8.1). Apparently his opponents affirmed precisely the opposite, namely, that by living according to Judaism one does receive grace. Indeed, Trypho's advice to Justin is that he should be circumcised, observe the Sabbath, feasts, and new moons, "in brief, fulfill the whole written law, and then probably, you will experience the mercy of God" (*Dial.* 8). Similarly, rabbinic literature is replete with passages that consider circumcision and Sabbath observance to be qualifiers for the world to come. Indeed teachers were expected to instruct their disciples on how to achieve the world to come. It is told of a late-first-century rabbi, R. Eliezer, that his students pleaded, "Our Master, teach us the ways of life that we may merit the life of the world to come" (*b. Ber.* 28b; see *'Abot R. Nat.* A, 19, ed. Schechter, p. 70), and his own teacher, R. Yohanan b. Zakkai, is reported as telling his disciples, "Go out and see what is a good way for a man to cleave to so that through it he will enter the world to come" (*'Abot R. Nat.* A, 14, ed. Schechter, p. 58). Also his teacher, Hillel, said: "Whoever has acquired words of Torah has acquired life in the world to come" (*m. 'Abot* 2:4). They would all concur with Trypho that scripture "compels us to wait for him who, as son of man [i.e., as a human being] receives from the Ancient of days the everlasting kingdom" (*Dial.* 32, see 89). Both religions were focused on the quest for salvation and everlasting life.

From a Johannine perspective and what became the Pauline perspective, nothing could be more blasphemous than the denial of the exclusive salvific power of Christ, especially by former adherents. Even though the doctrine of the exclusive salvation by Christ may not have been made explicit until

---

want to live according to the Law of the Jews like the multitude of the Jews" (Origen *Contra Celsum* 5.61).

Cyprian in 256 C.E. (*Epistle* 73.21), Mark 16:16 already correlates belief and baptism with salvation, and nonbelief with damnation.

For Ignatius, "it is monstrous to talk of Jesus Christ and to practice Judaism. For Christianity did not base its faith on Judaism, but Judaism on Christianity" (Ign. *Magn.* 10.3). Clearly his opponents believed that professing Jesus as the Christ and practicing Judaism was a wining combination to achieve salvation.[29] Unlike him, they held that if Christianity is the fulfillment of Judaism then Christians should fulfill Judaism.[30] After all, who would ever consider a law to be fulfilled by its abandonment or transgression? As always, it is only the position of a former adherent that can become blasphemous. And nothing is more irking than the traitorous blasphemy of insiders who should know better.

This interpretation also explains the punishment. According to Revelation, the condemned apparently exalted themselves over their Gentile Christian brethren by virtue of their compliance with biblical injunctions. Accordingly, their punishment is to prostrate themselves before those they sought to be lord over, following standard measure-for-measure schemes of retribution that characterize so much of the Bible. Such quid pro quo ideas are theological commonplaces. Although many understand this politically, it is better understood eschatologically. At the time of judgment, claims Revelation, those who relied exclusively on the grace of Christ will lord it over those who did not.

It is possible that the harshness against Law-abiding Christians was due to the fact that the author of Revelation was an apostate Jew to Christianity. In the same vein, Justin notes (*Dial.* 122.2) that the Jews who were harshest on Christians were Jewish proselytes. Justin also makes note of Gentiles who abandoned Christianity for Judaism. If these are the same, then there were cases where the hostility between Christianity and Judaism was fanned by crossovers.

Ignatius ostensibly addressed a similar problem in Asia Minor and/or his own locale of Antioch.[31] In the *Epistle to the Magnesians*, he warns his readers against living in accordance with Judaism (*kata Ioudaismon;* 8.1) and against Judaizing (*ioudaizein;* see Barrett 1982) whereas, in the *Epistle to the Philadelphians*, he states:

> If anyone interprets Judaism to you do not listen to him, for it is better to hear Christianity from the circumcised than Judaism from the uncircumcised. (Ign. *Phld.* 6.1)

29. So Acts 15:1: "Unless you have yourselves circumcised in the tradition of Moses you cannot be saved."

30. According to Jerome, Judaizers believe the time is coming when all the precepts of the Law will be observed and "Jews will no longer become Christians but Christians will become Jews" (*Commentary to Zechariah* 14:10–11).

31. For the various issues and resolutions, see J. T. Sanders 1993: 159–60, 315 n. 39; and Wilson 1995: 361 nn. 92–96.

Again we have a case of Gentiles advocating compliance with biblical Law. Ignatius of course would prefer to hear born Jews advocate the salvific power of Christ than Gentiles advocating the advantages of complying with biblical Law. "Judaism" here means simply biblical Law, for Ignatius reports in 8.2:

> For I have heard some say: "If I do not find it in the archives [*archeioi* — apparently the OT] I do not believe it in the Gospel."[32] And when I said to them, "it is written," they replied, "That is just the issue." But for me "the archives" are Jesus Christ.

Ignatius seeks to persuade these people that whatever is written in the Gospels is written in the archives, holding as he does that the archives are Jesus Christ. They, however, limit the archives to the Bible.

Barnabas (4.6) also makes it clear that it was sinful to claim that 'the covenant is both theirs and ours' (*he diatheken ekeinon kai hemon*). For him, the covenant is 'ours or theirs' (*eis hemas e eis ekeinous*, 13.1). And since Christ appeared to perfect the sins of the Jews so that through him Christians might receive the covenant (14.5), the covenant belongs exclusively to Christians. Since the author and readers of *Barnabas* were apparently Gentile Christians (see *Barn.* 3.6, 16.7; and Alon 1957: 1.310), the work confirms the existence of a Gentile Christian position known from the *Pseudo-Clementine Homilies* (8.6–7) and *Pseudo-Clementine Recognitions* (4.5) as well as from the final rescension of the *Testaments of the Twelve Patriarchs* of a two-covenant notion. This notion claimed that 'the covenant is both theirs and ours' (*he diatheken ekeinon kai hemon*); 'theirs' through Moses and 'ours' through Jesus.[33] Of special note is the fact that the aforementioned Clementine literature is by all accounts of Syro-Palestinian provenance and that its begrudging positive attitude to Jewish leadership parallels that of Matthew (see Baumgarten 1992: 47–50).

In any event, for Ignatius a Christianizing Jew is better than a Judaizing Christian Gentile. The social reality is that Gentile Judaizers were promoting Judaism to Christians (see Wilson 1995: 164). These Gentiles had not yet taken the step of no return, namely, circumcision.[34] That Judaizing Gentile Christians should be promoting Judaism among Christians follows the logic noted by Eusebius, in *Praeparatio Evangelica* 15, that the Greeks cannot

---

32. For this reading, see J. T. Sanders 1993: 325 n. 172. Note that, according to Chrysostom, his Judaizing parishioners frequent synagogues because "the Law and the books of the prophets can be found there" (*Homilies against the Jews* 1.5).

33. So *Pseudo-Clementine Homilies* 8.5–7. For the way that this literature relates to rabbinic Judaism and patristic Christianity, see Wilson 1995: 127–42.

34. As Metilius, the Roman garrison commander in Jerusalem in 66 C.E., said he was prepared to behave as a Jew (*ioudaisein*) even as far as undergoing circumcision (Josephus J.W. 2.454). Even Juvenal describes a man who, fearing the Jewish god, kept the Sabbath and some dietary laws, had a son who went as far as denying pagan cults and undergoing circumcision (*Satires* 14.96–106). While admitting to a wide range of Jewish practices adopted by Judaizing Christians (see Wilken 1983: 75), Chrysostom concedes that those who underwent circumcision are "not present" (*Homilies against the Jews* 2.2).

understand why Christians claim to be faithful to the Jewish heritage without adhering to Jewish rites. According to him, the straightforward Greek mind assumes that claiming the Bible entails complying with it. Similarly Celsus has his Jewish interlocutor say: "Why do you [Christians] take your origin from our religion [Judaism], and then, as if you are progressing in knowledge, despise these things, although you cannot name any other origin for your doctrine than our Law" (*Contra Celsum* 2.4). Such mind-sets were not easily given to explaining away the need of complying with biblical Law. After all, the Church itself preserved the fourth book of Maccabees with its celebration of the martyrdom of the seven sons for their refusal to transgress the Law of Moses.

There is thus a sense in which such Law-abiding Christians are better dubbed "biblicizers" than "Judaizers." Having been won over to Christianity by its claim to have fulfilled the Bible, it occurred to them to do so. For them, it would appear strange to claim a book as one's own and empty it of so much of its content. Such biblicizing phenomena can exist without proximity to a Jewish community, as they have throughout the history of Christianity up to the Seventh Day Adventists of modern times. It is not necessary to postulate the presence of a Jewish community that was attracting them to Judaism.

There is also a sense in which people may have been called Judaizers because they took Matt 5:17–19 seriously, as noted above. In any event, the position opposed by Ignatius may simply have been that God's covenant is open to all who comply with its stipulations, such as the Sabbath (*Magn.* 8.1) and circumcision, since these are both considered the biblical signs of the covenant. Since Ignatius is promoting the thesis that "Christianity did not believe in Judaism, but Judaism in Christianity" (*Magn.* 10.3), it follows that his opponents believed that Christianity did indeed believe in Judaism. For them, Christianity was Judaism-plus, not Judaism-minus.

Ignatius's concerns are echoed in the Gospel of John, whose final redaction took place in his lifetime. John lambasts those who practiced Judaism but believed in Jesus (3:1–2, 7:50, 9:22, 12:42–43, 19:38, 20:19). Since he was seeking to persuade them to leave the synagogue, they must have held that belief in Jesus entails following, not abandoning, his way of life, a way of life that includes the practice of Judaism and synagogue attendance. Indeed, the intensity of John's opposition may have been in proportion to his failure. Apparently his either/or ultimatum was only heeded by a minority. Jews, despite John's harangues to the contrary, were not excluding Jews for believing in Jesus, as long as such a belief did not preclude loyalty to the People Israel and their mode of living. John seeks to "out" them in both senses of the word. Either they refused to come out of the closet or remained unconvinced that their world was the world that John presents.

The social reality in the Gospel of John is that Jewish leadership could no more prevent Jews from being devoted to Jesus than Christian leadership could prevent such Jews from being devoted to Jewish life. When push came to shove, many preferred linkage with their fellow Jews over linkage with Johannine Christians. They apparently saw their primary loyalty to the People Israel rather than to those followers of Jesus who were not part of Israel.

Since, according to Ignatius, Christianity has to define itself in contrast to Judaism, he rejects any attempt at blurring the boundaries between them. He may have promoted Sunday as the Christian Sabbath precisely for this reason (see *Magn.* 8.1),[35] just as later authorities fixed the days of Christian fasts and feasts in contrast to the Jewish days of fasting and feasting.[36] His opponents, however, held that Christianity was inclusive, not exclusive, of Judaism.

Around the same time Barnabas also expressed his apprehension of the attractiveness of the Law. He warns Christians away, saying, "lest we be shipwrecked as proselytes (Sinaitic text: *epelutoi* ['imitator']) to their law" (*Barn.* 3.6). Like Ignatius, Barnabas wants a clear division. He lambasts those who continued to pile up sins by claiming that the 'covenant is both theirs and ours' (*he diatheken ekeinon kai hemon*) [*Barn.* 4.6, 13.1]. Their blasphemy consisted in denying that belief in Jesus precluded sharing in the Jewish covenant or at least precluded complying with biblical Law. If the two groups overlap, then there were Christian Gentiles who by virtue of their belief in a double covenant adopted Jewish ways. Barnabas responds by going on the offensive and denying that the Jews were ever meant to have a share in the covenant (4.7–8). This seems to confirm the theory that the anti-Jewish animus of the leader correlates well with the pro-Jewishness of his constituents.

Similarly, Justin, in the middle of the second century, was aware of Christians who had gone over to the polity of the Law (*metabantas a ennomospoliteia; Dial.* 47.4), that is, a Jewish way of life. These were Christian Gentiles as opposed to Christian Jews, such as the Ebionites, who were described a generation later by Irenaeus as ones who "practice circumcision, persevere in the customs which are according to the Law and practice a Jewish way of life" (*Against Heresies* 1.26.2). Irenaeus also knows of the Christian convert Cerinthus, who in the time of Ignatius insisted that Christians comply with biblical Law, including circumcision.[37]

The *Martyrdom of Pionius*, which has been dated from the end of the third to the middle of the fourth century, also records Pionius (d. 250, Smyrna) as saying: "I hear that the Jews call some of you to the synagogues" (13.1; see Gero 1978: 164). Apparently some acceded to their invitation (see *The Acts of the Christian Martyrs* 13.1, 14.1).

---

35. Unless of course this is the insertion of a later editor; see Kraft 1965: 24.

36. *Didascalia* 21 urges that the Christian Pasch be distinct from the Jewish Passover, for as Rouwhorst argues, "there are strong indications that the Syriac churches till the Council of Nicea were Quartodecimans and that they celebrated Easter on the Jewish date, in the night from the fourteenth to the fifteenth Nisan, just as the Christians of Asia did in the second century"(Rouwhorst 1997: 82). The problem of Judaizing Christians peaked with the outbursts of Chrysostom, as discussed below.

37. See discussion in Unger 1992: 243–44.

The Syrian author of the early-third-century *Didascalia* (26) also deemed heretical the practice of the dietary laws, circumcision, the Sabbath, and ritual bathing after menstruation. Note that most of these are precisely the practices that are prerequisites for salvation according to Trypho (*Dial.* 46).

Origen, a mid-third-century resident of Caesarea, formerly of Egypt, knows of Egyptians who frequented both synagogue and church (*Homilies on Lev.* 5.8). Origen also alludes to Jewish missionaries who induced Christians to practice Jewish rites (see *Contra Celsum* 5.61, 2.1; and Krauss 1893–94: 147 n. 2). Indeed, he complains of pagans who went over to Judaism without considering Christianity (*Contra Celsum* 1.55; *Sermons on Matthew* 16).

In the late fourth century, Jerome stressed that Christians imitated the rites of the synagogue, probably as a result of familiarity with synagogue practice (see Krauss 1894–95: 238 nn. 2 and 9). In his recent study on "Jewish Liturgical Traditions in Early Syriac Christianity," Rouwhorst attributes the adoption of Jewish liturgical practice to local Jewish Christians. Murray also contends that Syrian Christianity contains "some features which can only be accounted for by an origin in a thoroughly Jewish form of Christianity" (1975: 7; see pp. 7–24). In light of the amount of Judaizing Christian material, however, I find that it may well have been due to the Judaizers' influence or the influence of Christian clergy who, seeking to wean Jewish Christians away from synagogue attendance, attracted them by offering fare similar to the synagogue's (see Kimelman 1982: 240 n. 83; Murray 1975: 140–41). This may also constitute a contributing factor to the commonality of biblical motifs in synagogue and church. The frequency of contact between the two groups can also be gauged from Jerome's chagrin at the number of Christian recipients of Jewish charity. He even urged their refusal lest it attract them to Judaism (*Epistle to Nepotion* 52).

Christian observance of the Law was so widespread that councils had to prohibit it. Christians were resting on the Sabbath and reading scripture, but not the Gospels, as well as participating in the feasts and ceremonies of the Jews. The Council of Laodecia in Asia Minor held in the mid–fourth century thus forbade resting on the Sabbath (Canon 29); required those worshiping on the Sabbath to read the Gospel along with scripture (Canon 16); and prohibited participation in Jewish feasts and ceremonies (Canons 27 and 28).[38] Even more startling are the prohibitions against clergy partaking of Jewish rites, such as celebrating Easter with the Jews (Council of Antioch in 341) or using phylacteries (Council of Laodicea, Canon 36) or entering a synagogue to pray or to fast or to feast or to receive unleavened bread (*Apostolic Constitutions* 8.47, 62, 65, 70, 71; *Apostolic Canons*, Canon 69). Even Apollinaris, the bishop of Laodicea, was attacked by Basil for advocating "the observance of worship according to the Law" (*Epistle* 265.2, 263.4; for these rulings, see Wilken 1983: 72).

---

38. Compare the *Apostolic Constitutions*, where Christians are called upon to observe Saturday as the day on which creation is commemorated (7.23.2; 7.36.15; and 8.33.2).

The fourth-century Syrian Father, Ephrem of Nisbis, is another good example of the theory that, the more attractive Judaism[39] is to Christians, the greater the animus of Christian leaders. In his *Hymns on the Unleavened Bread* number 19, he states:

· Do not take, my brethren that unleavened bread
  From a People which defile its hand with blood.
  . . .
  How unclean, therefore is the unleavened bread
  Which was kneaded by the hands which killed the Son (16–17)
  For the blood of Christ is mixed and dwells
  In the unleavened bread of the People and in our Eucharist.
  He who takes it in through our Eucharist, takes the medicine of life;
  He who eats it with the People, takes the medicine of death. (23–24)
  And he who takes part in their festivals
  The sprinkling of the blood come to him as well. (26)

                                    (cited in Hayman 1985: 432)

This is a clear example of Christians eating unleavened bread and taking part in the Jewish festivals. Indeed, some apparently went all the way and converted, because Ephrem is aware of Christians who underwent circumcision and prayed in synagogues.

Finally, the evidence from Ephrem's younger compatriot, John Chrysostom of Antioch, is overwhelming. In the *Homilies against the Jews*, he harangues against the Judaizing activities of Christians in general and their frequenting of synagogues in particular. The latter was so serious that he felt impelled to denounce it more than 15 times (*Homilies* 1.3.3–4; 1.4.6; 1.5.2; 1.5.7; 1.6.2; 1.8.1; 2.3.5; 4.7.3–4; 4.7.7; 5.12.12; 6.6.6; 6.7.3–4; 6.7.7; 7.6.10; 8.8.7–9). His vituperative attacks indicate that the aforementioned Christian legislation against Judaizing was ineffective. Chrysostom himself notes that Christians who frequented synagogues urged their household, friends, and neighbors not to report them to the priests (*Homilies* 8.8.8; see also 3.6.11). Even fear of the priests, however, did not deter synagogue attendance.

Significantly, in an effort to dissuade Christians from rushing off to the synagogue to beg the Jews to help them, Chrysostom asserts that the Jews laugh and scoff at them. Then, most revealingly, he concedes: "Even if they do not do it openly . . . they are doing this deep down in their hearts" (*Homilies* 8.8.9). Apparently, Chrysostom could not point to any evidence of Jews scoffing, and clearly not cursing, at Christians. Add this to the previously cited evidence from Jerome, and the result is a situation wherein the Jews must have been quite receptive to Christians' seeking their assistance and the succor of the synagogue.

39. On Nisibus as a Jewish center throughout Late Antiquity, see Gafni 1990: 67 n. 53, and p. 77.

Like Ephrem, Chrysostom is also aware of those who underwent circumcision, for he notes that they chose to absent themselves from church during the Lenten fast *(Homilies against the Jews* 2.2.4, see 2.3.5). Such a phenomenon may explain his countenancing of violence to recover a fellow Christian from the fellowship of "the Christ-killers" (1.4.5). According to Chrysostom, "there is so much harm in circumcision because it makes Christ's whole plan of redemption useless" (2.1.6), for circumcision is not just a single command; rather, as he emphasizes, "it is that very command which imposes on you the entire yoke of the Law" *(Homilies* 2.2.4, see 2.3.5; for these sources, see Kinzig 1991: 37).

How then shall we define a synagogue-going, church-going, circumcised Antiochean: as Christian or Jew? An either/or mentality just will not do here. Too many scholars follow Chrysostom in adopting the Pauline distinction between Law and Grace in defining such people. Whether or not this makes for good theology, it hardly makes for good sociology. The social reality contains significant numbers (see *Homilies* 8.4.5–10) of Gentile Antiocheans who simply rejected the dichotomy between Christ and Torah. Dubbing them syncretists does little to enhance our understanding of the phenomena. After all, what in Christianity is not syncretistic from some perspective? From Marcion's perspective, even the acceptance of the Hebrew Bible was.

This both/and perspective is not unique to Jewish Christianity or, if you prefer, Christian Judaism. Rather, from the time of Ignatius, if not as far back as Galatians (2:4, 5:1), through Chrysostom, there were Christian Gentiles who felt that the completion of their salvation required abiding by the Bible. Such a feeling could be buttressed by a belief that they were imitating their savior, as Justin notes: "those Gentiles who have been circumcised from error by Christ to observe the same things as himself, telling them that they will not be saved unless they do so" *(Dial.* 47.2). This sentiment may be reflected in the Sinaitic text of Barnabas, which lambastes those who are *"epelutoi* ['imitators'] to their law" (3.6). It is clearly reflected in Origen ("imitators of Christ"—*Commentary on Matthew,* sermon 79) in the third century, and in Epiphanius ("Since Christ lived according to the law; therefore you do the same," *Panarion* 28.5.1–2) in the fourth, as well as in Chrysostom, who reports the claim that if Christ celebrated the Jewish Pasch, his followers should do likewise *(Homilies against the Jews* 3.4).

The claims that Jesus is the fulfillment of the Law or that the Law was never meant to be observed or that the Law was only given because of Jewish sinfulness just did not ring true. Law-abiding Christians likely concurred with the sentiment, cited by Eusebius, that Christians were misappropriating scripture and dispossessing Jews from their inheritance:

> The sons of the Hebrews also would find fault with us, that being strangers and aliens we misuse their books, which do not belong to us at all, and because in an impudent and shameless way, as they would say, we thrust ourselves in, and

try violently to thrust out the true family and kindred from their own ancestral rights. (*Praep.* 1.2)

Law-abiding Christians simply found it implausible that the reward of those who break the Law should exceed those who keep it. Even Eusebius conceded the unreasonability of such a claim. He says:

> The most unreasonable thing of all is, that though we do not observe the customs of their Law as they do, but openly break the Law, we assume to ourselves the better rewards which have been promised to those who keep the Law. (*Praep.* 1.2)

Such Christians assumed that God's bounty corresponds with human compliance to his Law. This is precisely Trypho's astonishment at non–law-abiding Christians:

> You yet expect to obtain some good things from God, while you do not obey His commandments [*entolas*]. (*Dial.* 10.3)

For them, there is no Christian dispensation for the abrogation of the Law. The Law stands for all time. When told the contrary, they probably retorted as did Julian. Writing in Antioch in the 360s, Julian stated:

> That they say this falsely I will clearly show by quoting from the books of Moses not merely ten but ten thousand passages where he says that the Law is for all time. (*Against the Galileans* 319d–320a)

So much of Christian argumentation about and interpretation of the Bible, starting with Paul, goes against its grain that one wonders whether its persuasiveness was due to the fact that the Bible was only heard and not read. The inability to retrieve a text to confirm an interpretation can enhance the receptivity of such claims. The spread of claims about the nonoperative nature of biblical law may also attest to the fact that the community lacks members who comply with or have access to the Bible, who could have served to restrain such claims.

On the Jewish side, Origen noted Jews who "want to accept Jesus as the one prophesied and to observe the law of Moses just as much as before" (*Contra Celsum* 2.3). Faced with the choice of scripture as the source of eternal life (see *b. Ber.* 28a, above) or only a witness to Christ (Matt 1:45, 5:39), they opted for both.

Apparently the protestations of Ephrem and Chrysostom were ineffective, since the situation perdured for another four centuries. In his *Disputation against a Jew* (22.1), Sergius the Stylite reports that his Jewish disputant retorted:

> But now I am amazed how, after knowing [all] this, there are among you some Christians who associate with us in the synagogue, and who bring offerings and alms and oil, and at the time of the Passover send unleavened bread [and], doubtless, other things also. They are not entirely Christians, and some of our

men have said that, if they were truly Christians, they would not associate with us in our synagogue and law.

In the eighth century(!), Christians were still frequenting synagogues and concerned with unleavened bread on the Passover, except that it was understood that "true Christians" did not express their religiosity this way. Despite the fact that the Catholic understanding of Christianity had become normative, some still refused to forgo their link with Judaism, as noted in Sergius's response:

> So also you, wicked sons of impious fathers, have failed to wonder and be amazed at the signs of Jesus, and have seized on a pretext in weak Christians who, doubtless, are the children of heathen and their mind has not yet been cleansed from the fear of their father's idols. Or they are the children of Hebrews, and the former custom still prevails over them. (22.5; cited by Hayman 1985: 435)

Sergius is frustrated that the wonders of Jesus lacked impact on the Jews (from which I infer that Jesus was still being marketed as a miracle-maker)[40] and that Christians were still attracted to Judaism.

Noteworthy is the type of Christian attracted: "the children of Hebrews" and "the children of heathens." The children of heathens indicates second-generation Christian Gentiles. Extending their parent's path from heathendom into Christianity, they took the next step into Jewish practice. The children of Hebrews indicates the children of Jews who adopted Christianity without abandoning Jewish practice. Not feeling that apostasy in belief demands apostasy in action, they maintained Jewish practice.

The logic behind this lay attitude that Judaism and Christianity were not mutually exclusive is also cited by Sergius.

> If Christianity is good, behold, I am baptised as a Christian. But if Judaism is also useful, behold I will associate with Judaism that I might hold on to the Sabbath. (22.15)

Thus as late as the eighth century in Syria there is evidence

> that ordinary Syrian Christians . . . could still not distinguish clearly between Judaism and Christianity. We can trace this uncertainty about the exact boundary between the two religions virtually from the emergence of the Syriac-speaking Church right down to its effective demise as a major cultural force in the Middle East. The intellectual elite, the theologians, clergy, and the shock troops of the Syriac Church, the monks, knew where the boundaries lay. But the ordinary lay people did not. They appear to have taken a more tolerant attitude to the differences between the two religions despite all the attempts of the Christian elite to create an image of the Jews which would frighten lay people from having any contact with them. (Hayman [1985: 440], who also cited the previous source)

40. On the role of miracles and exorcism in making the Christian case, see MacMullen 1985: 25–30.

As already noted, the Canons of Laodicea, a fourth-century collection of ecclesiastical regulations, was considerably agitated by the problem of Judaizing. Canon 29 prohibits Judaizing and being idle on the Sabbath; indeed, "if they are found Judaizing, they shall be shut out from Christ." In fact the *Apostolic Constitutions* (cited above), which emanated from the Syrian Church probably around the turn of the fourth century, deemed synagogue attendance to be forsaking God.

> See that you never leave the Church of God; if one overlooks this, and goes either into a polluted temple of the heathens, or a synagogue of the Jews or heretics, what apology will such a one make to God in the day of judgment, one who has forsaken the living God?

Clearly, Christians were both resting on the Sabbath and attending synagogues of both Jews and Christian heretics(!), which must mean Judaizing Gentile Christians or Jewish Christians; otherwise, they would not be designated heretics and clearly would not have synagogues. Recall the expression in Revelation above with regard to the synagogue of Satan.

Even more important from the point of view of the fluidity of identity is the fact that some Christians are frequenting pagan temples. Clearly, allegiance to Christianity was not perceived to be exclusionary. The situation is comparable to people whose primary allegiance is to modern medicine but will try out alternative medicine when needed. These people frequently decline to inform their physician, just as Christians kept their synagogue attendance from their priests. In both cases, there is the apprehension that the normative authority figure will cast aspersions on or mock their belief in the alternative — or even worse, cut them off. Salvific establishments, be they religious or medicinal, are exclusivists about cure/salvation. Outside of them there is no salvation. In any event, protestations of allegiance to the one does not preclude for many the seeking out of relief from the other.

The attitude of the Church to Judaizing Christians was matched by a hardening of attitude toward Christian Jews. As the legal power of the Church grew, so grew the capacity to expel boundary-confusing groups — as did Church Councils to other dissenting Christian groups. Justin was willing to tolerate them as long as they did not seek to foist their ways on Gentile Christians. Cyril of Jerusalem, in 348, wondered why Jews who worshiped Jesus Christ stuck to the old name, *ioudaioi*, rather than adopting the new name of *christianoi* (*Cat.* 10.16, cited from Stroumsa 1996: 28). But a generation later, Epiphanius says of the Nazarenes: "They are Jews and nothing else" (*Panarion* 29.9.1). And in the next generation, Jerome says that the Nazarenes who "believe in Christ . . . want to be both Jews and Christians, but are neither Jews nor Christians" (*Epistle to Augustine* 112.13).

The last three sources all point to a fourth-century Palestinian group whose belief in Jesus did not preclude them from considering themselves Jewish. It is generally thought that, since they did not require Christian Gentiles to follow their example of compliance with the Law, they did not regard the Law as necessary for salvation and only observed it out of tradition.[41] Only one who has no experience with complying with the demands of the Law could entertain the possibility that such compliance could be thought bereft of salvific qualities. It is more plausible to assume that their position paralleled that of the rabbis, namely, that compliance was necessary for Jewish salvation, but not for Gentile salvation. In that sense, they viewed Gentile acceptance of Jesus as the rabbis viewed the Gentile acceptance of the Noachide laws.[42]

In sum, for at least four centuries, and up to eight in Syria, many Christians adhered to things Jewish. Rather than heed the warnings of Church authorities about forsaking the living God, they deemed compliance with scripture and other Jewish practices as attaching themselves further to the living God. For Chrysostom the stakes were ultimate: "If the Jewish rites are holy and venerable, our way life must be false" (*Homilies against the Jews* 1.6). For many Christian Antiocheans, however, observing the Jewish rites of Saturday and the Christian rites of Sunday enhanced one's religiosity. This latitude so infuriated the great boundary marker, Chrysostom, however, that he demanded their exclusion from the church/Church: "If one who has this sickness [Judaizing] is a catechumen, let him be barred from entering the church doors; if he is one of the faithful and baptized, let him be barred from the Eucharist" (*Homilies against the Jews* 2.3). And so it was.

Rabbis and Church Fathers

Let us now turn to the Jewish side of the equation. We shall start with that sometime Galilean, Josephus. In the *Antiquities* (18.63–64) the following appears:

> At this time there appeared Jesus, a wise man (sophos aner). . . . For he was a performer of startling deeds [paradoxon ergon poietes], a teacher of people who receive the truth with pleasure. And he gained a following both among many Jews and among many of Greek origin.

Whether or not this is authentic Josephan material, its position is confirmed by the *Talmud*:

> On the eve of Passover they hung Jeshu. And the crier went forth before him forty days, saying, "He goes forth to be stoned because he practices magic and deceived and led Israel astray." (*b. Sanh.* 43a)

Similarly, *b. Sanh.* 107b says: "Jesus the Nazarene practiced magic and led astray and deceived Israel." Common to both sources is the image of Jesus as

---

41. See Kinzig (1991: 33), who also offers a scholarly survey of the Nazarenes (1991: 30–35).

42. Unless they in fact did impose the Law on Gentiles (see Kinzig 1991: 49 n. 56).

a wonder-worker, either as a performer of startling deeds or as a practitioner of magic. Both are two sides of the same coin and would be perceived this way by an outsider. Both sources also agree that Jesus induced Jews to follow him, whether they termed it "gained a following" or "led Israel astray." Justin also reports that Jews deemed Jesus a "Galilean deceiver [*planos*]" (*Dial.* 108.2) and "a magician and deceiver of the people" [*magos kai laoplanos*] (*Dial.* 69.7), charges found already in Matthew (Stanton 1992: 101–8). The Christian claim of Jesus as miracle-worker and the Jewish claim of Jesus as magician or demon-possessed both point to the perception of Jesus as a doer of unusual deeds.

Note that Josephus casts no aspersions on the Jewishness of the followers of Jesus. The gaining of a following among both Jews and Greeks elicits no editorial comment. It could be that the messiahship of Jesus was initially no more exclusionary than that of Bar Kokhba. That at least seems to have been the attitude of R. Gamaliel as recorded in Acts.

Let us now turn to rabbinic literature. There we shall also find evidence of the porous nature of Jewish–Jewish Christian relations. The rabbis sought to plug up this situation in a manner resembling that of the Church fathers. We shall focus on incidents that purportedly occurred in Galilee. The first goes as follows:

> The case of R. Eliezer who was arrested for *minut*. And they brought him to the tribunal for judgment. When he had been released from the tribunal he was troubled that he had been arrested for *minut*. His disciples came in to console him, but he would not accept (it). R. Akiba entered and said to him, "Rabbi, shall I tell you something that might relieve your distress?" He said to him, "Speak." He said to him," Perhaps one of the *minim* told you a word of *minut* and it pleased you." He replied, "By Heaven, you have reminded me! Once I was walking along a street of Sepphoris, and chanced upon [the Munich MS of *b. ʿAbod. Zar.* 17a adds: "one of the disciples of Jesus the Nazarene"] Jacob of Kfar Sichnin, and he spoke to me a word of *minut* in the name of Jesus ben Pantiri, and it pleased me." (*t. Ḥul.* 2.24)[43]

What is remarkable from the perspective of the boundary between rabbinic Jewish and Christian Jewish identity is that it was credible for a rabbi to be accused of *minut*, here Jewish Christianity,[44] and for a Roman tribunal (*hegemon*) to mistake a rabbi for a Christian Jew. Even a rabbi could not easily dispute the claim, especially were he spotted conversing with one. Moreover, a Christian Jew could teach a rabbi a thing or two about the Bible. Finally, there was nothing exceptional about chancing upon a *min*, especially one from a nearby village.[45]

---

43. For the text, parallels, and comments, see Neusner 1973: 1.400–403, 2.366–67; and Miller 1993: 380 nn. 13–15.

44. On *min* in Palestinian rabbinic sources as Jewish Christian, see Kimelman 1982: 228–32.

45. See Kimelman 1982: 232 and 241. For the most recent evidence of Jews, Christians, and pagans mixing in northern Israel, see Gregg 1996: 318. The evidence also points

While Rabbi Eliezer could derive pleasure from this kind of exegetical illumination without compunction, as Trypho did from Justin's words (*Dial.*
118.5), for R. Akiba these kinds of exchanges were portentous for the partici-
pant. The redactor has adopted R. Akiba's perspective and uses the story to
stifle intercourse with *minim*. Indeed, in the later talmudic version of the
story, R. Eliezer is cited as conceding that he was arrested for transgressing
the scriptural words "remove your way far from her—which refers to *minut*,
and do not approach the door of her house (Prov 5:8)—which refers to the
ruling power" (*b. ʿAbod. Zar.* 17a). This part is clearly added, because only it
is paralleled by *ʾAbot R. Nat.* 3, versions A and B (see Finkelstein 1950: 128–
29). R. Akiba's attitude is comparable to the attitude of his colleague, R. Tar-
fon, who proclaimed that he would prefer refuge in a house of idolators over
that of *minim*, since the former "do not know Him and deny Him whereas
the latter know Him and [still] deny Him" (*t. Šabb.* 13.5). This idea, that
Christian Jews who should know better are most condemned, is also the position of the *Didascalia*: "The heathen are judged because they have not
known (Him) but the heretics [namely, Christian Jews] are condemned because they withstand God" (23). The same logic stands behind Chrysostom's
hatred of the Jews: "They have the prophets but do not believe in them, and
they read these book but do not accept their testimonies [namely, about
Christ]" (*Homilies against the Jews* 3.4).

R. Akiba's colleague R. Ishmael also adopted a strict position on relationships with *minim* as reflected in the above Tosepta and in the following incident with regard to R. Eliezer ben Dama:

> A case (in point was that) of R. Eliezer ben Dama. A snake bit him and one Ja-
> cob of the village of Sama (in Galilee) came to cure him in the name of Jesus
> ben Pantera, but R. Ishmael would not allow it. He said: "You are not permit-
> ted, ben Dama." He said, "I will bring you a proof that he may heal me." But
> before he could finish his proof he died. R. Ishmael said, "Happy are you, ben
> Dama, for you have departed in peace, and have not broken the ordinances of
> the wise." (*t. Ḥul.* 2.22)

When read against its rhetoric, this story provides a wealth of information
about relations with *minim* (pace Maier 1978: 130–82). Of course, when read
with its rhetoric, it seeks to prevent healing at the hands of a *min*. Against its
rhetoric, it tells us that Jews sought out healing even from *minim* using the
name of Jesus.[46] In contrast, R. Ishmael condemned healing through Jesus, as
Chrysostom condemned healing through rabbis. Authorities in both systems
preferred death over a cure by the other. On the Christian side, Chrysostom
said: "If they truly heal, it is better to die than to run to the enemies of God

---

to mixed burial among the groups, as pointed out to me by Byron R. McCane of Converse
College, who is writing on the subject.

46. The different cognomens probably reflect various oral variants; see Bauckham
1990: 114–19.

and be healed in this way" (*Homilies against the Jews* 8). On the Jewish side, R. Joshua ben Levi, upon finding out that his grandson had been helped by a man who whispered the name of Yeshu ben Pandira to him, said: "It would have been better had he died than need your whisper [of spells]" (*y. Šabb.* 14, 3, 14d and parallels).

The whispering of spells with the name of Jesus and the uttering of incantations in order to cure characterized the image of Jesus and Christianity. Appeals to the effectiveness of exorcisms made in the name of Jesus was a common motif (see, e.g., Justin *Apol.* 2.6; *Dial.* 76, 85; Origen *Contra Celsum* 1.6, 2.49, 6.40, 7.4, 7.67, 8.39, 8.58).

For most, the issue was cure, not theology. Holy men and healers are always attracting the persons seeking healing regardless of religious convictions. Healers transcend religious identities especially when they are effective. Magic, incantations, and exorcisms, like belief in angels and demons, are ecumenical. They constitute the "religious *koine*" of Late Antiquity (Stroumsa 1989: 21). Most of antiquity would agree with R. Yohanan that "whatever works as a remedy is not [considered] 'the way of the Amorite'" (*y. Šabb.* 6.9, 8c; see *b. Šabb.* 67a). This must have been R. Eliezer's position. Nonetheless, Eliezer was prepared to justify his practice by citing (biblical?) proof. R. Ishmael does not counter with a verse but a rabbinic ruling ("ordinances of the wise"), thereby conceding the lack of biblical support. In the absence of a biblical prohibition, many Jews had no compunctions against such healing.

The problem of the Gentile observance of the Sabbath was serious enough to spark the ire of both Church fathers and rabbis. The patristic material is cited above. With regard to the rabbis, a third-century rabbi, Resh Laqish, states: "A Gentile that 'Sabbatizes' deserves death" (*b. Sanh.* 58b), which is probably an elliptical version of the statement cited in the name of his older contemporary R. Yose b. Hanina, "A Gentile that 'Sabbatizes' before undergoing circumcision deserves death" (*Deut. Rab.* 1:21). The word שבת is deliberately translated here as 'Sabbatizes' to correspond to its use in patristic literature (namely, *sabbatizein*; *Dial.* 46.2, 47.4).

Both Justin and the rabbis tried to exclude others by virtue of their beliefs about redemption. Justin (*Dial.* 80) deems Christians who do not subscribe to his belief in the millennium heretical, just as rabbis (*m. Sanh.* 10:1; *t. Sanh.* 13.5) deny the world to come to those who do not subscribe to their beliefs about revelation and resurrection. Both Jerome (*Epistle to Nepotion* 52) and *'Abot de Rabbi Nathan* (A, 2, ed. Schechter, p. 14 with n. 76) sought to keep their constituency from benefiting from the generosity or hospitality of the other, lest they be taken in religiously. A manuscript of *'Abot de Rabbi Nathan* is explicit about this point:

> When people come and enter their (sc. Minim) houses, they feed him, give him to drink, dress, cover, and give him food. Once satiated, he agrees with them, heeds their counsel, denies the Root, and transgresses many sins. (cited in Kister 1998: 256; see Lieberman 1973: 756)

A general interdiction against social intercourse is also mentioned:

> The sacrifice of a *min* is idolatry. Their bread is the bread of a Samaritan, and their wine is deemed the wine of idolatry, and their produce is deemed wholly untithed, and their books are deemed magical books, and their children are *mamzerim*. People should not sell or buy anything from them. Neither should they take wives from them or give them children in marriage. And they should not teach their sons a craft nor seek assistance from them, either financial or medical. (*t. Ḥul.* 2.20–21)

This statement is as interesting for what is not stated as for what is. Despite its effort to prevent all social intercourse between rabbinic Jews and *minim*, it makes no disparaging remark about belief or character. Its sole concern is with excluding the *min* from intra-Jewish exchanges, much as a Gentile would be. In other words, Christian Judaism or Jewish Christianity came to be seen as a branch of Gentile Christianity and no longer a branch of Judaism.

According to Justin (*Dial.* 38.1), Jewish teachers sought to ban associating with Christians or conversing with them about scripture. The Talmud, however, reports that Palestinian rabbis, at least in the fourth century, were more proficient in biblical studies than their Babylonian counterparts, because "we who are always found in your midst have taken it upon ourselves to study [Bible]" (*b. 'Abod. Zar.* 4a). Eusebius also credits Jews with superior knowledge of scripture (*Praep.* 11.5, 12.1.4)—indeed he claims to have learned biblical interpretations from a rabbi (*Commentary on Isaiah* 23:15, 39:3). Similar claims are made by Jerome, who notes that Clement, Origen, and Eusebius were all students of Jewish interpreters (Jerome *Against Rufinus* 1.13).

Conclusion

Whereas many rabbis and Church fathers promoted a policy of either/or, many Jews and Christians acted as if it was both/and. As the rabbis and Church fathers gained control over their constituencies, their policy of either/or prevailed. Simon sums up the situation, saying, "The rabbinic authorities were just as hostile to Christianizing tendencies as the Church was to its Judaizers" (Simon 1996: 401).

It is easy to see such people as crossovers from Judaism to Christianity or from Christianity to Judaism, but this would be adopting the perspective of the victors in this issue, who of course opposed the blurring of boundaries. From the perspective of the participants, it was clear that the alternative to either/or was both/and, especially if the best of both worlds was attainable. There were many in Syria, and probably in Asia Minor and Caesarea and thus, likely, also in between them, in Galilee, who did not see allegiance to Jesus and the Law as mutually exclusive but as mutually reinforcing. They were not so much crossovers as combiners. If their opponents dub their synthesis syncretism, so be it.

Church fathers affected by this phenomena were more likely to activate the traditional Christian anti-Judaism material and apply it with vitriol to put an end to it. It was of little avail until Catholic Christianity achieved sufficient political power to impose its view during the fifth and sixth centuries. On the rabbinic side, in contrast to the extensive *Adversus Iudaeos* literature, there is no Jewish anti-Christian tract extant, nor is one mentioned in patristic literature. Nonetheless, there is considerable evidence of rabbinic retorts to the claims of Christianity (see Hirshman 1996).

There is no single theory that covers all Christian anti-Judaism (see Stroumsa 1996). There are cases of ideologies intensifying social conflict as there are cases of proximity intensifying conflict—all the more so when competing groups lay claim to the same geography or overlapping salvific schemes. The theory that most of Christian anti-Judaism can be attributed to competition over converts explains some but not much. This "conflict theory" cannot explain Christian anti-Judaism in places bereft of major contact between the Jewish and Christian community, such as North Africa. The excoriation of Judaism by Church fathers from North Africa, such as Tertullian, Cyprian, and Augustine, is not explicable on this basis. Nor can conflict theory explain why Church fathers rarely refer to actual Jews or Judaism instead of to OT and NT realities when inveighing against Jews or Judaism. Even the infamous antisemitic venom of Melito of Sardis precedes by generations the evidence for the presence of an imposing Jewish community in Sardis. Finally, the absence of significant mention of conflict over converts between Judaism and Christianity in pagan literature militates against it being the decisive issue. Moreover, the theory fails to explain the surface irenic spirit of a document like Justin's *Dialogue*, which is so aware of Christians crossing over into Judaism. It is just not true that Christian anti-Judaism is generally accentuated by proximity and attenuated by distance.

The discourse theory of anti-Judaism Christian rhetoric holds that this rhetoric had little to do with any actual Jewish Christian reality. Rather, it served internal Christian needs. These needs were based on the Christian confiscation of the Jewish heritage and the constant struggle of Christian authorities to dissuade Christians from reappropiating aspects of Jewish heritage by becoming Law-abiding or crossing over. Albeit not explaining the whole phenomenon, this theory has more explanatory power than any alternative (as Taylor [1995] has shown). In any event, it is clear that there was an ever-available tradition of anti-Judaism Christian discourse that, like dry gun powder, only needed an explosive situation to ignite it. The explosive situation was less caused by competition over converts than the fear of Christians adding Jewish, or just biblical, patterns of behavior, or even worse, crossing over totally. The incendiary issue for so many Church leaders, as we have seen, was not so much the failure to gain a convert as it was the fear of losing one.

Bibliography

Albeck, Ḥanokh
   1969   *Seder Nashim*. Jerusalem: Bialik.
Alon, Gedaliahu
   1957   *Studies in Jewish History in the Times of the Second Temple, the Mishna and the Talmud*. Tel Aviv: Hotsaʿat ha-Kibuts ha-Meuḥad. [Hebrew]
Barrett, C. K.
   1982   Jews and Judaizers in the Epistles of Ignatius. Pp. 133–58 in *Essays on John*, ed. C. K. Barrett. London: SPCK.
Bauckham, R.
   1990   *Jude and the Relatives of Jesus in the Early Church*. Edinburgh: T. & T. Clark.
Baumgarten, Albert I.
   1992   Literary Evidence for Jewish Christianity in the Galilee. Pp. 39–50 in *The Galilee in Late Antiquity*, ed. Lee I. Levine. New York: Jewish Theological Seminary of America.
Brown, Raymond
   1983   Not Jewish Christianity and Gentile Christianity, but Types of Jewish/Gentile Christianity. *Catholic Biblical Quarterly* 46: 74–79.
Cohen, S. D.
   1989   Crossing the Boundary and Becoming a Jew. *Harvard Theological Review* 82: 13–33.
Collins, Adela Yarbro
   1985   Insiders and Outsiders in the Book of Revelation and Its Social Context. Pp. 187–218 in *"To See Ourselves As Others See Us": Christians, Jews, "Others" in Late Antiquity*, ed. Jacob Neusner and Ernest S. Frerichs. Chico, California: Scholars Press.
Dodds, E. R.
   1965   *Pagan and Christian in an Age of Anxiety*. New York: Cambridge University Press.
Epstein, J. N.
   1964   *Mavo le-Nusa ha-Mishnah*. Jerusalem: Magnes.
Feldman, Louis H.
   1993   *Jew and Gentile in the Ancient World*. Princeton: Princeton University Press.
Fine, Steven
   1996   From Meeting House to Sacred Realm: Holiness and the Ancient Synagogue. Pp. 21–47 in *Sacred Realm: The Emergence of the Synagogue in the Ancient World*, ed. S. Fine. New York: Oxford University Press.
Finkelstein, Louis
   1950   *Mabo le-Masektot Abot ve-Abot d'Rabbi Natan*. New York: Bet ha-Midrash le-Rabanim ba-Amerikah.
Freyne, Sean
   1985   Vilifying the Other and Defining the Self: Matthew's and John's Anti-Jewish Polemic in Focus. Pp. 117–43 in *"To See Ourselves As Others See Us": Christians, Jews, "Others" in Late Antiquity*, ed. Jacob Neusner and Ernest S. Frerichs. Chico, California: Scholars Press.

Friedmann, M.
  1880   *Pesikta Rabbati.* Vienna, 1880. Repr. Tel Aviv, 1963.
Gafni, Isaiah M.
  1990   *The Jews of Babylonia in the Talmudic Era: A Social and Cultural History.*
         Jerusalem: Zalman Shazar Center. [Hebrew]
Gager, John G.
  1992   Jews, Christians and the Dangerous Ones in Between. Pp. 249–57 in *Inter-*
         pretation in Religion, ed. S. Biderman and B. A. Scharfstein. Leiden: Brill.
  1983   *The Origins of Anti-Semitism: Attitudes toward Judaism in Pagan and Chris-*
         tian Antiquity. New York: Oxford University Press.
Garnsey, P.
  1984   Religious Toleration in Classical Antiquity. Pp. 1–27 in *Persecution and Tol-*
         eration in Classical Antiquity, ed. W. J. Sheils. Oxford: Blackwell.
Gero, S.
  1978   Jewish Polemic in the *Martyrium Pionii* and a "Jesus" Passage from the Tal-
         mud. *Journal of Jewish Studies* 29: 164–68.
Goodman, Martin
  1994   *Mission and Conversion: Proselytizing in the Religious History of the Roman*
         Empire. Oxford: Oxford University Press.
Gregg, Robert C., and Urman, Dan
  1996   *Jews, Pagans, and Christians in the Golan Heights: Greek and Other Inscrip-*
         tions of the Roman and Byzantine Eras. Atlanta: Scholars Press.
Harnack, Adolph
  1908   *The Mission and Expansion of Christianity in the First Three Centuries.* New
         York: Putnam.
Hayman, A. P.
  1985   The Image of the Jew in the Syriac Anti-Jewish Polemical Literature.
         Pp. 423–41 in *"To See Ourselves As Others See Us": Christians, Jews, "Oth-*
         ers" in Late Antiquity, ed. Jacob Neusner and Ernest S. Frerichs. Chico,
         California: Scholars Press.
Hirshman, Marc
  1996   *A Rivalry of Genius: Jewish and Christian Biblical Interpretation in Late An-*
         tiquity. Albany: State University of New York.
Horbury, William
  1998   *Jews and Christians in Contact and Controversy.* Edinburgh: T. & T. Clark.
Irshai, Oded
  1995   Constantine and the Jews: The Prohibition against Entering Jerusalem—
         History and Hagiography. *Zion* 60: 129–78. [Hebrew with English summary,
         p. x]
Kimelman, Reuven
  1980   Rabbi Yohanan and Origen on the Song of Songs: A Third Century Jewish
         Christian Disputation. *Harvard Theological Review* 76: 567–95.
  1982   *Birkat Ha-Minim* and the Lack of Evidence for an Anti-Christian Jewish
         Prayer in Late Antiquity. Pp. 226–44, 391–403 in *Judaism from the Macca-*
         bees to the Mid–third Century c.e., ed. E. P. Sanders. Vol. 2 of *Jewish and*
         Christian Self-Definition. Philadelphia: Fortress.

Kinzig, Wolfram
1991   "Non-separation": Closeness and Co-operation between Jews and Christians in the Fourth Century. *Vigiliae Christianae* 45: 27–53.

Kister, Menahem
1998   *Studies in Avot de-Rabbi Nathan: Text, Redaction and Interpretation.* Jerusalem: Yad Izhak Ben-Zvi. [Hebrew]

Klijn A. J., and Reinink, G. J.
1973   *Patristic Evidence for Jewish-Christian Sects.* Leiden: Brill.

Kraemer, R. S.
1989   On the Meaning of the Term "Jew" in Greco-Roman Inscriptions. *Harvard Theological Review* 82: 35–53.

Kraft, Robert A.
1965   Some Notes on Sabbath Observance in Early Christianity. *Andrews University Seminary Studies* 3: 18–33.

Krauss, Samuel
1893–94 The Jews in the Works of the Church Fathers. *Jewish Quarterly Review* 5: 122–57.

1894–95 The Jews in the Works of the Church Fathers. *Jewish Quarterly Review* 6: 82–99, 225–61.

Lieberman, Saul
1973   *Seder Nashim.* Vol. 8 in *Tosefta Ki-feshutah.* New York: Jewish Theological Seminary of America.

Luedemann, Gerd
1989   *Opposition to Paul in Jewish Christianity.* Minneapolis: Fortress.

MacMullen, Ramsay
1984   *Christianizing the Roman Empire: A.D. 100–400.* New Haven: Yale University Press.

Maier, J.
1978   *Jesus von Nazareth in der talmüduschen Überlieferung.* Darmstadt: Wissenschaftliche Buchgesellschaft.

Miller, Stuart S.
1993   The *Minim* of Sepphoris Reconsidered. *Harvard Theological Review* 86: 377–402.

Murray, Robert
1975   *Symbols of Church and Kingdom: A Study in Early Syriac Tradition.* Cambridge: Cambridge University Press.

Neusner, Jacob
1973   *Eliezer Ben Hyrcanus: The Tradition and the Man.* 2 Volumes. Leiden: Brill.

Nock, Arthur Darby
1933   *Conversion.* Oxford: Clarendon.

North, John
1992   The Development of Religious Pluralism. Pp. 174–93 in *The Jews among Pagans and Christians in the Roman Empire,* ed. J. Lieu, J. North, and T. Rajak. London: Routledge.

Overman, Andrew
1988   The God-Fearers: Some Neglected Features. *Journal for the Study of the New Testament* 32: 17–26.

Rouwhorst, G.
   1997   Jewish Liturgical Traditions in Early Syriac Christianity. *Vigiliae Christi-
           anae* 51: 72–93.
Saldarini, Anthony
   1991   The Gospel of Matthew and Jewish-Christian Conflict. Pp. 36–59 in *Social
           History of the Matthean Community*, ed. David Balch. Minneapolis: For-
           tress.
   1992   Jews and Christians in the First Two Centuries: The Changing Paradigm.
           Shofar 10: 16–35.
   1994   *Matthew's Christian-Jewish Community.* Chicago: University of Chicago
           Press.
Sanders, E. P.
   1983   *Paul, the Law, and the Jewish People.* Philadelphia: Fortress.
Sanders, Jack T.
   1993   *Schismatics, Sectarians, Dissidents, Deviants: The First One Hundred Years
           of Jewish-Christian Relations.* Valley Forge, Pennsylvania: Trinity.
Segal, Alan F.
   1992   Jewish Christianity. Pp. 326–51 in *Christianity, Eusebius, and Judaism*,
           ed. H. Attridge and G. Hata. Leiden: Brill.
Setzer, Claudia
   1994   *Jewish Responses to Early Christians: History and Polemics, 30–150 C.E.*
           Minneapolis: Fortress.
Simon, Marcel
   1996   *Verus Israel: A Study of the Relations between Christians and Jews in the Ro-
           man Empire (A.D. 135–425).* London: Vallentine Mitchell.
Smallwood, E. Mary
   1981   *The Jews under Roman Rule: From Pompey to Diocletian.* Leiden: Brill.
Smith, Jonathan E.
   1980   Fences and Neighbors: Some Contours of Early Judaism. Pp. 1–25 in vol. 2
           of *Approaches to Ancient Judaism*, ed. W. S. Green. Chico, California:
           Scholars Press.
Stanton, Graham N.
   1992   Matthew's Christology and the Parting of the Ways. Pp. 99–116 in *Jews and
           Christians: The Parting of the Ways A.D. 70 to 135*, ed. James D. G. Dunn.
           Tübingen: Mohr, Siebeck.
Stroumsa, Guy G.
   1996   From Anti-Judaism to Antisemitism in Early Christianity. Pp. 1–26 in *Con-
           tra Iudaeos: Ancient and Modern Polemics between Christians and Jews.* Tü-
           bingen: Mohr, Siebeck.
   1989   Religious Contacts in Byzantine Palestine. *Numen* 36: 16–42.
Sussman, Yaakov
   1989   The History of *Halakha* and the Dead Sea Scrolls: Preliminary Observa-
           tions on *Miqṣat Maʿase Ha-Torah* (4QMMT). *Tarbiz* 59: 11–76. [Hebrew,
           with English summary, pp. i–ii]
Taylor, J. E.
   1990   The Phenomenon of Early Jewish Christianity: Reality or Scholarly Inven-
           tion. *Vigiliae Christianae* 44: 313–34.

Taylor, Miriam S.
  1995   *Anti-Judaism and Early Christian Identity: A Critique of the Scholarly Consensus*. Leiden: Brill.
Tiede, David L.
  1984   Religious Propaganda and the Gospel Literature of the Early Christian Mission. Pp. 1705–29 in *Aufstieg und Niedergang der Römischen Welt* II:25.2. Berlin: de Gruyter.
Trebilco, P. R.
  1991   *Jewish Communities in Asia Minor*. Cambridge: Cambridge University Press.
Unger, Dominic J.
  1992   *St. Irenaeus of Lyons against the Heresies*, vol. 1. New York: Paulist.
Werner, M.
  1957   *The Formation of Christian Dogma*. New York: Harper.
Wilken, Robert L.
  1983   *John Chrysostom and the Jews: Rhetoric and Reality in the Late 4th Century*. Berkeley: University of California Press.
  1984   *The Christians As the Romans Saw Them*. New Haven: Yale University Press.
Wilson, Stephen G.
  1995   *Related Strangers: Jews and Christians, 70–170* C.E. Minneapolis: Fortress.

Joseph of Tiberias Revisited
Orthodoxies and Heresies in Fourth-Century Galilee

STEPHEN GORANSON

Durham, North Carolina

This title, "Joseph of Tiberias *Revisited*," arises in part because some years ago I wrote about Joseph, the fourth-century Galilean, but the study is all carefully hidden away in a dissertation, so I will not assume familiarity with his story and the historical disputes about it. I thought the published version of this paper would provide the occasion for me to gather the relevant new bibliography of the last six years, and to list corrections and additions. But it turned out that there is so much relevant new literature and there are so many corrections and additions to my dissertation and to the bibliography that it would not all fit in an article. Revisiting my dissertation research after six years reminds me how many questions I deferred to future research. But for now, I will sketch his story, note some questions it raises, comment on two groups of heretics known as *minim* and Anthropomorphites, and provide speculation, questions, and suggestions for study of the history of these so-called heretics.[1]

1. My 1990 Duke University dissertation is *The Joseph of Tiberias Episode in Epiphanius: Studies in Jewish and Christian Relations*.

I hope to publish revisions of at least portions of the dissertation. The dissertation bibliography (pp. 173–202), includes most of the relevant older bibliography, and in this article I have drawn on arguments made in the dissertation without repeating all of the documentation given there. In addition to literature in the following notes, relevant literature since the dissertation includes: Marinus de Jong, "Robert Grosseteste and the Testaments of the Twelve Patriarchs," *JTS* 42 (1991) 115–25; and idem, "The Transmission of the Testaments of the Twelve Patriarchs," *Vigiliae Christianae* 47 (1993) 1–27 (both of which discuss the Cambridge University manuscript codex in which *Hypomnestikon* by Joseph, discussed below, appears); Frédéric Manns, "Joseph de Tibériade, un judéo-chrétien du quatrième siècle," in *Archaeological Essays in Honour of Virgillio C. Corbo, ofm* (ed. G. C. Bottini et al.; Studium Biblicum Franciscanum Collectio Maior 36; Jerusalem: Franciscan Press, 1990) 553–60; Bargil Pixner, "Die Kirchen der Brotvermehrung: Die Kirche des Joseph von

The story of Joseph of Tiberias comes to us from Epiphanius, a writer
scholars love to hate. Epiphanius wrote a huge book, the *Panarion*, which
laboriously reports on 80 heresies. The fourth century was a great time for disputes about orthodoxies and heresies—and for Jewish and Christian self-
definitions. Epiphanius was born in Judea (in or near Beth Guvrin) and wrote
Panarion, intended as a source of remedies for heresies, after he became a
bishop in Cyprus. He was abundantly confident in his ability to defend his
version of orthodox Christianity and to prove all heretics wrong. As freely and
as fully as he could, he described and quoted the literature of his opponents
(such as Marcionites, Gnostics, Montanists, Ebionites, and Nazarenes). In
many cases, ironically, he has preserved for us disapproved literature that
would otherwise be lost. He was a plodding, unimaginative writer, unless one
counts as clever his invention of a snake or lizard or insect name for each of
his opponents. But Epiphanius reported what he found in his extensive research; this includes hearsay. Fortunately, his own speculations are often distinguishable from his sources.

He met Joseph of Tiberias when the latter was living in Scythopolis (Beth-
Shean, the one Decapolis city west of the Jordan river) in about the year 353,
which was after the Gallus revolt and before the reign of Julian the Apostate
and the big earthquake. Joseph told Epiphanius his life story. Joseph evidently
embellished his story, but Epiphanius reports, as well as he can remember,
approximately two decades later, in 375. Historians frequently begin by declaring that they find Epiphanius insufferable but then go on to use some of
his uniquely-valuable information. There does not yet exist a good, comprehensive study of Epiphanius (which my dissertation did not attempt). However, we can say the *Panarion* is not the sort of book that later scribes could
easily emend to change its point of view. Consequently, we have a good
account of what Joseph claimed.

Joseph claimed that he had been a close assistant of the patriarch, the *nasi*,
or the leading rabbi in Tiberias, namely Judah III. Judah III is called *katan*
(small) in the Palestinian Talmud (*y. B. Bat.* 8, 2, 16a), indicating that he was
not highly regarded. After Judah died, Joseph worked for his young son, the
next *nasi*, Hillel II. (Hillel II is the one who fixed the calendar, bypassing cer-
tified lunar sightings in 358.) Joseph was sent to collect money from synagogues; he was an *apostolos*, apostle (*shaliaḥ* in Hebrew). Apparently he was
not a rabbi himself. In the Tiberias genizah, he found some Christian books
in Hebrew. These books were kept in order to dispute Christian claims.

Tiberias," in *Wege des Messias und Stätten der Urkirche: Jesus und das Judenchristentum im
Licht neuer archäologischer Erkenntnisse* (ed. R. Riesner; Giessen/Basel: Brunnen, 1991)
102–13, esp. 102–3; Aline Pourkier, *L'hérésiologie chez Épiphane de Salimine* (Christian-
isme antique 4; Paris: Beauchesne, 1992); Joan E. Taylor, *Christians and the Holy Places:
The Myth of Jewish-Christian Origins* (Oxford: Oxford University Press, 1993); and T. C. G.
Thornton, "The Stories of Joseph of Tiberias," *Vigiliae Christianae* 44 (1990) 54–63.

Epiphanius includes Joseph's story in his chapter (Heresy 30) on the Ebionites, one of the so-called Jewish-Christian heresies, because Epiphanius reports that the Ebionites use a Hebrew version of the Gospel of Matthew, and
this provides the link to the Joseph story.

Joseph himself was not an Ebionite. Joseph was a Jew who became an orthodox Christian, probably one of the few such converts or apostates at the
time in Galilee. On the other hand, Galilee included numerous Ebionites
and Nazarenes.[2] The presence of Jewish-Christians (meaning here those who
observed Jewish religious law as well as Christian belief) is attested both by
Christian writers like Epiphanius (and Origen, Eusebius, and Jerome) and in
many rabbinic texts. Though historians have to face the deep presuppositions
of the writers, the Jewish-Christians were rejected by both sides and in ways
that overlap. One can follow the dual trajectories of developing rabbinic Judaism and orthodox Christianity. For example, Epiphanius regarded the
Ebionites as the more heretical group of the two because they were more Jewish (in practice) than the Nazarenes. A rabbinic story (in *b. Šabb.* 116a and
b) has exactly the opposite opinion. In an argument about whether to save
books from a fire (allowing for a very slight and intentional misspelling to dis-
guise the referents, *Be Abadan* and *Be Niṣrepe*), all the rabbis cited say that
they would let books in the house of the Nazarenes burn, but Shmuel says
maybe one should save Ebionite books. In other words, this view is the opposite and confirming preference of the view in Epiphanius.

Of course, speaking about religious approvals and disapprovals and conversion and apostasy runs the risk of stirring contemporary presuppositional
differences. But it may help if we can agree that in the broad context of the
early years of what is now called Christianity, even Paul was called (in Acts
24:5) a Nazarene; in the fourth century, the word *Nazarenes* (*Nazarēnoi* and
Nazoraioi in Greek, *Noṣrim* in Hebrew, and *Naṣrayya* in Aramaic, etc.) had
more than one meaning. In the late Second Temple Period, the first century
C.E., the Greek word for heresy (*hairesis*) was a neutral term for a chosen
group; at the same time, the Hebrew term *min* retained its biblical sense of
merely a kind or a species (only later referring to a kind, a disapproved kind,
of Jew). The terms *minim*, with the sense of heretics, and *minut* (heresy) do
not appear, for instance, in the Qumran or Dead Sea Scrolls. There is an interrelated calculus of change in the Greek and Hebrew terms and perspectives over time. In the twentieth century there is no group or individual who
stands in a continuous historical tradition with the fourth-century Jewish
Christian varieties. They did not triumph, which obviates at least one motive
for tendentiousness.

Using rabbinic literature for history is surely difficult, given problems of
dating and attribution, and because the interests of the rabbis focused elsewhere. But there is a cumulative attestation of disputes between Jews and

---

2. See my "Ebionites" and "Nazarenes," in *ABD* 2.260–61 and 4.1049–50.

Christians in Galilee. We need to begin, not with atomistic studies, but with the overlapping trends. For example, Rabbi Yoḥanan is known from *several* accounts to have disputed with minim who were Jewish-Christians (as well as perhaps with Origen). According to the Palestinian Talmud, Rabbi Yoḥanan, who lived in Sepphoris and then in Tiberias in the third century, said, "Israel did not go into exile until there were twenty-four sects [*kitot*] of minim." This is presented as part of a discussion of Ezekiel but is often regarded as referring to the Second Temple destruction. Yoḥanan is not conducting a census or counting groups here but using symbolism (as suggested in Talmud commentary). The number 24 represents, to Yoḥanan, the 12 tribes of Israel, divided. If we look at the Jewish-Christian book Apocalypse of John we see that 24 is presented in a favorable light; there are 24 elders around the throne in heaven, and the new Jerusalem, it says, will have not only the 12 gates representing the 12 tribes but an additional 12 foundations representing the 12 apostles. Here we have two sides of an argument: Christianity represents either Judaism divided or Judaism augmented.[3]

The story of Joseph of Tiberias is of a conversion from one orthodoxy to another, skipping over middle groups, more numerous at the time in Galilee. Joseph was made a count (*komes* 'companion') by Constantine and was given permission (and presumably money, which could have been a motivating factor in Joseph's visit to Constantine) to build churches in Sepphoris, Tiberias, Capernaum, and Nazareth, none of which, according to *Panarion*, had Christian churches, that is, Catholic churches. Epiphanius did not credit Nazarenes and Ebionites as Christians. First, they had synagogues not churches, he says. Of the Nazarenes he writes, "they are nothing but Jews themselves."[4] Then he asserts that (other) Jews "stand up . . . three times a day when they recite their prayers in synagogues, and curse and anathematize them."[5] This is the earliest extant reference to the version of the *Birkat ha-Minim*, the Blessing or Curse on Heretics, which explicitly includes Noṣrim, which is also known from six Cairo Genizah manuscripts and an Oxford manuscript of Seder Rav Amran. Of course, Epiphanius has a category problem: Jews are cursing Jews. But he preserves this tension. Here are two related examples. First, in Heresy 53, he describes Sampsaeans and wrongly speculates that their name has to do with sun-worship rather than being Aramaic for 'servant' (*šamaš* not *šemeš*). The Samspaeans use the book of the Elkesaites, as do the Ossenes, Nazarenes, and Ebionites, he writes. Then he

---

3. For further discussion of Jewish-Christian aspects of the Apocalypse, see my "Text of Revelation 22.14," *NTS* 43 (1997) 154–57; idem, "The Exclusion of Ephraim in Rev. 7:4–8 and Essene Polemic against Pharisees," *Dead Sea Discoveries* 2 (1995) 80–85; and idem, "Essene Polemic in the Apocalypse of John," in *Legal Texts and Legal Issues: Proceedings of the Second Meeting of the International Organization for Qumran Studies, Published in Honour of Joseph M. Baumgarten* (ed. M. Bernstein et al.; Leiden: Brill, 1997) 453–60.

4. Epiphanius, *Panarion*, Heresy 29.9.1.

5. Epiphanius, *Panarion*, Heresy 29.9.2.

declares that "Sampsaeans . . . are neither Christians, Jews nor pagans; since they are merely in the middle, they are nothing."[6] Second, Epiphanius describes the flight of early Christians before the war with Rome, from Jerusalem to Pella, east of the Jordan. The next thing we hear from him about Pella, despite the divinely delivered warning to get out of Jerusalem, is that it is a hotbed of Ebionite and Nazarene heresies.[7] Epiphanius does not recognize that the church has in the interim, from the first to the fourth centuries, decided that Ebionites and Nazarenes are heretical.

Sepphoris, Tiberias, and Capernaum—three of the four places mentioned by Epiphanius as Joseph's church-building goals—all had Jewish-Christian *minim*, according to the rabbis. Why Nazareth is not mentioned in early rabbinic literature remains speculative: perhaps it was small (though it did have a priestly course at least by ca. 300, the date of the *mishmarot* [priestly courses] inscription from Caesarea), perhaps it had two names, perhaps it was named after Jesus rather than vice versa, perhaps it was censored out by Jews, perhaps it was censored out by Christians, or perhaps it is accidental. But three of Joseph's four locations had *minim*, and perhaps the fourth, Jesus' hometown, did as well.

Now, parts of Joseph's story can be questioned. There is not enough space here to recount his long adventures before becoming a Christian, including his healing (exorcising) a naked maniac and having contests of magic with Jews in Tiberias and at the Gader hot baths, stories that resemble others in the Palestinian Talmud (for example, *y. Sanh.* 25d). The element of his story that most invites doubt is his claim that the *nasi* Judah III converted to Christianity on his deathbed. Hearsay accounts of deathbed conversions, though surely not impossible, are approximately as certain as, say, new hearsay claims on an intended change of will in the estate of Doris Duke. Epiphanius reported this hearsay. But Joseph's attempt to build the first Catholic churches in these four towns is credible, even if we do not know precisely how far he succeeded; it appears likely that his foundations were not long-lasting, partly because the congregations of Catholic Christians to fill them did not yet exist.

What then about the population in Sepphoris at the time? It was a place where the *Birkat ha-Minim*, including the type that added *Noṣrim* ("may the *noṣrim* and *minim* speedily perish," to exclude Jewish-Christians from synagogue), would fit. This was not in Asia Minor, to bother the final author of the Gospel of John.[8]

---

6. Epiphanius, *Panarion*, Heresy 53.1.2.

7. Epiphanius, *Panarion*, Heresy 29.7.7–8; Heresy 30.2.7; and *Weights and Measures* 15.

8. Reuven Kimelman has provided a very helpful study of *minim*, showing, among other things, that the term refers only to kinds of *Jewish* heresy until Amoraic Babylonian literature, making some of Adolf Büchler's efforts to dismiss Jewish-Christian *minim* identifications as really "Bible-reading heathen" impossible. See Büchler, "The Minim of Sepphoris and Tiberias in the Second and Third Centuries," in *Studies in Jewish History: The*

Stuart Miller has gathered many sources and provided useful philological observations on some of the relevant rabbinic literature, but—and it is no surprise to him that I think this—historically, he has worked minimalism on *minim*. He argues for the smallest number of *minim* possible and presents this as a corrective. But what does it correct? A corrective is not history; a historian must strive for the most plausible reconstructions. Miller at first considers only the accounts that explicitly name Sepphoris and *minim*, putting aside many related accounts. If we wanted to know about, for example, American Colonial Jews in Providence, Rhode Island, would we limit ourselves and our research only to the texts that explicitly include the words "Jews" and "Providence"? I do not think we would. The rabbis do not always give the location. Rabbinic literature does not mention everything of historical interest; for example, the writers *never* mention the theater in Sepphoris. By Miller's method, there are four relevant stories. Three of these he dismisses as not Jewish-Christian *minim*, because they involve magic, gnosticism, and disrespect for authority, as if these were unknown in Christianity. To the contrary, having four explicit Sepphoris *minim* stories identifies Sepphoris, relatively, as a mecca for *minim*, along with Tiberias and Capernaum, among the most frequently named places. As for the fourth story, of Jacob the *min*, who is ineluctably presented by the rabbis as a Jewish Christian, we read in Miller's treatments, including the museum catalog,[9] that he was merely *visiting* (his

---

Adolph Büchler Memorial Volume (ed. I. Brodie; London: Oxford University Press, 1956) 245–74.

In my view, one of the best published studies of *minim* is Kimelman's *"Birkat Ha-Minim* and the Lack of Evidence for an Anti-Christian Prayer in Late Antiquity," in *Jewish and Christian Self-Definition*, vol. 2: *Aspects of Judaism in the Graeco-Roman Period* (ed. E.P. Sanders et al.; Philadelphia: Fortress, 1981) 226–44 and 391–403. My unpublished dissertation, *The Joseph of Tiberias Episode in Epiphanius*, discusses *minim* and related terms on pages 74–97. See also Kimelman's 1977 Yale Univ. Ph.D. dissertation, *Rabbi Yoḥanan of Tiberias: Aspects of the Social and religious History of Third Century Palestine*.

However, I would question two aspects of Kimelman's *"Birkat Ha-Minim"* article, taken together with his paper read at this conference. First, though he demonstrated that *minim* evolved, and that the term had a different range of meaning for writers of differing times and places, he does not fully take into account the fact that the meaning of the terms *noṣrim* and *Nazarenes* also evolved; and that the group *noṣrim* referred to in some forms of the *Birkat ha-Minim* must have been large enough to justify being mentioned in the liturgy. Second, in emphasizing the welcome early Christians may have received in some synagogues, I think that he underestimates the amount of regional variation and that he overestimates as universally-clear a dividing line between Jewish and Gentile Christians. For example, Antioch was different than Sepphoris; Pauline Christianity arrived at Sepphoris much later than in Antioch, which Paul himself visited. Also, his conference paper might lead one to think that in a given ancient synagogue, Gentile Christians were heartily welcomed at the same time Jewish Christians were officially invited "to speedily perish." If such a sharp distinction was the case in some time and place, it, nonetheless, I would think, could not have been universal at any time.

9. Stuart Miller, "Jewish Sepphoris: A Great City of Scholars and Scribes," in *Sepphoris in Galilee: Crosscurrents of Culture* (ed. R. M. Nagy et al.; Raleigh: North Carolina Museum

italics), as though being from Kfar Shiḥin were like being from Timbuktu or Chicago. But Shiḥin, as James Strange and colleagues have persuasively demonstrated, was the pottery-making village a kilometer or two distant from Sepphoris, and near the St. Anne property. Sepphoreans put out a fire there. Rabbi Yose of Sepphoris consulted on their questions. There is dispute about the spellings of the town name, but the location closest to Sepphoris is the most probable.[10] It is not a question, in my view, whether *minim* lived in Sepphoris, but whether we can recognize them and their material remains.[11]

Early Jewish Christians, *minim*, Ebionites, and Nazarenes are difficult to find in early material remains, which look like Jewish material culture. It was many decades before distinctive Christian iconography developed (present for instance in Dura-Europos in the third century). But we are not likely to find them if we do not ask questions. For instance, the reading of the so-called Maria ostracon is not certain; it is misspelled (and, please note, the catalog entry has four typographical errors[12]). It is not only uncertain but late.

---

of Art, 1996) 59–63, here p. 61. See also Stuart Miller, "The *Minim* of Sepphoris Reconsidered," *HTR* 86 (1993) 377–402, esp. 380–81, 399, and 400; and idem, "Further Thoughts on the *Minim* of Sepphoris," in *Proceedings of the Eleventh World Congress of Jewish Studies*, division B / vol. 1: *The History of the Jewish People* (Jerusalem: World Union of Jewish Studies, 1994) 1–8, esp. p. 4.

10. James F. Strange, Dennis E. Groh, and Thomas R. W. Longstaff, "Excavations at Sepphoris: The Location and Identification of Shikhin," *IEJ* 44 (1994) 216–27 and 45 (1995) 171–87. There are many spelling variations and confusions between the town names Shiḥin, Shiḥnin, Sikhaya, Sikhania. See, e.g., Marcus Jastrow, A *Dictionary of the Targumim* . . . (New York: Judaica, 1985) 992 (two entries) and 1559; and Frédéric Manns, "Jacob, le Min, selon la Tosephta Hulin 2, 22–24: Contribution à l'étude du christianisme primitif," *Cristianesimo nella storia* 10 (1989) 449–65. I suggest that the name Shiḥin became confused with the town better known to later rabbis, Sikhanya, which is a few miles farther north.

11. Furthermore, the rabbinic accounts do *not* say Jacob was visiting Sepphoris. Though he may have been visiting, he may also have been going to a daily job in Sepphoris, say, selling pottery. Or he may have moved to Sepphoris and was known from his place of origin. (This often occurs with ancient names; e.g., the Stoic philosopher Posidonius of Apamea, Syria, actually lived in Rhodes during much of his adult life.) We do not know how often Jacob was to be encountered in Sepphoris, despite Stuart Miller's choosing to insist that he was "visiting," a choice which tends to reify the minimal interpretation. Then Miller uses this minimalist assertion to support another unfounded assertion. On p. 400 of "The *Minim* of Sepphoris Reconsidered," Miller wrote that Jacob, ". . .a visitor himself to Sepphoris, can hardly be regarded as a member of a Jewish-Christian community in the city. . . ." But, if Jacob lived nearby, he *could* indeed have been a member of such a community. The rabbis do not explicitly tell us whether he was or not, but either is possible. And, given the fact that such communities existed, and given the fact that people learn a religious tradition, ordinarily, from others in some sort of community, Miller's conclusion is not persuasive.

12. Stephen Goranson, "Ostracon with Maria(?) Graffito," in *Sepphoris in Galilee: Crosscurrents of Culture* (ed. R. M. Nagy et al.; Raleigh: North Carolina Museum of Art, 1996) 69. The transcription of the ostracon should have a *rho*, not a *pi*. The phonetic representation was mārēa, not m_r_a. The bibliographic reference, truncated in the catalog,

An earlier uncertain question concerns the Late Hellenistic or Herodian shard that may read in Aramaic letters *epimeletes* (a common Greek word for 'overseer' or 'administrator').[13] This may relate to one of the five Synhedria of Gabinius, one of which was located in Sepphoris in the first century B.C.E.[14] Gabinius appointed Antipater *epimeletes* at the "Judean" Sanhedrin in Sepphoris. But here is an alternate possibility that perhaps you will consider after you reject it: Josephus calls the Essene *mebaqqer* an *epimeletes*.[15] Do I think it is an Essene inscription? No. It was more likely addressed to a Roman employee by a Jew. But Josephus and Philo do say that Essenes lived in various towns in Syria–Palestine, possibly including, for example, Sepphoris and/or Shihin.[16] Would we recognize them? At the early end of the trajectory, some Essenes became Christian or Nazarene and were later called *minim*.

The St. Anne Greek inscription reading is not settled.[17] I do not claim to have the final reading, and it has frequently been remarked how difficult it is. (For instance, where is the verb?) It is indeed anomalous in some of its collocations. But we can ask: is it from a synagogue or a burial lintel? Why is it said to come from the same synagogue as the Rabbi Yudan Aramaic inscription? It includes the word *archisynagogos* 'head of a synagogue' three times. Epiphanius wrote, "Ebionites have elders and *archisynagogoi*, and they call their church a synagogue, not a church."[18] The inscription apparently includes the term *komes* (abbreviated) twice. Joseph was a *komes* (or 'count'). When did Jews stop receiving that honorific title from Roman emperors? In other words, is the proposed fifth-century date possible? Avi-Yonah said that the *chi-rho* on this inscription abbreviates the end of the word *lamprotatos* ('illustrious'). Perhaps so, but he gives no parallels, and it is differently abbreviated the first time.[19] *Chi-rho* surely can be an abbreviation for words other than

---

is Bellarmino Bagatti, *Gli Scavi di Nazaret* (SBF Collectio Maior 17/1; Jerusalem: Franciscan Press, 1967) 150–52.

13. Joseph Naveh, "Jar Fragment with Inscription in Hebrew," in *Sepphoris in Galilee: Crosscurrents of Culture* (ed. R. M. Nagy et al.; Raleigh: North Carolina Museum of Art, 1996) 170.

14. According to Josephus *Ant.* 14.127 and 14.139, Gabinius gave Antipater the title of *epimeletes*. Note that Sepphoris here is conceived as part of Judea, in a Roman administrative sense. For an example of Judea used as including Judea proper and Galilee and Perea, see Pliny *Natural History* 5.70.

15. Josephus *J.W.* 2.123, 129, and 134.

16. Philo *Every Good Man Is Free* 75 and *Apology for the Jews* 1; Josephus *J.W.* 2.119.

17. See F. Hüttenmeister and G. Reeg, *Die Antiken Synagogen in Israel* (Wiesbaden: Reichert, 1977) 1.400–407; and Lea Roth-Gerson, *The Greek Inscriptions from the Synagogues in Eretz-Israel* (Jerusalem: Yad Yitshak ben-Tsvi, 1987) 105–10 [Heb.]. See also Tessa Rajak and David Noy, "*Archisynagogoi*: Office, Title and Social Status in the Greco-Jewish Synagogue," *JRS* 83 (1993) 75–93, esp. 91.

18. Epiphanius *Panarion*, Heresy 30.18.1.

19. Michael Avi-Yonah, *Abbreviations in Greek Inscriptions (The Near East, 200 B.C.–A.D. 1100)* (Quarterly of the Department of Antiquities of Palestine Supplement to vol. 9; Jerusalem: Government of Palestine / London: Oxford University Press, 1940).

christos, though more often for the beginning of a word than the end of one.[20] Also, what rabbinic Jew in Sepphoris (or in Tyre or Sidon, which, in some readings, are mentioned in the inscription) would not know about and avoid this possible association in the fifth century? There may be more than two buildings represented on the St. Anne property, property near Shihin. Did Shihin have a synagogue? Or did its residents walk to Sepphoris?

More on the Christian side of heresies, I would be remiss not to mention an important new book that I regard as relevant to Joseph. Robert Grant and Glen Menzies have edited and translated a text called *Hypomnestikon*, which they also call *Joseph's Bible Notes*.[21] It includes discussions of heresies, obviously based in part on Epiphanius, but with interesting differences. Grant and Menzies have done a good service providing a critical Greek text and translation. I say that the *Hypomnestikon* was written approximately 380 and possibly by our Joseph. They say I am wrong. I respond that, though I could be mistaken, their arguments for a later dating are not persuasive. The dating involves the Anthropomorphite heresy, the last and maybe latest heresy mentioned by Joseph. Epiphanius may have been an Anthropomorphite; at least he was accused of this. He had already tried to finesse the issue in *Panarion*, written approximately 375.[22] And he was also an iconoclast, before that term existed. The author Joseph may have been an Apollinarian, one with an excessively high Christology. Both considered themselves orthodox. To be brief, it is my view that Grant and Menzies date the beginning of the Anthropomorphite heresy too late.[23] They also propose Alexandria as the place of writing, perhaps under-appreciating the literary and cultural possibilities of Scythopolis. We do agree that it is interesting that this book by Joseph says that the Anthropomorphite heresy had its origin in Eleutheropolis, that is, Beth Guvrin, where Epiphanius was born and set up a monastery.[24]

There is more, I think, for historians of religion in Galilee to learn from Epiphanius and the newly-edited book by Joseph. In conclusion, Shihin and the St. Anne property, I would think, are promising excavation sites.[25]

20. Pasquale Colella, "Les abbréviations *taw* and *chi-rho*," *RB* 80 (1973) 547–58.

21. Robert M. Grant and Glen W. Menzies (ed. and trans.), *Joseph's Bible Notes (Hypomnestikon)* (Texts and Translations 41, Early Christian Series 9; Atlanta: Scholars Press, 1996).

22. In *Panarion*, Heresy 70.2, where Epiphanius made a gingerly attempt to correct their views about "the image of God" without being too severely condemning.

23. I hope to return to this issue in a future study.

24. *Hypomnestikon* 140.62; see Grant and Menzies (eds.), *Joseph's Bible Notes (Hypomnestikon)*, 302 for the Greek text and 303 for an English translation.

25. A related article, which came to my attention after this essay was written, is Simon C. Mimouni, "L'*Hypomnesticon* de Joseph de Tibériade: Une oeuvre du IVeme siècle?" *Studia Patristica XXXII* (12th International Conference on Patristic Studies, Oxford, 1995; ed. Elizabeth A. Livingstone; Leuven: Peeters, 1997) 346–57.

Pilgrims to the Land
Early Christian Perceptions of the Galilee

BLAKE LEYERLE

University of Notre Dame

When early Christian pilgrims first began traveling to the Holy Land, they were vividly aware of traveling through unfamiliar terrain. Their accounts, therefore, encode a variety of geographic perceptions of the Land. These comments invite careful attention, not so much for what they say about environmental "reality" or even the development of pilgrimage shrines and services (though these will also be our concern), but primarily about the pilgrim's own orientation. In this sense, these comments form a kind of map[1]—a map not like those drawn by professional cartographers but, rather, like the well-known cover of *The New Yorker* portraying a Manhattanite's view of the world.[2] Such maps resemble the partial, idiosyncratic, and distorted maps each of us develops of his or her own world. We construct these maps, according to Kevin Lynch, through a process of building up simplified images, first of landmarks, then of the routes connecting them, and then finally of entire districts or regions.[3] We should expect, therefore, that as pilgrimage

1. D. J. Walmsley and J. M. Jenkins, "Tourism Cognitive Mapping of Unfamiliar Environments," *Annals of Tourism Research* 19/2 (1992) 269; Allan Pred, "Place as Historically Contingent Process: Structuration and the Time-Geography of Becoming Places," *Annals of the Association of American Geographers* 74 (1984) 279; idem, *Making Histories and Constructing Human Geographies: The Local Transformation of Practice, Power Relations, and Consciousness* (Boulder, Colo.: Westview, 1990) 16; Blake Leyerle, "Landscape as Cartography in Early Christian Pilgrimage Narratives," *JAAR* 64 (1996) 119–43.

2. The March 29, 1976, cover art by Saul Steinberg shows Manhattan disproportionately large and the rest of the world figuring as vague bumps on the horizon.

3. Kevin Lynch, *The Image of the City* (Cambridge, Mass.: M.I.T. Press, 1960); Walmsley and Jenkins, "Tourism Cognitive Mapping," 280; Timothy P. McNamara, "Mental Representation of Spatial Relations," *Cognitive Psychology* 18 (1986) 91, 115–16; Robert Lloyd, "Cognitive Maps: Encoding and Decoding Information," *Annals of the Association of American Geographers* 79 (1989) 103; Reginald Golledge and A. Spector, "Comprehending the Urban Environment: Theory and Practice," *Geographical Analysis* 10 (1978) 125–52.

to Galilee increased, a corresponding richness of detail should mark perceptions of the land. Yet, as the cover of *The New Yorker* suggests, partiality is not necessarily the result of ignorance. Visibility tends, rather, to index value.

Value in the Holy Land, however, can never be divorced from history. For there, geographic features derive their importance from their status as the place where scriptural events were enacted. The Holy Land thus illustrates with particular sharpness that the past has its own geography. Pilgrims' perceptions of the environment always encode a prior sense of history.[4] What then do the earliest accounts of Christian pilgrimages to Galilee tell about the construction of a privileged geography of the past?

The Bordeaux Pilgrim

The first extant pilgrimage account comes from an anonymous traveler from Bordeaux, who visited the Land in 333.[5] Its format is initially that of an itinerary, where the most prominent feature, as Lynch's work suggests, is the road itself. Page after page records the number of miles traveled, milestones passed, horses changed, and nights spent on the road.[6]

A similar focus on the road marks a fascinating set of cylindrical goblets dating from the first century. On each cup, a slightly different itinerary from Cadiz to Rome is inscribed.[7] If O. A. W. Dilke is right that these variations reflect new construction on the route, these cups celebrate the experience of travel.[8] In a similar sense, I suggest, the easy rhythm of the Bordeaux itinerary proclaims the extraordinary achievement of the system of roads that linked the Roman Empire. Like travel on a well-paved highway, there seem to be no impediments on the Bordeaux itinerary: each day represents another segment traveled.

Punctuating this smooth procession, however, are natural obstacles, such as mountains or large bodies of water. These are examples of what Lynch terms "edges." Other, more arbitrary edges (for example, regional borders) are also registered. Among these, Mt. Gerizim represents a particularly important geographic and cultural edge, for here the list format of the Bordeaux pilgrim ends abruptly, to be replaced by sustained prose. From then on, apparently, environs are meaningful: after Mt. Gerizim, the Land is holy and therefore worthy of description. This sudden shift in style and perspective

---

4. Victor Turner, "The Center out There: The Pilgrim's Goal," *HR* 12 (1973) 221.

5. *Itinerarium Burdigalense* (hereafter abbreviated *It. Burd.*) 549–617. The critical edition used is edited by P. Geyer and O. Cuntz (CCSL 175; Turnhout: Brepols, 1965) 1–26.

6. *It. Burd.* 549–87, 600–617 (CCSL 175 1–13, 20–26).

7. Four goblets were discovered among votive offerings at *Aquae Apollinares*, modern Lake Bracciano. They are made of silver of varying height. Raymond Chevallier dates them 7 B.C.E.–47 C.E. (*Roman Roads* [trans. N. H. Field; Berkeley: University of California Press, 1976] 47–50).

8. O. A. W. Dilke, *Greek and Roman Maps* (Ithaca: Cornell University Press, 1985) 122–24.

reveals, moreover, that the previous concentration on the route marked not simply a celebration of travel but also the real-life connectedness of the world back "home" in Bordeaux to the sacred places of Palestine.

But if the sober list of miles spent on the road insists that the Land is as "real" as the familiar places of Gaul, its peculiar status sets it apart. A sharp boundary divides land that is simply foreign from that which is holy. Nowhere is this more evident than in this pilgrim's choice of route from Caesarea Palestina to Jerusalem. Instead of taking the more direct coastal route, he went up by way of Jezreel Scythopolis (modern Beth-Shean). No reason is given for this choice of route, but it may have been prompted by a desire to complete a tour of sites connected with the prophet Elijah. And there would be nothing odd in that.[9] But it is striking how this detour brought him within a day's journey of the Galilee, and yet he did not go there. Nazareth and Capernaum were not worth a side trip.[10] There was time enough, since he and his party took nearly seven months to walk to the Holy Land from the Bosporus, take in the sights, and return.[11] Apparently it was interest in the Galilee that was lacking. How are we to understand this?

I turn again to Lynch's theory, which suggests that we first learn landmarks and only then the routes connecting them. Elsewhere in the Bordeaux pilgrim's account, monuments feature prominently.[12] Indeed, his most sustained descriptions concern the impressive edifices in Jerusalem.[13] At this time, however, Galilee was still undeveloped. Shrines had yet to mark off specific sites as holy.[14] Where there are no landmarks, routes also go unrecorded

---

9. From the importance of sites connected with the Hebrew Bible, Robert L. Wilken suggests that this pilgrim may have had a Jewish guide or perhaps followed a Jewish itinerary (*The Land Called Holy: Palestine in Christian History and Thought* [New Haven: Yale University Press, 1992] 110–11).

10. Joan E. Taylor suggests that patterns of ethnic settlement may have influenced the itinerary. "Central Galilee," she writes, "was almost entirely Jewish in character in the second and third centuries, apart from a pagan presence in Sepphoris/Diocaesarea and Tiberias." When bishops from Palestine attended the Council of Nicaea in 325, none came from the Jewish towns of Galilee, a fact suggesting that there were no churches there (*Christians and the Holy Places: The Myth of Jewish-Christian Origins* [Oxford: Oxford University Press, 1993] 225–26, 57). While Eusebius mentions Nazareth in his *Onomasticon* (138.24–140.2), he notes nothing of interest about the place.

11. Dilke, *Greek and Roman Maps*, 129. C. W. Wilson, "Introduction" to the "Itinerary from Bordeaux to Jerusalem," in *The Library of the Palestine Pilgrims' Text Society* (London: Palestine Exploration Fund, 1887) 1.viii.

12. Yoram Tsafrir notes the similarity between this itinerary and the work of Theodosius, especially in the descriptions of Jerusalem and the Jordan ("The Maps Used by Theodosius: On the Pilgrim Maps of the Holy Land and Jerusalem in the Sixth Century C.E.," *Dumbarton Oaks Papers* 40 [1986] 135).

13. Solomon's palace is the parade example (*It Burd.* 590.4–591.3 [CCSL 175 15–16]).

14. Wilson, "Introduction," ix; Stephen Nichols speaks of the Bordeaux pilgrim "welcoming" the "intrusion" of "Constantine's monumental basilicas" ("The Interaction of Life and Literature in the *Peregrinationes ad loca sancta* and the *Chansons de Geste*," *Speculum* 44 [1969] 53–54).

because, according to Lynch, the learning of routes depends upon land-marks. Still further from perception is any sense of the general geographic area: the fields and trees, lake and hills. On this map, Galilee is quite blank.

But blankness is not the same as emptiness. Silences such as these have little to do with terrain or population, since Galilee, we can assume, was as geographically formed and populated as any region to the south. Instead, si-lences are prime indexes of value and, as such, encode political or social mes-sages.[15] Our pilgrim's silence on Galilee is thus a parade example of the selectivity with which any society commemorates its past.[16] While some events are highlighted, others are slighted or altogether ignored. The Bor-deaux pilgrim bypassed Galilee not simply because it was undeveloped but for precisely the reason that it was undeveloped: it was not valued. Interest in the scriptural events of this region had yet to be aroused. In this sense, it is a region without history. Because it has no history, it also has no geography.

Egeria

By the end of the fourth century, Galilee had both history and geography. In the early 380s, our next pilgrim, a woman named Egeria, traveled from the West to the Holy Land.[17] Among her various tours, she traveled to the Gali-lee. Her comments on this region, however, survive only in a medieval digest of information on the holy places.[18] Yet, even these spare remarks reveal a shift in perspective on the Land.

After the silence of the Bordeaux pilgrim, the sheer quantity of landmarks visited by Egeria in the Galilee is striking. In the village of Shunem, for ex-ample, she visits the house of Abishag and the woman who sheltered Elisha. The field in which Jesus plucked ears of wheat on the Sabbath is shown to her, as well as the grassy slope where he fed the five thousand. In Nain, she

15. J. B. Harley, "Maps, Knowledge and Power," in *The Iconography of Landscape: Essays on the Symbolic Representation, Design, and Use of Past Environments* (ed. Dennis Cosgrove and S. Daniels; Cambridge: Cambridge University Press, 1988) 290; idem, "Silence and Secrecy: The Hidden Agenda of Cartography in Early Modern Europe," *Imago Mundi* (1988) 57–76. For a different reading of this "impression of scenic emptiness," see Mary B. Campbell, "The Scriptural East: Egeria, Arculf, and the Written Pilgrimage," in *Discovering New Worlds: Essays on Medieval Exploration and Imagination* (ed. Scott Westrem; New York: Garland, 1991) 4–15.

16. Maurice Halbwachs, *On Collective Memory* (ed. and trans. Lewis A. Coser; Chicago: University of Chicago Press, 1992) 86.

17. Paul Devos, "La Date du voyage d'Égérie," *Analecta Bollandiana* 85 (1967) 165–94. John Wilkinson usefully summarizes the controversy over the dating of this text (*Egeria's Travels to the Holy Land* [Warminster: Aris & Phillips, 1981] 237–39). The critical edition is edited by Pierre Maraval, *Journal du voyage: Itinéraire Égérie* (Sources chrétiennes 296; Paris: du Cerf, 1982).

18. Peter the Deacon, *De Locis Sanctis*, dedicated to the abbot of Monte Cassino in 1137 (*PL* 173 1115–34). A partial translation, including the Galilean portion, with commentary, may be found in Wilkinson, *Egeria's Travels*, 179–210.

sees the burial place where the widow intended to lay her son; in Endor, she looks at the house of the wise woman visited by Saul; in Nazareth, she visits the garden where Jesus played as a child, as well as the cave that had formed part of Mary's home; in Capernaum, she is shown Peter's house and the site on the nearby highway of Matthew's tollbooth.[19]

The dense clustering of these places, although no doubt intensified by the compression inherent to any summary, conveys a simple yet powerful message: in this region there is a great deal to see. Even more impressive than the quantity of sites, however, is Egeria's excitement over their quality. She is thrilled, for example, that the house in which Elisha stayed is "still there today," that the foundations of the witch of Endor's house "are still to be seen," and that the "original walls" of Simon Peter's house in Capernaum "are still standing."[20] Such phrasing insists that pleasure in these sites cannot be separated from assurance of their authenticity.[21] Even the field, presumably so like any other, is singled out and legitimized by a landmark: a stone "you can still see . . . on which [Jesus] rested his arm."[22] Scripture mentions no such stone (nor indeed that Jesus rested his arm), but the omission does not impede her willingness to bestow meaning on place. This willingness is illustrated nowhere better than in the empty burial vault at Nain, where the sight itself is absence.[23] What then allows her to bestow such an excess of meaning on crumbling foundations, agricultural fields, hollow concavities, and stray rocks?

In answer, we might turn to some recent work on tourism that distinguishes between sites and what Dean MacCannell terms their "markers."[24]

---

19. *De Locis Sanctis* (PL 173 1127A–B, 1128A). Epiphanius tells us of the labors of the *comes* Joseph of Tiberias, who received permission from Constantine to build churches in Jewish strongholds like Nazareth. Taylor believes that Joseph was responsible for the church built on this location about 335 C.E. (*Christians and the Holy Places*, 227, 265–67).

20. "Quae domus usque hodie permanet. . . . de qua domo adhuc fundamenta apparent.. . . qui parietes usque hodie ita stant sicut fuerunt" (*De Locis Sanctis* [PL 173 1127A, 1128A-B]), trans. Wilkinson, *Egeria's Travels*, 192, 194.

21. Dean MacCannell, extending the work of Erving Goffman, would place this kind of authenticating rhetoric in the category of "staged authentic." While the attraction has been staged for the pilgrim, she is not aware of it and therefore accepts it as real ("Staged Authenticity: Arrangements of Social Space in Tourist Setting," *American Journal of Sociology* 79 [1973] 595–98; idem, *The Tourist: A New Theory of the Leisure Class* [New York, 1976] 44–45; cf. Erving Goffman, *Relations in Public: Microstudies of the Public Order* [New York: Basic Books, 1971] 62).

22. "Ibi lapis est, in quo cubitum fixit Dominus, qui usque hodie videtur" (*De Locis Sanctis* [PL 173 1127A]), trans. Wilkinson, *Egeria's Travels*, 192.

23. *De Locis Sanctis* (PL 173 1127A–B). Similarly, Egeria is "shown even the place from which Rachel stole the idols of her father" as well as the spot where Lot's wife had once stood as a pillar of salt (*It. Eg.* 21.4, 12.7 [SC 296 224, 178]).

24. This distinction is based on the semiotic principle that "a sign represents something to someone" (MacCannell, *Tourist*, 109–10). See also Jonathan Culler, "The Semiotics of Tourism," *American Journal of Semiotics* 1 (1981) 127–42.

While a site remains fixed, its markers come in many forms, such as bro-
chures, placards, souvenirs, and books. A traveler's first contact with a site is,
therefore, usually not with the site itself, but with one of its markers. The act
of recognition involves a process of connecting and then replacing the
marker with the site.[25] We see this same process replicated in Egeria's account. Over and over she describes how she looks at a site, recalls the scriptural passage, and then looks again. In her words, we see her eyes moving
continuously from scriptural locus to geographic place, connecting, and then
finally replacing marker with site.[26]

No wonder then that mountains prove so exciting. Their peaks afford un-
paralleled opportunities for locating places mentioned in the Bible. In the
Galilee, she climbs Mt. Tabor and its smaller neighboring hill, which she
calls Hermon.[27] From its top, she claims that "the whole of Galilee and the
Sea of Tiberias can be seen."[28] Yet it is precisely in these sections that we feel
most acutely the excerpting hand of the medieval copyist. For where her own
words are preserved in their fullness, she invariably replicates for her readers
the experience of panoptic biblical vision. But even then, certain silences
persist. While noting, for example, all the geographic features that could be
seen from Mt. Nebo or Mt. Sinai, she rarely describes what any of them look
like.[29] It is enough, apparently, that the places exist and are seen to do so.
Their specific geographic disposition is unimportant.[30] Dean MacCannell's
work helps us to understand why. A viewer's pleasure or satisfaction in any
given site, he argues, depends upon the level of emotional investment in the
marker, rather than in the site. For, like the field in which Jesus ate with his
disciples, sites can often seem disappointingly ordinary—too like any other
place.[31] Egeria's high investment in the Bible as a marker, however, guaran-
tees her satisfaction and explains why the only quality of a site that interests
her is its scriptural status. From Mt. Tabor, the significance of the Galilean

25. Sights are therefore often described as "looking just like the picture" (MacCannell,
Tourist, 121–23).

26. Leo Spitzer, "The Epic Style of the Pilgrim Aetheria," *Comparative Literature* 1
(1949) 225–58. Jonathan Z. Smith notes how Egeria uses "scripture as a Guide Bleu" to
bring together place and text (*To Take Place: Toward Theory in Ritual* [Chicago: University
of Chicago Press, 1987] 88–95).

27. Psalm 89, which links "Tabor and Hermon," led to an association of a hill in the
neighborhood of Tabor, probably Jebel Duhi, with the name Hermon (Wilkinson, *Egeria's
Travels*, 192 n. 4; cf. Jerome, *Epp.* 46.12, 108.13). It was not until the mid–fourth century
that Mt. Tabor was identified as the site of the Transfiguration (R. W. Thomson, "A Seventh-
Century Armenian Pilgrim," *JTS* n.s. 18 [1967] 28–29).

28. *De Locis Sanctis* (PL 173 1128A).

29. Cf. *It. Eg.* 12.4–10 (SC 296 176–80). Yet of Mt. Hermon, she writes: "it is very lofty
and from it there is a view over the whole of Galilee, unequalled for beauty, since the
whole vast plain is vineyards and olive-groves" (*De Locis Sanctis* [PL 173 1127A], trans.
Wilkinson, *Egeria's Travels*, 192).

30. Spitzer, "Epic Style," 238–42.

31. Noted by MacCannell, *Tourist*, 112–15.

terrain lies in its legibility: beneath her eyes it spreads out as deeply layered as the text of scripture.[32] Nonetheless, in Egeria's account there is an important shift in perception: simple geographic features like hills and fields are becoming distinct. This marks the beginning of the process of social framing through which terrain becomes infused with meaning. Once meaningfully organized, terrain becomes newly visible as landscape.[33]

With Egeria, however, the value of this land remains almost exclusively scriptural: the only significant time is past time.[34] Contemporary additions are unimportant, unless they serve, like the church built over Peter's house in Capernaum, to designate a specific spot as holy. For this reason, she gives no description of these buildings, apart from assurances of their authenticity. Like icons painted on the lids of ancient reliquaries, they function to preserve the fragmentary jumble of remnants from the status of junk: without markers they would subside into being emblems only of the disposable.[35]

This concentration on the past, in turn, controls Egeria's experience with the inhabitants. They too seem caught in a time warp, where only the past can make the present meaningful. Consider, for example, the story she tells about a synagogue near the northern end of the Sea of Galilee.

> While the Jews were building it, [Jesus] passed by and asked them, "What are you doing?" "Nothing," they replied. To which he said, "If nothing is what you are doing, then nothing it will be forever!" And thus it remains to this day. For afterwards, whenever the Jews attempted to build the synagogue, whatever work they accomplished during the day, collapsed in the night, and in the morning their building was at just the height it had been at the moment it was cursed.[36]

Here the present state of disrepair is explicable only in the light of history. Its significance is given by the past. But it is not just the ruin, of course, that is dignified by prophecy. The echoes of Penelope's fruitless labor insist upon the human conflict embedded in such stories. The rejection of a Jewish house of worship by the land itself voices a triumphalist theology: that Judaism has been superseded and therefore invalidated by Christianity. Egeria's blindness

32. Noted also by Marjo Westra, "The Pilgrim Egeria's Concept of Place," forthcoming in *Mittellateinisches Jahrbuch*.

33. Dennis Cosgrove, *Social Formation and Symbolic Landscape* (London: Croom Helm, 1984) 1–38. Alan R. Baker, "On Ideology and Landscape," in *Ideology and Landscape in Historical Perspective: Essays on the Meanings of Some Places in the Past* (ed. A. R. Baker and Gideon Biger; Cambridge: Cambridge University Press, 1992) 1–14. This process resembles the "framing and elevation" of attractions. Cf. MacCannell, "Staged Authenticity," 595–98; idem, *Tourist*, 44–45.

34. Wilken, *Land Called Holy*, 120.

35. Susan Stewart, *On Longing: Narratives of the Miniature, the Gigantic, the Souvenir, the Collection* (Durham N.C.: Duke University Press, 1993) 132–51. For examples, see Anton Legner (ed.), *Reliquien—Verehrung und Verklärung: Skizzen und Noten zur Thematik und Katalog zur Ausstellung der Kölner Sammlung Louis Peters im Schnütgen Museum* (Cologne: das Museum, 1989) esp. 70, 268, pls. 26 and 158.

36. *De Locis Sanctis* (PL 173 1128C).

to contemporary Jewish life is thus doubly endorsed by her perception of the testimony of the land as well as that of apocryphal scripture.

If uninterested in local inhabitants, Egeria does show some concern for the contemporary experience of other pilgrims. It is a present marked largely by devotional practices. She reports, for example, that there is a stone in the field where Jesus fed the five thousand with five loaves and two fishes, from which people take away small chips. The chips are reputed to bring "well-being" to their possessors, presumably because they retain some of the multiplying power that once made much out of little. "They are," Egeria adds, "helpful for everyone."[37] Close to Mt. Hermon is a spring "which the Savior blessed." Like Jesus, it too "strengthens sick people of all kinds," either, we may assume, through bathing or drinking.[38] In both of these devotions, we see how geographic features were used to make biblical events local and, therefore, present and accessible to pilgrims. Other gestures actually changed the face of the terrain. At the tomb of Jezebel, Egeria tells us, pilgrims customarily threw stones.[39] And, on the road to Gaza, a similar gesture, according to the Piacenza pilgrim, had heaped up such a mountain of stones over the tomb of Goliath that, "there was not a moveable stone to be found for twenty miles."[40] Through such actions, we see particularly vividly how the past acquires its own geography.

Egeria's prose, therefore, reveals the region's rapid architectural development. The many sites to visit in Galilee point, in turn, to a new value placed on Jesus' early ministry and the background of his apostles. Perhaps more strikingly, however, we also glimpse the incipient organization of the terrain into "landscape," as relatively unmarked terrain is gradually infused with meaning.[41] In this respect, Egeria's "map" of the Galilee is not unlike maps produced by Roman land surveyors of the same era. On these sketches, landmarks (both natural and manufactured) stand out against a relatively blank background.[42] A crucial difference, however, distinguishes the survey maps from Egeria's account: the time frame. For the land surveyors, a region's value lies in its present shape and development, but for Egeria, the value of the land depends on its biblical past. So strongly is this the case, that even her remarks about contemporary reality—the story of the half-built synagogue

37. "Salus," *De Locis Sanctis* (PL 173 1128B).

38. *De Locis Sanctis* (PL 173 1127A).

39. *De Locis Sanctis* (PL 173 1128D).

40. *Antonini Placentini Itinerarium* 5 (CCSL 175 144) [hereafter abbreviated *It. Plac.*].

41. Elsewhere, Egeria is explicit that it was the local monastic communities who were responsible for this development (*It. Eg.* 3.1, 4.8, 5.12, 11.1 [SC 296 128, 142, 148, 170]; cf. Hagith Sivan, "Pilgrimage, Monasticism and the Emergence of Christian Palestine in the 4th Century," in *The Blessings of Pilgrimage* [ed. Robert Ousterhout; Urbana: University of Illinois Press, 1990] 54–65).

42. Dilke, *Greek and Roman Maps*, 565. Robert K. Sherk notes the similarity in concept and composition between these surveyors' manuscripts and the Peutinger Table ("Roman Geographical Exploration and Military Maps," ANRW II.1 [1974] 534–62).

and the devotional practices of other pilgrims—derive their meaning from their relationship to the past.

The Piacenza Pilgrim

In 570, another anonymous pilgrim traveled from Piacenza, Italy to Palestine. In his richly textured account of the Galilee, the large areas left blank by the Bordeaux pilgrim or given a scriptural wash by Egeria are now filled in with crops and animals, peoples and customs. In Lynch's terms, districts have at last become meaningful and are therefore visible.

The prime feature of the Galilee is its fertility. This pilgrim describes the region around Nazareth as "a paradise: like Egypt in its wheat and fruit . . . but surpassing even Egypt in its wine, oil, and apples." Millet grows abnormally tall there, well above human height.[43] So lavish is this land that it influences even the people. Not only are the women of Nazareth exceptionally beautiful but, he adds, they are also "truly full of every kindness."[44]

This appreciation for regional diversity leads him, in turn, to record geographic contours with a new precision. He records that Mt. Tabor is six miles around at its base, three miles up, and has a level place at its top a mile long. Around the sea of Tiberias (or Galilee), it is sixty miles.[45] Suddenly, the entire region seems to have popped into focus.

An ancient analogue to this pilgrimage might therefore be the sixth-century mosaic map of the Land found in Madaba.[46] Like this pilgrim's careful measurements, this map is drawn with attention to contour and scale.[47] Figures populate the blank areas not, I suggest, out of *horror vacui*[48] ('a terror

---

43. "Provincia similis paradiso" (*It. Plac.* 5 [CCSL 175 131]). Mt. Tabor, he writes, has "fertile soil" and, in the place where the five thousand were fed, there "is a wide plain with olive and palm groves" (accepting Wilkinson's emendation that lines 20–21 have been misplaced and belong after 12 at the end of section 6; *It. Plac.* 6, 9 [CCSL 175 131, 133]). The region around Tabor was celebrated for its fertility by a seventh-century pilgrim and still famous for its wine in the thirteenth (Thomson, "Seventh-Century Armenian Pilgrim," 30; cf. Taylor, *Christians and the Holy Places*, 230–31).

44. "They say," he continues, "that this is Mary's gift to them, for they claim her as their ancestor (*parentem*)" (*It. Plac.* 5 [CCSL 175 131]).

45. *It. Plac.* 4, 6, 7 (CCSL 175 130–132).

46. Herbert Donner suggests that "the mosaic map looks like a cartographic illustration of two pilgrims' reports from the sixth century: the first one written by the archdeacon Theodosius (between 518 and 530), the other one by an anonymous pilgrim from Piacenza (shortly after 570)." It dates, therefore, from the second half of the sixth century (*The Mosaic Map of Madaba: An Introductory Guide* [Kampen: Kok Pharos, 1992] 14).

47. Donner notes that it "is the most exact map of Palestine before modern cartography" (ibid., 17–18). Yoram Tsafrir, however, objects that the Madaba map does not exhibit a high degree of exactitude, noting especially the distortion in the relationship between settlements ("The Maps Used by Theodosius," 136, 143).

48. Pace Donner, *Mosaic Map*, 29. Wilken agrees that these additions "helped create a sense of the region as a territory, a land, not simply as an assemblage of holy places" (*The Land Called Holy*, 177–78).

of emptiness') but rather from an enriched perception of the region. For if the artist had simply wished to fill in blank areas, surely any type of decoration would have done. But here the flora and fauna are typical of the region: date trees grow around Jericho, as do thorn bushes and Sodom apples, but at Mamre there is a terebinth. Fish swim downstream in the Jordan, except for the one closest to the Dead Sea, which wisely struggles against the current. A gazelle runs from a lion in the eastern Jordan Valley, but in the Nile Delta, a crocodile sports.[49]

Regrettably, the map is damaged and breaks off at Neapolis, just before the Galilee. But, from the flora and fauna around Jericho, we might suspect that the fertility of Galilee was once similarly expressed.[50] Indeed, the one small fragment of the Galilean portion of the map that has been recovered shows, not simply the town of Akbara, but also its location in the hills of Galilee and the generous plain stretching before it.[51]

Accuracy in representation seems such a self-evident good—a righteous concern with facticity—that we might easily overlook the crucial question of why this pilgrim was so concerned with precise delineation. It is a precision, furthermore, that has clear limits. After Egeria, the vague thinness of this pilgrim's scriptural knowledge is striking. Of Mt. Tabor, for example, he recalls only that it was the place where "one of the disciples said, 'Let us make three booths.'" Egeria would have known those were Peter's words. And, regarding the view from its peak, the Piacenza pilgrim simply observes, "various biblical cities with names from the book of Kings."[52] Given the selectivity of his precision, why is he so concerned with the measurement of holy places? He himself gives us the answer: measurement is connected to miracles. To possess the dimensions of a holy place, whether in strips of cloth or in standard units, promises the possessor access to that place's power.[53] The quantity of

49. Donner, *Mosaic Map*, 17–18. The Piacenza pilgrim saw crocodiles in the Nile (*It. Plac.* 45 [CCSL 175 152]). The human occupations are also realistic: on the Dead Sea, one boat rows against the wind carrying what appears to be a heap of salt; the other sails downwind with a load of wheat; the Piacenza pilgrim mentions that "sulphur and pitch are collected from the sea" (*It. Plac.* 10 [CCSL 175 134]).

50. The region around Jericho is also described as "a paradise" (*It. Plac.* 13 [CCSL 175 136]).

51. ΑΓΒΑΡΩΝ. Donner suggests that this is identical with ʿAkbara, located about 2.5 km south of Safad in Upper Galilee, mentioned by Josephus (*J.W.* 2.573) under the name Ἀκχαβάρων πέτρα 'the rock of the Akabarites'. If so, then the three circles below the representation might be the waters of Merom (Josh 11:5–7), and the plain the plateau west of Safad (Donner, *Mosaic Map*, 97).

52. *It. Plac.* 6 (CCSL 175 131; cf. 22, CCSL 175 140). Similarly, on their route down through the Galilee to Scythopolis, which he rightly notes is the capital (*metropolis*) of Galilee, he comments simply that they "passed through many cities mentioned in Scripture" (*It. Plac.* 8 [CCSL 175 133]).

53. *It. Plac.* 22–23 (CCSL 175 140). For a discussion of "measures," see Robert Ousterhout, "Loca Sancta and the Architectural Response to Pilgrimage," in his *Blessings of Pilgrimage*, 109–24.

measurements in Galilee, therefore, underscores this pilgrim's perception of the region as a place of miracles. And the miracles, in turn, reinforce his perception of the prodigiousness of the Land. Nowhere is this clearer than in the miracles he records, because all are examples of astonishing fertility: not only the virginal conception but also the water becoming wine and the five loaves feeding five thousand people. Those that do not stress the fertility of the region he passes over in silence. Unlike Egeria, he has no interest in Jesus' walking on the water, exorcising a demoniac or healing the paralytic.

But if scripture and geography combine to proclaim a region of supernatural abundance, the question of access becomes acute. Measurement, as we have seen, is one means, but it is not the most common. Bathing, as in the spring at Cana and the hot sea baths at Tiberias, is more common and shares with measurements a strongly curative dimension.[54] The relationship between scripture and the Land, however, is mediated most often through specific objects that serve to direct the pilgrim's attention to place.[55] In Sepphoris, for example, our pilgrim "venerated what they said was the flagon and bread-basket of Saint Mary," as well as the chair on which she was reputedly sitting when the angel came to her.[56] At Cana, he fills one of the two jars left from Jesus' day with wine and offers it at the altar. On the couch where Jesus had lain to eat, he not only reclines but actually scratches into its surface the names of his parents.[57] In Nazareth, he goes into the synagogue and lifts the bench on which Jesus sat as a child and peers into the book in which he wrote his ABCs.[58]

The purpose of such collections is not, as we might initially suppose, simply to preserve the past. For even this pilgrim seems to register some doubt over the authenticity of these objects when he writes that the pitcher and bread-basket were only "reputed to be" those used by Mary. Instead, the objects seem specifically designed to prompt the kind of action he does indeed take. Their purpose, in other words, is to access the past. As Maurice Halbwachs observes, religious memory must always be "reconstructed" by means, not only of the material traces and traditions of the past, but also by means of recent social and psychological data—that is, the present.[59] By lifting jars at

---

54. *It. Plac.* 4, 7 (CCSL 175 130, 132).

55. J. Z. Smith, *To Take Place*, 103–6; cf. 24–46, 86–87.

56. *It. Plac.* 4 (CCSL 175 130). The Marian associations of Galilee are striking. Taylor concludes from her study of graffiti at Nazareth that "pilgrims came to Nazareth to venerate Mary" (*Christians and the Holy Places*, 259–60).

57. *It. Plac.* 4 (CCSL 175 130). For graffiti on the walls of sanctuaries, see Pierre Maraval, *Lieux saints et pèlerinages d'orient* (Paris: du Cerf, 1985) 232–33.

58. *It. Plac.* 5 (CCSL 175 130–31). For a discussion of the possible Jewish-Christian origins of this shrine, see Taylor, *Christians and the Holy Places*, 221–67, esp. p. 229.

59. Maurice Halbwachs, *On Collective Memory*, 119. See also David Lowenthal, *The Past Is a Foreign Country* (Cambridge: Cambridge University Press, 1985) esp. pp. 185–259. Wilken coins the happy phrase "tactile piety" to describe these ritual reenactments (*The Land Called Holy*, 115–16).

Cana, the Piacenza pilgrim locates sacred history not only in a place, but also in his present, thereby "memorizing" it anew.

These objects provide a space for the interaction of past and present in yet another way: these gestures promote group identity by excluding others. If Christians can lift the synagogue bench on which Jesus sat "and move it about," "the Jews are unable to move it by any means and cannot carry it outside."[60] The quality of this information is strongly reminiscent of Egeria's story of the half-built synagogue: both stress the inability of the Jews and their superseded status. A couple of lines later, the Piacenza pilgrim writes frankly that "there is no love lost between Jews and Christians."[61] Nevertheless, his comments show none of the dislike reserved for the Samaritans. Of them, he writes, that

> whenever we passed along the streets [of their villages] they burned away our footprints with straw, whether we were Christians or Jews, they have such a horror (*execratio*) of both. This is what they tell Christians, "Don't touch what you want to buy until you have paid the money. If you do touch anything without buying it there will soon be trouble (*scandalum*)." Outside each village there is a guard to give this warning. You must put your money into water, since they will not take it from your hand. When you arrive they curse you. Nor must you spit. If you do, you start trouble, and later they have to purify themselves with water before entering their village or city.[62]

Yet, even this record of ill will attests an almost ethnographic interest in the indigenous peoples: how they form a group delineated from others through distinctive customs and gestures.[63] They exist for this pilgrim in the present; their interest is not solely in the gift of the past.

The Piacenza pilgrim's perceptions of the Land, therefore, show everywhere a vivid blend of past and present. Unlike Egeria's serene encounter with the past, this pilgrim describes a terrain in which the past jostles against the present on every side.[64] It is a region where the contemporary beauty of Nazarene women makes present the distant loveliness of Mary and where the long-ago miracle of the multiplication of loaves is ratified each year in the abundant yields of the land. This temporal jostling is, moreover, responsible for giving this account its crowded feel: the sense that there is simply too much to see in a land where every fragment bears abundant meaning. Once the entire region

60. *It. Plac.* 5 (CCSL 175 131).
61. *Ibid.*
62. *It. Plac.* 8 (CCSL 175 13), trans. John Wilkinson, *Jerusalem Pilgrims before the Crusades* (Warminster: Aris & Phillips, 1977) 81.
63. See also his remarks on the Ethiopians and a Saracen rite (*It. Plac.* 35, 38 [CCSL 175 147, 148]).
64. Compare Rehav Rubin, "Ideology and Landscape in Early Printed Maps of Jerusalem," in *Ideology and Landscape in Historical Perspective: Essays on the Meanings of Some Places in the Past* (ed. A. R. Baker and Gideon Biger; Cambridge: Cambridge University Press, 1992) 15–30, esp. pp. 24–28.

has become holy, everything it contains takes on value. As Jonathan Smith observes, "sacrality is, above all, a category of emplacement."[65]

Conclusion

The partial and idiosyncratic maps sketched by early Christian pilgrims allow a glimpse, not only of the ongoing transformation of the Land, but also of the changing interests and social formation of the viewers. The earliest account concentrates on the road itself and on architectural landmarks. Having no such markers, the Galilee was not worth a visit. In Egeria's text, we see not only the rapid development of the region, as shrines increasingly marked off sites as holy, but also the incipient organization of the terrain into meaningful landscape. Theories of "marker-sight" interaction, borrowed from the sociology of tourism, explain Egeria's participation in this process. It is her willingness to connect scripture with relatively unmarked geographic sites that infuses the Galilean terrain with meaning. By the time of the Piacenza pilgrim, the whole region has become meaningful as a place of miraculous fertility and therefore, finally, visible.

Even these few pilgrim accounts attest how profoundly a sense of the geography of the Galilee was shaped by and, in turn, expressed a vivid sense of history. From the silence of the Bordeaux pilgrim to the rich jumble of the Piacenza pilgrim, we see the shifting geography of the past.

65. Smith, *To Take Place*, 104.

Visible Ghosts and Invisible Demons
The Place of Jews in Early Christian *Terra Sancta*

ANDREW S. JACOBS
Duke University

In 351 C.E., Cyril, bishop of Jerusalem, dashed off an eager letter to the young Emperor Constantius to report a dazzling miracle that had lit up Jerusalem's Easter skies:

> A gigantic and luminous cross was seen in the sky above holy [*hagios*] Golgotha, extending as far as the holy Mount of Olives. . . . Immediately the whole population, overcome with joy mingled with fear of the heavenly vision, hastened to the Holy Church: young and old, people of both sexes and every age, even to the maidens closeted in their homes, local and foreign Christians, as well as visiting pagans.[1]

Cyril's description of both the city and its inhabitants is noteworthy. As in his more famous *Catecheses*, Cyril has configured Jerusalem as contiguous pockets of "holy" sites. The "luminous cross" stretches appropriately from the Mount of Olives, where Jesus' passion began, to Golgotha, where it ended. Furthermore, Jerusalem's "whole population" numbers the old, young, men, women, locals, foreigners, Christians, and pagans.

A later homily composed in Cyril's name evidently found this diverse catalogue of inhabitants wanting. A Coptic "Homily on the Virgin"[2] has

---

1. Cyril of Jerusalem, *Epistula ad Constantium* 4; text in J. Rupp (ed.), *Cyrilli Hierosolymum Archiepiscopi Opera* (2 vols.; Munich: Stahl, 1860) 2.434–41, here 2.436. Translation by Leo P. McCauley, *The Works of Saint Cyril of Jerusalem* (2 vols.; Fathers of the Church 61 and 64 [hereafter FC];Washington: Catholic University of American Press, 1968–70); here FC 64 232–33. On the date of the letter, see P. W. L. Walker, *Holy City, Holy Places? Christian Attitudes to Jerusalem and the Holy Land in the Fourth Century* (Oxford: Clarendon, 1990) 410.

2. Three versions of this homily are extant: two in the Pierpont Morgan collection (MS 583 and 597: see Leo Depuydt, *Catalogue of Coptic Manuscripts in the Pierpont Morgan*

incorporated this miraculous moment from the authentic Cyril's career, flesh-ing in some demographic detail with more appropriate "native" populations:

> You heard about the honor of the cross and its appearance for the conversion of
> Gentiles to the true knowledge of Christ; how Castor, prince of the Jews, be-
> lieved with his whole family and became a chosen Christian. I also baptized a
> host of Samaritans, among them Isaac the Joppite whom I converted in this
> way.[3]

For the pseudonymous homilist of the seventh or eighth century, Jews and Samaritans naturally supplement the sacred landscape of Jerusalem as "na-tives" who would be swayed by the power of Jesus manifest at Easter.

This disjunction between our two "Cyrils" demonstrates how the percep-tion of the Christian holy land in antiquity could be altered or transformed, irrespective of demographic "reality." We shall see that material and literary evidence leave little doubt that Jews populated areas of the Palestinian prov-inces in Late Antiquity. When we interrogate the texts that delineate Christian *terra sancta*, however, we shall find many authors reticent to acknowledge this presence (as in this letter of Cyril's). This reticence is further coupled with a sense that Jews hover on the fringes of Christian reality, an ethnic and theolog-ical danger to the holy land. Sifting through physical and literary remains of the post-Constantinian holy land, I shall analyze this tension between Jews' material visibility and conceptual "presence" as a way of studying how late an-cient Christians configured their religious, historical, and spatial subjectivity.

"Bound in a Certain Region":
Establishing Jewish Visibility

Possibly when Cyril wrote his letter to Constantius, Hadrian's ban on Jews in Aelia Capitolina remained in force and not a single Jew was to be found in or near the holy city.[4] Elsewhere Cyril is quite loquacious on the subject of Jews, as well as Samaritans, making the cryptic remark in his catechetical lec-tures that, "while the Jews are within the bounds of a certain region, the Christians reach to the ends of the earth."[5] Since Jews at that time probably extended as far into the diaspora as Christians, Cyril may be referring here to the "bounded" habitation of Jews in the Palestinian provinces of his day.[6]

Library [Leuven: Peeters, 1993] 2.325–28, 2.205–7, respectively) and a third in the British Museum collection (see E. A. Wallis Budge, *Miscellaneous Coptic Texts in the Dialect of Upper Egypt* [London: British Museum, 1915] 49–73, 626–51). Pierpont Morgan MS 583 is cited here, in my own translation.

3. Cyril, "Homily on the Virgin," MS 583, folio 140 recto.

4. For reconstructions of Hadrian's ban, see Walker, *Holy City*, 8 and note.

5. Cyril of Jerusalem, *Catecheses* 10.16 (Rupp 1.282).

6. On the troublesome omnipresence of Jews in the diaspora in this period, see Fergus Millar, "The Jews of the Graeco-Roman Diaspora between Paganism and Christianity, A.D.

Specific population numbers for Jews in late ancient Palestine remain elu-
sive,[7] but more certain is their demographic restriction to certain regions:
Galilee, the Golan, the cities of Lydda/Diospolis and Jamnia/Yavneh west of
Jerusalem, and the southern district known as the "Darom."[8] Scholars also
tend to emphasize "the segregation and ethnic seclusion that characterized
Roman-Byzantine Palestine in general,"[9] envisioning mixing only in dense
urban centers. Given the relatively close distances in Palestine in this period,
however, it is possible that even a village made up entirely of Jews would
never be too far from the habitations, and thus the "visibility," of Christians,
Gentiles, or Samaritans.[10]

It is also generally agreed that, despite an increase in the overall Byzantine
Period population of Palestine, the Jewish population dropped markedly.[11]
Even Michael Avi-Yonah's notably optimistic study of Roman-Byzantine Jews
concedes that "a sharp decline had occurred in the number of Jews in Palestine, both absolutely and in proportion to the rest of the inhabitants. This fact
was to have important political consequences."[12] One would also imagine
consequences on the cultural construction of the Christian sacred landscape:
surely such factors as highly-concentrated regions of Jewish habitation and
dwindling numbers of Jews would influence how Christians conceived of
their holy land? As we shall see when examining the relevant literature, however, "real" numbers have little impact on the cultural imaginary.

To focus more sharply on the question of Jewish "visibility" in the holy
land, we should consider the specific matter of Jews in or near sites that were
designated as *loca sancta* by Christians. Excavations of key centers of Christian worship reveal a late ancient physical presence that many would not

---

312–438," in *The Jews among Pagans and Christians in the Roman Empire* (ed. Judith Lieu,
John North, and Tessa Rajak; London: Routledge, 1992) 97–123.

7. For various estimates, see M. Broshi, "The Population of Western Palestine in the
Roman-Byzantine Period," *BASOR* 236 (1979) 1–10; Y. Tsafrir, "Introduction," in *Tabula
Imperii Romani—Iudaea, Palaestina: Eretz Israel in the Hellenistic, Roman, and Byzantine
Periods—Maps and Gazetteer* (ed. Y. Tsafrir, L. Di Segni, and J. Green; Jerusalem: Israel
Academy of Sciences and Humanities, 1994) 18; M. Avi-Yonah, *The Jews of Palestine* (New
York: Schocken, 1976) 19.

8. Ibid., 17; Tsafrir, *Tabula Imperii Romani*, 18–19; Joan E. Taylor, *Christians and the
Holy Places: The Myth of Jewish-Christian Origins* (Oxford: Clarendon, 1993) 48–56.

9. Zvi U. Maʿoz, "Comments on Jewish and Christian Communities in Byzantine
Palestine," *PEQ* 117 (1985) 59–68, here 65. See also Tsafrir, *Tabula Imperii Romani*, 18–19;
Dennis Groh, "Jews and Christians in Late Roman Palestine: Towards a New Chronology," *BA* 51 (1988) 80–96. E. W. Saunders ("Christian Synagogues and Jewish Christianity
in Galiee," *explor* 3 [1977] 70–77) argues for stricter segregation, even in urban centers;
Eric M. Meyers ("Early Judaism and Christianity in the Light of Archaeology," *BA* 51
[1988] 69–79) proposes a broader "religious pluralism."

10. See the comments of Taylor, *Christians and the Holy Places*, 84.

11. Safrai, *Economy*, 436–58, esp. p. 442; Tsafrir, *Tabula Imperii Romani*, 19.

12. Avi-Yonah, *Jews of Palestine*, 241; see also pp. 25–29.

hesitate to label "Jewish." Mamre, for example, presents both archaeological and literary signs of a sustained intermingling of Jews and Samaritans, as well as "pagans" and eventually Christians. The cultural and economic mixing at Mamre's popular fair testifies to the atmosphere of "religious pluralism" suggested by Eric Meyers.[13] As rabbis denounce the contamination by "idolaters" and Constantine attempts to exclude non-Christians in order to "restore" an ancient Christian shrine, we have the sense that Jews, Christians, and "pagans" at Mamre remained through this period "visibly" in each other's sights.[14]

Two other sites that might suggest high Jewish "visibility," however, have undergone a subtle academic shading that has relegated them to a nebulous field of religious and cultural uncertainty. Both are villages that claim to be "hometowns" of Jesus: Nazareth, where he grew up, and Capernaum, which acted as the base of his Galilean ministry in the Synoptic Gospels.[15] I present them here as indicative of the difficulties modern scholars find (and manufacture) in reconciling their preconceptions about the place of Jews in the rise of the Christian holy land and reasons why a more careful treatment of material visibility and cultural presence is in order.

Since the late 1960s, the village of Nazareth has been held up as the classic site of "Jewish-Christianity," a Palestinian phenomenon hypothesized by Italian scholars Bellarmino Bagatti and Emmanuele Testa.[16] Jewish-Christians are central to their particular reconstruction of the Christian holy land, insofar as they supposedly preserved many *loca sancta* from the death of Jesus until the advent of Constantine. The archaeological report of Nazareth's Franciscan excavator, Bagatti himself, is thus geared toward demonstrating the very early date of the Mary-shrine there, protected by these Jewish-Christians.[17] This historiographic framework has its difficulties on many fronts, one complication being the near erasure of Jews in ancient Nazareth. By labeling a structure found beneath the Byzantine basilica a "Jewish-Christian synagogue," Bagatti can practically dismiss with very little discussion a *Jewish* synagogue uncovered elsewhere.[18] In addition, finds that might otherwise be labeled "Jewish" (such as burial remains) are transformed into

---

13. See above, n. 9; on the Mamre fair as a religious mixing, see Taylor, *Christians and the Holy Places,* 86–95; on the fair as economic mixing, see Safrai, *Economy,* 243–62.

14. Rabbinic injunctions: Safrai, *Economy,* 253–54; Constantine's "restoration": Taylor, *Christians and the Holy Places,* 92–94. Archaeological reports in E. Mader, *Mambre: Die Ergebnisse der Ausgrabungen im heiligen Bezirk, Ramat el-Halil in Süd-Palästina, 1926–1928* (2 vols.; Frieburg in Breisgau: Erich Wewel, 1957) esp. 1.95–103.

15. See, for example, Mark 1:9 and 2:1.

16. For a summary of their argument, see B. Bagatti, *The Church from the Circumcision* (trans. E. Hoade; Studium Biblicum Franciscanum Collectio Minor 2; Jerusalem: Franciscan Press, 1971) 3–60; Taylor, *Christians and the Holy Places,* 1–47.

17. B. Bagatti, *Gli Scavi di Nazaret, Volume I: Dalle Origini al Secolo XII* (Studium Biblicum Franciscanum Collectio Maior 17/1; Jerusalem: Franciscan Press, 1967).

18. Ibid., 111 and 226.

evidence of this continued Jewish-Christian presence dating back to the crucifixion.[19]

The entire "Bagatti-Testa hypothesis" and its attendant conclusions have been incisively critiqued by Joan Taylor. Taylor reexamines the significance of Nazareth's material remains without assuming the presence of "Jewish-Christians" and finds no evidence for Christians before the fourth century—the date of the earliest Christian structure in the grove of the Annunciation—after Constantine began his Christian building projects. She goes so far as to assert that "the town was clearly Jewish until the seventh century."[20] While perhaps her supposition of Jewish *control* over the Christian pilgrimage site may be exaggerated (and her explanation that Jews in Nazareth tolerated Christian building and pilgrimage "for the sake of the appreciative 'tourist dollar'"[21] may be subject to unfortunate interpretation), Taylor's rereading of the evidence stands as a useful corrective to Bagatti's predetermined archaeological "findings."

Capernaum also stands as an excellent case study in the deleterious muddling of historiographic "common senses." The remains of a monumental Jewish synagogue and an impressive church dedicated to Peter have been uncovered there "on opposite sides of the street."[22] Dating of the church has proceeded without much ado, with the monumental octagonal structure assigned to the fifth century; a less securely-dated fourth-century "house-church" marked by international graffiti has been uncovered beneath it.[23] The synagogue, on the other hand, has been the object of rancorous debate. In the 1970s two Franciscan archaeologists challenged the dating of the synagogue to the second or third century C.E. and proposed a date in "the last decade of the fourth to the mid–fifth century C.E."[24] Opponents reiterated their architectural, stylistic, and historical arguments against this late date: architecturally, this synagogue was of the "Galilean" type, traditionally assigned to the second and third centuries;[25] stylistically, the façade seemed more Roman than the "interiorized" Byzantine structures of a later date;[26] and historically,

19. Ibid., 230–38, esp. p. 236.

20. Taylor, *Christians and the Holy Places*, 221–67, here 228.

21. Ibid., 228–29. Taylor clearly seeks to empower late ancient Jews, but such easy explanations as "commercial gain" (p. 228) may mask more complex cultural and political issues involved in the appropriation of Jewish space by pilgrims.

22. Meyers, "Early Judaism and Christianity," 76.

23. For a detailed summary of the archaeological reports see Taylor, *Christians and the Holy Places*, 268–74.

24. S. Loffreda, "The Late Chronology of the Synagogue of Capernaum," *IEJ* 23 (1973) 37–43, here 37.

25. On the tripartite chronological division of synagogue types, see M. Avi-Yonah, "Synagogue Architecture in the Late Classical Period," in *Jewish Art: An Illustrated History* (ed. Cecil Roth; New York: McGraw-Hill, 1961) 157–90.

26. G. Foerster, "Notes on Recent Excavations at Capernaum," *IEJ* 21 (1971) 207–11, esp. p. 207. Foerster relies on art historian Richard Krautheimer, whose own opinions on Byzantine "stylistics" have been critiqued: see Annabel Wharton, *Refiguring the Post Classical*

the contemporaneous construction of a monumental synagogue and church seemed unlikely, if not fanciful. As Avi-Yonah dryly commented: "Such a state of affairs might be conceivable in our own ecumenical age, but it seems almost impossible to imagine that it would have been allowed by the Byzantine authorities."[27]

Over the past decades two of these supports have been undermined: the chronological division of synagogue types has been superseded by a regional categorization,[28] while the notion of historically fixed artistic "styles," such as Roman exteriority versus Byzantine interiority, has likewise been deflated.[29] This leaves as the principal argument for early dating of the synagogue the historiographic presuppositions of "how things were" in ancient Capernaum. Despite Avi-Yonah's concern with overly "archaeologizing" history ("we should avoid staring, as if hypnotized, at the five-meter squares of a locus and basing all of our arguments on the finds in such a small area"),[30] there is a certain circularity involved in dismissing archaeological evidence because a situation *seems* historically "impossible." Joan Taylor's response has been to reverse Avi-Yonah's presumed power structures in early Byzantine Capernaum:

> The contemporaneity of two buildings is only a problem if we insist that the Christian authorities exercised an effective absolute rule over Capernaum. There is no real evidence to show that they did. The situation may well have been quite the reverse; *only this would account for the archaeological evidence.* The Jewish authorities of Capernaum permitted the construction of a small Christian pilgrimage site.[31]

Taylor's reassignment of political agency would certainly allow for Jews to build whatever they pleased in Capernaum, but unfortunately the evidence for such sustained autonomy into the Byzantine Period is lacking. Taylor moves quickly from still-contested moments of Jewish emancipation in the fourth century, such as the "Gallus revolt" and Julian the Apostate's brief, abortive promise of Jewish resettlement in Jerusalem,[32] to Jewish autonomy

---

City: Dura Europos, Jerash, Jerusalem and Ravenna (Cambridge: Cambridge University Press, 1995) 70–72 and 96–97.

27. M. Avi-Yonah, "Some Comments on the Capernaum Excavations," in *Ancient Synagogues Revealed* (ed. Lee Levine; Jerusalem: Israel Exploration Society, 1981) 60–62, here 62.

28. Rachel Hachlili, "Synagogues in the Land of Israel: The Art and Architecture of Late Antique Synagogues," in *Sacred Realm: The Emergence of the Synagogue in the Ancient World* (ed. Steven Fine; Oxford: Oxford University Press / New York: Yeshiva University Museum, 1996) 99–102 and notes (p. 180); Steven Fine and Eric Meyers, "Synagogues," *OEANE* 5.118–23.

29. See above, n. 26.

30. Avi-Yonah, "Some Comments," 61.

31. Taylor, *Christians and the Holy Places*, 293, emphasis mine. Ironically, Taylor is playing Avi-Yonah's optimistic vision of Byzantine Jewry (see Avi-Yonah, *Jews of Palestine,* 237–40, cited by Taylor, p. 292) against his archaeological pessimism.

32. Taylor, *Christians and the Holy Places*, 292–93, again relying on Avi-Yonah.

and freedom from Byzantine (essentially Christian) authority into the fifth century. This ignores, to name but one stumbling block, Theodosius's declaration of Christianity as the official imperial religion in 391, as well as subsequent legislation against Jews in the East. In extending her argument against Bagatti's Jewish-Christians, Taylor has ended up transposing one set of over-determined historiographic assumptions for another. Yet if we cannot explain the tension between "visibility" and "presence" in terms of simple power structures—minority subjugation = invisibility/absence or the reverse—we should then reevaluate the complexity of these issues in the construction of the Christian holy land. Having established at least a bare Jewish "visibility" at key sites of Christian *sanctitas*, I shall now attempt to outline how and when such visibility translated into a conceptual "presence."

"They Mourn and Rend Their Garments": *Constructing Jewish Presence*

Recently Blake Leyerle has explored the cultural construction of a Christian landscape with the understanding that "we make our own geography in much the same way that we make our own history."[33] Her astute study outlines a cognitive shift whereby naked routes and cartographic edges become filled in by pilgrims with a "real interest in local flora, fauna, and peoples."[34] I would like to build on Leyerle's work by particularizing this inclusion of "peoples" in the evolving Christian holy land. Specifically, through reading the literary productions of post-Constantinian Christians I want to ask how Jews were incorporated into this sacred space *as* Jews. It will become clear that the presence or nonpresence of Jews in the Christian holy land has little to do with "real" Jewish visibility and shifts instead within a framework of biblical succession and proximal anxiety typified by two fourth-century Palestinian bishops.

Eusebius of Caesarea exemplifies what I call a more relaxed "successionist" conception of Jews. Early in his career Eusebius attempted to align biblical place-names with contemporary topography in his *Onomastikon*.[35] This tract was fourth in a series that had so far included a Greek translation of Hebrew names, a register of ancient Judea by tribe, and a plan of Jerusalem and the Temple.[36] As Dennis Groh points out, the *Onomastikon* also fits conceptually into Eusebius's larger historiographic project:

---

33. Blake Leyerle, "Landscape as Cartography in Early Christian Pilgrim Narratives," *JAAR* 64 (1996) 119–43, here 120. As will be clear, I am greatly indebted to the theoretical and historical ground that Leyerle has broken in this piece.

34. Ibid., 138.

35. On the date of the *Onomastikon*, see T. D. Barnes, "The Composition of Eusebius' *Onomasticon*," *JTS* n.s. 26 (1975) 412–14.

36. Eusebius *Onomastikon* 2.5–12 (text edited by E. Klostermann; GCS 11.3; Leipzig: Hinrichs, 1904). References are to page and line numbers in the critical edition.

In the *Onomasticon* Eusebius is doing spatially (and alphabetically) what he has already done chronologically in the *Chronicon* and what he will go on to do narratively in the *History*—namely, bring biblical, Roman, and Christian realities together in such a way that Christianity in his own day can be seen to be the successor of the biblical realities in the Roman world.[37]

This judicious reading of Eusebius's world-view consigns such contemporary Jews as are listed in the *Onomastikon*[38] to the disappearing "biblical reality" now supplanted by the Christian present. Later, in his *Ecclesiastical History* Eusebius will depict Jews in this same ghostly half-light, slowly vanishing from Christian reality. The list of bishops of Jerusalem given in Book Four demonstrates this evanescent Jewish presence:

> Up to Hadrian's siege of the Jews there had been a series of fifteen bishops there. All are said to have been Hebrews in origin. . . . For at that time their church consisted of Hebrew believers who had continued from apostolic times down to the later siege in which the Jews, after revolting a second time from the Romans, were overwhelmed in a full-scale war. As that meant the end of the bishops of the circumcision, *this is the right moment* to list their names from the first.[39]

Because the history of these Jews has ended, it is now appropriate to make them historically "visible" to the reader: this historicizing makes the Jews both present yet "safe" by framing them in an irrevocable past-tense. We can imagine Eusebius performing a similar task topographically in the *Onomastikon*, crowding Jews into a space that, through biblical place-names, in fact encrypts them into a scriptural past, making way for a triumphant Christian present. In this way, Jews achieve a measure of "visible absence" in the Eusebian holy land as vague, fleeting ghosts.

Next to Eusebius's translucent phantoms we can juxtapose the demonic, yet invisible "presences" found in the alarmist *Catecheses* of Cyril of Jerusalem.[40] While absent from Cyril's "miraculous" holy land, as we saw above, Jews nonetheless linger unseen at the door of the catechetical lecture hall, waiting to lead Cyril's vulnerable catechumens into apostasy. From the first lecture Cyril sets a tone of holy warfare for his would-be "Christian soldiers": "You are taking up arms against heresies, against Jews, against the Samaritans, against the Gentiles. Your enemies are many: take plenty of ammunition."[41]

---

37. Dennis Groh, "The *Onomasticon* of Eusebius and the Rise of Christian Palestine," *Studia Patristica* 18 (1983) 23–31, here 29.

38. 'Jewish towns' (*kômai tôn Ioudaiôn*) described by Eusebius are: Accaron (22.9), Anab/Anea (26.9), Dabeira (78.6), Engaddi (86.18), Esthemo (86.22), Eremmon (88.17), Zeib/Zif/Carmelis (92.21), Thalcha (98.26), Jettan (108.9), Nineveh of Arabia (136.2), and Naaratha (136.25).

39. Eusebius *Historia Ecclesiastica* 4.5.2–5 (GCS 2.1). Translation by G. A. Williamson, *Eusebius: The History of the Church from Christ to Constantine* (London: Penguin, 1989) 107, emphasis mine.

40. Probably delivered while Cyril was still a priest: Walker, *Holy City*, 410.

41. Cyril *Procatechesis* 10 (Rupp 1.14; FC 61 78).

Jews are often lumped into this horde of "enemies," but they also merit special attention as the paradigmatic unbelievers, "ever ready to object and slow to believe."[42] When his charges roam unattended between lectures, Cyril imagines these devious Jews will attack and sully their incomplete formation. His thus frames his advice for "if the Jews ever trouble you," and he announces curtly that his Trinitarian exposition, for example, is being given "because of the Jews."[43] Inscribing this invisible demonic presence spatially, Cyril indicates to his "hearers" the empty space occupied just moments before by these villains: "Because of these words of Jesus, 'There will not be left here one stone upon another' (Matt 24:2) the Temple of the Jews just opposite us is fallen."[44] The proximate desolation of the Temple Mount stands in all its naked glory as a reminder of a shattered and angry presence, waiting in shadows to burst in: "For if he [the Antichrist] is to come as Christ to the Jews and wants their worship . . . he will manifest the great zeal for the Temple; he will create the impression that he is the descendent of David who is to restore the Temple of Solomon."[45] Jews for Cyril are "present" by their menacing invisibility;[46] they linger on the edges of Christian reality "bound" away in their particular regions of Palestine, committing acts so shameful that Cyril will not even speak of them.[47] Between these two poles of Christian inculturation—Eusebian "succession," in which visibility is domesticated into a historicized absence, and Cyrilian "alarm," in which invisibility betokens a threatening presence—literary productions of the Christian holy land by travelers and others will seek to encode Palestinian Jews into sacred Christian geography.

The earliest extant pilgrimage text comes from an early-fourth-century traveler from Bordeaux. As Leyerle points out, "His account lacks any real interest in the native terrain, flora, fauna, or people,"[48] focusing instead on the ardor of travel and the difficult yet attainable goal of pilgrimage. What people we do encounter in the Bordeaux pilgrim's holy land resonate with the scripturally-encrypted ghosts of Eusebius's *Onomastikon*: just as Eusebius reconfigured a contemporary space into a historical land of biblical tribes and villages, so too the Bordeaux pilgrim arrives through his spatial journey to a distinctly historicized reality. Most of the "Jews" he encounters are entombed or legendary figures from the Old Testament: at Neapolis, for instance, the

42. Cyril, *Catecheses* 13.7 (Rupp 2.58; FC 64 8–9).
43. Cyril, *Catecheses* 4.12, 10.8 (Rupp 1.102, 270; FC 61 125, 200).
44. Cyril, *Catecheses* 10.11 (Rupp 1.277; FC 61 203).
45. Cyril, *Catecheses* 15.15 (Rupp 2.172–73; FC 64 62). Cyril ironically anticipates the threatened resettlement by Julian in 363; perhaps Jews were vocal enough about their desire, or Christians about their fear, for Julian to exploit.
46. On the simultaneously reassuring and menacing "erasure" left as visible *spolia* in Christian Jerusalem, see Wharton, *Refiguring the Post Classical City*, 94–104.
47. Cyril, *Catecheses* 12.17 (Rupp 2.24; FC 61 238), specifically the shameful "doings concerning those who are nowadays called 'patriarchs' among them."
48. Leyerle, "Landscape as Cartography," 123–24.

landscape is peopled by the conjured ghosts of Abraham sacrificing, Joseph being buried, Jacob bestowing land, and Dinah being abducted.[49]

This temporal distortion is most evident as the pilgrim moves across the Temple Mount, where we get the nearest glimpse of nonbiblical Jews. The complex folding of time and space necessitates a long citation:

> In Jerusalem beside the Temple are two large pools, one to the right and the other to the left, built by Solomon, and inside the city are the twin pools with five porches called Bethsaida. . . . There is also a vault there where Solomon used to torture demons, and the corner of a very lofty tower, which was where the Lord climbed and said to the Tempter, "Thou shalt not tempt the Lord thy God, but him only shalt thou serve." . . . Below the pinnacle of this tower are very many chambers where Solomon had his palace. . . . And in the sanctuary itself, where the Temple stood which Solomon built, there is marble in front of the altar which has on it the blood of Zacharias—you would think it had only been shed today. All around you can see the marks of the hobnails of the soldiers who killed him, as plainly as if they had been pressed into wax. Two statues of Hadrian stand there and, not far from them, a pierced stone which the Jews come and anoint each year. They mourn and rend their garments and then depart. There too is the house of Hezekiah, king of Judah.[50]

Mostly, the Temple grounds are linked to their most ancient proprietor, Solomon; but as the empty space signifying the invisible presence of the Jews grows nearer, time loops in on itself. Suddenly, we are spectators at Jesus' temptation, and the murder of John the Baptist's father by Herod's soldiers (an apocryphal tale derived from confusion between John's father and an Old Testament Zechariah; the site and manner of murder here are more appropriate to the apocryphal account).[51] Mention of Hadrian's statues brings us one step away from the biblical era, evoking the final desolation and exile of the Jews. At the heart of the empty Temple Mount we "see" the invisible phantoms themselves, exiled Jews mourning in true Old Testament style. It is significant that the pilgrim himself does not witness this strange

49. *Itinerarium Burdigalense* 587.2–588.2 (text edited by P. Geyer and O. Cuntz; CCSL 175; Turnhout: Brepols, 1965) 13–14. Numbering follows the edition of P. Wesseling (see CCSL 175, *monitum*). Translated by John Wilkinson, *Egeria's Travels to the Holy Land* (Jerusalem: Ariel, 1981) 153–63; here 154–55. See now the valuable overview and suggestions of Laurie Douglass, "A New Look at the *Itinerarium Burdigalense*," *Journal of Early Christian Studies* 4 (1996) 313–33, including discussion of the Bordeaux pilgrim's class and gender.

50. *Itinerarium Burdigalense* 589.7–591.7 (CCSL 175 14–16; Wilkinson, *Egeria*, 155–57).

51. The Old Testament Zechariah, son of Jehoiada, was stoned to death in the court (2 Chr 24:20–22), not stabbed on the altar. Confusion derives from Luke 11:50–51, which contrasts Abel and Zechariah (the first and last murder victims in the Hebrew Bible) while elsewhere discussing Zechariah, the Baptist's father. Matt 23:5 clumsily introduces a third Zechariah, the minor prophet. The story of the murder of the Baptist's father by Herod's soldiers was circulated from the second century C.E. on in the *Protevangelium of James* 23.1–3 (in J. K. Elliott, *The Apocryphal New Testament* [Oxford: Clarendon, 1993] 66).

rite, but having heard tell of it, imaginatively evokes a ghostly presence in a way that highlights the Jews' material absence from Christian space. Once the Jews "depart," the biblical ambience is restored by mention of Hezekiah. Like Jacob Marley before a repentant Ebenezer Scrooge, the phantom Jews have receded into their biblical penumbra, relegated to their safe, historical invisibility.

A more engaging tone energizes the text of the pilgrim possibly named Egeria who later in the fourth century made a sweeping tour of the Christian East and recorded her journey for "sisters" back home in the West. Even her animated prose, however, constructs an ethnographic landscape not dissimilar from the Bordeaux pilgrim's.[52] Although this account now has live, active bodies inserted into it, we must attend to *who* these live bodies are and how they are presented. They are mostly the Christian monks and clergy who inhabit *loca sancta* and act as guides and escorts for Egeria's group. At Sinai, where the fragmentary diary begins *in medias res*, Egeria is received "hospitably" by local monks, some of whom escort her group up the mountain; upon reaching the summit, they are greeted by "a healthy old man, a monk from his boyhood and an 'ascetic' (*ascitis*) as they call it here — in fact, just the man for the place (*qualis dignus est esse in eo loco*)."[53] Apart from these monastic caretakers, Egeria's landscape is as bare and ghostly as the Bordeaux pilgrim's: "All there is on the actual summit of the central mountain is the church and the cave of holy Moses. No one lives there."[54] Moses, like Solomon on the Temple mount, is an invisible "presence," a shadow who has been succeeded by the ascetic monk who is now "just the man for the place."

Throughout Egeria's diary, contemporary Christians stand over and next to the ghosts of sainted biblical heroes: where "holy Melchizedek met Abraham" Egeria meets "an oldish man with an excellent knowledge of the Bible . . . in charge of the place from the time when he was a monk"; where "holy John baptized," there now live "a great many brothers, holy monks from different parts, who come here to wash"; inquiring after the cell of a lone monk in the Jordan Valley, Egeria is told that "the holy prophet Elijah the Tishbite stayed here in the reign of King Ahab."[55] In all of these holy sites, Old Testament figures hover like benign shades, resonant alter egos who provide a justification and identity for the monks who now move in their footsteps. Any contemporary Jews remain invisible,[56] while Jewish "presence" is encoded by phantom figures inscribed onto holy land through scriptural correlation.

---

52. See Leyerle, "Landscape as Cartography," 126–28.

53. *Itinerarium Egeriae* 3.1–4 (CCSL 175 39–40; Wilkinson, *Egeria*, 93–94).

54. *Itinerarium Egeriae* 3.5–6 (CCSL 175 40; Wilkinson, *Egeria*, 94).

55. *Itinerarium Egeriae* 14.2, 15.1–4, 16.3–4 (CCSL 175 55–57; Wilkinson, *Egeria*, 110–12).

56. The surviving portions of Egeria's diary contain no references to nonbiblical Jews. In the summaries of her reports contained in the twelfth-century work by Italian monk Peter the Deacon, *Book on the Holy Places*, mention is made of the synagogues in Capernaum

Jerome, the multilingual scholar from the West who founded a monastery in Bethlehem near the end of the fourth century, could also at times write in the style of a visiting pilgrim. In his *Epistle* 108, written in 404 to Eustochium on the death of her mother and Jerome's longtime companion Paula, Jerome narrates Paula's first tour of the holy land.[57] Like the journeys of Egeria and the Bordeaux pilgrim, Paula's tour is structured by the Bible as Jerome names "only such places as are mentioned in the sacred books (*sacris volumini-bus*)."[58] These sites are also populated by scriptural ghosts: at New Testament locales Paula uses her own imagination, as at Bethlehem where "she could behold with the eyes of faith . . . the star shining overhead, the virgin mother, the attentive foster-father, the shepherds coming by night";[59] in contrast, Old Testament figures are generally made manifest by their venerated tombs.[60] Paula passes through a densely populated land that has the power to make the past appear in the present; like Egeria, Paula moves through a country of shadows and ghosts that welcome her and graciously cede place to her.[61]

While able to bask in this comfortable position of Eusebian "succession," Jerome can also withdraw into the "alarmism" characteristic of Cyril. For Jerome, too, less friendly Jews can hover at the edge of Christian existence, not cozy in their pleasant historicity but menacingly evil and demonic. His interaction with Palestinian Jews employed to teach him Hebrew for his biblical translation project was at first portrayed as a safe journey into the biblical past. In the preface to his translation of the book of Job, accomplished around 392, Jerome describes how he learned Hebrew: "I remember that, for the sake of understanding this book, I paid over quite a few coins to have a certain Lyddan as my teacher (*praeceptorem*), one who among the Hebrews was thought to be held in first rank (*primus*)."[62] Naturally one of these "ghostly" Jewish presences would be much more in touch with the biblical past than the contemporary Christian and therefore eminently qualified to act as *praeceptor* in unmasking the ancient language of scripture. This casual contact with local Jews causes Jerome trouble some years later when embroiled in an international controversy. Jerome's nemesis Rufinus, once his schoolmate,

---

and Nazareth but only as sites where Jesus performed miracles (*De locis sanctis Petri Diaconi* 15–16 [CCSL 175 275–76]). See Wilkinson, *Egeria*, 179–210, for those parts of Peter's book believed to come from Egeria's diary.

57. Jerome, *Ep*. 108 (text edited by I. Hilberg; CSEL 55; repr. Vienna: Österreichischen Akademie der Wissenschaften, 1996) 306–51.

58. Jerome, *Ep*. 108.8 (CSEL 55 313).

59. Jerome, *Ep*. 108.10 (CSEL 55 316).

60. Paula visits the tombs of Rachel (*Ep*. 108.10), Abraham, Isaac, Jacob, and Adam (or Caleb) at Hebron (*Ep*. 108.11), Joshua (*Ep*. 108.13), Elijah, Obadiah, and John the Baptist (*Ep*. 108.13), and Micah (*Ep*. 108.14) (CSEL 55 316, 319, 322, 323, 324).

61. Earlier, Jerome had also promised his friend Marcella that she would 'see' (*videre*) a host of biblical characters if she visited from Rome: *Ep*. 46.13 (CSEL 54 343–44). See the comments of Leyerle, "Landscape as Cartography," 130–31.

62. Jerome, *Praefatio in translatione libri Job* (PL 28 1140a).

latches onto this "master from the Jews" to question Jerome's loyalty to Christianity. Rufinus's jibe is based on a "misunderstanding" of the name of Jerome's teacher, Baraninas or Bar Haninah: "Now we did not receive *Barabbas* as he did, as a teacher (*magistrum*) from the synagogue. . . . Pardon me that I have preferred to listen on as unskilled and unlearned rather than to be called the disciple of Barabbas!"[63] Prudently Jerome then withdraws from the casual position that solidified this faded Jewish phantom into a religiously and culturally threatening reality. To some friends he writes reassuringly:

> What trouble and expense it cost me to have Baraninas as my teacher (*praeceptorem*) under cover of night. He so feared the Jews that he showed himself to me as a second Nicodemus (cf. John 3.1–2). . . . If it is expedient to hate any men and to loath any race, I have a remarkable dislike for the circumcised.[64]

His Jewish teacher is transformed from "the first of his rank" among his fellow Lyddans to a covert instructor, "a second Nicodemus" smuggled out "under cover of night" for fear of the Jews. When a nonchalant rhetoric of succession causes the scriptural echo of Jews to materialize into a too-present presence, it is necessary to invoke the more alarmist language of Cyril and cast Jews as a lingering, marginal threat.

The cultural interplay of Jewish visibility and presence is more subtly narrated in a curious anecdote in the massive heresiological tract *Panarion* (or "Medicine Chest against Heresies"), composed by Epiphanius of Salamis near the end of the fourth century. While decrying the Jewish-Christian heresy of the Ebionites, Epiphanius is reminded by a reference to a Hebrew translation of the Gospels about an encounter with a certain "Count Joseph of Tiberias." This Joseph had once been a "man of rank" in service to the Jewish patriarch in Palestine.[65] When this patriarch had himself secretly baptized on his deathbed, Joseph began protracted years of confused exploration of the Christian faith.[66] His long spiritual struggle (during which he discovered the Hebrew translations of the New Testament prompting this digression) is punctuated by the heinous deeds of the secretly-converted patriarch's successor. This young ne'er-do-well not only engages in "seductions of

---

63. Rufinus *Apologia contra Hieronymum* 2.15 (text edited by M. Simonetti; CCSL 20; Turnhout: Brepols, 1961) 95. See also 2.38 (CCSL 20 112–13), where Rufinus sardonically portrays the Church as a faithless woman calling upon "Barabbas from the synagogue" when Peter and Paul no longer satisfy her.

64. Jerome, *Ep.* 84.3 (CSEL 55 123).

65. Epiphanius, *Panarion* 30.4.2 (text edited by Karl Holl; GCS 25.1; (Leipzig: Hinrichs, 1915) 338. Translated by Frank Williams, *The Panarion of Epiphanius of Salamis: Book I (Sects 1–46)* (Nag Hammadi Studies 35; Leiden: Brill, 1987) 122. For an excellent discussion of the Joseph of Tiberias story, see Stephen Goranson, *The Joseph of Tiberias Episode in Epiphanius: Studies in Jewish and Christian Relations* (Ph.D. diss., Duke University, 1990); and T. C. G. Thornton, "The Stories of Joseph of Tiberias," *Vigiliae Christianae* 44 (1990) 54–63.

66. Epiphanius, *Panarion* 30.4.5–7 (GCS 25.1 339–40; Williams, *Panarion*, 122–23).

women and unholy sexual unions," but even attempts to seduce a Christian maiden through magic.[67] At this moment the Jew stands as a real and monstrous threat to Christians of the holy land, acting unseen through sorcery on the fringes of Christian sanctity (exemplified by a virgin). Later, Joseph converts and requests a special commission from Constantine to construct churches in towns "where no one had ever been able to found churches."[68] Joseph engages the Jewish menace at the precise Constantinian moment of building the Christian holy land. He goes first to Tiberias, his hometown, where the Jews provide resistance: "The ingenious Jews, who are ready for everything, did not spare their continual sorcery. Those natural-born Jews wasted their time on magic and jugglery to put a spell on the [lime-pit] fire, but did not entirely succeed."[69] Of course, Joseph's Christian faith triumphs over Jewish chicanery, and several small churches are built in Galilee under his supervision.[70]

Epiphanius does not, however, permit these Palestinian Jews to linger as a threat on the borders of Christian reality in his own day: he makes several rhetorical moves to historicize their demonic activity, transforming them into harmless ghosts. First, Epiphanius reiterates that he heard this tale long ago; he cannot remember the names of the patriarchs, for instance, "because of the time."[71] Next, he emphasizes that Joseph's construction of these churches was itself long before Epiphanius met him and heard his story.[72] In this way, the villainous Jews are already situated in the pluperfect past. Finally, Epiphanius makes it clear that Jews are no longer the "enemy" within the borders of the holy land, but that this role has been assumed by various heretics, most notably the Arians:

> Joseph was not only privileged to became a faithful Christian, but a despiser of Arians as well. In that city, Scythopolis, he was the only orthodox Christian — they were all Arian. Had it not been that he was a count, and the rank of count protected him from Arian persecution, he could not even have undertaken to live in that town. . . . There was another, younger man in town too, an orthodox believer of Jewish parentage. He did not even dare [to associate] with me in public.[73]

The hounding Jews of Tiberias stand merely as phantoms behind the harassing Arians of Scythopolis. Epiphanius even hammers his point home with a supplementary Orthodox victim, once a Jew but now an "orthodox believer"

67. Epiphanius, *Panarion* 30.7.3 (GCS 25.1 342; Williams, *Panarion*, 124).
68. Epiphanius, *Panarion* 30.11.7 (GCS 25.1 347; Williams, *Panarion*, 128).
69. Epiphanius, *Panarion* 30.12.4 (GCS 25.1 347–48; Williams, *Panarion*, 128).
70. Epiphanius, *Panarion* 30.12.9 (GCS 25.1 348; Williams, *Panarion*, 129). Taylor (*Christians and the Holy Places*, 288–90) suggests that the earlier "house-church" in Capernaum might in fact be the structure built by Joseph.
71. Epiphanius, *Panarion* 30.4.3 (GCS 25.1 338–39; Williams, *Panarion*, 122).
72. Epiphanius, *Panarion* 30.5.1–2 (GCS 25.1 339–40; Williams, *Panarion*, 123).
73. Epiphanius, *Panarion* 30.5.5–7(GCS 25.1 340; Williams, *Panarion*, 123).

fearful of Arian recrimination, to mark the defunct "visible absence" of Jewish antagonism.

Epiphanius allows the Jewish threat several paces closer to his own time and place than earlier authors of the Christian holy land; after all, these sorcerous patriarchs are practically within living memory, and the anecdote itself is embedded in a tract on still-operating Jewish-Christian heretics. This willingness to allow the danger so much closer suggests a new sensibility on Epiphanius's part, although still inchoate. Epiphanius's narrative about the former Jew who has become an orthodox Christian represents the first step in actively transforming the cultural existence of contemporary Jews into the experience of Christian identity. Leaping ahead more than a century to our final pilgrimage text, we can witness this cultural colonization being fully realized.

"The Most Beautiful Jewesses in the Country": Christian Culture and the Other

In the last third of the sixth century, an anonymous pilgrim from Piacenza traveled to the Byzantine holy land. As much as anything, his account reads like later mediaeval and early modern European travelogues made on voyages to the East; we find the same attitude of comfortable colonizing curiosity on the part of the knowledgeable touristic subject.[74] There are far fewer attempts to narrate the Palestinian present as an echo of the scriptural past and even fewer precautions against the lingering malefaction of dangerously displaced marginal populations. Instead the Jews of Palestine are permitted to move and act in a sort of cultural display case, remotely connected with the events that have made the land holy but living their contemporary lives for the edification and entertainment of our author. One of the first regions the Piacenza pilgrim visits is Galilee, whose Jewish population is now both visible and present:

> We traveled on to the city of Nazareth, where many miracles take place. In the synagogue there is kept the book in which the Lord wrote his ABCD, and in this synagogue there is the bench on which he sat with the other children. Christians can lift the bench and move it about, but the Jews are completely unable to move it, and cannot drag it outside. The house of Saint Mary is now a basilica, and her clothes are the cause of frequent miracles. The Jewesses (*mulierum Hebraeis*) of that city are better looking than any other Jewesses in the whole country. They declare that this is Saint Mary's gift to them, for they also say that she was a relation of theirs. Though there is no love lost between Jews and Christians, these women are full of kindness (*caritate plenae*).[75]

74. See the remarks of Leyerle, "Landscape as Cartography," 132–37.
75. *Antonini Placenti Itinerarium* 5 (CCSL 175 130–31). Translated by John Wilkinson, *Jerusalem Pilgrims before the Crusades* (Warminster: Aris & Philips, 1977) 79–89, here 79–80.

This richly textured description positions the pilgrim as spectator in direct visual and oral contact with the Jews, something impossible for the cheerful scriptural ghosts of Egeria or the looming demons of Cyril or Jerome. While vague scriptural references establish the site's sanctity (although restriction to canon seems unimportant, since much weight is given to the apocryphal "ABC-book" of little Jesus),[76] there is more interest in the present remains of Jesus' hometown. The pilgrims enter a Jewish synagogue, rearrange the furniture, and leaf through the books; moreover, they allow this space to be coded as "still Jewish," challenging the "locals" to move the furniture back. They talk to (and even "chat up") the "pretty girls" of the village. While a level of ethnographic interest coheres with the Piacenza pilgrim's general attention "to the native peoples,"[77] this pleasant interaction with the Jewish population and the acknowledgment that they still move and act within the confines of the Christian holy land is striking when contrasted with the earlier silence of pilgrimage texts, as well as the actual demographic "shrinkage" of Jews in the Early Byzantine Period. Even more striking is the presentation of a Jewish response: the Jewish women are flirtatious and the men willing to humor the Christian pilgrims in their inability to move Jesus' bench. Taylor sees evidence of Jewish autonomy in this and believes that they in fact operated the pilgrimage site.[78] For the pilgrim, however, these Jews are not so much proprietors as part of the "exhibit" itself. It is difficult to imagine Jews having much choice under the thumb of Christian Byzantine rule than to smile and go along with waves of intrusive tourists.

Similarly the Jews paying homage at the shrine of the patriarchs are portrayed as congenially "sharing" their sacred space. We recall how Egeria juxtaposed the cadavers and shades of Old Testament figures with the lively, "fitting" bodies of Christian monks who had taken their place; at Mamre, Christians and Jews occupy opposite sides of the same basilica, a mere screen (*cancellus*) dividing their prayerful encounter. But while the Christians (like our author) come from far and wide, the Jews are specifically "the people of this area," coming from "all over that land (*omni terra illa*)" to put on a show with lights and incense for Christian spectators.[79] As in Nazareth, the customs of the Jews are as much on display as are the bodies of their dead ancestors or the miraculous artifacts of their "cousins" Mary and Jesus. Not only has their history been incorporated into the Christian holy land, their present experience has been culturally appropriated as well.

76. Jesus' learning to read is most famously portrayed in the *Infancy Gospel of Thomas* 6.2–7.1 (in Elliott, *Apocryphal New Testament*, 77). Leyerle generously describes the pilgrim's knowledge of scripture as "modest" ("Landscape as Cartography," 134).

77. Leyerle, "Landscape as Cartography," 135. The pilgrim comments on the lewd Tyrians (2), the hostile Samaritans (8; to be discussed below), the hospitable monks (10, 12), and the serene border patrols (40) (CCSL 175 129, 133, 134–36, 149–50).

78. Taylor, *Christians and the Holy Places*, 228–29.

79. *Antonini Placenti Itinerarium* 30 (CCSL 175 144).

The Piacenza pilgrim also juxtaposes the "good" cooperative natives with the "bad," spiteful ones, the latter role now filled by Samaritans encountered "on the way down" from Scythopolis to Sebaste; significantly they are not part of the pilgrimage exhibit as are the Jews of *loca sancta* but are instead a harrowing roadside danger:

> There were several Samaritan cities and villages on our way down through the plains, and wherever we passed along the streets they burned away out footprints with straw, whether we were Christians or Jews, they have such a horror of both. This is what they tell Christians, "Don't touch what you want to buy till you have paid the money. If you do touch anything without buying it there will soon be trouble." Outside each village there is a guard to give this warning.[80]

The threat once lingering in the "bound" populations of the Jews is now relocated to the strange and inhospitable customs of the Samaritans. The Jews now are explicitly part of the civilized sphere of the Christians, lumped with them as objects of Samaritan hatred. Even this danger, however, can be ameliorated by the advice of a cosmopolitan traveler: the Samaritans are discussed in the context of wayside provisioning and can be appeased by appropriate negotiation tactics.

By this later date, Christians have such firmly established mechanisms of power and display that Jews may be perceived as materially "visible" and culturally "present." No longer blurred into the scriptural past or dissolved into threatening shadows, the Jew in the holy land is now an appropriate aspect of Christian spatial and historical identity. It is worth noting that the delimitation of Christian reality within the most particular of sacred spaces still requires the negative "other," a new cultural "edge" to the Christian experience of *sanctitas*, which is provided by the cranky Samaritans.

My survey of material and literary remains has been necessarily short, but my intention has not been to wring *realia* and text dry of historical interest. Rather, by dislocating bare physical visibility from the construction of cultural "presence," I have tried to suggest that as Christians became more comfortable within their sacred spaces (and more aligned with the political reassurance of the Byzantine *imperium*) they found more creative ways to ameliorate the dangers posed by the distressing "other." By the sixth century this is accomplished by incorporating the "local" experience of Jews into the universality of sacred Christian time and space. Otherness still marks the limits of Christian experience—inscribed in the roadside Samaritans—but "real" Jews can at last emerge from the murky realms of scriptural obscurity and proximal peril.

80. *Antonini Placenti Itinerarium* 8 (CCSL 175 133; Wilkinson, *Jerusalem*, 81).

The Advent of Islam at Sepphoris and at Caesarea Maritima

FRED L. HORTON, JR.
Wake Forest University

An *"Easy Conquest"*

Philip K. Hitti, in his classic work *History of the Arabs*, uses al-Balādhuri's phrase "easy conquest" to describe the fall of Byzantine Syria to the Moslem armies that began in 633/634 c.e.[1] According to Hitti, the ease of the Islamic conquest derived from the cultural and ethnic differences between the Greek-speaking Byzantine rulers of Syria and their Semitic subjects. In his view, the Semitic populace of Syria welcomed the sudden appearance of Semitic invaders from Arabia as a relief from the Hellenistic culture Alexander the Great had imposed upon it some nine centuries previously. Furthermore, the tolerance of the invaders for the Monophysite and Monothelite Christianity of the Semitic majority, in contrast to their Byzantine overlords' insistence on uniform Chalcedonianism, distanced the populace from their Greek masters just at the crucial juncture.

The Byzantinist Romilly Jenkins arrives at a similar conclusion, explaining that "Syria, Palestine, and Egypt were ripe for the sickle,"[2] having been compelled for nearly a millennium to live under Hellenistic culture. Jenkins further contends that the Monophysite views of the Syrians and Egyptians represented a mystical monotheism of Semitic culture that found resonance in the monotheism of the Saracen invaders.[3]

This "easy conquest" was not, however, as Jenkins avers, "relatively bloodless."[4] Both Byzantine and Arabic literary sources attest the bloodiness of the

---

1. Philip K. Hitti, *History of the Arabs from the Earliest Times to the Present* (10th ed.; London: Macmillan, 1970) 153.
2. Romilly Jenkins, *Byzantium: The Imperial Centuries* (rev. ed.; New York: Barnes and Noble, 1993) 28.
3. Ibid., 28–29.
4. Ibid., 29.

great battles of the conquest such as Ajnādayn, Marj al-Ṣuffar, and most importantly Yarmūk. What was "easy" to secure in most cases was the submission of walled cities to the Arab armies in instances where the Byzantine garrison had departed, as in Damascus, or was totally inadequate to the defense of the city, as in Fihl. Kāhlid's terms for the city of Damascus,[5] payment of the poll tax in return for personal security and the preservation of homes, property, and churches set a precedent for the negotiated surrender of walled cities in Syria–Palestine. In Gaza, however, which surrendered in 637, sixty members of the Byzantine garrison suffered imprisonment for failure to convert to Islam and faced martyrdom in the following year at Beit Guvrin.[6] Although this account may have received embellishment and most certainly lies behind the fictional account of the martyrdom of sixty pilgrims to Palestine, the incident at Gaza is likely based on fact. Robert Schick's suggestion that the crime for which the soldiers met their deaths may not have been simply refusal to convert[7] is possible but amounts to a conjecture unsupported by the literary sources. In addition, even in Damascus itself, the terms of Khālid's generosity did not survive into the Umayyad Period, as is shown by the fact that the present Umayyad mosque not only occupies the site of the former Church of St. John the Baptist but boasts possession of the Baptist's head, the chief relic of the Byzantine structure. Nevertheless, there is general agreement among the literary sources about the generally peaceable transfer of walled cities from Byzantine to Arab hands.

The countryside is another matter. In his sermon "On Holy Baptism,"[8] dated to Epiphany of 635,[9] the Patriarch Sophronius complained of the "ceaseless" flow of human blood at the hands of the invaders, the burning of villages, desecration of churches, ruin of monasteries, and devastation of cultivated fields. A Syriac chronicle reports a massacre of some four thousand noncombatants associated with the defeat of Sergius near Gaza.[10] The very

---

5. As reported by al-Balādhuri. See Hitti, *History of the Arabs*, 150.

6. Robert Schick, *The Christian Communities of Palestine from Byzantine to Islamic Rule: A Historical and Archaeological Study* (Princeton: Darwin, 1995) 171–12. See also Walter E. Kaegi, *Byzantium and the Early Islamic Conquests* (Cambridge: Cambridge University Press, 1992) 95–96.

7. Ibid., 172.

8. Sophronius, "On Holy Baptism," in Athanasios Papadopoulos-Kerameu (ed.), *Analekta Hierosolymitikes Stachyologias* 4.151–68, as cited in Schick, *Christian Communities of Palestine*, 70.

9. Bat Ye'or (*The Decline of Eastern Christianity under Islam: From Jihad to Dhimmitude* [trans. Miriam Kochan and David Littman; Madison, N.J.: Fairleigh Dickinson University Press, 1995] 44) cites the year as 636 and mentions a communication from Sophronius to Sergius, patriarch of Constantinople, that contains reference to "ravages" of the Arabs.

10. *Chronicon miscellaneum ad Annum Domini 724 pertins* (ed. and trans. E. W. Brooks and Jean-Baptiste Chabot; CSCO 3–4; Paris: Durbecq, 1904), as cited in Schick, *Christian Communities of Palestine*, 71.

late account of Michael the Syrian (1126–99)[11] reports that Khālid, after the surrender of Damascus, sent an army to the region of Aleppo and Antioch that murdered large numbers of people.[12]

Over against the views of Hitti and Jenkins, there is some justification in the literature for the more sanguine interpretations of scholars such as Bat Ye'or that portray the coming of Islam as an altogether murderous affair, at least outside of walled cities.[13] Such also is the view of Moshe Gil, who contends that the visit of ʿUmar to Jerusalem to receive the city's surrender in 638 was an effort to bring an end to the bloodshed and destruction of the conquest.[14] Walter Kaegi contends that some atrocities may well have stood behind the stories of Arab brutality and created an "atmosphere of terror" that actually made the work of conquest easier for the invaders than it might otherwise have been.[15]

Schick rightly says that the issue for the modern historian is which sources to believe.[16] If one follows the Christian sources, then the conquest in the countryside was attended by the horrors of massacre and wholesale looting. If, on the other hand, one follows the Islamic sources, the Arab armies adhered to the Prophet's requirement that women, children, and the elderly were to be spared, as well as field and building.[17] Bat Ye'or, for instance, understands the conquest to involve elements both of the religiously motivated *jihad* as well as the older Arab tribal practice of raids for booty, or *razzia*, while Jenkins stands at the other extreme to proclaim the conquest "relatively bloodless."[18]

We might expect the archaeological discoveries in this century to decide the issue for us, to arbitrate, as it were, between the Christian and the Islamic literary documents and the widely divergent historical analyses each supports. If we do not know which literary corpus to favor, perhaps the record in the soil will establish the truth of one side or another or put the lie to both. As I shall show, however, this expectation has made the task of archaeological interpretation of the period of transition from Byzantine to Islamic rule extremely difficult and has in some cases even obscured the meaning of the data. I hold this certainly to be true for Caesarea Maritima, where I have labored, and see it as a potential danger for my colleagues at Sepphoris.

11. F. L. Cross and E. A. Livingston (eds.), *The Oxford Dictionary of the Christian Church* (2d ed.; London: Oxford University Press, 1983) 913b.

12. *Chronica de Michel le Syrien* (ed. and trans. Jean-Baptiste Chabot; Paris: Leroux, 1899–1905) 2.421, as cited in Ye'or, *Decline of Eastern Christianity*, 47.

13. Ibid., 47.

14. Moshe Gil, *A History of Palestine 634–1099* (trans. Ethel Broido; Cambridge: Cambridge University Press, 1992) 61.

15. Kaegi, *Byzantium*, 94.

16. Schick, *Christian Communities of Palestine*, 69.

17. Ibn ʿAsākir, *Taʾirkh madinat Dimashq*, 1.390–94, 396–37, as cited by Schick, *Christian Communities of Palestine*, 69. Schick points out that Eutychius puts this instruction in the mouth of Abū Bakr on the eve of the Syrian invasion.

18. Ye'or, *Decline of Eastern Christianity*, 39 and Jenkins, *Byzantium*, 29.

The Fall of Caesarea Maritima

The city of Caesarea in Heraclius's day was the capital of Palestine, as well as a commercial and maritime center of great importance to Byzantine fortunes in the East. As such, no victory of the Arab armies in Syria–Palestine, whether the decisive victory at Yarmūk or the submission of Jerusalem, could be complete without the subjection of the imperial capital. This subjection, however, was very difficult to achieve. Like Jerusalem, Caesarea boasted effective defenses against hostile armies, but, unlike Jerusalem, Caesarea could be resupplied almost at will by the Byzantines from the sea. That Caesarea held out two years longer than Jerusalem is no surprise. What is a surprise is that it was taken at all. Like Alexandria in Egypt, this Palestinian port city appeared to have had the ability to resist the forces of Islam indefinitely. Strikingly, the Arabian general who finally succeeded in entering Alexandria in 641, ʿAmr ibn-al-ʿĀṣ, was the very general who had failed to conclude his on-again, off-again siege of Caesarea Maritima. He had been required to leave this task to be accomplished in 640 by Muʿāwiyah.

According to the written sources, both Alexandria and Caesarea finally fell to Islamic rule, not because of weaknesses in their defenses, but because of treachery from within their walls. In the case of Alexandria, the city was sold out by its bishop, the redoubtable Cyrus, whose earlier concessions to the Arabs at Babylon had resulted in his exile at the hands of Heraclius. As spokesman for and relentless enforcer of the claims of Constantinople, and later of Heraclius's Monothelitism, Cyrus was utterly estranged from the majority of the Christians in his city.[19] It is little wonder that he sought accommodation with the Arab invaders, who had less cause than his own people to despise him.

In the case of Caesarea, according to al-Balādhuri, who provides our earliest Arabic account (from the middle of the ninth century), a Jew named Yusef is supposed to have conducted some of Muʿāwiyah's troops through a "tunnel" into the city, shouting "God is great!" These troops in turn opened the gates of the city to the remainder of the Arab army.[20]

Gil is unconvinced by this tale, pointing out its similarity to the story of the capture of Caesarea in Cappadocia by Maslamah ibn-ʿAdb-al-Malik in 729. Most interpreters, however, have chosen to regard this story as having at least a kernel of truth. Kenneth Holum and others, for instance, accept the historicity of al-Balādhuri's account and suggest the "tunnel" in question could have been the city's low-level aqueduct.[21] The aqueduct, however,

---

19. See Hitti, *History of the Arabs*, 164.

20. The full text in English translation is available as Ahmad ibn Yahya Baladhuri, *The Origins of the Islamic State* (trans. Philip K. Hitti and Francis Clark Murgotten; New York: Columbia University Press, 1916) 1.215–17.

21. Kenneth G. Holum et al., *King Herod's Dream: Caesarea on the Sea* (New York: Norton, 1988) 203.

seems an unlikely referent for "tunnel," and the reference might be better taken to be the extensive Byzantine sewer system, which would have provided more immediate access to the center of the city. It is unreasonable to suppose that the lower aqueduct would require anyone to lead the Arab warriors through it, but the sewer system would indeed require a certain expertise to navigate. Gil's point is well taken, however. Clearly, the historian's problem in this case is to account for the fall of a city that should not have fallen; and it is not completely unprecedented to grasp for whatever historical straw might be available in the form of a believable story.

Whatever the occasion for the fall of the city, there is no doubt that it passed into Arab hands at the end of Mu'āwiyah's siege. Al-Balādhuri says enigmatically that the city was "reduced" after its capture with little clue as to the exact meaning of this term. The seventh-century Coptic bishop John of Nikiu, who gives our earliest description of 'Amr's conquest of Egypt, mentions "the horrors committed on the city of Caesarea in Palestine."[22] The next earliest Christian account of the conquest of Caesarea is that of Theophanes, who composed a chronicle of the years 284–813. He records that Caesarea fell to the Moslems after a siege of seven years[23] but says nothing about the nature of the conquest or the severity of the conquerors. In the eleventh century, Michael the Syrian refers to the city as being devastated upon its capture.[24]

Early excavations by the Joint Expedition to Caesarea Maritima (JECM) in the heart of the Byzantine city found destruction layers that were taken at the time to be a single phase dated to the conquest of the city in 640. In the excavation manual this was termed "Phase 4," distinguished both from the "Latest Byzantine" (614–40) and Phase 3c, which included the pre-Umayyad and Umayyad Periods at the site.[25]

Field A, north of the Byzantine Esplanade, was a north–south street with a heavy stone pavement, houses and shops to the east, and an industrial area to the west. Above the last Byzantine construction layer, the excavators found a thin layer of bricks, ash, architectural fragments, and a high concentration of Byzantine pottery. Lawrence E. Toombs, field director for the JECM, assigned this destruction layer to the time of the Arab conquest in 640. Below

---

22. As quoted by Schick, *Christian Communities of Palestine*, 76. In 1916, R. H. Charles published an English translation of the Ethiopian version of John's work: *The Chronicle of John Bishop of Nikiu* (London: William & Norgate, 1916). See also Herman Zotenberg, (ed.), *Chronique de Jean, Evéque de Nikiou* (Paris: Imprimerie nationale, 1879).

23. Cherie Joyce Lenzen, *The Byzantine/Islamic Occupation at Caesarea Maritima as Evidenced through the Pottery* (Ph.D. diss., Drew University, 1983) 73. See also the translation by Harry Turtledove, *The Chronicle of Theophanes* (Philadelphia: University of Pennsylvania Press, 1982).

24. As quoted by Schick, *Christian Communities of Palestine*, 76.

25. Olin J. Storvik, "The Joint Expedition to Caesarea Maritima Dig Manual" (circulated privately, 1987) appendix 16.

this material Toombs found a "thin layer of worked-over destruction debris," which he assigned with "less certainty" to the Persian invasion of 614.[26]

Holum strongly attacked Toombs's conclusions about Field A after a review of the field books.[27] Although he questions Toombs's interpretation of the "worked-over destruction debris" because he can find no reference to it in the field books,[28] he fails to give reasons for his doubt about the evidence for the Arab conquest. Cherie Lenzen, however, appears to have located the "Persian" layers in question but contends that they do not really show evidence of burning.[29] Her conclusion, however, is that the evidence favors an extended period of use in the Arab Period with no need to relate the post-Byzantine debris to the Arab conquest of 640.[30]

In Field B, south of the Byzantine Esplanade, thick deposits of ash and burned pottery just above identifiably Byzantine structures suggested a clear relationship to the literary history of the site. Indeed, in his report on the first seasons in the field, Toombs contended that Field B offered clear evidence, not only for the Arab conquest of 640, but also for the Persian occupation of 614 in the form of a layer of wood ash above the Byzantine floor of Structure O in the northeast corner of the field.[31] The conquest of 640 was represented in his view by the breakup of the tesselated surface overlying Ramp C and the thick layers of ash above them.[32] Closely following the 640 conquest, Toombs envisioned a robber phase in which residents of the site exploited the destroyed Byzantine remains for useful materials.[33]

Lenzen, however, in her review of the Field B excavations, shows that the assignment of these layers to the Arab conquest and the period immediately thereafter was founded on a misidentification of the pottery they contained. She correctly locates the glazed wares from these layers in the Fatamid Period

26. L. E. Toombs, "The Stratigraphy of Caesarea Maritima," in *Archaeology in the Levant: Essays for Kathleen Kenyon* (ed. P. R. S. Moorey and Peter Parr; Warminster: Aris & Phillips, 1978) 224.

27. Kenneth G. Holum, "Archaeological Evidence for the Fall of Byzantine Caesarea," *BASOR* 286 (1992) 73–85.

28. Ibid., 75. The lack of mention of this layer in the field books says more about the way in which the books were kept than it does about the evidence Toombs brings forward. Toombs was the senior archaeologist, and there is no reason not to accept his report of the matter—which was, after all, based on firsthand observation. What is regrettable is that the observation did not result in the assignment of a new locus number and the opening of a new pottery bucket. In a similar matter, relating to an observation in Field B, Holum (ibid., 83 n. 4) defers to Toombs's observation but laments that he cannot find the data in the field books.

29. C. Lenzen, "Byzantine/Islamic Occupation," 214.

30. Ibid., 236.

31. Lawrence E. Toombs, "Field B: 1971–1974," in *Caesarea Maritima Preliminary Reports in Microfiche* (ed. Robert J. Bull; Madison N.J.: Drew University, 1987) chap. 4, p. 15. The general stratigraphy of the site was proposed by Toombs, in "Stratigraphy," 223–32.

32. Ibid., 16.

33. Ibid., 17.

rather than in the pre-Umayyad.[34] In other words, the most cherished evidence of conquest and immediate postconquest remains in Field B actually dates from much later. Whatever the cause of the destruction containing the pottery, it cannot derive from the events of 640 and the period immediately thereafter. Lenzen would grant the possibility that Ramp 1023 might derive from an early Umayyad date but admits that the evidence only supports a date after 618.[35]

The Ambiguity of Evidence at Caesarea

In 1976 and 1978, excavations were carried out in JECM's Field E, a Late Byzantine bath complex that was almost certainly part of a larger suburban villa about a kilometer from the northern wall of the Byzantine city.[36] These excavations sought to complement and extend the work done in 1964 by the Italian Archaeological Mission.[37] It was immediately apparent to all concerned that the bath structure belonged to the general design of sixth-century domestic baths. This fact was confirmed by the recovery of coins and fine wares datable to the middle of the sixth century underneath the floors of Area 5. What was most frustrating about this structure was the fact that there was no clearly identifiable terminus for its desertion. Obviously, the structure had not been destroyed intentionally, although most of its marble facing and flooring had been removed. Certain coarse wares from the levels above the floors were sometimes called "Early Arabic" in field readings, but my review of the pottery of Areas 1 and 5 has disclosed nothing that must be assigned to the late seventh century or later. Indeed, even the pottery found in the drain of the latrine in Area 5, presumably pottery associated with the latest usage of the structure as a bath, disclosed nothing that could not be termed "Late Byzantine." Given its date of construction and the fact that the structure was allowed to fall into dilapidation rather than be destroyed, we must conclude that this was a domestic structure, far from the defensive walls of the Byzantine city, that clearly survived the Persian conquest of 614 and the Islamic conquest of 640. Evidence of repair and rebuilding even suggests that the facility was made over at least once in less-than-elegant fashion to serve the

34. Lenzen, "Byzantine/Islamic Occupation," 410.

35. Ibid., 416.

36. See Fred L. Horton, Jr., "Bathing in the Face of the Enemy: A Late Byzantine Bath Complex in Field E of the Joint Expedition to Caesarea Maritima," *The Yahweh/Baal Confrontation and Other Studies in Biblical Literature and Archaeology: Essays in Honor of Emmett Willard Hamrick* (ed. Julia M. O'Brien and Fred L. Horton, Jr.; Lewiston N.Y.: Mellen, 1995) 150–73; and Fred L. Horton, Jr., "A Sixth-Century Bath in Caesarea's Suburbs and the Transformation of Bathing Culture in Late Antiquity," *Caesarea Maritima: A Retrospective after Two Millennia* (ed. Avner Raban and Kenneth G. Holum; Leiden: Brill, 1996) 177–89. I was a volunteer in the 1976 campaign and an area supervisor in 1978 under the field supervision of Robert C. Wiemken.

37. Antonio Frova, *Scava di Caesarea Maritima* (Rome: L'Erma di Bretschneider, 1966) 14.

bathing needs of an undisclosed population.[38] The buckled floor of Area 5 now suggests to me damage associated with the earthquakes of the eighth century rather than failure of the hydraulic system, as I earlier supposed.[39] This, of course, does not mean that the facility was necessarily in use at the beginning of the eighth century, but it seems unlikely that it was in use after that time.

Nothing at all in Field E reflects the seven-year siege and final conquest of Caesarea Maritima as represented in the literary sources, nor is there a shred of evidence to connect it with the Persian conquest of 614. Neither enemy burned it or caused recognizable damage to it. Were it not for the lateness of its construction, the Field E bath would simply be listed as an unremarkable Late Byzantine domestic structure. Yet, it almost certainly witnessed the coming of the Persians and the extended sieges of the Arabs and likely functioned as a bath during some or all of that time. Of all that might be imagined from both the Christian and Islamic literary sources, the survival of this complex seems least likely.

Another instance of ambiguity relating to the seventh century derives from the excavation of a Byzantine church on Herod's temple platform within the Crusader city, first identified by Abraham Negev[40] and excavated by the Combined Caesarea Expeditions (CCE) as Area TP.[41] Like the bath complex in Field E, the octagonal Byzantine church is a construction of the sixth century that survived both the Persian conquest of 614 and the Arab takeover of 640.[42] Like the Field E bath, the church shows no evidence of intentional destruction. Indeed, the next phase of occupation in Area TP is indicated by a series of silos that cannot be dated before the tenth century. They are dug into and, in some cases, right through the foundations of the Byzantine church. These silos existed for the storage of perishable foodstuffs, as is shown by the care taken to waterproof them, and reflect a period of agricultural storage in

---

38. Horton, "Bathing," 161–62. See also my conjectures on the matter, in "Sixth-Century Bath," 189.

39. Horton, "Bathing," 160.

40. See Abraham Negev, *Caesarea* (Tel Aviv: Lewin-Epstein, 1967) 61–62.

41. Holum et. al. (*King Herod's Dream*, 177–78) suggest identification of this structure with the *martyrium* of St. Procopius mentioned in literary sources. This worthy suggestion has yet to meet with adequate evidence for its correctness in the excavation of the site.

42. Jodi Magness has found the latest material associated with the construction of the church to be a "Jerusalem" bowl from 4073, which she dates to the second half of the sixth century, and three unguentaria from TP/1 and TP/2 that could date from the first quarter of the sixth century to the middle of the seventh century. Because there is about a century's difference between the terminus post quem for these vessels and the latest date for the Late Roman fine ware from these loci, perhaps the last word has not been said. Nevertheless, we are currently operating under the belief that the Octagonal Structure was constructed around the middle of the sixth century of our era. See Jodi Magness, "Late Roman and Byzantine Pottery: Preliminary Report," in *Caesarea Papers* (ed. Robert Lindley Vann; Journal of Roman Archaeology Supplementary Series 5; Ann Arbor: University of Michigan Press, 1992) 130, 132, 134, 139 and figs. 58.9 (p. 136); 59.14, 59.16 (p. 138).

the area. The puzzle in this case is what might have happened on the acropolis from the late sixth century to the new agricultural phase of the Fatimid Period. The Crusader building and rebuilding on the acropolis disturbed much of the evidence, but there seem to be no new phases between the latest Byzantine and the tenth century. Perhaps this means that the church continued in use over those centuries or that the Fatimid agricultural phase began with a general scraping of the site.

Even more curious, however, is the evidence from the great cistern that lay underneath the western entrance to the church. This cistern had a plain, white tesselated floor and sides plastered with pottery shards. The cistern was fed by a large drain that ran underneath the entrance and that was part of a larger drainage system changed and repaired at least once during its service. The only probe of the cistern fill, undertaken in the 1991 season, produced the surprising result that showed the drain continued to pour fill into the cistern from the Byzantine Period right up through the Crusader Period—that is, even after the area had been turned to agricultural use and even later, after the Crusaders had established their large north–south street across the site. The layers of fill are helpful in assuring that the site was in continuous use. Not too much more should be made of these results until further probing of the cistern can be accomplished. Nevertheless, we note that in the limited sample now available, the pottery of the fill appears to shift from Byzantine content in the bottom levels quickly to Abassid, Fatamid, and a profusion of Crusader forms at the upper levels. This does not mean, of course, that the site was not in use during the Umayyad Period, only that the cistern fill gives no independent attestation of that occupation.

A final excavation at Caesarea that bears directly on the question at hand is the small eighth JECM season that explored Field K, which lies along Cardo II between the public buildings of Field C and the Theater.[43] Robert C. Wiemken and Holum reported considerable evidence for a Phase 4 in this field, consisting of a burn layer some 10–15 cm thick in Area 1, and evidence of destruction but no burning in Area 3.[44] Ceramic and coin evidence favored a date in the middle of the seventh century or later for this destruction and construction, as well as for the octagonal church and the Field E bath, possibly in the time of Justinian.

Wiemken and Holum connected the burn layers and other evidence of destruction with the Arab invasion of 640,[45] but this identification is brought into question by their own pottery analysis, authored by Wiemken. For instance, in "deposit 1," taken from atop the Byzantine tessellation in Area 1, Wiemken noted a proliferation of CRS forms and a complete lack of African

43. Robert C. Wiemken and Kenneth G. Holum, "The Joint Expedition to Caesarea Maritima: Eighth Season, 1979," *BASOR* 244 (1981) 27–52. Appendix B (pp. 46–49) on coins in this article was written by Robert L. Hohlfelder.

44. Ibid., 244.

45. Ibid., 40.

and LRC wares. He paid special attention to two bowl rims[46] he found similar to Hayes CRS form 9[47] as well as to forms found at Dhiorius, Cyprus,[48] from the eighth century and at Kellia, in Egypt, from the end of the seventh century.[49] This evidence at best makes it possible that the deposit was made sometime in the seventh century, but this result is by no means guaranteed. By way of attempting to narrow the period in which the deposit was made, Wiemken wrote that there was a "conspicuous lack of Islamic pottery *beyond a few Umayyid glazed shards*" (emphasis mine). This seems to settle the matter. The existence of glazing clearly puts these unpublished shards into the post-Umayyad Period.[50]

Similar problems exist with the dating of the other deposits of destruction debris in Field K. The evidence is consistent with destruction anytime after the middle of the seventh century, but nothing requires a date within that century. Indeed, mention of glazed shards in reference to deposit 1 makes it possible to believe that the burned material might even reflect a date in the post-Umayyad Period, as Lenzen was forced to conclude in the case of the destruction layers in Field B.[51]

Holum, coauthor with Wiemken on the 1979 season at Caesarea,[52] later repudiated its conclusions, contending in one article that it is not even correct to say that the city "fell" to the Arab armies—at least not on the basis of the archaeological evidence presently available.[53] This is a strangely worded conclusion. It seems rather certain that the city "fell." All of the historical sources attest this, and the Christian sources, further, contend that the fall was attended by destruction and loss of life. It was not unreasonable for Toombs to expect that Caesarea's archaeological remains would show evidence of what was, in some ways at least, a cataclysmic end to the Byzantine capital of Palestine. The reasons for positing a Phase 4 were very solid at the time. Nevertheless, subsequent sophistication in reading Arabic pottery, and a judicious review of the evidence must lead to the striking conclusion that the historical claims are not yet matched by archaeological data.

In closing this review of the Caesarea materials, it may be worthwhile to ask whether we can offer any other (admittedly conjectural) explanation for

46. Ibid., 41 and fig. 13.2, 3.
47. J. W. Hayes, *Late Roman Pottery* (London: British School at Rome, 1972) 379–82 and figs. 81 and 82.
48. See H. W. Catling, "An Early Byzantine Pottery Factory at Dhiorios in Cyprus," *Levant* 4 (1972) 1–82.
49. See M. Egloff, *Kellia*, vol. 3: *La poterie copte* (Geneva: Georg, 1977).
50. Lenzen, "Byzantine/Islamic Occupation," 375–91.
51. Ibid.
52. Wiemken and Holum, "The Joint Expedition to Caesarea Maritima."
53. The definitive repudiation is in "Archaeological Evidence." But Holum et al. (*King Herod's Dream*, 202–4) shows significant doubt about the matter of the conquest. See also Holum, "The End of Classical Urbanism at Caesarea Maritima, Israel," *Studia pompeiana & classica in Honor of Wilhelmina Jashemski* (ed. R. Curtis; New Rochelle, N.Y.: Caratzas, 1989) 2.87–103.

the destruction layers discussed here. Although fires may break out for any number of reasons in a community, it is notable just how often the destruction layers in question have been associated by their excavators with industrial complexes, especially kilns and glass and metal shops. These inherently dangerous installations offer ample opportunity for the fiery destructions found in association with them.

Into the Galilee:
Capernaum in the Seventh Century

The principal difficulty encountered in these archaeological tales of woe is actually the result of the expectation that something as historically important as the Islamic conquest should leave some record in the soil and should, indeed, represent a division point between strata. The creation of a special phase, Phase 4, at Caesarea is but one example of this expectation in action, when goaded by the slightest piece of archaeological evidence—in this case the destruction layers in Fields A, B, C, H, and K. For Caesarea, if for no other walled city in Syria–Palestine, there was good historical evidence for a sacking of the city in 640. The recovery of large amounts of destruction debris within the walled areas should, it seemed, correlate with that cataclysmic event for the city.

As we have seen, however, there is good reason to locate much of this debris as being laid at a time subsequent to the conquest. Furthermore, in the case of the Field E bath, both the Persian conquest of 614 and the Arab conquest of 640 appear to have left the structure intact and even functioning, despite the total lack of defense for it. Finally, the large church building in Area TP, surely a tempting target for any army, appears to have continued to function in some capacity and to have fallen into dilapidation only later in the Islamic Period. Nothing, of course, in these finds contradicts the literary sources, but nothing clearly confirms them either; and we are left to our imaginations in attempting to relate the two.

The excavations in the Greek Orthodox compound of Capernaum provide two clear strata that bridge the period of interest. Stratum V is defined as the early seventh century through 650, and Stratum IV ranges from 650 to 750.[54] Stratum IV is especially well controlled by coin evidence, especially the Umayyad gold hoard found in Building A, Room 1.[55] Stratum V is less well defined than Stratum IV because of a lack of Byzantine coins and Arab/Byzantine coins associated with this level, but it certainly contains the expected Late Byzantine imported fine wares associated with "transitional" strata throughout Syria–Palestine as well as the distinctive Galilean bowls.[56] Stratum V

---

54. Vassilios Tzaferis, *Excavations at Capernaum*, vol. 1: *1978–1982* (Winona Lake, Ind.: Eisenbrauns, 1989) xxi.
55. Ibid., 17, 145–79.
56. Ibid., 32–42, 49–51.

represented a new settlement for Capernaum, a movement away from the synagogue and church area now in the possession of the Franciscans.

When one investigates the "early seventh century" terminus of Stratum V, one finds neither coin nor ceramic evidence to support it. The reason for the dating appears to be Vassilios Tzaferis's reading of the excavation reports of the Franciscan excavators.[57] Although Virgilio Corbo describes a gradual abandonment of the area around the synagogue and church, continuing through most of the seventh century,[58] Tzaferis complains of the lack of "substantial architectural evidence" to support the claim for continued occupation in the seventh century.[59] Pottery and coins are not enough to make Tzaferis believe in a continued occupation. For him, these items must be associated with structures in unspecified ways. Having questioned the evidence for a seventh-century occupation in the area of the synagogue and church, Tzaferis then concludes that this area was abandoned earlier and that Stratum V in the Greek Orthodox compound represents a new pre-Moslem settlement stemming from the brief period of Byzantine revival after 629. During this time, Tzaferis conjectures, the Jews might have been expelled and the synagogue demolished, in accordance with the pattern of anti-Jewish violence during this period.[60]

This historical reconstruction is fascinating, but to support his interpretation Tzaferis must discount the strong evidence for continued occupation of the synagogue-church area in the seventh century and search for a very brief period of Byzantine revival in the seventh century for the founding of the new settlement in the Greek compound. It is more likely that the synagogue-church area continued to be occupied in the seventh century and that there was new building in the present area of the Greek compound at the same time. Indeed, the results of the two excavations actually favor such a view. The disadvantage for the historian, however, is that this reconstruction, although more likely than Tzaferis's, makes no provision for the catastrophes and upheavals of the seventh century.

Contrary to our expectation, there is no evidence in the excavations at Capernaum that requires a correlation with the Persian invasion, the Byzantine revival, or the Arab conquest. Stratum V is a continuation of Byzantine settlement and life in the general area, which also appears to have included the area of the modern Franciscan compound. Gradually, residents abandoned the older settlement in favor of the new, but there is no particular reason to believe that this gradual movement was occasioned by the great events of the seventh century.

57. Especially V. Corbo, *Cafarnao: Gli Edifici della Citta* (SBF Collectio Maior 19/1; Jerusalem: Franciscan Press, 1975).

58. Ibid., 220.

59. Tzaferis, *Capernaum I*, 214.

60. Ibid., 216.

Implications for Sepphoris

It may be of some comfort to excavators at Sepphoris that al-Balādhuri records the surrender of Sepphoris on the usual terms and with little additional information.[61] This may incline interpreters away from attempts to associate the record in the earth too closely with historical reconstructions of the period of transition. If Caesarea and Capernaum can be of any help, no sudden disturbance of the Late Byzantine layers should be expected, only a continuation of general Byzantine remains, some of which clearly extend into the seventh century. The excavator may trust that the signs of Islamic culture will make their appearance at an appropriate point in the excavation, but these signs may not be like the seamless movement into the Early Umayyad Period seen in Stratum IV at Capernaum. It may be more like the situation in Area TP at Caesarea, where the next clear phase is much later, for reasons that will not always be apparent. Or, it may be the case that the Late Byzantine stands as the last phase before the present, as it is in Field E at Caesarea, in a context in which the structures clearly stood beyond the political end of Byzantine rule.

The so-called pre-Umayyad phase, where it can actually be isolated in excavation, is a continuation of Byzantine life and civilization. As of now, the evidence from the only city supposedly extensively damaged by the Arabs, Caesarea Maritima, favors an interpretation of a largely nonviolent transition to Arab rule. If the city lost population after the conquest, it was neither enough to close the great church on the acropolis nor enough to end a demand for bathing facilities in the city's northern suburbs. It is most likely that Caesarea's population fell the gradual victim to the reorientation of Palestinian life away from Byzantium and the sea toward Syria, Arabia, and Mesopotamia. The archaeological record suggests that for the remainder of the century the city was a Byzantine city in Arab hands, with a population not much less Christian and Jewish than it was in 640.

The Sepphoris 1994 report to the Israel Antiquities Authority mentions the excavation of Area 84.5 and the completion of excavations in Areas 84.1 and 84.4.[62] The authors describe these areas as comprising "an intensively used commercial district" of the late sixth to early seventh centuries that came to a "disastrous end" in the middle of the seventh century, owing perhaps to the earthquake of 633 or 659. Evidence for this disaster consisted of a significant burn layer, some 30–40 cm thick. The report also mentions quantities of glass

61. Baladhuri, *Origins of the Islamic State*, 1.179. Cf. Seth Ward, "Sepphoris in the Arab Period," in *Sepphoris in Galilee: Crosscurrents of Culture* (ed. Rebecca Martin Nagy et al.; Raleigh, N.C.: North Carolina Museum of Art, 1996) 91–99.

62. Eric M. Meyers, Carol L. Meyers, and Kenneth G. Hoglund, "Report on the 1994 Field Season of the Sepphoris Regional Project Excavations in the Residential Quarter of Roman Sepphoris," Report to Israel Antiquities Authority.

slag and metalworking. Kenneth Hoglund and Eric Meyers, in the catalog of the Sepphoris exhibit at the North Carolina Museum of Art, raise the possibility of light metallurgical industry in the area during the Early Byzantine Period.[63] The excavators mention the reuse of the area in the eighth century and refer to what they term an "Early Arabic water jar" from Locus 5053. Sensibly, there is no effort to force the data into the historical molds created by the seventh-century conquests.

I would caution only that in an industrial/commercial area such as the one described, disaster by fire is very possible and need not be associated with historical events such as earthquakes or conquests. Indeed, earthquakes leave a very clear pattern of destruction (one I should have noticed in my early interpretation of the buckled floor in Caesarea's E.5). Furthermore, the use of pottery to determine a terminus post quem for a layer is a dangerous business, especially in the present instance, because one effect of the Arab conquest was to reduce the importation of the very fine wares we often use to make such determinations. Thus, some loci will insist on looking early seventh century, even when there is evidence to suggest that they belong to a time later in the century. The characteristic coinage of the post-Byzantine administrations was slow in making its way beyond the mint cities.[64] Only in the Umayyad Period did Sepphoris have its own mint.[65] Work on the construction phase of the Byzantine industrial/commercial district should clarify the time of construction for the complex, but the discovery of an appropriate terminus ad quem may be a great challenge.

---

63. Kenneth G. Hoglund and Eric M. Meyers, "The Residential Quarter on the Western Summit," in *Sepphoris in Galilee: Crosscurrents of Culture* (ed. Rebecca Martin Nagy et al.; Raleigh, N.C.: North Carolina Museum of Art, 1996) 42.
64. See John F. Wilson, "The Bronze and Silver Coins," in *Excavations at Capernaum*, vol. 1: *1978–1982* (ed. V. Tzaferis; Winona Lake, Ind.: Eisenbrauns, 1989) 139.
65. Schick, *Christian Communities of Palestine*, 451.

Sepphoris in Sacred Geography

SETH WARD

University of Denver

Sepphoris was a major population center in Galilee during the Roman and Byzantine Periods. The objects that have been recovered from recent excavations there, especially the mosaic floors of rare beauty and quality, illustrate its high level of material culture and prosperity during the early centuries of the Christian era. Sepphoris ceased to be a major urban center, however, sometime in the first half of the seventh century, probably as a result of the Arab conquest in 635. Nevertheless, Sepphoris was blessed with a strategic location and especially with sites revered by multiple religious traditions. If it no longer had major economic importance or demographic significance, it and its environs in Lower Galilee still played an important role in what may be called *sacred geography*: itineraries, maps, and travelogues describing tombs and holy sites. This paper first briefly reviews the history of Sepphoris from the end of the Byzantine Period to modern times, then offers some perspectives on the "sacred geography" of Sepphoris and the surrounding region, based primarily on Medieval material.

This survey is offered with a caveat: the "sacred geographers" who have been surveyed did not always have adequate familiarity with the geography and topography of the area; they may not have recorded everything correctly or may have had local guides whose identifications and explanations varied from one to another. Perhaps most important, we must try to keep in mind that the individuals who created this material, be it travel accounts, maps, or whatever, found primarily "what they were looking for"—and what they were looking for was most likely informed by the goals of their pilgrimage and travels and not necessarily or often by the critical spirit and rigor of modern academic research.[1]

The first half of the seventh century was one of great political upheaval for Lower Galilee. In 614, the Persians wrested control of Galilee from the

---

1. Blake Leyerle, "Landscape as Cartography in Early Christian Pilgrimage Narratives," *JAAR* 64 (1996) 119–43.

Byzantines. Many towns, including Sepphoris, appear to have opened their gates to the Persians without a fight.[2] Thirteen years later, Byzantines defeated the Persians decisively just outside their capital city of Ctesiphon, in what is today Iraq. The Persians agreed to return all the land they had conquered, and Heraclius returned to Palestine triumphantly, marching through Tiberias to Jerusalem in 629.

About six years later, Galilee was conquered by the Muslims.[3] Muslim historians indicate that Sepphoris was a city conquered by force, as were most of the towns and villages of Galilee, except for Tiberias. In many areas, conquest by force meant battles leading to the total destruction of the town, with residents who did not manage to flee being killed or forced into slavery; this too is the scenario envisioned by Islamic Law.[4] There is, however, no literary indication of protracted fighting or reconquests at Sepphoris or, indeed, any further details of conquest for this or or any other immediately neighboring locale.[5] Perhaps this was the occasion of fire damage noted at the site, but the cause or exact date of the fire cannot be established with certainty. It may well have resulted from an earthquake such as the one that rocked the area about two years before the conquest, or it may have resulted from the "Year of Ashes" (in 639 c.e.), which was marked by extended drought, widespread fires, and especially a deadly plague throughout Palestine.[6] In any case, in the 630s a combination of natural, military, and other factors had a dramatic effect, and the population of Sepphoris,

---

2. For maps of the Persian-Byzantine wars, noting cities that opened their gates to the Persians, see *Carta's Atlas of the Jewish People in the Middle Ages* (ed. Haim Beinart; Jerusalem: Carta, 1981) 15 [Heb.].

3. F. M. Donner has suggested that Damascus and other locales changed hands several times, in order to reconcile the various sources, but does not suggest this for Galilee (*The Early Islamic Conquests* [Princeton: Princeton University Press, 1981]). For example, Sepphoris was conquered in A.H. 15, according to al-Suyūṭī (*Ta'rīkh al-khulafā al-madanī* [Cairo, 1964] = *History of the Caliphs* (trans. H. S. Jarret; Amsterdam: Oriental, 1970; repr. of Calcutta, 1881] 135). Balādhurī (below) places the conquest in A.H. 13, and al-Yaʿqūbī in A.H. 14 (*Dār iḥyā al-turāth al-ʿarabī* [1988] 88–89, trans. G. Wiet, *Les Pays* [Cairo, 1937] 327–28 [Arabic pagination]). For other sources and discussions, see M. Gil, *Palestine during the First Muslim Period (634–1099)* (3 vols.; Tel Aviv: Tel Aviv University/Ministry of Defense, 1983) [Heb.]; English translation: *A History of Palestine 634–1099* (trans. E. Broido; Cambridge: Cambridge University Press, 1992) §56 (section numbers are the same in Hebrew and in English translation; documents only in Hebrew); and Donner, *Early Islamic Conquests*, 112ff.

4. For a review of the dire circumstances that can result from the legal status of capture by force, see Bat Yeʾor, *The Decline of Eastern Christianity under Islam: From Jihad to Dhimmitude* (trans. Miriam Kochan and David Littman; Madison, N.J.: Fairleigh Dickinson, 1996).

5. Donner, *Early Islamic Conquests*, 153.

6. Other sources date the Year of Ashes a year or two earlier. Donner, *Early Islamic Conquests*, 152 and 245, 322 n. 286 (mostly on plague). Gil, *Palestine 634–1099*, §74. Theophanes (*The Chronicle of Theophanes* [trans. H. Turtledove; Philadelphia: University of Pennsylvania Press, 1982] 35) dates an earthquake to 632/633.

like the population of other locales in the area, must have experienced a sharp decline.

Archaeology, literary sources, travelers' reports, oral traditions, and other evidence all indicate that Sepphoris was not permanently abandoned. A few coins were found there from around the time of the Arab conquest,[7] and some artifacts and structural remains found there appear to postdate the conquest. It appears to have continued to be the center of a district in Jund al-Urdunn, the Umayyad Jordan province.[8] There is literary evidence that the Umayyads minted copper coins there as part of their reform of the coinage in 697;[9] recently, coins from this period were uncovered by the University of South Florida excavation team.[10] A few references to individuals from Sepphoris among the many thousands of documents from the Cairo Geniza indicate that there probably was a tiny Jewish community there at least until the eleventh century;[11] in the twelfth century, travelers Yaʿakov b. Netanʾel and Benjamin of Tudela did not find any Jewish community in Sepphoris. Their contemporary, Petachyah of Regensburg, mentions in the context of his report on Sepphoris a spice-seller and physician named Nehoray, who had a written family pedigree tracing his ancestry back to Judah the Prince and had named his son Judah in honor of his ancestor.[12] Presumably, Nehoray stayed in Sepphoris because of his family connection; quite possibly his genealogy

---

7. Catherine S. Bunnel, "Catalogue of the Coins," in *Preliminary Report of the University of Michigan Excavation at Sepphoris, Palestine in 1931* (ed. L. Waterman; Ann Arbor: University of Michigan Press, 1937) 77, coins 387–90.

8. For example, Yāqūt refers to the Sepphoris district (*kūra*) in *Muʿjam al-Buldan: Yacut's Geographisches Wörterbuch* (5 vols.; ed. F. Nüstenfeld; Leipzig: Brockhaus, 1866–73) 3.402.

9. Ibn Taghrī Birdī, *al-Nujūm al-Zāhira fi mulūk Miṣr wal-Qāhira* (12 vols.; Cairo: Ministry of Culture and National Guidance, 1929–56) 1.177; Ibn al-Athīr, *al-Kāmil fi al-Taʾrīkh* (13 vols.; ed. Tornberg; Leiden: Brill, 1870; repr. Beirut: Dār Ṣadr-Dār Bayrūt, 1965) 4.416–17.

10. As of this writing, these finds have not been published. My thanks to Prof. Strange for bringing this to my attention. Copper coins minted in Sepphoris are described in J. Walker, *A Catalogue of the Arab-Byzantine and Post-Reform Omaiyad Coins* (London: British Museum, 1956) lxxxii, 266; one is included in the illustrations.

11. J. Mann, *The Jews in Egypt and Palestine under the Fatimid Caliphs* (2 vols.; London: Oxford University Press, 1920; repr., New York, 1969) 2.357. Gil, *Palestine 634–1099*, §323 n. and document 190, line 14 [Hebrew] 2.326. Gil dates this document to 1039. As Gil notes, the shelf mark reported by Mann is incorrect; Stuart Miller has informed me that he has been able to locate the document.

12. The travels of Benjamin, Petachyah, and Yaʿakov have been translated into English in E. N. Adler, *Jewish Travellers in the Middle Ages: 19 Firsthand Accounts* (London: Routledge, 1930; repr., New York, 1987). Abraham David recently published a new text of R. Petachyah's travels, with references to previous editions: "Sivuv R. Petachyah me-Regensburg be-nusach chadash," *Qobets ʿal-Yad* n.s. 13 (23; Jerusalem: Mekitzei Nirdamim, 5756/1996) 237–69; this passage appears on p. 268. All three texts were also published in Hebrew by J. D. Eisenstein, *Ozar Massaoth: A Collection of Itineraries by Jewish Travelers to Palestine, Syria, Egypt and Other Countries* (New York, 1926; repr. Tel Aviv, 1969). A discussion of these contemporaries may be found in Y. Levanon, *The Jewish Travellers in the Twelfth*

served to demonstrate his family's continuous residence there since the time of his illustrious ancestor.[13] Oral traditions of contemporary Arab Sepphoreans published by Tzvika Tzuk explicitly posit continuous settlement in Sepphoris throughout this period, with the multi-religious character of the city continuing until Crusader times.[14] Nevertheless, the population could not have been large: Arab geographical dictionaries and atlases usually ignore Sepphoris in lists of major towns;[15] Geniza references do not seem to indicate anything about the life of the community there.

In 1099, Sepphoris was captured by the Crusaders. They called it Le Saphorie, made it one of 16 *bourgs* in the Kingdom of Jerusalem, and fortified its citadel. In 1187, the Crusaders gathered what may have been their largest army ever at Sepphoris to make war against Saladin. Presumably this site was chosen in part because of its strategic location along important roads and in part because of the availability of fresh water and the fertility of the surrounding valley. The Arab historian al-ʿUlaymī wrote that "they were about 50,000 and more."[16] Although the number is surely exaggerated (Christian sources, also probably exaggerating, reported only 30,000 or 40,000),[17] it was clearly the largest army ever raised by the Latin Kingdom.[18] After Saladin's conquest, "its people fled and no one was found there," although they left behind "wealth and treasures."[19] Saladin himself visited the area after the battle, and, as al-ʿUlaymī noted, left "buried treasures (*al-athqāl*)" behind in Sepphoris. ʿImād al-Dīn al-Iṣfahānī noted that after the Crusader defeat "Ṣaffūriyya was empty (*ṣafirat*) of its inhabitants; no one who could whistle (*ṣāfir*)," that is, no one was left alive.[20] Apparently the Arab historians all refer here to Christian

---

Century (Lanham, Md.: University Press of America, 1980). Many travelogues are also published in A. Yaʿari, *Masot Eretz Yisrael shel Olim Yehudim* (Ramat Gan: Masada, 1976).

13. It should be noted, however, that the text does not explicitly say that Nahoray made his home in Sepphoris!

14. Tsvika Tsuk, *Tsippori ve-atareha* (Jerusalem: Misrad ha-Hinukh veha-Tarbut, Agaf ha-Noar, 1987) 117.

15. For example, it is not found in the works of Ibn Hawkal, al-Muqaddasī, and al-Istakhrī. See M. de Goeje (ed.), *Indices, Glossarium, et addenda et emendanda* (Bibliotheca Geographorum Arabicorum 4; Leiden: Brill, 1879).

16. Mujīr al-Dīn al-ʿUlaymī, *Al-Uns al-Jalīl bi-taʾrīkh al-Quds wal-Khalīl* (Cairo, 1866) 284.

17. Peter W. Edbury has published various documents in English translation in *The Conquest of Jerusalem and the Third Crusade: Sources in Translation* (Brookfield, Vt.: Scolar, 1996). The Old French Continuation of William of Tyre puts the number at 40,000 (p. 35) and the letter to Archumbald at 30,000 (p. 160).

18. P. H. Newby, *Saladin in His Time* (Boston: Faber and Faber, 1983) 113–14. Newby totals 13,200 knights, turcopoles, and infantry. S. Runcimann reconstructs an earlier assemblage of Crusader forces at Sepphoris, in 1183 (*History of the Crusades* [London: Cambridge University Press, 1952] 2.439).

19. al-ʿUlaymī, *Al-Uns*, 287.

20. ʿImad al-Dīn al-Kātib al-Iṣfahānī, *al-Fatḥ al-qussī fi al-fatḥ al-qudsī* (Conquête de la Syrie et de la Palestine; ed. Carl Landberg; Leiden: Brill, 1888) 33.

abandonment of the town, apparently leaving behind both valuables and the bodies of the dead.[21] Le Saphorie returned to Crusader hands in 1240 and was reconquered by the Mamluks under Baybars in 1263.[22]

The Crusader Period is better attested in traveler's reports than any previous period since the Islamic conquest. While we know of several individuals who visited Sepphoris, except for Petachya's reference to Nehoray, we hear of few individuals who actually lived there during the twelfth and thirteenth centuries. As noted above, Benjamin of Tudela (about 1165) and Ya'akov (1180s) visited Sepphoris and did not find a Jewish community there. Christian travelers also remarked on Sepphoris's small population: John of Würzburg (1170) described it as sparsely populated, and John Phocas (1185) wrote that Sepphoris "has almost no houses and displays no trace of its original prosperity."[23] The place was important enough, however, for a John Semes to be appointed by the Crusaders in Nazareth to be "Rais of Saphorie." Semes was probably a native-born Christian or Muslim landholder, surnamed al-Shams in Arabic.[24]

We know little about the town in Mamluk times — it is rarely mentioned in travelogues, lists of major cities, or other sources;[25] nevertheless, it seems reasonable to assume there was steady growth in the Muslim community up to the time of the Ottoman conquest of Palestine in 1516. In early Ottoman times, at least a dozen Muslim individuals who were born in or lived in Sepphoris are known from Islamic biographical literature.[26] This represents a rise in the level of Islamic education of Sepphorean Muslims, since this literature is more likely to record the names and lives of members of the educated class. While some were born in Sepphoris and left and others born elsewhere came to live there only later in life, these individuals in general received their Islamic higher education elsewhere.[27]

The Jewish community of the Land of Israel experienced substantial growth in the fifteenth century and especially in the sixteenth century, after the expulsion from Spain and the Ottoman conquest. Yet there is no indication of a Jewish presence in Sepphoris at any time after the twelfth-century

21. al-ʿUlaymī, *Al-Uns*, 318.

22. Meron Benvenisti, *Crusaders in the Holy Land* (Jerusalem: Israel Universities Press, 1970) 260ff.

23. John Wilkinson, *Jerusalem Pilgrimage, 1099–1185* (London: Haklyut, 1988) 64, 319.

24. Benvenisti, *Crusaders in the Holy Land*, 260; J. Prawer, *The Latin Kingdom of Jerusalem* (London: Wiedenfeld and Nicolson, 1972) 368.

25. It is not mentioned, for example, in a survey by Maurice Gaudefroy-Demombynes of places in Syria (including the Land of Israel) under the Mamluks based on literary sources; see his *La Syrie à l'époque des Mamelouks* (Paris: Geuthner, 1923) index. For the area, see index "Nacira" (Nazareth), "Akka" (Acre), etc., and esp. pp. 118ff.

26. Described in Muṣṭafā Murād al-Dabbāgh, *Bilāduna Filasṭīn* (Kafr Qarʿ: Manshurat al-Yasar, 1988) 7:2, pp. 93ff.

27. One of the few Sepphoreans from this period to have achieved sufficient prominence to be noted in Western encyclopedias is Badr al-Dīn Ḥasan al-Būrīnī al-Ṣaffūrī (d. 1615). See C. Brockelman, "Al-Būrīnī," *EI*[2] 1.1333.

visit of Petachyah. It is also unlikely that there were Christians after the Crusades except for those connected with the Church of St. Anne.

In the eighteenth century, Sepphoris came under the control of the Bedouin Shaykh Ḍāhir al-ʿUmar, as did much of the Galilee. Ḍāhir al-ʿUmar rebuilt the citadel at Sepphoris in 1745.[28] The Citadel was repaired again during the reign of the Ottoman Sultan ʿAbd al-Ḥamīd, probably shortly after 1889,[29] and served as a school until the Israeli War of Independence in 1948.

Sepphoris in Sacred Geography

Sepphoris figured in the sacred geography and itineraries of Judaism, Christianity, and Islam. For Christians, the most important associations at Sepphoris are with the mother and grandmother of Jesus. Muslims noted the location of numerous grave-sites associated with biblical figures, primarily Jacob's children and individuals associated with Moses' family. Jewish travelers also noted many of these locations, especially the ones associated with various sons of Jacob; Jews also knew Sepphoris as the home of Judah ha-Nasi for his last seventeen years, and a nearby mausoleum was usually identified as his burial site.

Christian Sacred Geography

Sepphoris is said to be the location of a house owned by Joachim and Anne, Mary's mother, and is said to be where Mary was born, where she lived for a time, or where her mother was born. A well nearby, sometimes called the "well of roses," is sometimes said to be where Mary first realized she was pregnant with Jesus.[30] Petachyah reports that a "sweet smell" proceeded from the Tomb of Rabbenu ha-Kadosh which could, however, only be perceived at some distance;[31] although Petachyah notes (presumably in explanation) that graves in the Land of Israel are dug deeper than those of Babylonia because the water table is lower, the description strikes one as more in line with the roses around the spring than smells one might usually associate with a tomb!

The Church of St. Anne may have been in continual use from Byzantine times. In the sixth century, visitors to Sepphoris "adored with reverence the flagon and breadbasket of blessed Mary," as well as the chair upon which she was sitting when the angel came to her with the news that she was to bear

---

28. For a study of the career of Ḍāhir al-ʿUmar (Ẓāhir al-ʿUmar al-Zaydānī), see Ahmad Hasan Joudah, *Revolt in Palestine in the Eighteenth Century* (Princeton: Kingston, 1987).

29. Tsuk, *Tsippori ve-atareha*, 32.

30. Ibid., 116.

31. See David, "Sivuv R. Petachyah me-Regensburg," 268.

Jesus.[32] It is not clear, however, that this tradition was associated with Sepphoris in later times, because the site is often identified as being in Nazareth itself. In the twelfth century, John of Würzburg knew about the connection of Anne and Mary to the city,[33] as apparently did the Russian Abbot Daniel (1113–15) who visited the "Well of Mary," about a bowshot away from Nazareth (apparently this is to be understood as 1.5 versts, the same distance from Nazareth as Kfar Cana and thus consonant with Sepphoris).[34] Jacques de Vitry (ca. 1240) also described the well there.[35] But later on, Burchard (1280) passed through the village with a reference to the birth of Joachim, Mary's father, and to its geographical qualities and the fertility of the valley, but not to its sacred sites.[36] Mario Sanuto (1321) and Ludolph von Suchem (1350) knew it as the birthplace of St. Anne and, according to Sanuto, some said of Joachim as well, but neither mentioned any sites there.[37] Nevertheless, in modern times, the town was again said to be the birthplace of Mary herself.[38]

Like many important urban centers, Hellenized Sepphoris was renamed in the second century.[39] There never seems to have been any use of the Greek name, Diocaesarea, by Jews or, later, by Arabs; indeed Samuel Krauss suggested long ago that the use of Diocaesarea had disappeared at the time of the rebellion under Gallus (mid–fourth century), when "the old native name was restored."[40] The sixth-century Antoninus, the Piacenza pilgrim, apparently used this name,[41] although later Christian travelers generally did not. The Byzantine name, however, continued to be used by the Christian hierarchy; a "Bishop of Diocaesaria" is referred to in a list of bishops dependent

32. John Wilkinson (trans.), *Jerusalem Pilgrims before the Crusades* (Warminster: Aris & Phillips, 1977); Piacenza Pilgrim, 79, cited in Vilnay, *The Guide to Israel* (Jerusalem: Ahiever, 1969) 429; and in Leyerle, "Landscape as Cartography." This pilgrim text is often associated with the name of Antoninus and was one of dozens of such texts included in Palestine Pilgrims' Text Society, *The Library of the Palestine Pilgrims' Text Society*, originally published in London, 1887–97 (repr. New York: AMS, 1971). Several books were often bound together in individual volumes of this series; hereafter cited as PPTS, including a, b, c, or d, with the volume number to indicate numeration series within a volume. For Antoninus/Piacenza on Sepphoris, see PPTS 2d.4.

33. Ibid., 5b.4.

34. Ibid., 4c.71. If my reading is correct, the reference in F. Buhl [C. E. Bosworth], "al-Nāṣira" (*EI*² 7.1008–9) needs to be corrected to read that the well is "near" Nazareth.

35. PPTS 11b.37, 100.

36. Ibid., 12a.39, 41.

37. Ibid., 12b.37, 12c.64.

38. The editor of PPTS, writing in 1896 as a comment on Antoninus, said, "the traditional birthplace of the Virgin is still shown" (2d.4 n. 2).

39. On the history of the introduction of this term and for an overview of the history of Sepphoris, see S. Miller, *Studies in the History and Traditions of Sepphoris* (Leiden: Brill, 1984) 1–5, esp. p. 3.

40. S. Krauss, "Sepphoris," *The Jewish Encyclopedia* (New York: Funk & Wagnalls, 1907) 11.199.

41. PPTS 2d.4.

on the Patriarch of Jerusalem. This list was probably drawn up in the ninth century, based on earlier sources, and included episcopates that existed in name only, whose bishops served in Jerusalem in the Patriarch's Court. In the twelfth century it was still considered appropriate to translate it into Latin, even though the Crusader conquests had changed the situation quite substantially.[42] Latin maps often mark the city, usually denoting it as Sephora or Saphora; occasionally the Greek name is given.

Muslim and Jewish Sites Associated with Biblical Personalities

Muslims venerate Jesus as a prophet, and Mary figures in the Qur'ān. In Islamic sources, Mary's father is called ʿImrān; her mother, Ḥanna.[43] Miriam, the sister of Moses, is also called Maryam bint ʿImrān by the Muslims. The grandfathers of the two Maryams are different; it is not true that Islam cannot distinguish between the two. Nevertheless, while the association of Jesus with Nazareth and the towns in its environs is well known to Muslims, the Muslim holy places generally reported in this region (except for Nazareth itself) have to do with the family of the earlier Maryam bint ʿImrān, Moses' sister. These include Hebrew Bible figures such as Moses, his wife and father-in-law, occasionally the mother of Moses and Miriam, and the tribes of Israel. Kfar Manda, near Sepphoris, is sometimes given as the location of the tomb of Ṣafūra (Zipporah), the wife of Moses.[44] The editor and translator of the travelogue of ʿAlī al-Harawī (thirteenth century) supposed that this was because of the similarity of the names of the biblical figure and the village of Sepphoris.[45] Yaʿakov b. Netanʾel also reports a tradition that Zipporah is buried at Kfar Cana, also not far from Sepphoris.[46]

Indeed, there is an interesting association of Lower Galilee with the biblical Midian and Moses' family: Kfar Manda is sometimes identified as the city of Midian.[47] Shuʿayb, the prophet of Midian in the Qur'ān[48] and usually identified since Medieval times with Jethro, Zipporah's father, is buried in Kfar Ḥaṭṭin near Tiberias (a site sacred to today's Druse community).[49] Other

42. See A. Linder, "Christian Communities in the City," in *The History of Jerusalem: The Early Islamic Period (638–1099)* (Jerusalem: Yad Izhak ben-Zvi, 1987) 101, esp. n. 21 [Heb.]. English translation: *The History of Jerusalem: The Early Muslim Period, 638–1099* (New York: New York University Press / Jerusalem: Yad Izhak ben Zvi, 1996) 125–26.

43. A. J. Wensinck (Penelope Johnstone), "Maryam," *EI*[2] 6.628–32. Qur'ān: 3:31–42, 29:1–35, 23:52.

44. ʿAlī al-Harawī, *Kitab Al-Ishārāt ilā maʿrifat al-ziyārāt* (Damascus: al-Mahad al-Faransi di-Dimashq, 1953) 21, 96; ed. and trans. Janine Sourdel-Thomine, *Guide des lieux de pelerinage* (Damascus: al-Mahad al-Faransi di-Dimashq, 1957) 54.

45. Ibid., translation, 54 nn. 4–5.

46. Yaʿari, *Masot Eretz Yisrael*, 59–60.

47. Guy le Strange, *Palestine under the Moslems: A Description of Syria and the Holy Land from* A.D. *650 to 1500* (Beirut: Khayats, 1965 [repr.]) 470.

48. Qur'ān 7:83–91, 11:85–98, 29:35–36.

49. On the association of Shuʿayb with Jethro and Qur'ānic references, see, e.g., F. Buhl, "Shuʿaib" and "Madyan Shuʿaib," *EI* 7.388–89 and 5.104.

"Midianite" and biblical desert locales have been located here, including Se'ir as Nazareth[50] (biblical Mt. Se'ir is in the southern desert), and Ṭūr as Mount Tabor (in the Qur'ān, Ṭūr is Mt. Sinai).[51] The biblical Mt. Se'ir was the home of Esau and Edom; the rabbis associated Edom with Rome and Christianity. The location of "Sā'ir" in or near Nazareth no doubt reflects this usage; note also that some Arab authors have the "Injīl," that is, the Christian scriptures, revealed to 'Īsā (Jesus) on Sā'ir (paralleling the Sinaitic revelation of the Torah), and the Qur'ān revealed in Paran, paralleling Deut 33:2.[52]

In the sources we have surveyed in this section, Muslims connect a number of biblical personages and locales not so much with Sepphoris itself but with other locations in the area: Tiberias, Nazareth, Tabor, and Manda, alongside a small number of references to Christian sites, including the birthplace of Mary and the place where she received the "good news." However, even in describing Nazareth, the use of Se'ir reminds us of the biblical connection; other locales are associated with Moses' family and with Midian.[53] Ultimately, although traditions deriving from the Jews are clearly in play, we must consider these sites to reflect Islamic veneration of sacred sites and individuals mentioned or hinted at in the Qur'ān.

The same is probably true of the tombs of Jacob's children that have been located in this area, again, especially by Muslims. There is little unanimity on where the sons of Jacob lie buried. 'Alī al-Harawī found Reuben and Simeon buried in Kābul,[54] while Ya'akov b. Netan'el says that Reuben and Simeon are buried together with Levi and Dinah in Arbela.[55] Ibn Baṭṭūṭa found a mosque called "Prophets' Mosque" in Tiberias, wherein were buried Shu'ayb and his daughter Zipporah, Solomon, Reuben, and Judah.[56] Ya'akov b. Netan'el located the tomb of a "Judah the King" "half a parasang away" from Sepphoris at Kfar Cana; as J. D. Eisenstein notes, this may well be a

50. Le Strange, *Palestine under the Moslems*, 301–2.

51. Qur'ān chapter 52 as well as, for example, 23:20 and 95:2.

52. Nazareth is only one of several locations for "Se'ir"; for geographical references and references to Se'ir as a place of revelation, see le Strange, *Palestine under the Moslems*, 301–2 and 440.

53. Can the genesis of the association of this area with Midian have anything to do with the Midianite Wars in the book of Judges (chaps. 6ff.)? The biblical text seems to indicate that the Midianites came to the Jezreel Valley rather than to Lower Galilee. Moreover, the Midianites of Judges 6–8 were hostile and were defeated by a federation of adjacent tribes, including tribes in whose area the sites are located, led by Gideon. It is not the Judges-period Midianites who are recalled in Lower Galilee, but the Midianites depicted in the first five books of the Bible. Perhaps this association reflects migrations of Arab tribes with "Midianite" associations, such as the 'Āmila, who came to this region from the southern desert areas adjoining the holy land. In pre-Islamic times, they would have been living near a "Madyan Shu'ayb" located not far from Eilat (see Buhl, "Shu'ayb" and "Madyan Shu'ayb").

54. 'Alī al-Harawī, *K. Al-Ishārāt* [Arabic], 96; trans., 54.

55. Following Ya'ari's reading, *Masot Eretz Yisrael*, 59.

56. Ibn Baṭṭūṭa, *Riḥlat Ibn Baṭṭūṭa* (Beirut: Dār Ṣadr-Dār Bayrūt, 1964) 62.

reference to "Judah the King of the Tribes," that is, the son of Jacob.[57] ʿAlī has
Benjamin "not far away" from Kfar Manda; others found Benjamin in the village itself or in Rama or Rumi (for example, according to a student of the
Ramban).[58] Asher and Zebulon or Ashir and "Nafshālī" were in Manda, according to ʿAlī and to other sources surveyed by Guy le Strange.[59] Zebulon's
grave is also found near Sidon[60] or in Arbel, according to Yākūt, with Dan, Issachar, and Gad;[61] note that Yākūt's list is completely different from the list of
Yaʿakov b. Netanʾel. Nāṣir Khuṣraw (eleventh century) found four tombs
there and called this location "sons of Jacob . . . the brothers of Joseph."
"Moses' mother" was there as well, in a separate tomb.[62] Jacob, the messenger of R. Yechiel (ca. 1240) finds three sons of Jacob and Dinah there.[63] The
Jewish traveler and author of a Crusade chronicle, Samuel ben Samson (writing in 1210), also calls it the "Graves of the Tribes" and locates Dinah there.[64]
In a variation on this theme, the graves of Bilhah and Zilpah, the concubines
of Jacob, are located with Jochebed and Miriam, the mother and sister of
Moses; these four women were "near the walls of Tiberias," probably on the
way to Arbel.[65]

Most of the sites are associated with specific sons of Jacob, except for
tombs at Arbel, which as we have seen were often anonymous (for example,
"Sons of Jacob" or "tombs of the tribes"). Another anonymous location is
cited on the authority of a *History of Ṣafad* by Muḥammad b. ʿAbd al-
Raḥmān al-ʿUthmānī (d. 1378), who located the "*maqām* of the children of
Jacob, a famous place of pilgrimage" in al-shāghūr al-gharāba, part of a "region of many villages with no seat of government" bounded by Ṣafad, Acre,
and Nazareth.[66]

Given the frequency with which tombs of diverse biblical figures, especially various children of Jacob, are encountered in Lower Galilee, it is astonishing that there is no explicit reference to any such locations in Sepphoris in
the material so far surveyed. In recent times, however, local Arabs identified

57. Yaʿari, *Masot Eretz Yisrael*, 59; Eisenstein, *Ozar Massaoth*, 60. Adler, however, assumed that it was Judah the Maccabee (*Jewish Travellers in the Middle Ages*, 96).

58. Yaʿari, *Masot Eretz Yisrael*, 93. See also Adler, R. Jacob the Messenger of R. Yechiel
of Paris, in *Jewish Travellers in the Middle Ages*, 125.

59. Le Strange, *Palestine under the Moslems*, 470. ʿAlī al-Harawī, K. *Al-Ishārāt* [Arabic]
96; trans., 54.

60. Eliyahu Ashtor, "Sidon," *EncJud* 14.1508.

61. Yāqūt, *Muʿjam al-Buldām*, 1.184.

62. PPTS 4a.16.

63. Adler, *Jewish Travellers in the Middle Ages*, 125.

64. Ibid., 106.

65. Yaʿari, *Masot Eretz Yisrael*, 63; Adler, *Jewish Travellers in the Middle Ages*, 125.

66. As cited by Gaudefroy-Demombynes (*La Syrie à l'époque des Mamelouks*, 122), presumably on the basis of al-Qalqashandī. I have not been able to check this passage with the
Arabic original. There are other locations known as *Shāghūr*, for example, in Damascus.

the mausoleum near Sepphoris associated with "Rabbenu ha-Kadosh" as *qabr banāt Ya'qūb* 'the grave of the daughters of Jacob'.[67] Presumably these are the same daughters who crossed the the Jordan River on the bridge near Rosh Pina, which today bears their name. In neither location can the case be made for the antiquity of the association with Jacob's daughters. The Sepphoris site does not appear to have been specifically associated with Jacob or any children of Jacob in Medieval times. The river crossing, however, may have been associated with Jacob himself in earlier times: it appears to be identical to a site called simply Jacob's Bridge in earlier Arabic and Hebrew sources.[68] Arabic sources mention a *maskan Ya'qūb* 'Jacob's residence' or *qaṣr Ya'qūb* 'Jacob's Castle', often said to be twelve miles from Tiberias on the way to Banias or Damascus; some mentioned that it was near *jubb Yūsuf* 'Joseph's pit'.[69] These sites may also have been at or near the bridge.

Apart from the lack of tombsites in Sepphoris, the biblical tombs of Lower Galilee present additional curiosities. Some of the children buried together reflect children of the same mother: Reuben, Simeon, Levi, Judah, and Dina were all children of Leah. Other groupings do not. Moreover, Jews were clearly aware of the traditional borders of tribal patrimonies, yet the sons of Jacob are not often found buried within the frontiers of the lands their descendants held. It seems unlikely that these tombs would so regularly ignore both tribal geography and maternal lines if they were directly based on Jewish traditions. No doubt it was obvious to Jewish travelers that the burial of the children of Jacob in the holy land seems to contradict the biblical text of Genesis and Exodus and many midrashim, which only mention Jacob and Joseph as having had their remains taken back to the holy land. Indeed, the midrash expands on Moses' finding and taking Joseph's casket in the Exodus, and even the travel of this casket alongside the Holy Ark, with no details given for the remains of any of Joseph's brothers. Nevertheless, the *Midrash Rabbah* and *Mek. Exod.* 13:19 interpret the words of Joseph's deathbed charge as requiring not only the transfer of his remains but those of his family back to the holy land.[70] Moreover, the tomb of the daughters of Jacob may reflect biblical and midrashic justifications for reference to Jacob's daughters,[71] yet most

---

67. See N. Avigad, "*Kever Bnot Ya'akov* near Sepphoris," *ErIsr* 11 (Dunayevsky Volume; 1971) 41–44 [Heb.].

68. Ibn al-Farrā' of Malaga, writing in 1441, in *Ya'ari Masot Eretz Yisrael*, 110; le Strange, *Palestine under the Moslems*, 53, citing Dimashkī.

69. Ibn Ḥawkal, *Ṣurat al-'arḍ* (Beirut: Khayyāt, n.d.) 160; Ibn Baṭṭūṭa, *Riḥlat Ibn Baṭṭūṭa*, 62; le Strange, *Palestine under the Moslems*, 465–66.

70. *Gen. Rab.* 100:11, *Mekilta de-Rabbi Ishmael* (Horowitz-Rabin, 80), and see notes there for parallels.

71. Jacob's daughters are referred to in Gen 37:35 and 46:7. There are midrashim that state that most of Jacob's children were born as twins (e.g., *Pirqe R. El.* chap. 36; *Gen. Rab.* 84:21). Other commentators assume that the reference is to Jacob's daughters-in-law. See, for example, Rashi and other commentators on Gen 37:35.

Jewish sources recognized only one daughter of Jacob, Dinah, even explaining away seemingly contradictory biblical texts.[72]

These gravesites are noted by Muslim travelers as well as Jews. A fifteenth-century Jewish traveler, Isaac b. al-Farrā of Malaga, found tombs of Jacob's children Reuben, Simeon, Levi, Judah, Dinah, and Benjamin within a walk of a day or two of each other in the vicinity of Sepphoris, noting that they were "all guarded by non-Jews."[73] Indeed, it seems that Jews visited these tombs but that for the most part they were managed by Muslims. Although Muslims had access to Bible stories through the Qurʾān and other sources, the biblical text itself was not a part of their culture. Thus they could and did locate "Nabī Mūsā" on the road from Jerusalem to Jericho, not east of the Jordan, in seeming contradiction to Deut 34:6.[74] The Joseph story features prominently in the Qurʾān (Sūra 12), and Joseph's brothers are mentioned several times in it. Their names would have been available to Muslims via extra-Qurʾānic sources, such as histories and Qurʾān commentaries, and as Qurʾānic figures it is not surprising that Muslims venerated and maintained their tombs. Moreover, Muslim tradition located Jacob's home and Joseph's pit (among other places) in this region. In short, we may conclude that during this period the various Galilean tombs of Jacob's sons were primarily Muslim sacred sites that were also recognized and venerated by Jews. It seems, therefore, that the many associations of sites in Galilee with the family of Jacob were venerated by Jews (and Christians) as well as Muslims but may reflect Islamic sensibilities as well as and perhaps more than Jewish.

The Tomb of Rabbenu ha-Kadosh and Its Peregrinations

Jewish travelers generally associated the site of Sepphoris not with biblical but with Rabbinic-Period individuals. Almost all Jewish sources identify it as the home of Rabbenu ha-Kadosh 'our Holy Rabbi', that is, Rabbi Judah ha-Nasi, the editor of the Mishnah, who lived in Sepphoris for the last seventeen years of his life. Most believed that he was buried at the mausoleum just outside the village, and some even identified this tomb as Beth Sheʿarim, where according to the Talmud R. Judah's tomb is located. In fact, the archaeologist N. Avigad accepts the dating of the mausoleum to the Roman Period, although he does not think that Rabbi Judah was buried there.[75] The problematics of this identification were apparent even in Medieval times. As Eshtori ha-Parḥi notes, while the grave considered to be that of Rabbenu was only half an hour from the village, Beth Sheʿarim was two hours away.[76] (It is not

---

72. See, e.g., Ibn Ezra and Hizquni on Gen 46:7. (These commentaries may be found, e.g., *Torat Hayyim* [Jerusalem: ha-Rav Kook, 5752/1991–92]).

73. Ibn al-Farrā, in Yaʿari, *Masot Eretz Yisrael*, 109–10.

74. See, e.g., most guidebooks, and J. W. Parkes, R. Posner, and S. P. Colbi, "Holy Places," *EncJud* 8.935.

75. Avigad, *"Kever Bnot Yaʿakov."*

76. E. ha-Parḥi, *Kaftor wa-ferah* (ed. Tzvi Hirsch Edelman; Berlin: Sittenfeld, 1852) 48b.

clear to me, however, that Eshtori contests that this is in fact the grave of Judah the Prince; the text might be read as acknowledging that Rabbenu had had a grave prepared in Beth She'arim even though he was buried in the Rabbenu site). Beth She'arim was definitively identified only in our own times, by B. Mazar and Avigad, as a site near Kiryat Tiv'on,[77] although the mausoleum at Sepphoris continues to be identified by some (including the Israeli Chief Rabbinate) as Judah ha-Nasi's grave.[78]

Rabbi Judah is often said to be buried with his wife; some had their graves together, others had her buried in a separate tomb, in one source described as 40 cubits lower down the mountain.[79] He is often joined by his students or his sons Simeon and Gamaliel, or ten *geonim*. Eshtori ha-Parhi had Simeon and Gamaliel half an hour away to the northeast.[80] In recent times, this site has been identified as the tomb of his grandson Yehuda Nesi'a, whose name also translates to 'Judah the Prince'; his name is on the sign over the entrance. Benjamin of Tudela notes the graves of Jonah the Prophet and Rabbi Hiyya the Babylonian in his description of Sepphoris, although probably both were shown in neighboring villages, not in Sepphoris itself.[81] Ya'akov b. Netan'el identified the "the assembly of our lord King Hezekiah" in a garden on the mountain at Sepphoris.[82] He also reported a multiple tomb, a cave within a cave, just outside of the village; although this may well be a reference to the Rabbenu tomb, Ya'akov did not report who was supposed to have been buried there.

Events associated with the less famous are often transferred in the retelling to more famous individuals. The peregrinations of the reported burial site of Judah the Prince illustrate a similar phenomenon in sacred geography. Throughout the Middle Ages, reports of Judah ha-Nasi's grave almost always located it at the mausoleum just outside of Sepphoris. In more recent times, however, his grave was reported in other spots: Simcha b. Yehuda of Zatozce (1764–65) reported Yehuda Nesi'a's grave in Safed.[83] Moshe Basola and Moshe Yerushalmi (writing in Yiddish) located the grave in a village in Upper Galilee.[84] However, Rahamim Joseph of Oplatka, writing in 1876, returned Rabbi Judah's final resting place to Lower Galilee, locating the grave of Judah the Prince "just outside the wall of Tiberias."[85] Just as some acts seem to be

77. The archaelogists' findings were published in Hebrew and English. English: B. Mazar et al., *Beth She'arim* (3 vols.; Jerusalem: Israel Exploration Society / New Brunswick, N.J.: Rutgers University Press, 1971–76).

78. I am grateful to Stuart Miller for bringing this to my attention.

79. See, e.g., Adler, *Jewish Travellers in the Middle Ages*, 115, 125.

80. Ha-Parhi, *Kaftor wa-ferah*, 48b. Compare also Isaac b. Chelo (Adler, *Jewish Travellers in the Middle Ages*, 145).

81. Jonah and Hiyya are identified by Benjamin of Tudela and may have been located near, rather than in, Sepphoris, based on identifications by other travelers.

82. Ya'ari, *Masot Eretz Yisrael*, 59.

83. Ibid., 412.

84. Ibid., 434, 439.

85. Ibid., 631.

ascribed to ever-more-famous individuals, the case of Rabbi Judah's sepul-
chral migration illustrates a tendency to locate sacred spaces in or near more
accessible, heavily populated and sacred areas. As time went on, Jews recognized Safed and Tiberias as the two "holy cities" of Galilee, and perhaps it is
not surprising that Rabbi Judah's gravesite was located in the same general region as the traditional graves of many other rabbis said to rest there.

Location Names

Sepphoris is not a biblical place-name. In pre-Islamic times, the Talmud
(b. Meg. 6a) identified Sepphoris with Qitron, a city of the tribe of Zebulon
(Judg 1:30),[86] and in the Middle Ages, Eshtori ha-Parhi visited Sepphoris and
noted that it is within the territory of the tribe of Zebulon, very near the border of Issachar.[87] The Christian Eusebius identified Diocaeasarea with Lod
and noted that this city had an entirely Jewish population. Possibly he confused Diocaesarea with Diospolis, the Byzantine name for Lod, a city of the
tribe of Benjamin mentioned in Ezra, Nehemiah, and Chronicles. Eusebius
identifies Diospolis with a city in Egypt.[88] In the Islamic Period, Sepphoris
may have been identified by Jews as the biblical Tirza, as shown in an
eleventh-century Geniza document, mentioned above, and in a Judeo-Arabic
chronicle.[89]

I have been able to examine only a limited number of maps and itineraria;
in general Sepphoris is missing from these items. Traditional Jewish maps of
Eretz Israel focus on biblical place-names; thus they may include Qitron but
not usually Sepphoris. The cartography is not meant to be sufficiently accurate to tell whether "Qitron" is located by the map-maker exactly where Sepphoris is situated. Itineraria, stylized depictions of sacred places centering
around the holy sites of Jerusalem, include many tombs and graves—but usually not the tomb of Rabbenu ha-Kadosh.

---

86. Miller, *Studies in the History and Traditions of Sepphoris*, 25ff. Miller rejects the
identification.

87. Ha Parhi, *Kaftor wa-ferah*, 48b.

88. Y. Ne'eman, *Sepphoris in the Days of the Second Temple, Mishna and Talmud*
(Jerusalem: Shem, 1993) 53–55 [Heb.]. Ne'eman cites William Cureton, *History of the
Martyrs of Palestine by Eusebius* (London: Williams & Norgate, 1861) 29, a Syriac version
of this work with English translation. I have not had access to Cureton and have been unable to locate this or a similar passage in the index to Eusebius's *Martyrs* in Migne, *Patrio-
logiae Cursus Completus . . . series Graeca* (Paris, 1841–66; repr., Turnhout: Brepols, 1977–
84) vol. 20, cols. 1457–1519; or in Eusebius's *Onomasticon*, which identifies place-names
in the Bible with names of places existing in his day, in Jerome's Latin translation, *PL*
23.903ff. On Diospolis, see *PL* 23.938.

89. Mann, *The Jews in Egypt and Palestine*, 2.357. Gil (*Palestine 634–1099*, §323, note)
reports that the shelfmark listed by Mann for the fragment mentioning Yefet is incorrect;
Stuart Miller has indicated that he has located the manuscript and confirmed Mann's reading and found an additional reference to Sepphoris as Tirzah.

Despite the phenomenal growth in overall Jewish population in Galilee and in Palestine as a whole in the fifteenth and sixteenth centuries, there is no indication that Jews lived in Sepphoris at this time. So the mention of Sepphoris in a number of Jewish responsa in the fifteenth through eighteenth centuries may be considered another example of "sacred geography." These references have been shown not to reflect the existence of a Jewish community there but, rather, the conventional use of well-known cities from the Mishna and Talmud to refer to arbitrary place-names.[90]

Conclusion

The sources we have surveyed present a picture of Sepphoris as a small village after the Islamic conquest. A large city under the Byzantines, it may have escaped damage in 614 when it opened its gates to the Persians in the Persian-Byzantine wars. But many of its people may have fled or were killed at that time or in the 630s, when it was conquered by force and the plague and natural disasters hit Galilee. Sepphoris was one of many locales that never regained the population and importance it had had in ancient times. Sepphoreans earned their living from crafts and trade, including textiles. For a short time under the Umayyads they minted copper coins. No doubt some residents were involved in providing services to travelers and especially to pilgrims, since the town was located along major routes, with sites of interest to Muslims, Christians, and Jews. At first, the Muslims were not a majority but grew in size as the old families converted to Islam. Nevertheless, Sepphoris and its district would not lose its multireligious character until after the Crusader Period. The Crusaders recognized Sepphoris as a site of some strategic and religious importance, with a small fortified citadel and a church; Sepphoris was one of sixteen *bourgs* and a major staging point for war in 1187. Yet the civilian population in the village clearly remained quite small. Its population seems to have increased in the Early Ottoman Period, and in the eighteenth century, Ḍāhir al-ʿUmar accorded it some secondary strategic importance. Yet it never regained the prominence it had held in Byzantine times.

Christians sought to locate Sepphoris within the story of Mary and her parents. In Roman times, Sepphoris was a far larger city than Nazareth, but after the Byzantine Period, Nazareth became more important and Sepphoris a small village; even when travelers went there, they might locate Mary's spring as being near Nazareth, rather than just outside Sepphoris.

For Muslims and Jews, Sepphoris was in the middle of a region in which they sought to find biblical figures and locales. The children of Jacob are especially prominent and perhaps surprising from the standpoint of Jewish tradition; some Muslims, however, placed Jacob's home and Joseph's pit not far

---

90. Meir Benayahu, "Was There a Jewish Settlement in Sepphoris after the Talmud?" *Melilah* 3–4 (1949–50) 103–9 [Heb.]. Benayahu counters the suggestion of Baruch Toledano, "Jewish Settlement in Sepphoris, 1525–1874" *Tarbiz* 17 (1946) 190–93.

away, near Tiberias. Also frequent are place-names and tombs associated with Moses' family, including his father-in-law, and the Israelite's desert wanderings, such as Ṭūr and Seʿir. For the most part, these places and personages were mentioned in the Qurʾān (explicitly or by inference); in the case of Seʿir as Nazareth, an Islamic polemic is clearly visible. It is curious that neither the children of Jacob nor other biblical associations have been reported for Sepphoris, except in recent times, when Arabs have associated Sepphoris with the tomb of the "daughters of Jacob."

Jews sought to locate places in the Land of Israel in the framework of the tribal land allocations and biblical toponyms: many Jews writing about Sepphoris were aware of its tribal assignment, and it was associated with the biblical place-names Qitron and Tirzah. The major "sacred geography" of this region for Jews, however, were the tombsites of rabbinic figures. Most Jews located the tomb of Judah the Prince at Sepphoris; although other individuals are often said to be buried in Sepphoris, they are associated closely with Judah: his wife, his sons, named or unnamed, or his students or the *geonim*, left unnamed; sometimes the tomb is associated with his grandson instead. Although many other rabbis lived in Sepphoris and it was a prominent Jewish center in the Roman and Byzantine Periods, Rabbenu's presence here is overwhelmingly felt; virtually no unrelated tomb or Sepphorean sacred site was recorded by Jews. Perhaps this reflects Judah's commanding role in the Mishnah. With such good evidence from multiple passages in rabbinic literature, there was great awareness of Rabbenu's ties to Sepphoris and no reason to find other rabbinic graves there. This is somewhat ironic. Rabbenu is assumed by most scholars today not to have been buried in Sepphoris; moreover, Sepphoris itself had a Jewish burial place, and it is possible that various Sepphorean rabbis were indeed interred there.

The process of Sepphoris's losing its central importance in the region had begun prior to the Islamic conquest; as time went on, the administrative center of the region shifted to Tiberias, to Acre, and to Safed. The sacred geography of Sepphoris reflects not only what Jews, Christians, and Muslims were looking for, but where they were looking for it. As populations shifted, other routes became more important, and even Rabbenu was sometimes located far away from Sepphoris.

Today's travelers are often looking for stunning art, archaeology with wonderful achievements of esthetics and engineering, and sites of historical importance, which put contemporary society into an age-old context. The contemporary Sepphoris National Park has all these and more; no doubt it will continue to attract and hold the interest of the contemporary successors of the Medieval travelers whose works were surveyed here.

Index of Authors

Index of Scripture

Hebrew Bible

New Testament

Deuterocanonical and Apocryphal Works

Index of Sites and Geographical Names

Index of Ancient and Medieval Sources

Early Jewish, Christian, and Classical Sources

Rabbinic Sources

Qur'ān